Szycher's Practical Handbook of Entrepreneurship and Innovation

T0320262

Szycher's Practical Handbook of Entrepreneurship and Innovation

By
Michael Szycher, PhD

CRC Press
Taylor & Francis Group
Boca Raton London New York

CRC Press is an imprint of the
Taylor & Francis Group, an **informa** business

CRC Press
Taylor & Francis Group
6000 Broken Sound Parkway NW, Suite 300
Boca Raton, FL 33487-2742

First issued in paperback 2020

© 2019 by Taylor & Francis Group, LLC
CRC Press is an imprint of Taylor & Francis Group, an Informa business

No claim to original U.S. Government works

ISBN-13: 978-1-138-73599-6 (hbk)
ISBN-13: 978-0-367-65701-7 (pbk)

Library of Congress Cataloging-in-Publication Data

Names: Szycher, M. (Michael), author.
Title: Szycher's practical handbook of entrepreneurship and innovation/
Michael Szycher.
Description: Boca Raton, FL : CRC Press, [2019] | Includes bibliographical references
and index.
Identifiers: LCCN 2018005786 (print) | LCCN 2018006711 (ebook) | ISBN
9781351736374 (Adobe PDF) | ISBN 9781351736367 (ePub) | ISBN 9781351736350
(Mobipocket) | ISBN 9781138735996 (hardback) | ISBN 9781315186191 (ebook)
Subjects: LCSH: Entrepreneurship. | Technological innovations.
Classification: LCC HB615 (ebook) | LCC HB615 .S993 2018 (print) | DDC
658.4/21–dc23
LC record available at https://lccn.loc.gov/2018005786

Visit the Taylor & Francis Web site at
http://www.taylorandfrancis.com

and the CRC Press Web site at
http://www.crcpress.com

This book is dedicated to my wife, Laurie; my son, Mark, and his wife, Rachel; my son, Scott, and his wife, Diane; and my wonderful grandchildren, Arielle and Jason.

Contents

Section II   Entrepreneurial Self-Assessment

Section III Entrepreneurial Environment

Section IV   Classical Initial Decisions

Section V   Exit Strategies, AKA Harvesting

Author

A successful serial entrepreneur, Dr. Michael Szycher conceptualized, financed, took public, and ran three public companies and has founded a fourth over the past few years. As chairman and/or CEO of companies, he was responsible for road shows, public offerings, acquisitions, product launches, and spin-outs.

A prolific author of several books and over 140 technical papers, Dr. Szycher holds a B.S. in chemical engineering from the University of New Hampshire, a PhD in cardiac physiology from Boston University School of Medicine, and an MBA from Suffolk University.

He literally "wrote the book"—*Szycher's Handbook of Polyurethanes*, which has become the polyurethane industry's bible.

He currently serves on the Board of Directors/Advisors of several international companies engaged in the biopharma/medical device industry.

Among his professional accomplishments, we cite

- Founder, chairman, CEO, Sterling Biomedical Inc., venture-backed company established to develop and commercialize silver-based antimicrobial products.

- Founder, chairman, CEO, Cardiotech International, Inc. (CTE), now called AdvanceSource Biomaterials. Under SBIR grants, developed CardioPass, a small bore vascular graft, currently undergoing clinical trials in Europe. Under SBIR grants, developed ChronoFlex, a third-generation medical-grade polyurethane.

- Founder, Board Chairman, Polymedica Corp (sold to Medco Healthcare Solutions [MHS]). Under SBIR grants, developed CarboThane, universally used in indwelling catheters.

- Co-founder, Thermedics Inc. (sold to Thoratec [THOR]). Under NIH contracts, developed Heartmate, the world's largest-selling left ventricular–assisting assist device.

Section I

Startups under the Microscope

1

Entrepreneurship and Innovation

"Entrepreneurial vision is the act of seeing the invisible."

1.1 Introduction

According to the *Business Dictionary*, entrepreneurship is

> the capacity and willingness to develop, organize and manage a business venture along with any of its risks in order to make a profit. The most obvious example of entrepreneurship is the starting of new businesses.
>
> In economics, entrepreneurship combined with land, labor, natural resources and capital can produce profit. Entrepreneurial spirit is characterized by innovation and risk-taking, and is an essential part of a nation's ability to succeed in an ever changing and increasingly competitive global marketplace.[1]

Entrepreneurs and entrepreneurship are universally held in the highest esteem. Worldwide attention to entrepreneurs as agents of economic value was bolstered in the early 1940s by the seminal work of Joseph Schumpeter.[2] The Austrian economist's concepts helped establish entrepreneurship as a substantive economic activity linking entrepreneurship to a theory of national economic benefit. Schumpeter argued that the essence of entrepreneurial activity lay in the creation of "new combinations" that disrupted the competitive equilibrium of existing markets, products, processes, and organizations.[3]

In theory, entrepreneurship is a business venture where an individual is able to turn an innovative idea into a profitable commercial reality. In practice, entrepreneurship is multifaceted, ranging from operating a small business from a garage, to solving an unmet market need, to turning a new and unique idea into a high-growth company. Entrepreneurship can involve starting a business that brings a new cure for a disease, offering a product or service previously unavailable, or acquiring an existing business with an established market presence and helping it evolve to reflect the entrepreneur's own vision and personality.

As a business venture, the founder/entrepreneur should be able to unambiguously answer the following key "vision" questions:

- What is your target market?
- How large is your total addressable market?
- Who will be your first customer?
- What problem can you solve for them?
- How do you design and manufacture your product?
- How do customers acquire your product?
- How do you scale your production?
- How do you make a profit?
- How do you intend to "exit"?

1.2 What Makes Startups Successful?

The prospect of starting a new business is exciting for any entrepreneur. But industry statistics consistently report a 90% startup failure rate over a two-year period. When you embark on a trip, it is prudent to plan your route on a map to ensure that you do not get lost. You might think of an overall strategy as a type of map that plans the best and quickest route for your new startup.

In the author's experience, the concept of the *opportunity window* for ensuring startup success is as it is shown in Figure 1.1.

- **Funding:** You may start by bootstrapping the organization, but eventually you will need external *funding* to expand your operation. If the company looks like a success, it will attract capital.
- **Business model:** Your *business model* is your overall plan to propel the startup from concept to profitability. It is your master road map for penetrating the market and becoming a market leader.
- **Team:** While you are the undisputed leader, you must hire the best affordable talent to round your *team* and make sure you hire people with complementary skills to yours.
- **Timing:** Your *timing* refers to the receptivity of the market to your innovation. If the market is ready, it will embrace your product without much delay or resistance.
- **Disruptive idea:** Your *disruptive idea* should be your market innovation. The idea is your sensational answer to an unmet need in the market. It should provide you with a distinct business advantage.

Success factors in startups

Your disruptive idea at the right market time is your "business opportunity window"

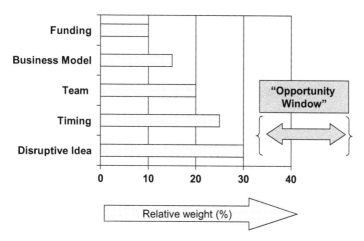

FIGURE 1.1
A disruptive idea (at the right time) is the best predictor of startup success.

The early stage of a startup company is the most important phase of the firm's life because it will determine the evolution of its whole structure. In the early stages, a startup must clearly and decisively define the following cornerstones:

- **Founder's group expertise:** Any weakness in the founder's group should be remedied by seeking outside talent and input from a dedicated board of trustees.
- **Commitment by entrepreneurial team:** The startup team must be willing to make many personal sacrifices to ensure success. It is crucial to enlist this kind of commitment as early as possible.
- **Secure supply sources of critical raw materials:** Does the startup have safe and available sources of critical raw materials, or is that a company vulnerability?

1.3 What Makes Startups Fail?

Small business statistics show that 9 out of 10 startups are doomed to fail within the first two years of business. And amazingly, the figure is the same not just for technological startups but for other small enterprises as well.

Failure factors in startups

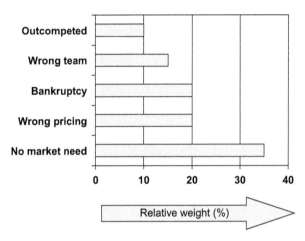

FIGURE 1.2
No demand or wrong pricing are the best predictors of startup failures.

Although there is a surplus of reasons that contribute toward startup failure, there are a few core reasons that are common across all failed startups, no matter the niche. Let us consider the five most common reasons of failure witnessed across almost all unsuccessful business startups, as shown in Figure 1.2.

The biggest single reason for startup failure is *no market need* or poor fit. This underscores the importance of researching whether or not the market needs your product. Literature surveys state that 35%–42% of failed startups are due to "lack of a market (need) for their product" as the prime reason for their failure.[4]

Wrong pricing means either too high or too low product pricing. If the product is priced too high, it will fail to capture adequate market share, thus opening an opportunity for lower-priced competitors to gain a foothold in the innovative product.

Conversely, failing to keep the costs of producing the product low ultimately forces startups to increase their price point. It becomes especially problematic if the startup is offering a "free trial" product in the first place.

Most entrepreneurs finance their startups with their own savings combined with small to medium-size loans from friends and family. Add some failed starts, mismanagement, and employment issues and you've got the perfect recipe for a financial disaster. This phenomenon is commonly termed as being *underfunded*, leading to *bankruptcy*.

An astonishing 15% of startups claim they failed because they did not have the right people in their executive *team*. Inability to find, or afford, the perfect candidate for the job will lead to bad hiring decisions.

Finally, no matter what is your niche, you will have competitors vying for your audience/market. Unless, your startup has the financial strength to establish itself as the go-to product in your niche, you will start to lose ground to competitors and eventually become *outcompeted* in your selected market.

1.4 Types of Entrepreneurs

According to the *Entrepreneurship and Resource Guide*[5] the following definitions provide cross-sections of the different types of entrepreneurial types as follows:

- **Community entrepreneurs:** Community entrepreneurs often involve a number of people in a community working together to address a critical community need. This type of entrepreneurship is particularly effective in rural areas where no one family or person may have the financial resources to help establish a much-needed business or service. Community entrepreneurs may also be involved in nonprofit projects, such as building a community swimming pool, community center, or public library.

- **High-growth entrepreneurs:** During every major economic growth period in history, the majority of jobs created resulted from entrepreneurs operating high-growth businesses. Therefore, communities should not only continue efforts to recruit established firms and branch plants, but also make the expansion of high-growth businesses a top priority. High-growth entrepreneurs connect local communities to national and international markets more effectively than nearly any other existing industry. In addition, entrepreneurial businesses are likely to reinvest their wealth in local communities, while a branch plant may instead send money back to a corporate office or to an administrative headquarters.

- **Hobby entrepreneurs:** Hobby entrepreneurs often develop businesses related to activities they enjoy as pastimes. Hobby entrepreneurs are important to rural Nebraska because they provide services that may be otherwise unavailable to local communities due to the low population. While larger-scale entrepreneurs may look for pools of skilled labor, hobby entrepreneurs often work alone and may engage in their entrepreneurial venture part-time in addition to another occupation.

- **Lifestyle entrepreneurs:** As well as bringing more jobs and increased consumer spending, a lifestyle entrepreneur will often

bring a unique product or service to a community. Lifestyle entrepreneurs often develop a business simply from something they
enjoy doing, which could be anything from producing and selling
crafts to painting murals in baby nurseries.

- **Minority entrepreneurs:** Minorities and immigrants throughout
history have served as vital sources of entrepreneurial spirit that
have led to the creation of numerous enterprises throughout the
United States. Whether creating businesses to provide culturally
specific goods or services or to address a need in the larger economy,
minority entrepreneurs fill critical roles in local economies.

- **Social entrepreneurs:** Social entrepreneurs operate both within
the for-profit and nonprofit sectors. They use business skills and
resources to provide solutions to community and national needs.

- **Student entrepreneurs:** Student entrepreneurs use their abilities to
apply classroom skills in non-academic settings. Entrepreneurship offers
students at both the high school and college levels the opportunity to
create jobs that are more flexible and more tailored to their interests and
time than if they were to enter the general job market. Students may also
be able to provide insight into a market that would otherwise be overlooked and present fresh new ideas for improving existing businesses.

- **Women entrepreneurs:** While many younger women may not think
twice about starting a business, women who grew up in an earlier
time may find the prospect daunting. Women often have special
insight into the marketplace and bring unique skills and interests to
a business venture.

1.5 Entrepreneurial DNA

Entrepreneurs are business opportunists who, through their knowledge,
creativity, drive, and vision, create economic value. Entrepreneurs challenge
conventional wisdom by practicing disruptive innovation—that is, innovation that creates new markets through the application of a novel set of principles. Entrepreneurs change the rules of the game by challenging the status
quo in return for commensurate financial returns.

Successful entrepreneurs guide their fledgling organization in a variety of
methods, such as[6]

- **Clearly articulating your organizational vision**
  - A meaningful vision and long-term plan of action. Organizational
  vision acts as a constant point of reference in what is otherwise a
  chaotic working environment.

- Your organization's vision acts as a powerful motivator for employee behavior,[7] creating a common purpose that helps pull people in a desired direction and increasing performance and commitment.[8] The specific content of the vision will vary with the organization, but your job as the founder/entrepreneur is to formulate an inspiring narrative and then to articulate that narrative clearly, unambiguously, and regularly.

- As well as clearly articulating and regularly communicating your organization's vision, entrepreneurs need to make that vision concrete in terms of values and expected behaviors—motivating their people by reinforcing entrepreneurial behaviors (e.g., dependability, truthfulness, openness, honesty, courage, etc.) and promoting entrepreneurial values (e.g., creativity, confidence, capability, excellence, etc.).

- **Empowering your team**
  - In the entrepreneurial organization, leaders need to understand when to adopt a directive leadership style and when to empower their staff.[9] While overly directive and authoritarian leadership cripples creativity, being too unstructured can result in projects never being realized.

  - At the inception of a project, entrepreneurs may grant high levels of autonomy but set clear expectations in terms of deadlines and deliverables. If the leader micro-manages and displays pessimistic attitudes, entrepreneurial behavior will be stifled.[10]

  - However, as projects progress and ideas and strategies become more concrete, leaders should adopt a more direct approach to consolidate ideas and ensure that the project is completed and delivered on time.

- **Specifying your organizational risk tolerance**
  - When making decisions, it is important to specify the amount of organizational risk the entrepreneur is willing to tolerate. Leaders who work for established organizations tend to be less aggressive than entrepreneurs (founders) and as a result tend to favor evolutionary rather than revolutionary developments.[11]

  - Inevitably, this leads to the concept of *risk management*. Risk management is not the total avoidance of risks but rather the reduction of negative deviation from plans, instead placing emphasis on business opportunities. The focus is on anticipating future potential issues and taking a conscious decision on how best to proceed.

- **Your organizational culture**
  - Every organization has a "culture"—the shared values and beliefs of an organization that influence its experience, behavior,

and interaction with others.[12] And as an organization's culture shapes behavior, in turn, it is vital that the culture facilitates entrepreneurial behavior among the staff.[13]

- An entrepreneurial culture is a culture where motivation and enthusiasm are incentivized and valued. Leaders are to be given the time and opportunity to develop ideas that may fail (the corollary of leaders tolerating controlled levels of risk). Most people become self-employed[14] because they are not given the opportunity to develop their ideas or because their ideas are not valued by their organization.[15] With this in mind, any entrepreneurial organization needs to ensure the culture supports its *intrapreneurs* (existing employees that have entrepreneurial potential).[16]

- **Your chain of command**
  - The *chain of command* describes the line of authority from the top of the organizational hierarchy to the bottom, military style. An organization's span of control is related to the number of subordinates a manager can effectively and efficiently direct.
  - Successful entrepreneurs are able to react and exploit opportunities quickly and effectively.[17] A long chain of command coupled with a large span of control (as in larger, established companies) makes it harder to seize opportunities quickly. Conversely, successful entrepreneurs operate with a low chain of command and grant high autonomy to their subordinates,[18] thus creating a "flat" hierarchy that facilitates fast decision making.[19]

- **Your entrepreneurial team: Composition and dynamics**
  - Contrary to the popular conception of the lonely, creative genius, most people are actually more innovative and effective when they are part of a larger social group and within a supportive workplace that is likely to be their own department or team.[20]
  - Entrepreneurial teams are defined as a small a number of individuals who work together to innovate and exploit opportunities. Venture capital firms rarely consider venture proposals based on individual entrepreneurs but favor proposals from team-based ventures[21] because team-based ventures, overall, have a better track record.[22] In sum, "Entrepreneurial teams are at the heart of any new venture."[23]

- **Intraorganizational communication**
  - Research has conclusively shown that the more an idea is shared with other experts, the more feasible and applicable the idea

becomes.[24] For example, it is common to find that engineers are preoccupied with technical details yet fail to pay attention to the benefits the consumer wants from a product. By increasing the level of communication between marketers and engineers, consumer demand can be met while reducing the possibility of "dead on arrival" product releases.[25]

- Understanding is the essence of communication. Communication is a two-way process of reaching mutual understanding in which participants not only exchange (encode/decode) information but also create and share meaning and direction. Your startup success may depend on how well you communicate your mission/vision to your staff.

1.6 Discovery, Invention, and Innovation

For the founder/entrepreneur, it is important to understand that discovery, invention, and innovation have very different incentive systems.

1. **Discovery or basic research:** An increment to preexisting knowledge. For example, pure scientists aspire to become famous (not necessarily wealthy). Such fame brings them praise, peer admiration, and a place in history. With fame as an incentive system, scientists have powerful incentives to immediately publish their results, thus creating a free flow of ideas.

   Basic research has the goal of advancing or increasing the understanding of a fundamental principle. It has no immediate expectation to yield a product; its intent is to advance knowledge.[26]

2. **Invention:** A non-obvious new device or process. To qualify for a patent, an invention must pass a test of originality—that is, being sufficiently different (non-obvious) from previous inventions. It must be understood that patented inventions do not have any economic value until the invention results in a saleable product. Thus, the incentive is to commercialize inventions.

3. **Innovation:** A market-disrupting way of doing business. Innovations can occur in all goal-directed behaviors such as product introductions, profit maximization, and increased personal wealth. Thus an innovation improves performance in goal-directed behavior as measured by a criterion. An example would be profit maximization in business.

Table 1.1 presents a summary of these concepts.

TABLE 1.1

Summary of Concepts

	Discovery	Invention	Innovation
Definition	Scientific finding	First occurrence of a concept	First attempt to commercialize
Requirements	Hitherto unknown knowledge	Prior theoretical understanding	Market needs Demographic trends
Examples	Electricity Nuclear physics	Computers genetics	Mobile devices Decoding DNA

1.6.1 Distinctions between Invention and Innovation

The literature makes an important distinction between invention and innovation.[27] Invention and innovation are closely linked, to the extent that it is hard to distinguish one from another—biotechnology and pharmaceuticals, for instance.

In many cases, there is a considerable time lag between the two. In fact, a lag of several decades or more is not uncommon.[28] Such time lags reflect the different requirements for working out ideas and commercializing a product. While inventions may be carried out primarily in universities, innovations occur mostly in small entrepreneurial firms. To be able to turn an invention into an innovation, a firm normally needs to combine several types of knowledge, capabilities, skills, and resources. For instance, the firm may require production knowledge, adequate facilities, market knowledge, a distribution system, promotional capabilities, and sufficient financial resources to reach profitability.

Another complicating factor is that, frequently, inventions and innovations are a continuous process. For instance, the modern car is radically improved compared with the first Model T Ford, through the incorporation of a very large number of different inventions/innovations. In fact, the first versions of virtually all significant innovations, from the computer to the World Wide Web, were primitive, unreliable versions of the products that eventually succeeded in the marketplace. In an influential 1986 paper,[29] Kline and Rosenberg point out the following:

> It is a serious mistake to treat an innovation as if it were a well-defined, homogenous thing that could be identified as entering the economy at a precise date—or becoming available at a precise point in time. [...] The fact is that most important innovations go through drastic changes in their lifetimes—changes that may, and often do, totally transform their economic significance. The subsequent improvements in an invention after its first introduction may be vastly more important, economically, than the initial availability of the invention in its original form.

Nonetheless, innovation occurs when an invention is used to change how we live, work, feel, or behave, as depicted mathematically in Figure 1.3.

Mathematical relationship between innovation and invention

INNOVATION = (INVENTION) (COMMERCIALIZATION)

According to the equation if there is no invention (value -0), or there is no viable commercialization (value=0) there is no innovation (value = 0).

> ## Innovation is a process, not an event
> ## A marathon, not a sprint

FIGURE 1.3
Mathematical relationship between innovation and invention.

1.7 Entrepreneurship and Innovation

The terms *entrepreneurship* and *innovation* are often used interchangeably, but this is misleading. Innovation is often the basis on which an entrepreneurial business is built because of the competitive advantage it provides. On the other hand, the act of entrepreneurship is only one way of bringing an innovation to the marketplace. Knowledge-intensive entrepreneurs often choose to build a startup company around a technological innovation. This will provide the financial and skill-based resources needed to exploit the opportunity to develop and commercialize the innovation.

Once the entrepreneur has established a new organization, the focus is to develop and commercialize an innovative product.[30] An innovative product or service must add value to customers or perceive an improvement. An important part of the exploitation process is to ensure that the innovation adequately fulfills prospective customers' needs. The better the innovation fulfills customer needs, the more likely customers are to adopt it. A common mistake technology companies make is to focus on the technological capability of their product rather than on how that technology can satisfy customer needs.

1.7.1 Four Drivers of Innovation

Four factors encourage an entrepreneurial organization to innovate. These four drivers can be summarized as follows:

- Emerging technologies
- Competitor actions

- New requirements from customers, suppliers, and governments
- Emerging changes in the external environment

1.7.1.1 Emerging Technologies

Emerging technologies are by nature risky undertakings. In the past, established organizations developed technologies in large R&D laboratories; however, in today's environment, entrepreneurial companies are best positioned to exploit innovation, since entrepreneurial companies accept high risks in exchange for potentially large rewards.

1.7.1.2 Competitor Actions

Competitors can provide a benchmark regarding which projects and initiatives to pursue. Copying competitor innovations reduces risk because the products may have already been adopted by the market. Although such behavior is unlikely to increase market share, it can be effective in maintaining the status quo by counteracting some competitor advantages.

1.7.1.3 New Requirements

Historically, innovations were developed from the insights of a small number of designers and engineers. Now, however, with greater technological complexity and market segmentation, modern organizations are engaging as many stakeholders as possible in the innovation process.

1.7.1.4 External Environment

All organizations are affected by changes in their external environment; these changes can be another driver of innovation. Environmental changes can occur because of competitor actions that have revolutionized the business environment or through macro shifts in the political, economic, cultural, or technological environment. As organizations struggle to realign with their new business environment, they must innovate their products, processes, and services accordingly.

Example: After the terrorist attacks of September 2001 in the United States, governments across the globe imposed greater security requirements on the airline industry. The initial impact of this new environment was chaos at airports, long lines, and customer exasperation. Airlines and airport authorities had to innovate their processes to meet these new customer requirements to remain competitive.

Innovation came in the form of explosives detectors, capable of detecting trace quantities of explosive vapors in the air surrounding baggage. Explosives detectors are now ubiquitous in every concourse of domestic and international airports.

1.7.2 Innovation Pitfalls

Innovation is critical to any company that wants to build or sustain a competitive advantage. But the *wrong* kind of innovation can destroy profits and annihilate companies. For example, Enron was proclaimed the "most innovative" company from 1996 to 2001 by *Fortune* magazine.

But many of its innovations were illusory. Enron's leaders formed autonomous corporate venturing units, novel partnerships, and spinouts. They substituted recognized accounting, financial, and valuation rules and instead relied on *real options* approaches and *mark-to-market* accounting to create fictitious profits that existed only on paper. We could call that "innovative" accounting.

1.7.3 Replication from Previous Employment

Particularly in the high-tech industry, many successful entrepreneurs spend little time researching and analyzing their markets. In addressing the area of the entrepreneurial origins of high-tech firms, it is hard to ignore the importance of new ventures that spin off from more established firms.

According to Bhide,[31] however popular it may be in the academic world, a comprehensive analytical approach to planning does not suit most high-tech startups. Entrepreneurs typically lack the time and money to interview a representative cross-section of potential customers, let alone analyze substitutes, reconstruct competitors' cost structures, or project alternative technology scenarios. In fact, too much analysis can be harmful; by the time an opportunity is investigated fully, it may no longer exist in the fast-paced high-tech world.

Examples from the electronics industries (e.g., semiconductors, lasers, and hard disk drives) are legendary. Spin-offs of Fairchild Semiconductor (e.g., Intel, Advanced Micro Devices, and National Semiconductor) and the Xerox Corporation (e.g., 3Com and Adobe) are examples of this intriguing phenomenon.

1.7.4 Impact of Geographic Location

Geographic location is also important to new venture creation for reasons other than knowledge replication. Certain geographic areas may be associated with different cultures of risk-taking and career norms, which may differ even within technology-intensive regions (e.g., Silicon Valley vs. Boston's Route 128 area).[32]

According to GEM's "2016 Global Report,"[33] we can assess innovation activity according to two dimensions—geographic region and economic development level—among the participating economies in the survey, as depicted in Table 1.2.

TABLE 1.2

Nexus between Geographic Location and Innovation (Excluding Kuwait, Latvia, and Turkey)

	Innovation-driven economies • Business sophistication • Innovation	Factor-driven economies • Institutions • Infrastructure • Macroeconomic stability • Health and primary education	Efficiency-driven economies • Higher education and training • Goods market efficiency • Labor market efficiency • Financial market sophistication • Technological readiness • Market size
North America	United States, Canada		
European Union	Austria, Belgium, Denmark, Estonia, Finland, France, Germany, Greece, Ireland, Italy, Luxembourg, the Netherlands, Portugal, Slovenia, Slovakia, Spain, Sweden, United Kingdom	None	Croatia, Hungary, Lithuania, Poland, Romania
Latin America and Caribbean	Puerto Rico, Trinidad, Tobago	Bolivia	Argentina, Barbados, Belize, Brazil, Chile, Colombia, Costa Rica, Ecuador, El Salvador, Guatemala, Jamaica, Mexico, Panama, Peru, Suriname, Uruguay
Asia and Oceania	Australia, Japan, Singapore, Taiwan, Qatar		
Non–European Union	Norway, Switzerland		
Africa	None	Angola, Botswana, Cameroon, Uganda	South Africa

The GEM report proposes that entrepreneurship dynamics can be linked to conditions that enhance (or hinder) new business creation. In the GEM's methodology these conditions are known as *entrepreneurial framework conditions* (EFCs). EFCs are one of the most important components of any entrepreneurship ecosystem and constitute "the necessary oxygen of resources, incentives, markets and supporting institutions for the creation and growth of new firms."[34]

The EFCs can be considered an essential part of the puzzle that understanding businesses' creation and growth represents. The state of these conditions directly influences the existence of entrepreneurial opportunities, capacities, and preferences, which in turn determines business dynamics. Hence, it is expected that different economies and regions have different structures and qualities of EFCs or different "rules of the game"[35] that directly affect entrepreneurial activities. This is summarized in Table 1.3.

Entrepreneurship typically operates within an entrepreneurship ecosystem that often includes

- Government programs and services that promote entrepreneurship and support entrepreneurs and startups

TABLE 1.3

GEM's Nine Key Entrepreneurial Framework Conditions (EFCs)

1. **Entrepreneurial Finance:** The availability of financial resources—equity and debt—for small and medium enterprises (SMEs) (including grants and investments).
2. **Government Policy:** The extent to which public policies support entrepreneurship. This EFC has two components:
   2a. Entrepreneurship as a relevant economic issue
   2b. Taxes or regulations that encourage new SMEs
3. **Government Entrepreneurship Programs:** The presence and quality of programs directly assisting SMEs at all levels of government (national, regional, municipal).
4. **Entrepreneurship Education:** The extent to which training in creating or managing SMEs is incorporated within the education and training system at all levels. This EFC has two components:
   4a. Entrepreneurship education at basic school (primary and secondary) level
   4b. Entrepreneurship education at post-secondary levels (higher education such as vocational, college, business schools, etc.)
5. **R&D Transfer:** The extent to which national research and development will lead to new commercial opportunities and is available to SMEs.
6. **Commercial and Legal Infrastructure:** The presence of property rights, commercial, accounting, and other legal and assessment services and institutions that support or promote SMEs.
7. **Entry Regulation:** This EFC contains two components:
   7a. Market dynamics: the level of change in markets from year to year
   7b. Market openness: the extent to which new firms are free to enter existing markets
8. **Physical Infrastructure:** Ease of access to physical resources—communication, utilities, transportation, land or space—at a price that does not discriminate against SMEs.
9. **Cultural and Social Norms:** The extent to which social and cultural norms encourage or allow actions leading to new business methods or activities that can potentially increase personal wealth and income.

- Nongovernmental organizations such as small business associations and organizations that offer advice and mentoring to entrepreneurs (e.g., through entrepreneurship centers or websites)
- Small business advocacy organizations that lobby the government for increased support for entrepreneurship programs and more small business-friendly laws and regulations
- Entrepreneurship resources and facilities (e.g., business incubators and seed accelerators)
- Entrepreneurship education and training programs offered by schools, colleges, and universities
- Financing (e.g., bank loans, venture capital financing, angel investing, private foundation grants)

Not surprisingly, the strongest entrepreneurship ecosystems are those found in top entrepreneurship hubs such as Silicon Valley, New York City, Boston, Singapore, and other such locations where there are clusters of leading high-tech firms, top research universities, and venture capitalists.[36]

1.8 Search for a Suitable Definition of Entrepreneurship

The literature provides a confusing array of definitions for entrepreneurship. There are as many definitions as there are academics in the business field. For this reason, Table 1.4 provides some important definitions by different authors.

1.9 Market Leadership

According to most business startup experts,[37] market leadership is desirable not only for the obvious reasons of revenue and profit but also because it also enables lower sales costs, makes it easier to access decision makers, increases publicity, lengthens product lifecycles, facilitates recruiting, and more. Yet one of the most frustrating issues for a sales force in a startup company is the enormous discrepancy between where the company is today ("Nobody has heard of us!") and actually dominating the market.

The key is to very carefully define a small but important market, build a plan to dominate your market segment, execute your plan, and then target adjacent markets by systematically building a share in a continuously larger market.

TABLE 1.4

Entrepreneurship: Definitions

Author and Reference	Definition of Entrepreneurship
Miller, D. (1983). The correlates of entrepreneurship in three types of firms. *Management Science*, 29(7): 770–791.	A firm's actions relating to product–market and technological innovation
Kanter, R. (1985). Supporting innovation and venture development in established companies. *Journal of Business Venturing*, 1(1): 47–60.	The creation of new combinations
Gartner, W.B. (1985). A conceptual framework for describing the phenomenon of new venture creation. *Academy of Management Review*, 10(4): 696–706.	The process of new venture creation; the process by which new organizations come into existence
Gartner, W.B. (1989). "Who is an entrepreneur?" is the wrong question. *Entrepreneurship: Theory & Practice*, 13(4): 47–68.	
Schuler, R.S. (1986). Fostering and facilitating entrepreneurship in organizations: Implications for organization structure and HRM practices. *Human Resource Management*, 25(4): 607–629.	The practice of creating or innovating new products or services within existing businesses or within newly forming businesses
Stevenson, H.H. & Jarillo, J.C. (1990). A paradigm of entrepreneurship: Entrepreneurial management. *Strategic Management Journal*, 11(special issue): 17–27.	The process by which individuals, either on their own or inside organizations, pursue opportunities without regard to the resources they currently control
Jones, G.R. & Butler, J.E. (1992). Managing internal corporate entrepreneurship: An agency theory perspective. *Journal of Management*, 18(4): 733–749.	The process by which firms notice opportunities and act to creatively organize transactions between factors of production so as to create surplus value
Krueger, N.F. & Brazeal, D.V. (1994). Entrepreneurial potential and potential entrepreneurs. *Entrepreneurship: Theory & Practice*, 18(3): 91–104.	The pursuit of an opportunity irrespective of existing resources
Kouriloff, M. (2000). Exploring perceptions of a priori barriers to entrepreneurship: a multidisciplinary approach. *Entrepreneurship: Theory & Practice*, 25(2): 59–79.	The process of creating a new venture
Shane, S. & Venkataraman, S. (2000). The promise of entrepreneurship as a field of research. *Academy of Management Review*, 25(1): 217–226.	The discovery, creation, and exploitation (including by whom and with what consequences) of opportunities to bring into existence future goods and services
Low, M.B. (2001). The adolescence of entrepreneurship research: specification of purpose. *Entrepreneurship: Theory & Practice*, 25(4): 17–25.	The creation of a new enterprise
Yetisen, A.K., Volpatti, L.R., Coskun, L.R., Cho, S., Kamrani, E., Butt, H., Khademhosseini, A., & Yun, S.H. (2015). Entrepreneurship. *Lab on a Chip*, 15(18): 3638–60.	The process of designing, launching, and running a new business, which typically begins as a small business, such as a startup company, offering a product, process, or service for sale or hire, and the people who do so (entrepreneurs)

By choosing your target market, working diligently to dominate that segment, then carefully choosing adjacent markets and working diligently to dominate them, you can eventually reach the position to which you aspire. This reasoning may sound counterintuitive and risky. Many startup entrepreneurs feel that they cannot afford to ignore any potential buyer and that the more markets they cover the better. Unfortunately, experience shows that such a strategy almost always leads to failure—failure to "own" a market, failure to achieve significant traction in a specific market, and inevitably failure to produce a "must-have" product.

1.9.1 Choosing Your Target Market

Choosing your target market is one of the hardest strategic tasks, yet many startups ignore this crucial step and rush to market with a product that they feel is suited to anyone. Choose instead to introduce a highly differentiated product that can lead to early victories. Steps in choosing your target market are shown in Table 1.5.

1.9.2 Expected Growth

Be prepared for the first period in operation to be strenuous. Not just for a few weeks, but maybe for months and years. Then you'll really notice the benefits of having worked thoroughly with the business plan. But you also have to be able to take action on the fly and get help when this is wise.

As a newly established business, export and expansion are probably not the first things you think of. But in the medium term, it may be worth looking a bit beyond the market you have established yourself in. It may be regional, national, or international expansion. Do not consider a geographic expansion before you have fully exploited the potentials of the domestic market.

TABLE 1.5

Sequential Steps in Choosing Your Target Market

- Select your optimal candidate industries/markets.
- Segment your markets based on objective criteria.
- Define the key characteristics of each segment.
- Determine your optimal category and focus on the selected category.
- Shortlist and size the segments.
- Select your first target market and segment.
- Project your market share and competitors' shares.
- Understand your customer and their needs.
- Develop the go-to-market strategy: sales.
- Develop the go-to-market strategy: marketing.
- Determine your optimal price strategy.
- Finalize your market size and share projections.

Ideally, you should have available production, capital, and management capacity before you concentrate on other geographical markets. You should have a strong position on the domestic market in terms of customer loyalty and profitability. Today, exports and imports are far more than the trade and import of goods to and from abroad. In an increasingly globalized world, even very small and newly established businesses can engage in cross-border trading without major problems. In some cases, international trade can be a part of the business concept of the establishment. With the Internet as a communication channel, it is feasible to buy services in countries with high competence and low labor costs.

1.10 What is Your Exit DNA?

The truth about investors is that they are a pain the neck. They will want a never-ending amount of financial data, to be named on the Board of Directors, to get their investment back in record time, but most of all they want an *exit strategy* before they even look at you. This is illustrated in Figure 1.4.

There are basically two types of exit strategies: either you go public or you are acquired. The media will always focus on the big exits, worth billions of dollars, but exits are generally not that spectacular.

Your Exit DNA

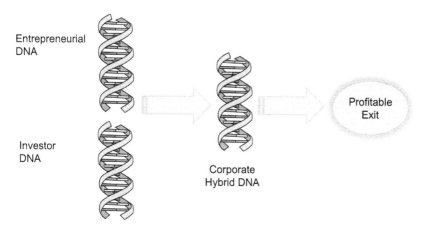

FIGURE 1.4
Your most profitable exit will depend on a mixture of your entrepreneurial approach, coupled with your investor's demands.

Most exits are in the order of $100 million or lower. According to the Mergerstat database, the following high-tech exits were under $30 million.

- Google bought Adscape for $23 million (now AdSense).
- Google bought Blogger for $20 million.
- Google bought Picasa for $5 million.
- Yahoo bought Oddpost for $20 million.
- Ask Jeeves bought LiveJournal for $25 million.
- Yahoo bought Flickr for $30 million.
- AOL bought Weblogs for $25 million.
- Yahoo bought del.icio.us for $30–35 million.
- Google bought Writely for $10 million.
- Google bought MeasureMap for less than $5 million.
- Yahoo bought WebJay for around $1 million.
- Yahoo bought Jumpcut for $15 million.

A common misunderstanding about exits is that you have to grow the company to be profitable or grow it to be larger than $X million of revenue before you can exit. The real threshold is to "prove your business model." In a recurring revenue business, for example, you have a history that clearly shows actual results for

1. Revenue per customer
2. Gross margin per customer
3. Customer lifetime (or churn)
4. Cost of customer acquisition

In other words, how much is a customer worth to the business, and what do they cost to acquire?

With that data, you can clearly prove a credible projection that shows that

- if the new owners can add $X million of capital, the business
- Will have Y customers
- Will generate $YY revenue
- Will be worth $Z million on a discounted cash flow basis

Bottom line: When you can have a reasonable negotiation on enterprise value, you can sell your business at an optimal price.

Notes

1. *Business Dictionary.* (2018). Entrepreneurship. http://www.businessdictionary. com/definition/entrepreneurship.html.
2. Schumpeter, J. (1942). *Capitalism, Socialism, and Democracy.* New York: Harper.
3. Schumpeter, J. (1947). The creative response in economic history. *The Journal of Economic History,* 7: 149–159.
4. https://www.inventorsdigest.com/articles/many-start-ups-fail-two-surveys-highlight-common-factors/.
5. T. Osborne. (2005). Entrepreneurship and resource guide. https://www.scribd. com/document/268021545/Entrepreneur-Handbook.
6. META. (2013). The entrepreneurial organization: What it is and why it matters. http://www.metaprofiling.com/docs/The-Entrepreneurial-Organization.pdf.
7. Bennis, W., and Nanus, B. (1985). *Leaders: The Strategies for Taking Charge.* New York: Harper & Row.
8. Kirkpatrick, S. A., and Locke, E. A. (1996). Direct and indirect effects of three core charismatic leadership components on performance and attitudes. *Journal of Applied Psychology,* 81(1), 36–51.
9. Hmieleski, K. M., and Ensley, M. D. (2007). A contextual examination of new venture performance: Entrepreneur leadership behavior, top management team heterogeneity, and environmental dynamism. *Journal of Organizational Behavior,* 28(7), 865–889.
10. Kim, H., and Yukl, G. (1995). Relationships of managerial effectiveness and advancement to self-reported and subordinate-reported leadership behaviors from the multiple-linkage mode. *The Leadership Quarterly,* 6(3), 361–377.
11. Busenitz, L. W., and Barney, J. B. (1994). Biases and heuristics in strategic decision making: Differences between entrepreneurs and managers in large organizations. *Academy of Management Proceedings,* (1), 85–89.
12. Pettigrew, A. M. (1979). On studying organizational cultures. *Administrative Science Quarterly,* 24, 570–81.
13. Schneider, B., Ehrhart, M. G., and Macey, W. H. (2013). Organizational climate and culture. *Annual Review of Psychology,* 64, 361–388.
14. Beugelsdijk, S., and Noorderhaven, N. (2005). Personality characteristics of self-employed: An empirical study. *Small Business Economics,* 24(2), 159–167.
15. Pinchot, G., and Pinchot, E. (1978). Intra-corporate entrepreneurship. Tarrytown School of Entrepreneurs. http://www.intrapreneur.com/MainPages/History/IntraCorp.html (retrieved August 17, 2013).
16. Menzel, H. C., Aaltio, I., and Ulijn, J. M. (2007). On the way to creativity: Engineers as intrapreneurs in organizations. *Technovation,* 27(12), 732–743.
17. Chell, E. (2008). *The Entrepreneurial Personality: A Social Construction.* New York: Routledge.
18. Gupta, A., Cozza, R., Nguyen, T. H., Milanesi, C., and Lu, C. K. (2013). *Market Share Analysis: Mobile Phones, Worldwide, 4Q12 and 2012.* Stamford, CT: Gartner.
19. Anderson, C., and Brown, C. E. (2010). The functions and dysfunctions of hierarchy. *Research in Organizational Behavior,* 30, 55–89.
20. Leenders, R. T. A., Van Engelen, J. M., and Kratzer, J. (2003). Virtuality, communication, and new product team creativity: A social network perspective. *Journal of Engineering and Technology Management,* 20(1), 69–92.

21. Kamm, J. B., and Nurick, A. J. (1993). The stages of team venture formation: A decision-making model. *Entrepreneurship Theory and Practice*, 17, 17–28.
22. Timmons, J. (1994). *New Venture Creation: Entrepreneurship for the 21st Century*. Irwin.
23. Cooper, A. C., and Daily, C. M. (1997). Entrepreneurial teams. In D. L. Sexton and R. W. Smilor (Eds.), *Entrepreneurship 2000* (pp. 127–150). Chicago, IL: Dearborn Publishing.
24. Sáenz, J., Aramburu, N., and Rivera, O. (2009). Knowledge sharing and innovation performance: A comparison between high-tech and low-tech companies. *Journal of Intellectual Capital*, 10(1), 22–36.
25. Menzel, H. C., Aaltio, I., and Ulijn, J. M. (2007). On the way to creativity: Engineers as intrapreneurs in organizations. *Technovation*, 27(12), 732–743.
26. Wikipedia. Basic research. https://en.wikipedia.org/wiki/Basic_research.
27. Fagerberg, J. Innovation: A guide to the literature. Working Papers on Innovation Studies 2003. Centre for Technology, Innovation and Culture, University of Oslo, Norway.http://folk.uio.no/janf/downloadable_papers/03fagerberg_innovation_ottawa.pdf.
28. Rogers, E. (1995). *Diffusion of Innovations*, 4th ed. New York: The Free Press.
29. Kline, S. J., and Rosenberg, N. (1986). An overview of innovation. In R. Landau and N. Rosenberg (Eds.), *The Positive Sum Strategy: Harnessing Technology for Economic Growth*. Washington, DC: National Academy Press (pp. 275–304).
30. O'Sullivan. (2008). Defining innovation. https://www.scribd.com/document/283731003/Defining-innovation-O-Sullivan-2008.
31. Bhide, A. (1994). How entrepreneurs craft strategies that work. *Harvard Business Review*, 72, 150–161.
32. Saxenian, A. (1994). *Regional Advantage Culture and Competition in Silicon Valley and Route 128*. Cambridge, MA: Harvard University Press.
33. GEM. 2016 global report. http://www.babson.edu/Academics/centers/blank-center/global-research/gem/Documents/GEM%202014%20Global%20Report.pdf.
34. Bosma, N., Acs, Z. J., Autio, E., Coduras, A., and Levie, J. (2009). Global Entrepreneurship Monitor 2008 executive report. London Business School, London; Universidad del Desarrollo, Santiago; and Babson College, Wellesley, MA. http://entreprenorskapsforum.se/wp-content/uploads/2010/02/GEM-Global-Report_2008.pdf.
35. Baumol, W. J. (1990). Entrepreneurship: Productive, unproductive, and destructive. *Journal of Political Economy*, 98(5), Part 1, 893–921. http://www.colorado.edu/ibs/es/alston/econ4504/readings/Baumol%201990.pdf.
36. National Venture Capital Association and PricewaterhouseCoopers. (2016). Venture investment: Regional aggregate data. https://nvca.org/research/venture-monitor/.
37. Candia, T. (2012). *Starting Your Start-Up: Book 2*. E-book edited by Georgia C. Stelluto, IEEE-USA Publishing Manager. IEEE-USA.

2

External Factors Affecting the Entrepreneurial Ecosystem

2.1 Introduction

The concept of the *entrepreneurial ecosystem* can be traced back to the study of industry clustering and the development of national innovation systems in the 1990s. Since then, the term has been used by researchers to describe the conditions that helped to bring people together and foster economic prosperity and wealth creation.[1]

In 2010, Professor Daniel Isenberg[2,3,4] from Babson College published an influential article in the *Harvard Business Review* that helped boost awareness of the concept. Table 2.1 shows the major elements considered important to the generation of an entrepreneurial ecosystem.

Most economists agree that entrepreneurship is essential to the vitality of any economy, developed or developing. Entrepreneurs create new businesses, generating jobs for themselves and those they employ. In many cases, entrepreneurial activity increases competition and, with technological or operational changes, can increase productivity as well.[5]

In the United States, for example, small businesses provide approximately 75% of the net new jobs added to the U.S. economy each year and represent over 99% of all U.S. employers. Most small businesses in the United States are founded by entrepreneurs.

Entrepreneurs innovate, and innovation is a crucial ingredient in economic growth. Entrepreneurs are credited for the commercial introduction of many new products and services and for opening entirely new markets. History shows that entrepreneurs were essential to many of the most significant innovations, ones that revolutionized how people live and work. From the automobile to the airplane to personal computers to wireless communications, individuals with vision and determination developed these commercial advances.

Small firms in the United States, for instance, innovate far more than large ones do. According to the Small Business Administration (SBA), small technology companies produce nearly 13 times more patents per employee

TABLE 2.1

Components of Entrepreneurial Ecosystems

Accessible Markets	**Human Capital/Workforce**
Domestic market: large companies as customers	Management talent
Domestic market: small/medium-sized	Technical talent
companies as customers	Entrepreneurial culture
Domestic market: governments as customers	Outsourcing availability
Foreign market: large companies as customers	Access to immigrant workforce
Foreign market: small/medium-sized companies	
as customers	
Foreign market: governments as customers	
Funding and Finance Sources	**Support Systems**
Friends and family	Mentors/advisors
Angel investors	Professional services
Private equity	Incubators/accelerators
Venture capital	Network of entrepreneurial peers
Access to public markets	
Regulatory Framework and Infrastructure	**Education and Training**
Ease of starting a business	Vocational training
Tax incentives	Available workforce with pre-university
Business-friendly legislation/policies	education
Access to basic infrastructure (e.g., water,	Available workforce with university
electricity)	education
Access to telecommunications/broadband	Entrepreneur-specific training
Access to transport	
Major Universities as Catalysts	**Cultural Atmosphere and Support**
Major universities promoting a culture of respect	Tolerance of risk and failure
for entrepreneurship	Preference for self-employment
Major universities playing a key role in idea	Success stories/role models
formation for new companies	Research culture
Major universities playing a key role in providing	Positive image of entrepreneurship
graduates for new companies	Celebration and reward of innovation
Major universities as technology transfer source	

than large firms. They represent one-third of all companies in possession of 15 or more patents. International and regional institutions, such as the United Nations and the Organisation for Economic Co-operation and Development (OECD), agree that entrepreneurs can play a crucial role in mobilizing resources and promoting economic growth and socioeconomic development. This is particularly true in the developing world, where successful small businesses are the primary engines of job creation and poverty reduction.

The SBA is a U.S. government agency[6] that provides support to entrepreneurs and small businesses. The mission of the SBA is "to maintain and strengthen the nation's economy by enabling the establishment and viability of small businesses and by assisting in the economic recovery of communities after disasters." The agency's activities are summarized as the "three Cs" of capital, contracts, and counseling.

SBA loans are made through banks, credit unions, and other lenders who partner with the SBA. The SBA provides a government-backed guarantee on part of the loan. Under the Recovery Act and the Small Business Jobs Act, SBA loans were enhanced to provide up to a 90% guarantee in order to strengthen access to capital for small businesses. SBA helps lead the federal government's efforts to deliver 23% of prime federal contracts to small businesses. Small business contracting programs include efforts to ensure that certain federal contracts reach woman-owned and service-disabled veteran-owned small businesses as well as businesses participating in programs such as 8(a) and HUBZone.

2.2 Crucial Importance of Government Policies

The desire to stimulate economic and job growth via the application of entrepreneurship and innovation has been a common theme in government policy since at least the 1970s. The origins of this interest can be traced to the 1979 report produced by Professor David Birch of MIT, "The Job Generation Process."[7]

A key finding from this work was that job creation in the United States was not coming from large companies but small, independently owned businesses. It recommended that government policy should target indirect rather than direct strategies, with a greater focus on the role of small firms.

Over the past 45 years, the level of government interest in entrepreneurship and small business development as potential solutions to flagging economic growth and rising unemployment has increased. This has helped to spawn a new field of academic study and research.

This trend has been boosted by the success of iconic *technopreneurs*—that is, entrepreneurs involved with high technology.[8] Technopreneurs such as Steve Jobs of Apple, Bill Gates of Microsoft, Jeff Bezos of Amazon, or Larry Page and Sergey Brin of Google have become the "poster children" of the entrepreneurship movement.

2.2.1 Business Ecosystems

Starting in the early 1990s, James F. Moore originated the strategic planning concept of a *business ecosystem*,[9,10] now widely adopted in the high-tech community. The basic definition comes from Moore's book *The Death of Competition: Leadership and Strategy in the Age of Business Ecosystems*. Moore defined a business ecosystem as

> an economic community supported by a foundation of interacting organizations and individuals—the organisms of the business world.

The economic community produces goods and services of value to customers, who are themselves members of the ecosystem. The member organisms also include suppliers, lead producers, competitors, and other stakeholders. Over time, they co-evolve their capabilities and roles, and tend to align themselves with the directions set by one or more central companies. Those companies holding leadership roles may change over time, but the function of ecosystem leader is valued by the community because it enables members to move toward shared visions to align their investments, and to find mutually supportive roles.[11]

Using ecological metaphors to describe business structure and operations is increasingly common, especially within the field of information technology (IT). For example, J. Bradford DeLong, a professor of economics at the University of California, Berkeley, has written that the term *business ecosystem* describes "the pattern of launching new technologies that has emerged from Silicon Valley." DeLong defines *business ecology* as "a more productive set of processes for developing and commercializing new technologies" that is characterized by the "rapid prototyping, short product development cycles, early test marketing, options-based compensation, venture funding, early corporate independence."[12]

One of the best-known ecosystems of high-tech entrepreneurial activity has been California's Silicon Valley. Although it is not the only place in which innovation and enterprise have flourished, it has served as a role model for many governments seeking to stimulate economic growth. Silicon Valley was a pioneer of the science/technology park due to its proximity to large government defense facilities and a major university, thus creating a unique industry–university ecosystem.

Today, science or technology parks can be found scattered around the world. They usually follow a similar format, with universities and R&D centers co-located with the park and venture financiers hovering nearby looking for deals. Science/technology parks are strategically planned, purpose-built work environments. They are located in close physical proximity to universities or government and private research bodies involved in a particular field of endeavor.[13] This is so that knowledge can be shared, innovation promoted, and research outcomes progressed to viable commercial products. Most have been supported by government policies.

Governments throughout the world want to replicate Silicon Valley and the formation and growth of what have been described as entrepreneurial ecosystems. However, despite significant investments by governments into such initiatives, their overall success rate is mixed.

Entrepreneurial activity leads to economic growth and helps to reduce poverty, create a middle class, and foster stability. It is in the interest of all governments to implement policies to foster entrepreneurship and reap the benefits of its activity.

Among the most successful strategies for encouraging entrepreneurship and small business are provisions in tax policy, regulatory policy, access to capital, and the legal protection of property rights, as follows:

- **Tax policy:** Governments use taxes to raise money. But taxes increase the cost of the activity taxed, discouraging it somewhat. Therefore, policymakers need to balance the goals of raising revenue and promoting entrepreneurship. Corporate tax rate reductions, tax credits for investment or education, and tax deductions for businesses are all proven methods for encouraging business growth.

- **Regulatory policy**: The simpler and more expedited the regulatory process, the greater the likelihood of small business expansion. Reducing the cost of compliance with fewer government regulations is essential. Governments can, for example, provide one-stop service centers where entrepreneurs can find assistance and electronically file and store forms.

- **Access to capital:** Starting a business takes a lot of money. There are required procedures and fees as well as the initial costs of the new enterprise itself. Therefore, an important government activity is to assist potential entrepreneurs with finding money for startups.

  In the United States, the SBA helps entrepreneurs get funds. The SBA is a federal agency whose main function is guaranteeing loans. Banks and other lenders that participate in SBA programs often relax strict loan requirements because the government has promised repayment if the borrower defaults. This policy makes many loans available for risky new businesses.

- **Legal protection of property rights:** Small business can thrive where there is respect for individual property rights and a legal system to protect those rights. Without property rights, there is little incentive to create or invest.

  For entrepreneurship to flourish, the law needs to protect intellectual property. If innovations are not legally protected through patents, copyrights, and trademarks, entrepreneurs are unlikely to engage in the risks necessary to invent new products or new methods. According to the World Bank report "Doing Business 2007: How to Reform," new technologies are adopted more quickly when courts are efficient. "The reason is that most innovations take place in new businesses—which unlike large firms do not have the clout to resolve disputes outside the courts."

2.2.2 Creating a Friendly Business Culture

The primary role of the public sector in supporting *venture capital* is to reduce the risk and cost of private equity finance, complementing and encouraging the development of the private capital industry. There is major variation across OECD countries in the use of funding methods for SMEs, but the provision of *equity financing* to startup companies is more advanced in the United States and Canada than elsewhere.

Governments can also show that they value private enterprise by making it easier for individuals to learn business skills and by honoring entrepreneurs as well as small business owners. Policymakers can

- **Offer financial incentives for the creation of business incubators:** These usually provide new businesses with an inexpensive space in which to get started and services such as a copier and a fax machine, which most new businesses couldn't otherwise afford. Often, business incubators are associated with colleges, and professors offer their expertise.

- **Make information available:** In the United States, for example, the SBA has many offices, making publications widely accessible. Its Answer Desk (telephone: 800-827-5722) and its website (www.sba.gov) answer general business questions. Its online business tutorials are available to anyone with Internet access (https://www.sba.gov/learning-center).

- **Enhance the status of entrepreneurs and businessmen in society:** Governments might create local or national award programs that honor entrepreneurs and call on business leaders to serve on relevant commissions or panels.

2.2.3 Fostering Growth of Entrepreneurial Ecosystems

Entrepreneurial ecosystems cannot be started merely by the availability of researchers, capital, or modern business infrastructure. Through the 1950s and early 1960s, large corporations dominated R&D efforts and new product introductions while ignoring the contributions of small firms. This model dominated both the East and West Coast approaches to technology startups[14] and government-sponsored venture capital initiatives.[15]

From the 1960s, however, Silicon Valley started a unique West Coast approach to high-tech entrepreneurship, where young, highly educated engineers (both native and foreign born) shared an incomparable, laid-back, intensely competitive work environment conducive to risk-taking for high rewards and focused on mass production and vertically integrated organizations. Speed to market was highly coveted, since it brought first-mover advantage, compared with the lethargic, no-risk industrial behemoths of the time.

The supporting ecosystem sprang from adventurous venture capital investors, more willing to accept risks than their East Coast colleagues. The first wave of successful founders/entrepreneurs in turn invested heavily in the startups of friends and even competitors. The fluidity of employees recycled between firms further facilitated additional venture capital investments that resulted in an open, collaborative environment.

2.2.4 Government Policies and Entrepreneurial Ecosystems

The challenge for government policy is to develop policies that work but avoid the temptation to try to effect change via direct intervention. A 2014 study of entrepreneurial ecosystems[16] undertaken by Colin Mason at the University of Glasgow and Ross Brown at the University of St Andrews for OECD developed a set of general principles for government policy in relation to these ecosystems.

In summary, the key recommendations for government policy in the fostering of entrepreneurial ecosystems are as follows:

1. **Make the formation of entrepreneurial activity a government priority:** The formulation of effective policy for entrepreneurial ecosystems requires the active involvement of government ministers working with senior public servants who act as *institutional entrepreneurs* to shape and empower policies and programs.

2. **Ensure that government policy is broadly focused:** Policy should be developed that is holistic and encompasses all components of the ecosystem rather than seeking to "cherry pick" areas of special interest.

3. **Allow for natural growth, not top-down solutions:** Build from existing industries that have formed naturally within the region or country rather than seeking to generate new industries from green field sites.

4. **Ensure all industry sectors are considered, not just high-tech:** Encourage growth across all industry sectors, including low-, mid-, and high-tech firms.

5. **Provide leadership but delegate responsibility and ownership:** Adopt a top-down and bottom-up approach, devolving responsibility to local and regional authorities.

6. **Develop policy that addresses the needs of both the business and its management team:** Recognize that small business policy is *transactional*, while entrepreneurship policy is *relational* in nature.

2.3 Regional Clusters of Innovation

A cluster is a geographic concentration of related companies, organizations, and institutions in a particular field that can be present in a region, state, or nation. Clusters arise because they raise a company's productivity, which is influenced by local assets and the presence of like firms, institutions, and infrastructure that surround it. Innovation clusters are sector and spatial concentrations of business and non-business enterprises that allow the exchange of ideas and information across product or service networks.[17] State-based and regional innovation clusters are geographic concentrations of firms and industries that do business with each other and have common needs for talent, technology, and infrastructure.

Innovation clusters build on the unique strengths of a region rather than trying to copy other regions.[18] Examples include the life sciences clusters found in the Boston/Cambridge, Raleigh/Durham, and Pittsburgh/Akron/Cleveland regions, and the IT and aerospace cluster found in the Seattle/Tacoma/Olympia region. Clusters draw on the expertise of local universities and related institutions, which serve as centers of innovation and drivers of regional growth, as illustrated in Figure 2.1.

State-anchored clusters are dominated by public or nonprofit entities such as universities, R&D labs, defense installations, or government offices that "play the role of a key anchor tenant in a district" (e.g., the supply web network: Wright-Patterson Air Force Base, SEMATECH Austin, and the Los Alamos Laboratory).

State-anchored clusters are concentrated in a few key states. In 2015, the 10 states with the largest R&D expenditure levels accounted for about 65% of U.S. state-based R&D expenditures: California, New Jersey, Texas, Massachusetts, Washington, Maryland, New York, Michigan, Pennsylvania, and Illinois. California alone accounted for 22% of the U.S. total, exceeding each of the next three highest states by about a factor of four.

The Innovation Cluster System

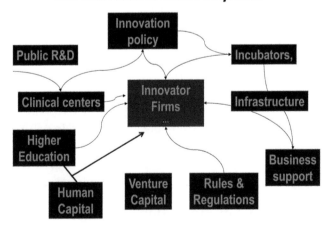

FIGURE 2.1
Innovation exists as part of an interlocking "ecosystem."

2.4 Entrepreneurship and the Internet

The Internet—a vast computer network linking smaller computer networks—has revolutionized commerce by bringing together people from all over the globe. Many of its features can be used to shape a new business. The following paragraphs describe the most salient features of the Internet.

2.4.1 Communications

An entrepreneur must communicate with many people—suppliers, distributors, and customers, for example. A quick and relatively inexpensive way to send letters, reports, photographs, and so on to other Internet users is with e-mail. E-mail can be used even for marketing. Various forms of computer software are available to protect documents from unauthorized access or alteration so that they can be securely shared and easily authenticated.

2.4.2 Research

Starting a business takes lots of research. An entrepreneur can find information on almost any subject very rapidly by using the Internet's World Wide Web. (The Web is a collection of text and multimedia documents linked to create a huge electronic library.) Many government agencies, universities, organizations, and businesses provide information on the Internet, usually at no cost.

The easiest way to find information on the Web is by using a search engine—a data retrieval system. The user types key words for a subject on the computer, clicks the enter button, and receives a list of materials—often within seconds. The items are linked electronically to the actual documents so that Internet users can read them on their computer screens. Among the most popular search engines are Yahoo! (http://yahoo.com) and Google (http://google.com).

2.4.3 Promotion

Websites (pages of print and visual information that are linked together electronically) offer an opportunity for entrepreneurs to introduce a new business and its products and/or services to a huge audience. In general, Websites can be created and updated more quickly and inexpensively than printed promotional materials. Moreover, they run continuously!

To create a website for their business, entrepreneurs can hire a firm to create one or purchase computer software to create it on their own. Many universities also offer courses that teach how to build a website.

A website needs a name and an address. On the Internet, the two are usually the same. Website names and addresses must be registered. InterNIC (https://internic.net) is a website that lists registrars by country and language used. The address of the online business is expressed as a uniform resource locator (URL). It usually ends in dot com (.com), which indicates a "commercial" site. Dot net (.net), an alternate ending, is often used when a specific website name ending in .com has already been registered. Good business website names are easy to remember and evoke the firm and its products or services.

Entrepreneurs also need a piece of property in cyberspace, where the website will reside. Many commercial *hosting services*, called Internet service providers (ISPs), rent space on their large computers (called servers) for a small monthly or annual fee.

Website promotion is critical. A website address can be put on business cards, stationery, brochures—anything having to do with the new firm. Otherwise, entrepreneurs can pay to place a colorful advertisement on noncompetitive websites, such as ones for complementary products. Advertising banners usually link back to the advertised firm's website.

Entrepreneurs also can provide information about their websites to well-known Internet search engines. For a fee, most search engines will promote a website when a selected set of search terms is used. Online shoppers, for instance, often use search engines to find businesses that provide specific products and services.

2.4.4 Safe Use

Just as shopkeepers lock their storefronts, entrepreneurs who use the Internet need to take steps to keep their computer systems safe from the potential hazards of security breaches and viruses. One of the most effective steps is installing security software. Another is setting up an Internet firewall to screen and block undesired traffic between a computer network and the Internet. A technology consultant on contract can install these and other computer defenses. There is a lot of information about computer safety available, and often for free. For example, the National Cyber Security Alliance (http://www.staysafeonline.info), an organization devoted to raising Internet security awareness, offers educational materials and other resources.

As Julian E. Lange,[19] associate professor of entrepreneurship at Babson College, states, "For creative entrepreneurs with limited resources, the Internet offers significant opportunities to build new businesses and enhance existing enterprises." New businesses will develop solutions to enhance the Internet user's experience. Existing businesses will take advantage of myriad Internet applications—from customer service to order processing to investor relations. Lange suggests that, for many entrepreneurs, the challenges posed by the Internet are "opportunities to delight customers and create exciting entrepreneurial ventures."

2.5 Facilitated Sources of Financing

Many entrepreneurs struggle to find the capital to start a new business. There are many sources to consider, so it is important for entrepreneurs to fully explore all financing options. They should also apply for funds from a wide variety of sources. The facilitated sources of financing are as follows.

2.5.1 Personal Savings

Experts agree that the best source of capital for any new business is the entrepreneur's own money. It is easy to use, quick to access, has no payback terms, and requires no transfer of equity (ownership). Also, it demonstrates to potential investors that the entrepreneur is willing to risk his or her own funds and will persevere during hard times.

2.5.2 Friends and Family

These people believe in the entrepreneur, and they are the second easiest source of funds to access. They do not usually require the paperwork that other lenders require. However, these funds should be documented and treated like loans. Neither part ownership nor a decision-making position should be given to these lenders, unless they have expertise to provide. The main disadvantage of these funds is that, if the business fails and money is lost, a valuable relationship may be jeopardized.

2.5.3 Credit Cards

The entrepreneur's personal credit cards are an easy source of funds to access, especially for acquiring business equipment such as photocopiers, personal computers, and printers. These items can usually be obtained with little or no money paid up front and with small monthly payments. The main disadvantage is the high rate of interest charged on credit card balances that are not paid off in full each month.

2.5.4 Banks

Banks are superconservative lenders. As successful entrepreneur Phil Holland explains,[20] "Many prospective business owners are disappointed to learn that banks do not make loans to startup businesses unless there are outside assets to pledge against borrowing." Many entrepreneurs simply do not have enough assets to get a secured loan from a lending institution.

However, if an entrepreneur has money in a savings account, he or she can usually borrow against that money. If an entrepreneur has good credit, it is also relatively easy to get a personal loan from a bank. These loans tend to be short term and not as large as business loans.

2.6 Other Funding Sources

The myth is that entrepreneurship is "the pursuit of opportunity without regard to resources currently controlled."[21] But the reality is that you have been underground for months with your team, turning your idea into a real product with real users. Now you need money to hire more engineers, acquire more users, and scale your company into the billion-dollar behemoth you know it is. It is time to pitch to investors and raise your first round of funding.

If it were as easy as setting up meetings and pitching your idea, everybody would hit their fundraising targets. But the truth of the matter is that most entrepreneurs do not get any funding, much less hit their targets. The following are your best targets for raising your needed capital.

2.6.1 Angel Investors

These tend to be successful entrepreneurs who have capital that they are willing to risk. They often insist on being active advisers to businesses they support. Angel funds are quicker to access than corporate venture funds, and they are more likely to be invested in a startup operation. But they may make smaller individual investments and have fewer contacts in the banking community.

In most deals, angels do not compete with venture capitalists to fund entrepreneurs. Most venture capitalists are later-stage investors and are not looking to make investments in the range of $250,000 to $1,000,000. Angels dominate this early-stage market.

2.6.2 Venture Investors

This is a major source of funding for startups that have a strong potential for growth. However, venture investors insist on retaining part ownership in any new businesses that they fund.

Formal institutional venture funds are usually limited partnerships in which passive limited partners, such as retirement funds, supply most of the money. These funds have large amounts of money to invest. However, the process of obtaining venture capital is excruciatingly slow. Several books, such as *Galante's Venture Capital and Private Equity Directory*,[22] give detailed information on these funds.

2.6.3 Corporate Venture Capital Funds

These are large corporations with funds for investing in new ventures. These often provide technical and management expertise in addition to large monetary investments. However, these funds are slow to access compared with other sources of funds. Also, they often seek to gain control of new businesses.

Corporate venture capital (CVC) is the investment of corporate funds directly in external startup companies. CVC is defined by the *Business Dictionary* as the "practice where a large firm takes an equity stake in a small but innovative or specialist firm, to which it may also provide management and marketing expertise; the objective is to gain a specific competitive advantage."[23]

The definition of CVC often becomes clearer by explaining what it is not. An investment made through an external fund managed by a third party, even when the investment vehicle is funded by a single investing company, is not considered CVC. Most importantly, CVC is not synonymous with venture capital (VC); rather, it is a specific subset of venture capital.

In essence, it is best to think of CVC as a subset of VC whereby a company is investing, without using a third-party investment firm, in an external startup that it does not own. Examples of CVC investors include Google Ventures and Intel Capital.[24]

2.6.4 Government Programs

Many national and regional governments offer programs to encourage small and medium-sized businesses. In the United States, the SBA assists small firms by acting as a guarantor of loans made by private institutions for borrowers who may not otherwise qualify for a commercial loan.

2.7 Strengths of Small Business Entities (SBEs)

Any entrepreneur who is contemplating a new venture should examine the strengths of small businesses as compared with large ones and make the most of those competitive advantages. With careful planning, entrepreneurs can lessen the advantages of large businesses vis-à-vis their operations and thereby increase their chances for success.

The strengths of large businesses are well documented. They have greater financial resources than small firms and therefore can offer a full product line and invest in product development and marketing. They benefit from economies of scale because they manufacture large quantities of products, resulting in lower costs and potentially lower prices. Many large firms have the credibility that a well-known name provides and the support of a large organization.

2.7.1 How Can a Small Business Entity Possibly Compete?

In general, small startup firms have greater flexibility than larger firms and the capacity to respond promptly to industry or community developments. They are able to innovate and create new products and services more rapidly and creatively than larger companies that are mired in bureaucracy. Whether reacting to changes in fashion, demographics, or a competitor's advertising, a small firm usually can make decisions in days—not months or years.

A small firm has the ability to modify its products or services in response to unique customer needs. The average entrepreneur or manager of a small business knows his customer base far better than one in a large company. If a modification in the products or services offered—or even the business's hours of operation—would better serve the customers, it is possible for a small firm to make changes. Customers can even have a role in product development.

Another strength derives from the involvement of highly skilled personnel in all aspects of a startup business. In particular, startups benefit from having senior partners or managers working on tasks below their highest skill level. For example, when entrepreneur William J. Stolze helped start RF Communications in 1961 in Rochester, New York, three of the founders came from the huge corporation General Dynamics, where they held senior marketing and engineering positions.

In the new venture, the marketing expert had the title of president but actually worked to get orders. The senior engineers were no longer supervisors; instead, they were designing products. As Stolze said in his book *Start Up*, "In most start-ups that I know of, the key managers have stepped back from much more responsible positions in larger companies, and this gives the new company an immense competitive advantage."[25]

An additional strength of a startup is that the people involved—the entrepreneur, any partners, advisers, employees, or even family members—have a passionate, almost compulsive, desire to succeed. This makes them work harder and better.

Finally, many small businesses and startup ventures have an intangible quality that comes from people who are fully engaged and doing what they want to do. This is the "entrepreneurial spirit," the atmosphere of fun and excitement that is generated when people work together to create an opportunity for greater success than is otherwise available. This can attract workers and inspire them to do their best.

2.8 Clearly Define Your Potential Market

Market research provides data and information about the industry and its customers, market analysis helps the business owner understand the business environment and the basis on which they must compete.[26]

Market research tells you who are your customers, where they are, and how large is the potential market. Through market research, you will be able to gather certain information and data, such as:

- Demographics
- Size of your potential market
- Customer lifestyles and buying behavior
- Specifically who the customer is
- Demand for your product or service

Market research is a way of getting an overview of consumers' wants, needs, and beliefs. It can also involve discovering how they act. The research can be used to determine how a product could be marketed. Peter Drucker believed market research to be the quintessence of marketing.[27] There are two basic types of market research: primary and secondary.

2.8.1 Primary Research

This is research gathered firsthand through techniques such as surveys, questionnaires, focus groups, or in-depth interviews. Primary research can be time-consuming and possibly expensive. However, it provides the business owner with the opportunity to hear customer feedback and act accordingly (Table 2.2).

2.8.2 Secondary Research

This is research that has already been published. It includes sources such as directories, industry journals, and association publications. Secondary research is accessible and less expensive, can be conducted on a continuous basis, and can be combined with the business owner's knowledge of the business, geographical conditions, and customer base. The business owner can informally tailor the research findings to meet the needs of the business (Table 2.3).

TABLE 2.2

Primary Research Sources

- Surveys
- In-depth interviews
- Competitor analysis
- Questionnaires
- Focus groups

TABLE 2.3

Secondary Research Sources

Available at many libraries

- Business directories
- Industry reports
- Newspapers
- Business magazines
- Trade publications
- Market analysis
- Tracking customer response to advertising and promotion
- Website and social media metrics

Examples of secondary print research sources
- *Demographics USA*
- *Encyclopedia of American Industries*
- *Encyclopedia of Emerging Industries*
- *Encyclopedia of Associations*
- *Household Spending*
- *Lifestyle Market Analyst*
- *Market Share Reporter*
- *Standard & Poor's Industry Surveys*
- *US Industry & Trade Outlook*

2.8.3 Market Analysis

Market analysis helps business owners understand the business climate in which they must compete. It is through market analysis that a business owner determines whether a certain business or industry provides an attractive opportunity (Table 2.4).

Market analysis provides competitive analysis, which includes

- **Industry analysis:** Evaluates the industry's overall opportunity and attractiveness, including ease of entry, availability of substitutes, and buyer/supplier issues.

TABLE 2.4

Sources of Market Analysis

Business Directories
- ACCESSNC: http://accessnc.commerce.state.nc.us
- Hoover's Company Profiles: http://search.proquest.com.prox.lib.ncsu.edu

Demographics
- SimplyAnalytics: http://simplyanalytics.com/
- U.S. Census Bureau's American Fact Finder: http://factfinder2.census.gov

Industry Analysis
- BizMiner: http://www.bizminer.com
- Hoover's Industry Analysis: http://www.hoovers.com/industry-analysis.html
- MarketResearch.com: http://www.marketresearch.com
- SEC Filings (for competitor analysis): http://www.sec.gov/edgar.shtml

- **Competitor analysis:** Who are the primary competitors, and what are their strengths and their weaknesses?
- **Business analysis:** Identifies the strengths, weaknesses, opportunities, and threats (SWOT) of your identified market.

2.9 Selecting Your Optimal Business Location

Location is more important to some businesses than to others. The importance of the location is determined by certain characteristics of the business. These questions represent some of the issues that need to be answered before making a business site selection (Table 2.5).

2.10 Workplace and Environmental Regulations

Limited space in this handbook prevents us from identifying and describing all the workplace and environmental regulations that could potentially affect your business. A few common agencies you may encounter are as follows:

- **Occupational Safety and Health Administration (OSHA):** This agency sets guidelines for worker safety. Failure to comply with OSHA regulations can result in severe financial penalties. Compliance with these regulations are not optional.
- **Americans with Disabilities Act:** As an employer, you cannot discriminate against the disabled. This applies to your workforce as

TABLE 2.5

Considerations for Optimal Business Locations

- How will you ship your product?
- Is convenience a key factor in relationship to what your business offers the customer?
- Is your business offering a special product with little accessible competition?
- Will your product or service require a specific location?
- Will proximity to vendors and customers play an important role in your location?
- Are transportation, labor, utilities, state and local taxes, zoning, and other regulations critical factors to consider in your site selection?
- Do traffic flow, parking, and other business establishments impact your site selection?
- How much space is required?
- Do you need expansion capability?
- Should you lease or buy a facility?
- What are the terms of your lease (if leasing)?
- How is your rent determined? (Rent = cost of space + utilities.)
- What are the insurance requirements?
- Do you understand the local zoning and code requirements?

well as your facilities if you are open to the public. You are encouraged to get copies of the regulations and determine which sections apply to your business.

- **Harassment:** The government and the courts are taking a strong position in trying to discourage harassment in the workplace. Harassment, including sexual harassment, can take many forms. An employee policy that specifically addresses these issues and provides for enforcement can help you avoid problems in this area.

- **Consumer protection:** Federal and state governments have passed laws to protect the consumer. These regulations affect everything from consumer credit to warranties. The North Carolina Attorney General's Office can provide information and assistance regarding these regulations.

- **Environmental laws:** Over the past 30 years, several environmental acts have been passed that impact virtually every business and real estate transaction.

Notes

1. Mazzarol, T. (2014) 6 ways governments can encourage entrepreneurship. World Economic Forum, December 29. https://www.weforum.org/agenda/2014/12/6-ways-governments-can-encourage-entrepreneurship.
2. Isenberg, D. J. (2010) How to start an entrepreneurial revolution. *Harvard Business Review*, June. Reprint R1006A.
3. Isenberg, D. (2011) The entrepreneurship ecosystem strategy as a new paradigm for economy policy: Principles for cultivating entrepreneurship, Babson Entrepreneurship Ecosystem Project, Babson College, Babson Park, MA.
4. Isenberg, D. (2013) When big companies fall, entrepreneurship rises. *Harvard Business Review*, March 18. http://blogs.hbr.org/2013/03/when-big-companies-fall-entrep.
5. US Department of State/Bureau of International Information Programs. Principles of entrepreneurship. https://www.ait.org.tw/infousa/zhtw/DOCS/enterp.pdf.
6. https://en.wikipedia.org/wiki/Small_Business_Administration.
7. https://papers.ssrn.com/sol3/papers.cfm?abstract_id=1510007.
8. https://www.merriam-webster.com/dictionary/technopreneur.
9. Moore, J. (1993). Predators and prey: A new ecology of competition. *Harvard Business Review*, 71(3), 75.
10. https://en.wikipedia.org/wiki/Business_ecosystem.
11. Moore, J. F. (1996). *The Death of Competition: Leadership & Strategy in the Age of Business Ecosystems*. New York: HarperBusiness.
12. https://www.youtube.com/watch?v=0m2c75ohs3s.
13. https://en.wikipedia.org/wiki/Science_park.

14. Vallas, S. P., Kleinman, D. L., and Biscotti, D. (2011). Political structures and the making of U.S. biotechnology. In F. L. Block and M. R. Keller (Eds.) *State of Innovation: The U.S. Government's Role in Technology Development*. Boulder, CO: Paradigm (pp. 57–76).
15. Keller, M. R. (2011). The CIA's pioneering role in public venture capital initiatives. In F. L. Block and M. R. Keller (Eds.) *State of Innovation: The U.S. Government's Role in Technology Development*. Boulder, CO: Paradigm (pp. 109–132).
16. Mason, C., and Brown, R. Entrepreneurial ecosystems and growth oriented entrepreneurship. Background paper prepared for the workshop organized by the OECD LEED programme and the Dutch Ministry of Economic Affairs on Entrepreneurial Ecosystems and Growth Oriented Entrepreneurship, The Hague, The Netherlands, November 2013.
17. Porter, M. E. 2001. *Clusters of Innovation: Regional Foundations of U.S. Competitiveness*. Washington, DC: Council on Competitiveness. http://www.usistf.org/download/documents/Clusters-of-Innovation/Clusters-of-Innovation.pdf.
18. US Economic Development Administration, Regional Innovation Clusters, 2011. https://eda.gov.
19. http://blogs.babson.edu/leadership/2012/02/29/on-analytics-and-entrepreneurs/.
20. https://www.scu.edu/mobi/about/.
21. Eric Shurenberg. http://www.inc.com/eric-schurenberg/the-best-definition-of-entepreneurship.html.
22. http://www.worldcat.org/title/galantes-venture-capital-private-equity-directory/oclc/37106726.
23. http://www.businessdictionary.com/definition/corporate-venturing.html.
24. https://en.wikipedia.org/wiki/Corporate_venture_capital.
25. Stolze, W. J. (1999) *Start Up. An Entrepreneur's Guide to Launching and Managing a New Business*. 5th ed. Franklin Lakes, NJ: Career Press.
26. Birch, D. G. W. Business start-up and resource guide, University of Illinois at Urbana–Champaign's Academy for Entrepreneurial Leadership, Historical Research Reference in Entrepreneurship.
27. Drucker, P. F. (1974). *Management: Tasks, Responsibilities, Practices*. New York: Harper & Row (pp. 64–65).

3

Government Impact on Technology-Based Innovation

3.1 Introduction

Theoretically, invention is the creation of a product or the introduction of a process for the first time. Innovation, on the other hand, occurs when someone *improves on* or *makes a significant contribution to* an existing product, process, or service.

In this chapter, we use *invention* as shorthand for a commercially promising product or service idea, based on new science or technology that is protectable (patents, copyrights, trade secrets, etc.). By *innovation*, we mean the successful entry of a new science- or technology-based product into a particular market. By *early-stage technology development* (ESTD), we mean the technical and business activities that transform a commercially promising invention into a business plan that can attract enough investment to enter a market successfully and through that investment become a successful innovation.

A technological-based innovation system is a concept developed within the scientific field of innovation studies that serves to explain the nature and rate of technological change.[1] A technological innovation system is defined as "a dynamic network of agents interacting in a specific economic/industrial area under a particular institutional infrastructure and involved in the generation, diffusion, and utilization of technology."[2]

Technological innovation is critical to the long-term economic growth of all nations. Most technological innovation consists of incremental change in existing industries. As the pace of technical advance quickens and product cycles compress, established corporations have strong incentives to seek opportunities for such incremental technological change.

However, incremental technical change alone is not adequate to ensure sustained growth and economic security. Sustained growth can occur only with the continuous introduction of truly new goods and services—radical technological innovations that disrupt markets and create new industries.

The capacity to turn science-based inventions into commercially viable innovations is critical to radical technological innovation. As economist Martin Weitzman noted, "The ultimate limits to growth may lie not as much in our ability to generate new ideas, so much as in our ability to process an abundance of potentially new seed ideas into usable forms."[3]

Understanding the invention-to-innovation transition is essential in the formulation of both public policies and private business strategies designed to convert the nation's research assets more efficiently into economic assets.

3.2 The Poster Child of Technological Innovation

If ever there were a poster child for innovation, it would be former Apple CEO Steve Jobs. And when people talk about innovation, Jobs's iPod is cited as an example of innovation at its best.[4]

Let us analyze: The iPod wasn't the first portable music device (Sony had popularized the "music anywhere, anytime" concept 22 years earlier with the Walkman); the iPod was not even the first device to put hundreds of songs in your pocket (dozens of manufacturers had MP3 devices on the market when the iPod was released in 2001); and Apple was actually *late* to the party when it came to providing an online music-sharing platform. (Napster, Grokster, and Kazaa all preceded iTunes.)

Given these sobering facts, is the iPod's distinction as a defining example of innovation warranted? Absolutely. What made the iPod and the music ecosystem it engendered innovative wasn't that it was the *first* portable music device. It wasn't that it was the *first* MP3 player. And it wasn't that it was the *first* company to make thousands of songs immediately available to millions of users.

What made Apple innovative was that it *combined* all of these elements— design, ergonomics, and ease of use—in a single device and then tied it directly into a platform that effortlessly kept that device updated with music.

Apple invented nothing. Its technological innovation was in creating an easy-to-use ecosystem that unified music discovery, delivery, and device. And, in the process, they revolutionized the music industry. It also created an entirely new genre of portable products that ushered in the advent of the smartphones.

So how do you know if you are inventing or innovating? Consider this analogy: If invention is a pebble tossed in the pond, innovation is the rippling effect caused by the pebble. Someone has to toss the pebble. That is the inventor. Someone has to recognize that the ripple will eventually become a wave. That is the successful entrepreneur, as depicted in Figure 3.1.

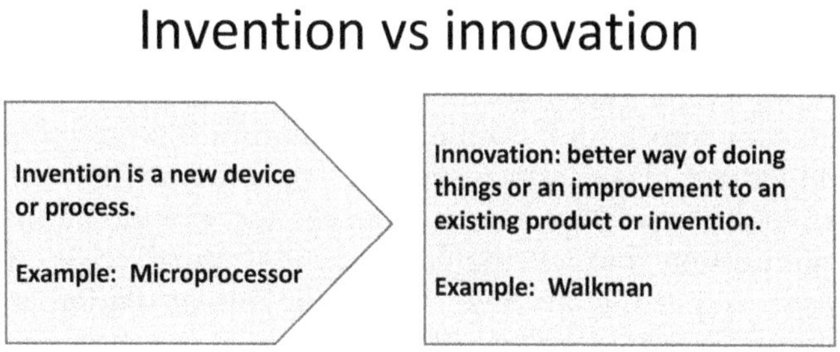

Invention vs innovation

Invention is a new device or process.

Example: Microprocessor

Innovation: better way of doing things or an improvement to an existing product or invention.

Example: Walkman

FIGURE 3.1
Crucial differences between invention and innovation.

3.3 Poster Boy of Technological Failure

Staid, conservative, Eastern IBM was a corporation where executives could "wear any shade of white shirt they chose," where new employees were taught songs of company loyalty, where unquestioned success had been built on a platform of room-sized, climate-controlled, multimillion-dollar mainframe computers.

IBM enjoyed an astonishing 62% share of the mainframe computer market in 1981.[5] Its share of the overall computer market, however, declined from 60% in 1970 to 32% in 1980.[6] Perhaps distracted by a long-running antitrust lawsuit, the "Colossus of Armonk"[7] completely missed the fast-growing minicomputer revolution during the 1970s and was behind such rivals as Wang, Hewlett-Packard, and Control Data in other areas. The importance of microcomputers to a company so prestigious could not be underestimated; a popular saying in American companies stated, "No one ever got fired for buying an IBM personal computer."

The IBM Personal Computer, commonly known as the IBM PC, is the original version and progenitor of the IBM PC compatible-hardware platform. Its legendary model number, 5150, was introduced on August 12, 1981. It was created by a team of engineers and designers under the direction of Don Estridge of the IBM Entry Systems Division in Boca Raton, Florida. It ushered in the era of personal computers, which would revolutionize desktop publishing, word processing, spreadsheet calculations, data processing, graphing tools, and so on.

Nonetheless, despite its predominance, IBM stumbled badly in the early 1990s. At the depth of the crisis, the company suffered its first ever operating loss and eliminated nearly 200,000 jobs. What went wrong? According to Mills and Friesen,[8] IBM disregarded its customers and misled its employees. In their book *Broken Promises*, the authors draw on extensive interviews with IBM executives, access to company files, and surveys of the company's customers to explain why, despite its advantages, IBM's executives failed to maintain their market leadership.

The authors contend that IBM developed an overly optimistic strategic plan based more on pride than on reality; made a financing decision that eventually crippled its industry-leading marketing franchise; destroyed its long-term relationship with customers, to whom it had guaranteed high-quality product and close service support; broke its implied commitment to employees of lifetime employment security; and executed a massive corporate reorganization that left the subsequent strategic crisis unresolved. *Broken Promises* is a cautionary tale of strategic miscalculation, managerial error, and a loss of confidence that demonstrates for executives at any large company the risks of neglecting customer and employee relationships in the face of large-scale change.

3.4 National Institute of Standards and Technology Study of Invention versus Innovation

In 2002, the National Institute of Standards and Technology (NIST) published a report from a comprehensive study of the differences between invention and innovation. The purpose of the project was to support informed design of public policies regarding technology entrepreneurship and the transition from invention to innovation by providing a better understanding of the sources of investments into ESTD projects.[9]

Most of the federal investment into R&D supports basic scientific research carried out in university-affiliated research laboratories. While such investment may lead to science-based inventions and other new product ideas, it is primarily intended to support basic research with potential to generate fundamental advances in knowledge. In contrast, most venture capital and corporate investment into R&D exploits science-based inventions that have already been translated into new products and services, with specifications and costs matching well-defined market opportunities.

The basic science and technology research enterprise of the United States—sources of funding, performing institutions, and researcher incentives and motivations—is reasonably well understood by academics and policymakers alike. Similarly, corporate motivations, governance, finance, strategy, and competitive advantage have been much studied and are relatively well understood.

3.4.1 Transitioning from Invention to Innovation

But the process by which a technical idea of possible commercial value is converted into one or more commercially successful products—the transition from invention to innovation—is highly complex, poorly documented, and not well studied. The NIST project aimed for a better understanding of this important transition, by seeking the answers to two sets of questions:

1. What is the distribution of funding for ESTD across different institutional categories? How do government programs compare with private sources in terms of magnitude?
2. What kinds of difficulties do firms face when attempting to find funding for early-stage, high-risk R&D projects? To what extent are such difficulties due to structural barriers or market failures?

The 31 companies interviewed by Booz Allen Hamilton represented a cross-section of large and medium-sized firms from among the 500 U.S. firms with the highest R&D expenditures, distributed between eight industry sectors—electronics, biopharmaceutical, automotive, telecommunications, computer software, basic industries and materials, machinery and electrical equipment, and chemicals—since these companies jointly fund approximately 7% of all U.S. corporate R&D spending. An additional eight interviews were with representatives from leading venture capital firms.

NIST found the following conditions to be indicative of success.

- Conditions for success in science-based, high-tech innovation were strongly concentrated in just a few geographical regions, indicating the importance in the process of innovator–investor proximity and networks of supporting people and institutions.
- If ESTD investments from all sources are distributed as non-uniformly as venture capital investments, then they are concentrated in a few states and a few industries.
- Angel investments are even more locally focused than venture capital.
- Theory suggests that the quality of social capital in the locality where inventions are being exploited is an important determinant of success.
- Where the social capital is strongly supportive, in places such as Route 128 in Boston or Silicon Valley near San Francisco, one might expect not only strong venture capital and angel investments, but a concentration of federal support for ESTD and industry-supported high-tech ventures as well.
- Since angel investors make the vast majority of their investments close to home, ESTD activities, particularly those of smaller firms, are likely to be concentrated in regions with active communities of tech-savvy angels.

3.5 Role of State Governments

State governments, while providing a relatively small portion of total ESTD funding, play a critical role in establishing regional environments that help bridge the gap from invention to innovation.

State governments facilitate university–industry partnerships, leverage federal academic research funds by providing both general and targeted grants, build a technically educated workforce through the support of public colleges and universities, and ease regulatory burdens to create a more fertile ground for technology startups. While Route 128 and Silicon Valley arose with little local- or state-level political support (in part because they had developed the required networks, stimulated by defense funding, in the 1950s), a number of states have created many of the environmental features needed for successful innovation. Research Triangle Park in North Carolina, for example, was conceived and initiated by Governor Luther Hodges.

These geographical concentrations create additional challenges to champions of ESTD projects located outside of favored geographical or market spaces. Such challenges may be of considerable importance to public policy. The implications for public policy will depend heavily on whether the federal government attempts to compensate for such tendencies toward concentration or chooses instead to accept them as reflecting the flow of resources to geographical and market areas in which expected economic returns are highest. In subsequent work, we will further explore the causes and implications of inter-regional and inter-industry differences in funding for ESTD projects.

3.6 Early-Stage Technology-Based Innovation

A natural starting point for a study of early-stage technology-based innovation is to seek coherent, consistent definitions of the terms *innovation, early stage,* and *technology based.* Let us begin with innovation: "Technological innovation is the successful implementation (in commerce or management) of a technical idea new to the institution creating it," as depicted in Figure 3.2.

According to Investopedia,[10] the following are the two funding sources of innovation.

1. Angel investors are most often individuals (friends, relations, or entrepreneurs) who want to help other entrepreneurs get their businesses off the ground—and earn a high return on their investment. The term *angel* comes from the practice in the early 1900s of wealthy businessmen investing in Broadway productions. Usually, they are the bridge from the self-funded stage of the business to the point that the business needs true venture capital. Angel funding usually ranges from $150,000 to $1.5 million. They typically offer expertise, experience, and contacts in addition to money.

Early stage innovation and funding

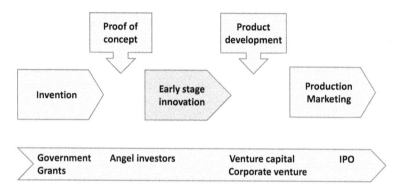

FIGURE 3.2
Your funding source(s) depend on your development stage.

2. Venture capital is a source of financing for new businesses. Venture capital funds pool investors' cash and loans it to startup firms and small businesses with perceived long-term growth potential. This is a very important source of funding for startups that do not have access to other capital, and it typically entails high risk (and potentially high returns) for the investor.

3. Most venture capital comes from groups of wealthy investors, investment banks, and other financial institutions that pool such investments or partnerships. This form of raising capital is popular among new companies, or ventures, with a limited operating history that cannot raise capital though a debt issue or equity offering. Often, venture firms will also provide startups with managerial or technical expertise. For entrepreneurs, venture capitalists are a vital source of financing, but the cash infusion often comes at a high price. Venture firms often take large equity positions in exchange for funding and may also require representation on the startup's board.

3.6.1 Application of Technical, Market, or Business Model Strategy

An early-stage commercial innovation is the result of the application of a technical, market, or business model strategy to create a new or improved product, process, or service that is successfully introduced into the market. An invention is thus distinguished from an innovation by its character as pure knowledge. The direct products of a technological invention are not goods or services per se, but the recipes used to create the goods and services. These new recipes may ultimately be embodied narrowly in patents or more broadly in new firms or business units within existing firms; they may eventually (and in some cases immediately) be associated with products (through a successful innovation).

However, the essence of technology-based innovation (as distinct from both market-based innovation and routine technology-based product development) is the systematic and successful use of science to create new forms of economic activity.

Technology-based innovation thus represents a subset of all innovation, but it is an important one, for it has the potential to create entire new industries. The theoretical distinction between technology-based innovation and incremental product enhancement is based on the extent of novelty in the science or technology being used in the product, where technical risk is greater than market risk. Of course, the most radical technology-based innovations are often accompanied by unique capabilities that allow new markets to be created, thus introducing high levels of both market and technical risks.

Technology-based innovations are also common to certain business models. Thus, a company that defines its business by specializing in a specific area of technology, which it then brings to many markets, will expect to introduce many technology-based innovations. A company that defines itself by its market or its products will be less able to specialize in an area of science or engineering and is less likely to produce radical, technology-based innovations on its own (e.g., Microsoft).

Venture economics defines the stages of project development as follows:

- Seed financing usually involves a small amount of capital provided to an inventor or entrepreneur to prove a concept. It may support product development but is rarely used for production or marketing.
- Startup financing provides funds to companies for use in product development and initial marketing. This type of financing is usually provided to companies that are just getting organized or to those that have been in business just a short time but have not yet sold their products in the marketplace. Generally, such firms have already assembled key management, prepared a business plan, and made market studies.
- First-stage financing provides funds to companies that have exhausted their initial capital and need funds to initiate commercial manufacturing and sales.

3.6.2 Stage of Technology Development

A parallel set of definitions emphasizes the stage of technology development, abstracted from institutional development, although any division of the innovation process into temporal stages is bound to be arbitrary and imperfect. One distinction that has often been employed by practitioners is that between *proof of principle* and *reduction to practice*.

Proof of principle means that a project team has demonstrated its ability, within a research setting, to meet a well-defined technological challenge: to show in a laboratory setting that a model of a possible commercial product, process, or service can demonstrate the function that, if produced in quantity at low enough cost and high enough reliability, could meet an identified market opportunity. It involves the successful application of basic scientific and engineering principles to the solution of a specific problem.

Reduction to practice means that a working model of a product has been developed in the context of well-defined and unchanging specifications, using processes not unlike those that would be required for scaled-up production. Product design and production processes can be defined that have sufficient windows for variability to validate the expectation that a reliable product can be made through a high-yield, stable process.

3.6.3 Vital Infrastructure Requirements

Another vital obstacle facing champions of most radical innovations in the process of getting from invention to innovation is the absence of necessary infrastructure. By infrastructure we mean not only the large-scale infrastructure required for final products in the marketplace (e.g., gas stations for internal combustion automobiles or software to run on a new operating system) but also all of the complementary assets that may be required for market acceptance: suppliers of new kinds of components or materials, new forms of distribution and service, training in the use of the new technology, auxiliary products, and software to broaden market scope. Another example of a complementary asset is availability of critical equipment, either for research, development, or pilot production.

The following is a list of critical infrastructure requirements for innovation.

1. Establishing an innovation-friendly governmental system
2. Establishing a set of attainable goals to focus development and investment
3. Strengthening links between academia and industry
4. Encouraging innovation transfer between research and industry
5. Providing R&D tax (investment) incentives to encourage investments
6. Nurturing local and regional innovation funding
7. Supporting innovation development through public and private investments
8. Ensuring responsive/suitable protection of intellectual property (IP)

In some cases, the requirement for infrastructure sets a prohibitive market entry barrier. For example, an automobile powered by fuel cells burning hydrogen gas would have to have a network of stations able to fuel the cars.

In this special case, the innovation may require government action in order to proceed on a timely basis.

3.7 Critical Role of Government in Innovation

Consider all of the innovations that had to take place for you to read this sentence. There are lots: computers, semiconductors, the Internet, and the World Wide Web just for starters. Where did this innovation come from? Many firms have played important roles in these breakthrough innovations. But another important player, in the United States at least, has been the government. Nearly all of the major innovations relating to computers and the Internet have been the result of government-funded and often government-directed research.

The origins of many technological innovations can be traced to at least an initial investment by U.S. federal R&D support and funds.[11] The following examples illustrate the extent of federal technology innovation support.

3.7.1 Information Technology

3.7.1.1 Google Search Engine

With $4.5 million in grants from the National Science Foundation (NSF), Larry Page and Sergey Brin began work on an Internet search engine dubbed BackRub in 1996 as academic research at the Stanford Integrated Digital Library Project, with an algorithm called Page Rank. After proof-of-concept testing on equipment partially supported by the NSF, the two students sought private financing and founded the now legendary company Google.

In 1998, Brin and Page published a paper that began, "In this paper, we present Google, a prototype of a large-scale search engine." The paper says that Google is "designed to crawl and index the Web efficiently and produce much more satisfying search results than existing systems." The pair succeeded: there are currently billions of searches on the Google search engine. On page 16 of their paper, Brin and Page wrote that their research was supported by the NSF, with funding also provided by the Defense Advanced Research Projects Agency (DARPA) and the National Aeronautics and Space Administration (NASA).

3.7.1.2 Global Positioning System (GPS)

Following the shock of Sputnik orbiting the earth, the U.S. Department of Defense (DoD) realized that orbiting satellites could be used to determine "an accurate position on earth from Doppler signals received from a satellite on a known orbit.["12](The DoD utilized atomic clocks developed by NIST and lighter GPS receivers developed by DARPA to create a military-based system. Later, DoD opened the system for civilian use, creating an entirely new market.

3.7.1.3 Artificial Intelligence and Speech Recognition

The Air Force and DARPA initially funded these related technologies in the early 1950s. Dragon Systems commercialized a speech recognition program in the late 1990s, drawing on years of research and participation in DARPA's SUR program. The popular iPhone speech recognition assistant dubbed "Siri" branched from the DARPA-funded CALO project in the late 2000s.

3.7.1.4 ARPANET: Progenitor of the Internet

First envisioned by J.C.R. Licklider in the late 1960s as a "Galactic Network," ARPANET, a network of only five computers, went online in 1969 with research support and leadership from DARPA. While still a DARPA project, key innovations to ARPNET such as TCP/IP and e-mail paved the way for today's global Internet. TCP/IP became dominant and is now the standard Internet protocol.

3.7.1.5 Smartphones

Much of the technology currently found in smartphones is the direct result of federal procurement and research grants. From underwriting the microchip revolution to supporting the University of Delaware's research project on touchscreens, funding from the NSF's Experimental Program to Stimulate Competitive Research made the smartphone possible. Wayne Westerman, a doctoral student at the university, launched FingerWorks in 1998. FingerWorks was bought by Apple in early 2005. Touchscreen surfaces are an essential feature of smartphones.

The market for semiconductor devices—recognized as a key driver behind the IT revolution—was enhanced by a public–private partnership known as SEMATECH that DARPA cost-shared for its crucial first 5 years. Microchips are foundational components for smartphones, allowing the amplification of signals, the physical movement of data, and computational analysis. Without microchips your smartphone would cost over $15,000 and be the size of a refrigerator.

3.7.2 Energy

3.7.2.1 Visible LED Lighting Technology

The Air Force funded Nick Holonyak at General Electric in the early 1960s to develop the first red LED. The next breakthrough occurred in the 1990s with the development of blue LEDs, which made the creation of white light possible.

The U.S. Department of Energy (DoE)'s Next Generation Lighting initiative helped the development of brighter, smaller, and more efficient LEDs, making them a cost-competitive and energy-efficient alternative to the older fluorescent and incandescent lighting.

3.7.2.2 Shale Gas

In 1980, two U.S. government employees named Leo Schrider and Robert Wise published a paper in which they described work by the DoE to extract natural gas from shale rock. Noting "declining gas reserves" in the United States, the two argued that U.S. shale formations "contain a vast, essentially unexplored volume of natural gas" and highlighted a "DOE–industry partnership [...] that will produce the technology required to stimulate commercial development" of shale gas. Last year, shale provided roughly 23% of U.S. natural gas—a figure that's expected to grow. A leading U.S. natural gas producer recently said: "Early DOE R&D in [...] gas shales [...] helped to catalyze the development of technologies that we are applying today. The Department of Energy was there with research funding when no one else was interested and today we are all reaping the benefits."

3.7.3 Health Care

3.7.3.1 Magnetic Resonance Imaging

Magnetic resonance imaging (MRI) is a medical imaging technique used in radiology to create pictures of the anatomy and the physiological processes of the body in both health and disease.

At Columbia University in the 1930s, Isidor Rabi developed an apparatus that succeeded in detecting and measuring single states or atom rotation and in determining the magnetic moments of the nuclei. In the 1040s, Felix Bloch at Stanford and Edward Purcell at Harvard independently found nuclear magnetic resonance, the phenomenon where nuclei absorb and then readmit electromagnetic resonance. All these programs were federally funded. The National Institutes of Health (NIH) has played a long-term role in the development of MRI.

3.7.3.2 Human Genome Project

This project was jointly conceived and executed by the NIH and the DoE. Federal grants to university-affiliated genome centers were critical to the project's eventual success, fueled by clinical needs.

The NIH was spurred into action by Leroy Hood and Lloyd Smith at the California Institute of Technology, where they invented the first automated sequencing machine in 1986 to facilitate more rapid analysis of DNA. Prior to this development, one scientist required an entire day to sequence about 50 bases. The automated sequencer enabled the sequence of 10,000 bases per day without the need for constant human supervision.

A rapidly developing class of genomics and bioinformatics research was launched. The United States spearheaded genome sequencing and opened new vistas in the study of medicine and biotechnology.

3.7.4 Agriculture

3.7.4.1 Hybrid Corn

As a result of NSF, DOE, and United States Department of Agriculture (USDA) funding, improvements in corn genome technology allowed the United States to produce about 35% of the world's corn production. Breeding and genetic modifications continue to increase yields.

The complex process of sequencing the corn genome (corn has 12,000 more genes than humans) was led by the Genome Center at Washington University School of Medicine in St Louis. While genetically modified foods remain controversial in many parts of the world, the complete corn genome may help improve traditional breeding, leading to more drought- and infestation-resistant varieties with improved yields.[13]

3.7.4.2 Lactose-Free Milk

In the 1980s, while working at the USDA Agricultural Research Center, Virginia Harris developed a method to break down the lactose into simple sugars in milk. This innovative process allowed millions of lactose-intolerant people to enjoy the nutritional benefits of milk.

In the United States, about 21% of Caucasian Americans are lactose intolerant, and up to 80% in Asian and Native American populations. A company called Lactaid commercialized the development, and it shared the 1987 Industrial Achievement Award from the Institute of Food Technologists.

3.8 Fostering Innovation by Government

3.8.1 Ways to Foster Innovation

Governments can foster innovation four basic ways: (1) buying it, (2) reducing its risk, (3) collaborating on it, and (4) using standards or encouraging regulations.[14]

3.8.1.1 Buying Innovation

In many instances, the government's key role in fostering innovation is as the lead customer. The government itself acquires the required systems, products, and services, generally after following a prescribed procurement procedure that provides free competition. As very large and concentrated purchasers, governments have major opportunities to promote innovation.

For example, the U.S. Postal Service and other postal administrations worldwide have fostered innovation through their purchases of advanced long-life vehicles and advanced optical scanning technologies. In many countries, military and space agency procurement has triggered major innovations, including Teflon, advanced composite materials, and advanced sensor technology.

Departments of energy and public utilities have used procurement to foster innovation in nuclear power generation, solar and renewable energy technologies, and environmental technologies. In some cases, states and regions have also targeted specific areas of energy-related innovation to accelerate commercialization and business development within their regions (e.g., the solar industry in the Tennessee Valley, the electric vehicle industry in California, and the packaged nuclear plant industry in France).

Public health departments and hospitals have also led the innovation effort. In Canada, for example, there have been considerable efforts to use procurement to support innovation in healthcare products—particularly for the elderly—with the dual objectives of supporting independent living for the elderly at lower public cost and supporting innovation in a nascent high-tech industry.

3.8.1.2 Reducing the Risks of Innovation

The government can also help reduce the technical, commercial, and financial risks associated with industrial innovation. To reduce technical risk (i.e., the chance that effective solutions to problems being addressed will not be found), the government funds R&D programs and demonstration projects.

Under a project called PATH at the University of California, federal and state governments are providing funding for the development of advanced vehicle control systems as part of the Intelligent Vehicle Highway System (IVHS) program. Similarly, governments are providing R&D funding for magnetic levitation (maglev) transportation systems in Japan, Europe, and the United States. In this case, the U.S. Department of Transportation (DoT) conducted a survey to determine whether the private sector would be willing to finance the development of an American maglev system to compete with the Japanese and German systems. When the response was generally negative, public sector funds were released.

Governments also fund demonstration programs that help to reduce not only technical risk but commercial and financial risks as well, while the private sector gets a much better idea of potential demand for the innovation. Examples include government funding for consumer equipment purchases to support the development of videotext services in France. Another way governments can help reduce financial risk is through insurance liability caps. In the highly litigious United States, many innovations will not be commercialized unless some relief is provided on liability issues.

3.8.1.3 Collaboration on R&D to Support Innovation

Governments facilitate innovation by collaborating on advanced R&D and product development, usually at the precompetitive stage but increasingly at the competitive stage as well. Often a government agency coordinates R&D efforts or innovative technology applications. For example, the two major public sector entities involved in transportation in the United States are the DoT and the Transportation Research Board (TRB), a unit of the National Research Council that serves the National Academy of Sciences and the National Academy of Engineering. The DoT and TRB coordinate the dissemination of information on innovative concepts and practices in transportation systems, services, or infrastructure financing and development through conferences, publications, and symposia. As previously noted, similar programs have long existed in the agriculture and health fields.

The U.S. government also provides funding and support for consortium research efforts such as SEMATECH ($100 million matched by private industry)—efforts that have parallels in both Japan (through the Ministry of International Trade and Industry) and Europe (through the European Council). In addition, cooperative research and development agreements (CRADAs) are relatively new tools that are now being used aggressively to accelerate innovation, with collaborative efforts among the national labs in the United States and private businesses or industry consortia. Governments are also entering into collaborative agreements with their suppliers to develop new technologies and product applications and to share the costs and returns.

3.8.1.4 Using Standards or Regulations

Government regulations and standards serve as important barriers and incentives for innovation. For example, efforts to accelerate innovation in broadband telecommunications capabilities and intelligent network services in the United States and Europe are being driven or held back primarily by government regulatory policy on rates and investments. Patent policy and healthcare regulation drives pharmaceutical and medical equipment innovation in most countries.

Electric vehicle technology and automobile engine technology are being driven by the Corporate Average Fuel Economy (CAFE) and zero-emissions vehicle (ZEV) regulations in the United States as regions recognize the dual benefits of environmental enhancement and economic development. Similarly, environmental, health, and safety regulations are driving numerous innovations in environmental technologies for power plants, automobiles, environmental clean-ups, and recycling.

3.8.2 Broadening Role of Government

Like them or not, believe in them or not, government agencies at all levels and in all parts of the world are broadening their roles and expanding their efforts to encourage innovation and enhance industrial competitiveness. They are partnering more closely with whole industries (e.g., SEMATECH) and with individual businesses. They are also providing more government resources: technical expertise from government laboratories, financial resources, targeted tax benefits for R&D and innovation, and access to government patents, as in the United Kingdom, for example. They are loosening antitrust regulations and not only permitting but actively supporting the formation of consortia of otherwise competing firms.

And they are aggressively purchasing more advanced technologies and providing purchase guarantees. Many projects fall into more than one of these categories. For example, the recent agreement by the DoE to help Cray Research develop software for its supercomputers exemplifies both close partnering and the provision of government resources. This move, a part of the National Technology Initiative, will help the firm with its rivals at the top end of computing power. At the same time, the project will attempt to transfer defense-based technologies supported by national laboratories to commercial uses in areas such as environmental modeling, material design, and advanced manufacturing.

According to the agreement, the DoE and Cray will share the costs of software development. Additional participants in the project will include two national laboratories (Lawrence Livermore in California and Los Alamos in New Mexico) and many private firms.

In the area of technology transfer, a number of laws written over the past decade not only allow but also promote such transfer to the private sector. In the United States, the Stevenson–Wydler Technology Innovation Act (1980), the Federal Technology Transfer Act (1986), and the National Competitive Technology Transfer Act (1989) allow and encourage federal laboratories to enter into cooperative R&D with private companies, to license technology directly to them, and to provide private firms with direct access to the personnel, services, and equipment of federal laboratories to pursue joint efforts in technology development. For many national laboratories in the United States, the recent reductions in defense spending have created a sense of urgency.

Cooperative arrangements play a dual role, both increasing private sector competitiveness and providing a new mission for national laboratories. For example, the idea of using the national laboratories to help the American automotive industry become more competitive is currently being explored.

The Advanced Research Projects Agency (ARPA) was involved in several innovative—and sometimes controversial—ways to foster private sector innovations. For example, ARPA provided $4 million to Gazelle Manufacturing, a private firm involved in making gallium arsenide computer chips for fiberoptic communications systems. This award was an investment under which ARPA became an equity partner and was allowed to keep returns and use them on other projects. In effect, ARPA acted as a venture capital firm. ARPA also pursued projects related to high-definition television (HDTV) as a *dual-use* technology for military and civilian applications.

Additional examples of technology transfer and novel ways of funding are provided by NASA, which has backed more than a dozen industry–university partnerships known as Centers for the Commercial Development of Space. Using NASA funding as seed money, the centers are expected to gradually become financially self-sufficient as their university sponsors and industrial partners develop processes and technologies that can be used both in space and in earth-based applications. The centers deal with a wide variety of subjects: advanced materials, remote sensing, macro-molecular crystallography, crystal growth, space vacuum epitaxy, space automation/robotics, mapping, cell research, space power, and space propulsion.

Yet another form of industry–government partnering is exemplified by a collaboration of industrial organizations with the state of South Carolina, established in response to federal initiatives undertaken by the Department of the Navy. Under the authority and leadership of the South Carolina Research Authority (SCRA), several consortia of industrial firms are working on advanced technology development programs. The American Manufacturing Research Consortium—composed of the SCRA, Arthur D. Little, the Battelle Memorial Institute, Grumman Data Systems, and the Systems Engineering Analysis Corporation—is working under a $93 million navy contract for the Rapid Acquisition of Manufactured Parts (RAMP) program. RAMP's objective is to develop manufacturing technology capable of revolutionizing the way the Naval Supply Systems Command manufactures and delivers replacement parts. Its goal is to design, procure, test, and install computer-integrated systems that can process and manufacture several small-lot orders for new products daily. Aimed at developing the "factory of the future" for the navy, the RAMP technology is reducing the time spent waiting for spare parts by 90%—from 300 days and more to just 30 days.

The industry–government partnership represented by the association of the SCRA with its industrial partners has more than technology development as its operating objective. Like other industry–government partnership models described earlier, the RAMP program has technology transfer as a major goal. Once its technology is proven successful at the RAMP Test and Integration Facility in Charleston, South Carolina, the navy intends to introduce RAMP technology at the Charleston Naval Shipyard, the Cherry Point Naval Aviation Depot in North Carolina, and the Naval Avionics Center in Indianapolis. The army has also expressed interest in RAMP technology and is looking at possible applications for activities in Anniston, Alabama, and Warren, Michigan.

In addition, many defense and aerospace companies, including Westinghouse, General Dynamics, and McDonnell Douglas, have expressed serious interest in the technology and intend to participate in the technology transfer process. This venture exemplifies the potential for state government, federal government, and the private sector to work together to develop technology that is both immediately useful and transferrable.

Unlike the German government, which has actively promoted the formation of consortia of otherwise competing firms to perform precompetitive research—for example, the Jessie consortium for semiconductor research—the U.S. government has generally looked askance at such consortia as potentially anticompetitive. Recently, however, Robert Bartholemy, project manager of the National Aerospace Plane (NASP), decided that the United States had enough competition without pitting American companies against each other. When the 1990 budget for NASP was slashed from $427 to $254 million, Bartholemy won approval from the DoD secretary to pull all contractors from the six competing teams into a joint venture in which individual firms have agreed to share data and to facilitate the transfer of technology to other industries.

3.9 Five Reasons Government Is Important to Innovation

In a speech at Yale University, David Sandalow, assistant secretary for policy and international affairs at the DoE, stated the following:[15]

Why is government important to innovation? For at least five reasons:

First and most basic—because government protects intellectual property, with patents and other tools. That protection helps ensure that innovators benefit from their hard work and creativity, inducing more innovation. In the United States, this role for government is deeply embedded in our Constitutional scheme. Article 1, Section 8 of the U.S. Constitution provides:

> *The Congress shall have power … To promote the progress of science and useful arts, by securing for limited times to authors and inventors the exclusive right to their respective writings and discoveries.*

In the academic literature on innovation, the number of patents issued in a country is often used as a proxy for the rate of innovation. At this most basic level, governments play a central role in innovation.

Second—because the private sector under-invests in fundamental research. That's natural. Time horizons in many businesses are short. Few companies are in a position to capture benefits from fundamental research they might fund on their own. In many fields, fundamental research requires resources available only to governments and the largest companies. As Prof. Henry Chesbrough documents in his book *Open Innovation*, the big corporate research labs of decades past have given way to more distributed approaches to innovation. That gets many technologies to market faster, but at the expense of fundamental research. Without government support for such research, the seed corn for future generations would be at risk.

Third—because innovation depends on an educated workforce, which is a job for governments. Biomedical research requires medical technicians. Energy research requires engineers. Computer research requires programmers. Although private companies often provide specialized training, an educated workforce is the essential starting point. Primary and secondary education is a vital precursor to much innovation. That's a job for governments everywhere. And universities play a central role, with training of promising young innovators often made possible by government funding.

Fourth—because market failures stifle innovative technologies. For example, lack of capital and information prevents homeowners from investing in energy-saving technologies with very short payback periods. Split incentives between architects, builders, landlords and tenants prevent widespread adoption of similar technologies in commercial buildings. Governments have a central role in overcoming these barriers and more.

Fifth—because government policies and standards can lay a strong foundation for innovation. Last century, the United States benefited from government policies requiring near universal access to electricity and telephone services, laying the groundwork for a vibrant consumer electronics industry. This century, Finland and Korea (among others) are benefitting from government policies to promote broadband access, helping position each country for global leadership in a vast global market. New technologies often require standards that allow them to operate within larger systems. The NTSC television broadcast standard and 110 V AC current, for example, each helped market actors coordinate, encouraging innovation. Or consider Israel, which has a teeming innovation culture in which the Israeli government plays a central role, providing the foundation for startups that commercialize civilian uses of military technologies in materials, semiconductors, medical devices and communications.

Notes

1. Smits, R. E. H. M. (2002). Innovation studies in the 21st century. *Technological Forecasting and Social Change*, 69, 861–883.
2. Carlsson, B., and Stankiewicz, R. (1991). On the nature, function, and composition of technological systems. *Journal of Evolutionary Economics*, 1, 93–118.
3. Weitzman, M. L. (1998). Recombinant growth. *Quarterly Journal of Economics*, 113(2), 33–360.
4. Grasty, T. (2017). The difference between "invention" and "innovation." *Huffington Post*, December 6. http://www.huffingtonpost.com/tom-grasty/technological-inventions-and-innovation_b_1397085.html.

5. Salmans, S. (1982). Dominance ended, I.B.M. fights back. *New York Times,* January 9.
6. Burton, K. (1983). Anatomy of a colossus, part II." *PC Magazine,* p. 316.
7. Sandler, C. (1984). IBM: Colossus of Armonk. *Creative Computing,* November. http://www.atarimagazines.com/creative/v10n11/298_IBM_colossus_of_Armonk.php.
8. Mills, D. Q., and Friesen, G. B. (1996). *Broken Promises: An Unconventional View of What Went Wrong at IBM.* Boston, MA: Harvard Business School Press.
9. Branscomb, L. M., and Auerswald, P. E. (2002). Between invention and innovation: An analysis of funding for early-stage technology development. NIST Publication GCR 02–841.
10. http://www.investopedia.com/exam-guide/cfa-level-1/alternative-investments/venture-capital-investing-stages.asp.
11. Singer, P. (2014). Federally supported innovations: 22 examples of major technology advances that stem from federal research support. The Information Technology & Innovation Foundation.
12. Bonnor, N. (2012). A brief history of global navigation satellite systems. *Journal of Navigation,* 65(1), 3.
13. Wilson, R. K. (2009). Amaizing: Corn genome decoded. *Science Daily,* November 21. https://www.sciencedaily.com/releases/2009/11/091119193636.htm.
14. Boghani, A. B., and Jonash, R. S. The role of government in fostering innovation. Arthur D. Little. http://www.adlittle.com/uploads/tx_extprism/1993_q1_23-27.pdf.
15. Sandalow, D. (2011). Thoughts on the role of government in innovation. Yale University, October 21. https://www.energy.gov/sites/prod/files/Sandalow%20innovation%20remarks%2010-21-11.pdf.

4

Entrepreneurial Venture Secret Sauce

4.1 Introduction

"Over the past 15 years, small businesses have created roughly 65% of new jobs in America," proclaimed President Obama in February 2010. Both sides of the aisle have consistently advocated for small business legislation, including the Small Business Jobs Act of 2010.[1]

Many other countries have enacted similar legislation encouraging the formation of small businesses, so it must be true.

Entrepreneurial small business ventures are the poster child of job formation in the modern world. Moreover, knowledge-intensive entrepreneurial small business ventures are the most desirable, since they produce high-paying jobs with unlimited earning potential.

There are three main types of competition faced by entrepreneurs in their ventures.

- **Type 1:** In type 1 competition, entrepreneurs compete with each other to establish firms. The many personal attributes of entrepreneurs that are critical include preferences, income, wealth, judgment, knowledge, ability, ideas, and opportunity costs.[2]

- **Type 2:** In type 2 competition, entrepreneurs compete with direct exchange between consumers. Entrepreneurs will be successful in establishing firms only if firms

- provide transaction benefits that cannot be achieved by consumer organizations.

- **Type 3:** In type 3 competition, entrepreneurs compete with established firms since the entrepreneurial startup must provide incremental economic benefits that incumbents are unable or unwilling to provide. To add value, the entrepreneur must launch a firm that can offer scarce capacity, more effective organizations, better market transactions, more efficient technologies, or differentiated goods and services.

4.2 Entrepreneurial Ventures and Small Businesses

In 1984, Carland et al. argued for the positive impact that small businesses have on the economy, but they also suggested that the impact of entrepreneurial ventures might be even greater. They defined two types of firms:

1. **Small business venture:** A small business venture is any business that is independently owned and operated, not dominant in its field, and does not engage in any new marketing or innovative practices.
2. **Entrepreneurial venture:** An entrepreneurial venture is one that engages in at least one of Schumpeter's four categories of behavior; that is, the principal goals of an entrepreneurial venture are profitability and growth and the business is characterized by innovative strategic practices.

Entrepreneurial ventures can be small, but not all small firms are entrepreneurial. A small firm that does not engage in entrepreneurial behavior is another small firm that lacks the additional impact that entrepreneurial behavior might generate through growth, profitability, and innovative practices. And although small businesses are a significant segment to almost every economy, the entrepreneurial ventures that exist within the overlap might wield a disproportionate influence behind the impact that the small business sector has on economic development.[3]

4.3 Silicon Valley and Entrepreneurship

The publicist Don Hoefler coined the nickname "Silicon Valley" in a 1971 article about computer chip companies in the San Francisco Bay Area.[4] Hoefler began his career in electronics journalism as a publicist for Fairchild Semiconductor in Mountain View, California. He subsequently worked as a reporter for Fairchild Publications, owner of *Electronic News*, and then held editorial positions with the RCA Corporation and McGraw-Hill.

Few areas compare to Silicon Valley as a center for scientific and technological innovation. The extraordinary growth led to lasers, microprocessors, personal computers, video and sound recording, integrated circuits, video game technology, aerospace/office automation, high-energy physics, recombinant DNA, social networks, cloud computing, and virtual reality.

4.3.1 History of a Legend

In 1939, with the encouragement of their professor and mentor, Frederick Terman, Stanford alumni David Packard and William Hewlett established a small electronics company in a Palo Alto garage. That garage would later be dubbed "the Birthplace of Silicon Valley."

In 1951, Varian Associates built a research and development lab on the edge of campus that would become the famed Stanford Industrial Park, now known as Stanford Research Park. In 1952, Stanford won its first Nobel Prize, which went to physics professor Felix Bloch; three years later, his colleague Willis Lamb, Jr also won a Nobel.

Under the leadership of Terman, a professor of electrical engineering who served as provost from 1955 to 1965, the university embarked on a campaign to build "steeples of excellence"—clusters of outstanding science and engineering researchers who would attract the best students.

His role in fostering close ties between Stanford students and the emerging technology industries has led some to consider him the father of Silicon Valley. He created an entrepreneurial spirit that today extends to every academic discipline at Stanford. By the 1970s, the Valley was home to many prominent chip businesses, such as Intel and AMD.

Coincidentally, all of these companies used silicon (as opposed to germanium)[5] to manufacture their chips and were primarily located in a suburban farming valley south of San Francisco. Hoefler combined these two facts to create a new name for the area that highlighted the success of these chip businesses.[6]

In the early 1970s, Professor Vinton Cerf, known as the "father of the Internet," developed with a colleague the TCP/IP protocols that would become the standard for Internet communication between computers. In the 1980s, John Cioffi and his students realized that traditional phone lines could be used for high-speed data transmission, leading to the development of digital subscriber lines (DSL).

In 1991, SLAC physicist Paul Kunz set up the first Web server in the United States after visiting Tim Berners-Lee, creator of the World Wide Web, in Geneva, Switzerland.[7] The Internet, of course, is central to the story of Silicon Valley. Google, the Web's most popular search engine and one of the world's most influential companies, got its start at Stanford when Sergey Brin and Larry Page developed their Page Rank algorithm as graduate students in the 1990s. Before them, alumni Jerry Yang and David Filo founded Yahoo. Other legendary Silicon Valley companies with strong ties to Stanford include Cisco Systems, Hewlett-Packard Company, Intuit, Silicon Graphics, and Sun Microsystems.

4.3.2 Silicon Prevails as Semiconductor

The name Silicon Valley originally referred to the large number of silicon chip innovators and manufacturers in the region, but the area is now the home to many of the world's largest high-tech corporations, including the headquarters of 39 businesses in the Fortune 1000 and thousands of startup companies.

Silicon Valley also accounts for one-third of all of the venture capital investment in the United States, which has helped it to become a leading hub and startup ecosystem for high-tech innovation and scientific development. It was in the Valley that the silicon-based integrated circuit (the microprocessor) and the microcomputer, among other key technologies, were developed. As of 2013, the region employed about a quarter of a million information technology workers.[8]

Silicon Valley is now the most famous technology hub in the world, but it was a very different place before these businesses developed. When the computer chip industry was emerging in the mid-1950s, there were no venture capital investors in the area.[9] Stanford University did not produce any research on computer chip components and the supply of local employees qualified to work with these high-tech devices was almost nonexistent.

Furthermore, the Bay Area was seemingly far behind cities such as Boston and New York in the chip industry.[10] No one expected the region to become a hub for these technology companies. While it is impossible to fully replicate the exact events that established the Valley, its development can provide qualified insights to leaders in communities across the world. Its story illustrates two important lessons for cultivating high-growth companies and industries.

1. **Great companies can develop in unlikely and challenging places:** When the first computer chip businesses were developing in the mid-1950s, the Bay Area was a difficult place for entrepreneurs in the industry. It did not have large sources of funding, significant pools of talented employees, or major research centers focused on the sector. Cities such as Boston and New York had a 6-year head start in the industry. Nevertheless, Fairchild managed to develop in the Bay Area and become one of the most successful computer chip companies.

2. **A few entrepreneurs can make a huge impact:** The story of Fairchild Semiconductor demonstrates how a small number of successful founders can spawn many fast-growing companies. The firm's eight co-founders were directly responsible for the development of over 30 local computer chip companies in less than 14 years. These new firms formed the core of a new local industry that employed a total of 12,000 people.

4.3.3 Silicon Valley Is the Only Place Not Trying to Become Silicon Valley

The rise of Silicon Valley has garnered worldwide attention because it seemed to offer the possibility that a region with no prior industrial history could make a direct leap to a leading-edge industrial economy, given the right set of circumstances, without the time and effort required to pass through any intermediate stages of development.

Here was "cowboy capitalism" in its most raw and dynamic form. The idea that so much growth could occur in so short a time within such a small geographic area sent planning bodies and governmental agencies from Albania to Zimbabwe scrambling to "grow the next Silicon Valley" in their own backyard.[11] Thus, the model of Silicon Valley quickly became the Holy Grail of economic development.[12]

However, this "model" has proven impossible to replicate elsewhere. The Valley seems unique in its formation, development, and proliferation. Ironically, Silicon Valley could not become itself today even if it tried. The Valley evolved under an exclusive set of circumstances:

1. An adjacent gigantic aerospace industry that devoured its innovative products
2. The open Californian entrepreneurial culture
3. Stanford University's supportive relationships with industry
4. A continual supply of inventions from Fairchild Semiconductor
5. A liberal immigration policy toward doctoral students
6. Mostly pure luck

These six factors combined launched a technological revolution that defies the definitive determination of cause and effect.

4.3.4 Immigrant Valley

Silicon Valley is the home of the integrated circuits or ICs; but when local technologists claim that Silicon Valley is "built on ICs" they do not refer to integrated circuits but to Indian and Chinese engineers.[13] According to a November 2016 report by *Bloomberg BusinessWeek*, 51% of Silicon Valley startups worth $1 billion or more were founded by one or more immigrant entrepreneurs. Table 4.1 shows the share of foreign-born employees living in the Silicon Valley counties of Santa Clara and San Mateo.

Historically, the Immigration and Nationality Act of 1965,[14] often referred to as the Hart–Cellar Act, had a huge impact on immigrant entrepreneurship in America, particularly in the West Coast. Before 1965, the U.S. immigration policy severely curtailed foreign entry by mandating small quotas according to national origin. Hart–Cellar, by contrast, allowed immigration based on both the possession of scarce skills and family ties to citizens or permanent residents.

The Hart–Cellar Act thus created significant new opportunities for foreign-born engineers and other highly educated professionals whose technical skills were in short supply, as well as for their families and relatives. The

TABLE 4.1

Immigrant Valley

Field	Share by Immigrants (%)
Computers and manufacturing	67.3
Architecture and engineering	60.9
Natural sciences	48.7
Medical and health services	413
Financial services	41.5
Other occupations	42.7

great majority of these new skilled immigrants were of Asian origin, and they settled disproportionately on the West Coast of the United States.

By 1990, one-quarter of all the engineers and scientists employed in California's technology industries were foreign born—more than twice that of other high-tech cluster states such as Massachusetts and Texas.[15]

4.3.5 Immigration and Startups

Immigrants are widely perceived as being highly entrepreneurial. Business ownership of startups is higher among the foreign born than the native born in many developed countries such as the United States, United Kingdom, Canada, and Australia.[16,17,18,19,20,21]

4.4 High-Impact Firms Universe

A 2008 report published by the U.S. Small Business Administration (SBA)'s Office of Advocacy, entitled *High-Impact Firms: Gazelles Revisited*, found that a relatively small class of firms was responsible for generating nearly all net new jobs in the U.S. economy from 1994 to 2006.

According to a subsequent 2011 report by the SBA,[22] there are, on average, about 350,000 high-impact companies in the United States alone, representing about 6.3% of all companies in the economy. These companies are younger and more productive than all other firms and are found in relatively equal shares across all industries, even declining and stagnant ones.

Though there is no universally agreed definition of *high-impact firms* (a.k.a. *high-growth firms*), many of the earliest definitions were based solely on revenue growth.[23] Currently, as shown in Table 4.2, from the many choices to calculate firm growth, the category can generally be defined in two major ways:

1. High growth as a percentage of growth over a given timeframe (i.e., 1%, 5%, or 10% of firms with the highest growth rate)

TABLE 4.2

High-Growth Firms Definitions

Basis	Authors	Timeframe (years)	Total Growth (Organic plus Acquisitions)
Sales	Siegel, R., Siegel, E., & Macmillian, I. C. (1993). Characteristics distinguishing high-growth ventures. *Journal of Business Venturing*, 8, 169–180.	3 years	Double sales annually.
	Birch, D. L., & Medoff, J. (1994). *Gazelles*. In L. C. Solomon, & A. R. Levenson (Eds.), *Labor Markets, Employment Policy and Job Creation* (pp. 159–167). Boulder, CO: Westview.	4 years	Sales growth $\geq$ 20% each year; base revenue $\geq$ $100,000.
	Acs, Z. J., Parsons, W., & Tracy, S. (2008). *High-Impact Firms: Gazelles Revisited*. Washington, DC: Small Business Administration.	4 years	Double sales growth.
Employment	Kirchhoff, B. A. (1994). *Entrepreneurship and Dynamic Capitalism*. Westport, CT: Praeger	6 years	In the top 10% annual sales growth.
	Organisation for Economic Co-operation and Development. (2007). *Eurostat–OECD Manual on Business Demography Statistics*. Paris, France: OECD. http://www.oecd.org/std/business-stats/eurostatoecdmanualonbusinessdemographystatistics.htm.	3 years	Average annualized growth >20% with 10 or more employees.
	Stangler, D. (2010). *High-Growth Firms and the Future of the American Economy*. Kansas City, MO: Ewing Marion Kauffman Foundation.	1 year	Top 5%.
	Clayton, R. L., Sadeghi, A., Spletzer, J. R., & Talan, D. M. (2013), High-employment-growth firms: Defining and counting them. *Monthly Labor Review*, June, 3–13.	3 years	Grow by 72.8% over 3 years with 10 or more employees. If <10, the number of employees must grow by 8 employees.
Sales and employment	Acs, Z. J., & Mueller, P. (2008). Employment effects of business dynamics: Mice, gazelles and elephants. *Small Business Economics*, 30 (1), 85–100.	4 years	Doubled sales growth with an EGQ $\geq$ 2.[a]
	Choi, T., Roberson, J. C., & Rspasingha, A. (2013). *High-Growth Firms in Georgia*. Atlanta, GA: Federal Reserve of Atlanta.	3 years	Average of 20% annualized sales growth with 10 or more employees.

[a] *Note:* The employment growth quantifier (EGQ) is the product of a firm's absolute and percent change in employment. The EGQ helps to mitigate the bias of computing change statistics solely on the basis of either absolute or percentage terms.

2. Firms that grow at or above a particular pace or threshold (either in absolute and/or relative), measured either as growth between the initial and final year or as annualized growth over a certain number of years.[24]

High-impact firms generate all net jobs in the economy, and their job creation capacity is largely immune from the expansions and contractions of the business cycle. The report also found that the number of women-owned high-impact companies is proportionate to the number of women-owned non-high-impact companies.

4.4.1 Gender and High-Impact Firms

Of the high-impact companies existing during the 2004–2008 period, 11.7% were owned by women. Of all other companies existing during the same period, 12.8% were owned by women. These findings indicate that the share of women-owned high-impact companies is virtually the same as that of women-owned non-high-impact firms. Thus, the success rate for women-owned firms achieving high-impact status shows negligible difference from their counterparts owned by men.

Women have created high-impact companies at virtually the same rate as men. But the larger the high-impact company, the lower the likelihood it will be women owned. This same pattern is observed for all other companies. In other words, women-owned firms generally succeed at the same rate as men-owned firms, but women ownership diminishes with increased size, regardless of growth. It seems that as firm size increases, the "glass ceiling" phenomenon takes a stronger hold.

4.4.2 Distribution of High-Impact Firms

One might expect a disproportionate share of high-impact companies to be found in high-tech industries where technological change has been rapid. But high-impact companies are relatively evenly distributed across all sectors of the economy. No industry dominates consistently in its share of high-impact companies, and no industry other than museums and membership organizations contains a disproportionately low share of high-impact companies.

Mounting evidence now suggests that the principal drivers of job creation are neither small firms nor large firms but rather a unique class of both small and large firms. Yet to focus on their size is to overlook their most important attributes: innovation and growth.

4.4.3 Gazelle Firms

The term *gazelle* was coined by David Birch of Cognetics, Inc. to describe the ability of certain firms to generate a large number of jobs in a very short period of time. (Cognetics commercialized the Interactive Encyclopedia

TABLE 4.3

Best Metro Areas for Gazelles

Top 10 Large Metro Areas	Top 10 Small Metro Areas
1. Phoenix, AZ	1. Las Vegas, NV
2. Salt Lake City–Provo, UT	2. Sioux Falls, SD
3. Atlanta, GA	3. Huntsville, AL
4. Raleigh–Durham, NC	4. Fort Wayne, IN
5. Birmingham–Tuscaloosa, AL	5. Lincoln, NE
6. Nashville, TN	6. Austin, TX
7. Orlando, FL	7. Savannah, GA
8. Indianapolis, IN	8. Springfield, MO
9. Denver–Boulder, CO	9. Boise, ID
10. Washington, DC-MD-VA	10. Mobile, AL

System as HyperTIES, the forerunner of the World Wide Web, and one of the first commercial hypertext systems.) Gazelle firms also display rapid sales growth in a short period of time. Microsoft, Intel, Yahoo, Google, and Tellabs are well-recognized examples. Classic growth companies would be IBM, Caterpillar, Abbott Labs, and Nucore Steel. But, unlike these examples, a gazelle need not grow to be a huge company.

In its fifth annual report[25] on the emergence of small, fast-growth companies, Cognetics identified the best metro areas for gazelles, as shown in Table 4.3.

4.4.4 Mice, Elephants, and Gazelles

Birch used the term *gazelle* to help him distinguish between three types of companies he was observing in his job generation data: fast-growth companies, stable companies, and companies that generated no jobs. Gazelles were the very small percentage (3%–5%) of the companies that were generating the most jobs in the economy. Opposite the gazelle is the *elephant*. These are the large ponderous companies who Birch argues employ thousands of people but create very few new jobs. To finish the analogy, Birch picked the lowly *mouse* to describe those companies with little or no potential for generating new jobs. The mice are essentially the single-location pizza parlors, pastry shops, or gourmet restaurants celebrating their 15th anniversary, as depicted in Figure 4.1.

4.4.5 Common Gazelle Misconceptions

Few segments of the entrepreneurial market generate as many misconceptions as gazelles. Among the most common, noted by John Case, are as follows:[26]

- **Gazelles are all in high tech:** Nope. Of course, many of the most visible small companies are. For example, a sizable percentage of the businesses that make *Fortune*'s annual list of the 100 fastest-growing small companies are in high tech. Those companies (by definition) are all publicly traded, which skews the list toward technology. Overall,

Mice, elephants and gazelles

- **Mice**
  Small, vulnerable, hardworking, little market influence, quick to change direction if needed, very few aspire to grow, maintain their profitability
- **Elephants**
  Large, command respect, cannot change direction quickly, can influence the market place and conditions, likely to be contracting in size
- **Gazelles**
  Growth oriented with above average profitability, seek growth and market share, ultimately become large employers, agile, **'at least 20% growth a year for 4 years'**

FIGURE 4.1
Entrepreneurial companies are jokingly classified as mice, elephants, and gazelles depending on their strategic intent.[32]

though, close to 30% of all gazelles are in wholesale and retail trade (not too "techy"), according to David Birch. Another roughly 30% are in services (some techy, some not). Of the gazelles on last year's Inc. 500, only 47% were in computers or other electronics.

Just as typical were companies such as HealthScribe, Inc. (number 20), a medical transcription service.

- **Gazelles get venture capital:** Well, yes, venture capital firms hope that all their investments will go to gazelles. But most gazelles don't get any formal venture capital at all. The proof is in the figures: gazelles as a group number some 350,000, and even in last year's venture capital boom, only about 5000 companies got funding.

- **Gazelles are all young:** Interestingly, Birch's research finds that as a group, gazelles are somewhat older than small companies in general. Sure, a few companies take off like rockets almost from birth. More common, says Cognetics in a study of gazelles, is a "gradual development phase followed by a robust (but not explosive) growth." Nearly one-fifth of gazelles have been in operation 30 years or more.

- **Gazelles are all small:** Small-business advocates like to make that claim—and certainly new gazelles are necessarily small—but gazelles as a group include companies of all sizes. The big ones (think Cisco Systems, which has grown its revenues at a compound annual growth rate of about 57% over the past 5 years) aren't significant in their numerical totals, but they account for a sizable share of the new jobs created by gazelles.

- **Gazelles operate in national or international markets:** Not necessarily. A study of fast-growing companies in Georgia a couple of years ago, published in the *Economic Development Review,* found that some gazelles did go national or global, but many didn't. Among those that didn't were a catering company and a seven-outlet fast-food franchise. "Most growth companies are in low-tech or traditional industries," concluded researchers Emil E. Malizia and Rebecca M. Winders. "Most serve local markets," says Winders.

4.5 Globalization and Entrepreneurial Ventures

First the good news: globalization has opened up new opportunities for entrepreneurial ventures, and an increasing number now consider trading internationally as an important business option. They are seen as a new generation of international traders. Now for the bad news: globalization has also created new challenges for the survival and sustainability of firms, especially small entities. As more small firms enter the emerging and growing markets domestically and overseas, many face challenges that arise from various sources—for example, the threat of competition from emergent entrants into their domestic markets, frequently competing strictly on price.

Entrepreneurial ventures characteristically have very flexible and lean governance structures. This enables them to make and implement decisions quickly. For instance, in comparison with their larger counterparts, small business entities (SBEs) take less time on decisions to modify systems and processes, produce new products and services, adopt new selling strategies, or reach new customers. Such decisions are usually dependent on technological capabilities, managerial competencies and incentives to invest in new approaches and innovations.

Most SBEs have limited access to finance and lack managerial and specialized skills and expertise needed to operate in a rapidly globalizing market. Often, they lack proper information about technologies and markets. SBEs are often informed about these technologies, markets, opportunities, and issues by their formal and/or informal network contacts, advisers, consultants, and accountants. The services provided by such professionals are costly and often beyond an SBE's budget.

4.5.1 Definitions of Entrepreneurial Ventures, SBEs, and SMEs

Entrepreneurial ventures are also called small business entities (SBEs) and small and medium-sized enterprises (SMEs). There is no generally accepted

TABLE 4.4

Firm Classification Based on the Number of Employees

Country	Name	Number of Employees
United States	Small entity Small firm Small manufacturing entity	<500
Canada	Small manufacturing firms	<500
European Union	Small manufacturing enterprises	<500
European Commission	Micro-enterprises	<10 (<€2 million annual sales)
Japan	Small firms	<250

definition of SBEs and SMEs. This implies that, depending on the criteria used, there could be a few definitions. Most countries use the number of employees as the key criteria to classify firms into the size categories indicated in Table 4.4.[27]

4.5.2 Mobility of Highly Skilled Personnel

There is interdependence between globalization and the international mobility of not only highly skilled professionals but also semi-skilled personnel.[28] Two general trends are noticeable for migrating workers. One trend relates to the highly skilled workers, such as academics, medical practitioners, engineers and scientists, who migrate to the West for better jobs, incomes, and professional recognition.[29]

There is a second trend that consists of technical and managerial personnel who have obtained education, training, and experience in the West and who return to their home countries for work or to create competitive and/or new business ventures.[30] This second type is now becoming more of a new generation of small business entrepreneurs in developing and transitional economies.

The term *highly skilled personnel* is used to refer to professional, managerial, and technically skilled workers who possess tertiary-level qualifications or their equivalent.[31] It can be argued that the global mobility of workers should be seen as *brain and skill circulation* rather than just a *brain drain* from one country to another. The indicated trends in the global migration of workers are both contributing to the intensification of globalization and new venture creation and becoming an inevitable result of globalization.

These mutually reinforced relationships (i.e., worker migration as a contributor to new startups in domestic and foreign economies and as a result of globalization), together with the continual economic, technological, and structural changes taking place in most of the economies, suggest that the phenomenon of brain and skill circulation is becoming more important and spreading out to many regions of the world. More globalization of workers is inevitable. This phenomenon should lead to the formation of more new SBEs and startups globally. The global mobility of workers, and particularly highly skilled personnel that seek jobs in the international markets, may be a social engineering issue. But it is becoming a new source of business entrepreneurs across many nations.

Many SBEs are owned and operated by such migrant workers. A number of the more entrepreneurially skilled and semi-skilled migrant workers set up their own business ventures in their host countries. Although data is not available to support this claim, it can be argued that the global mobility of workers contributes to the formation of new SBEs in many economies.

Developing a more clear understanding of this complex issue will certainly benefit policymakers. Most policymakers operate with policies that help to optimize the benefits of overseas training programs and the mobility of highly skilled personnel while at the same time preventing the loss of their best brains. How to leverage the entrepreneurial capabilities of skilled and semi-skilled migrant workers for new SBE startups is still a policy challenge.

4.5.3 Globalization Challenges to Small Ventures

Findings so far have indicated an overall lack of enquiry, researched discussions, and theoretical frameworks to explain the impact of globalization and international business on SBEs and SMEs. Most discussions relate to large businesses and multinational corporations. There is little discussion on the internationalizing or globalizing experiences of smaller firms, particularly SBEs. This is in spite of the fact that globalization has been intensifying for a few decades now and an increasing number of SMEs and SBEs are participating in it.

The findings indicated that, as new opportunities were unfolding in a constantly changing environment, many SBEs had challenges in identifying and leveraging new opportunities and operating their businesses for more gains. The challenges and opportunities were arising from both domestic and global sources. While there are opportunities for survival and growth for more innovative, entrepreneurial, and technology- and knowledge-based SBEs, there are issues and concerns for those that lack resources; innovative, entrepreneurial, and managerial skills; and other capabilities required to perform successfully in a globalizing environment.

There are constant changes in customers' needs, market expectations, compliance requirements, levels of competition, and technological changes in domestic and foreign economies. It is tempting to conclude that globalization has created more challenges than opportunities for many SBEs.

Factors that constrain an SBE's performance include

- Lack of financial and human resources
- Uncertainties arising from the ongoing globalization of markets and economies
- Management of cash flows

- Short-term planning
- Finding reliable business partners domestically and overseas
- Marketing and selling challenges in foreign markets
- Fluctuations in exchange rates
- Increasing regulatory requirements with associated compliance costs
- Difficulties arising from differences in culture, language, and business practices
- Inability to manage intellectual and intangible assets

4.6 What Is Your Secret Sauce?

Entrepreneurial ventures fail for a host of reasons. Bad luck surely plays a role, but disaster usually strikes because of a more fundamental flaw: in the original idea, the strategy, and the execution—that is, the "secret sauce." Your secret sauce is just like a complex recipe: it is the constellation of ingredients plus the cooking method that delivers.

What entrepreneurs can do is ask the core set of tough questions that govern the fate of any enterprise.

1. **What is your value proposition?** This is the single most important question of the bunch. If you can't explain—in three, jargon-free sentences or less—why customers need your product, you do not have a value proposition. Without a need, there is no incentive for customers to pay. And without sales, you have no business. Period.

2. **Does your product address a viable market?** Entrepreneurs are passionate to a fault. Many fall in love with an idea before confirming that there's any viable market for it, let alone one large enough to attract investment capital. If a market doesn't yet exist—the toxic term of art here is *white space*—they assume they can create one. (*Hint*: There may be a reason for all that white space.)

3. **What differentiates your product from those of competitors?** Few companies can rely on, let alone afford, clever marketing schemes to separate themselves from the competition. Yes, Starbucks made people believe they wanted $4 caffeinated concoctions, and Louis Vuitton lulled people into shelling out $1500 for denim handbags, but those are the exceptions that prove the rule. If you want to win in business, you need to offer something tangibly valuable that the competition doesn't.

4. **How big is the threat of new entrants?** If you're smart enough to spy a profitable business opportunity, you can bet the competition

isn't far behind. Some barriers to entry (e.g., patented technology, a storied brand) are more fortified than others, but eventually someone will find a way to do what you do faster, cheaper, and maybe even better. If not a direct competitor, then a substitute technology might take a chunk out of your hide. (Think what digital film did to Kodak.) The trick: building a loyal following before that happens.

5. **How much startup capital do you need?** Any early-stage investor or small business consultant will tell you that most businesses fail because they were undercapitalized. The lesson: figure out how much you think you need and then add plenty of extra cushion.

6. **How much cash do you need to survive the early years?** In case you didn't pay attention to the previous question, take this one to heart. It doesn't matter how much money your business might make down the road if you can't get out of your garage. Plenty of business plans boast hockey stick–style financial projections but run out of cash before the good times kick in. (Remember all those busted dotcom companies from the tech boom?) Three words: mind the cash.

7. **How will you finance the business?** You have a few choices: Aunt Sally, credit cards (dangerous), angel investors, and if you're really onto something, venture capital. Forget bank loans (at least until the cash is flowing in a positive direction). As for selling shares to the public, what with all the regulatory hurdles, you might find the price of that exposure a tad steep. If you can bootstrap your business, do it; raising money is difficult and distracting. If you plan on stumping for capital, consider how much equity and control you're willing to give up. (The more you need the money, the stiffer the terms will get, so ask for it sooner rather than later.) Finally, always remember to match the timing of cash inflows from your assets and the outflows to cover liabilities. A mismatch can sting.

8. **What are your strengths?** Google writes powerful search algorithms; Steinway works wonders with wood; Cisco sniffs out promising new technologies and buys them. Figure out what you're good at and stick to it. An obvious notion, perhaps, but plenty of zealous entrepreneurs lose their way—especially when the world seems so full of possibilities.

9. **What are your weaknesses?** You may know how to design a widget but not know a thing about running an efficient manufacturing plant. Apple designs and markets its nifty iPods and iPhones but lets someone else slap them together. Countless webpreneurs farm out the design of their sites and back-office payment systems. Wasting resources just to be mediocre is suicide. Stick to core competencies and find trusted partners to handle the rest.

10. **How much power do your suppliers have?** Convincing customers to buy your products is tough enough without suppliers giving you a hard time. A basic rule of thumb: The fewer the number of suppliers, the more sway they have. Take the steel industry, which relies on a handful of companies for its iron feedstock. If two of those big guys should get together—as BHP Billton and Rio Tinto have been discussing—they would have significant pricing power, potentially crimping steel producers' margins. On the flipside, beware getting hooked on low-cost providers who don't keep an eye on quality. (Lead-laced Barbie, anyone?)

11. **How much power do your buyers have?** Take a lesson from Delphi, the giant autoparts supplier stuck in Chapter 11 bankruptcy despite its $26 billion in annual sales: It's no fun to be in a business where a few big customers can demand price cuts with each passing year. Meanwhile, movie theaters—even while besieged by video on demand and other services—still manage to push higher prices on the disaggregated masses. The cost of a seat at a Regal Entertainment Group theater in lower Manhattan is now $12—up 20% in less than 3 years.

12. **How should you sell your product?** There is no one-size-fits-all solution to wooing customers. For two decades, Dell bypassed retailers and sold directly to customers, with limited tech support. General Motors and Coca Cola rely on distributors to move their cars and cans. Clothing companies such as Ralph Lauren work both internal and external channels. And thanks to daily, intensive sales training, privately held Lazy Days moves some $800 million worth of RVs out of one sprawling location near Tampa, Florida. Whatever sales method you choose, make sure it aligns with your overall business strategy.

13. **How should you market your product?** Young companies have to get the word out, but they also can go broke doing it. A decade ago, America Online spent so much money flooding the planet with free trial software that it tried to mask the bleeding by capitalizing those expenses on its balance sheet. (Regulators later nixed that accounting treatment, wiping out millions in accounting profits.) What percentage of sales should go toward marketing? As with sales, there is no one rule of thumb.

14. **Does the business scale?** Bill Gates plowed piles of money into developing the first copy of Microsoft Office. The beauty: each additional copy of that software program costs next to nothing to produce. That's called scale, and it's the difference between modest wealth and obscene riches. What models don't scale? Think service businesses, where the need for people grows along with revenues.

15. **What are your financial projections?** You can't lead if you don't have a destination. Two critical milestones: (1) the point where more cash is coming into the business than going out in a given period, and (2) the point at which you finally recuperate your cumulative initial investment (including an adjustment for the time value of money). Financial projections should be reasonable. Paint too rosy a picture and seasoned investors will run; more to the point, you might run out of cash.

16. **What price will consumers pay?** Get this answer wrong and you could leave bags of money on the table—or worse, send customers running into the arms of the competition. When Apple sliced the price of its iPhone by one-third after only 2 months on the market, even loyal customers screamed, forcing chief Steve Jobs to apologize and offer a partial rebate. Consultants get paid handsomely to help companies arrive at the right price.

17. **How do you protect your intellectual property?** Imagine slaving for years on a new cell phone battery that lasts more than 2 days, only to watch it reverse engineered and patented by someone else. Before you ask anyone to crank out a few prototypes, file for a provisional patent. It protects your idea for a year while you work out the kinks.

18. **How do you keep the help happy?** What's Google worth without its super-geeks? Goldman Sachs without its number crunchers (and their golden Rolodexes)? The local bar without old Jim manning the tap? Not much, which is why attracting and retaining talent is critical to so many businesses. For starters, that means crafting the right benefits package. Starbucks sets a fairly high standard: health benefits are available to any Starbucks employee who works at least 20 hours a week and has been with the company for more than 90 days.

19. **How committed are you to making this happen?** About a year ago, Chuck Prince, recently resigned chief executive of Citigroup, addressed a group at New York University's Stern School of Business. An audience member asked what life looked like at the helm of such a colossal firm. Prince responded that, save for a few exceptions, every evening for the next 5 months was already accounted for. Fair warning: if you want to run the show, get ready to give everything— and then some.

20. **What is your end game?** Running a business with an eye toward flipping it to a strategic buyer is a lot different than digging in for the long haul. (Will YouTube ever turn a profit? Who knows, but that's Google's problem now; the same goes for MySpace and News Corp.). Not sure whether you want to build the next great empire or just make a decent buck?

Notes

1. Small Business Jobs Act of 2010. Public Law 111–240. September 27, 2010.
2. Spulber, D. F. (2008). The economic role of the entrepreneur. Northwestern University. June. http://lawlab.org/EconomicRoleoftheEntrepreneur.pdf.
3. Carland, J., Hoy, F., Boulton, W., and Carland, A. (1984). Differentiating entrepreneurs from small business owners: A conceptualization. *The Academy of Management Review* (pre-1986), 9, 000002; Entrepreneurship, p. 354.
4. Hoefler, D. (1971). Silicon Valley U.S.A, *Electronic News*.
5. Seidenberg, P. (1997). From germanium to silicon: A history of change in the technology of the semiconductors. In A. Goldstein and W. Aspray (Eds.), *Facets: New Perspectives on the History of Semiconductors*. New Brunswick: IEEE Center for the History of Electrical Engineering, p. 67.
6. Morris, R., and Mariana Penido, M. (2014). How did Silicon Valley become Silicon Valley? Three surprising lessons for other cities and regions. Endevor Insight report. http://endeavor.org.tr/wp-content/uploads/2016/01/How-SV-became-SV.pdf.
7. Stanford University, History of Silicon Valley. https://www.stanford.edu/about/history/history_ch3.html.
8. Wikipedia (2018). Silicone Valley. https://en.m.wikipedia.org/wiki/Silicon_Valley.
9. Rao, A. (2013). *A History of the Silicon Valley: The Greatest Creation of Wealth in the History of the Planet*, 2nd Edition. Palo Alto, CA: Omniware Group, p. 96.
10. Tilton, J. (1971). *International Diffusion of Technology*. Washington D.C.: Brookings Institution, p. 52; Klepper, S., Silicon valley a chip off the old Detroit bloc. In Z. Acs et al. (Ed.), *Entrepreneurship, Growth and Public Policy*. Cambridge, UK: Cambridge University Press, pp. 79–116; Endeavor Insight analysis.
11. Miller, R., and Cote, M. (1985). Growing the next Silicon Valley. *Harvard Business Review*, July–August, pp. 114–123.
12. Sturgeon, T. J. (2000). How Silicon Valley came to be. In M. Kenney (Ed.), *Understanding Silicon Valley: Understanding an Entrepreneurial Region*. MIT-IPC-00-014.
13. Saxenian, A. (1999). *Silicon Valley's New Immigrant Entrepreneurs*. San Francisco, CA: Public Policy Institute of California, p. 9. http://www.ppic.org/content/pubs/report/R_699ASR.pdf.
14. H. R. 2580; Pub L 89-236, 79 Stat 911, enacted June 30, 1968.
15. Alarcon, R. (1997). From servants to engineers: Mexican immigration and labor markets in the San Francisco Bay Area. University of California at Berkeley, Chicano/Latino Policy Project Working Paper, California Policy Seminar, Vol. 4, No. 3, January.
16. Borjas, G. (1986). The self-employment experience of immigrants. *Journal of Human Resources*, 21, Fall, 487–506.
17. Lofstrom, M. (2002). Labor market assimilation and the self-employment decision of immigrant entrepreneurs. *Journal of Population Economics*, 15(1), 83–114.
18. Clark, K., and Drinkwater, S. (2000). Pushed out or pulled in? Self-employment among ethnic minorities in England and Wales. *Labour Economics*, 7, 603–628.

19. Clark, K., and Drinkwater, S. 2010. Patterns of ethnic self-employment in time and space: Evidence from British Census microdata. *Small Business Economics*, 34(3), 323–338.
20. Schuetze, H. J., and Antecol, H. (2007). Immigration, entrepreneurship and the venture start-up process. In S. Parker (Ed.), *The Life Cycle of Entrepreneurial Ventures: International Handbook Series on Entrepreneurship*, Vol. 3. New York: Springer.
21. Fairlie, R. W., Zissimopoulos, J., and Krashinsky, H. A. (2010). The international Asian business success story: A comparison of Chinese, Indian, and other Asian businesses in the United States, Canada, and United Kingdom. In J. Lerner and A. Shoar (Eds.), *International Differences in Entrepreneurship*. Chicago: University of Chicago Press and National Bureau of Economic Research (pp. 179–208).
22. Tracy, S. L, Jr. (2011). Accelerating job creation in America: The promise of high-impact companies. Report, July. Washington, DC: SBA. https://www.sba.gov/sites/default/files/HighImpactReport.pdf.
23. Birch, D. L., and Medoff, J. (1994). Gazelles. In L. C. Solmon and A. R. Levenson (Eds.), *Labor, Employment Policy, and Job Creation*. Boulder, CO: Westview Press (pp. 159–168).
24. Piazza, M., and Austrian, Z. (2016). High-growth firms: Delineating definitions, industries, and business cycle. Technical Report, Cleveland State University, prepared for the Ewing Marion Kauffman Foundation, May. https://www.researchgate.net/profile/Merissa_Piazza/publication/310627318_High-Growth_Firms_Delineating_Definitions_Industries_and_Business_Cycle_Performance/links/583469ae08ae004f74c875c2.pdf?origin=publication_detail.
25. David Birch (1994). *Entrepreneurial Hot Spots: The Best Places in America to Start and Grow a Company*. Cambridge, MA: Cognetics. The report ($45) is available from Cognetics: http://www.cogonline.com or 617 661 0300.
32. Mouse photo public domain; source: National Cancer Institute (NCI); creator: Leidos Biomedical Research, Inc. Elephant photo released under Creative Commons license, attribution to nickandmel2006. Gazelle photo released under Creative Commons license, attribution to Energo.
26. Case, J. (2001). The gazelle theory: Are some small companies more equal than others? *Inc.*, May 15. http://www.inc.com/magazine/20010515/22613.html.
27. Deo, S. (2013). The impact of globalisation on small business enterprises (SBEs). *Proceedings of the Small Enterprise Association of Australia and New Zealand 26th Annual SEAANZ Conference*, Sydney.
28. Xiaonan, C. (1996). Debating "brain drain" in the context of globalisation. *Compare: A Journal of Comparative International Education*, 26(3), 269–285.
29. Tinguy, A., and Wenden, C. (1993). Eastern Europe: What benefits from the brain drain? *The OECD Observer*, 184, 33–36.
30. Engardio, P. (1994). Have skills, will travel—homeward. *Newsweek*, special bonus issue, pp. 164–165.
31. Salt, J. (1992). Migration processes among the highly skilled in Europe. *International Migration Review*, 26, 484–505.

Section II

Entrepreneurial
Self-Assessment

5

Entrepreneurial Self-Starters

Your attitude will determine your altitude.

5.1 Introduction

Best wishes! Your decision to start your own business can be one of the most exhilarating and consequential decisions you will ever make in your life. Owning your own business should be an invigorating, inspiring, grand adventure. The journey will be full of new sights and experiences, thrilling highs, sporadic lows, tricky paths, and hopefully big monetary rewards. But to ensure that your business journey will be a fruitful one, it is important to understand all that becoming an entrepreneur entails.

In self-employment there are no guarantees, and yes, there are many obstacles to overcome. But if you do it right, if you start the right small business—one suited to your strengths, one that you are passionate about, one that epitomizes your highest aspirations, dreams and values, and certainly one that rewards you with a nice profit—then there is no telling how high it can take you.

Successful entrepreneurs rely on two core principles, as shown in Table 5.1.

5.2 Self-Employment Pros and Cons

According to Steven Strauss, senior business columnist,[1] many entrepreneurs start their business adventure dreaming of riches and freedom. And while both are certainly possible, the crucial thing to understand is that there are trade-offs once you decide to start a business. Difficult bosses, annoying co-workers, peculiar policies, demands on your time, and limits on how much money you can make are traded for independence, creativity, opportunity, and power.

But by the same token, you also swap a regular paycheck and predictable benefits for no paycheck and no benefits. A life of security, comfort, and

TABLE 5.1

Core Principles of Self-employment

1. Your Vision	2. Contingency Planning
• Visions are more than ideas. They are your reachable dreams. • Visions link the present to the future. • Use visions to inspire your followers to achieve the impossible and unexpected • Make your visions positive. Everyone wants to make the world a better place.	• Plan for every contingency, and remember that you cannot plan for every contingency. • Build flexibility in your plans. When things go wrong, you can adjust. • Make certain you have adequate resources. Cash is your key to survival. • Plan for change. Be prepared when it arrives.

economic reliability is traded for uncertainty. There are definitely pros and cons to starting your own business. To be more precise, the balances of starting a business are shown in Table 5.2.

5.3 Are You Infected by the Self-Employment "Bug"?

Considering the pros and cons of your venture is not enough. Making the decision to leave your job and start a business is monumental. Even if starting a business seems like a great idea, despite the drawbacks, the question remains: How do you know if you are cut out for being an entrepreneur?

TABLE 5.2

Pros and Cons of Self-employment

	Pros	Cons
Control	Increased authority. Own boss.	Responsible for meeting payroll. Make sure clients pay on time.
Money	Unlimited ability to earn.	Lost security of a monthly paycheck. Can you raise the startup funds?
Creativity and Independence	You are the marketing wizard, salesman, accountant, secretary, and president all rolled into one.	Hectic life. Unlimited time demands.
Freedom	Final authority.	Are you qualified to make all the decisions?
Uncertainty	May be exhilarating.	May lead to nervous collapse.
Risk	You decide how much risk is acceptable. Risk acceptance is the hallmark entrepreneurship.	Risk is a four letter word. You could make a zillion or you could go bankrupt. Learning to manage risk.
Lack of Structure	You decide your own "culture." Flexibility of actions.	No written rules/regulations. Arbitrary decisions. Inconsistent directives.

Do you have what it takes? In order to assist you, answer the following quiz. It will help you evaluate your qualifications.

As you answer the questions, be sure to be perfectly honest. There is no need to get every question "right." Entrepreneurs come in all shapes, sizes, temperaments, and skill levels. Thus, this test is more informative than rigorous; that is, it should help you realize some of the skills necessary to start your own business. It does you no good to pretend to answer the questions correctly (Table 5.3).

5.4 Why Did You Start Your Startup?

Ask entrepreneurs why they started their startup and the common answer is "I wanted to bring a better product to the market." But that statement is quickly followed by the admission that fame and fortune are also important, as is the need to be their own boss and to prove that they are ready to face the next big challenge.

However, the overarching goal of a startup should be to gain the critical market share that will allow the company to reach the breakeven point. After breakeven, the goal should be to become insanely profitable. That is the secret to startup success.

First, establish your initial market share in a targeted segment of the market, and then you can annex adjacent market segments, continuing to grow until your company dominates a significant market share. Don't even enter a market unless you intend to dominate it. A startup will inevitably require a tremendous amount of hard work, long hours, and sacrifice. If you want to settle for second best, then your startup is not worth much to investors.

5.5 Generating Business Ideas from a Problem

You may have considered the prospect of starting your own business many times before. The thought of being your own boss—calling the shots, being responsible for your own financial rewards—is very alluring. You may have the drive, the experience, and the financial resources necessary to succeed. The only thing stopping you is figuring out what type of business you should start.

If this sounds familiar, you are in good company. Most entrepreneurs take a considerable amount of time investigating, analyzing, and agonizing about the right type of business for them. Self-starters may have a multitude of ideas but need to research the opportunity, as shown in Table 5.4.

TABLE 5.3

Self-Employment IQ

Are you a self-starter?	**a.** Yes, I like to think up ideas and implement them.	a = (5 points)
	b. If someone helps me get started, I will definitely execute the assignment.	b = (3 points)
	c. I would rather follow than lead.	c = (1 point)
How do you feel about taking risks?	**a.** I really like the feeling of being in the fast lane.	a = (5 points)
	b. Calculated risks are acceptable at times.	b = (3 points)
	c. I prefer the tried and true method.	c = (1 point)
Are you a leader?	**a.** Yes.	a = (5 points)
	b. Only when absolutely necessary.	b = (3 points)
	c. No, not really.	c = (1 point)
Can you and your family live without a regular paycheck?	**a.** Yes, if that is what it takes.	a = (5 points)
	b. I would rather not, but I understand that is part of the process.	b = (3 points)
	c. No, not at all.	c = (1 point)
Could you fire someone who really depends on you?	**a.** Yes. I may not like it, but that is the best for the company.	a = (5 points)
	b. I would do it reluctantly.	b = (3 points)
	c. I really cannot see myself doing that.	c = (1 point)
Are you willing to work 60 hours a week or more for a long time?	**a.** Yes, if that is what it is required to succeed.	a = (5 points)
	b. Only in the beginning.	b = (3 points)
	c. I think many other things (such as family) are more important than work.	c = (1 point)
Are you self-confident?	**a.** Absolutely.	a = (5 points)
	b. Most of the time.	b = (3 points)
	c. Unfortunately, that is not one of my strong suits.	c = (1 point)
Can you live with uncertainty?	**a.** Yes, of course.	a = (5 points)
	b. Reluctantly, but I don't like it.	b = (3 points)
	c. No, I like predictability.	c = (1 point)
Can you persevere once you have put your mind to something?	**a.** I usually will not let anything get in the way.	a = (5 points)
	b. Most of the time, if I like what I am doing.	b = (3 points)
	c. Not always.	c = (1 point)
Are you creative?	**a.** Yes, I do get a lot of good ideas.	a = (5 points)
	b. I could be if properly supervised.	b = (3 points)
	c. No, not really.	c = (1 point)
Are you competitive?	**a.** Sometimes too much so.	a = (5 points)
	b. Sure, when it is necessary.	b = (3 points)
	c. Not really, my nature is more passive.	c = (1 point)
Do you have a lot of willpower and self-discipline?	**a.** Yes.	a = (5 points)
	b. I am self-disciplined when I need to be.	b = (3 points)
	c. Not really.	c = (1 point)

(Continued)

TABLE 5.3 (CONTINUED)

Self-Employment IQ

Are you individualistic or would you rather go along with the status quo?	**a.** I like to think things through myself and do things my way.	a = (5 points)
	b. I am sometimes an original thinker.	b = (3 points)
	c. I think strongly individualistic people are difficult to work with.	c = (1 point)
Can you live without a formal structure?	**a.** No problem.	a = (5 points)
	b. Actually, the idea of living without a regular paycheck makes me nervous.	b = (3 points)
	c. No, I like routine and predictability in my job.	c = (1 point)
Do you have all the necessary business skills?	**a.** Yes, I do, and those I don't have, I'll learn.	a = (5 points)
	b. I have some.	b = (3 points)
	c. No, not really.	c = (1 point)
Are you flexible and willing to change course when things are not going your way?	**a.** Yes.	a = (5 points)
	b. I like to think so, but others may disagree.	b = (3 points)
	c. No, I have a fairly rigid personality.	c = (1 point)
Do you have experience in the business you are thinking of starting?	**a.** Yes.	a = (5 points)
	b. Some.	b = (3 points)
	c. No.	c = (1 point)
Could you competently perform multiple business tasks: accounting, sales, marketing, and so on?	**a.** I sure would like to try!	a = (5 points)
	b. I hope so.	b = (3 points)
	c. That sounds intimidating.	c = (1 point)
Are you willing to really hustle for clients and customers?	**a.** Sure.	a = (5 points)
	b. If I have to.	b = (3 points)
	c. I would rather not.	c = (1 point)
How well do you handle pressure?	**a.** Quite well.	a = (5 points)
	b. It's not my strongest trait, but I can do it	b = (3 points)
	c. Not well at all.	c = (1 point)

Scoring (suggested by your answers)
80–100: You have both the temperament and the skills to become an entrepreneur.
60–79: You are not a natural entrepreneur, but may become one over time.
Below 60: You would be wise to think of something else to do besides self-employment.

TABLE 5.4

Research Opportunities

- Read everything about the unmet need.
- Go to trade shows.
- Surf the Internet.
- Attend conferences.
- Never stop learning.

Your research should uncover whether or not this opportunity has been discovered before. If it has, investigate who is successful at it to find out what they are doing right and if there is any room for you to do it better. You need something to differentiate your business from the competition. This is a critical part of deciding whether or not your idea could turn into a viable business.

The opposite is equally common: they do not have a business idea, but know they want to be an entrepreneur. How do entrepreneurs come up with ideas to start businesses and how do you know if an idea would make a good business? The *Business Start-Up Handbook*[2] recommends the following sequence:

Often, business ideas are generated from a **problem** in the market place:

A group of people have needs that are not being properly satisfied.

This leads to an idea for the solution to the problem.

If the idea can be proven to be viable, a business **opportunity** has been created.

As an entrepreneur, you must learn to look at situations from a whole new perspective. You must look beyond what is there and imagine what could be there. The possibilities are endless. The opportunities surround you.

5.6 The Business Environment

Table 5.5 highlights factors in the environment that may provide you with ideas for a business opportunity. Remember that when something changes, the result usually has an effect on something or somebody, often creating new needs or shifting the demand for products or services. Hence, the possibility for you to develop a creative solution.

5.7 Preparing for a Visit from "Angels"

Due to the crucial importance of angels as a key source of startup capital for entrepreneurs, this section has been developed to provide some additional information and tips that relate specifically to "angel investors." In the startup marketplace, this particular source has been widely used by the technology industry to secure investment in the early stages of business operations. It is also suitable for other business sectors, provided that the growth of the business allows for annual expected returns in the range of 30%–40% per annum.

Figure 5.1 summarizes the appropriate time for seeking angel investments.

TABLE 5.5

Environmental Factors Leading to Business Opportunities

Changes	Comments
Changes in the Market	When consumers change their buying habits and preferences, there are always new opportunities. For example, the shift from going outside of the home for entertainment to staying at home and watching videos created a whole new opportunity for the growth of video stores, the manufacturing of larger home entertainment centers, and the building of smaller (more intimate) movie theaters.
Changes in an Industry	When governments change regulations, there is often an effect on many industries. Opportunities arise to help provide solutions to companies to deal with these changes or to service new needs created by them.
Technological Influences	The impact of technological growth has had an influence on almost all sectors in business, from car maintenance to photo radar to videoconferencing. New opportunities that exploit new technologies develop at an incredibly fast rate.
Competitive Pressures	The demand for certain products has created a very competitive marketplace in some industries. The personal computer industry is an example where competitive pressures have greatly influenced this market.
Demographic Shifts	Changes in the age, income, and status of the population have contributed to increased demand in many sectors such as health care, financial planning, and travel advice.

5.7.1 The Funding Gap Blues

Entrepreneurs who approach private investors must be thoroughly prepared. This involves completing your business plan and assembling the management team. Shortcomings that according to angels have led to decisions to decline investment opportunities include a lack of management competence, an incomplete management team, a lack of understanding of the market for product(s)/service(s), inadequate market research and competitive positioning, weak/unrealistic business plans, and unrealistic expectations of the investment-raising process.

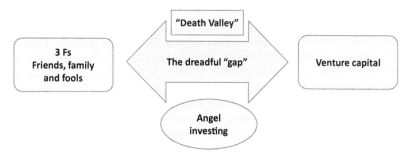

Preparing for a visit from Angels

"Death Valley"

3 Fs
Friends, family
and fools

The dreadful "gap"

Venture capital

Angel
investing

FIGURE 5.1

Angels help bridge the funding "gap" between the modest initial funding and the larger venture capital funding.

TABLE 5.6

The Funding Gap Blues: Angels to the Rescue

- It is difficult to raise >$100,000–$200,000 from the three Fs beyond seed stage.
- Angel deals typically require <$150,000 at startup stage.
- Angel capital fills the gap in startup financing between the three Fs and venture capitalists.
- Venture capitalists will not usually consider investments <$10 million.
- Angel investment is a common second round of financing for high-growth startups and accounts in total for more money invested annually than all VC funds combined.
- There is a large variety of structures:
  - Umbrella LLCs with each angel as a member
  - Independent LLCs formed specifically for an investment
  - Nonprofit organizations with individuals making independent investments
  - Some form of management company acting as a general partner
  - A hybrid of some or all of these

Modified from: Jay Schwartz (2007). Preparing for a visit from angels. Available from: https://www.massmedic.com/wp-content/uploads/2007/06/schwartz07.ppt.

Conversely, key factors that have prompted investment include confidence in the management team, strong product sales potential, knowledge of key players in the business, clear differentiation of the product in the market, and the entrepreneur's commitment to personal development and willingness to take advice (Table 5.6).

5.8 Characteristics of Angel Investors

Business angel investors, often simply referred to as *angels* are high–net worth, non-institutional, private equity investors who have the desire and sufficiently high net worth to enable them to invest part of their assets in high-risk, high-return entrepreneurial ventures in return for a share of voting, income, and ultimately capital gain.

Historically, angel investors were high–net worth individuals who privately invested in new startup firms or in the early formative stage of emerging ventures with little publicity of their involvement. They typically kept quiet about their wealth and discretely searched for deals to invest in. Angels were very wealthy individuals who invested widely across many ventures.[3]

Over the past 50 years, the number of angels has greatly increased. Some of this increase has come from greater spending power in the established professions; much has come from cashed-up entrepreneurs from the explosive growth in high-tech industries and some from the golden handshakes of senior executives retiring or being made redundant. This wave of potential, but mostly naive, angels resulted in a large number of poor investments, especially during the dotcom boom. However, over the past few years, the situation has changed markedly. Today, most angels are linked either formally or informally to networks of fellow angels. This has come about because of the need to band together to share deal investigations, the time required to undertake due diligence, and the costs of administration, professional accounting, and legal services associated with investments.

Both angels and venture capital (VC) funds invest in private firms through what is termed *private equity*, often referred to as *patient money*. It is called patient money because investments in private companies are usually quite illiquid and the private equity investor has to wait for a liquidity event, typically a trade sale or an initial public offering (IPO), to harvest their money.

While both parties participate in similar investments, although often at different stages in the venture growth, the VC sector is better organized, far more rigorous in approach, and much more standardized in the conditions under which it invests. It is this lack of rigor and deal-screening sophistication that has been the most serious deficiency of the angel sector.

Angels generally invest across a wide range of investment categories of which private equity represents, on average, only a few per cent of their total portfolio. They typically invest within an hour's journey of their residence and usually only for a period of 3–7 years before exiting the investment or when the venture fails. Rates of return on angel investments vary depending on the year of the calculation and the period over which the returns are estimated. Some speculate that the returns are similar to the VC sector, others that the returns are higher due to the greater risks of earlier stages. In achieving their returns, their lack of sophistication in investing is balanced by the commercial knowledge that they provide to their investee firms.

The following are some tips that you may find useful if you believe your investment opportunity is suitable for angels and wish to approach this type of investor.

- **Demographic:** Entrepreneurs, professionals, and business executives, well educated and can be described as self-made successes
- **Preferred investment size:** <$50,000: 75%; $50,000–$150,000: 25%
- **Preferred stage of company development:** Seed (concept stage): 53%; startup (near market ready): 32%
- **Preferred business sectors:** Software, wireless, telecommunications, health care, biotechnology
- **Focus on knowledge-intensive investments**
- **Average length of investment:** <3 years
- **Expected return on investment (annualized):** <30%: 35%; 30–40%: 22%; >40%: 43%
- **Areas of active involvement in investee companies:** Finance: 35%; marketing: 35%; general: 75%; strategic planning: 55%
- **Preferred exit horizon from investment:** <3 years: 15%; 3–5 years: 57%; <5 years: 54%

- **Tenfold return 3–7 years after investment**
- **Clearly articulated exit strategy**

5.9 Approaching Angel Investors

An emerging company that has constructed an experienced management team, a robust competitive position and strong gross margins usually has little need for angel investment. The same might be said of early stage ventures with strong profit and growth potential, which can attract formal VC. The angel plays the middle role: funding the business that has yet to stand on its own feet and not yet mature enough or with enough potential to attract VC. Angels typically invest in seed, start-up or early stage businesses.

The following definitions help to describe various stages at which an angel may make investments. Keep in mind that angels typically participate in late-seed or early-stage startups.

- **Seed:** Product is in development; usually in business less than 18 months.
- **Early:** Product in pilot production; usually in business less than 30 months.
- **Expansion:** Product in market; significant revenue growth.
- **Turnaround:** Current products stagnant; financing provided to a company at a time of operational or financial difficulty.
- **Late:** New product or product improvement; continued revenue growth.
- **Buyout:** Leveraged buyout (LBO), management buyout (MBO), or management buy-in—a fund investment strategy involving the acquisition of a product or business from either a public or private company, utilizing a significant amount of debt.

If you feel your startup meets the investment requirements of the typical angel, you are ready to approach your potential investors.

- Sell yourself first by emphasizing and demonstrating your managerial competence and vision.
- Be clear and concise when describing your investment opportunity and when answering questions; you may "lose" the investor if you are unfocused and use language that may be confusing (i.e., technical).
- Be honest at all times and openly discuss the strengths and weaknesses of your venture; investors expect all companies to have weaknesses and will dig until they find yours.

- Be prepared to discuss valuation, exit strategy, and rate of return. Obtain professional advice in these areas if needed.
- Be prepared to meet with as many qualified investors as possible and never stop meeting new investors until you have secured the required funding.
- Remember that personal chemistry is a two-way street and that it is critical that you share the same visions and plans for the company.
- Bad investor relationships can lead to the demise of your company.
- Always keep in mind that an investor is in business for the same reason that you are: to make a profit.
- Don't forget to run your business. Seeking investment is an important function, but it should not completely consume you.

In seeking equity investors, give preference to those who can add value to the enterprise in the form of management assistance.

5.10 Investment Drivers and Resistance Points

Angel investment is normally the first round of external independent investment. Angels usually invest in early-stage ventures where the founding team has exhausted their personal savings and sources of funding from family and friends. These ventures are not sufficiently developed to stand on their own or sufficiently attractive to gain VC funding.

These ventures exist in a halfway state, often between possible failure and takeoff. Typically, the management team lacks experience in a growth venture and the business needs not only additional funding but also mentoring to take it to the next stage of development. Investing in early-stage private companies has many drawbacks, which is why this form of investment is typically undertaken by individuals who can afford to lose the money and/or are willing to wait some years before they see a return on their money.

To put this into context, private early-stage ventures have the following attributes:

- The shares are not freely traded and no established market exists for them. An investor is forced to wait for a liquidity event such as a trade sale or a public listing.
- Novel business concepts and inventions are often associated with emerging and untried markets. The risks in the venture are likely to be higher and some aspects of the business subject to high levels of uncertainty.

- Products may be new and/or under development and still subject to technical and market risks.
- The knowledge of the product and its design may be highly dependent on a small number of key staff who may not necessarily have proven business experience.
- The small size of new ventures and their lack of presence in the market mean they may be highly susceptible to changes in market conditions. Timing may be critical to survival. Small delays in product release or in achieving revenue milestones may be sufficient to cause the failure of the enterprise.
- There is limited access to further finance if the business encounters delays or undertakes operations that require additional funds.
- Early-stage ventures typically have little collateral to pledge for loans.
- Early-stage ventures often have a high cash burn rate as they have yet to reach a critical mass where they are self-funding.
- Funding for acquisitions or expansion can be limited.
- Valuations are problematic, if not speculative. Shares are not readily traded and so no public market value exists for the firm. Often there is little historical performance and future revenues and profits are uncertain.
- Minority shareholders have little power unless it is through an investment agreement. Even if they disagree with management actions, they have little power and can't sell their shares easily.

Figure 5.2 summarizes the investment drivers and resistance points normally encountered when seeking angel investments.

Investment drivers and resistance points

> Team
  - Several specialties with strong leadership
> Product
  - Radical new product
  - Patent protected
> Market
  - $500M market potential
  - Regulatory status
    - e.g. FDA 510k already in progress, or approved
> Competition
  - Current: large players with older technology
  - Future: large players will adapt, but will take 5 years to retool
> Financials
  - Seeking <$2M,
  - Cash-flow break even in 3 years

FIGURE 5.2
Classical resistance points encountered by entrepreneurs.

5.11 Angel's Investment Stipulations

The new venture entrepreneur may find angel investment very useful as a bridge to VC finance. The angel can provide much-needed finance as well as assist in developing the business further to prove the business model. When they do invest, angels will likely stipulate similar conditions to their investments as VCs. Typically they will require

- A position on the Board of Directors
- Remuneration for their time spent on the business
- Veto power over the issue of new shares
- Adjustment of the number of shares issued to the investor if milestones are missed and/or a lower valuation is set in a subsequent round of investment
- Veto power over further long-term debt
- Approval rights over executive remuneration
- Approval rights over issue of options
- The right to put the business up for sale if certain milestones are not achieved
- The right to replace the CEO if certain milestones are not achieved

Angels are normally active "hands-on" investors. They expect and often enjoy being directly involved in the management of the venture. In fact, this is often one of their prime reasons for investing. They typically spend time with each of their investments on a regular basis.

Lastly, angel investors need to see a path to liquidity for their investment. Few angels invest for dividends; most will be investing for capital gains. However, whether they invest for dividends or capital gains, they still need to have a mechanism for releasing their original investment. The normal form of harvesting is either a sale to another business (trade sale) or a listing on a public stock exchange (an IPO). Many investment proposals use such exit phrases as "Sell to a corporation in 3–5 years" or "List on the stock exchange in 5 years" with no substance behind the statement. They have neither identified who the potential buyer might be nor how they would be an ideal candidate for an IPO.

The business proposal needs to demonstrate to the angel a well-articulated exit strategy that is meaningful. A trade sale strategy should have identified potential buyers and have convincing arguments as to why the selected corporations should buy the business. An IPO strategy should show how similar businesses, with comparable products, services, and growth patterns, were able to list on the target exchange.

Notes

1. Strauss, S. D. (2002). *The Business Start-Up Kit*. Chicago, IL: Dearborn Trade. https://www.amazon.com/Business-Start-Up-Kit-Steven-Strauss/dp/07931 60278.
2. Centre D'Entrepreneurship de Prescott-Russell (2018). *Business Start-Up Handbook*. Hawkesbury, ON: CEPR. http://prec-cepr.com/images/guides/business_start-up_handbook.pdf.
3. McKaskell, T. (2009). *An Introduction to Angel Investing: A Guide to Investing in Early Stage Entrepreneurial Ventures*. Melbourne, Australia: Breakthrough.

6

Entrepreneurial Personalities

6.1 Introduction

According to the U.S. Office of Advocacy's Small Business Profiles 2016, U.S. small businesses (fewer than 500 employees) employed 56.8 million people (48.0% of the private workforce) in 2013. In contrast, firms with fewer than 100 employees produced the largest share of small business employment.

The U.S. Census Bureau's Business Dynamics Statistics (BDS) reported that small businesses created 1.1 million net jobs in 2013. Among the seven BDS size classes, firms employing 250–499 employees experienced the largest gains, adding 257,245 net jobs. The smallest gains were in firms employing 5–9 employees, which added 84,020 net jobs, as shown in Figure 6.1.

The median income[1] for individuals who were self-employed at their own incorporated businesses was $49,204 in 2014. For individuals self-employed at their own unincorporated firms, the income was $22,209.

U.S. small businesses are truly an "equal opportunity" community that incorporates practically every demographic group found in the country. There are few barriers to entry into this community, other than a willingness to work long hours, accept financial risks, and focus your efforts into making the enterprise successful. This is clearly seen in Table 6.1, which lists the business ownership by demographic group in 2016.

U.S. small businesses comprise a surprisingly large portion of the labor market. Small businesses employed over 28 million people in 2013 (the last reported government statistics), as shown in Table 6.2.

More to the point, the small business employment share in the United States is surprisingly high, with some sectors (e.g., construction) as high as 82.7%, with an overall employment share of 49%, as seen in Table 6.3.

6.2 Entrepreneurial "Personality Characteristics"

In spite of the fact that theoretically anyone can start up a company, entrepreneurs share certain personality characteristics and behavior patterns that seem

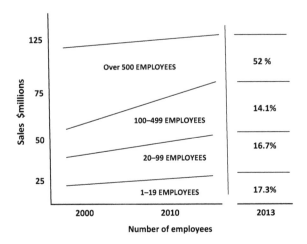

FIGURE 6.1
U.S. employment by firm size.

to benefit running an enterprise. Entrepreneurs as individuals differ from other people. An entrepreneur's personality differs from the average, at least statistically. Entrepreneurs in widely different fields appear connected by certain characteristics. There might not be one "true" or "universal" personality type of entrepreneurs, but certain personalities emerge as being "more" enterprising.[2]

In the 1920s and 1930s, a *theory of personality* was proposed by Carl Jung.[3,4] The theory proved quite popular, particularly when applied to entrepreneurs. Jung's theory of psychological types was designed to categorize people in terms of various personality patterns, focusing on four basic psychological functions:

1. Extraversion versus Introversion

2. Sensation versus Intuition

3. Thinking versus Feeling

4. Judging versus Perceiving

TABLE 6.1

U.S. Business Ownership by Demographic Group

Hispanic	46.3%
Hawaiian/Pacific Islander	45.3%
Minority	38.1%
African American	34.5%
Asian	23.8%
Non-minority	−5.5%

Source: Small Business Profile 2016, https://www.sba.gov/sites/default/files/advocacy/United_States.pdf.

TABLE 6.2

U.S. Small Firms by Industry, 2013[18]

Industry	1–499 Employees	1–19 Employees	Non-employer Firms	Total Small Firms
Professional, scientific, and technical services	778,090	731,341	3,235,906	4,013,996
Other services (except public administration)	670,468	626,850	3,583,742	4,254,210
Retail trade	649,764	595,280	1,906,597	2,556,361
Construction	645,479	598,039	2,368,442	3,013,921
Health care and social assistance	642,586	561,706	1,959,723	2,602,309
Accommodation and food services	502,076	397,330	346,280	848,356
Administrative, support, and waste management	325,474	289,799	2,032,516	2,357,990
Wholesale trade	309,568	267,370	406,469	716,037
Real estate, rental and leasing	275,298	262,850	2,448,282	2,723,580
Manufacturing	248,155	188,964	343,025	591,180
Finance and insurance	233,184	216,130	706,394	939,578
Transportation and warehousing	167,496	149,262	1,102,255	1,269,751
Arts, entertainment, and recreation	116,159	100,867	1,256,694	1,372,853
Educational services	85,151	67,144	616,952	702,103
Information	70,792	61,051	326,526	397,318
Mining, quarrying, and oil and gas extraction	21,594	18,222	106,610	128,204
Agriculture, forestry, fishing and hunting	21,323	19,997	239,863	261,186
Utilities	5,715	4,511	19,344	25,059
Total	5,768,372	5,156,713	23,005,620	28,773,992

Note: Sorted by small employer firms.

6.2.1 Personality Characteristics or Types

In 1992, Isabel Briggs Myers and her mother, Katherine Cook Briggs, developed the *Myers–Briggs Type Indicator* (MBTI) in response to Carl Jung's theory. After years of research and testing, the resulting instrument—the MBTI—differentiated 16 different types or preferences.[5] The MBTI is the most commonly used personality assessment being used today. It is widely considered a valid and reliable instrument and has been used extensively in research into entrepreneurial characteristics.[6,7,8]

TABLE 6.3

U.S. Employment by Industry and Firm Size, 2013 (Sorted by Small Firm Employment)

Industry	Small Business Employment	Total Private Employment	Small Business Employment Share
Health care and social assistance	8,515,106	18,598,711	45.8%
Accommodation and food services	7,454,788	12,395,387	60.1%
Retail trade	5,370,419	15,023,362	35.7%
Manufacturing	5,059,759	11,276,438	44.9%
Professional, scientific, and technical services	4,869,277	8,275,350	58.8%
Other services (except public administration)	4,536,340	5,282,688	85.9%
Construction	4,526,389	5,470,181	82.7%
Administrative, support, and waste management	3,523,802	10,185,297	34.6%
Wholesale trade	3,463,622	5,908,763	58.6%
Finance and insurance	1,918,122	6,063,761	31.6%
Transportation and warehousing	1,585,539	4,287,236	37.0%
Educational services	1,532,214	3,513,469	43.6%
Real estate and rental and leasing	1,361,352	1,972,105	69.0%
Arts, entertainment, and recreation	1,315,721	2,112,000	62.3%
Information	871,065	3,266,084	26.7%
Mining, quarrying, and oil and gas extraction	288,789	732,186	39.4%
Agriculture, forestry, fishing and hunting	132,812	154,496	86.0%
Utilities	110,352	638,575	17.3%
Total	**56,435,468**	**115,156,089**	**49.0%**

Accordingly, the MBTI typology is primarily concerned with the valuable differences in people that result from where they like to focus their attention, the way they process information, the way they decide, and the way they like to "adopt." Usually one pole dominates another. The eight preferences are identified in 16 types, each representing a certain preference order,[9,10] as shown in Table 6.4.

Typically, an entrepreneur will discover an opportunity, marshal resources, and organize these into a venture that offers some innovation in the market. Entrepreneurs essentially act as agents for change and wealth creation.[11] Entrepreneurs face many significant challenges, not the least of which is generating or recognizing ideas that have the potential to be developed into

TABLE 6.4

The Eight Preferences or Dimensions

Extraversion (E) (action-oriented)	Interested in people and things in the world around them. People who prefer Extraversion tend to focus on the outer world of people and activity.
Introversion (I) (contemplative)	Interested in the ideas in their minds that explain the world. People who prefer Introversion tend to focus on the inner world of ideas and impressions.
Sensing (S) (pragmatic)	Interested in what is real and can be seen, heard, and touched. People who prefer Sensing tend to take in information through the five senses and focus on the here and now.
Intuition (N) (visionary)	Interested in what can be imagined and seen with the "mind's eye." People who prefer Intuition tend to take in information from patterns and the big picture and focus on future possibilities.
Thinking (T) (logical)	Interested in what is logical and works by cause and effect. People who prefer Thinking tend to make decisions based primarily on logic and on objective analysis.
Feeling (F) (compassionate)	Interested in knowing what is important and valuable. People who prefer Feeling tend to make decisions based primarily on values and on the subjective evaluation of person-centered concerns.
Judging (J) (plan-centric)	Interested in acting by organizing, planning, and deciding. People who prefer Judging tend to like a planned and organized approach to life and want to have things settled.
Perceiving (P) (adaptable)	Interested in acting by watching, trying out, and adapting. People who prefer Perceiving tend to like a flexible and spontaneous approach to life and want to keep their options open.

Caution: MBTI words used to describe preferences in psychology do not mean the same thing as they do in everyday life.
- *Extravert* does not mean talkative or loud.
- *Introvert* does not mean shy or inhibited.
- *Feeling* does mean emotional.
- *Judging* does not mean judgmental.
- *Perceiving* does not mean perceptive.

Modified from: E. Hirsh, K. W. Hirsh, and S. Krebs, *Teambuilding Program (2nd Edition)*.

appealing goods and services. Successful ideas are often a balance between novelty and familiarity.

Deo[12] defines an entrepreneur from two different viewpoints: those of an economist and a psychologist.

1. To an economist, an entrepreneur is one who brings resources, labor, materials and other assets into combinations that makes their value greater than before, and also one who introduces changes, innovations, and a new order.

2. To a psychologist, such a person is typically driven by certain forces—the need to "obtain or attain."

6.3 Careers Suggested by MBTI Typology

Your MBTI personality type can direct you to work in some occupations.[13] As a result, certain personalities are attracted to certain types of occupations and workplace characteristics. In turn, certain occupations attract certain personality characteristics.

In order to maximize your career potential, it is vital to match your chosen occupation and work environment to your personality type. According to MBTI typology, your job satisfaction and success is at its highest when your job is in line with your personality traits. Similarly, your professional fulfillment is at its highest when your job is in line with your attitude, values, and preferences.

Research has shown that many of the different personality types tend to have distinct preferences in their choice of careers. We have incorporated observations of each type's character traits that affect career choice along with some suggestions for possible directions.[14]

This material is being provided for your reference and is intended to be an informational guide. It does not comprise a complete analysis of ideal careers for individuals and does not guarantee success or failure at any occupation.

For example, INTJs, ENTJs, ENFJs, and ESTJs often find themselves in engineering roles within technology-focused organizations. Likewise, these four personality types frequently engage in leadership roles within their organizations, as shown in Table 6.5.

As can be seen from Table 6.5, ESFP, ESTP, INTP, ISTP, ENTP, and ENFP are the six most entrepreneurial types based on the occupation statistics of the sample. What is common to all of them? The common preference is Perceiving (P); that is, they all are spontaneous, interested in acting by watching, trying out, and adapting.

The typical managerial types are ISTJ, ESTJ, and ENTJ.[15] What is common to all of them? The common preference is Thinking (T); that is, they all tend to make decisions slowly and deliberately based on logic and analysis.

6.4 Most and Least Entrepreneurial Types Compared

Based on the MBTI concept, we can statistically predict the most and least entrepreneurial personalities, as shown in Table 6.6.

TABLE 6.5

Careers Suggested by MBTI Typology

ESTJ: Natural leaders, they work best when they are in charge and enforcing the rules.	Military personnel, business administrators, managers, police, detectives, judges, financial officers, teachers, sales representatives, government workers, insurance agents, underwriters, nursing administrators, trade and technical teachers
ISTJ: Similar to ESTJs, they have a knack for detail and memorization but work more behind the scenes instead of up front as a leader.	Business executives, administrators and managers, accountants, police, detectives, judges, lawyers, medical doctors, dentists, computer programmers, systems analysts, computer specialists, auditors, electricians, math teachers, mechanical engineers, laboratory technicians
ESFJ: Do best in jobs where they can apply their persuasion abilities at building relationships with other people.	Physicians, dental assistants, radiological technologists, office managers, home economics, nurses, teachers, administrators, child care workers, family practice clergy, counselors, social workers, bookkeepers, accountants, secretaries, organization leaders, receptionists, religious educators, speech pathologists
ISFJ: Tradition oriented and down to earth, they do best in jobs where they can help people achieve their goals or where structure is needed.	Family practice physicians, administrators, managers, health service workers, medical technologists, interior decorators, designers, nurses, secretaries, child care/early childhood development workers, social workers, counselors, paralegals, clergy, office managers, shopkeepers, bookkeepers, gardeners, clerical supervisors, curators, librarians, typists
ESTP: Have a gift for reacting to and solving immediate problems and persuading other people.	**Entrepreneurs**, sales representatives, marketers, police, detectives, paramedics, medical technicians, computer technicians, computer technical support agents, firefighters, military personnel, auditors
ISTP: Have the ability to stay calm under pressure and excel in any job that requires immediate action.	**Entrepreneurs**, police, detectives, forensic pathologists, computer programmers, system analysts, computer specialists, engineers, carpenters, mechanics, pilots, drivers, athletes, firefighters, paramedics, construction workers, dental hygienists, electrical engineers, farmers, military, probation officers, steelworkers, transportation operatives
ESFP: Optimistic and fun-loving, their enthusiasm is great for motivating others.	Actors, painters, comedians, sales representatives, teachers, counselors, social workers, child care workers, fashion designers, interior decorators, consultants, photographers, musicians, human resources managers, clerical supervisors, coaches, factory supervisors, food service workers, receptionists, recreation workers, religious educators, respiratory therapists
ISFP: Tend to do well in the arts, as well as in helping others and working with people. Follow instructions to the letter.	Artists, musicians, composers, designers, child care workers, social workers, counselors, teachers, veterinarians, forest rangers, bookkeepers, carpenters, personal service workers, clerical supervisors, secretaries, dental and medical staffers, waiters and waitresses, chefs, nurses, mechanics, physical therapists, X-ray technicians

(Continued)

TABLE 6.5   (CONTINUED)

Careers Suggested by MBTI Typology

ENFJ: Have the gift of encouraging others to actualize themselves and provide excellent leadership.	Teachers, consultants, psychiatrists, social workers, counselors, clergy, sales representative, human resources, managers, events coordinators, politicians, diplomats, writers, actors, designers, musicians, religious workers, writers.
INFJ: Blessed with an idealistic vision, they do best when they seek to make that vision a reality.	Basic scientists, counselors, clergy, missionaries, teachers, medical doctors, dentists, chiropractors, psychologists, psychiatrists, writers, musicians, artists, psychics, photographers, child care workers, education consultants, librarians, marketers, social workers.
ENFP: Very creative and fun-loving, they excel at careers that allow them to express their ideas and spontaneity.	**Entrepreneurs**, actors, journalists, writers, musicians, painters, consultants, psychologists, psychiatrists, teachers, counselors, politicians, television reporters, marketers, scientists, sales representatives, artists, clergy, public relations, social scientists, social workers
INFP: Driven by a strong sense of personal values, they are also highly creative and can offer support from behind the scenes.	Scientists, social scientists, writers, artists, counselors, social workers, language teachers, fine arts teachers, child care workers, clergy, missionaries, psychologists, psychiatrists, political activists, editors, education consultants, journalists, religious educators
ENTJ: Born to lead and can steer the organization toward their vision, using their excellent organizing abilities. Clear understanding of what needs to get done.	**Organization founders**, **entrepreneurs**, business executives, CEOs, business administrators, managers, judges, lawyers, computer consultants, university professors, politicians, credit investigators, labor relations workers, marketing department managers, mortgage bankers, systems analysts, scientists
INTJ: They have a particular skill at grasping difficult, complex concepts and building strategies.	**Organization founders**, scientists, engineers, professors, teachers, medical doctors, dentists, corporate strategists, business administrators, managers, military, lawyers, judges, computer programmers, system analysts, computer specialists, psychologists, research department managers, researchers, university instructors
ENTP: Extremely freedom oriented. Need a career that allows them to act independently and express their creativity and insight. Excellent at cause-and-effect relationships.	**Entrepreneurs**, engineers, scientists, inventors, lawyers, psychologists, photographers, consultants, sales representatives, actors, marketers, computer programmers, comedians, computer analysts, credit investigators, journalists, psychiatrists, public relations, designers, writers, artists, musicians, politicians
INTP: Highly analytical, they can discover connections between two seemingly unrelated things and work best when allowed to use their imagination and critical thinking. Best when working on intellectual projects.	Physicists, chemists, biologists, photographers, strategic planners, mathematicians, university professors, computer programmers, computer animators, technical writers, engineers, lawyers, forensic researchers, writers, artists, psychologists, social scientists, systems analysts, researchers, surveyors

Note: This is a guide to which careers utilize the natural talents of each MBTI type (entrepreneurial personalities highlighted).

TABLE 6.6

Most Entrepreneurial and Least Entrepreneurial Types Compared

Most Entrepreneurial Types	Least Entrepreneurial Types
ESFP • Prefers a flexible, spontaneous, and changing environment • Realistic adapter of human relationships • Likes action and making things happen	**ISFJ** • Prefers a structured, organized, and planned environment • Relies on facts and details, based on written manuals and handbooks
ESTP • Prefers a flexible, spontaneous, and changing environment • Realistic adapter in the world of material things • Good at on-the-spot problem-solvingLikes action, enjoys whatever comes along	**INFP** • Prefers a structured, organized, and planned environment • Relies on stability and predictability
INTP • Prefers a flexible, spontaneous, and changing environment • Inquisitive analyzer • Likes solving problems quickly	**INFJ** • Prefers a structured, organized, and planned environment • People-oriented innovator of ideas • Respected for their firm principles
ISTP • Prefers a flexible, spontaneous, and changing environment • Practical analyzer, values exactness • Excels at getting to the core of a practical problem and finding a suitable solution	**ENFJ** • Prefers a structured, organized, and planned environment • Imaginative harmonizer • Shows real concern for what others think or want and tries to handle things with due regard for their feelings
ENTP • Prefers a flexible, spontaneous, and changing environment • Inventive, analytical planner of change • Quick, ingenious, good at many things	**INTJ** • Prefers a structured, organized, and planned environment • Logical, critical, decisive innovator • Skeptical, critical, independent, determined
ENFP • Prefers a flexible, spontaneous, and changing environment • Warmly enthusiastic planner of change • Able to do almost anything that interests themQuick with a solution to any difficulty and ready to help anyone with a problem	**ISTJ** • Prefers a structured, organized, and planned environment • Analytical manager of facts and details • Sees to it that everything is well organized

As the table indicates, the most entrepreneurial types all prefer a flexible, spontaneous, and changing environment. On the contrary, all the least entrepreneurial types prefer a structured, organized, and planned environment. The typical managerial types prefer a structured, organized, and planned environment. These individual tendencies explain why some types prefer unstable, risky, chaotic working environments and why some types avoid them completely.

6.5 MBTI Dichotomies

The four letters of the MBTI are one-half of the four dichotomies.[16] The four preferences or dichotomies are

- Introversion (I) versus Extroversion (E)
- Sensing (S) versus Intuition (N)
- Thinking (T) versus Feeling (F)
- Judging (J) versus Perceiving (P)

Introversion versus Extroversion: Assume you have an orange with you. Are you more likely to eat it by yourself silently (I) or, having located a group of people afar, join them and crack jokes about oranges and share the orange with the whole group (E)? I and E represent how you gain or lose energy in an environment. Introverts need some alone time to get back on their feet, while extroverts become bubbly when surrounded by people.

Sensing versus Intuition: Assume you still have the same orange. Are you more likely to smell, touch, and taste the orange (S) or imagine the orange as a ball and play baseball with it (N)? This dichotomy deals with the level of abstraction or concreteness in perception.

Thinking versus Feeling: Again, assume the same orange. Are you more likely to ponder about the macro-economical impact of sales of oranges (T) or the sorry plight of farmers toiling under the hot sun just to feed us (F)? This dichotomy is about your approach to decision making. One is a rational approach, while the other is a moral/ethical approach.

Judging versus Perceiving: You still have the orange. Are you more likely to peel the orange right now with the Swiss Army knife you have brought anticipating such a circumstance (J) or are you more likely to put it away in your bag for later because you do not feel like eating and you do not have sharp nails or a knife to peel it (P)? This dichotomy deals with the decision-making process itself. Some people like to act as the situation arises, while others prefer to wait it out.

TABLE 6.7

The Four Dichotomies

	Subjective Characteristics	Objective Characteristics
Perception	Intuition/Sensing (How do you prefer to take in information?)	Introversion/Extraversion (Where do you prefer to focus your attention and get your energy?)
Judging	Feeling/Thinking (How do you make decisions?)	Introversion/Extraversion (Where do you prefer to focus your attention and get your energy?)
Deductive	Intuition/Sensing (How do you prefer to take in information?)	Introversion/Extraversion (Where do you prefer to focus your attention and get your energy?)
Inductive	Feeling/Thinking (How do you make decisions?)	Perception/Judging (How do you deal with the outer world?)

Table 6.7 summarizes the four MBTI dichotomies.

Table 6.8 presents the preferences exhibited by the personality types.

6.6 High-Level Description of Personality Types

The following is an in-depth description of the 16 personality types[17] along with their descriptive names. Which one represents you best? Or are you best represented by some combination?

6.6.1 ISTJ: The Duty Fulfiller

- Serious and quiet, interested in security and peaceful living
- Extremely thorough, responsible, and dependable
- Well-developed powers of concentration
- Usually interested in supporting and promoting traditions and establishments
- Well-organized and hard working; work steadily toward identified goals
- Can usually accomplish any task once they have set their mind to it

As an ISTJ, your primary mode of living is focused internally, where you take things in via your five senses in a literal, concrete fashion. Your secondary mode is external, where you deal with things rationally and logically.

ISTJs are quiet and reserved individuals who are interested in security and peaceful living. They have a strongly felt internal sense of duty, which lends

TABLE 6.8

Preferences Exhibited by the Meyers–Briggs Dichotomies

E–I Dichotomy: Source of Energy

Most people who prefer Extraversion	**Most people who prefer Introversion**
• Prefer action over reflection • May act quickly without thinking • Are attuned to external environments • Prefer to communicate by talking • Learn best through doing or discussing • Are sociable and expressive • Enjoy working in groups	• Prefer reflection over action • May not take action at all • Are attuned to the inner world • Prefer to communicate in writing • Learn best through thorough mental practice and reflection • Are private and contained • Enjoy working alone or in pairs

S–N Dichotomy: Take in Information

Most people who prefer **Sensing**	Most people who prefer **Intuition**
• Emphasize the pragmatic • Prefer facts and details/specific information • Are oriented to present realities • Value realism • Observe and remember specifics through the five senses • Build carefully and thoroughly to conclusions • Trust experience	• Emphasize the theoretical • Prefer general concepts/high-level plans • Are oriented to future possibilities • Value imagination • See trends and patterns in specific data • Use a "sixth" sense • Move quickly to conclusions; follow hunches • Trust inspiration

T–F Dichotomy: Decision-Making

Most people who prefer **Thinking**	Most people who prefer **Feeling**
• Are analytical • Use cause-and-effect reasoning • Solve problems with logic • Strive for objective standards of truth • Described as reasonable • Search for flaws in an argument • Fair; want everyone treated equally	• Empathetic • Guided by personal values • Assess impact of decisions on people • Strive for harmony and positive interactions • Described as compassionate • Search for point of agreement in an argument • Fair; want everyone treated as an individual

J–P Dichotomy: Lifestyle

Most people who prefer **Judging**	Most people who prefer **Perceiving**
• Are scheduled/organized • Strive to finish one project before starting another • Like to have things decided • May decide things too quickly • Try to avoid last-minute stresses; finish tasks well before deadline • Try to limit surprises • See routines as effective	• Are spontaneous/flexible • Start many projects but may have trouble finishing them • Like things loose and open to change • May decide things too slowly • Feel energized by last-minute pressures; finish tasks at the deadline • Enjoy surprises • See routines as limiting

them a serious air and the motivation to follow through on tasks. Organized and methodical in their approach, they can generally succeed at any task they undertake.

ISTJs are very loyal, faithful, and dependable. They place great importance on honesty and integrity. They are "good citizens" who can be depended on to do the right thing for their families and communities. While they generally take things very seriously, they also usually have an offbeat sense of humor and can be a lot of fun—especially at family or work-related gatherings.

ISTJs tend to believe in laws and traditions, and expect the same from others. They're not comfortable with breaking laws or going against the rules. If they are able to see a good reason for stepping outside of the established mode of doing things, the ISTJ will support that effort. However, ISTJs more often tend to believe that things should be done according to procedures and plans. If an ISTJ has not developed their Intuitive side sufficiently, they may become overly obsessed with structure and insist on doing everything "by the book."

ISTJs are extremely dependable on following through with things that they have promised. For this reason, they sometimes get more and more work piled on them. Because ISTJs have such a strong sense of duty, they may have a difficult time saying "no" when they are given more work than they can reasonably handle. For this reason, they often work long hours and may be unwittingly taken advantage of.

ISTJs will work for long periods of time and put tremendous amounts of energy into doing any task that they see as important to fulfilling a goal. However, they will resist putting energy into things that don't make sense to them or for which they can't see a practical application. They prefer to work alone but work well in teams when the situation demands it. They like to be accountable for their actions and enjoy being in positions of authority. ISTJs have little use for theory or abstract thinking, unless the practical application is clear.

ISTJs have tremendous respect for facts. They hold a tremendous store of facts within themselves, which they have gathered through their Sensing preference. They may have difficulty understanding a theory or idea that is different from their own perspective. However, if they are shown the importance or relevance of the idea to someone who they respect or care about, the idea becomes a fact, which the ISTJ will internalize and support. Once the ISTJ supports a cause or idea, he or she will stop at no lengths to ensure that they are doing their duty of giving support where support is needed.

ISTJs are not naturally in tune with their own feelings and the feelings of others. They may have difficulty picking up on emotional needs immediately, as they are presented. Being perfectionists themselves, they have a tendency to take other people's efforts for granted, like they take their own efforts for granted. They need to remember to pat people on the back once in a while.

ISTJs are likely to be uncomfortable expressing affection and emotion to others. However, their strong sense of duty and the ability to see what needs to be done in any situation usually allows them to overcome their natural reservations, and they are usually quite supporting and caring individuals with the people that they love. Once ISTJs realize the emotional needs of those who are close to them, they put in effort to meet those needs.

ISTJs are extremely faithful and loyal. Traditional and family-minded, they will put in great amounts of effort to making their homes and families running smoothly. They are responsible parents, taking their parenting roles seriously. They are usually good and generous providers to their families. They care deeply about those close to them, although they usually are not comfortable with expressing their love. ISTJs are likely to express their affection through actions, rather than through words.

ISTJs have an excellent ability to take any task and define it, organize it, plan it, and implement it through to completion. They are very hard workers who do not allow obstacles to get in the way of performing their duties. They do not usually give themselves enough credit for their achievements, seeing their accomplishments simply as the natural fulfillment of their obligations.

ISTJs usually have a great sense of space and function, and artistic appreciation. Their homes are likely to be tastefully furnished and immaculately maintained. They are acutely aware of their senses and want to be in surroundings that fit their need for structure, order, and beauty.

Under stress, ISTJs may fall into "catastrophe mode," where they see nothing but all of the possibilities of what could go wrong. They will berate themselves for things that they should have done differently or duties that they failed to perform. They will lose their ability to see things calmly and reasonably and will depress themselves with their visions of doom.

In general, ISTJs have a tremendous amount of potential. As capable, logical, reasonable, and effective individuals with a deeply driven desire to promote security and peaceful living, ISTJs have what it takes to be highly effective at achieving their chosen goals—whatever they may be.

6.6.2 ISTP: The Mechanic

- Quiet and reserved; interested in how and why things work
- Excellent skills with mechanical things
- Risk-takers who live for the moment
- Usually interested in and talented at extreme sports
- Uncomplicated in their desires
- Loyal to their peers and to their internal value systems but not overly concerned with respecting laws and rules if they get in the way of getting something done
- Detached and analytical; excel at finding solutions to practical problems

As an ISTP, your primary mode of living is focused internally, where you deal with things rationally and logically. Your secondary mode is external, where you take things in via your five senses in a literal, concrete fashion.

ISTPs have a compelling drive to understand the way things work. They're good at logical analysis and like to use it on practical concerns. They typically have strong powers of reasoning, although they're not interested in theories or concepts unless they can see a practical application. They like to take things apart and see the way they work.

ISTPs have an adventuresome spirit. They are attracted to motorcycles, airplanes, skydiving, surfing, and so on. They thrive on action and are usually fearless. ISTPs are fiercely independent, needing to have the space to make their own decisions about their next step. They do not believe in or follow rules and regulations, as this would prohibit their ability to "do their own thing." Their sense of adventure and desire for constant action makes ISTPs prone to becoming bored rather quickly.

ISTPs are loyal to their causes and beliefs and are firm believers that people should be treated with equity and fairness. Although they do not respect the rules of the "system," they follow their own rules and guidelines for behavior faithfully. They will not take part in something that violates their personal laws. ISTPs are extremely loyal and faithful to their "brothers."

ISTPs like and need to spend time alone, because this is when they can sort things out in their minds most clearly. They absorb large quantities of impersonal facts from the external world and sort through those facts, making judgments, when they are alone.

ISTPs are action-oriented people. They like to be up and about, doing things. They are not people to sit behind a desk all day and do long-range planning. Adaptable and spontaneous, they respond to what is immediately before them. They usually have strong technical skills and can be effective technical leaders. They focus on details and practical things. They have an excellent sense of expediency and grasp of the details, which enables them to make quick, effective decisions.

ISTPs avoid making judgments based on personal values; they feel that judgments and decisions should be made impartially, based on the fact. They are not naturally tuned in to how they are affecting others. They do not pay attention to their own feelings, and even distrust them and try to ignore them, because they have difficulty distinguishing between emotional reactions and value judgments. This may be a problem area for many ISTPs.

ISTPs who are overstressed may exhibit rash emotional outbursts of anger, or on the other extreme, may be overwhelmed by emotions and feelings that they feel compelled to share with people (often inappropriately). ISTPs who are down on themselves will foray into the world of value judgments—a place that is not natural for ISTPs—and judge themselves by their inability to perform some task. They will then approach the task in a grim emotional state, expecting the worst.

ISTPs are excellent in crisis situations. They're usually good athletes and have very good hand–eye coordination. They are good at following through with a project and tying up loose ends. They usually don't have much trouble with school because they are introverts who can think logically. They are usually patient individuals, although they may be prone to occasional emotional outbursts due to their inattention to their own feelings.

ISTPs have a lot of natural ability, which makes them good at many different kinds of things. However, they are happiest when they are centered in action-oriented tasks that require detailed logical analysis and technical skill. They take pride in their ability to take the next correct step.

ISTPs are optimistic, full of good cheer, loyal to their equals, and uncomplicated in their desires. They are generous, trusting, and receptive people who want no part in confining commitments.

6.6.3 ISFJ: The Nurturer

- Quiet, kind, and conscientious
- Can be depended on to follow through
- Usually puts the needs of others above their own needs
- Stable and practical; value security and traditions
- Well-developed sense of space and function
- Rich inner world of observations about people
- Extremely perceptive of other's feelings
- Interested in serving others

As an ISFJ, your primary mode of living is focused internally, where you takes things in via your five senses in a literal, concrete fashion. Your secondary mode is external, where you deal with things according to how you feel about them or how they fit into your personal value system.

ISFJs live in a world that is concrete and kind. They are truly warm and kindhearted and want to believe the best of people. They value harmony and cooperation and are likely to be very sensitive to other people's feelings. People value the ISFJ for their consideration and awareness and their ability to bring out the best in others by their firm desire to believe the best.

ISFJs have a rich inner world that is not usually obvious to observers. They constantly take in information about people and situations that is personally important to them and store it away. This tremendous store of information is usually startlingly accurate, because the ISFJ has an exceptional memory about things that are important to their value systems. It is not uncommon for ISFJs to remember a particular facial expression or conversation in precise detail years after the event occurred, if the situation made an impression on them.

ISFJs have a very clear idea of the way things should be, which they strive to attain. They value security and kindness and respect traditions and laws.

They tend to believe that existing systems are there because they work. Therefore, they're not likely to buy into doing things in a new way, unless they're shown in a concrete way why it's better than the established method.

ISFJs learn best by doing, rather than by reading about something in a book or applying theory. For this reason, they are not likely to be found in fields that require a lot of conceptual analysis or theory. They value practical application. Traditional methods of higher education that require a lot of theorizing and abstraction are likely to be a chore for the ISFJ. The ISFJ learns a task best by being shown its practical application. Once the task is learned, and its practical importance is understood, the ISFJ will faithfully and tirelessly carry through the task to completion. The ISFJ is extremely dependable.

The ISFJ has an extremely well-developed sense of space, function, and aesthetic appeal. For that reason, they're likely to have beautifully furnished, functional homes. They make extremely good interior decorators. This special ability, combined with their sensitivity to others' feelings and desires, makes them very likely to be great gift-givers—finding the right gift that will be truly appreciated by the recipient.

More so than other types, ISFJs are extremely aware of their own internal feelings, as well as other people's feelings. They do not usually express their own feelings, keeping things inside. If they are negative feelings, they may build up inside the ISFJ until they turn into firm judgments against individuals that are difficult to unseed once set. Many ISFJs learn to express themselves and find outlets for their powerful emotions.

Just as ISFJs are not likely to express their feelings, they are also not likely to let on that they know how others are feeling. However, they will speak up when they feel another individual really needs help, and in such cases they can truly help others become aware of their feelings.

ISFJs feel a strong sense of responsibility and duty. They take their responsibilities very seriously and can be counted on to follow through. For this reason, people naturally tend to rely on them. ISFJs have a difficult time saying "no" when asked to do something and may become overburdened. In such cases, the ISFJ does not usually express their difficulties to others because they intensely dislike conflict and because they tend to place other people's needs over their own. ISFJ need to learn to identify, value, and express their own needs, if they wish to avoid becoming overworked and taken for granted.

ISFJs need positive feedback from others. In the absence of positive feedback, or in the face of criticism, ISFJs become discouraged and even depressed. When down on themselves or under great stress, ISFJs begin to imagine all of the things that might go critically wrong in their lives. They have strong feelings of inadequacy and become convinced that "everything is all wrong" or "I can't do anything right."

ISFJs are warm, generous, and dependable. They have many special gifts to offer in their sensitivity to others and their strong ability to keep things running smoothly. They need to remember to not be overly critical of themselves, and to give themselves some of the warmth and love that they freely dispense to others.

6.6.4 ISFP: The Artist

- Quiet, serious, sensitive, and kind
- Do not like conflict and not likely to do things that may generate conflict
- Loyal and faithful
- Extremely well-developed senses and aesthetic appreciation for beauty
- Not interested in leading or controlling others
- Flexible and open-minded
- Likely to be original and creative
- Enjoy the present moment

As an ISFP, your primary mode of living is focused internally, where you deal with things according to how you feel about them or how they fit into your value system. Your secondary mode is external, where you take things in via your five senses in a literal, concrete fashion.

ISFPs live in the world of sensational possibilities. They are keenly in tune with the way things look, taste, sound, feel, and smell. They have a strong aesthetic appreciation for art and are likely to be artists in some form, because they are unusually gifted at creating and composing things that will strongly affect the senses. They have a strong set of values, which they strive to consistently meet in their lives. They need to feel as if they're living their lives in accordance with what they feel is right and will rebel against anything that conflicts with that goal. They're likely to choose jobs and careers that allow them the freedom of working toward the realization of their value-oriented personal goals.

ISFPs tend to be quiet and reserved and are difficult to get to know well. They hold back their ideas and opinions except from those who they are closest to. They are likely to be kind, gentle, and sensitive in their dealings with others. They are interested in contributing to people's sense of well-being and happiness and will put a great deal of effort and energy into tasks they believe in.

ISFPs have a strong affinity for aesthetics and beauty. They're likely to be animal lovers and to have a true appreciation for the beauties of nature. They're original and independent and need to have personal space. They value people who take the time to understand them and who support them in pursuing their goals in their own unique way. People who don't know them well may see their unique way of life as a sign of carefree lightheartedness, but the ISFP actually takes life very seriously, constantly gathering specific information and shifting it through their value systems in search for clarification and underlying meaning.

ISFPs are action-oriented individuals. They are "doers" and are usually uncomfortable with theorizing concepts and ideas, unless they see a practical application. They learn best in a "hands-on" environment and may consequently become bored with traditional teaching methods that emphasize abstract thinking. They do not like impersonal analysis and are uncomfortable with the idea of making decisions based strictly on logic. Their strong value systems demand that decisions are evaluated against their subjective beliefs, rather than against some objective rules or laws.

ISFPs are extremely perceptive and aware of others. They constantly gather specific information about people and seek to discover what it means. They are usually penetratingly accurate in their perceptions of others.

ISFPs are warm and sympathetic. They genuinely care about people and are strongly service-oriented in their desire to please. They have an unusually deep well of caring for those who are close to them and are likely to show their love through actions rather than words.

ISFPs have no desire to lead or control others, just as they have no desire to be led or controlled by others. They need space and time alone to evaluate the circumstances of their life against their value system and are likely to respect other people's needs for the same.

ISFPs are likely to not give themselves enough credit for the things they do extremely well. Their strong value systems can lead them to be intensely perfectionist and cause them to judge themselves with unnecessary harshness.

The ISFP has many special gifts for the world, especially in the areas of creating artistic sensation and selflessly serving others.

6.6.5 INFJ: The Protector

- Quietly forceful, original, and sensitive
- Tend to stick to things until they are done
- Extremely intuitive about people and concerned for their feelings
- Well-developed value systems that they strictly adhere to
- Well-respected for their perseverance in doing the right thing
- Likely to be individualistic, rather than leading or following

As an INFJ, your primary mode of living is focused internally, where you take things in primarily via intuition. Your secondary mode is external, where you deal with things according to how you feel about them or how they fit with your personal value system.

INFJs are gentle, caring, complex, and highly intuitive individuals. Artistic and creative, they live in a world of hidden meanings and possibilities. Only

1% of the population has an INFJ personality type, making it the most rare of all the types.

INFJs place great importance on having things orderly and systematic in their outer world. They put a lot of energy into identifying the best system for getting things done and constantly define and redefine the priorities in their lives. On the other hand, INFJs operate within themselves on an intuitive basis that is entirely spontaneous. They know things intuitively, without being able to pinpoint why and without detailed knowledge of the subject at hand. They are usually right, and they usually know it. Consequently, INFJs put a tremendous amount of faith into their instincts and intuitions. This is something of a conflict between the inner and outer worlds and may result in the INFJ not being as organized as other Judging types tend to be. Or we may see some signs of disarray in an otherwise orderly tendency, such as a consistently messy desk.

INFJs have uncanny insight into people and situations. They get "feelings" about things and intuitively understand them. As an extreme example, some INFJs report experiences of a psychic nature, such as getting strong feelings about there being a problem with a loved one and discovering later that they were in a car accident. This is the sort of thing that other types may scorn and scoff at, and INFJs themselves does not really understand their intuition at a level that can be verbalized. Consequently, most INFJs are protective of their inner selves, sharing only what they choose to share, when they choose to share it. They are deep, complex individuals, who are quite, private, and typically difficult to understand. INFJs hold back part of themselves and can be secretive.

But INFJs are as genuinely warm as they are complex. INFJs hold a special place in the heart of people who they are close to, who are able to see their special gifts and depth of caring. INFJs are concerned for people's feelings and try to be gentle to avoid hurting anyone. They are very sensitive to conflict and cannot tolerate it very well. Situations that are charged with conflict may drive the normally peaceful INFJ into a state of agitation or charged anger. They may tend to internalize conflict into their bodies and experience health problems when under a lot of stress.

Because the INFJ has such strong intuitive capabilities, they trust their own instincts above all else. This may result in stubbornness and a tendency to ignore other people's opinions. They believe that they're right. On the other hand, INFJs are perfectionists who doubt that they are living up to their full potential. INFJs are rarely at complete peace with themselves; there's always something else they should be doing to improve themselves and the world around them. They believe in constant growth and don't often take time to revel in their accomplishments. They have strong value systems and need to live their lives in accordance with what they feel is right. In deference to the Feeling aspect of their personalities, INFJs are in some ways gentle and easygoing. Conversely, they have very high expectations of themselves and frequently of their families. They don't believe in compromising their ideals.

INFJs are natural nurturers—patient, devoted, and protective. They make loving parents and usually have strong bonds with their offspring. They have high expectations of their children and push them to be the best that they can be. This can sometimes manifest itself in the INFJ being hard-nosed and stubborn. But generally, children of an INFJ receive devoted and sincere parental guidance, combined with deep caring.

In the workplace, the INFJ usually shows up in areas where they can be creative and somewhat independent. They have a natural affinity for art, and many excel in the sciences, where they make use of their intuition. INFJs can also be found in service-oriented professions. They are not good at dealing with minutia or very detailed tasks. The INFJ will either avoid such things or else go to the other extreme and become enveloped in the details to the extent that they can no longer see the "big picture." An INFJ who has gone the route of becoming meticulous about details may be highly critical of other individuals who are not.

The INFJ individual is gifted in ways that other types are not. Life is not necessarily easy for the INFJ, but they are capable of great depth of feeling and personal achievement.

6.6.6 INFP: The Idealist

- Quiet, reflective, and idealistic
- Interested in serving humanity
- Well-developed value system, which they strive to live in accordance with
- Extremely loyal
- Adaptable and laid-back, unless a strongly held value is threatened
- Usually talented writers
- Mentally quick and able to see possibilities
- Interested in understanding and helping people

As an INFP, your primary mode of living is focused internally, where you deal with things according to how you feel about them or how they fit into your personal value system. Your secondary mode is external, where you take things in primarily via your intuition.

INFPs, more than other intuitive Feeling types, are focused on making the world a better place for people. Their primary goal is to find out their meaning in life. What is their purpose? How can they best serve humanity in their lives? They are idealists and perfectionists who drive themselves hard in their quest for achieving the goals they have identified for themselves.

INFPs are highly intuitive about people. They rely heavily on their intuitions to guide them and use their discoveries to constantly search for value in life. They are on a continuous mission to find the truth and meaning underlying things. Every encounter and every piece of knowledge gained gets sifted through the INFP's value system and is evaluated to see if it has any potential to help define or refine the INFP's own path in life. The goal at the end of the path is always the same: the INFP is driven to help people and make the world a better place.

Generally thoughtful and considerate, INFPs are good listeners and put people at ease. Although they may be reserved in expressing emotion, they have a very deep well of caring and are genuinely interested in understanding people. This sincerity is sensed by others, making the INFP a valued friend and confidante. INFPs can be quite warm with people they know well.

INFPs do not like conflict and go to great lengths to avoid it. If they must face it, they will always approach it from the perspective of their feelings. In conflict situations, INFPs place little importance on who is right and who is wrong. They focus on the way that the conflict makes them feel and indeed don't really care whether or not they're right. They don't want to feel badly. This trait sometimes makes them appear irrational and illogical in conflict situations. On the other hand, INFPs make very good mediators and are typically good at solving other people's conflicts, because they intuitively understand people's perspectives and feelings and genuinely want to help them.

INFPs are flexible and laid-back, until one of their values is violated. In the face of their value system being threatened, INFPs can become aggressive defenders, fighting passionately for their cause. When INFPs adopt a project or job that they're interested in, it usually becomes a "cause." Although they are not detail-oriented individuals, they will cover every possible detail with determination and vigor when working for their "cause."

When it comes to the mundane details of life maintenance, INFPs are typically completely unaware of such things. They might go for long periods without noticing a stain on the carpet but carefully and meticulously brush a speck of dust off of their project booklet.

INFPs do not like to deal with hard facts and logic. Their focus on their feelings and the "human condition" makes it difficult for them to deal with impersonal judgment. They don't understand or believe in the validity of impersonal judgment, which makes them naturally rather ineffective at using it. Most INFPs will avoid impersonal analysis, although some have developed this ability and are able to be quite logical. Under stress, it's not uncommon for INFPs to misuse hard logic in the heat of anger, throwing out fact after (often inaccurate) fact in an emotional outburst.

INFPs have very high standards and are perfectionists. Consequently, they are usually hard on themselves and don't give themselves enough credit. INFPs may have problems working on a project in a group because their standards are likely to be higher than those of other members of the group. In group situations, they may have a "control" problem. INFPs need to work on balancing their high ideals with the requirements of everyday living. Without resolving this conflict, they will never be happy with themselves, and they may become confused and paralyzed about what to do with their lives.

INFPs are usually talented writers. They may be awkward and uncomfortable with expressing themselves verbally but have a wonderful ability to define and express what they're feeling on paper. INFPs also appear frequently in social service professions, such as counseling or teaching. They are at their best in situations where they're working toward the public good and in which they don't need to use hard logic.

INFPs who function in their well-developed sides can accomplish great and wonderful things, which they will rarely give themselves credit for. Some of the great, humanistic catalysts in the world have been INFPs.

6.6.7 INTJ: The Scientist

- Independent, original, analytical, and determined
- Have an exceptional ability to turn theories into solid plans of action
- Highly value knowledge, competence, and structure
- Driven to derive meaning from their visions
- Long-range thinkers
- Have very high standards for their performance and the performances of others
- Natural leaders but will follow if they trust existing leaders

As an INTJ, your primary mode of living is focused internally, where you take things in primarily via your intuition. Your secondary mode is external, where you deal with things rationally and logically.

INTJs live in the world of ideas and strategic planning. They value intelligence, knowledge, and competence, and typically have high standards in these regards, which they continuously strive to fulfill. To a somewhat lesser extent, they have similar expectations of others.

With Introverted Intuition dominating their personality, INTJs focus their energy on observing the world and generating ideas and possibilities. Their mind constantly gathers information and makes associations about it. They are tremendously insightful and usually are very quick to understand new ideas. However, their primary interest is not *understanding* a concept but rather *applying* that concept in a useful way. Unlike INTPs, they do not follow an idea as far as they possibly can, seeking only to understand it fully. INTJs are driven to come to conclusions about ideas. Their need for closure and organization usually requires that they take some action.

The tremendous value INTJs place on systems and organization, combined with their natural insightfulness, makes them excellent scientists. An INTJ scientist gives a gift to society by putting their ideas into a useful form for others to follow. It is not easy for the INTJ to express their internal images, insights, and abstractions. The internal form of the INTJ's thoughts and concepts is highly individualized and is not readily translatable into a form that others will understand. However, INTJs are driven to translate their ideas into plans or systems that are usually readily explainable, rather than to directly translate their thoughts. They usually don't see the value of a direct transaction and will also have difficulty expressing their ideas, which are non-linear. However, their extreme respect of knowledge and intelligence will motivate them to explain themselves to another person who they feel is deserving of the effort.

INTJs are natural leaders, although they usually choose to remain in the background until they see a real need to take the lead. When they are in leadership roles, they are quite effective, because they are able to objectively see the reality of a situation and are adaptable enough to change things that aren't working well. They are the supreme strategists—always scanning available ideas and concepts and weighing them against their current strategy, to plan for every conceivable contingency.

INTJs spend a lot of time inside their own minds and may have little interest in the other people's thoughts or feelings. Unless their Feeling side is developed, they may have problems giving other people the level of intimacy that is needed. Unless their Sensing side is developed, they may have a tendency to ignore details that are necessary for implementing their ideas.

The INTJ's interest in dealing with the world is to make decisions, express judgments, and put everything that they encounter into an understandable and rational system. Consequently, they are quick to express judgments. They often have very evolved intuitions and are convinced that they are right about things. Unless they complement their intuitive understanding with a well-developed ability to express their insights, they may find themselves frequently misunderstood. In these cases, INTJs tend to blame misunderstandings on the limitations of the other party, rather than on their own difficulty in expressing themselves. This tendency may cause the INTJ to dismiss others' input too quickly and to become generally arrogant and elitist.

INTJs are ambitious, self-confident, deliberate, long-range thinkers. Many INTJs end up in engineering or scientific pursuits, although some find enough challenge within the business world in areas that involve organizing and strategic planning. They dislike messiness and inefficiency and anything that is muddled or unclear. They value clarity and efficiency and will put enormous amounts of energy and time into consolidating their insights into structured patterns.

Other people may have a difficult time understanding an INTJ. They may see them as aloof and reserved. Indeed, the INTJ is not overly demonstrative of their affections and is likely to not give as much praise or positive support as others may need or desire. That doesn't mean that they don't truly have affection or regard for others, they simply do not typically feel the need to express it. Others may falsely perceive INTJs as being rigid and set in their ways. Nothing could be further from the truth; they are committed to always finding objectively the best strategy to implement their ideas. The INTJ is usually quite open to hearing an alternative way of doing something.

When under a great deal of stress, the INTJ may become obsessed with mindless, repetitive, Sensate activities, such as over-drinking. They may also tend to become absorbed with minutia and details that they would not normally consider important to their overall goal.

INTJs need to remember to express themselves sufficiently, so as to avoid difficulties with people misunderstanding them. In the absence of properly developing their communication abilities, they may become abrupt and short with people and isolationist.

INTJs have a tremendous amount of ability to accomplish great things. They have insight into the big picture, and are driven to synthesize their concepts into solid plans of action. Their reasoning skills give them the means to accomplish that. INTJs are almost always highly competent people and will not have a problem meeting their career or education goals. They have the ability to make great strides in these arenas. On a personal level, INTJs who practice tolerance and put effort into effectively communicating their insights to others have every chance of leading a rich and rewarding life.

6.6.8 INTP: The Thinker

- Logical, original, creative thinkers
- Can become very excited about theories and ideas
- Exceptionally capable and driven to turn theories into clear understandings
- Highly value knowledge, competence, and logic
- Quiet and reserved; hard to get to know well
- Individualistic; have no interest in leading or following others

As an INTP, your primary mode of living is focused internally, where you deal with things rationally and logically. Your secondary mode is external, where you take things in primarily via your intuition.

INTPs live in the world of theoretical possibilities. They see everything in terms of how it could be improved or what it could be turned into. They live primarily inside their own minds, having the ability to analyze difficult problems, identify patterns, and come up with logical explanations. They seek clarity in everything and are therefore driven to build knowledge. They are "absentminded professors" who highly value intelligence and the ability to apply logic to theories to find solutions. They are typically so strongly driven to turn problems into logical explanations that they live much of their lives within their own heads and may not place as much importance or value on the external world. Their natural drive to turn theories into concrete understanding may turn into a feeling of personal responsibility to solve theoretical problems and help society move toward a higher understanding.

INTPs value knowledge above all else. Their minds are constantly working to generate new theories or to prove or disprove existing theories. They approach problems and theories with enthusiasm and skepticism, ignoring existing rules and opinions and defining their own approach to the resolution. They seek patterns and logical explanations for anything that interests them. They're usually extremely bright and able to be objectively critical in their analysis. They love new ideas and become very excited over abstractions and theories. They love to discuss these concepts with others. They may seem "dreamy" and distant to others because they spend a lot of time inside their minds musing over theories. They hate to work on routine things; they would much prefer to build complex theoretical solutions and leave the implementation of the system to others. They are intensely interested in theory and will put forth tremendous amounts of time and energy into finding a solution to a problem with has piqued their interest.

INTPs do not like to lead or control people. They're very tolerant and flexible in most situations, unless one of their firmly held beliefs has been violated or challenged, in which case they may take a very rigid stance. INTPs are likely to be very shy when it comes to meeting new people. On the other hand, they are very self-confident and gregarious around people they know well or when discussing theories that they fully understand.

INTPs have no understanding or value for decisions made on the basis of personal subjectivity or feelings. They strive constantly to achieve logical conclusions to problems and don't understand the importance or relevance of applying subjective emotional considerations to decisions. For this reason, INTPs are usually not in tune with how people are feeling and are not naturally well equipped to meet the emotional needs of others.

INTPs may have a problem with self-aggrandizement and social rebellion, which will interfere with their creative potential. Since their Feeling side is their least developed trait, INTPs may have difficulty giving the warmth and support that is sometimes necessary in intimate relationships. If INTPs don't realize the value of attending to other people's feelings, they may become overly critical and sarcastic with others. If they are not able to find a place for themselves that supports the use of their strongest abilities, they may become generally negative and cynical. If INTPs do not develop their Sensing side sufficiently, they may become unaware of their environment and exhibit weakness in performing maintenance-type tasks, such as bill paying and dressing appropriately.

For INTPs, it is extremely important that ideas and facts are expressed correctly and succinctly. They are likely to express themselves in what they believe to be absolute truths. Sometimes, their well-thought-out understanding of an idea is not easily understandable by others, but INTPs are not naturally likely to tailor the truth so as to explain it in an understandable way to others. INTPs may be prone to abandoning a project once they have figured it out, moving on to the next thing. It's important that INTPs place importance on expressing their developed theories in understandable ways. In the end, an amazing discovery means nothing if you are the only person who understands it.

INTPs are usually very independent, unconventional, and original. They are not likely to place much value on traditional goals such as popularity and security. They usually have complex characters and may tend to be restless and temperamental. They are strongly ingenious and have unconventional thought patterns, which allows them to analyze ideas in new ways. Consequently, a lot of scientific breakthroughs in the world have been made by INTPs.

INTPs are at their best when they can work on their theories independently. When given an environment that supports their creative genius and possible eccentricity, INTPs can accomplish truly remarkable things. These are the pioneers of new thoughts in our society.

6.6.9 ESTP: The Doer

- Friendly, adaptable, action-oriented
- "Doers" who are focused on immediate results
- Living in the here and now; risk-takers who live fast-paced lifestyles
- Impatient with long explanations
- Extremely loyal to their peers, but not usually respectful of laws and rules if they get in the way of getting things done
- Great people skills

As an ESTP, your primary mode of living is focused externally, where you take things in via your five senses in a literal, concrete fashion. Your secondary mode is internal, where you deal with things rationally and logically.

ESTPs are outgoing, straight-shooting types. Enthusiastic and excitable, ESTPs are "doers" who live in the world of action. Blunt, straightforward risk-takers, they are willing to plunge right into things and get their hands dirty. They live in the here and now and place little importance on introspection or theory. They look at the facts of a situation, quickly decide what should be done, execute the action, and move on to the next thing.

ESTPs have an uncanny ability to perceive people's attitudes and motivations. They pick up on little cues that go completely unnoticed by most other types, such as facial expressions and stance. They're typically a couple of steps ahead of the person they're interacting with. ESTPs use this ability to get what they want out of a situation. Rules and laws are seen as guidelines for behavior rather than mandates. If ESTPs decide that something needs to be done, then their "do it and get on with it" attitude takes precedence over the rules. However, ESTPs tend to have their own strong beliefs in what's right and what's wrong and will doggedly stick to their principles. The rules of the establishment may hold little value to ESTPs, but their own integrity mandates they will not under any circumstances do something they feel to be wrong.

ESTPs have a strong flair for drama and style. They're fast-moving, fast-talking people who have an appreciation for the finer things in life. They may be gamblers or spendthrifts. They're usually very good at storytelling and improvising. They typically makes things up as they go along rather than following a plan. They love to have fun and are fun people to be around. They can sometimes be hurtful to others without being aware of it, as they generally do not know and may not care about the effect their words have on others. It's not that they don't care about people, it's that their decision-making process does not involve taking people's feelings into account. They make decisions based on facts and logic.

ESTPs are least developed in their intuitive side. They are impatient with theory and see little use for it in their quest to "get things done." An ESTP will occasionally have strong intuitions that are often way off base but sometimes very lucid and positive. ESTPs do not trust their instincts and are suspicious of other people's intuition as well.

ESTPs often have trouble in school, especially higher education that moves into realms where theory is more important. ESTPs get bored with classes in which they feel they gain no useful material that can be used to get things done. ESTPs may be brilliantly intelligent, but school will be a difficult chore for them.

ESTPs need to keep moving, and so do well in careers where they are not restricted or confined. ESTPs make extremely good salespersons. They will become stifled and unhappy dealing with routine chores. ESTPs have a natural abundance of energy and enthusiasm, which makes them natural entrepreneurs. They get very excited about things and have the ability to motivate others to excitement and action. The can sell anyone on any idea. They are action-oriented and make decisions quickly. All in all, they have extraordinary talents for getting things started. They are not usually so good at following through and might leave those tasks to others. Mastering the art of following through is something ESTPs should pay special attention to.

ESTPs are practical, observant, fun-loving, spontaneous risk-takers with an excellent ability to quickly improvise an innovative solution to a problem. They're enthusiastic and fun to be with and are great motivators. If ESTPs recognize their real talents and operate within those realms, they can accomplish truly exciting things.

6.6.10 ESTJ: The Guardian

- Practical, traditional, and organized
- Likely to be athletic
- Not interested in theory or abstraction unless they see the practical application

- Have clear visions of the way things should be
- Loyal and hardworking
- Like to be in charge
- Exceptionally capable in organizing and running activities
- "Good citizens" who value security and peaceful living

As an ESTJ, your primary mode of living is focused externally, where you deal with things rationally and logically. Your secondary mode is internal, where you take things in via your five senses in a literal, concrete fashion.

ESTJs live in a world of facts and concrete needs. They live in the present, with their eye constantly scanning their personal environment to make sure that everything is running smoothly and systematically. They honor traditions and laws and have a clear set of standards and beliefs. They expect the same of others and have no patience for or understanding of individuals who do not value these systems. They value competence and efficiency and like to see quick results for their efforts.

ESTJs are take-charge people. They have such a clear vision of the way that things should be that they naturally step into leadership roles. They are self-confident and aggressive. They are extremely talented at devising systems and plans for action and at being able to see what steps need to be taken to complete a specific task. They can sometimes be very demanding and critical because they have such strongly held beliefs and are likely to express themselves without reserve if they feel someone isn't meeting their standards. But at least their expressions can be taken at face value, because ESTJs is extremely straightforward and honest.

ESTJs are usually model citizens and pillars of the community. They take their commitments seriously and follow their own standards of "good citizenship" to the letter. ESTJs enjoy interacting with people, and like to have fun. ESTJs can be very boisterous and fun at social events, especially activities that are focused on the family, community, or work.

ESTJs need to watch out for the tendency to be too rigid and to become overly detail-oriented. Since they put a lot of weight in their own beliefs, it's important that they remember to value other people's input and opinions. If they neglect their Feeling side, they may have a problem with fulfilling other's needs for intimacy and may unknowingly hurt people's feelings by applying logic and reason to situations that demand more emotional sensitivity.

When bogged down by stress, an ESTJ often feels isolated from others. They feel as if they are misunderstood and undervalued and that their efforts are taken for granted. Although ESTJs are normally very verbal and don't have any problem expressing themselves, when under stress they have a hard time putting their feelings into words and communicating them to others.

ESTJs value security and social order above all else and feel obligated to do all that they can to enhance and promote these goals. They will mow the lawn, vote, join the PTA, attend homeowners' association meetings, and generally do anything that they can to promote personal and social security.

ESTJs put forth a lot of effort in almost everything that they do. They will do everything that they think should be done in their job, marriage, and community with a good amount of energy. They are conscientious, practical, realistic, and dependable. While ESTJs will dutifully do everything that is important to work toward a particular cause or goal, they might not naturally see or value the importance of goals that are outside of their practical scope. However, if they are able to see the relevance of such goals to practical concerns, you can bet that they'll put every effort into understanding them and incorporating them into their quest for clarity and security.

6.6.11 ESFP: The Performer

- People-oriented and fun-loving; make things more fun for others by their enjoyment
- Live for the moment; love new experiences
- Dislike theory and impersonal analysis
- Interested in serving others
- Likely to be the center of attention in social situations
- Well-developed common sense and practical ability

As an ESFP, your primary mode of living is focused externally, where you take things in via your five senses in a literal, concrete fashion. Your secondary mode is internal, where you deal with things according to how you feel about them or how they fit with your personal value system.

ESFPs live in the world of people possibilities. They love people and new experiences. They are lively and fun and enjoy being the center of attention. They live in the here and now and relish excitement and drama in their lives.

ESFPs have very strong interpersonal skills and may frequently find themselves in the role of peacemaker. Since they make decisions by using their personal values, they are usually very sympathetic and concerned for other people's well-being. They're usually quite generous and warm. They are very observant about other people and seem to sense what is wrong with someone before others might, responding warmly with a solution to a practical need. They might not be the best advice-givers in the world, because they dislike theory and future planning, but are great for giving practical care.

ESFPs are definitely spontaneous, optimistic individuals. They love to have fun. If ESFPs do not develop their Thinking side by giving consideration to rational thought processing, they tend to become overindulgent and place more importance on immediate sensation and gratification than on their duties and obligations. They may also avoid looking at the long-term consequences of their actions.

For the ESFP, the entire world is a stage. They love to be the center of attention and perform for people. They're constantly putting on a show for others to entertain them and make them happy. They enjoy stimulating other people's senses and are extremely good at it. They would love nothing more than for life to be a continual party in which they play the role of the fun-loving host.

ESFPs love people, and everybody loves an ESFP. One of their greatest gifts is their general acceptance of everyone. They are upbeat and enthusiastic and genuinely like almost everybody. An ESFP is unfailingly warm and generous with their friends, and they generally treat everyone as a friend. However, once crossed, an ESFP is likely to make a very strong and stubborn judgment against the person who crossed them. They are capable of deep dislike in such a situation.

ESFPs under a great deal of stress become overwhelmed with negative thoughts and possibilities. As optimistic individuals who live in the world of possibilities, negative possibilities do not sit well with them. In an effort to combat these thoughts, they're likely to come up with simple, global statements to explain away the problem. These simplistic explanations may or may not truly get to the nature of the issue, but they serve ESFPs well by allowing them to get over it.

ESFPs are likely to be very practical, although they hate structure and routine. They like to "go with the flow," trusting in their ability to improvise in any situation presented to them. They learn best with "hands-on" experience, rather than by studying a book. They're uncomfortable with theory. If ESFPs haven't developed their intuitive side, they may tend to avoid situations that involve a lot of theoretical thinking or are complex and ambiguous. For this reason, ESFPs may have difficulty in school. On the other hand, ESFPs do extremely well in situations where they're allowed to learn by interacting with others or in which they "learn by doing."

ESFPs have a very well-developed appreciation for aesthetic beauty and an excellent sense of space and function. If they have the means, they're likely to have to have many beautiful possessions and an artfully furnished home. In general, they take great pleasure in objects of aesthetic beauty. They're likely to have a strong appreciation for the finer things in life, such as good food and good wine.

ESFPs are great team players. They are not likely to create any problems or fuss and are likely to create the most fun environment possible for getting the task done. ESFPs will do best in careers in which they are able to use their excellent people skills, along with their abilities to meld ideas into structured formats. Since they are fast-paced individuals who like new experiences, they should choose careers that offer or require a lot of diversity, as well as people skills.

ESFPs usually like to feel strongly bonded with other people and have a connection with animals and small children that is not found in most other types. They're likely to have a strong appreciation for the beauties of nature as well.

ESFPs have a tremendous love for life and know how to have fun. They like to bring others along on their fun rides and are typically a lot of fun to be with. They're flexible, adaptable, genuinely interested in people, and usually kindhearted. They have a special ability to get a lot of fun out of life, but they need to watch out for the pitfalls associated with living entirely in the moment.

6.6.12 ESFJ: The Caregiver

- Warm-hearted, popular, and conscientious
- Tend to put the needs of others over their own needs
- Feel a strong sense of responsibility and duty
- Value traditions and security
- Interested in serving others
- Need positive reinforcement to feel good about themselves
- Well-developed sense of space and function

As an ESFJ, your primary mode of living is focused externally, where you deal with things according to how you feel about them or how they fit in with your personal value system. Your secondary mode is internal, where you take things in via your five senses in a literal, concrete fashion.

ESFJs are people persons; they love people. They are warmly interested in others. They use their Sensing and Judging characteristics to gather specific, detailed information about others and turn this information into supportive judgments. They want to like people and have a special skill at bringing out the best in others. They are extremely good at reading others and understanding their point of view. Their strong desire to be liked and for everything to be pleasant makes them highly supportive of others. People like to be around ESFJs, because the ESFJ has a special gift of invariably making people feel good about themselves.

ESFJs take their responsibilities very seriously and are very dependable. They value security and stability and have a strong focus on the details of life. They see before others do what needs to be done, and do whatever it takes to make sure that it gets done. They enjoy these types of tasks and are extremely good at them.

ESFJs are warm and energetic. They need approval from others to feel good about themselves. They are hurt by indifference and don't understand unkindness. They are very giving people who get a lot of their personal satisfaction from the happiness of others. They want to be appreciated for who they are and what they give. They're very sensitive to others and freely give practical care. ESFJs are such caring individuals that they sometimes have a hard time seeing or accepting a difficult truth about someone they care about.

With Extraverted Feeling dominating their personality, ESFJs are focused on reading other people. They have a strong need to be liked and to be in control. They are extremely good at reading others and often change their own manner to be more pleasing to whoever they're with at the moment.

ESFJs' value systems are defined externally. They usually have very well-formed ideas about the way things should be and are not shy about expressing these opinions. However, they weigh their values and morals against the world around them rather than against an internal value system. They may have a strong moral code, but it is defined by the community that they live in rather than by any strongly felt internal values.

ESFJs who have had the benefit of being raised and surrounded by a strong value system that is ethical and centered around genuine goodness will most likely be the kindest, most generous souls, who will gladly give you the shirt off their back without a second thought. For these individuals, the selfless quality of their personality type is genuine and pure. ESFJs who have not had the advantage of developing their own values by weighing them against a good external value system may develop very questionable values. In such cases, the ESFJ most often genuinely believes in the integrity of their skewed value system. They have no internal understanding of values to set them straight. In weighing their values against society, they find plenty of support for whatever moral transgression they wish to justify. These types of ESFJs are dangerous people indeed. Extraverted Feeling drives them to control and manipulate, and their lack of Intuition prevents them from seeing the big picture. They're usually quite popular and good with people, and good at manipulating them. Unlike their ENFJ cousin, they don't have Intuition to help them understand the real consequences of their actions. They are driven to manipulate others to achieve their own ends, yet they believe that they are following a solid moral code of conduct.

All ESFJs have a natural tendency to want to control their environment. Their dominant function demands structure and organization and seeks closure. ESFJs are most comfortable with structured environments. They're not likely to enjoy having to do things that involve abstract, theoretical concepts or impersonal analysis. They do enjoy creating order and structure and are very good at tasks that require these kinds of skills. ESFJs should be careful about controlling people in their lives who do not wish to be controlled.

ESFJs respect and believe in the laws and rules of authority and believe that others should do so as well. They're traditional and prefer to do things in the established way, rather than venturing into unchartered territory. Their need for security drives their ready acceptance and adherence to the policies of the established system. This tendency may cause them to sometimes blindly accept rules without questioning or understanding them.

An ESFJ who has developed in a less than ideal way may be prone to being quite insecure and focusing all of their attention on pleasing others. He or she might also be very controlling or overly sensitive, imagining bad intentions when there aren't any.

ESFJs incorporate many of the traits that are associated with women in our society. However, male ESFJs will usually not appear feminine at all. On the contrary, ESFJs are typically quite conscious about gender roles and will be most comfortable playing a role that suits their gender in our society. Male ESFJs will be quite masculine (albeit sensitive when you get to know them), and female ESFJs will be very feminine.

ESFJs at their best are warm, sympathetic, helpful, cooperative, tactful, down to earth, practical, thorough, consistent, organized, enthusiastic, and energetic. They enjoy tradition and security, and will seek stable lives that are rich in contact with friends and family.

6.6.13 ENFP: The Inspirer

- Enthusiastic, idealistic, and creative
- Able to do almost anything that interests them
- Great people skills
- Need to live life in accordance with their inner values
- Excited by new ideas but bored with details
- Open-minded and flexible, with a broad range of interests and abilities

As an ENFP, your primary mode of living is focused externally, where you take things in primarily via your intuition. Your secondary mode is internal, where you deal with things according to how you feel about them or how they fit in with your personal value system.

ENFPs are warm, enthusiastic people, typically very bright and full of potential. They live in the world of possibilities and can become very passionate and excited about things. Their enthusiasm lends them the ability to inspire and motivate others, more so than we see in other types. They can talk their way in or out of anything. They love life, seeing it as a special gift, and strive to make the most out of it.

ENFPs have an unusually broad range of skills and talents. They are good at most things that interest them. Project-oriented, they may go through several different careers during their lifetime. To onlookers, the ENFP may seem directionless and without purpose, but ENFPs are actually quite consistent, in that they have a strong sense of values that they live with throughout their lives. Everything that they do must be in line with their values. An ENFP needs to feel that they are living their lives as their true self, walking in step with what they believe is right. They see meaning in everything and are on a continuous quest to adapt their lives and values to achieve inner peace. They're constantly aware and somewhat fearful of losing touch with themselves. Since emotional excitement is usually an important part of their lives, and because they are focused on keeping "centered," ENFPs are usually intense individuals with highly evolved values.

ENFPs need to focus on following through with their projects. This can be a problem area for some of these individuals. Unlike other Extraverted types, ENFPs need time alone to center themselves and make sure they are moving in a direction that is in sync with their values. ENFPs who remain centered will usually be quite successful at their endeavors. Others may fall into the habit of dropping a project when they become excited about a new possibility, and thus they never achieve the great accomplishments that they are capable of achieving.

Most ENFPs have great people skills. They are genuinely warm and interested in people and place great importance on their interpersonal relationships. ENFPs almost always have a strong need to be liked. Sometimes, especially at a younger age, ENFPs will tend to be "gushy" and insincere, and generally "overdo" in an effort to win acceptance. However, once ENFPs learn to balance their need to be true to themselves with their need for acceptance, they excel at bringing out the best in others and are typically well liked. They have an exceptional ability to intuitively understand a person after a very short period of time and use their intuition and flexibility to relate to others on their own level.

Because ENFPs live in the world of exciting possibilities, the details of everyday life are seen as trivial drudgery. They place no importance on detailed, maintenance-type tasks and will frequently remain oblivious to these types of concerns. When they do have to perform these tasks, they do not enjoy themselves. This is a challenging area of life for most ENFPs and can be frustrating for family members.

ENFPs who have "gone wrong" may be quite manipulative, and very good it. The gift of the gab that they are blessed with makes it naturally easy for them to get what they want. Most ENFPs will not abuse their abilities, because that would not jive with their value systems.

ENFPs sometimes make serious errors in judgment. They have an amazing ability to intuitively perceive the truth about a person or situation, but when they apply judgment to their perception, they may jump to the wrong conclusions.

ENFPs who have not learned to follow through may have a difficult time remaining happy in marital relationships. Always seeing the possibilities of what could be, they may become bored with what actually is. The strong sense of values will keep many ENFPs dedicated to their relationships. However, ENFPs like a little excitement in their lives and are best matched with individuals who are comfortable with change and new experiences.

Having an ENFP parent can be a fun-filled experience but may be stressful at times for children with strong Sensing or Judging tendencies. Such children may see the ENFP parent as inconsistent and difficult to understand, as the children are pulled along in the whirlwind life of the ENFP. Sometimes ENFPs will want to be their child's best friend, and at other times they will play the parental authoritarian. But ENFPs are always consistent in their value systems, which they will impress on their children above all else, along with a basic joy of living.

ENFPs are basically happy people. They may become unhappy when they are confined to strict schedules or mundane tasks. Consequently, ENFPs work best in situations where they have a lot of flexibility and where they can work with people and ideas. Many go into business for themselves. They have the ability to be quite productive with little supervision, as long as they are excited about what they're doing.

Because they are so alert and sensitive, constantly scanning their environments, ENFPs often suffer from muscle tension. They have a strong need to be independent, and resist being controlled or labeled. They need to maintain control over themselves, but they do not believe in controlling others. Their dislike of dependence and suppression extends to others as well as to themselves.

ENFPs are charming, ingenuous, risk-taking, sensitive, people-oriented individuals with capabilities ranging across a broad spectrum. They have many gifts that they will use to fulfill themselves and those near them, if they are able to remain centered and master the ability of following through.

6.6.14 ENFJ: The Giver

- Popular and sensitive, with outstanding people skills
- Externally focused, with real concern for how others think and feel
- Usually dislike being alone
- See everything from the human angle and dislike impersonal analysis
- Very effective at managing people issues and leading group discussions
- Interested in serving others and probably place the needs of others over their own

As an ENFJ, you're primary mode of living is focused externally, where you deal with things according to how you feel about them or how they fit into your personal value system. Your secondary mode is internal, where you take things in primarily via your intuition.

ENFJs are people-focused individuals. They live in the world of people possibilities. More so than any other type, they have excellent people skills. They understand and care about people, and have a special talent for bringing out the best in others. Their main interest in life is giving love, support, and a good time to other people. They are focused on understanding, supporting, and encouraging others. They make things happen for people and get their best personal satisfaction from this.

Because their people skills are so extraordinary, ENFJs have the ability to make people do exactly what they want them to do. They get under people's skins and get the reactions that they are seeking. Their motives are usually unselfish, but ENFJs who have developed less than ideally have been known to use their power over people to manipulate them.

ENFJs are so externally focused that it's especially important for them to spend time alone. This can be difficult for some ENFJs, because they have the tendency to be hard on themselves and turn to dark thoughts when alone. Consequently, ENFJs might avoid being alone and fill their lives with activities involving other people. ENFJs tend to define their life's direction and priorities according to other people's needs and may not be aware of their own needs. It's natural to their personality type that they will tend to place other people's needs above their own, but they need to stay aware of their own needs so that they don't sacrifice themselves in their drive to help others.

ENFJs tend to be more reserved about exposing themselves than other extraverted types. Although they may have strongly felt beliefs, they're likely to refrain from expressing them if doing so would interfere with bringing out the best in others. Because their strongest interest lies in being a catalyst of change in other people, they're likely to interact with others on their own level, in a chameleon-like manner, rather than as individuals.

Which is not to say that ENFJs do not have opinions. ENFJs have definite values and opinions that they're able to express clearly and succinctly. These beliefs will be expressed as long as they're not too personal. ENFJs are in many ways expressive and open, but more focused on being responsive and supportive of others. When faced with a conflict between a strongly held value and serving another person's need, they are highly likely to value the other person's needs.

6.6.15 ENTP: The Visionary

- Creative, resourceful, and intellectually quick
- Good at a broad range of things
- Enjoy debating issues and may be into "one-upmanship"
- Get very excited about new ideas and projects but may neglect the more routine aspects of life
- Generally outspoken and assertive
- Enjoy people and are stimulating company
- Excellent ability to understand concepts and apply logic to find solutions

As an ENTP, your primary mode of living is focused externally, where you take things in primarily via your intuition. Your secondary mode is internal, where you deal with things rationally and logically.

With Extraverted Intuition dominating their personality, ENTPs' primary interest in life is understanding the world that they live in. They are constantly absorbing ideas and images about the situations they are presented in their lives. Using their intuition to process this information, they are usually extremely quick and accurate in their ability to size up a situation. With the exception of their ENFP cousin, the ENTP has a deeper understanding of their environment than any of the other types.

This ability to intuitively understand people and situations puts ENTPs at a distinct advantage in their lives. They generally understand things quickly and with great depth. Accordingly, they are quite flexible and adapt well to a wide range of tasks. They are good at most anything that interests them. As they grow and further develop their intuitive abilities and insights, they become very aware of possibilities, and this makes them quite resourceful when solving problems.

ENTPs are idea people. Their perceptive abilities cause them to see possibilities everywhere. They get excited and enthusiastic about their ideas and are able to spread their enthusiasm to others. In this way, they get the support that they need to fulfill their visions.

ENTPs are less interested in developing plans of actions or making decisions than they are in generating possibilities and ideas. Following through on the implementation of an idea is usually a chore to the ENTP. For some ENTPs, this results in the habit of never finishing what they start. The ENTP who has not developed their Thinking process will have problems with jumping enthusiastically from idea to idea, without following through on their plans. The ENTP needs to take care to think through their ideas fully in order to take advantage of them.

ENTPs' auxiliary process of Introverted Thinking drives their decision-making process. Although ENTPs are more interested in absorbing information than in making decisions, they are quite rational and logical in reaching conclusions. When they apply Thinking to their Intuitive perceptions, the outcome can be very powerful indeed. A well-developed ENTP is extremely visionary, inventive, and enterprising.

ENTPs are fluent conversationalists, mentally quick, and enjoy verbal sparring with others. They love to debate issues and may even switch sides sometimes just for the love of the debate. When they express their underlying principles, however, they may feel awkward and speak abruptly and intensely.

The ENTP personality type is sometimes referred to the *lawyer* type. ENTP lawyers quickly and accurately understand a situation and objectively and logically act on it. Their Thinking side bases their actions and decisions on an objective list of rules or laws. If ENTPs were to defend someone who had actually committed a crime, they would be likely to take advantage of quirks in the law that would get their client off the hook. If they were to actually win the case, they would see their actions as completely fair and proper to the situation, because their actions were lawful. The guilt or innocence of their client would not be as relevant. If this type of reasoning goes completely unchecked by ENTPs, it can result in a character that is perceived by others as unethical or even dishonest. ENTPs who do not naturally consider the more personal or human element in decision making should take care to notice the subjective, personal side of situations. This is a potential problem for ENTPs. Although their logical abilities lend them strength and purpose, they may also isolate them from their feelings and from other people.

The least developed area for ENTPs is the Sensing–Feeling arena. If the Sensing areas are neglected, ENTPs may tend to not take care of details in their lives. If the Feeling part of themselves is neglected, ENTPs may not value other people's input enough or may become overly harsh and aggressive.

Under stress, ENTPs may lose their ability to generate possibilities and become obsessed with minor details. These details may seem to be extremely important to ENTPs, but in reality they are usually not important to the big picture.

In general, ENTPs are upbeat visionaries. They highly value knowledge and spend much of their lives seeking a higher understanding. They live in the world of possibilities and become excited about concepts, challenges, and difficulties. When presented with a problem, they're good at improvising and quickly coming up with a creative solution. Creative, clever, curious, and theoretical, ENTPs have a broad range of possibilities in their lives.

6.6.16 ENTJ: The Executive

- Assertive and outspoken; driven to lead
- Excellent ability to understand difficult organizational problems and create solid solutions
- Intelligent and well informed; usually excel at public speaking
- Value knowledge and competence; usually have little patience with inefficiency or disorganization

As an ENTJ, your primary mode of living is focused externally, where you deal with things rationally and logically. Your secondary mode is internal, where you take things in primarily via your intuition.

ENTJs are natural born leaders. They live in a world of possibilities, where they see all sorts challenges to be surmounted and they want to be the ones responsible for surmounting them. They have a drive for leadership, which is well served by their quickness to grasp complexities, their ability to absorb a large amount of impersonal information, and their quick and decisive judgments. They are take-charge people.

ENTJs are very career-focused and fit into the corporate world quite naturally. They are constantly scanning their environment for potential problems that they can turn into solutions. They generally see things from a long-range perspective and are usually successful at identifying plans to turn problems around—especially problems of a corporate nature. ENTJs are usually successful in the business world, because they are so driven to leadership. They're tireless in their efforts on the job and driven to visualize where an organization is headed. For these reasons, they are natural corporate leaders.

There is not much room for error in the world of ENTJs. They dislike to see mistakes repeated and have no patience with inefficiency. They may become quite harsh when their patience is tried in these respects, because they are not naturally tuned in to people's feelings and more than likely don't believe that they should tailor their judgments in consideration for people's feelings. ENTJs, like many types, have difficulty seeing things from outside their own perspective. Unlike other types, ENTJs naturally have little patience with people who do not see things the same way as they do. ENTJs need to consciously work on recognizing the value of other people's opinions, as well as the value of being sensitive toward people's feelings. In the absence of this awareness, ENTJs will be forceful, intimidating, and overbearing individuals. This may be a real problem for ENTJs, who may be deprived of important information and collaboration from others. In their personal world, it can make some ENTJs overbearing as spouses or parents.

ENTJs have a tremendous amount of personal power and presence, which will work for them as a force toward achieving their goals. However, this personal power is also an agent of alienation and self-aggrandizement, which ENTJs would do well to avoid.

ENTJs are very forceful, decisive individuals. They make decisions quickly and are quick to verbalize their opinions and decisions to the rest of the world. ENTJs who have not developed their Intuition will make decisions too hastily, without understanding all of the issues and possible solutions. On the other hand, ENTJs who have not developed their Thinking side will have difficulty applying logic to their insights and will often make poor decisions. In that case, they may have brilliant ideas and insight into situations, but they may have little skill at determining how to act on their understanding, or their actions may be inconsistent. ENTJs who have developed in a generally less than ideal way may become dictatorial and abrasive—intrusively giving orders and direction without a sound reason for doing so and without consideration for the people involved.

Although ENTJs are not naturally tuned in to other people's feelings, these individuals frequently have very strong sentimental streaks. Often these sentiments are very powerful to ENTJs, although they will likely hide it from general knowledge, believing the feelings to be a weakness. Because the world of feelings and values is not where ENTJs naturally function, they may sometimes make value judgments and hold on to submerged emotions that are ill-founded and inappropriate, and will cause them problems—sometimes rather serious ones.

ENTJs love to interact with people. As Extroverts, they're energized and stimulated primarily externally. There's nothing more enjoyable and satisfying to ENTJs than having a lively, challenging conversation. They especially respect people who are able to stand up to them and argue persuasively for their point of view. There aren't too many people who will do so, however, because ENTJs are a very forceful and dynamic presence and have a tremendous amount of self-confidence and excellent verbal communication skills. Even the most confident individuals may experience moments of self-doubt when debating a point with an ENTJ.

ENTJs want their home to be beautiful, well furnished, and efficiently run. They're likely to place much emphasis on their children being well educated and structured, and to desire a congenial and devoted relationship with their spouse. At home, ENTJs need to be in charge as much as they are in their career. ENTJs are likely best paired with someone who has a strong self-image, who is also a Thinking type. Because ENTJs are primarily focused on their careers, some have a problem with being constantly absent from home, physically or mentally.

ENTJs have many gifts that make it possible for them to have a great deal of personal power, if they don't forget to remain balanced in their lives. They are assertive, innovative, long-range thinkers with an excellent ability to translate theories and possibilities into solid plans of action. They are usually tremendously forceful personalities and have the tools to accomplish whatever goals they set out for.

Notes

1. Median income represents earnings from all sources. Unincorporated self-employment income includes unpaid family workers, a very small percentage of the unincorporated self-employed.
2. Routamaa, V., and Miettinen, A. *Knowing Entrepreneurial Personalities: A Prerequisite for Entrepreneurial Education.* http://www.intent-conference.de.
3. Cherry, K. (2016). Learning styles based on Jung's theory of personality. Verywellmind, January. https://www.verywell.com/jungs-theory-of-personality-learning-styles-2795160.
4. McLeod, S. (2014). Carl Jung. Simply Psychology. http://www.simplypsychology.org/carl-jung.html.
5. Kroeger, O. (1992). *Type Talk at Work.* New York: Dell.
6. Honaker, S. L. (2003). True colors: New implications from convergent validity research with the Myers–Briggs Type Indicator. Paper presented at the National Career Development Conference, Westminster, CO.
7. Carlson, J. G. (1985). Recent assessment of the Myers–Briggs Type Indicator. *Journal of Personality Assessment,* 49(4): 356–465.
8. Myers, et al. (1998). *MBTI Manual: A Guide to the Development and Use of the Myers–Briggs Type Indicator.* Palo Alto, CA: Consulting Psychologists Press.
9. Myers, I., and McCaulley, M. H. (1990). *Manual: A Guide to the Development and Use of the Myers–Briggs Type Indicator.* CA: Consulting Psychologists Press.

10. https://www.iccb.org/iccb/wpcontent/pdfs/adulted/tdl_bridge_curriculum/tdl_career_awareness/tdl_career_aware_resource_file/Suggested_Careers_for_MBTI.pdf

11. Rwigema, H., and Venter, R. (2004). *Advanced Entrepreneurship*. Oxfird, UK: Oxford University Press.

12. Deo, S. (2005). Challenges for small business entrepreneurs: A study in the Walka region of New Zealand. Small Business Advancement National Centre, University of Arkansas. http://www.sbaer.uca.edu/research/icsb/2005/056.pdf.

13. Human Metrics. Career choices for your type. http://www.humanmetrics.com/personality/career-choices.

14. Personality Page. Common careers for personality types. https://www.personalitypage.com/careers.html.

15. Routamaa, V., and Vesalainen, J. (1987). Types of entrepreneur and strategic level goal setting. *International Small Business Journal*, 5(3): 19–29.

16. Ramabhadran, R. What do the 4 parts of Myers–Briggs mean? Quora. https://www.quora.com/What-do-the-4-parts-of-Myers-Briggs-mean.

17. Personality Page. High-level description of the sixteen personality types. http://www.personalitypage.com/high-level.html.

18. All profiles, source data, methodology notes, and county-level employment statistics are available at http://go.usa.gov/cfKMd.

Section III

Entrepreneurial Environment

7

Leadership Qualities

Open the curtains behind any major innovation
and you will find an entrepreneur.

7.1 Introduction

An entrepreneur is one who envisions, organizes, directs, funds, and manages a new business. A successful business is one that will build lasting value for the founder as well as all the stakeholders. Figure 7.1 presents in graphical format what the "entrepreneurial animal" looks like.

Many skills have been identified as being crucial to entrepreneurs, including initiative, problem solving, perseverance, independent thinking, stamina, commitment, self-confidence, and above all, having an instinct for risk-taking—*not gambling but managing risks*. The entrepreneurial environment can be visualized as shown in Figure 7.2.

Lifelong employment in a large corporation is no longer considered the preferred objective of many college graduates. The corporate world is no longer perceived as the ultimate expression of individual success. The "self-made" person has a unique, romantic, and individualistic appeal, particularly if this leads to personal wealth while contributing to the nation's overall economic well-being. To become economically independent through individual effort—entrepreneurship—is the highest expression of the American dream.

Some individuals appeared entrepreneurial from a tender age, selling lemonade, cutting grass, selling cupcakes, and so on. Once the inherent entrepreneurial talent has been discovered, most learned entrepreneurs can tip the balance in their favor by following and studying the behavior patterns of experienced entrepreneurs. This chapter allows you to closely analyze the secrets behind winning founders and entrepreneurs and improve your chances of success.

The "entrepreneurial animal"

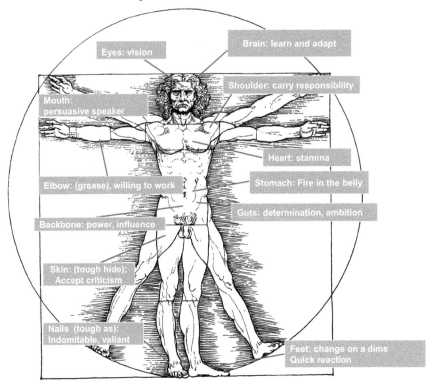

FIGURE 7.1
The mythical entrepreneur as depicted by anatomical features. (Photo released under Creative Commons license, attribution to Hans Bernhard.)

Entrepreneurial balance

FIGURE 7.2
Entrepreneurs are "risk managers" not "gamblers."

TABLE 7.1

Murphy's Eight Leadership Roles

1. Select the right people.
2. Connect them to the right cause.
3. Solve problems that arise.
4. Evaluate progress toward objectives.
5. Negotiate resolutions to conflicts.
6. Heal the wounds inflicted by change.
7. Protect their cultures from the perils of crisis.
8. Synergize all stakeholders to achieve improvements together.

7.2 Leadership Qualities: Startups Are Started by Leaders

Leadership can be defined as the knowledge and skills that enable a person to use reason, power, and influence to persuade others to follow a desired course of action. Murphy[1] discovered that leadership can be defined and measured as a form of intelligence, defined by eight specific roles, as shown in Table 7.1.

Visually, some of the most crucial leaderships skills found in founders and leaders are depicted in Figure 7.3.

7.2.1 Leaders versus Managers

There is a very big difference between a leader and a manager in their behavior patterns. The ability to raise capital, inspire confidence, and nurture a

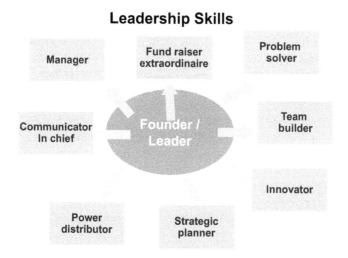

FIGURE 7.3

The eight leadership skills—crucial to founder/leaders.

TABLE 7.2

Differences between Leaders and Managers in Startups

Leaders	Managers (traditional roles)
Heroic figures	Planners and budgeteers
Strategist in chief, visionaries	Organizers (coping with complexity)
Change leaders, chaos managers	Directors (organizing and staffing)
Problem solvers	Controllers (monitoring activities)
Great negotiators	
Motivators, influencers, innovators	
Corporate spokespersons	
Resource finders	

"Managing is doing things right; leadership is doing the right things." — Warren Bennis and Peter Drucker

fledgling business is crucial to leader-entrepreneurs. Particularly in a startup organization, those differences are magnified. This is dramatically seen in Table 7.2.

Thus, according to *our* definition, Lee Iacocca (Ford Mustang), Carly Fiorina (Hewlett-Packard), and Jack Welch (General Electric) are *not* entrepreneurs. These individuals did not form new firms with innovations as they created new wealth for their shareholders. In contrast, business leaders like Bill Gates (Microsoft), Frederick W. Smith (FedEx), Sam Walton (Walmart), Arthur Blank and Bernie Marcus (Home Depot), Howard Schultz (Starbucks), Steve Jobs (Apple Computers), Andrew Carnegie (U.S. Steel), and Michael Dell (Dell Computer) were all entrepreneurs.

7.2.2 Centrality of Leadership in a Startup

A startup is a business that is in the early process of developing the infrastructure to operate as an ongoing business. The entrepreneur-leader is the person that (1) foresaw an opportunity, (2) assembled a startup team, (3) performed proof-of-principle studies, and (4) raised enough early-stage capital to initiate operations.

Starting a business "from scratch" takes a lot guts, hard work, and some luck. However, the leader does not rely on luck; they make their own luck by hard work. Thomas Alva Edison, one of the most prolific American inventors, quipped when asked to what he attributed his luck in inventing so many products, "The harder I work, the luckier I get." *Time* magazine dedicated an entire issue to Edison, the inventor.

Leadership entails convincing, motivating, inspiring, and above all, leading and controlling *change*. Veteran entrepreneurs will tell you that their most challenging aspect of a startup was preparing their staff to accept fast-paced technical and economic change, since we are all preprogrammed to resist change. This is illustrated in Figure 7.4.

The centrality of leadership

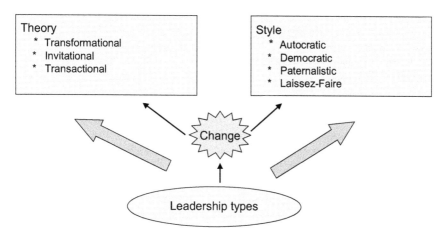

Theory
* Transformational
* Invitational
* Transactional

Style
* Autocratic
* Democratic
* Paternalistic
* Laissez-Faire

Change

Leadership types

FIGURE 7.4
Leadership is about change.

Transformational leadership introduces widespread changes to an organization; *invitational leadership* strives to build relationships and a general sense of belonging; *transactional leadership* focuses on management, efficiency rules, and regulations.

The *autocratic style* is when the leader makes all decisions without staff consultation or input. The *democratic* leader encourages consensus and majority rule. The *paternalistic style* fosters a "parent figure" that forgives the transgressions of the staff. Finally, the *laissez-faire* (French; "let it be") leader allows decisions to be made by everyone, relying on the ability and goodwill of the entire senior staff.

7.2.3 Leadership Is Situational

> *Leadership is a journey. Greatness is its destination.*

Leaders will find that every senior employee (follower) requires a different style of leadership, depending on their individual development level (maturity). Thus, leadership is situational.

To address this issue, Hersey and Blanchard[2] proposed that leaders should adapt their style to follower development style (or maturity) based on how ready and willing the follower is to perform required tasks (i.e., their competence and motivation).[3] This is presently known as the Situational Leadership® Model (SLM).

TABLE 7.3

Four Situational Leadership Styles (in Response to Follower Development Level)

S1: Telling/directing	S2: Selling/coaching
High task focus, low relationship focus	High task focus, high relationship focus
S3: Participating/supporting	S4: Delegating/observing
Low task focus, high relationship focus	Low task focus, low relationship focus
(follower lead)	(follower lead)

SLM is best used when a leader (1) engages in two-way communication with a follower and asks the follower for input, (2) listens and provides support and encouragement to the follower, (3) involves the follower in decision making to facilitate problem solving, and (4) encourages and promotes self-reliant follower behavior in the follower.

There are four leadership styles (S1 to S4) that match the development levels (D1 to D4) of the followers. The four styles suggest that leaders should put greater or less focus on the task in question and/or the relationship between the leader and the follower, depending on the development level of the follower. This is summarized in Tables 7.3 and 7.4.

Visually, SLM can be summarized in Figure 7.5.[4]

In summary, the SLM theory states that successful leaders adapt their leadership style to the needs of the situation. Effective leaders should know that there is no one best way to manage people. Leaders adapt their style according to the development level of the people they are leading.

7.3 Establishing Your Founder Team

The founder team is the group of founders, key personnel, and advisers that established the startup organization. Generally (50%–70%), the team is started by more than one individual, although not all team members have the same amount of initial stock ownership (founder's shares).

The characteristics of your team will have huge consequences on the manner in which your business will operate, including organizational structure, culture, power and influence, and business strategy and tactics.

You will need to decide whether the members of your founding team are *heterogeneous*, that is, diverse in terms of their abilities and experiences, or

TABLE 7.4

Four Development Levels of Followers

D1: Low competence, low commitment/ unable and unwilling or insecure	D2: Some competence, variable commitment/ unable but willing or motivated
D3: High competence, variable commitment/ able but unwilling or insecure	D4: High competence, high commitment/ able and willing or motivated

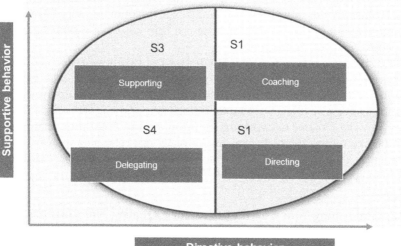

FIGURE 7.5
How you provide leadership depends on the situation.

homogeneous, that is, similar to one another in terms of their abilities and experiences.

The founder with a controlling share majority may easily ask, "Why do I need to build a team?" Because lenders and investors prefer an A team with a B product, rather than a B team with an A product. Table 7.5 summarizes the most important characteristics to consider.

TABLE 7.5

Characteristics of Founder Teams

- Founder has (1) higher education credentials, (2) prior successful entrepreneurial experience, (3) recognized expertise in a relevant technical area, and (4) professional contacts and has provided (5) "sweat equity" to the firm.
- Teams bring a combination of talents, resources, and experience unmatched by any single individual.
- Frequently, the team does not come together all at once. Instead, it is built as the new firm can afford to hire additional talent. At first, the firm may rely on non-paid volunteers willing the help get the organization "off the ground."
- The team also involves more than insiders. Most startup teams consist of BODs, BOAs, and professionals on whom they rely for direction and advice.
- New ventures have a high propensity to fail. The high failure rate is due in part to what researchers call the "liability of newness." Startups often falter because the people who start the firms cannot adjust quickly enough to their new roles and because the firm lacks a "track record" with investors, buyers, and suppliers.

Source: Modified after Barringer, B. R., Ireland RD building a new-venture team, http://wps. pearsoned.co.uk/wps/media/objects/8940/9155051/ema_ge_barringer_e3_ppt_09.ppt.

7.3.1 Elements of Skilled Teams

Skilled teams bring credibility and stability to the startup. The founder will quickly find that their area of expertise is not enough to ensure business success. Ironically, the founder starts an as expert (someone who knows more and more about less and less) but, after the firm has been established, needs to become the great "generalist."

The skilled team brings access to all areas of business expertise, such as marketing, sales, manufacturing, accounting, and finance. It is generally accepted that startups survive when standing on the shoulders of many persons, especially those with business, science, and engineering skills. The team provides greater networking (building and maintaining relationships with people whose interests are similar or whose relationships could bring advantages to a firm[5]) and a diverse knowledge base, thus providing the ability to specialize in specific tasks. This is illustrated in Figure 7.6.

7.3.2 Establishing Your Board of Directors: Quality, Not Quantity

If you have organized your venture as a corporation, you are legally required to have a Board of Directors (BOD). A BOD is a panel of individuals elected by a corporation to oversee the governance of the entity. Corporate governance involves regulatory and market mechanisms, and the roles and relationships between a company's management, board, shareholders, and other stakeholders, and the goals for which the corporation is governed.[6] The best boards do more than govern: they should ensure that your board adds value to your firm.

The Founder Team Elements

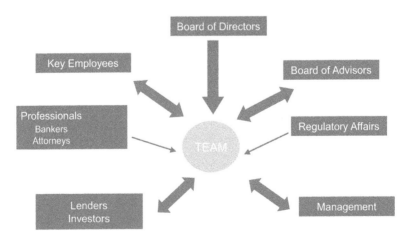

FIGURE 7.6
The seven most important elements of a founder team.

In addition to fulfilling the traditional roles of setting and monitoring the implementation of business strategy, boards are increasingly providing greater contributions in operations, succession planning, executive compensation, risk management, tactical decision making, marketing strategies, and so on.

Startups always want to start with an odd number of directors (typically three or five) to prevent potential deadlock on tricky issues. In addition to the founder, who usually serves as board chairman, there is a tendency to evenly split between inside directors (persons who work for the company) and outside directors (directors who are independent and unaffiliated with the firm), to ensure examination of issues from a balanced perspective.

The greatest benefit of a BOD is based on their knowledge and understanding of the industry. Good directors closely examine strategic plans, assumptions, aggressiveness, and current market realities. Lastly, as a group, the BOD should bring expertise in specialized areas, such as financial auditing, fundraising, regulatory experience, and overseas operations.

The BOD has primary responsibility for overseeing and implementing the company's governance system. While responsibility for implementing the various activities is delegated to isolated functional areas, the BOD connects all the activities into one coherent set of rules, as depicted in Figure 7.7.

A board of advisers (BOA) is a panel of experts convened by the founder to provide counsel, advice, and direction on an ongoing basis. Importantly,

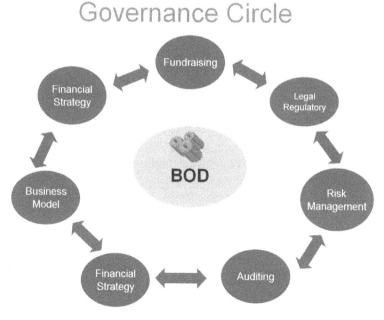

FIGURE 7.7
Corporate governance at a glance.

TABLE 7.6

Considerations When Choosing BOA Members

Does the candidate possess the technical skills relative to the firm?
Are they well known and respected in their field?
What is their success track record in similar small organizations?
Does the candidate have experience dealing with startups?
Has the candidate published papers in relevant technical journals?
Can the candidate get along with experts in other fields?

members of the BOA do not have legal liability to the firms, since their opinions are considered to be advisory and nonbinding in nature. Legally and operationally, BOAs are established for the purpose of providing expert opinions to management on specific issues, and thus less of their time is required.

Table 7.6 presents some important considerations when choosing your BOA members.

7.4 Authority, Power, and Influence

When we disagree I am right, and when we agree we are both right.

The word *authority* is derived from the Latin word *auctoritas*, meaning invention, advice, opinion, influence, or command. In an entrepreneurial context, the word *authority* is generally used to mean the persuasion capacity given by possession of formal academic knowledge.[7]

Power is the ability of a team member to produce or force desired effects on others.[8] It is the potential ability to change the course of events, change behavior, and overcome organizational resistance. *Influence* is the ability to effectuate desired change by virtue of authority and/or power. Both terms are derived from the Latin words *potere* ("to be able, capable") and *influere* ("to flow in, from within"). Thus, power is the ability to effectuate change, while influence is the practical exercise of power.[9]

In many startups, the founder exerts both authority and power.[10] Initially, the founder is the recognized and uncontested leader by virtue of the expert knowledge that allowed the establishment of the firm in the first place. Power is derived from five recognized sources: legitimate, reward, coercive, expert, and referent.[11] This is depicted in Figure 7.8.

- *Legitimate power* is conferred as a result of formal titles, that is, CEO, president, vice president, and so on. The founder starts with a great deal of legitimate power, since the dual titles of chairman of the board and president are at the top rung of the organization.

Types of power

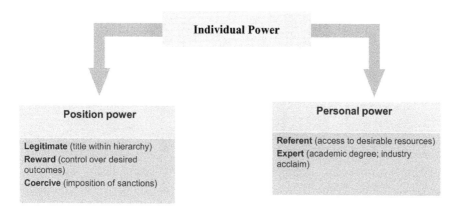

FIGURE 7.8
The two types of individual power.

- *Reward and coercive powers* are highly influential based on control over distribution of valuable compensation (salaries, awards, and recognition) or punishment of unwanted behavior.
- *Referent power* derives from the possession of or access to scarce resources (budgets, meeting schedules, and attendance to technical conferences).
- *Expert power* is based on advanced technical degrees, specialized skills, information, knowledge, and know-how ("knowledge is power").

At this point, we need to emphasize a crucial distinction between authority and power. Since authority and status are derived from personal knowledge, they are always and permanently relevant, unless made obsolete by new technology. Conversely, power is frequently dependent on reciprocity ("If you agree to do this for me, I will owe you one"); it constantly diminishes. It can be likened to a car battery that can provide a charge when needed, but it needs periodic recharging, as illustrated in Figure 7.9.

7.5 The Founder and Organizational Politics

It is not about who is in charge, but who takes charge.

Whether the founder wants it or not, organizational politics occurs in every business environment. In the business environment, politics is the informal

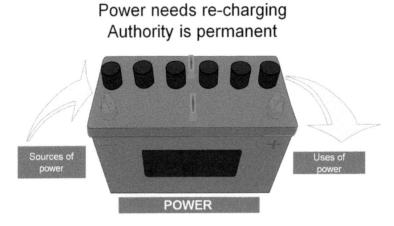

Power needs re-charging
Authority is permanent

Sources of power

Uses of power

POWER

FIGURE 7.9
Difference between power and authority.

struggle for personal dominance, where each player struggles to make their abilities and achievements known to the group.[12]

Anytime that humans associate in a group, politics will be part of the interaction, and the startup is no exception. In fact, startups are ripe for politics, since the official organizational chart may not accurately reflect who are the real leaders and who are the real followers. Figure 7.10 is an "official" generic organizational chart.

But in reality, there exists a phantom, parallel, unofficial chart that more accurately reflects who gets things done, shown in Figure 7.11.

A parallel organization differs from a traditional, hierarchical organization in that it reflects organizational politics. It is possible—and sometimes advantageous—to blend an official structure with a parallel structure. For example, a subset of employees can act as a parallel structure to develop solutions to specific problems (situational leadership).

Organizational politics are most acute in a startup setting when there is (1) high emotional insecurity, (2) a chaotic atmosphere, (3) a scarcity of resources, (4) a highly competitive and fluid work environment, (5) an impending financial or technological crisis, and (6) a continually evolving set of individual performance standards.[13] We will discuss organizational politics more fully in subsequent sections.

7.5.1 Szycher's Founder's Supremacy Theory

> Successful companies did not start from third base.

Startups must be built from the ground up. And the politically skilled, politically savvy employees are some of the most effective builders of the company. Ahearn defined political skill[14] as "the ability to effectively understand

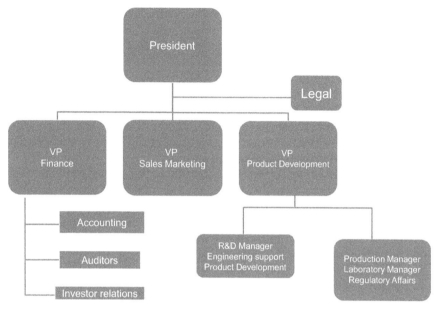

FIGURE 7.10
A typical entrepreneurial organization chart.

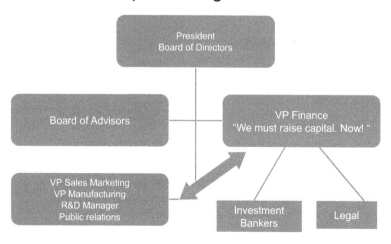

FIGURE 7.11
The Board of Directors must provide clear strategic direction to the organization.

others at work, and to use such knowledge to influence others to act in ways that enhance one's personal and/or organizational objectives." We will call the politically skilled/savvy "actors."

Politics is a fact of life, whether you want it or not. Actually, politics is one of the most important mechanisms that enable actors to get things done quickly and efficiently. The politics of the organization even helps to shape culture, and vice versa. Political moves are made so that managers can get things done with a minimum of resistance.

There is often a negative connotation when the word *politics* is whispered. But politics is far from being a negative; only bad actors give it a bad name. When properly applied, politics is an important managerial tool of the actor. The unpleasant name comes from the few unethical actors who play "dirty politics," mainly for their own benefit, not the organization as a whole. The best actors are seldom recognized by those around them.

To advance organizational objectives, politically skilled leaders form coalitions to secure their power bases and to protect their occupancy of powerful, central positions in the organization. The most powerful of these coalitions are called *dominant coalitions*,[15] and wield the highest amounts of power in the organization.

Politically skilled/savvy individuals share some important performance characteristics, summarized in Figure 7.12.

The main trick of politics is to make it appear rational and in the best interest of the organization (not the political actor). And, politics is best done in the shade. "The rattlesnake that survives is the one that doesn't rattle." Importantly, the founder is above all this maneuvering, having authority by virtue of title, knowledge, and voting power, as depicted in Szycher's founder's supremacy theory, illustrated in Figure 7.13.

As you can deduce from Figure 7.13, Szycher's founder supremacy theory relates to organizational politics. It can be summarized as politics is not something you do *to* people; politics is something you do *with* people.

Characteristics of politically skilled/savvy

- Actively promote their boss
- Correctly identify true power brokers
- Constantly improve their technical knowledge
- Volunteer to write meeting agendas and minutes
- Design and author business documents dealing with rules, regulations, procedures, etc.
- Are part of the dominant coalition
- Publicize their activities as "best for the company"
- Always seem ready to tackle the most difficult problems
- Are "doers" not "talkers"
- Develop a reputation for getting things done on time
- Their solutions to problems are practical and timely
- Are always there when you "most need them"

FIGURE 7.12
How to become a master business "politician."

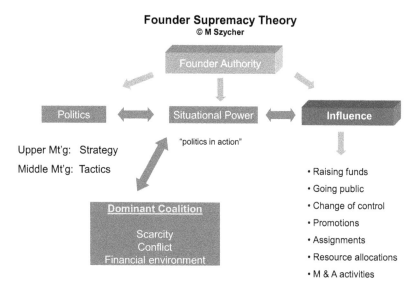

FIGURE 7.13
The founder starts with unlimited authority.

7.5.2 Organizational Persona

The founder sets the tone by their "imprimatur" not only for the political environment but also for the persona of the organization. In every respect, the firm reflects the personality of the founder, and the dominant coalition moves the company forward through organizational politics. Organizational politics can be defined as "intentional acts of influence to enhance, protect and advance the self-interests of individuals."[16]

The founder decides the organizational persona by their initial decisions, as presented in Figure 7.14.

Organizational persona as determined by founder

- **Hunting?**   **Or**   **Fishing?**
- **Manufacture?** **Or**   **Outsource?**
- **Gazelle?**   **Or**   **Turtle?**
- **Family?**   **Or**   **Harvest?**
- **Flexibility?** **Or**   **Control?**
- **Lifestyle entrepreneur (sacrifice income for relaxed work habits)** .... or
  ....
- **High value builder entrepreneur**

FIGURE 7.14
At first, the organization reflects the founder's personality and attitude.

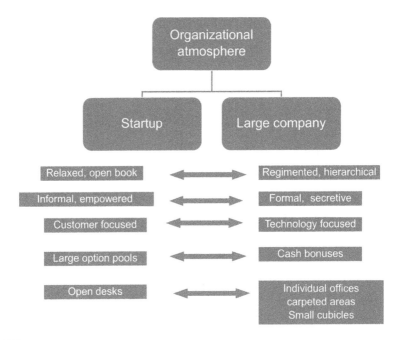

FIGURE 7.15
The atmosphere (culture) of a startup is very different compared to a large company.

Lastly, the founder decides *how* the organization will be managed, as shown in Figure 7.15.

7.6 The Dominant Coalition: Chaos Creates Opportunity

The dominant coalition is a select group of people within an organization—mostly the executive or senior management team—making all the important decisions regarding the direction and focus of the firm. The term *dominant coalition* was coined by James Thompson (who adopted the work of March and Cyert[17]) in his 1967 book entitled *Organizations in Action.*[18]

In business, coalitions have been present for many years as a means of bringing together people, departments within an organization, entire companies, or industries with some common purpose. Examples of such purposes include achieving an important corporate goal, lowering market entrance, regulating an industry action, or strategic planning. Coalitions are an exercise in power, whether in politics or business.[19]

Many managers form coalitions to (1) secure their power source, (2) protect their power positions, and (3) wield the maximum amount of power and influence. Dominant coalitions are formed through compromise, bargaining, and negotiation between managers from different functions.[20]

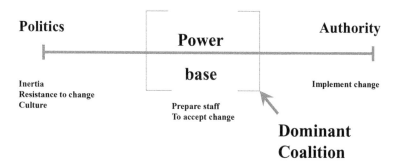

Dominant coalition
(1) must be aware of their power
(2) Must be willing to exercise power
(3) Power must be exclusive to the coalition

"Politics is power in action"

Politics   **Power**   **Authority**

base

Inertia   Implement change
Resistance to change
Culture   Prepare staff
To accept change

Dominant Coalition

FIGURE 7.16
Politics is frequently in the hands of a select group that form a coalition.

Figure 7.16 summarizes the modus operandi of a typical dominant coalition.

7.6.1 Dominant Coalition as Change Agent

> The great pleasure in life is doing what people say you cannot do.
> **—Walter Bagehot**

Any proposed change to the status quo will be fiercely resisted at all levels, no matter how desirable. General Motors, Sears, JC Penney, Wang Computers, and Polaroid all faced need for dramatic change, but they all failed to change. Those managers pushing for organizational or technological improvements were ignored or fired. The companies could not overcome the culture, power structure, and behavioral obstacles inherent in their organizations.

The main reasons for organizational resistance to change are presented in Table 7.7.

TABLE 7.7

Organizational Resistance to Change

- Fear of the unknown
- Renegotiations of employment/psychological contracts
- People are inherently "risk avoiders"
- Changes in role or power positions
- Age of the staff (the older, the more resistant)
- Need to retrain in new technology/systems

The dominant coalition must overcome the organizational resistance to change and explain necessary organizational challenges on an ongoing basis. This means that when change suddenly appears, employees will have the background and context they need to understand why the change is required. The following steps should be followed:[21]

- *Be as transparent as possible.* As part of the dominant coalition, the entrepreneur plays a pivotal role in how change is received. You may not be able to offer full transparency regarding the changes that lie ahead. However, whenever possible, share as much as reasonable. Employees appreciate honesty and respond well to it, even when it is difficult to hear.

- *Articulate specific changes and what is required of the team.* Nothing heightens anxiety as much as ambiguity. When changes are discussed in vague generalities, employees begin to expect the worst. They may become paralyzed as they wonder what effects the changes will have on them. As much as possible, try to articulate the specific steps employees need to take in response to the changes and what exactly is required of them.

- *Recognize emotional responses.* Change is an emotional experience for most people, especially in the beginning. It creates feelings of insecurity, uncertainty, and even anger. Ignoring the emotional side of the situation will only make you appear detached. Employees will not see you as one of the team, but rather as an outside force inflicting pain on them.

  Take the time to address emotions—good, bad, and indifferent. Do not resent the employee who voices dissent or resistance. Recognize that they are sharing valuable information. The emotions themselves are symptoms, but you ultimately want to get to the root cause.

- *Listen intently and sympathetically.* If you are following the strategies listed here, you have already started to ease the emotions, so now you just need to listen with empathy and compassion. Allow team members to vent, thank them for being honest, and then gently steer them toward acceptance. However, avoid outwardly agreeing with their feelings. Position yourself as a champion for the change and a supportive partner for the employee. Help team members see the opportunity that change presents for them and help them manage the disruption.

7.6.1.1 Theory of Change

To effectuate change productively, Kurt Lewin[22] proposed a three-stage theory of change commonly referred to as *unfreeze, change, freeze* (or refreeze). The dominant coalition could follow the Lewin sequence, as shown in Table 7.8.

TABLE 7.8

Productive Change Sequence

- Create dissatisfaction and crisis
  - Fear
  - Vision of a better tomorrow
  - Opportunity for all to advance
- Unfreeze the system
  - Separate from past practices
  - Reject old customs and approaches
  - Reduce support for old ways
  - Reward those engaged in new approach
- Change/psychological converting
  - Separation from the past
  - Rejection of the past
  - Practice until new system is internalized and understood
- Refreeze in new ways
  - Reward new behavior patterns
  - Reinforce new attitudes
  - Be consistent, predictable

The Lewin three-stage theory of change model can be more easily visualized as shown in Figure 7.17.

7.6.1.2 Force Field Analysis

When first proposed, the force field analysis (FFA) became an influential development in the field of social science. It provided a framework for looking

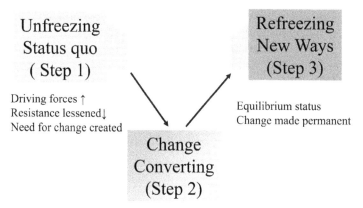

Lewin's Change Management Model

Unfreezing
Status quo
(Step 1)

Driving forces ↑
Resistance lessened↓
Need for change created

Change
Converting
(Step 2)

Refreezing
New Ways
(Step 3)

Equilibrium status
Change made permanent

Modified after :Managing Change Approaches to Change Management Lecture 4
http://dl.wecouncil.com/serfweb/User157/MC/Lesson4.ppt

FIGURE 7.17
Lewin's change management model to first unfreeze and then refreeze.

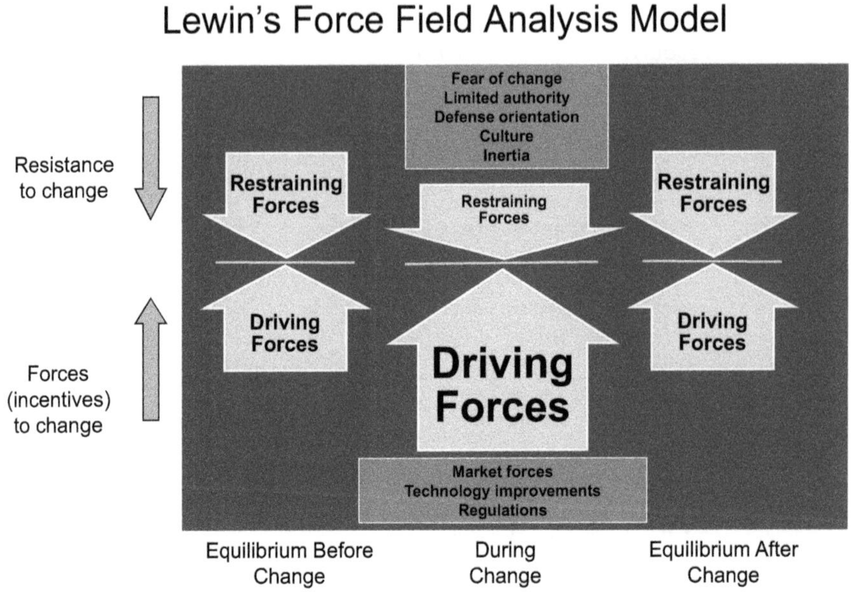

Lewin's Force Field Analysis Model

Resistance to change

Restraining Forces

Fear of change
Limited authority
Defense orientation
Culture
Inertia

Restraining Forces

Restraining Forces

Forces (incentives) to change

Driving Forces

Driving Forces

Driving Forces

Driving Forces

Market forces
Technology improvements
Regulations

Equilibrium Before Change | During Change | Equilibrium After Change

Modified after Organizational Change © McGraw Hill Companies 2009
http://faculty.salisbury.edu/~whdecker/MGMT425StudentSlidesbyChapter/Chap014.ppt

FIGURE 7.18
How to overcome the inevitable resistance to change, according to Lewin.

at the factors (forces) that influence a situation, originally social situations. It looks at forces that are either driving movement toward a goal (helping forces) or blocking movement toward a goal (hindering forces). The FFA principle, developed by Lewin,[23] was a significant contribution to the fields of organizational development, process management, and change management.[24]

The "field" was conceived as very dynamic, changing with time and experience. When fully constructed, an individual's field (Lewin used the term *life space*) describes that person's motives, values, needs, moods, goals, anxieties, and ideals.[25] Figure 7.18 presents an idealized conception of FFA.

7.7 Leaders Need Followers

> Leaders rarely use their power wisely or effectively over
> long periods unless they are supported by followers
> who have the stature to help them do so.
>
> **— power wisely or effectively over long periods
> unless they are suIra Chaleff**

Followership is the process of being purposely guided and directed by a leader in the business environment. Organizations are successful based on not only whether their leaders can lead, but also how decidedly followers are willing to follow. Followership is the reciprocal organizational process of leadership.[26]

The study of followership is integral to a better understanding of leadership, since the success or failure of groups, organizations, and teams is dependent on not only how well a leader can lead, but also how well the followers can follow. Specifically, followers play a crucial and active role in organization, group, and team successes and failures.[27]

The literature is deep on the subject of leadership but, not surprisingly, shallow on the subject of followership. The emergence of the field of followership in 1988 is widely credited to Kelly in his influential "In Praise of Followers" *Harvard Business Review* paper.[28] Kelly argued that what distinguishes an effective follower from an ineffective one is (1) intelligent, (2) responsible, and (3) enthusiastic participation in pursuit of an organizational goal. Kelly further described four main qualities of effective followers:[29]

1. *Self-management*: This refers to the ability to think critically, be in control of one's actions, and work independently. It is important that followers manage themselves well and leaders are able to delegate tasks to these individuals.

2. *Commitment*: This refers to an individual being committed to the goal, vision, or cause of a group, team, or organization. This is an important quality of followers as it helps keep one's (and other members') morale and energy levels high.

3. *Competence*: It is essential that individuals possess the skills and aptitudes necessary to complete the goal or task of the group, team, or organization. Individuals high on this quality often hold skills higher than their average coworker (or team member). Further, these individuals continue their pursuit of knowledge by upgrading their skills through classes and seminars.

4. *Courage*: Effective followers hold true to their beliefs and maintain and uphold ethical standards, even in the face of dishonest or corrupt superiors (leaders). These individuals are loyal, honest, and importantly, candid with their superiors.

7.7.1 Current Views of Followership

Followership has been popularized by Chaleff under the title "The Courageous Follower."[30] According to Chaleff, there are three things we need to understand in order to fully assume responsibilities as effective followers, as seen in Figure 7.19.

> *Followership intrinsic power.* Followers have far more power than generally acknowledged in the literature. Followership entails accepting

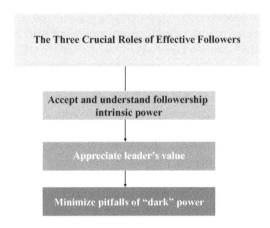

FIGURE 7.19
The crucial role of followers.

and understanding the sources of their power, working toward the common goal, and using their available tools to achieve the mission.

Appreciate leader's value. Understand the pressures placed on the leader and work to minimize those pressures, thus contributing to the common purpose.

Minimize pitfalls of "dark" power. This is done by helping the leader to stay on track. If power becomes corrupt, the follower should speak up and provide feedback to the leader in a constructive fashion.

Courageous followers share five characteristics, as shown in Figure 7.20.

7.7.2 The Followership Universe

Understanding followers as contributors to an organization implies that followers have equal status with leaders in sustaining and advancing organizational viability. Followers exist within knowledge-based organizations and are distinguishable at all organizational levels and activities. Figure 7.21 presents an accurate representation of the interactions between followers and their leader.

7.8 Time Management

> The entrepreneurial clock must tick faster than anyone else's.

Time is your most implacable enemy. We all have the same amount of time: 24 hours a day, 7 days per week. But entrepreneurs must break the "tyranny

The Five Dimensions of Courageous Followership

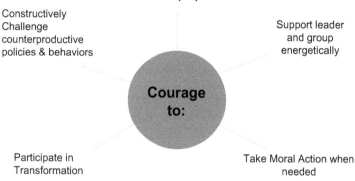

Assume Responsibility for common purpose

Constructively Challenge counterproductive policies & behaviors

Support leader and group energetically

Courage to:

Participate in Transformation

Take Moral Action when needed

Source: The Courageous Follower – © Ira Chaleff

FIGURE 7.20
Chaleff's roles of courageous followers.

of time." You must accomplish more per day or week than the big guys. In 1748, Ben Franklin exclaimed, "Remember that time is money." To accomplish that, you must practice time management.

The standard definition of time management is "the ability to plan and control how you spend the hours in your day to effectively accomplish your goals. Poor time management can be related to procrastination, as well as problems with self-control. Skills involved in managing your time include planning for the future, setting goals, prioritizing tasks, and monitoring where your time actually goes."[31]

The Followership Universe

Organizational Goals

Followership powera

Followership competence

Business Plan Uncertainty

Extrinsic Forces

Intrinsic Forces

Markets Regulations Competition

Dominant Coalition

Culture Politics

FIGURE 7.21
How followers fit into the successful organization.

TABLE 7.9

Time Management Principles

"Work expands so as to fill the time available for its completion." — Cyril Parkinson
1. Prioritize, prioritize, prioritize.
2. Organize your day around productive activities.
3. Say no to unnecessary commitments.
4. Manage your time like money.
5. Clarify goals and delegate as much as possible.
6. Do the ugliest things first.
7. Make and keep deadlines (no exceptions).
8. Keep teammates informed and involved.
9. Touch each document only once.
10. Keep meetings productive and short.

Table 7.9 summarizes some of the important principles behind practical time management.

7.8.1 The Urgent–Important Matrix

A technique that has been successfully used in business time management for a long time is the categorization of large data into groups. These groups are often marked quadrants 1–4. Activities are ranked on these general criteria:[32]

- Quadrant 1: Tasks that are perceived as being urgent and important
- Quadrant 2: Tasks that are urgent but not important
- Quadrant 3: Tasks that are not urgent but important
- Quadrant 4: Tasks that are neither urgent nor important

This is based on Pareto's law, or the 80-20 rule. The principle is that 80% of tasks can be completed in 20% of the disposable time. The remaining 20% of tasks will take up 80% of the time. This principle is used to sort tasks into two parts. According to this form of Pareto analysis, it is recommended that tasks that fall into the first category be assigned a higher priority.

The 80-20 rule can also be applied to increase productivity: it is assumed that 80% of the productivity can be achieved by doing 20% of the tasks. Similarly, 80% of results can be attributed to 20% of activity. If maximum productivity is the aim of time management, then these tasks should be prioritized higher. Thus, Quadrant 1 is reserved for critical activities, Quadrant 2 consists of important goals, Quadrant 3 may contain interruptions, and Quadrant 4 activities should be totally disregarded.

The Pareto principle depends on the method you adopted to complete the task. There is always a simpler and more efficient way to complete a task. If a complex way is utilized, then it will be time-consuming. So, the efficient entrepreneur should always try to find alternate ways to complete each task.[33] This is summarized in Figure 7.22.

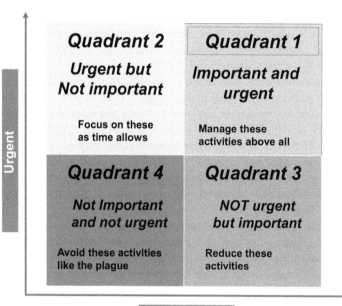

FIGURE 7.22
Quadrant IV: Quadrant of Waste. This quadrant represents activities that are not important and are not urgent. Here are examples of activities that fall into Q-IV: Trivia, busywork; Reviewing junk mail; Some phone calls; Escape activities; Viewing mindless TV shows. Most of us do not spend much time in this quadrant, because we simply don't have time to waste. The most common Q-IV activity I encounter in my work with busy people is escape activities. When the stress level gets high enough, some people escape from reality by doing activities that do not address or resolve the problem. This is considered wasteful. Note that the same activity can fall into Q-II or Q-IV. You are the only one who can determine which quadrant the activity belongs in. If you are treating yourself to true recreation and relaxation (resting and renewing yourself), you are in Q-II. If you are engaging in an escape activity (avoiding the problem and not finding a solution), you are in Q-IV. The motivation behind the activity determines which quadrant you are in.

7.9 Conflict Management

> Fight as if you are right; listen as if you are wrong.

If you are running a fast-paced organization, you will surely face organizational conflict. Conflict is a natural, recurring, and inevitable outcome of group dynamics. How will you manage the conflict?

Regarding organizational conflict, leaders come in two flavors: (1) the production or task-oriented leader and (2) the people-oriented or accommodative leader. Of course, these are two polar extremes, and many leaders fall somewhere in between. Neither preference is necessarily right or wrong, but will depend on the situation. It is useful for you to understand your inherent leadership characteristics so you can work out a suitable solution to the conflict and defuse the situation.

A useful framework for analyzing yourself is the Blake–Mouton managerial grid, also known as the leadership grid.[34] This model originally identified five different leadership styles based on *concern for people* and *concern for production*. The optimal leadership style in this model is based on Theories X and Y.[35] (In Theory Y, management assumes that employees may be ambitious and *self-motivated* and exercise *self-control*. In Theory X, which has been proven countereffective in most modern practice, management assumes that employees are inherently lazy and will avoid work if they can, and that they inherently dislike work.)

The grid plots your degree of task-centeredness versus your people-centeredness. By plotting concern for production in the abscissa against concern for people in the ordinate, the grid proposes that leaders who place too much emphasis in one area at the expense of all others will likely experience an overall lowering in productivity and prolongation of conflict. While the grid does not entirely address the question of which leadership style is best, it provides an excellent starting place for critically analyzing your own performance and improving your leadership skills.[36] This is shown in Figure 7.23.

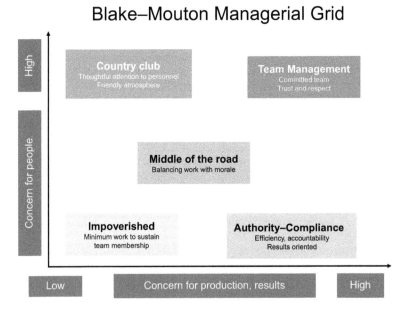

Blake–Mouton Managerial Grid

FIGURE 7.23
Blake–Mouton's view of balancing concern for people versus concern for production.

The Blake–Mouton managerial grid is based on two behavioral dimensions:

- *Concern for people*: The degree to which a leader considers the needs of team members, their interests, and their areas of personal development when deciding how best to accomplish a task
- *Concern for production*: The degree to which a leader emphasizes concrete objectives, organizational efficiency, and high productivity when deciding how best to accomplish a task

7.10 Entrepreneurial Rewards

> *My idea of risk and reward is for me to get the*
> *reward and others to take the risk.*

The American dream involves two characters: (1) the entrepreneurial hero and (2) the industrial drone or, as Robert Reich said, "the inspired and the perspired." This highlights the differences between the entrepreneur—the seeker of opportunity—and the administrator—the guardian of resources and procedures.

Ask any entrepreneurial hero and they will tell you that individual recognition is more important than salaries, bonuses, or promotions. For many people, the dream of charting their own destiny and being self-sufficient is enough to stimulate the pursuit of opportunity and investing time and money in that pursuit.

Figure 7.24 summarizes the most compelling rewards listed by entrepreneurs.

7.11 Entrepreneurial Types

> Find your sweet spot.

Not all entrepreneurs are born the same. In the pioneering studies, Cole[37] defined four distinctive types of entrepreneurs. Nowadays, by consensus the style categories are

1. Lifestyle
2. Innovator
3. Empire builder
4. Serial entrepreneur

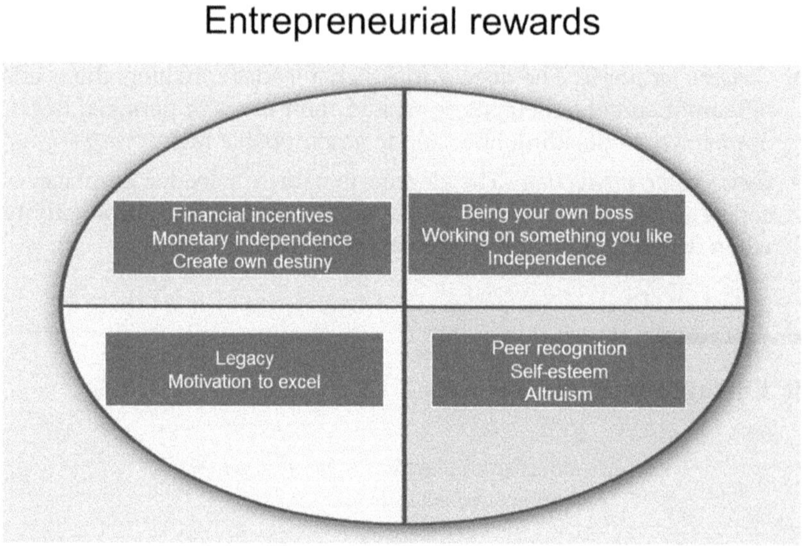

Entrepreneurial rewards

Financial incentives Monetary independence Create own destiny	Being your own boss Working on something you like Independence
Legacy Motivation to excel	Peer recognition Self-esteem Altruism

FIGURE 7.24
The many rewards of entrepreneurial success.

Lifestyle entrepreneur. This is someone who has decided to build a business strictly to make a living to satisfy their own personal motivations. This entrepreneur would like to create a successful company, but building a public company would definitely *not* be a necessity or a main driving force. The choice of businesses would generally be high-cash generative businesses. An example is Ben Cohen, co-founder of Ben & Jerry's ice cream.

Innovator entrepreneur. If you operate your business predominantly in the innovator mode, you are focused on using your company as a means to improve the world. A business owned and operated by an innovator is full of life, energy, and optimism. Your company is life energizing and makes customers feel that the company has a "get it done attitude." Examples include Gordon Moore, Intel founder, and Malcolm Forbes, founder and publisher of *Forbes* magazine.

Empire builder (also called a visionary). A business built by an empire builder will often be based on the future vision and thoughts of the founder. This person will have a high degree of curiosity to understand the world around them and will set up plans to avoid the land mines. Examples include Bill Gates, founder of Microsoft, Inc., and Steve Jobs, founder of Apple, Inc.

Serial entrepreneur. This entrepreneur's main motivation is the exit strategy (harvesting)—and usually this entrepreneur type is dismissed by many angel investors due to the fact they may have started a number of business ventures (and moved on) and therefore may have mixed priorities. Interestingly, some angel syndicates actually do prefer to invest in the serial entrepreneur, because this entrepreneurial type is focused on the exit or sale, and the cash payout is their main motivation.[38] An example is Donald Trump, founder and CEO of Trump Hotels and Casino Resorts.

7.12 Summary

Have you ever been in a corner desperately waving at taxis on a rainy day? Where are all the taxis? You need to get to the airport on time. It can be highly frustrating.

Well, entrepreneurial organizations experience the same frustration when they desperately need a leader on a "rainy day." Most organizations in troubled times tend to get more management and not enough leadership. Please do not misunderstand the message: I am not saying that management itself is bad, because both effective leadership and management are necessary to run an efficient organization, but too much management and not enough leadership can be catastrophic! In this chapter, we covered the most important aspects of and differences between leading and managing people.

Table 7.10 summarizes the leading/managing dichotomy.

Lastly, being a successful leader demands the following attributes:

- Achieve maximum levels of performance and productivity for every person and your whole team.

TABLE 7.10

Leading/Managing Dichotomy

Too much work to do: Such as when technical problems multiply as deadlines approach. The pressure to satisfy the schedule pushes capacity, systems, and people to their limits, causing mistakes and problems.	**Too little work to do:** Waiting for technical, manufacturing, or distribution issues to be resolved. When people have too little work to do over long periods, they start worrying about keeping their jobs.
Too few people to do the work: Such as when a company is growing quickly and cannot recruit the right people, or following people being made redundant due to the company cutting costs. When people have too much work to do over long periods of time, they struggle to cope, become exhausted, or even burn out.	**Too many people to do the work:** Such as following a merger between two companies. People become concerned or worried about their job security and meeting their personal technical and/or financial commitments.
Too many system or structural changes: Such as people suffering from initiative overload and becoming confused about what they should be doing and how they should be working. Little or no direction from top leaders. Decisions are not made, and problems are not being solved.	**Too few system or process changes:** Such as outdated and archaic systems not providing them with the right information at the right time to do their job well. People look for leadership and leaders in these situations because they are experts in how to solve them but need direction.

- Build a sense of team spirit and belonging that exceeds most common experience of teamwork.
- Unequivocally convey purpose, intentions, and direction to your team.
- Enable all people to find meaning in their work (also known as empowerment).
- Gain the commitment of all individuals through genuinely involving them in major decisions and actions to achieve stated objectives.
- Have a positive influence on the way people who work for and with you think, feel, and act.
- Encourage and continually develop knowledge, skills, and the expertise of your whole team.

7.13 Ten Commandments of Leadership[39]

1. Thou shall balance influence with good judgment.
2. Thou shall speak authoritatively and clearly.
3. Thou shall prioritize achievable goals.
4. Thou shall delegate to motivate.
5. Thou shall promote diversity of skills.
6. Thou shall clearly communicate your vision/mission.
7. Thou shall inspire confidence by example.
8. Thou shall focus on results, not activities.
9. Thou shall encourage mentoring at all levels.
10. Thou shall develop and publicize a succession plan.

7.14 Overcoming Organizational Resistance to Change

> Change is a constant.
> —**Heraclitus, Greek philosopher**

What was true more than 2000 years ago is just as true today. We live in a world where "business as usual" *is* change. New initiatives, project-based working, technology improvements, and staying ahead of the competition—these things come together to drive ongoing changes to the way we work.

However, nowhere is change more crucial than in an entrepreneurial environment, where everything is in constant flux. And corporate change inevitably brings ferocious organizational resistance. This has made organizational change management[40] an important focus of corporate management strategy, as described below.[41]

- *Change management* is a collective term for all approaches to preparing and supporting individuals, teams, and organizations in making organizational change.[42]
- Leaders and managers must cope with internal issues, such as an employee's job role change.[43]
- Major changes of the workplace location.[44]
- Implementing new processes or programs.[45]
- Sustainability programs and the need for change: organizational change and transformational vision.[46]
- Large-scale changes: whole-company reorganizations.[47]
- Moran and Brightman[48] stated that change is the process of continually renewing an organization's direction, structure, and capabilities to meet expectations from both external and internal customers and make an organization as successful as possible.
- Organizational leadership.[49] Competent leaders can be the difference between success and failure, not only for the organization itself, but also for internal projects, such as business or strategy development.
- Leaders and managers have important roles to fill, such as influencing and encouraging employees, ranking from top to middle management, in striving toward the fulfillment of the organization's stated vision.[50]
- Gill[51] states that the foundation of effective leadership involves defining and clearly communicating an appealing vision of the future within an organization.
- Leadership during the change process is vital for its success, but leaders must also have a specific goal to work toward, which should encompass the fulfillment of a clearly formulated organizational vision.[52]

7.14.1 Managing Change

While there is a business inevitability of internal and external change, people generally prefer the status quo and resist change to varying degrees. The organizational resistance to change is dramatically illustrated in Table 7.11.

7.14.2 Kotter's Eight-Step Process for Leading Change

Professor John P. Kotter, the Konosuke Matsushita Professor of Leadership Emeritus at Harvard Business School, developed the eight-step process for

TABLE 7.11

Quantifying the Organizational Resistance to Change

20-50-30 rule
- Only 20% of people are likely to embrace needed change.
- 50% of people are unconvinced and ambivalent about any change.
- 30% of people are ferociously opposed to *any* change and are generally willing to resort to sabotage and active interference to prevent change.

80-20 rule

The 80-20 rule implies that 80% of an organization's staff starts out as opposed to any needed change. The 30% is unalterably opposed, while the 50% is "persuadable."

According to Bill Quirke, *Communicating Change*, McGraw Hill Book Company, the following are some of the most common reasons for resistance to change:
- There is no need for change.
- The proposed change violates long-held core principles.
- The change implications are misunderstood and distrusted.
- The proposed change is not in the best long-term interest of the organization.
- There is a lack of trust in the change proponents.
- There is a belief that leadership is incapable of executing the change.
- There is a perception that change unfairly discriminates against them.
- No suitable alternatives are presented to the group.

leading change in his 1995 book, *Leading Change*. The process consists of eight stages,[53] shown in Table 7.12.

7.14.3 Beer and Nohria's "Cracking the Code of Change"

According to Beer and Nohria,[54]

> the new economy has ushered in great business opportunities—and great turmoil. Not since the Industrial Revolution have the stakes of dealing with change been so high. Most traditional organizations have accepted, in theory at least, that they must either change or die. And even Internet companies such as eBay, Amazon.com, and America Online recognize that they need to manage the changes associated with rapid entrepreneurial growth.
>
> Despite some individual successes, however, change remains difficult to pull off, and few companies manage the process as well as they would like. Most of their initiatives—installing new technology, downsizing, restructuring, or trying to change corporate culture—have had low success rates. The brutal fact is that about 70% of all change initiatives fail.

But why do 70% of initiatives fail? Managers flounder in an alphabet soup of change methods, drowning in conflicting advice. Change efforts exact a heavy toll—human *and* economic—as companies flail from one change method to another.

To effect successful change, Beer and Nohria proposed two basic theories of change:

1. Theory E	Change emphasizes economic value—as measured *only* by shareholder returns. This hard approach boosts returns through economic incentives, drastic layoffs, and restructuring. "Chainsaw Al" Dunlop's firing of 11,000 Scott Paper employees and selling several businesses—tripling shareholder value to $9 billion—is a stunning example.
2. Theory O	Change, through a softer approach, focuses on developing corporate culture and human capability, patiently building trust and emotional commitment to the company through teamwork and communication.

TABLE 7.12

Kotter's Eight Steps for Leading Change

1. Establish a sense of urgency	Examine market and competitive position Identify crises, potential crises, or major opportunities
2. Create the guiding coalition	Assemble a powerful group Empower the group to work as a team
3. Develop a vision and strategy	Clearly articulate the vision Develop strategies for achieving vision
4. Communicate the change vision	Frequently use memos, meetings, conferences, etc. Teach by example
5. Empower employees for broad-based action	Remove obstacles to change Change systems that undermine the vision Encourage out-of-the-box thinking
6. Generate short-term wins	Publicize team wins, no matter how small
7. Consolidate gains and produce more change	Develop and promote team members
8. Anchor new approaches in the culture	Articulate the connection between behavior and corporate success Explain what is meant by change success and how it will benefit the organization

TABLE 7.13

Theories E and O Compared

Dimensions of Change	Theory E	Theory O
1. Goals	Maximize shareholder value above all else	Develop organizational capabilities
2. Leadership	Manage change from the top-down (military style)	Encourage individual and team participation from the bottom-up
3. Focus	Emphasize and accentuate corporate structure and systems	Build up corporate culture and vision: employees' behavior and attitudes are paramount
4. Process	Plan and establish programs and implementation deadlines	Experiment and evolve as an iterative process; build consensus
5. Reward system	Motivate through financial incentives and individual advancement	Motivate through commitment—use pay as fair exchange
6. Use of consultants	As expert resources, consultants analyze problems and shape unique solutions	Consultants support both management and the team in shaping their own solutions

Their research showed that all corporate transformations can be compared along the six dimensions shown here. Table 7.13 outlines the differences between the E and O archetypes.

In summary, Theory E change strategies usually involve heavy use of economic incentives, drastic layoffs, downsizing, and restructuring. Shareholder value is the only legitimate measure of corporate success. Theory O change strategies are geared toward building up the corporate culture: employee behaviors, attitudes, capabilities, and commitment. The organization's ability to learn from its experiences is considered a legitimate yardstick.

Notes

1. Murphy, E. C. (1996). *Leadership IQ*. Hoboken, NJ: John Wiley & Sons.
2. Hersey, P. and Blanchard K. H. (1993). *Management of Organizational Behavior*, 6th ed. Englewood Cliffs, NJ: Prentice Hall.
3. Hersey and Blanchard's approach. http://changingminds.org/disciplines/leadership/styles/situational_leadership_hersey_blanchard.htm.
4. Situational leadership. http://web.usf.edu/airforce/AS300/SLD19_Situational_Leadership.ppt (accessed April 2013).
5. Building a new venture team. Chapter 6. http://foba.lakeheadu.ca/hart-viksen/3215/Management%20Team.ppt.
6. Corporate governance. http://en.wikipedia.org/wiki/Corporate_governance.
7. Authority. http://en.wikipedia.org/wiki/Authority.
8. Power and influence. http://web.usf.edu/airforce/AS300/SLD_26_Power_Influence_08.ppt.
9. Influence and influencing. Eyre district leaders (August 2007). http://www.decd.sa.gov.au/eyreandwestern/files/links/PPInfluence_Topic_Aug_07.ppt.
10. Pfeffer, J. (1992). *Managing with Power*. Boston: Harvard Business School Press.
11. French, J. P. R., Jr. and Raven, B. (1960). The bases of social power. In D. Cartwright and A. Zander (Eds.), *Group Dynamics*. New York: Harper and Row (pp. 607–623).
12. Gordon, C. Office politics and gossiping. http://www.careersmarts.com/shrm/media/office_politics.ppt.
13. Artra, L. Surviving office politics. http://www.sasag.org/2004/04/SA_2_OfficePolitics_v2.ppt.
14. Ahearn, K. K., Ferris, G. R., Hochwarter, W. A., Douglass, C. and Ammeter, A. P. (2004). Leader political skill and team performance. *Journal of Management*, 30, 309–327.
15. Cyert, R. M. and March, J. G. (1963). *A Behavioral Theory of the Firm*. Englewood Cliffs, NJ: Prentice-Hall.
16. Influence, power and politics: An organizational survival kit. Chapter 13. http://www.drluisortiz.com/PPT/ob09Chap013.ppt.
17. March, J. G. and Cyert, R. M. (1963). *A Behavioral Theory of the Firm*. Englewood Cliffs, NJ: Prentice-Hall.

18. Thompson, J. D. (1967). *Organizations in Action: Social Science Bases of Administrative Theory*. New York: McGraw-Hill.
19. http://www.enotes.com/coalition-building-reference/coalition-building.
20. The power-control model. http://www.iun.edu/~bnwcls/w430/orgpol.ppt.
21. Strategies for communicating change to your team. https://www.ivyexec.com/executive-insights/2017/university-birmingham-online-mba-strategies-communicating-change-team/.
22. Lewin, K. (1958). Group decision and social change. In E. E. Maccoby, T. M. Newcomb and E. L. Hartley (Eds.), *Readings in Social Psychology*. New York: Holt, Rinehart and Winston (pp. 197–211).
23. Lewin, K. (1943). Defining the "field at a given time." *Psychological Review*, 50, 292–310. Republished in Lewin, K. (1997). *Resolving Social Conflicts & Field Theory in Social Science*. Washington, DC: American Psychological Association.
24. Force-field analysis. http://en.wikipedia.org/wiki/Force_field_analysis.
25. Cartwright, D. (1997). Foreword to the 1951 edition. *Field Theory in Social Science and Selected Theoretical Papers—Kurt Lewin*. Washington, DC: American Psychological Association. Originally published by Harper & Row.
26. Riggio, R. E., Chaleff, I. and Blumen-Lipman, J. (2008). *The Art of Followership: How Great Followers Create Great Leaders and Organizations*. San Francisco: Jossey-Bass.
27. Baker, S. D. (2007). Followership: The theoretical foundation of a contemporary construct. *Journal of Leadership & Organizational Studies*, 14, 50–60. doi: 10.1177/0002831207304343.
28. Kelly, R. E. (1988). In praise of followers. *Harvard Business Review*, November–December, 142–148.
29. Followership. http://en.wikipedia.org/wiki/Followership.
30. Chaleff, I. The courageous follower: A new view of leader-follower relationships. http://www.tobiascenter.iu.edu/conferences/documents/UofINDIANA sharedfile.ppt.
31. Time management. http://en.wikipedia.org/wiki/Time_management.
32. Lakein, A. (1973). *How to Get Control of Your Time and Your Life*. New York: P.H. Wyden.
33. Time management. http://en.wikipedia.org/wiki/Time_management.
34. Blake, R. and Mouton, J. (1964). *The Managerial Grid: The Key to Leadership Excellence*. Houston: Gulf Publishing.
35. McGregor, D. (1960). *The Human Side of Enterprise*. New York: McGraw-Hill.
36. Zeida, H. (2009). The Blake Mouton managerial grid: The certified accountant. www.lacpa.org.lb/Includes/Images/Docs/TC/TC409.pdf.
37. Cole, A. An approach to the study of entrepreneurship. *Journal of Economic History*, 6(Suppl. 1), 1–15. Reprinted in Lane, F. C. and Riesmersma, J. C. (Eds.). 9146.
38. Anand, R. What type of an entrepreneur are you? http://www.venturegiant.com/news-channel-282-what-type-of-an-entrepreneur-are-you.aspx.
39. Inspired by Maxwell, J. C. (1998). *The Ten Irrefutable Laws of Leadership*. Nashville, TN: Thomas Nelson Publishers.
40. Rune, T. B. (2005). Organisational change management: A critical review. *Journal of Change Management*, 5(4), 369–380.
41. Mavromatis, M. and Olofsson, J. (2013). Leading organizational change. Master's thesis, Chalmers University of Technology. http://publications.lib.chalmers.se/records/fulltext/183830/183830.pdf.

42. Change management. https://en.wikipedia.org/wiki/Change_management.
43. Byrd, J. T. and Thornton, J. C. (2013). Job role change and leadership development. *Journal of American Academy of Business, Cambridge*, 18(2), 75–80.
44. Allard, L. E. and Barber, C. (2003). Challenges and opportunities in aligning real estate and the workplace with business strategy: A survey of leading CEOs. *Journal of Corporate Real Estate*, 5(3), 213–220.
45. Beer, M. (2003). Why total quality management programs do not persist: The role of management quality and implications for leading a TQM transformation. *Decision Sciences*, 34(4), 623–642.
46. Millar, C., Hind, P. and Magala, S. (2012). Sustainability and the need for change: Organisational change and transformational vision. *Journal of Organizational Change Management*, 25(4), 489–500.
47. Hayes, J. (2010). *The Theory and Practice of Change Management*, 4th ed. Palgrave MacMillan.
48. Moran, J. W. and Brightman, B. K. (2001). Leading organizational change. *Career Development International*, 6(2), 111–119.
49. Bass, B. M. and Bass, R. (2009). *The Bass Handbook of Leadership: Theory, Research, and Managerial Applications*. Free Press.
50. Daft, R. L. (2008). *The Leadership Experience*. South-Western Publications.
51. Gill, R. (2002). Change management—or change leadership? *Journal of Change Management*, 3(4), 307–318.
52. Woodward, S. and Hendry, C. (2004). Leading and coping with change. *Journal of Change Management*, 4(2), 155–183.
53. Mind Tools Content Team. (2016). Kotter's 8-step change model. https://www.mindtools.com/pages/article/newPPM_82.htm.
54. Beer, M. and Nohria, N. (2000). Cracking the code of change. *Harvard Business Review*, May–June.

8

Communicating Value to Investors

8.1 Introduction

In the startup world, validity is king. It would be nice if you had an established business record, such as 8 years of steady, spectacular growth in revenues and profits. But you are a startup, so how can you have a track record?

For any company—particularly startups—communications is a key driver to attaining capital for your business. This chapter provides you with the fundamental elements of the art of communicating value to your investors, thus allowing securing initial as well as follow-on funding.

While execution is key to a startup success, the way in which a company *communicates* the essential factors to a potential group of investors is central to the ability to raise initial and subsequent rounds of capital. If vital elements are omitted from a startup's story or they are not explained convincingly and with veracity, true value will go unrecognized, resulting in failure to raise needed capital.

Investor relations—the art of positioning and communicating a startup's story and investment proposition to investors—is the heart and soul of attaining fair value. However, if written or oral communications do not sufficiently explain the current value and potential opportunity for growth, more damage than good will result.

There is a method to communicating value to investors effectively, and it is accomplished in four basic steps:

1. Determine the investment proposition of your company.
2. Identify and target the appropriate investor audience.
3. Develop your communication platform specific to your targeted investor audience.
4. Maintain constant communications with your investor audience so that key drivers of business are current and obvious to investors.

8.2 Chasing Capital and Credibility

Your first step is to create a coherent and comprehensive business plan to communicate how you aim to achieve profitability.[1] Your plan should contain a few concrete, real-world examples of your strategy to move the business forward while also providing a bigger picture of your long-term goals and objectives.

For example, if you have a product or launch coming up, identify and communicate the positive outcomes from the launch (i.e., cost savings, time savings, efficiencies, etc.). Ideally, your business plan should communicate a well-thought-out value proposition for your investors and potential customers with the goal of ultimately securing monetary support or funding. Put yourself in the investor's shoes—your startup's product or service must create value.

8.2.1 Communicate a Viable Competitive Strategy

While investors are always on the prowl for the next "big thing," like a Google or an Apple, they also do not want to hear unrealistic pitches. Maintaining an opportunistic but realistic approach when communicating makes your startup appear more credible. An excellent way is to identify your startup's competitive landscape and define your competitive advantage to potential investors. The goal is to clearly and concisely convey the *why* behind the *what* and how your startup is more than qualified to meet your customer's needs above all other options.

8.2.2 Utilize Strategic Partnerships

There is no denying that paying customers are the best possible form of traction to receive funding; however, not all startups have paying customers. If your startup is especially young, partnering with an already established business will provide access to resources that may help advance your case for funding. Develop strategic partnerships with like-minded entrepreneurs who are a few steps ahead of you. Ideally, these partnerships should be with entrepreneurs or businesses that are experts in your industry, thus complementing each other.

Such collaboration can accelerate the business faster than just capital alone, but the key to success is finding harmony between both your goals and objectives. These strategic relationships have a robust framework that includes shared visions, a proper cultural fit, and mutual understanding to maintain autonomy. At the end of the day, the investor is investing in *you*, so come to the game prepared with a strategy.

8.3 Communication Process

What role does communication play in the many successes and failures of various organizations?

Let us take a look at one organization that has had phenomenal success and some notable failures: Facebook. Mark Zuckerberg was still a Harvard sophomore when he began operating Facebook for college and high school friends.[2]

Since its introduction, the site has gained close to 200 million active users. It doubled in size in less than 8 months and continued to grow at close to 1 million new users per day, which made Microsoft decide to invest $240 million for 1.6% ownership. To meet the needs of many people using the site for many purposes, Facebook continued to experiment with new policies and features. This has been widely accepted as a communications success.

But Facebook experienced communication failures as well. In 2006, Zuckerberg introduced a feature that is now highly used and even taken for granted by new users: the *news feed*, "which allows users to see their friends' most recent online activities." Customer backlash was immediate and considerable, but the new feature remained and customers were allowed to opt out if they wished.

In 2007, users again became angry when a new feature, called "Beacon," was implemented.[3]

Beacon formed part of Facebook's advertisement system that sent data from external websites to Facebook for the purpose of allowing targeted advertisements and allowing users to share their activities with their friends. Beacon would report to Facebook on its members' activities on third-party sites that also participate with Beacon. These activities would be published to users' news feed. This would occur even when users were not connected to Facebook and would happen without the knowledge of the Facebook user.

One of the main concerns was that Beacon did not give the user the option to block the information from being sent to Facebook. Beacon was launched on November 6, 2007, with 44 partner websites.[4] The controversial service, which became the target of a class action lawsuit, was shut down in September 2009. Zuckerberg characterized Beacon on the Facebook Blog in November 2011 as a "mistake."[5] Although Beacon was unsuccessful, it did pave the way for Facebook Connect, which has become widely popular.[6] The new approach remedied the previous complaints that information was being shared without their knowledge because users had to opt in before any sharing occurred.

8.3.1 Determining the Investment Proposition of Your Company

Before presenting a company's story to investors, your company must fully understand what type of investment opportunity it presents. Thus, a basic understanding of "market value" and "intrinsic value" is in order.[7]

The *Oxford Dictionary* defines valuation as "an estimation of something's worth." For a publicly traded company, where, in most cases, there is an opportunity to buy or sell stock in an open and liquid market, valuation is that company's *market value* or capitalization.

Market capitalization of a publicly traded company, valuation, is nothing more and nothing less than the current price a buyer is willing to pay and a seller is willing to accept for a liquid minority interest in a company. It is the company's "market value" as of today.

Intrinsic value, in contrast, is based on expectations of future profits, future growth, future cash flow, and future risk. Still, other investors focus on a combination of both present and future criteria to determine an appropriate price for a minority interest in a public company. While different investors will weigh each of these measures differently when analyzing a company, they all seek to reach the same conclusion. Is this company worth more than its market value today? Or, do I believe management will create additional value in the future so that my investment will appreciate as the market recognizes a greater worth?

Determining how investors reach their varying conclusions of intrinsic value is what drives the practice of investor communications and relations. And, the way in which a company communicates its story, in writing or verbally, is the basis upon which investors will calculate a company's intrinsic value.

Before communicating, it is necessary for a company to understand how investors calculate intrinsic value. This involves an analysis of a company's profitability, growth, cash flow, and risk—the focal points of valuation and the areas where management, through its future actions, has the ability to create value for its shareholders.

8.3.2 Targeting the Right Investors

Many startups with great investment propositions are not properly valued by the marketplace. These companies are definitely worthy of a higher valuation but, for some reason, are not able to raise capital. Often, the reason for this is quite simple. Management has not been proactive in its investor outreach, and as a result, no one knows the company even exists.

In the United States, there are many potential investors, such as angels, venture capitalists, mutual fund managers, hedge fund managers, and asset managers—each with separate and distinctive investment philosophies. And, with thousands of companies to invest in, how should an investor pick one over another? The company that developed a communications platform that clearly conveys its investment proposition and a management team that tells its story has the better chance of winning the investor race than the company that hibernates at its headquarters.

Once you determine your investment proposition, the next step is to determine the specific type of investor you should target. On one level, all investors are alike. Their central focus is how much reward they will reap from their investment and how quickly this will happen. While investors are interested in what a company does and the industry in which it exists, this information is only valuable if it helps to illuminate the likely return on their investment. The primary concern to investors is that the company in which they are investing is addressing a market opportunity that will increase the value of their investment commensurate with the risks.

To persuasively communicate future intrinsic value to a group of investors, it is essential to understand individual styles of investing. The following two general categories describe some of the most common investment approaches:

- *Growth investors.* Some individuals or firms invest only in companies they believe have potential for rapid growth. In selecting companies, they focus on the income statement and are usually looking for annual growth that outpaces the overall market as well as investments with similar risk profiles.

- *Value investors.* These investors look for companies whose share price is less than the company's asset value—well below the industry average. They focus on the total balance sheet and believe that if a company is financially sound, they will be rewarded over time for buying in at an undervalued or "cheap" level. These investors also care about growth—they want to know what is likely to get the market's attention and how this will push up market value. However, paying a discounted market price for the company's intrinsic value is their main goal.

8.3.3 Develop Your Communication Platform Specific to Your Targeted Investor Audience

For the company that only presents a growth investment proposition, that company's communications platform must exude growth. For the value proposition company, the communications platform must trumpet the undervalued song.

For the company that is growing by leaps and bounds, and at the same time is undervalued, it must tell its story in two different ways. (1) When meeting with growth investors, it must demonstrate to the investor how it plans to grow. (2) When meeting with value investors, it must explain the rationale for why it believes it is undervalued. While it is not necessary to have two separate sets of materials or presentations, it is important that when your company meets with each of these two types of investors, you know which one you are meeting and tailor your remarks to each of their respective needs for information.

Having a communications platform that provides a roadmap for success is therefore necessary to demonstrate how a company believes that it can successfully execute it and grow. A well-thought-out and comprehensive communications platform allows investors to realize that management is aware of its responsibility to provide as much information as possible to its current and prospective equity holders and to give them the confidence they need to feel comfortable parting with their cash and investing.

A company has various means in which to communicate how it intends to grow and why its current stock price or valuation is appropriate, or why it should have a higher value. Management can provide investors with a snapshot of their business in the form of a fact sheet that highlights how they have positioned the company to grow and the opportunity for growth that exists in the industry. They also have the ability to speak to investors at investor conferences or meet with them in one-on-one or group settings. At these meetings, your team can present a PowerPoint investor presentation that similarly highlights its growth potential.

8.3.4 Maintain Constant Communications with Your Investor Audience So That Key Drivers of Business Are Current and Obvious to Investors

With a sound investment proposition determined, an appropriate audience of investors targeted, and a well-articulated story found in your company's investment materials, the next step toward achieving success in a company's investor relations program is to secure a meeting with the right investor. Convince the investor why they should invest and begin the process of building a relationship that will lead to the investor maintaining their long-term investment in your company.

And, this is the challenging part: convince the investor that management is serious and for the long haul has no intention of squandering the investor's cash. While many entrepreneurs have the requisite presentation skills, many are new to representing their companies. Careful: The way you present yourself is crucial since you have only one opportunity to make your case.

A carefully conceived investor communications platform is at the heart of a company's effort to attain true value. What a company says about itself and how it says it is central to how that company will be perceived. The ability of a company to communicate persuasively depends on the company's ability to truly understand its strengths, where it is going, and what type of investment opportunity it represents, and therefore what type of investor to approach. While a company's financial fundamentals speak for themselves, what a company says and how it says it ultimately will determine how the market values your business.

8.3.5 Corporate Core Values Communications

Below are two examples of value communications from two powerful and highly respected American corporations, Pfizer and General Electric.[8]

8.3.5.1 Pfizer

The following is from a complex assignment during media training with different members of the oncology team at Pfizer. Their mission is to be a world leader in developing new medicines for the treatment of cancers where patients are without treatment or have limited or diminishing options.

The following three core values emerged from several hours of brainstorming and analysis:

- Pfizer is committing US$7.5 billion a year to pursue new medicines— a level unmatched in the industry.
- Pfizer has assembled the best and brightest cancer scientists from around the globe—a United Nations of recognized leaders in drug discovery and development.
- Pfizer scientists are committed to success, often pursuing cures for a decade or more until they find the one success out of a thousand promising compounds.

From those core values, the scientists had impressive research projects in the pipeline that would provide positive supporting evidence. In (1), the US$7.5 billion core value, they can add how much it costs to develop a drug, the rate of failure, the need for new technology to speed the discovery process, and other details on the cost of equipment and so forth. In (2), they can refer to published works of their scientific teams and successful new products. In (3), they can give personal anecdotes, such as one scientist who started pursuing a new compound to treat cancer when his first daughter was born.

That same compound is now entering Phase III (the last stage of clinical trials before applying to the Food and Drug Administration [FDA] for approval) as his daughter enters middle school! The scientists also talked about getting up early or staying up late for teleconference sessions with colleagues around the globe, or traveling inordinately to meet and advance the science.

8.3.5.2 General Electric

Core values are the foundation for benefits that are delivered to your different constituencies. They are the major ingredients of success. General Electric wants to be number one or two in each market it serves because of its culture of innovation, customer focus, and ability to deliver the highest quality on a consistent basis, using its internal process called Six Sigma. From those three pillars of the image, GE provides ongoing evidence for each core value. It introduces new products. It upgrades existing ones and replaces defective products. It also promotes its Six Sigma process to other companies as a means of raising their standards. GE is leading the field. More GE alumni run major corporations than those from any other Fortune 100 firm.

8.4 Less Sizzle—More Steak

To make your investor's communications more effective, write a company description in 50 words or less. The written description should emphasize how an investor will make money, and in what period of time. And together with a written description, investors expect to hear and see the entrepreneur in person. Like it or not, a company is judged by the first impression made by the entrepreneur. They are the responsible party for interacting with the investment community. As such, every aspect of appearance and demeanor is noticed, even if subconsciously. The statistics tell the story, as seen below.

- 95% of the queried rated one-on-one private meetings as their preferred method of learning about the company.
- 87% considered one-on-one conference-style meetings their second best method.
- Less than 65% favored general conference calls.
- Less than 50% liked to use a company website as a source of information.

In the "first impressions" category, your verbal impression is as important as the physical or visual one. You must demonstrate articulate speech, beautifully enunciated and delivered with enthusiasm. This is not something most of us consciously think about, but it is important. Make sure you always speak clearly and articulately. The words you say are also judged by the *way* you say them. The last thing you want to do is damage your presentation because of poor enunciation or delivery.

8.4.1 Personal Presentation Skills

Your personal presentation skills are being assessed each time you present your company to a potential investor or shareholder. The care you devote to your presentation will play a large role in determining whether investors will want to risk their hard-earned dollars with an investment in your company. Below are some of the best ways to quickly capture the imaginations of potential investors.[9]

8.4.1.1 Lead with Greed

In the best presentations, the person making the presentation adopts the perspective of a potential shareholder and proactively answers the question, "Why would I buy this stock?" It should come as no surprise to you that investors want to make money, and quickly. Thus, if you would like someone to invest in your company, tell them how they are going to make a reasonable profit.

8.4.1.2 Why Should They Invest in Your Company?

Have you ever really asked yourself why anyone should buy your stock. There are thousands of startup companies seeking funding. If you are lucky enough to be in a one-on-one, or are presenting to a large group, or are in the process of being interviewed by a reporter, remember that the person in front of you liked your story enough to take time from their busy schedule to meet with you and get the "official" scoop. Make it interesting and compelling for them. What are the secrets to being compelling? Ask yourself the following:

- Would I buy my company's stock? Did I invest myself?
- If I did, why? If I didn't, why not?
- What would make *me* reconsider?
- What objectives must be reached before I would put my own money behind the company?

Do not forget that investors want and need your investment vehicle. They want to find good companies because this is how they make a living, whether by trading, investing, selling on commission, performing research analyses, or filling editorial pages.

Think of the primary factors that support your company's growth outlook. For example, do you have the following?

- A large market potential
- A proprietary and innovative product
- Patent protection
- High margins
- Barriers to competitive entry
- Technological advantages
- Unique management in place

8.4.1.3 Match Your Presentation to Your Audience

If you are not being asked super-scientific questions, do not feel the compunction to be super-scientific. Keep in mind that even other PhDs and MDs might not be able to carry on high-level discussions about your technology. Think of ways to explain your company's products in everyday language. One of the most important considerations in making your presentation is that it needs to be understood.

You might be speaking to a partner of an investment firm. This person then has to explain the science to his superior, who must then explain it to the other partners. We have all played the telephone game, where the story gets more distorted as people tell other people.

On the other hand, if you are being asked highly scientific questions, this is your chance to shine. There are some really sharp investors, many of whom can hold their own against top scientific officers, even without a PhD or MD degree.

8.4.1.4 Do Not Try to Educate

You are not a professor talking to students. In one-on-one meetings, do not spend your time trying to educate your audience about your entire sector, the health problem you aim to solve, or your high-tech solutions, and again, do not use technical or scientific jargon. You will be making a serious error if you try to educate the person in front of you. You are assuming that they do not know what you know. Do not assume. This could be perceived as condescending, and can also leave you open to debate—never a winning formula in trying to gain investor interest. Keep in mind that the more technical and complex your presentation, the more you run the risk of losing your audience's attention.

The person in front of you is most likely not interested in the intricate details. What most investors want to hear from you is how they are going to make money if they invest in your stock. Keep your presentation simple and describe how your product, technology, research, patent, intellectual capital, location, or services are better than those of the competition. Reserve the deep technical explanations for subsequent meetings.

8.4.1.5 Ask for the Order

Always be closing. You want the person in front of you to invest in your company. Do you typically make sure that you specifically ask for the money at the end of your presentations? Or are you, instead, shaking hands and leaving the meeting with a big question mark in your mind as to whether or not you have a new investor? Once you finish presenting and the Q&A session has wound down, directly ask, "Will you start buying our stock?"

If you get a yes, that is great. Silently congratulate yourself and believe them. Most people react honestly in these situations, and it definitely pays to ask. If the answer is no, thank them for their candor and tell them it would be helpful if you knew why not. Listen closely and learn. When the investor says no, one way you might frame your next question is, "What factors need to be in place to make you feel more comfortable investing in our company?"

Again, listen closely. This is a dating process. Even when there is no immediate love connection, you are going to obtain valuable information to help you understand what will make the investor feel secure about a long-term relationship with you and your company.

The investor meeting is the time to put on your thickest skin. Be prepared for criticism and opposition, and listen closely. Assess if it is valid without becoming defensive. To get someone to say yes means they have to believe in the ideal of the product, the timeline, and the management. Even beyond that, people are wary of making a commitment because, as in all relationships, commitment is scary. They look to you for reassurance that they are making a sound decision by investing in you and your company.

8.5 Crisis Communications and Management

The question is not if you will encounter a problem that turns into a crisis, but when. The extensive news coverage that such events garner often results in intense public scrutiny that can affect your business, operations, and financials and subject your company to political, governmental, and legal consequences.[10]

Several recent crises at large corporations, including product safety issues, product recalls, and product injuries, have brought greater attention to risks and raised the potential for boards to be held legally responsible for failing to account for and address these risks. A developing crisis might not kill a major corporation, but the resulting legal liability and reputational damage may compromise the ability of many smaller companies to survive.

Indeed, it is not uncommon for companies in the biotech and life sciences sector to lack the corporate staffing and capital resources to plan for or weather the storm that a crisis can bring. As a result, entrepreneurial companies are at a heightened risk of events that could spin out of control and be memorialized and disseminated through the Internet, in a matter of hours.

Many crisis situations reflect a failure of management to be sufficiently prepared. In this chapter, we discuss how management and boards of entrepreneurial companies should plan for and deal with crises to mitigate adverse consequences. How can you prepare for the day when an unpredictable event morphs into a crisis, with all the potential negative repercussions for your company's reputation and financial standing? You will need to set up a crisis communication team, as discussed below.

8.5.1 Crisis Communication

Crisis communication is "the perception of an unpredictable event that threatens important expectancies of stakeholders and can seriously impact an organization's performance and generate negative outcomes."[11]

Many scholars have proposed other definitions, but despite assumptions to the contrary, there is imperfect agreement among them as to the preferred definition of the word. Table 8.1 provides a sampling of definitions; these highlight other important aspects of crises—for example, their effects on organizational processes such as decision making and on entities beyond the organization itself.

Four elements are common to a crisis: (1) a threat to the organization, (2) the element of surprise, (3) a short decision time, and (4) the need for change. If change is not needed, the event could more accurately be described as a failure or incident. Venette[12] argues that "crisis is a process of transformation where the old system can no longer be maintained."

According to Murphy's law, whatever can go wrong will go wrong (or, its corollary: whatever can go wrong will go wrong, at the worst possible time, and in the worst possible way). Every entrepreneur should keep a copy of Murphy's law prominently displayed on their desk to remind them that a crisis will occur sometime in the future.

The effect of Murphy's law regarding business crises is not simply an error or situation that has to be made right. It can lead to irreparable damage to the reputation of an organization. Such damage can have financial, business, and motivational implications that take years to redress.

While every issue or crisis has to be handled in a different way, there is one common factor: the need for an effective crisis communication strategy.

8.5.2 Crisis Management

Crisis management is a situational-based management system that includes clear roles and responsibilities and process-related organizational requirements company-wide. The response should include action in the following areas: crisis prevention, crisis assessment, crisis handling, and crisis termination. The aim of crisis management is to be well prepared for crisis and ensure a rapid and adequate response to the crisis, maintaining clear lines of reporting and communication in the event of a crisis and rules for crisis termination. Crisis management consists of different aspects, including[13]

- Methods used to respond to both the reality and perception of crises
- Establishing metrics to define what scenarios constitute a crisis and should consequently trigger the necessary response mechanisms

8.5.2.1 Situational Crisis Communications Theory

In 2002, Coombs and Holladay[14] proposed the situational crisis communication theory (SCCT) as a suitable strategy for managing a crisis. They suggested focusing on two factors, namely, severity and performance history. Severity refers to the amount of damage (financial, human, and environmental damage) generated by a crisis, while performance history refers to the previous actions of organizations, including their crisis history.

They further argued that determining a crisis response strategy to accommodate all stakeholders affected by crisis events, as well as being able to control such a crisis, is vital. By doing so, organizations demonstrate that they care for the injured and understand what steps they should undertake during crisis times. In turn, it would be possible for organizations to regain

TABLE 8.1

Definitions of Business Crises

Definition	Authors
"Any emotionally charged situation that, once it becomes public, invites negative stakeholder reaction and thereby has the potential to threaten the financial well-being, reputation or survival of the firm or some portion thereof."	Erica Hayes James and Lynn Perry Wooten, "Leadership as (Un)usual: How to Display Competence in Times of Crisis," *Organizational Dynamics*, 34, no. 2 (2005): 142.
"A low-probability, high-impact event that threatens the viability of the organization and is characterized by ambiguity of cause, effect, and means of resolution, as well as by a belief that decisions must be made swiftly."	Christine M. Pearson and Judith A. Clair, "Reframing Crisis Management," *Academy of Management Review*, 23 (1998): 60.
"A serious threat to the basic structure or the fundamental values and norms of a social system, which—under time pressure and highly uncertain circumstances—necessitates making critical decisions."	Uriel Rosenthal, Paul 't Hart, and Michael T. Charles, "The World of Crises and Crisis Management," in *Coping with Crises: The Management of Disasters, Riots and Terrorism*, ed. Uriel Rosenthal, Michael T. Charles, and Paul 't Hart (Springfield, IL: Charles C. Thomas), 1 10.
"A situation that threatens high-priority goals of the decision-making unit, restricts the amount of time available for response before the decision is transformed and surprises the members of the decision-making unit by its occurrence."	C. F. Hermann, *International Crises: Insights from Behavioral Research* (New York: Free Press, 1972), as quoted in Uriel Rosenthal and Alexander Kouzmin, "Crises and Crisis Management: Toward Comprehensive Government Decision Making," *Journal of Public Administration Research and Theory*, 7, no. 2 (1997): 279.

the public trust and quickly repair their reputation. Figure 8.1 shows several variables that need to be applied to SCCT.

8.5.3 Typology of Crises

Crises are a product of interacting technological, organizational, and human failures.[15] This typology stresses the differences between various types of events that trigger corporate crises.

Table 8.2 summarizes the internal versus external crises.[16]

It is important to further identify types of crises since each crisis necessitates the use of different crisis management strategies. Potential crises are enormous, but crises can be clustered. Lerbinger[17] categorized eight types of crises:

1. Financial disasters (business)
2. Technological crises (business)
3. Confrontations

Situational crisis communications theory

FIGURE 8.1
Crisis communications aims to preserve organizational reputation.

4. Malevolence

5. Organizational misdeeds

6. Workplace violence

7. Rumors

8. Terrorist attacks and man-made disasters

Technological crises are caused by human application of science and technology. Technological accidents inevitably occur when technology becomes complex and coupled and something goes wrong in the system as a whole (technological breakdowns). Some technological crises occur when human error causes disruptions.

TABLE 8.2

Events That Trigger a Crisis

Typology	Examples of Internal Crises	Examples of External Crises
Technical/ economic	Major industrial accidents Product injuries Computer breakdown Defective, undisclosed information	Widespread, environmental destruction Natural disasters Hostile takeover Societal crises Large-scale systems failure
Human/ organizational/ social	Failure to adapt to change Sabotage by insiders Organizational breakdown Communication breakdown On-site political tampering Illegal activities	Symbolic projection Sabotage by outsiders Terrorism Executive kidnapping Off-site product tampering Counterfeiting

The public tends to assign blame for a technological disaster because technology is subject to human manipulation, whereas they do not hold anyone responsible for natural disasters. When an accident creates significant environmental damage, the crisis is categorized as *megadamage*.[18] Samples include medical product strict liability, software failures, industrial accidents, and oil spills.

A crisis may happen following a failed takeover that causes the share price to plummet; toxic food, medicines, or drinks lead to mass hysteria. All attention focuses on the "guilty" parties.

Inevitably, these crises are made public and are often grossly exaggerated by the media. If an organization produces a defective product, or fails to demonstrate efficacy during a clinical trial, social media can be expected to make this headline news within a matter of hours.

Every day, organizations run the risk of being affected. The fact that we live in an age of transparency means that no company or organization is immune to the threat of a possible crisis. Companies have become glass houses in which nothing can remain hidden. Everything is expected to be visible.

A crisis does not necessarily have to turn into a disaster for the business or organization involved. This chapter discusses how to limit damage effectively by acting quickly and positively. Moreover, it explains how to turn a crisis into an opportunity by communicating properly and efficiently.

8.5.4 Crisis Communication Life Cycle

Understanding the pattern of a crisis can help communicators anticipate problems and respond appropriately. For communicators, it is vital to know that every emergency, disaster, or crisis evolves in four predictable phases. The communication, too, must evolve through these changes. By dividing the crisis into the following phases, the communicator can anticipate the information needs of the media, agencies, organizations, and the general public. For each of these four phases, specific types of information need to be created and delivered to your audience, as shown in Figure 8.2.

One of the best ways to limit public anxiety in a crisis is to provide useful information about the event and tell the public what they can do, if anything. During the initial phase of an event, organizational response and authorized spokespersons should take steps to establish their credibility.

Even when there is little information to offer, it is still possible to communicate how the organization is handling the event and when more information will be available. Commit to the public that you will continue to provide new information as it becomes available.

8.5.4.1 Initial Phase

In the initial phase, communication objectives include rapid communication to the general public and affected groups. These communication efforts seek to do the following:

Crisis communications lifecycle

Modified after Crisis Communications US Department Health and Human Services 2012 Edition

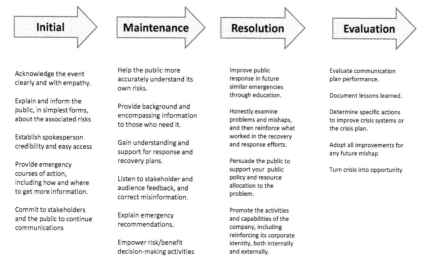

Initial

Acknowledge the event clearly and with empathy.

Explain and inform the public, in simplest forms, about the associated risks

Establish spokesperson credibility and easy access

Provide emergency courses of action, including how and where to get more information.

Commit to stakeholders and the public to continue communications

Maintenance

Help the public more accurately understand its own risks.

Provide background and encompassing information to those who need it.

Gain understanding and support for response and recovery plans.

Listen to stakeholder and audience feedback, and correct misinformation.

Explain emergency recommendations.

Empower risk/benefit decision-making activities

Resolution

Improve public response in future similar emergencies through education.

Honestly examine problems and mishaps, and then reinforce what worked in the recovery and response efforts.

Persuade the public to support your public policy and resource allocation to the problem.

Promote the activities and capabilities of the company, including reinforcing its corporate identity, both internally and externally.

Evaluation

Evaluate communication plan performance.

Document lessons learned.

Determine specific actions to improve crisis systems or the crisis plan.

Adopt all improvements for any future mishap

Turn crisis into opportunity

FIGURE 8.2
The four steps of crisis communications.

- Convey empathy and reassurance and reduce emotional turmoil
- Designate crisis or agency spokespersons and identify formal channels and methods of communication
- Establish general and broad-based understanding of the crisis circumstances, consequences, and anticipated outcomes based on available information
- Reduce crisis-related uncertainty as much as possible
- Help the public understand the responsibilities of the various organizations involved in the response
- Promote self-efficacy (explain to people that they can help themselves or reach a goal) through personal response activities and share how and where they can get more information

When communicating in the initial phases of an emergency, it is important to present information that is simple, credible, accurate, consistent, and delivered on time. The initial phase of a crisis is characterized by confusion and intense media interest. Information is usually incomplete, and the facts are sparse. An information deficit exists. Channels of communication are often disrupted. It is important to recognize that information from the media, other organizations, and even within response organizations may not be completely accurate. It is important to learn as much about what happened as possible, to determine the organization's communication responses, and to confirm the magnitude of the event as quickly as possible.

In the initial phase of a crisis, you must be accurate while recognizing that not having all the facts available early will not alleviate responders from the responsibility of communicating, even if that is an honest "we don't know." Accuracy in what is released and the speed with which response officials acknowledge the event are critical at this stage.

One of the best ways to limit public anxiety in a crisis is to provide useful information about the event and tell the public what they can do. During the initial phase of an event, response organizations and spokespersons should take steps to establish their credibility. Even when there is little information to offer, it is still possible to communicate how the organization is handling the event and when more information will be available. Commit to the public that you will continue to provide new information as it becomes available.

At the very least, messages should demonstrate that organizations are engaged and addressing the issues directly. This means that approaches are reasonable, caring, and timely, and all available information is being provided. At the same time, the pressure to release information prematurely can be intense. In most cases, all information must be cleared by the appropriate leaders or designated clearance personnel before it is offered to the media. If clearance procedures are too slow or cumbersome, they should be challenged during exercises and in planning.

Although the types of information that people need will vary according to the specific crisis, in the initial phase of a crisis, an information vacuum often exists. People want that vacuum filled. They want timely and accurate facts about what happened, what is being done, and most importantly, what they should do. People will question the immediate threat to them, the duration of the threat, and who is going to fix the problem. Communicators should be prepared to answer these questions as quickly, accurately, and fully as possible while acknowledging the uncertainty of the situation. At the same time, they will need to direct people to places where more information is available.

8.5.4.2 Maintenance Phase

Communication objectives during the crisis maintenance phase include talking with the general public and other stakeholders.

- Ensure that the public is updated, understands ongoing risks, and knows how to mitigate these risks.
- Provide background and supportive information to those who need it.
- Encourage broad-based support and cooperation with response and recovery efforts.
- Gather feedback from the affected public—listen, learn, and assess.

- Correct misunderstandings, rumors, or unclear facts.
- Continue to help people believe they can take steps to protect themselves, their families, and their community. Continue to explain those steps.
- Support informed decision making by the public based on their understanding of risks and benefits.

As the crisis evolves, anticipate sustained media interest and scrutiny. Unexpected developments, rumors, or misinformation may place further media demands on organization communicators. Other experts, professionals, and those not associated with the response will comment publicly on the issues. Sometimes they will contradict or misinterpret your messages. Criticism about the response is inevitable and to be expected.

Staying on top of the information flow and maintaining close coordination with others is essential. Processes for tracking communication activities and audiences become increasingly important as the workload increases. The crisis maintenance phase includes an ongoing assessment of the event and allocation of resources.

8.5.4.3 Resolution Phase

Communication objectives for the resolution phase will likely include continued communication to the general public and affected groups. During this phase, crisis communicators should do the following:

- Explain a product recall, failed clinical trial, botched product introduction, and so on, to your audience. Motivate your stakeholders to take action if needed.
- Facilitate broad-based, honest, and open discussion about causes, blame, responsibility, resolutions, and adequacy of the response.
- Improve individual understanding of new risks.
- Promote behaviors that avoid risks.
- Promote personal preparedness.
- Promote the activities and capabilities of the organization by reinforcing positive identities and images.
- Persuade the public to support your policy and resource allocation to the problem.

As the crisis resolves, there may be a return to the status quo, with a better understanding about what took place. Complete recovery systems are activated. This phase is depicted by much less public and media interest. Once the crisis is resolved, you may need to respond to intense media scrutiny of how the response was handled.

An opportunity may exist to reinforce public health messages while the issue is still current. The organization may need to start a public education campaign or change its website. A community is more likely to respond to safety and public health messages at this time.

8.5.4.4 Evaluation Phase

Objectives during the evaluation phase include communication directed toward the response community. Responders will evaluate and assess the effectiveness of responses, including the following:

- Discuss, document, and share lessons learned.
- Determine specific actions to improve crisis communication and crisis response capability.
- Evaluate the performance of the communication plan.
- Implement links to pre-crisis activities.

Typically, an after-evaluation report, sometimes called a "lessons learned" report, is generated through an exhaustive process of reviewing records and consulting the key people involved. No response is ever perfect, and there is always something to learn.

Crisis communication tactics during the evaluation phase may also include the following: reviewing and dissecting the successes and failures of the crisis management team in order to make any necessary changes to the organization or its employees, practices, or procedures, and providing follow-up crisis messages as necessary. Below are listed seven landmark communication case studies:

- Tylenol tampering crisis (1982 and 1986)[19]
- *Exxon Valdez* oil spill crisis (1989)[20]
- Bridgestone/Firestone and Ford tire crisis (1990s)[21]
- McDonald's hot coffee crisis (1992)[22]
- Pepsi syringe crisis (1993)[23]
- Dominos YouTube crisis (2009)[24]
- BP Gulf oil spill (2010)[25,26]

8.5.4.5 Social Media and Crisis Management

Social media has accelerated the speed with which information about a crisis can spread. The viral effect of social networks such as Twitter means that stakeholders can break news faster than traditional media, thus making managing a crisis much harder to manage.[27] This can be mitigated by having the right training and policy in place as well as the right social media monitoring tools to detect signs of a crisis breaking.[28] Social media also gives crisis management team's access to real-time information about how a crisis is impacting stakeholder sentiment and the issues that are of most concern to them.

The crisis management mantra of Lanny Davis, former legal counselor to Bill Clinton, is to "tell it early, tell it all, tell it yourself"—highly instructive. This was a strategy employed at the Clinton White House during 1996–1998 to any breaking news.[29] On a November afternoon in 1996, Mr. Davis got a phone call that would change his life. It was from a top aide at the White House, asking him if he was interested in joining the president's senior staff. Within a few short weeks, he had signed on as special counsel to the president. Fourteen months later, his tour of duty almost over, he got another phone call, this time from a *Washington Post* reporter who asked, "Have you ever heard the name Monica Lewinsky?"

In the time between those two phone calls, Davis received an extraordinary political education. As President Bill Clinton's chief spokesman for handling scandal matters, he had the unenviable job of briefing reporters and answering their pointed questions on the most embarrassing allegations against the president and his aides, from charges of renting out the Lincoln Bedroom to stories of selling plots in Arlington Cemetery, and from irregular campaign fundraising to sexual improprieties. He was the White House's first line of defense against the press corps and the reporters' first point of entry to an increasingly reticent administration. His delicate task was to remain credible to both sides while surviving the inevitable cross fire.

Upon entering the White House, Davis discovered that he was never going to be able to turn bad news into good news, but he could place the bad news in its proper context and work with reporters to present a fuller picture. While some in the White House grew increasingly leery of helping a press corps that they regarded as hostile, Davis moved in the opposite direction, pitching unfavorable stories to reporters and helping them garner the facts to write those stories accurately. Most surprisingly of all, he realized that to do his job properly, he sometimes had to turn himself into a reporter within the White House, interviewing his colleagues and ferreting out information. Along the way, he learned the true lessons of why politicians, lawyers, and reporters so often act at cross-purposes and gained some remarkable and counterintuitive insights into why this need not be the case.

Searching out the facts wherever he could find them, even if he had to proceed covertly, Davis discovered that he could simultaneously help the reporters do their jobs and not put the president in legal or political jeopardy. With refreshing candor, Davis admits his own mistakes and reveals those instances where he dug a deeper hole for himself by denying the obvious and obfuscating the truth. And in a powerful reassessment of the scandal that led to the president's impeachment, Davis suggests that if the White House had been more receptive to these same hard-won lessons, the Monica

Lewinsky story might not have come so close to bringing down an otherwise popular president. For as Davis learned above all, you can always make a bad story better by telling it early, telling it all, and telling it yourself.

8.5.4.6 Crisis Management Teams

Businesses should have a planned approach to releasing information to the media in the event of a crisis. A media reaction plan should include a company media representative as part of a "crisis management team." Since there is always a degree of unpredictability during a crisis, it is best that all crisis management team members understand how to deal with the media and be prepared to do so, should they be thrust into such a situation.[30]

In 2010, Procter & Gamble called reports claiming that its new Dry Max Pampers caused rashes and other skin irritations "completely false" as it aimed to contain a public relations threat to its biggest diaper innovation in 25 years. A Facebook group called "Pampers Bring Back the Old Cruisers/Swaddlers" rose to more than 4500 members. Pampers denied the allegation and stated that only two complaints had been received for every 1 million diapers sold.[31]

Pampers quickly reached out to people expressing their concerns via social media. Pampers even held a summit with four influential "mommy bloggers" to help dispel the rumor. Pampers acted quickly and decisively to an emerging crisis, before competitors and critics alike could fuel the fire any further. But not before the law firm Keller Rohrback, which was "investigating claims of diaper rash and chemical burns from Pampers Dry Max diapers," filed two lawsuits against Procter & Gamble seeking to create a class action suit.

8.6 The Crisis-Ready Organization

Crisis management is arguably one of the most important areas of organizational communications. While there are numerous views of crisis management, one of the most accepted models was developed by Pearson and Mitroff,[32] who are leading scholars in the area of organizational crises. These authors maintain that crisis management should proceed through five logical steps: (1) signal detection, (2) preparation and prevention, (3) containment damage limitation, (4) recovery, and (5) learning.

As best practice advice on crisis management, organizations should

- Not ignore low-probability, high-consequence events when developing their crisis management plans.
- Understand the limitations of risk analysis—namely, the fact that it does not usually include failures in multiple systems simultaneously.

- Dedicate one individual to crisis management. This individual does not need to be a "chief crisis officer" but does need to make crisis management (and avoidance) a full-time responsibility.

To use time effectively, management should identify the events that are most likely to occur and their potential impact on the company. A review of events that could have a major adverse impact on biotech companies may be useful. Further, an acceptable level of risk tolerance needs to be established by management so that resources are used efficiently. Table 8.3 summarizes the events that are most likely to be experienced by a biotechnology company.

8.6.1 Business Continuity Planning

Business continuity planning (BCP) is a technique that is designed to help organizations quickly return to normal operations after a crisis.[33] Originally, BCP largely focused on ensuring that an organization's data stores would be preserved in the event of a crisis. Now, however, many view BCP as including all essential aspects of the organization during and after a crisis.

The primary purpose of BCP is to "get critical functions up and running as soon as possible."[34] This activity appears to have roots in redundancy theory and is particularly relevant to technologically complex

TABLE 8.3

Events Most Likely to Occur to Biotechnology Companies

Type of Event	Examples
Inherent	Failure of a clinical trial relating to efficacy or safety concerns or preliminary release or leak of data
	FDA regulatory compliance issues
	Negative vote from an FDA advisory panel
	Product-related issues, such as impurities, counterfeits, and adverse events
	Adverse response from payers or doctors to the pricing of a drug
	Disappointing sales of a newly launched drug
Force majeure	Governmental investigations
	Unexpected departure of key personnel
	Failure to gain adequate reimbursement
	Negative business events, such as loss of key customer
	Supply chain issue or factory or other business catastrophe
	Natural disasters, extreme weather, or environmental events
	Incidents that threaten the lives or safety of employees
	"Bad acts" by rogue or disgruntled employees
	Negative reports from security analysts
	Shareholder activism
	Insider trading by employees
	Negative stock market event associated with company
	Bid for the company by potential suitor
	Cyberattacks and data security breaches

organizations. Frederickson and LaPorte write that "the full application of the logic of redundancy asks that the parts of the system be loosely coupled or sufficiently independent of each other, so that a failure in one part is an independent event that can be compensated for by the other parts of the system."[35] Thus, BCP can be seen as a critical aspect for the high-reliability organization and as a potential means of minimizing the "normal accidents" problem.

8.7 Practical Advice on Crisis Management

A crisis can create three related threats: (1) public safety, (2) financial loss, and (3) reputation loss. Some crises, such as industrial accidents and product harm, can result in injuries and even loss of lives. Crises can create financial loss by disrupting operations, creating a loss of market share or purchase intentions, or spawning lawsuits related to the crisis.[36]

Practical crisis management is a process designed to prevent or lessen the damage a crisis can inflict on an organization and its stakeholders. As a process, crisis management is not just one thing. Crisis management can be divided into three phases: (1) pre-crisis, (2) crisis response, and (3) post-crisis.

The pre-crisis phase is concerned with prevention and preparation. The crisis response phase is when management must actually respond to a crisis. The post-crisis phase looks for ways to better prepare for the next crisis and fulfills commitments made during the crisis phase, including follow-up information. This three-part view of crisis management serves as a practical framework, as discussed in the subsequent paragraphs.

8.7.1 Pre-Crisis Phase

Prevention involves seeking to reduce known risks that could lead to a crisis. This should be an integral part of an organization's risk management program. Preparation involves creating the crisis management plan, selecting and training the crisis management team, and conducting periodic exercises to test the crisis management plan and crisis management team.

It is well established that organizations are better able to handle crises when they have a crisis management plan that is updated at least annually, have a designated crisis management team, conduct exercises to test the plans and teams at least annually, and pre-draft some crisis messages that speak with one voice.[37]

Table 8.4 lists the crisis preparation best practices. The planning and preparation allow crisis teams to react faster and make more effective decisions, as shown below.

TABLE 8.4

Crisis Preparation Best Practices

Have a crisis management plan (CMP) and update it at least annually.	A CMP provides lists of key contact information, reminders of what typically should be done in a crisis, and forms to be used to document the crisis response. Preassigning tasks presumes that there is a designated crisis team. The team members should know what tasks and responsibilities they have during a crisis.
Have a designated crisis management team that is properly trained.	Management identifies the common members of the crisis team as public relations, legal, security, operations, finance, and human resources. Valuable time is saved because the team has already decided on who will do the basic tasks required in a crisis.
Conduct exercise at least annually to test the crisis management plan and team.	A key component of crisis team exercise is spokesperson training. Organizational members must be prepared to talk to the news media during a crisis. Media training should be provided *before* a crisis hits.
Pre-draft select crisis management messages, including content for dark websites and templates for crisis statements. Have the legal department review and preapprove these messages.	Crisis managers can pre-draft messages that will be used during a crisis. More accurately, crisis managers create templates for crisis messages. Templates include statements by top management, news releases, and dark websites.

8.7.2 Crisis Response Phase

The crisis response is what management does and says after the crisis hits. Public relations plays a critical role in the crisis response by helping to develop the messages that are sent to various publics. Management must be prepared to talk to the news media and all stakeholders during a crisis. Table 8.5 presents a summary of best practices for media responses.[38,39,40]

The literature has extensively examined the crisis response by different organizations. The responses were divided into two main sections: (1) the initial crisis response and (2) reputation repair and behavioral intentions, as discussed below.

8.7.2.1 Initial Response

Practitioner experience and academic research have combined to create a clear set of guidelines for how to respond once a crisis hits. The initial crisis response guidelines focus on three points:
(1) be quick, (2) be accurate, and (3) be consistent.

8.7.2.1.1 Be Quick

Be quick seems rather simple: provide a response in the first hour after the crisis occurs. That puts a great deal of pressure on crisis managers to have a

TABLE 8.5

Summary of Best Practices for Media Responses

1. Avoid the phrase "no comment" because people think it means the organization is actually guilty and trying to hide something.
2. Present information clearly by avoiding jargon or technical terms. Lack of clarity makes people think the organization is purposefully being confusing in order to hide something ("snow job").
3. Appear pleasant on camera by avoiding nervous habits that people interpret as deception. A spokesperson needs to have strong eye contact, limit disfluencies such as "ums" or "uhs," and avoid distracting nervous gestures, such as fidgeting, rubbing hands, or pacing. Spokespersons will be perceived as deceptive if they avoid eye contact, have a lot of disfluencies, or display obvious nervous gestures.
4. Brief all potential spokespersons on the latest crisis information and the key message points the organization is trying to convey to stakeholders.

message ready in a short period of time. Again, we can appreciate the value of preparation and templates. The rationale behind being quick is the need for the organization to tell its side of the story. In reality, the organization's side of the story is the key points management wants to convey about the crisis to its stakeholders.

When a crisis occurs, people want to know what happened. Crisis experts often talk of an information vacuum being created by a crisis. The news media will lead the charge to fill the information vacuum and be a key source of initial crisis information.

If the organization experiencing the crisis refuses to communicate with the news media, other people will be ready to talk to the media. These people may have inaccurate information or may try to use the crisis as an opportunity to attack the organization. As a result, crisis managers must have a quick response. An early response may not have much new information, but the organization positions itself as a source and begins to present its side of the story, since a quick response is active and shows an organization is in control.[41] Silence is too passive: it lets others control the story (narrative) and suggests the organization has lost control of the situation.[42]

A 2005 study convincingly documented how a quick, early response allows an organization to generate greater credibility than a slow response.[43] This study discusses an experiment that introduces the concept of "stealing thunder." Stealing thunder is when an organization releases information about a crisis before the news media or others release the information. The results found that stealing thunder results in higher credibility ratings for a company than allowing others to report the crisis information first. This is additional evidence to support the notion of being quick in a crisis and telling the organization's side of the story.

8.7.2.1.2 Be Accurate

Crisis preparation will make it easier for crisis managers to respond quickly. Obviously, accuracy is important anytime an organization communicates with the public. People want accurate information about what happened and how that event might affect them. Because of the time pressure in a crisis, there is a risk of inaccurate information. If mistakes are made, they must be corrected. However, inaccuracies make an organization look inconsistent. Incorrect statements must be corrected quickly, to prevent an organization from appearing incompetent. The strategy of speaking with one voice in a crisis is a way of maintaining accuracy and message control.

8.7.2.1.3 Be Consistent

However, speaking with one voice does not mean only one person speaks for the organization for the whole duration of the crisis. It may be impossible to expect one person to speak for an organization if a crisis lasts for more than a day. Watch news coverage of a crisis and you most likely will see multiple people speak. The news media want to question experts, so they may need to talk to a person in operations, another from regulatory affairs, one from marketing, and so on.

The crisis team needs to share information so that different people can still convey a consistent message. The spokespersons should be briefed on the same information and the key points the organization is trying to convey in the messages. The public relations department should be instrumental in preparing the spokespersons. Ideally, potential spokespersons are trained and practice media relations skills prior to any crisis. The focus during a crisis then should be on the key information to be delivered rather than how to handle the media. More preparation helps by making sure that the various spokespersons have the proper media relations training and skills.

The news media are drawn to crises and are a useful way to reach a wide array of publics quickly. So it is logical that crisis response research has devoted considerable attention to media relations. Media relations allow crisis managers to reach a wide range of stakeholders fast. Fast and wide ranging is perfect for public safety—get the message out quickly and to as many people as possible. Clearly there is waste as nontargets receive the message, but speed and reach are more important at the initial stage of the crisis. However, the news media is not the only channel crisis managers can and should use to reach stakeholders.

Websites, intranet sites, and mass notification systems add to the news media coverage and help to provide a quick response. Crisis managers can supply greater amounts of their own information on a website. Mass notification systems deliver short messages to specific individuals through a mix of phone, text messaging, voice messages, and e-mail. The systems also allow people to send responses. In organizations with effective intranet systems, the intranet is a useful vehicle for reaching employees as well. If an organization integrates its intranet with suppliers and customers, these stakeholders can be reached as well. As the crisis management effort progresses, the channels can become more selective.

More recently, crisis experts have recommended a third component to an initial crisis response, crisis managers should express concern or sympathy for any victims of the crisis. Victims are the people that are hurt or experienced financial loss due to the crisis. Victims might have become ill, had to evacuate, or suffered property damage.

Kellerman[44] details instances when it is appropriate to express regret and defines an apology as accepting responsibility for a crisis and expressing regret. The value of apologies is highlighted along with suggestions for when an apology is appropriate or inappropriate. An apology should be used when it serves an important purpose and the crisis has serious consequences. Table 8.6 summarizes the cost of an apology, according to Kellerman's view.

Expressions of concern help to lessen reputational damage and reduce financial losses. But the literature is far from a consensus on this issue, as discussed below.

> Experimental studies by Coombs and Holladay.[45] This publication uses an experimental design to document the negative effect of crises on an organization's reputation. The research also establishes that the type of reputation repair strategies managers use does make a difference on perceptions of the organization. An important finding is proof that the more an organization is held responsible for the crisis, the more accommodative a reputation repair strategy must be in order to be effective and protect the organization's reputation.
>
> Dean[46] found that organizations experienced less reputational damage when an expression of concern was offered versus a response lacking any expression of concern. This experimental study included a comparison of how people reacted to expressions of concern versus no expression of concern. Post-crisis reputations were stronger when an organization provided an expression of concern.
>
> Cohen[47] examined legal cases and found that early expressions of concern help to reduce the number and amount of claims made against an organization for the crisis. This scholarly article examines expressions of concern and full apologies from a legal perspective. He noted that California, Massachusetts, and Florida have laws that prevent expressions of concern from being used as evidence against defendants in a court case. The evidence from court cases suggests that expressions of concern were helpful because they helped to reduce the amount of damages sought and the number of claims filed.
>
> However, Tyler[48] admonishes us that there are limits to expressions of concern. Plantiffs' lawyers may try to use expressions of concern as admissions of guilt. For that reason, a number of states have laws that protect expressions of concern from being used against an organization

TABLE 8.6

Kellerman's Apology Cost

Apologize when the cost of an apology will be lower than the cost of remaining silent.

in court. Another concern is that as more crisis managers express concern, the expressions of concern may lose their effect on many people. Hearit[49] cautions that many expressions of concern seem too routine and sterile. Still, a failure to provide a routine response could hurt an organization. Hence, bland expressions of concern may provide little benefit when used, but can inflict damage when not used. In his book, Chapter 1 helps to explain the different ways the term *apology* is used and concentrates on how it should be treated as a public acceptance of responsibility. Chapter 3 details the legal and liability issues involved when an organization chooses to use an apology.

Table 8.7 provides a summary of the initial crisis response best practices. Form refers to the basic structure of the response. The initial crisis response should be delivered in the first hour after a crisis and be vetted for accuracy. Content refers to what is covered in the initial crisis response. The initial message must provide any information needed to aid public safety, provide basic information about what has happened, and offer concern if there are victims. In addition, crisis managers must work to have a consistent message between spokespersons.

8.7.2.2 Reputation Repair

Public relations, communication, and marketing experts have shed light on how to repair the reputational damage a crisis inflicts on an organization. At the center of this research is a list of reputation repair strategies. Benoit[50] has done the most research to identify the reputation repair strategies. He analyzed and synthesized strategies from many different research traditions that shared a concern for reputation repair.

The reputation repair strategies vary in terms of how much they accommodate victims of this crisis (those at risk or harmed by the crisis).[51,52] The master list arranges the reputation repair strategies from the least to the most accommodating, as shown in Table 8.8.

Your reputation is key to salvaging your company after a major crisis, as depicted in Figure 8.3.

TABLE 8.7

Summary of Initial Crisis Response Best Practices

- Be quick and try to have an initial response within the first hour.
- Name one person as the official crisis spokesperson.
- Be accurate and carefully check all known facts.
- Be consistent by keeping spokespeople informed of crisis events and key message points.
- Make public safety your number one priority.
- Use all your available communication channels, including the Internet, intranet, and mass notification systems.
- Provide some expression of concern/sympathy for victims.
- Include employees and other stakeholders in your initial response.
- Continue to provide timely information as it becomes available.

TABLE 8.8

Master List of Reputation Repair Strategies

1. *Attack the accuser*: Crisis manager confronts the person or group claiming something is wrong with the organization.
2. *Denial*: Crisis manager asserts that there is no crisis.
3. *Scapegoat*: Crisis manager blames some person or group outside of the organization for the crisis.
4. *Excuse*: Crisis manager minimizes organizational responsibility by denying intent to do harm and/or claiming inability to.
5. Control the events that triggered the crisis.
6. *Provocation*: Crisis was a result of response to someone else's actions.
7. *Defeasibility*: Lack of information about events leading to the crisis situation.
8. *Accidental*: Lack of control over events leading to the crisis situation.
9. *Good intentions*: Organization meant to do well.
10. *Justification*: Crisis manager minimizes the perceived damage caused by the crisis.
11. *Reminder*: Crisis managers tell stakeholders about the past good works of the organization.
12. *Ingratiation*: Crisis manager praises stakeholders for their actions.
13. *Compensation*: Crisis manager offers money or other gifts to victims.
14. *Apology*: Crisis manager indicates that the organization takes full responsibility for the crisis and asks stakeholders for forgiveness.

It should be noted that reputation repair can be used in the crisis response phase, post-crisis phase, or both. Not all crises need reputation repair efforts. Frequently, the instructing information and expressions of concern are enough to protect the reputation. When a strong reputation repair effort is required, that effort will carry over into the post-crisis phase. Or, crisis managers may feel more comfortable waiting until the post-crisis phase to address reputation concerns.

Not all crises may be attributed to actions (or inactions) by the organization. The organization's responsibility may be characterized as minimal, low, or strong. This attribution of crisis responsibility is summarized in Table 8.9.

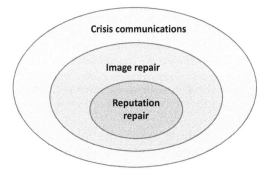

Reputation repair at a glance

Crisis communications

Image repair

Reputation repair

FIGURE 8.3
Reputation repair is the epicenter of crisis communication.

TABLE 8.9

Crisis Types by Attribution of Crisis Responsibility

Minimal Crisis Responsibility (provide and disseminate instructions)
- Rumors: False and damaging information being circulated about you organization
- Workplace violence: Attack by former or current employee on current employees on site
- Product tampering/malevolence: External agent causes damage to the organization

Low Crisis Responsibility (add excuses and justification to instructions)
- Challenges: Stakeholder claim that the organization is operating in an inappropriate manner
- Technical error accidents: Equipment or technology failure that causes an industrial accident
- Technical error product harm: Equipment or technology failure that causes a product to be defective or potentially harmful

Strong Crisis Responsibility (add compensation and/or care response to instructions)
- Human error accidents: Industrial accident caused by human error
- Human error product harm: Product is defective or potentially harmful because of human error
- Organizational misdeed: Management actions that put stakeholders at risk and/or violate the law

---

8.7.2.3 Post-Crisis Evaluation

In the post-crisis phase, the organization is returning to business as usual. The crisis is no longer the focal point of management's attention but still requires some attention. As noted earlier, reputation repair may be continued or initiated during this phase. There is important follow-up communication that is required.

> First, crisis managers often promise to provide additional information during the crisis phase. The crisis managers must deliver on those informational promises or risk losing the trust of the public wanting the information.
>
> Second, the organization needs to release updates on the recovery process, corrective actions, and/or investigations of the crisis. The amount of follow-up communication required depends on the amount of information promised during the crisis and the length of time it takes to complete the recovery process. If you promised a reporter a damage estimate, for example, be sure to deliver that estimate when it is ready.
>
> Third, as the Corporate Leadership Council[53] and the Business Roundtable[54] observe, intranets are an excellent way to keep employees updated, if the employees have ways to access the site. Continual and accurate information to all employees via intranets defuses rumors and empowers employees to feel they are part of the solution.

A crisis should be a learning experience for all crisis managers. More specifically, the crisis management effort needs to be evaluated to see what worked and what needs improvement. The same holds true for exercises. The organization should seek ways to improve prevention, preparation, and/or the response. As most books on crisis management note, those lessons are

TABLE 8.10

Post-Crisis Phase Best Practices

- Deliver all information promised to stakeholders as soon as that information is known.
- Keep stakeholders updated on the progression of improvement efforts, including any corrective measures being taken, and the progress of investigations.
- Analyze the crisis management effort for lessons and integrate those lessons into the organization's crisis management system.
---

then integrated into the pre-crisis and crisis response phases. That is how management learns and improves its crisis management process. Table 8.10 lists the post-crisis phase best practices.

Notes

1. Stoepler, J. Chasing capital: How to communicate your business' value when seeking funding. http://www.kcdpr.com/chasing-capital-how-to-communicate-your-business-value-when-seeking-funding/.
2. Hamilton, C. (2011). *Communicating for Results.* Boston: Wadsworth. http://www.pdfslibmanual.com/communicating-for-results-cheryl-hamilton.pdf.
3. Stone, B. (2007). Facebook executive discusses Beacon brouhaha. https://bits.blogs.nytimes.com/2007/11/29/facebook-responds-to-beacon-brouhaha/?_r=0.
4. Leading websites offer Facebook Beacon for social distribution (2007). Facebook Press Room.
5. Zuckerberg, M. (2011). https://newsroom.fb.com/news/2011/11/our-commitment-to-the-facebook-community/.
6. Facebook Beacon. https://en.wikipedia.org/wiki/Facebook_Beacon.
7. Corbin, J. (2004). *Investor Relations: The Art of Communicating Value.* Aspatore.
8. Anthonissen, P. F. (2008). *Crisis Communications.* London: Kogan Page. http://www.institutik.cz/wp-content/uploads/2012/03/Crisis-Communication-Peter-Anthonissen.pdf.
9. Griesel, D. (2002). *Capitalization Success.* New York: Investor Relations Group.
10. Kessel, M. and Masella, R. (2006). Preparing for crises. *Nature Biotechnology*, 34, 133–136. http://www.nature.com/nbt/journal/v34/n2/abs/nbt.3475.html.
11. Coombs, W. T. (2004). Impact of past crises on current crisis communications: Insights from: Situational crisis communication theory. *Journal of Business Communication*, 41, 265–289.
12. Venette, S. J. (2003). *Risk Communication in a High Reliability Organization: APHIS PPQ's Inclusion of Risk in Decision Making.* Ann Arbor, MI: UMI Proquest Information and Learning.
13. Crisis management. http://en.wikipedia.org/wiki/Crisis_management.
14. Coombs, W. T. and Holladay, S. J. (2002). Helping crisis manager protect reputational assets: Initial tests of the situational crisis communication theory. *Management Communication Quarterly*, 16(2), 165–186.
15. Shrivastava, P. and Mitroff, I. (1987). Strategic management of corporate crises. *Columbia World Journal of Business*, 22(1), 7.

16. Light, P. C. Predicting organizational crisis readiness: Perspectives and practices toward a pathway to preparedness. New York University. http://www.nyu.edu/ccpr/pubs/OrgPreparedness_Report_NYU_Light_8.18.08.pdf.
17. Lerbinger, O. (1997). *The Crisis Manager: Facing Risk and Responsibility*. Mahwah, NJ: Erlbaum.
18. Coombs, W. T. (1999). *Ongoing Crisis Communication: Planning, Managing, and Responding*. Thousand Oaks, CA: Sage.
19. Benson, J. A. (1988). Crisis revisited: An analysis of strategies used by Tylenol in the second tampering episode. *Central States Speech Journal*, 39(1), 49–66.
20. Williams, D. E. and Treadaway, G. (1992). Exxon and the Valdez accident: A failure in crisis communication. *Communication Studies*, 43(1), 56–64.
21. Blaney, J. R., Benoit, W. L. and Brazeal, L. M. (2002). Blowout! Firestone's image restoration campaign. *Public Relations Review*, 28(4), 379–392.
22. Sherowski, E. (1996). Hot coffee, cold cash: Making the most of alternative dispute resolution in high-stakes personal injury lawsuits. *Journal on Dispute Resolution*, 11(2), 521–536.
23. Crisis management/Pepsi syringe scare. http://iml.jou.ufl.edu/projects/Spring01/Morrison/Pepsi.html.
24. Jacques, A. (2009). Domino's delivers during crisis: The company's step-by-step response after a vulgar video goes viral. *The Strategist*, August 17.
25. De Wolf, D. and Mejri, M. (2013). Crisis communication failures: The BP case study. *International Journal of Advances in Management and Economics*, 2(2), 48–56.
26. McCarthy, E. (2013). Crisis management case study: BP oil spill. *The PR Code*, April 2.
27. Social media—Asset, threat or distraction during a crisis? (2013). Steelhenge Consulting. http://issuu.com/steelhenge/docs/socialmedia_crisis?mode=window&backgroundColor=%23222222.
28. Lewis, A. How to avoid a social media crisis. http://www.adamlewis.info/how-to-avoid-a-social-media-crisis/.
29. Davis, L. J. (2002). *Truth to Tell: Tell It Early, Tell It All, Tell It Yourself: Notes from My White House Education*. New York: Free Press.
30. Fischer, R. P., Halibozek, E. and Green, G. (2008). *Introduction to Security*, 8th ed. London: Butterworth-Heinemann (p. 256).
31. Geller, M. (2010). P&G dismisses Dry Max Pampers rash rumors. *Reuters*, May 6. http://www.reuters.com/article/2010/05/07/us-procter-pampers-idUSTRE6457AH20100507.
32. Pearson, C. M. and Mitroff, I. I. (1993). From crisis prone to crisis prepared: a framework for crisis management. *Academic Management Perspective*, 7(1).
33. Britt, P. (2005). Taking steps for disaster recovery. *Information Today*, 22(9), 21.
34. Hofmann, M. A. (2007). Continuity plans key to business survival after disaster. *Business Insurance*, 41(4), 18.
35. Frederickson, G.H. and LaPorte T.T. Airport security, high reliability, and the problem of rationality. *Public Administration Review*, 62(1) 33–43.
36. Coombs, T. (2007). *Crisis Management and Communications*. Institute for Public Relations.
37. Barton, L. (2001). *Crisis in Organizations II*, 2nd ed. Cincinnati, OH: College Divisions South-Western.
38. Lerbinger, O. (1997). *The Crisis Manager: Facing Risk and Responsibility*. Mahwah, NJ: Lawrence Erlbaum.

39. Fearn-Banks, K. (2001). *Crisis Communications: A Casebook Approach*, 2nd ed. Mahwah, NJ: Lawrence Erlbaum.
40. Coombs, W. T. (2007). *Ongoing Crisis Communication: Planning, Managing, and Responding*, 2nd ed. Los Angeles: Sage.
41. Carney, A. and Jorden, A. (1993). Prepare for business-related crises. *Public Relations Journal*, 49, 34–35.
42. Hearit, K. M. (1994). Apologies and public relations crises at Chrysler, Toshiba, and Volvo. *Public Relations Review*, 20(2), 113–125.
43. Arpan, L. M. and Roskos-Ewoldsen, D. R. (2005). Stealing thunder: An analysis of the effects of proactive disclosure of crisis information. *Public Relations Review*, 31(3), 425–433.
44. Kellerman, B. (2006). When should a leader apologize and when not? *Harvard Business Review*, 84(4), 73–81.
45. Coombs, W. T. and Holladay, S. J. (2006). Halo or reputational capital: Reputation and crisis management. *Journal of Communication Management*, 10(2), 123–137.
46. Dean, D. H. (2004). Consumer reaction to negative publicity: Effects of corporate reputation, response, and responsibility for a crisis event. *Journal of Business Communication*, 41, 192–211.
47. Cohen, J. R. (1999). Advising clients to apologize. *South California Law Review*, 72, 1009–1131.
48. Tyler, L. (1997). Liability means never being able to say you're sorry: Corporate guilt, legal constraints, and defensiveness in corporate communication. *Management Communication Quarterly*, 11(1), 51–73.
49. Hearit, K. M. (2006). *Crisis Management by Apology: Corporate Response to Allegations of Wrongdoing*. Mahwah, NJ: Lawrence Erlbaum Associates.
50. Benoit, W. L. (1997). Image repair discourse and crisis communication. *Public Relations Review*, 23(2), 177–180.
51. Benoit, W. L. (1995). *Accounts, Excuses, and Apologies: A Theory of Image Restoration*. Albany: State University of New York Press.
52. Ulmer, R. R., Sellnow, T. L. and Seeger, M. W. (2006). *Effective Crisis Communication: Moving from Crisis to Opportunity*. Thousand Oaks, CA: Sage.
53. Corporate Leadership Council. (2003). *Crisis Management Strategies*. http://www.executiveboard.com/EXBD/Images/PDF/Crisis%20Management%20Strategies.pdf.
54. Business Roundtable's post-9/11 crisis communication toolkit. (2002). http://www.nfib.com/object/3783593.html.

9

Corporate Entrepreneurship

9.1 Introduction

> Sooner or later your competitors will slow your sales, and profits
> will begin to evaporate. The solution is intrapreneurship.

Corporate entrepreneurship, or *intrapreneurship*, is the act of behaving like an entrepreneur while working within a large organization. Intrapreneurship is known as the practice of a corporate management style that integrates risk-taking and innovation approaches, as well as the reward and motivational techniques that are more traditionally thought of as being the province of entrepreneurship.[1]

Some of the world's most successful companies, including 3M, Anaconda-Ericsson, GE, Lockheed, Intel, Apple Computers, Rubbermaid, Google, Facebook, Sony, Toyota, Thermo Electron, Medtronic, and IBM, are all enthusiastic supporters of intrapreneurship. Could that be their secret to success?

9.2 Definitions

An *intrapreneur* is an innovator within an existing, large company who does not incur the risks associated with those activities. Intrapreneurship is acting like an entrepreneur within a larger organization. Intrapreneurs are usually highly self-motivated, proactive, and action-oriented people who are comfortable with taking the initiative, even within the boundaries of an organization, in pursuit of an innovative product or service. The intrapreneur has the comfort of knowing that failure does not have the personal cost that it does for an entrepreneur, since the organization absorbs losses arising from failure.[2]

In their influential 1978 publication, Gifford Pinchot III and Elizabeth Pinchot[3] coined the term *intrapreneurship* to describe the marriage of an entrepreneurial spirit—complete with its fierce independence and lack of deference to established views and the confines of conventional wisdom—with the resources of a large corporation. Later the term was credited to Gifford Pinchot III by Norman Macrae in the April 17, 1982, issue of *The Economist*.[4]

In 1992, the *American Heritage Dictionary* officialized the popular use of intrapreneur to mean "a person within a large corporation who takes direct responsibility for turning an idea into a profitable finished product through assertive risk-taking and innovation." Intrapreneurship is now known as practicing a corporate management style that integrates risk-taking and innovation with reward and motivational techniques more traditionally associated with entrepreneurship.

In 1994, Pinchot and Pinchot published their "Intraprise Manifesto,"[5] summarized below.

- Employees are treated with independence, dignity, and responsibility.
- Employees make up their own minds about what to do, limited only by general rules and commitments.
- Employees have access to resources required by their ideas—and are held accountable.
- Employees have the authority to manage the resources of their business units without interference.
- Employees are free to select their associations (e.g., peer support and coaches).
- Employees are permitted, and even rewarded, for taking qualified risks and making mistakes.

Using the failed examples of Wang Computers, DEC, Polaroid, and Kodak, Investopedia[6] suggests that companies should encourage employees to explore ideas rather than waiting until the company is in a bind. If an idea looks profitable, the company provides the innovator an opportunity to become an intrapreneur. Intrapreneurs thus use their entrepreneurial skills without personally incurring financial risks associated with entrepreneurial activities.

More comprehensively, Sharma and Chrisman[7] suggested that corporate entrepreneurship "is the process whereby an individual or a group of individuals, in association with an existing organization, create a new organization or instigate renewal or innovation within that organization."

All these concepts appear to be summarized by Zahra[8] when he stated,

> Corporate entrepreneurship refers to formal and informal activities aimed at creating new business in established companies through product and process innovations and market developments. These activities may take place at the corporate, division (business), functional, or project

levels, with the unifying objective of improving a company's competitive position and financial performance. Corporate entrepreneurship also entails the strategic renewal of an existing business.

9.3 Kelly Johnson's 14 Rules of Skunk Works[9]

Johnson earned recognition for his contributions to noteworthy aircraft designs, including the Lockheed U-2 and SR-71 Blackbird spy planes, P-38 Lightning, P-80 Shooting Star, and F-104 Starfighter. Johnson's famed "down-to-brass-tacks" management style was summed up by his motto "Be quick, be quiet, and be on time." He ran Lockheed's Skunk Works using "Kelly's 14 Rules." (Note: Skunk Works means keeping a group of intrapreneurs separate from the rest of the firm.)

1. The Skunk Works manager must be delegated near complete control of all aspects of his program and should report to a division president or higher.
2. Strong but small project offices must be established by both the military and industry.
3. The number of people having any connection with the project must be strictly limited. Use a small number, 10%–25% of a typical project's staffing, of top-notch people.
4. A very simple drawing and drawing release system with great flexibility for making changes must be provided.
5. Require a small number of reports, but important work must be recorded thoroughly.
6. There must be a monthly cost review covering not only what has been spent and committed but also what expenditures are expected to complete the program. Do not prepare the books 90 days late, and do not surprise the customer with unexpected cost overruns.
7. The contractor must be delegated and must assume more than normal responsibility to get good vendor bids for subcontracts on the project. Commercial bid procedures are very often better than military ones.
8. The current inspection system used by the Skunk Works, approved by both the Air Force and Navy, meets the intent of existing military requirements and should be used on new projects. Push more basic inspection responsibility back to subcontractors and vendors, and do not duplicate such inspection.

9. The contractor must be delegated the authority to test his final product in flight. He can and must test it in the initial stages. If not, he rapidly loses his competency to design other vehicles.

10. The specifications applying to the hardware must be agreed to well in advance of contracting. The Skunk Works' practice of having a specification section stating clearly which important military specification items will not knowingly be complied with and reasons therefore is highly recommended.

11. Funding a program must be timely so that the contractor does not have to keep running to the bank to support government projects.

12. There must be mutual trust between the military project organization and the contractor, with very close cooperation and liaison on a day-to-day basis. This cuts down misunderstanding and correspondence to an absolute minimum.

13. Access by outsiders to the project and its personnel must be strictly controlled by appropriate security measures.

14. Because only a few people will be used in engineering and most other areas, ways must be provided to reward good performance by pay not based on the number of personnel supervised.

9.4 Theory of Intrapreneurship

Lead, follow, or get out of the way.

As we have seen, an entrepreneur is an independent person who starts a venture and bears the full risk of failure and enjoys the complete fruit of success, whereas an intrapreneur is partially independent and is sponsored by the corporation in which he works. Intrapreneurs are not liable for financial losses in case of failure (although they may risk dismissal). An entrepreneur raises the finances from various sources and also promises a substantial return, whereas an intrapreneur does not assume responsibility to raise capital or return it. An entrepreneur has no relation with any existing organization, whereas intrapreneurs operate within the organization where they work, as shown in Table 9.1.

Intrapreneurship involves vision, innovation, risk-taking, and creativity. Intrapreneurs imagine things in novel ways. Intrapreneurs have the capacity to take calculated risks and accept failure as a learning point. An intrapreneur thinks like an entrepreneur in seeking those opportunities that will ultimately benefit the organization. Intrapreneurship is a

TABLE 9.1

Significant Differences between Entrepreneurs and Intrapreneurs

Entrepreneur	Intrapreneur
Independent agent	Sponsored by their employer
Risk their own capital	Not financially liable for failures
Raises capital (either equity or debt)	Financed by employer
Establishes a new entity	Operate within an existing, large organization

novel way of making organizations more profitable by incubating imaginative employees' entrepreneurial thoughts. It is in the best interest of an organization to encourage intrapreneurs since doing so is an effective way for large companies to reinvent themselves and improve financial performance.

Large corporations such as IBM, General Mills, AT&T, and Apple have been amply rewarded by the market for their intrapreneurial prowess, although the ubiquitous Post-it® Note has become legendary in the annals of intrapreneurship. 3M's policy of allowing employees to use 15% of their time and resources on pet projects known as "bootleg time"[10] is more fully discussed in the following paragraphs.

9.4.1 The 3M Illustration

A Post-it Note (or sticky note) is stationery with a readherable strip of adhesive on the back designed for temporarily attaching notes to documents and other surfaces. In 1968, Dr. Spencer Silver, a chemist at 3M in the United States, was attempting to develop a super-strong adhesive; instead, he accidentally created a "low-tack," reusable, pressure-sensitive adhesive. For 5 years, Silver promoted his invention within 3M, both informally and through seminars, without much success. In 1974, a colleague of Silver's, Art Fry, who had attended one of Silver's seminars, used the adhesive to anchor his bookmark in his hymnbook. Fry then further developed the idea by taking advantage of 3M's officially sanctioned "permitted bootlegging" policy. While the intrapreneur did not receive any profits from his invention, he was rewarded with a promotion that included a pay raise and many company benefits. 3M launched the product in stores in 1977 in four cities under the name "Press 'n Peel," but its results were disappointing. A year later, 3M issued free samples to residents of Boise, Idaho, and 94% of the people who tried them said that they would buy the product. On April 6, 1980, the product debuted in U.S. stores as "Post-it Notes." In 1981, Post-it Notes were launched in Canada and Europe.

There were actually two accidents that led to the invention of the Post-it Note. The first was Spencer Silver's creation of the Post-it Note's adhesive. According to the former vice president of technical operations for 3M,

Geoff Nicholson (now retired), in 1968 Silver was working at 3M trying to create super- strong adhesives for use in the aerospace industry in building planes. Instead of a super-strong adhesive, though, he accidentally created an incredibly weak, pressure-sensitive adhesive agent called Acrylate Copolymer Microspheres.

This adhesive did not interest 3M management, as it was seen as too weak to be useful, but nonetheless had two interesting features. First, when stuck to a surface, the adhesive could be peeled away without leaving any residue. Specifically, acrylic spheres only stick well to surfaces where they are tangent to the surface, thus allowing weak adhesion to be peeled easily. Second, the adhesive is reusable, thanks to the spheres' incredible strength and resistance to breaking, dissolving, or melting. Despite these notable features, no one, not even Silver himself, could devise a good marketable use. Thus, even with Silver's promotion to various 3M employees for 5 years, the adhesive was shelved.

Finally, in 1973, when Geoff Nicholson was named 3M's products laboratory manager, Silver approached him immediately with the adhesive and provided samples to play with. Silver also suggested his best idea for adhesive: a bulletin board with the adhesive sprayed on. One could then stick pieces of paper to the bulletin board without tacks, tape, or the like; the paper could subsequently be easily removed without any residue left on the sheets. While a decent idea, the sticky bulletin board was not deemed by Nicholson as sufficiently profitable, principally because annual bulletin board sales are fairly low.

Enter the second accident, this one courtesy of chemical engineer Arthur Fry. Fry was a 3M product development engineer and was familiar with Silver's adhesive thanks to attending one of Silver's seminars. Fry sung in a church choir in St. Paul, Minnesota, and while he sang, the page marker kept falling out of the hymnal. Fry eventually had the stroke of genius—he used Silver's adhesive to keep the slips of paper in the hymnal. Fry then suggested to Nicholson and Silver that they were using the adhesive backward. That is, instead of sticking the adhesive to the bulletin board, they should "put it on a piece of paper and then we can stick it to anything."

Doing so proved easier said than done, in terms of practical application. Although it was easy enough to get the adhesive onto the paper, the adhesive would often detach from the paper and stay on the object the paper was stuck to. Silver's bulletin boards did not suffer from the problem as he fabricated the boards to bond better with the yellow stickers than with the paper substrate. Two other 3M employees now entered the scene: Roger Merrill and Henry Courtney. Merrill and Courtney were tasked with devising a coating that would remain on the paper and not on whatever the paper was stuck to when the paper was removed; the two engineers ultimately succeeded.

Nonetheless, since 3M's management still did not think the product would be commercially successful, the idea was more or less shelved for 3 years; ironically, Post-it Notes were extremely popular internally at 3M labs during that time. As mentioned previously, in 1977 3M began running test sales in four cities of the Post-it Note, at that time called "Press 'n Peel." The test sales were disappointing, which confirmed in the executives' view that the product was not commercially viable.

Fortunately for offices the world over, Nicholson and Joe Ramey, Nicholson's boss, did not give up; they felt the marketing department had dropped the ball, as businesses and individuals were not provided a sufficient number of samples to see for themselves how useful the notes could be. A year after the initial flop, 3M introduced the Post-it Note to the world, providing a huge number of free samples in Boise, Idaho, in a marketing campaign labeled "The Boise Blitz." This time, the reorder rate went from almost nil in the previous attempt to 90% of the people and businesses that had received the free samples. For reference, a 90% reorder rate was double the best initial rate 3M had ever achieved for any other product introduction. Two years later, the Post-it Note was marketed throughout the United States.

Thus, after 5 years of rejection and another 7 years in development and initial marketing failures, Sliver and 3M finally had a hit in Post-it Notes, which have since become a mainstay in offices the world over. In fact, Post-it Notes remain one of top-five-selling office supply products in the world,[11,12] and 25 years later, Post-it Notes are still one of 3M's top-grossing products.

Over the years, 3M has had a policy that at least 25% of its revenue should come from products introduced within the last 5 years. That encourages a culture of innovation and intrapreneurship.

Table 9.2 summarizes 3M's rules for innovators.

Large companies may encourage intrapreneurship by:

1. Providing encouragement to innovators
2. Tolerating failures
3. Reducing the need for periodic explanations
4. Circumventing procedures, red tape, and micromanaging
5. Targeting real market needs

TABLE 9.2

3M's Rules for Bootlegging

- Don't kill a project
- Tolerate failure
- Keep divisions small
- Motivate the champions
- Stay close to the customer
- Share the wealth

6. Providing "innovation time" to research, discuss, and execute projects
7. Rewarding successful intrapreneurs in ways visible to all employees

Table 9.3 presents some important strategies that encourage intrapreneurial activity.

9.5 Characteristics of Intrapreneurs

Only one animal in the world is willing to endure peer ridicule, work pro bono, and face continual rejection and prolonged mental anguish in the hope of making a great contribution to his or her company: the intrapreneur. Intrapreneurs are pioneers with full knowledge that "pioneers have all the tomahawks in their backs."

Table 9.4 summarizes important characteristics of intrapreneurs.[13]

Corporate entrepreneurship is a constellation of processes utilized by existing large organizations to create new business opportunities. Individuals who perform these services are known as corporate entrepreneurs, intra-corporate entrepreneurs, or intrapreneurs. In this chapter, we refer to corporate entrepreneurs, intra-corporate entrepreneurs, or intrapreneurs interchangeably.

TABLE 9.3

Strategies That Encourage Intrapreneurial Activity

Support idea generation. Grant project ownership.	"Make intrapreneurial heroes out of managerial robots."
Make risk-taking and failure nonfatal.	"Failure is a station on the way to success."
Train employees on creating and selling innovation.	"Intrapreneurs are managers of managers."
Celebrate and reward intrapreneurial behavior.	"To be a realist you must be a dreamer."
Encourage networking and collaboration.	"Peer recognition is more important than salary, bonuses or promotions."
Provide access to data and business intelligence.	"Keep your friends close, and your enemies even closer."
Contain the stifling bureaucracy.	"Size is the enemy of innovation."
Create a common fund for intrapreneurial initiatives.	"Raising cheap money is very expensive."

Source: Modified after 10 tips for turning employees into 'intrapreneurs', SmartPlanet, http://www.smartplanet.com/blog/bulletin/10-tips-for-turning-employees-into-intrapreneurs/11368 (accessed March 2013).

TABLE 9.4

Recognized Characteristics of Intrapreneurs: "Lions Don't Need to Roar"

- Goal oriented, impactful, focused
- Ambitious, brilliant
- Competitive, activist for change
- Questioning, defiant, ready to do battle
- Self-motivated, inspiring
- Spurns bureaucracy, rebellious
- Comfortable with change, determined
- Adept at internal politics
- Good at conflict resolution
- Able to lead others

9.6 External and Internal Business Environment

The *business environment* is the totality of factors affecting an ongoing business, consisting of the external and internal environments. The *external environment* encompasses competitive trends, government regulations, and economic factors, whereas the *internal environment* relates to all organizational activities under the direct control of the business, as summarized in Figure 9.1.

- Economic factors: Overall health and vitality of the economic environment in which the organization operates.
- Technological factors: Proprietary techniques to convert resources into valuable products or services.

Business Environments

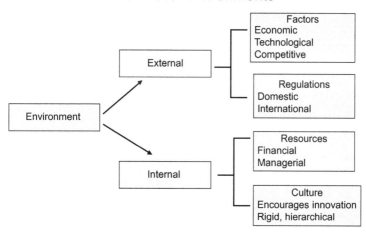

FIGURE 9.1
Intrapreneurs face both internal and external challenges.

- Regulations: All governmental and trade constraints imposed on the business.
- Financial resources: Monetary funds available to a business for spending in the form of cash, liquid securities, and credit lines.
- Managerial resources: Portfolio of capabilities and strategies to create maximum value for the organization.
- Organizational culture: Constellation of values, believes, behaviors, customs, attitudes, and history that guides members to understand what is expected and what the organization considers important. "How we do things around here."

Business environments are constantly changing, and a business capacity to adapt, to innovate, and to respond to competitive pressures may be directly impacted by intrapreneurs. If given the chance, intrapreneurs can lower production costs, improve quality, create new products, and open new markets, but to do so, large companies need to establish the right culture, which will be explored in greater detail in the next section.

9.7 Culture Regarding Innovation

Innovation is taking a creative idea and providing benefits to the user. Innovation is a pretty elusive activity and a never-ending task, especially since strategic objectives are constantly changing. Intrapreneurs can openly explore, express, and undertake their creative insights in a culture of innovation. Therefore, management is challenged with creating incentives that are consistent with an innovation-friendly culture. Table 9.5 presents the primary differences between traditional corporate and intrapreneurial cultures.

TABLE 9.5

A Clash of Cultures: "Be a Coach, Not a Judge"

Corporate Culture	Intrapreneurial (Innovation) Culture
Rewards ultraconservative decisions.	Trial and error: "You will miss 100% of the shots you don't take."
Demands to wait for instructions: "It usually takes 3 weeks to prepare a good impromptu speech."	Rewards quick actions: "Don't punish failure; reward success."
Expects "no surprises."	Encourages new approaches that may fail: "Starting up is hard to do."
Collects information: "Paralysis of the analysis."	Expects decisions even under imperfect information: "Take risks, not chances."
Controls information: "Information is power."	Encourages open discussion: "Gentlemen do read each other's mail."

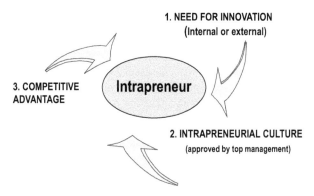

FIGURE 9.2
The intrapreneur's balance of three requirements.

In an established company, the intrapreneur can be a *change agent*, providing a much-needed competitive advantage. This is depicted in Figure 9.2.

9.8 Corporate Support for Internal Business Creation

> Don't fund the problem; fund the solution.

Surprisingly, the biggest barrier to intrapreneurship is corporate culture. *Culture* is the set of shared attitudes, values, goals, practices, and expectations that characterize an organization. Culture is the crucial intrapreneurial ingredient. Without a corporate culture supportive of internal innovation, there can be no intrapreneurship.

An intrapreneurial culture

1. Identifies sources of opportunities
2. Codifies the process of initiation, development, and introduction of opportunities
3. Selects individuals most likely to discover, evaluate, and exploit opportunities

Top management can encourage intrapreneurship in many ways. Table 9.6 provides a summary of some established methods of encouraging and fostering intrapreneurship.

TABLE 9.6

Encouraging Intrapreneurship: "Uncertainty Makes Innovation Less Expensive"

Parameters	Measures	Factors
Regular compensation, job security, innovation time	Personal rewards Specific goals	Promotions, autonomy, peer recognition, bonuses, empowerment
High-level support Executive encouragement	Top management buy-in under corporate umbrella	Public commitment, space, semiautonomy
Materials, budgets, data analysis, attendance to trade meetings Competitive intelligence	Establish well-defined project resources Feedback and positive reinforcement	Know-how, knowledge, access to competitive intelligence
Hierarchy Clearly defined organizational chart	Formal control structure	Skunk Works, brainstorming, cross-functional teams
Tolerance of failure	Risks, grieving period Support system	No penalties or dismissal

Formal steps that lead to the creation of a more innovative culture within an existing corporate organization.

9.9 Critical Issues in Intrapreneurship

> From know-how to innovation.

Intrapreneurship within a large organization starts with an idea and ends with commercial application. An innovation must be new, better, and cost-effective and solve a screaming need in the market. The intellectual process of transforming an idea into know-how can be summarized by the acronym DIKK (data, information, knowledge, and know-how), as shown in Figure 9.3.

9.9.1 DIKK Approach

The DIKK acronym is an approach to understanding how knowledge evolves as it travels through the organizational structure, as summarized below.

- *Data*: Individual elements.
- *Information*: Categorization, summarization, classification.
- *Knowledge*: Analysis, comprehension, relationships, acquaintance with the facts, and information. You know it, *in your head*.
- *Know-how*: Competitive intelligence; ability to perform a task or action in a highly competitive environment.

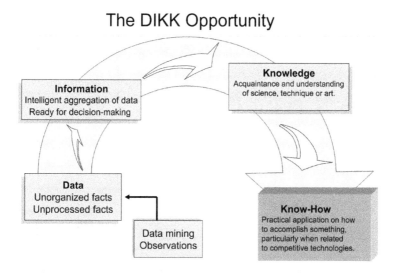

The DIKK Opportunity

FIGURE 9.3
Data is first transformed into information. Information is subsequently used to attain knowledge and eventually knowhow.

It should be understood that data are raw statistics, prior to any attempt to apply them to an organization's needs. The clever intrapreneur uses the DIKK to identify and then propose a unique solution to a corporate problem, as depicted in Table 9.7.

In plain English, information is what you store in your desk; knowledge is what you carry in your head. While everyone else in drowning in a sea of information, the intrapreneur uses knowledge as a life raft. The process of innovation generally starts with a single visionary, as shown in Figure 9.4.

9.10 Spin Zone

> Killing two stones with one bird.

There are two types of corporate venturing: external and internal. *External corporate venturing* is the creation a semiautonomous entity, known as a *spin-out*, separate from the parent organization. External ventures, known as

TABLE 9.7

Data versus IKK

Data	Information, Knowledge, Know-How
Parts per hour manufacturing or assembly	Maximizing profits
Receiving governmental approvals	Entering new market; new product launch
Reducing device-associated infections	Greater market share

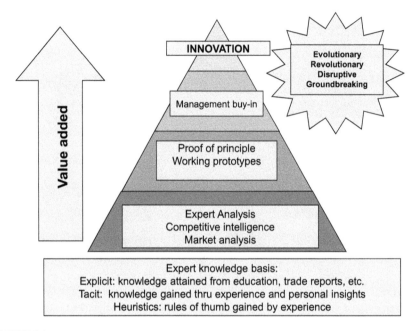

FIGURE 9.4
Innovation is the process used to increase the value of the enterprise.

spin-offs, also include divestitures, that is, selling assets, divisions, or subsidiaries to another corporation, or combination of corporations, or individual. A variation on the spin-off is an *equity carve-out*.

Internal corporate venturing is the creation of an entity residing within the existing organization, for example, a new division, and is often run by managers-turned-intrapreneurs.

Clearly, a spin-out is not the same as a spin-off, as spin-out is a type of spin-off whereby a company "splits" a section to be operated as a separate business. The common definition of spin-out is when a division of a company or organization becomes an independent business. The spun-out entity takes assets, intellectual property, technology, and/or existing products from the parent organization but remains firmly within the *corporate umbrella.*

9.10.1 Spin-Out

> Making the children behave.

The poster child of the spin-out technique was Thermo Electron (Thermo), now known as Thermo Fisher Scientific.[14] While most companies spin off their failures, Thermo demonstrated in the early 1980s how to spin out their successes. Thermo contributed seed capital, but when a new business started requiring significant capital, the venture was permitted to "go public." At the time Thermo sold minority shares to the public in one of its emerging businesses, those operations were marginally profitable or running at an operating loss. But under the Thermo corporate umbrella and reputation, the fledgling company commanded an enviable initial valuation.

This was a surprising method of turning to the public markets to finance certain promising operations while retaining a majority interest in the public entity post-IPO (initial public offering). Simultaneously lowering its cost of capital and establishing a higher valuation for its majority stake made the sum of the parts much greater than the whole.

For example, in August 1983, Thermedics (the first of Thermo's IPO spin-outs) raised a total of $6 million. At the time, Thermedics had several research contracts from the National Heart, Blood, and Lung Institute (NHLBI) to develop a surgically implantable left ventricular assist device (artificial heart) for patients in irreversible congestive heart failure. However, NHLBI funding was decreasing and the future looked bleak. Indeed, Thermedics' offering prospectus clearly warned of "substantial operating losses" to come. Nonetheless, Thermo retained 4.2 million shares (86.6% of the total share issuance) of Thermedics, whose post-IPO market value was an astounding $40 million.

Thermedics' intrapreneurs who developed the technology were given senior managing positions in the public entity and substantial share options, thus bonding them to the Thermo "family" and discouraging them from leaving to form competing firms. Thermo's culture encouraged intrapreneurship by helping intrapreneurs take their divisions public. If an employee had innovative products and intrapreneurial drive to create his or her own business, Thermo would be there to help.

Table 9.8 summarizes the spin-outs engineered by Thermo between the years 1983 and 1995.[15]

TABLE 9.8

Spin-Out Culture Thermo Children and Grandchildren

Spin-Out Company Name	IPO Date (month/year)	IPO Price ($/share)
Thermedics	8/83	9.50
Thermo Instrument	8/86	8.00
Thermo Process	8/86	6.00
Thermo Power	6/87	8.50
Thermo CardioSystems	1/89	8.50
Thermo Voltek	3/90	1.12
Thermo Trex	7/91	12.00
Thermo Fibertek	11/92	8.00
Thermo Remediation	12/93	12.50
ThermoLase	7/94	6.00
Thermo Ecotek	2/95	12.75
ThermoSpectra	8/95	14.00

For every new spin-out technology, Thermo created an intrapreneur's paradise by providing the innovators with administrative, financial, legal, marketing, and organizational backing. The intrapreneurs and technical talent of the public companies gained autonomy, stock ownership, and control without adult supervision. Investors bought into a clear and focused venture whose strategic and financial potential was not diluted by the labyrinthine hierarchy of the parent organization. Thermo was white hot.

At the time of the 12 spin-outs, Thermo was still being run by the original founders, the Hatsopoulos brothers, who were not afraid of being outshined by their intrapreneurs or losing their jobs to a younger crowd. Perhaps professional managers would be worried of losing control or their power base.

From 1993 to 1996, Thermo stock price tripled in price. However, by 1998, equity analysts were confused by so many "Thermo children and grandchildren." Each child had its own board, products, and target market. Businesses overlapped and customers became confused—Thermo had gone too far with this model. Many of the spin-outs contained core businesses that should have remained within the parent, while others were noncore businesses that should have been completely spun off by traditional methods. In 1998, Thermo stock lost $40/share in a single year, hitting bottom at $10/share. By the end of 2001, all the spin-outs were stopped. Their early success had turned into late excess.

Notwithstanding, the Thermo spin-out model still remains a viable alternative for many large companies wishing to reward divisional intrapreneurs who aspire to become independent businesspeople.

9.10.2 Spin-Off Reorganization

> Every battle is won before it is fought.

AT&T/Lucent, GM/Delphi, DuPont/Conoco, and R. J. Reynolds/Targacept did not follow the Thermo model. Instead, they followed the spin-off model. The parents granted outright ownership of all intellectual property and divested themselves from controlling interests,[16] as shown in Figure 9.5.

Spin-offs are the low-hanging fruit of the investment world. In a spin-off, the parent corporation distributes on a pro-rata basis all the shares it owns in the unit (subsidiary or division) to its own shareholders, thus creating a new public company. This divestiture is typically undertaken for the reasons shown in Table 9.9.

Recipients of the new company's equity usually greet their arrival with great expectations, since the newly independent management—freed of corporate yokes—often thrive and generally outperform the Standard & Poor's stock indexes in the early years. But on many occasions, stockholders dump their new shares, unwilling to hold a position in a smaller company. Institutions may be forced to sell, since their charters forbid owning new issues or small businesses.[17]

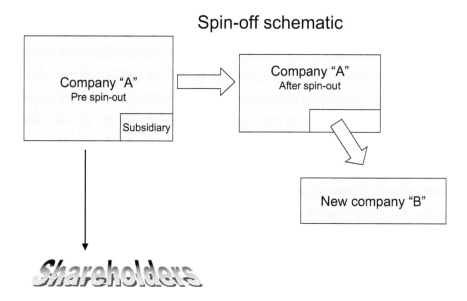

Spin-off schematic

(1) Shareholders receive shares of new company "B".
(2) Shareholders still own shares of company "A", which now only represent ownership of "A" without "B".

FIGURE 9.5
A typical spin-off process.

9.10.3 Equity Carve-Out

Everyone is entitled to be wrong. At least once.

An *equity carve-out*, also known as financial engineering, is a variation of a spin-off. Many companies have chosen to spin off a single subsidiary by means of an equity carve-out; others go further and use the carve-out as a basic organizing principle, repeatedly selling stakes in business units. The

TABLE 9.9

Reasons for Spin-Outs

• Unit spun off no longer had "strategic fit"	• Reduction of corporate asymmetries
• Parent's wish to return to its core business model	• Greater customer focus
	• Promote innovation
• Unit creates "pure play" in the market	• Retain and motivate brightest talent
• Unit unprofitable	• Attract new blood and ideas
• New management compensation directly tied to unit's performance	• Reduce decision-making time
	• Faster introduction of new products
• Improved management focus	

"Business has only two basic functions: marketing and innovation. Marketing and innovation produce results. All the rest are costs." —Peter F. Drucker private equity industry grew up around corporate carve-outs. Buyout firms believe that the strategy, involving the purchase of unloved divisions of big corporations, provides a clear way to add value through strategic and operational improvements.[18]

An equity carve-out, split-off IPO, or partial spin-off is a form of corporate reorganization in which a company creates a new subsidiary and IPOs it later while retaining control. Usually up to 20% of subsidiary shares are offered to the public. The transaction creates two separate legal entities—parent company and daughter company—each with its own boards, management team, financial team, and CEO. Equity carve-outs increase the daughter company's access to capital markets, enabling the new subsidiary to exploit stronger growth opportunities while avoiding the negative signaling associated with a seasoned offering of the parent equity.[19] Table 9.10 summarizes the most common types of restructuring associated with a carve-out.[20]

The overarching purpose of a corporate center is to do for the subsidiaries what they cannot do effectively for themselves. Many structures serve this purpose: operating companies, multibusiness companies, holding companies, conglomerates, and even investment firms such as Berkshire Hathaway. All are different ways for a centralized parent organization to deliver value to its individual business units. The newcomer to the list is the equity carve-out. Like its predecessors, the carve-out enables a subsidiary to draw on the wisdom, experience, and practical assistance of the executive center while offering something new—a degree of independence that appears to foster innovation and growth.[21]

Equity carve-outs, that is, IPOs of subsidiaries, are not unusual. AT&T is the poster child for equity carve-outs, having tried almost every restructuring method known in this galaxy. AT&T underwent a government-mandated carve-out of each "Baby Bell," whereby each shareholder received 1 share of the new company for every 10 AT&T shares.

Pharmacia carved out 14% of Monsanto in 2000. In late 1998, DuPont raised $4.4 billion by undertaking an equity carve-out equal to 30% of its oil subsidiary Conoco. Later the same year, CBS raised $3 billion in a carve-out of 16% of subsidiary Infinity Broadcasting. In August 1998, Cincinnati Bell sold 15 million shares in an IPO of subsidiary Convergys. Later that year, Cincinnati Bell distributed the remaining 137 million Convergys shares to its shareholders.

TABLE 9.10

Carve-Out Methods

---

* First stage of a broader divestiture, preceding
  Sale of subsidiary to a third party
  Spin-off of remaining ownership to shareholders
* Total or partial company splits
* Tracking stock by creation of new stock class based on divisional valuation

Equity carve-outs offer several advantages to a company and its shareholders. In general, management of the parent firm believes the market value of the separated companies will be greater than the market value of the combined firm prior to the carve-out. Perhaps the investment community has been overlooking the real value of the subsidiary that produces good financial results but is overshadowed by the other parts of the firm. Another plus is that a separately traded stock allows the former subsidiary to use its own stock as a currency for acquisitions and management incentives. The new publicly traded company will have access to the equity markets that can provide capital for expansion.[22]

9.11 Intrapreneurship in Academia

All forms of academic research are inherently intrapreneurial. Many world-class universities, such as MIT, Stanford, and Harvard, have technology transfer offices designed to commercialize worthy academic research. Unknowingly, the professors who worked on the grants and developed the technology are intrapreneurs.

Technology transfer, or transfer of technology and technology commercialization, is the process of transferring skills, knowledge, technologies, methods of manufacturing, and samples of manufacturing and facilities among universities and other institutions. Such a transfer ensures that scientific and technological developments are accessible to a wider range of users who can then further develop and exploit the technology into new products, processes, applications, materials, or services.[23]

The process of commercially exploiting research varies widely, including licensing agreements and establishing joint ventures and partnerships to share both the risks and rewards of bringing new technologies to market. Other corporate actions, for example, spin-outs, are used where the host organization does not have the necessary will, resources, or skills to develop a new technology. Often, these approaches are associated with raising venture capital (VC) to fund the development process; VC is more common in the United States than in the European Union, which has a more conservative approach to VC funding.[24] Research spin-off companies are popular vehicles of commercialization in Canada, where the rate of licensing of Canadian universities research remains far below that of the United States.[25]

There has been a marked increase in technology transfer intermediaries specialized in their fields since 1980, stimulated in large part by the Bayh-Dole Act (and equivalent legislation in other countries), which provided additional incentives for research exploitation. The U.S. Bayh-Dole Act of 1980 allows universities and nonprofit institutions, under specific circumstances, to retain intellectual property rights to discoveries resulting from

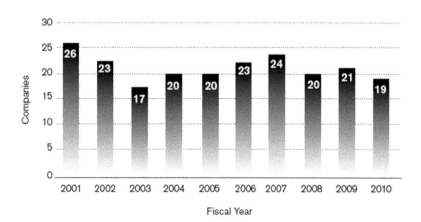

FIGURE 9.6
The number of startups has remained high since the start of the year 2000.

federally funded research (such as Small Business Innovation Research grants). The act has been credited with stimulating interest in technology transfer activities while generating increased educational opportunities and commercial development.

For example, MIT intrapreneurs have started an average of 20 companies per year, based on licenses to MIT technology. Successful startups include A123, Akamai, Alnylam, Brontes, E Ink, Ember, Luminus Devices, Momenta Pharmaceuticals, OmniGuide, QD Vision, Xtalic, and Z Corporation.[26] Figure 9.6 presents the MIT new company startup statistics since 2001.

A typical university-based technology transfer process is shown in Figure 9.7.

9.12 Obstacles to Intrapreneurship

The main obstacle to intrapreneurship is the traditional organization structure. In hierarchical organization, intrapreneurs are frustrated because they promote unending permissions at different levels. The traditional organizations stifle creativity and internal innovation; the organizations are resistant since they are risk-adverse. Decentralized organizations and smaller-power-distance organizations are better suited for intrapreneurs.

In spite of all obstacles, successful intrapreneurial ventures have been developed in many different companies.[27] While some researchers have concluded that intrapreneurship and bureaucracies are mutually exclusive and cannot coexist,[28,29] others have described successful intrapreneurial ventures within the enterprise framework.[30–33] In addition, many authors talked about

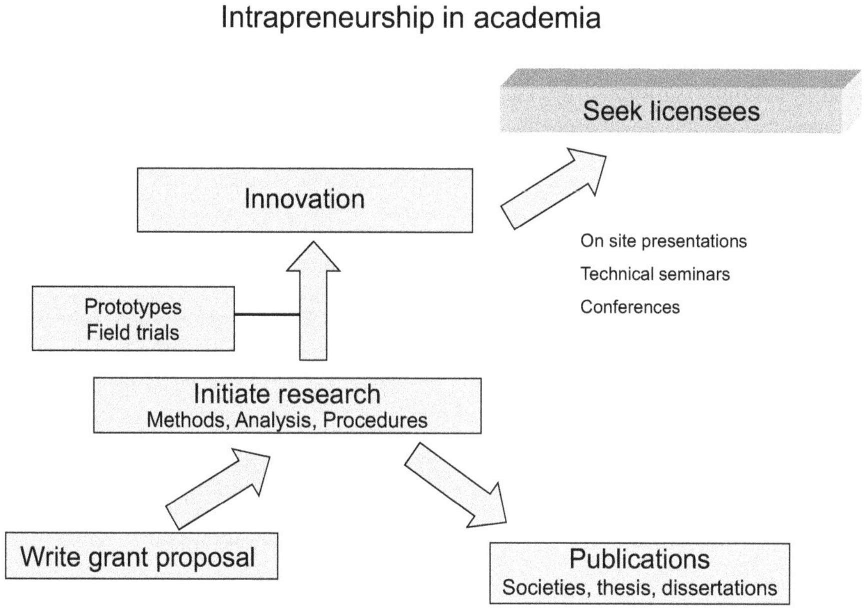

Intrapreneurship in academia

FIGURE 9.7
Academia is a perfect platform for intrapreneurship.

corporate entrepreneurship as an important growth strategy for enhanced competitive advantage.[34,35]

Table 9.11 summarizes the five most important obstacles against the establishment of intrapreneurship in many established organizations.

9.13 Intrapreneurial Life Cycle

Established companies are fundamentally in conflict with the concept of new ventures in general and intrapreneurship in particular.[36] Established companies are built on management requirements that are rigid, routine, and structured, according to the maxim "no surprises." Accordingly, intrapreneurship is considered too radical, too risky, and too unstructured to be accepted.

Nevertheless, market demands force the organization to explore the development of superior products for its existing customer base. Hill and Birkinshaw[37] identified two typologies of intrapreneurship, as shown in Table 9.12.

Internal explorer. The purpose of internal explorer units is to invest in new opportunities that arise inside the parent firm, and to actively nurture and grow them so that over time they become sources of growth for the firm.

TABLE 9.11

Obstacles Arrayed Against Intrapreneurship

Organizational features	Obstacles
Established organizational structure	• Oppressive corporate control • Arbitrary cost allocation • Rigid, obtrusive planning • Lack of reward systems
Organization chart	• Many hierarchical levels • Responsibility without authority • Too many control points • Restricted or absent communication channels
Culture	• No vision • Absence of internal innovation goals • No formal strategy • No priorities • No fit with established rules
Autocratic procedures	• Complex approval cycles • Stifling documentation • Obstructionist established rules
Staff	• Resistance to change • Complacency • Fear of failure

Source: Modified after Morris, M. H. and Kuratko, D. F., *Corporate Entrepreneurship*, South-Western College Publishers, Mason, OH, 2002.

This is probably the most well-known form of corporate venturing, comparable to Burgelman's New Venture Division[38,39] or the internal venturing models of Sykes[40] and Miles and Covin.[41] The emphasis of such units is on exploration in the early years of development of a new opportunity.

Internal exploiter. The purpose of such units is to "generate cash from harvesting spare resources"[42] The overall effect is to lower the cost of capital. Internal exploiters take existing assets within the firm, such as patents, technologies, innovative products, and managerial talent, and they attempt to monetize these within a short time frame, frequently by spinning them out.

Thus, while there is an inevitable element of exploration in such units, their dominant logic is one of exploiting existing assets and turning them into cash. While the logic of harvesting assets through spin-offs has been

TABLE 9.12

Typologies of Intrapreneurship

1. Internal explorer units	Invest in opportunities that arise inside the parent firm and actively nurture and develop these so that, over time, they become sources of growth for the firm
2. Internal exploiter units	Endeavor to monetize existing assets (such as patents, technologies, raw ideas, and managerial talent) of the parent firm within a short time frame, eventually spinning them out as new partially owned businesses (the Thermo Electron model)

Intrapreneurship life-cycle

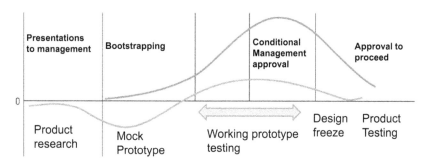

FIGURE 9.8
Intrapreneurial life cycle within an established organization.

recognized in the literature for many years, the creation of "dedicated har-vesting units" or "venture harvesting units" appears to have emerged dur-ing the most recent wave of corporate venturing activity.[43]

Figure 9.8 presents a typical intrapreneurship life cycle schema, where the intrapreneur performs the preliminary steps of researching, prototyping, and testing the concept, while the organization provides minimal internal capital (bootstrapping) and eventually approves the internal new venture, as either an internal explorer unit or internal exploiter unit.

9.14 Ten Commandments of Intrapreneurship[44,45]

1. Build your team—intrapreneuring is not a solo activity.
2. Share credit widely.
3. Ask for advice before you ask for resources.
4. Underpromise and overdeliver—publicity triggers the corporate immune system.
5. Do any job needed to make your dream work, regardless of your job description.
6. Remember that it is easier to ask for forgiveness than for permission.
7. Keep the best interests of the company and its customers in mind, espe-cially when you have to bend the rules or circumvent the bureaucracy.
8. Come to work each day willing to be fired.
9. Be true to your goals, but be realistic about how to achieve them.
10. Honor and educate your sponsors.

Notes

1. Intrapreneurship. https://en.wikipedia.org/wiki/Intrapreneurship.
2. Intrapreneurship. https://www.investopedia.com/terms/i/intrapreneurship. asp.
3. Pinchot, G. and Pinchot, E. (1978). Intra-corporate entrepreneurship Tarrytown School for Entrepreneurs. http://www.intrapreneur.com/MainPages/History/ IntraCorp.html (accessed March 2013).
4. McCrae, N. (1982). Intrapreneurial now. *The Economist*, April 17.
5. Pinchot, G. and Pinchot, E. (1994). *The End of Bureaucracy & the Rise of the Intelligent Organization*, 1st ed. San Francisco: Berrett-Koehler Publishers.
6. Investopedia is a premiere resource for investing in education, personal finance, market analysis, and free trading simulators. www.investopedia.com.
7. Sharma, P. and Chrisman, J. J. (1999). Toward a reconciliation of the definitional issues in the field of corporate entrepreneurship. *Entrepreneurship Theory and Practice*, 23(3), 11–28.
8. Zahra, S. A. (1991). Predictors and financial outcomes of corporate entrepreneurship: An exploratory study. *Journal of Business Venturing*, 6, 259–286.
9. Kelly Johnson (engineer). http://en.wikipedia.org/wiki/Kelly_Johnson_(engineer).
10. 3M: A Century of Innovation. Included in the accompanying CD.
11. Post-it Note. www.wikipedia.org/wiki/Post-it_note.
12. Post-it Notes were invented by accident. www.todayifoundout.com/index. php/2011/11/post-it-notes-were-invented-by-accident (accessed March 27, 2013).
13. Burns, P. Corporate entrepreneurship. In *Building an Entrepreneurial Organisation*, 2nd ed. New York: Palgrave Macmillan (chap. 8).
14. *Forbes*, October 9, 1995.
15. Source: Thermo Electron SEC filings.
16. Modified after Thompson, T. A. Sell offs, spin offs, carve outs and tracking stock. http://www.kellogg.northwestern.edu/faculty/thompsnt/htm/d48/ftp/ divest_2001.ppt.
17. Luxenberg, S. (1999). Prince of spin-offs. *Individual Investor*, April.
18. Lewis, T. (2010). Corporate carve-outs return to the table. *Financial News*, April 18. http://www.efinancialnews.com/story/2010-04-19/corporate-carve-outs-return-to-the-table.
19. Equity carve-out. http://en.wikipedia.org/wiki/Equity_carve-out.
20. Modified after Corporate restructuring and divestitures, chap. 11. http:// myweb.clemson.edu/~maloney/855/ch11.ppt.
21. http://www.mckinseyquarterly.com/Equity_carve-outs_A_new_spin_on_ the_corporate_structure_203.
22. *The American Heritage Dictionary of Business Terms*. (2010). Houghton Mifflin Harcourt Publishing Company. http://business.yourdictionary.com/equity-carve-out.
23. Technology transfer. http://en.wikipedia.org/wiki/Technology_transfer.
24. EU Report on EU/global comparisons in the commercialisation of new technologies.
25. State of the Nation 2008—Canada's Science, Technology and Innovation System.

26. An MIT inventor's guide to startups: For faculty and students. http://web.mit.edu/tlo/documents/MIT-TLO-startup-guide.pdf

27. Kuratko, D. F. and Hornsby, J. S. Developing an entrepreneurial perspective in contemporary organizations. https://www.researchgate.net/publication/242541731_DEVELOPING_AN_ENTREPRENEURIAL_PERSPECTIVE_IN_CONTEMPORARY_ORGANIZATIONS.

28. Morse, C. W. (1986). The delusion of intrapreneurship. *Long Range Planning*, 19, 92–95.

29. Duncan, W. J., Ginter, P. M., Rucks, A. C. and Jacobs, T. D. (1988). Intrapreneurship and the reinvention of the corporation. *Business Horizons*, 31(3), 16–21.

30. Kuratko, D. F. and Montagno, R. V. (1989). The intrapreneurial spirit. *Training and Development Journal*, 43(10), 83–87.

31. Burgelman, R. (1984). Designs for corporate entrepreneurship. *California Management Review*, 26, 154–166.

32. Burgelman, R. A. (1983). Corporate entrepreneurship and strategic management: Insights from a process study. *Management Science*, 29(12), 1349–1363.

33. Kanter, R. M. (1985). Supporting innovation and venture development in established companies. *Journal of Business Venturing*, 1(1), 47–60.

34. Kuratko, D. F., Hornsby, J. S., Naffziger, D. W. and Montagno, R. V. (1993). Implementing entrepreneurial thinking in established organizations. *Advanced Management Journal*, 58, 28–33.

35. Morris, M. H., Kuratko, D. F. and Covin, J. G. (2011). *Corporate Entrepreneurship & Innovation*. Mason, OH: South-Western Cengage Learning.

36. Sykes, H. B. and Block, Z. (1989). Corporate venturing obstacles: Sources and solutions. *Journal of Business Venturing*, 4(3), 159–167.

37. Hill, S. A. and Birkinshaw, J. Strategy–organization configurations in corporate venture units: Impact on performance and survival. http://faculty.london.edu/jbirkinshaw/assets/documents/63corp_venture_units.pdf.

38. Burgelman, R. A. (1984). Designs for corporate entrepreneurship in established firms. *California Management Review*, 26(3), 154–166.

39. Burgelman, R. A. (1985). Managing the new venture division: Research findings and implications for strategic management. *Strategic Management Journal*, 6(1), 39–54.

40. Sykes, H. B. (1986). The anatomy of a corporate venturing program: Factors influencing success. *Journal of Business Venturing*, 1(3), 275–293.

41. Miles, M. P. and Covin, J. G. 2002. Exploring the practice of corporate venturing: Some common forms and their organizational implications. *Entrepreneurship Theory and Practice*, 26(3), 21–40.

42. Campbell, A., Birkinshaw, J., Morrison, A. and van Basten Batenburg, R. (2003). The future of corporate venturing. *Sloan Management Review*, 45(1), 30–37.

43. Chesbrough, H. W. (2000). Designing corporate ventures in the shadow of private venture capital. *California Management Review*, 42(3), 31–49.

44. http://casnocha.com/2009/11/the-intrapreneurs-10-commandments.html

45. http://motivationfo Strategy–organization configurations in corporate venture units.

10

Marketing and Marketing Research on a Shoestring

Advertising is what you pay for; publicity is what you pray for.

10.1 Introduction

10.1.1 What Is Marketing?

The concept of marketing is confusing to many people. Is marketing sales, PR, branding, or advertising? The simple answer is that marketing is a mix of all these things. Marketing encompasses everything you do to put your product or service in front of your *potential* customers.[1]

We do not emphasize the word *potential* without reason. One thing that many companies and business owners do wrong in their marketing efforts is to think of the entire world (universe) as their potential client base. This is an inappropriate way to go about marketing your company or yourself.[2]

It is also important to recognize that in marketing, there are two major forms of advertising and promotion: one that is directed to individuals (business to consumer [B2C]) and one that is directed to businesses (business to business [B2B]).

B2C is when a company wants to sell a product or a service directly to a consumer (an individual person). B2B, on the other hand, is when a company wants to sell a product or service to another company.[3]

10.1.2 Marketing Research

Marketing research is any organized effort to gather information about target markets or customers. It is a very important component of business strategy.[4] Marketing research is a key factor in maintaining competitiveness over competitors. Marketing research provides critical information to identify and analyze the market need, market size, and your competition.

Information is power. Marketing research, which includes social and opinion research, is the systematic gathering and interpretation of information about individuals or organizations using statistical and analytical methods and techniques of the applied social sciences to gain insight or support decision making.

Startups and small, underfunded companies are often stuck in a chicken-or-egg-type dilemma when it comes to marketing research: they need good marketing research information in order to make key decisions to grow the company; however, they need money to do the research to get good market information to make the fundamental decisions on how to commercialize products and turn profitable.

It is a common dilemma that confounds many startup founders. They have great ideas, great products, and great people. They need actionable marketing information in order to move their companies forward, but they lack the resources to obtain that information. Fortunately, startups and small, resource-poor companies can obtain good, usable marketing information inexpensively through a number of unconventional methods and sources, discussed in this chapter.

10.2 A Small Business Is Not a Little Big Business

In their article in the *Harvard Business Review*, Welsh and White remind us that a small business is not a little big business.[5] An entrepreneur is not a multinational conglomerate but a struggling, underfinanced, and understaffed individual. To survive, an entrepreneur must apply different principles than a president of a large and established corporation.

The authors argue that the traditional assumption among managers has been that small businesses can use essentially the same managerial principles "as the big boys," only on a suitably reduced scaled. The basic assumption is that small businesses are like big businesses except that small companies have lower sales, smaller assets, and fewer employees.

Nothing could be further from the truth. Smallness creates what the authors call a special condition referred to as *resource poverty*. Resource poverty distinguishes small firms from their larger counterparts and thus requires critically different management styles and strategies. This can be summarized as shown in Table 10.1.

As we can see from Table 10.1, small businesses do not have the resources that big businesses do, so how can they operate and survive? The owners of small businesses need to wear many hats and have multiple skill sets. From finance to accounting, from marketing to human resources, from operations to negotiations, the small business person needs to understand all the elements of doing business.

TABLE 10.1

"Resource Poverty" Applicable to Small Companies

Executive salaries	Represent a much larger percentage of overall costs
Human resources	Difficulty in attracting expensive but necessary talent
	Salaries versus stock options, "skin in the game"
Business activities	Cannot afford large personnel expenditures in accounting, finance,
	marketing, sales, promotions, etc. Product launch expenses
External environment	Government regulations, industry standards
	Seasonal sales variations
	Insurance and banking needs
	Stakeholder demands
Internal environment	Cash flow management
	Reaching breakeven point

So where and how does the small business owner have the time to fulfill all these fundamental needs and functions, while at the same time creating the necessary innovations? Churchill and Lewis[6] is identified eight factors, four related to the enterprise and four related to owner, as follows:

A. Company-related factors

1. Financial resources, including cash and borrowing power
2. Personnel resources, relating to numbers, depth, and quality
3. Systems resources, relating to information, planning, and control
4. Business resources, relating to customer relations, market share, supplier relations, manufacturing, technology, and company position in its industry

B. Owner-related factors

1. Personal goals and business goals
2. Operational abilities relating to marketing, inventing, producing, and distribution
3. Managerial ability and willingness to delegate responsibility
4. Strategic abilities in matching strengths and weaknesses of the company

Also, the entrepreneur's salary in a small business represents a much larger fraction of revenues than in a big company, often such a large fraction that little is left over to pay additional managers or to reward investors. Similarly, small businesses cannot usually afford to pay for the kind of accounting and bookkeeping services they need, nor can new employees be adequately tested and trained in advance.

10.2.1 Difference between Marketing, Advertising, and Public Relations

Marketing, advertising, and *public relations*—what do all these even mean? Although we could break these terms down into stodgy textbook definitions, we think noted humorist and marketing professional S. H. Simmons put it in a more relatable context by analyzing these related fields through the prism of wooing a foxy lady:

> If a young man tells his date she is intelligent, looks lovely, and is a great conversationalist, he's saying the right things to the right person and that is *marketing*. If the young man tells his date how handsome, smart, and successful he is, that is *advertising*. If someone else tells the young woman how handsome, smart, and successful her date is, that's *public relations*.

According to Chron,[7] marketing is the overall process of communicating and delivering products to a target audience through the marketing mix of product, price, place, and promotion. Promotion is a combination of communication activities that include advertising and public relations. Deciding on what resources to apply to each of these promotion areas is a result of other factors identified in an overall marketing plan.

> Advertising is a means of communication to a target audience using mostly paid media, such as television, radio, the Internet, and print publications. Successful advertising programs include themes that communicate company mission, branding, and services, as well as specific product information. The media for advertising are chosen based on what market research has identified as the most successful way of reaching a target audience and the financial resources that can be applied to advertising based on the marketing budget.
>
> Public relations is a communication method used by businesses to convey a positive image to a target audience and the general public. Public relations methods can include press releases, community involvement, and speaking at public forums on issues important to a target audience. Small companies with small advertising budgets can use public relations as an inexpensive medium to establish the company name and communicate a brand image. Successful public relations programs highlight company accomplishments and positive contributions to the community.

To summarize, advertising is paid media and public relations is earned media. This means you convince reporters or editors to write a positive story about you or your client, your candidate, brand, or issue. It appears in the editorial section of the magazine, newspaper, TV station, or website, rather than the "paid media" section, where advertising messages appear. So your story has more credibility because it was independently verified by a trusted third party, rather than purchased.[8]

10.3 Marketing Research Fundamentals

Marketing research is the best way to get an overview of consumers' wants, needs, and beliefs. The research can be used to determine how a product should be marketed. Peter Drucker[9] eloquently argued that marketing research is the "quintessence of the marketing effort."

There are two major types of marketing research. Primary research is subdivided into quantitative/qualitative research and secondary research.

- *Primary research.* This is research you compile yourself or hire someone to gather for you.
- *Secondary research.* This type of research is already compiled and organized for you. Examples of secondary information include reports and studies by government agencies, trade associations, or other businesses within your industry. Most of the research you gather will most likely be secondary.

Regardless of whether you perform primary or secondary marketing research, the following are the critical factors that should be investigated:

- *Market information.* Through marketing information, you can uncover the prices of different products in the market, as well as the supply and demand situation. Market researchers have a wider role than previously recognized by helping their clients to understand social, technical, and even legal aspects of markets.[5]
- *Market segmentation.* Market segmentation is the division of the market or population into subgroups with similar motivations. It is widely used for segmenting on geographic differences, personality differences, demographic differences, technographic differences, use of product differences, psychographic differences, and gender differences. For B2B segmentation, firmographics is commonly used.
- *Market trends.* Market trends are the upward or downward movement of a specific market, during a period of time. Determining the market size may be more difficult if one is starting with a new innovation. In this case, you will have to derive the figures from the number of potential customers, or customer segments.
- *SWOT analysis.* SWOT is a written analysis of the strengths, weaknesses, opportunities, and threats to a business entity. Not only should a SWOT be used in the creation stage of the company, but also it could be used throughout the life of the company. A SWOT may also be written up for the competition to understand how to develop the marketing and product mixes.

- *Marketing effectiveness.* Marketing effectiveness is the quality of how marketers go to market with the goal of optimizing their spending to achieve good results for both the short term and long term. It is also related to marketing return on investment (ROI) and return on marketing investment (ROMI).[10] Marketing effectiveness includes
  - Customer analysis
  - Choice modeling
  - Competitor analysis
  - Risk analysis
  - Product research
  - Advertising the research findings
  - Marketing mix modeling
  - Simulated test marketing[6]
  - Clearly identifying your target market
  - Determining your target market potential
  - Preparing, communicating, and delivering satisfaction to your customers

10.4 Marketing Research for Business/Planning

Needs, wants, and demands. Jack Welch, a former CEO of General Electric, said, "Companies can't give job security. Only customers can." Marketing theory divides human necessities into three basic parts: needs, wants, and demands. *Needs* comprise some of the most basic and fundamental necessities of life, such as food, shelter, protection, and good health. These needs are not created by marketing, since they already exist in society.

Wants are desires for things that satisfy deeper requests, such as gourmet foods, sports cars, and vacations to exotic locales. Advanced societies are continually reshaping wants by societal forces such as schools, families, business corporations, and healthcare alternatives. Entrepreneurial companies are very active in satisfying consumer wants with innovative solutions and approaches. Needs are few; wants are many. Remember the old adage that "people don't know what they want, only what they know."

Demands are wants for specific high-quality, high-priced products or services that deliver superior performance. Entrepreneurial firms shine in this marketing sphere. Most of the innovations carry a hefty price tag, thus satisfying the demands of affluent customers, who are willing and able to buy these offerings. If we use the 80-20 rule, 20% of customers purchase 80% of the demand offerings.

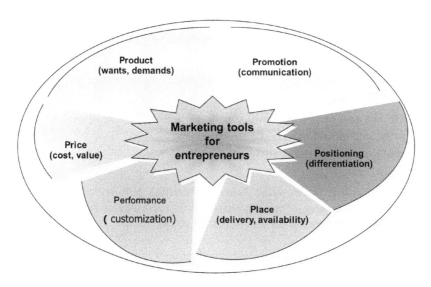

FIGURE 10.1
Marketing program tools.

Startups can market and promote their products by utilizing the marketing program tools shown in Figure 10.1.

10.5 Acquiring Marketing Research Information

You can use various methods of market research to find out information about markets, target markets and their needs, competitors, market trends, and customer satisfaction with products and services. Your businesses can learn a great deal about your customers, their needs, how to meet those needs, and how your business is doing to meet those needs.

10.5.1 Primary Research Information

Acquire your marketing research information from all the following sources:

- Set your marketing budget.
- Determine what information you need.
- Set a timeline for your research.
- Analyze the secondary research material you locate.

- Locate, read, and learn what information already exists about the target market, industry, competition, and product or service.
- Find all relevant facts.
- Organize a lot of critical information that was missing.
- Conduct primary research.
- Design research tools and determine who you would talk to and what you would ask them.
- Analyze the results of the primary research and secondary research data.
- Integrate this information into the business plan by adjusting the marketing strategy (pricing, advertising, product or service alterations) to give credibility to your sales projections.

Did you use any of the following tools to conduct your primary research?

- Telephone surveys
- Interviews
- Focus groups
- Mailed questionnaires

Did you find out the answers to any of these questions from your primary market research?

- Is there a need for your product?
- What price will your customers pay?
- How often do they buy a product or service like yours?
- How do they buy it now?
- What makes them want to buy it?
- What company do they usually buy it from?
- What do they like about the product or service?
- What don't they like about it?

Did you include the following information on your competitors through competitive analysis?

- List of all key competitors
- Location
- Years in business
- Product or service sold
- Pricing schedule

- Hours of operation
- Customer profile
- Description of their marketing strategies
- Size of company
- Marketing or promotional strategy
- Your observations
- Analysis of their strengths and weaknesses
- Strategy on how you will deal with these competitors

Where did you get the information on your competitors?

- I hit the pavement and visited my competition personally, and I observed their setup, customers, staff, and professionalism.
- I collected any material I could find from them.
- I asked their customers (primary research).
- I used secondary sources such as the yellow pages, trade associations, and newspapers to gather information.
- I looked at their website.

What steps did you take to conduct a strategic competitive analysis? Did you

- Develop a thorough list of all the competition you will face in the industry?
- Search for direct competitors who offer products or services that are essentially the same as yours?
- Search for indirect competitors who are businesses that offer products or services that can be substituted for yours?
- Identify each competitor's strengths?
- Identify each competitor's weaknesses?
- Identify your top three competitive advantages?
- Identify your top three weaknesses?
- Develop a strategy for dealing with competitors?
- Work out some best-case and worst-case scenarios on paper?
- Make sure your pricing, positioning, and marketing strategies are flexible enough to deal with these situations?

10.5.2 Secondary Research Information

The vast majority of research you can find will be secondary research. While large companies spend huge amounts of money on market research, the good news is that plenty of information is available for free to entrepreneurs on a tight budget. The best places to start? Your local library and the Internet.[11]

Secondary data are outside information assembled by government agencies, industry and trade associations, labor unions, media sources, chambers of commerce, and so forth, and found in the form of pamphlets, newsletters, trade and other magazines, newspapers, and so on. It is termed secondary data because the information has been gathered by another, or secondary, source. The benefits of this are obvious—time and money are saved because you do not have to develop survey methods or do the interviewing.

Secondary sources are divided into three main categories:

1. *Public.* Public sources are the most economical, as they are usually free and can offer a lot of good information. These sources are most typically governmental departments, business departments of public libraries, and so on.

2. *Commercial.* Commercial sources are equally valuable but usually involve costs such as subscription and association fees. However, you spend far less than you would if you hired a research team to collect the data firsthand. Commercial sources typically consist of research and trade associations, organizations like SCORE (Society Corps of Retired Executives) and Dun & Bradstreet, banks and other financial institutions, publicly traded corporations, and so on.

3. *Educational.* Educational institutions are frequently overlooked as viable information sources, yet there is more research conducted in colleges, universities, and polytechnic institutes than virtually any sector of the business community.

Government statistics are among the most plentiful and wide-ranging public sources of information. Start with the Census Bureau's helpful *Hidden Treasures! Census Bureau Data and Where to Find It!* In seconds, you will learn where to find federal and state information. Other government publications that are helpful include

- *Statistical and Metropolitan Area Data Book.* Offers statistics for metropolitan areas, central cities, and counties.
- *Statistical Abstract of the United States.* Data books with statistics from numerous sources, government to private.
- *U.S. Global Outlook.* Traces the growth of 200 industries and gives 5-year forecasts for each.

Do not neglect to contact specific government agencies such as the Small Business Administration (SBA). They sponsor several helpful programs, such as SCORE and Small Business Development Centers (SBDCs), which can provide you with free counseling and a wealth of business information.

The Department of Commerce not only publishes helpful books like the *U.S. Global Outlook* but also produces an array of products with information regarding both domestic industries and foreign markets through its International Trade Administration (ITA) branch. The above items are available from the U.S. Government Printing Office.

One of the best public sources is the business section of public libraries. The services provided vary from city to city, but usually include a wide range of government and market statistics, a large collection of directories including information on domestic and foreign businesses, and a wide selection of magazines, newspapers, and newsletters.

Almost every county government publishes population density and distribution figures in accessible census tracts. These tracts will show you the number of people living in specific areas, such as precincts, water districts, or even 10-block neighborhoods. Other public sources include city chambers of commerce or business development departments, which encourage new businesses in their communities. They will supply you (usually for free) with information on population trends, community income characteristics, payrolls, industrial development, and so on.

Among the best commercial sources of information are research and trade associations. Information gathered by trade associations is usually confined to a certain industry and available only to association members, with a membership fee frequently required. However, the research gathered by the larger associations is usually thorough, accurate, and worth the cost of membership. Two excellent resources to help you locate a trade association that reports on the business you are researching are *Encyclopedia of Associations* (Gale Research) and *Business Information Sources* (University of California Press) and can usually be found at your local library.

Research associations are often independent but are sometimes affiliated with trade associations. They often limit their activities to conducting and applying research in industrial development, but some have become full-service information sources with a wide range of supplementary publications, such as directories.

Educational institutions are very good sources of research. Their research includes faculty-based projects, often published under professors' bylines to student projects, theses, and assignments. Copies of student research projects may be available for free with faculty permission. Consulting services are available either for free or at a cost negotiated with the appropriate faculty members. This can be an excellent way to generate research at little or no cost, using students who welcome the professional experience either as interns or for special credit.

Look in the *Encyclopedia of Associations* (Gale Cengage Learning), found in most libraries, to find associations relevant to your industry. You may also want to investigate your customers' trade associations for information that can help you market to them. Most trade associations provide information free of charge.

Did you use any of the following tools in your secondary research?

- Census information
- Trade associations
- Chambers of commerce
- Market profiles
- Libraries and lifestyles profiles
- Local magazines and newspapers
- Online sites

10.5.2.1 Marketing Research Online

You may already be conducting online market research for your business—but you may not know it. Some of the easiest and most common tools to use are located right at your fingertips. Web searches, online questionnaires, customer feedback forms—they all help you gather information about your market, your customers, and your future business prospects.

The advent of the Internet has presented small businesses with a wealth of additional resources to use in conducting free or low-cost market research. The following pages will describe the different types of tools to conduct online market research, go over the general categories of market research, and advise you on how to create the best online searches and questionnaires.[12]

These days, entrepreneurs can conduct much of their market research without ever leaving their computers, thanks to the universe of online services and information. Start with the major consumer online services, which offer access to business databases. Here are a few to get you started:[13]

- *KnowThis.com* is a marketing virtual library that includes a tab on the site called "Weblinks." The tab contains links to a wide variety of market research web resources.
- *BizMiners.com* lets you choose national market research reports for 16,000 industries in 300 U.S. markets, local research reports for 16,000 industries in 250 metro markets, or financial profiles for 10,000 U.S. industries. The reports are available online for a nominal cost.
- *MarketResearch.com* has more than 250,000 research reports from hundreds of sources consolidated into one accessible collection that is updated daily. No subscription fee is required, and you pay only for the parts of the report you need with its "Buy by the Section" feature. After paying, the information is delivered online to your personal library on the site.

10.6 Your Startup Marketing Plan

Without marketing, no one will ever know your business exists—and if customers do not know you are in business, you will not record any sales. When your marketing efforts are working, however, and customers are streaming through the door, an effective customer service policy will keep them coming back for more. So now it is time to create the plans that will draw customers to your business again and again.

A marketing plan consists of the strategies and devices you are going to use to effectively communicate to your target audience. A customer service plan focuses on your customers' requirements and the ways of filling those requirements. The two must work in concert.

Descriptions of your market and its segments, the competition, and prospective customers should be in your business plan. This is the start of your marketing plan. Based on this information, you can begin choosing the communication channels to use to get the word out about your business: social media, blogs, e-mail newsletters, web banners, pay-per-click ads, radio, TV, billboards, direct mail, fliers, print ads, seminars, technical conferences, live presentations to audiences, webinars, and other venues. Then prioritize your tactics and begin with the ones that your research has shown to be the most effective for your audience.

For your customer service plan, think about what it will take to develop relationships with your customers that can be mutually beneficial for years to come. Since repeat customers are the backbone of every successful business, in your customer service plan, you will want to outline just how you are going to provide complete customer satisfaction. Consider money-back guarantees, buying incentives, and the resolution of customer complaints. Determine what your customer service policy will say, how you will train your employees to attend to the needs of your customers, and how to reward repeat customers. Remember, this is just the beginning: your program should evolve as the business grows.

To begin attracting your first customers, it is helpful to create a profile of the end user of your product or service. Now is the time to get in the habit of "talking up" your business—telling everyone you know about it. Ask for referrals from colleagues, suppliers, former employers, and other associates. You can improve the quality of your referrals by being specific in your request. For example, an insurance broker developed a successful referral network by asking existing clients if they knew anyone who was "in a two-income professional family with young children," rather than just asking if they knew anyone who needed insurance.

Consider offering free consultations or an introductory price to first-time buyers. Consider joining forces with a complementary business to get them to help you spread the word about your new venture. For example, a carpet cleaner might offer incentives to a housecleaning service if they would recommend them to their regular customers. Once you have done work for a few satisfied customers, ask them for a testimonial letter to use in your promotions.

10.7 Guerrilla Marketing

The term *guerrilla marketing* is often used to describe the most inexpensive, small-scale, and short-term marketing techniques. It can be defined as marketing that uses creativity and effort to maximize sales impact at the lowest cost. It is a low-budget approach to marketing that relies on ingenuity, cleverness, and surprise rather than traditional techniques.[14]

The concept of guerrilla marketing was invented as an unconventional system of promotions that relies on time, energy, and imagination rather than a traditional big marketing budget. Typically, guerrilla marketing campaigns (1) are unexpected and unconventional, (2) are potentially interactive, and (3) target specific customers in unexpected places. The objective of guerrilla marketing is to create a unique, engaging, and thought-provoking concept to generate buzz, and consequently turn viral.

One way of differentiating your "resource-poor" startup company inexpensively is to use a marketing concept known as guerrilla marketing. This concept was introduced by Jay Conrad Levinson[15] with the intention of helping small companies make big marketing splashes using a very limited budget.

Levinson teaches that marketing encompasses everything you do to promote your business, from the moment of conception to the point at which customers buy your product or service and begin to patronize your business on a regular basis. The key words to remember are *everything* and *regular basis*.

The meaning is clear: marketing includes the name of your company, the determination of whether you will be selling directly or through distributors, your method of manufacturing, the location of your business headquarters, your advertising method, your sales training, your sales presentation, your telephone inquiries, your web address effectiveness, your customer-based problem-solving ability, your expected growth plan, and your follow-up. If you gather from this that marketing is a complex process, you are right. If you do not see guerrilla marketing as an iterative, circular process, it will be a straight line that leads directly to the nearest bankruptcy court.

According to Hutter and Hoffmann,[16] three aspects distinguish guerrilla marketing from traditional marketing: (1) surprise, (2) diffusion, and (3) low-cost effect. A guerrilla marketing campaign should be surprising to your competition, meaning it should not follow the traditional marketing norms. Guerrilla marketers create and execute seven "strategies," as follows:

1. Determine the purpose of your strategy.
2. Determine how you will achieve this purpose, focusing on the benefits to the consumer.

3. Define your target market or markets.
4. Define the guerrilla marketing weapons you will employ.
5. Clearly focus on your niche market.
6. Explain your identity (see below).
7. Calculate your budget, expressed as a percentage of your expected gross revenues.

Take a moment to understand the crucial difference between your *image* and your *identity*. Image implies something artificial, contrived, and not genuine. Conversely, identity describes what your business is really all about.

10.7.1 Guerrilla Marketing Tactics

Never *assume* that a large market exists for your wonderful new product. Create it! Guerrilla marketing is as different from conventional marketing as guerrilla warfare is from conventional warfare. Below are some tactics that are easy to understand, easy to implement, and outrageously inexpensive.

- Organize technical demonstrations.
- Develop sales script (your elevator speech).
- Sell at every opportunity.
- Sponsor memorable events.
- Speak at many technical occasions.
- Ask for referrals from colleagues.
- Create samples (touchy-feelies).
- Create specification sheets.
- Create an unforgettable award.
- Collect testimonials.
- Get a journalist to write about your company or technology.
- Show great interest in customer needs.
- Create and distribute timely white papers.
- Create a widely circulated newsletter.
- Cooperate with other businesses.
- Exhibit at important trade shows.
- Get yourself published. Write an e-book.
- Join and participate.
- Organize community hospital–oriented projects.
- Fake publicity stunts.
- Create attention-getting press releases.

10.7.2 Apple's Guerrilla Marketing

By any measure, Apple is unquestionably one of the world's most successful retailers. Even though Apple never sold directly to consumers before they opened their first store in a mall in Tyson's Corner, Virginia, Apple now boasts some incredible bragging rights for its retail channel.[17]

Apple operates more than 380 retail stores that employ over 40,000 people and play host to more than a million visitors every day. Amazingly, Apple's stores average more than $7000 per square foot, which is more than twice the former gold standard Tiffany & Company. It is estimated that Apple's Fifth Avenue store generates more than $35,000 per square foot, making it the highest-grossing retailer in New York City—ever! Apple Stores are now the highest-performing stores in retail history.

10.7.2.1 Humble Beginnings

It was not always this way. Apple experienced massive failures in the 1990s when selling its products through retailers such as Sears and CompUSA. Its computers were muscled out of view and its brand so weakened that many retailers refused to properly market or stock Apple's computers. Even though Apple entered the retail business largely as a defensive move to gain more control of the customer experience, the climate then was anything but welcoming. Gateway was operating direct-to-consumer retail stores and failing fast. Apple had to learn how to retail its products differently.

Less than 2 years after Apple opened its retail stores, Gateway declared bankruptcy, shut down all of its shops, and laid off more than 2500 workers. Three years later, CompUSA shuttered its 23-year-old chain of stores. So while there was little expectation and no guarantee that Apple might succeed in selling its own computers in this challenging retail climate, amazingly, it somehow managed to survive.

10.7.2.2 Unconventional Thinking

But how did Apple survive the disappearance of its two retail distributors? Consider the following questions:

- How did a company with no experience in retail become the fastest in U.S. history to reach annual sales of $1 billion during the worst financial crisis in modern times?
- How did a company with only four products become the most profitable retailer in history while creating an experience that is now the standard by which all others are measured?

- Why did a company that was losing money decide to enter the retail market against the recommendations of every expert and where all retail businesses were going out of business?
- How did Apple entice millions of people to visit their stores and pay full price when all their products are readily available at other retailers and even tax-free online at Amazon.com?

Clearly, the answer to these questions is that Apple had to think *differently* about retail and make their stores more than just a place people go to buy things. They had to devise a way to enrich the lives of the people who shop at the Apple Stores and do more than simply deliver a transactional experience. In short, they had to reinvent retail.

Did you know that Apple rarely invents anything new? Entire books are written about how Steve Jobs borrowed ideas for Apple from other places, like Xerox and Sony, famously embracing the motto "Good artists borrow. Great artists steal." Apple clearly did not invent the PC, the MP3 player, downloadable music, or the mobile phone. The Mac, iPod, iTunes, and iPhone were all successful because Apple had ample time to improve upon existing designs and functionality. As a consequence of being late to these markets, Apple was forced to do a stunningly different (guerrilla) marketing strategy than anyone else. And that is guerrilla marketing at its best!

10.8 Your Marketing Plan

Firms that are successful in marketing invariably start with a marketing plan. Large companies have plans with hundreds of pages; small companies can get by with a half-dozen sheets. Put your marketing plan in a three-ring binder. Refer to it at least quarterly, but better yet monthly. Leave a tab for putting in monthly reports on sales/manufacturing; this will allow you to track performance as you follow the plan.[18]

The guerrilla plan should cover 1 year. For small companies, this is often the best way to think about marketing. Things change, people leave, markets evolve, customers come and go. Later on, we suggest creating a section of your plan that addresses the medium-term future—2–4 years down the road. But the bulk of your plan should focus on the coming year.

You should allow yourself a couple of months to write the plan, even if it is only a few pages long. Developing the plan is the "heavy lifting" of marketing. While executing the plan has its challenges, deciding what to do and how to do it is marketing's greatest challenge. Most marketing plans kick off with the first of the year or with the opening of your fiscal year if it is different.

Who should see your plan? The answer: all the players in your company. Firms typically keep their marketing plans very private for one of two very different reasons: either they are too skimpy and management would be embarrassed to have them see the light of day, or they are solid and packed with information—which would make them extremely valuable to the competition.

You cannot do a marketing plan without getting many people involved. No matter what your size, get feedback from all parts of your company: finance, manufacturing, personnel, supply, and so on—in addition to marketing itself. This is especially important because it will take all aspects of your company to make your marketing plan work. Your key people can provide realistic input on what is achievable and how your goals can be reached, and they can share any insights they have on any potential, as-yet-unrealized marketing opportunities, adding another dimension to your plan. If you are essentially a one-person management operation, you will have to wear all your hats at one time—but at least the meetings will be short!

What is the relationship between your marketing plan and your business plan or vision statement? Your business plan spells out what your business is about—–what you do and do not do, and what your ultimate goals are. It encompasses more than marketing; it can include discussions of locations, staffing, financing, strategic alliances, and so on. It includes "the vision thing," the resounding words that spell out the glorious purpose of your company in stirring language. Your business plan is the U.S. Constitution of your business: if you want to do something that is outside the business plan, you need to either change your mind or change the plan. Your company's business plan provides the environment in which your marketing plan must flourish. The two documents must be consistent.

10.8.1 Benefits of a Marketing Plan

Based on marketing research, a marketing plan is replete with meaning. It provides you with several major benefits. Let's review them.

- *Rallying point*: Your marketing plan gives your troops something to rally behind. You want them to feel confident that the captain of the vessel has the charts in order, knows how to run the ship, and has a port of destination in mind. Companies often undervalue the impact of a marketing plan on their own people, who want to feel part of a team engaged in an exciting and complicated joint endeavor. If you want your employees to feel committed to your company, it is important to share with them your vision of where the company is headed in the years to come. People do not always understand financial projections, but they can get excited about a well-written and well-thought-out marketing plan. You should consider releasing your marketing plan—perhaps in an abridged version–company-wide.

Do it with some fanfare and generate some excitement for the adventures to come. Your workers will appreciate being involved.

- *Chart to success*: We all know that plans are imperfect things. How can you possibly know what's going to happen 12 months or 5 years from now? Isn't putting together a marketing plan an exercise in futility—a waste of time better spent meeting with customers or fine-tuning production? Yes, possibly, but only in the narrowest sense. If you do not plan, you are doomed, and an inaccurate plan is far better than no plan at all. To stay with our sea captain analogy, it is better to be 5° or even 10° off your destination port than to have no destination in mind at all. The point of sailing, after all, is to get somewhere, and without a marketing plan, you will wander the seas aimlessly, sometimes finding dry land but more often than not floundering in a vast ocean. Sea captains without a chart are rarely remembered for discovering anything but the ocean floor.

- *Company operational instructions*: Your child's first bike and your new VCR came with a set of instructions, and your company is far more complicated to put together and run than either of them. Your marketing plan is a step-by-step guide for your company's success. It is more important than a vision statement. To put together a genuine marketing plan, you have to assess your company from top to bottom and make sure all the pieces are working together in the best way. What do you want to do with this enterprise you call the company in the coming year? Consider it a to-do list on a grand scale. It assigns specific tasks for the year.

- *Captured thinking*: You do not allow your financial people to keep their numbers in their heads. Financial reports are the lifeblood of the numbers side of any business, no matter what size. It should be no different with marketing. Your written document lays out your game plan. If people leave, if new people arrive, if memories falter, if events bring pressure to alter the givens, the information in the written marketing plan stays intact to remind you of what you had agreed on.

- *Top-level reflection*: In the daily hurly-burly of competitive business, it is hard to turn your attention to the big picture, especially those parts that are not directly related to the daily operations. You need to take time periodically to really think about your business—whether it is providing you and your employees with what you want, whether there aren't some innovative wrinkles you can add, whether you are getting all you can out of your products, your sales staff, and your markets. Writing your marketing plan is the best time to do this high-level thinking. Some companies send their top marketing people away to a retreat. Others go to the home of a principal. Some do marketing plan development at a local motel, away from phones and fax machines, so they can devote themselves solely to thinking hard and drawing the most accurate sketches they can of the immediate future of the business.

Ideally, after writing marketing plans for a few years, you can sit back and review a series of them, year after year, and check the progress of your company. Of course, sometimes this is hard to make time for (there is that annoying real world to deal with), but it can provide an unparalleled objective view of what you have been doing with your business life over a number of years.

10.8.2 Researching Your Market

Whether you are just starting out or have been in business for years, you should always stay up-to-date with your market information. Below we discuss the best methods for finding your relevant data.[19]

The purpose of market research is to provide relevant data that will help solve marketing problems a business will encounter. This is absolutely necessary in the startup phase. Conducting thorough market surveys is the foundation of any successful business. In fact, strategies such as market segmentation (identifying specific segments within a market) and product differentiation (creating an identity for your product or service that separates it from your competitors') would be impossible to develop without market research.

Your market research should be designed to answer two major questions (as depicted in Figure 10.2): (1) What are your target market needs? (2) What are your proposed solutions to answer those needs?

Whether you are conducting market research using the historical, experimental, observational, or survey method, you will be gathering two types of data. The first is primary information that you will compile yourself or hire someone to gather. Most information, however, is secondary, or already compiled and organized for you. Reports and studies done by government agencies, trade associations, or other businesses within your industry are examples of the latter. Search for them and take advantage of them.

When conducting market research on a shoestring, there are basically two types of information that can be gathered: exploratory and specific. Exploratory research is open-ended in nature, helps you define a specific problem, and usually involves detailed, unstructured interviews in which lengthy answers are solicited from a small group of respondents. Specific research is broader in scope and is used to solve a problem that exploratory research has identified. Interviews are structured and formal in approach. Of the two, specific research is more expensive.

There are basically three avenues you can take: (1) direct mail, (2) phone surveys and (3) personal interviews. These are discussed below.

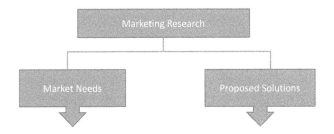

- Market share
- Market potential
- Forecasting & trend analysis
- Branding

- Market segmentation
- Pricing strategy
- Promotion
- Regulatory hurdles
- Distribution

Modified after Malhatra N. Marketing Research. An applied orientation. Pearson Education, NJ 200

FIGURE 10.2
Marketing research at a glance.

10.8.2.1 Direct Mail

If you choose a direct-mail questionnaire, be sure to do the following in order to increase your response rate:

- Make sure your questions are short and to the point.
- Make sure questionnaires are addressed to specific individuals and are of interest to the respondent.
- Limit the questionnaire's length to two pages.
- Enclose a professionally prepared cover letter that adequately explains what you need.
- Send a reminder about 2 weeks after the initial mailing. Include a postage-paid self-addressed envelope.

Unfortunately, even if you employ the above tactics, response to direct mail is always low, and is sometimes less than 5%.

10.8.2.2 Phone Surveys

Phone surveys are generally the most cost-effective, considering overall response rates; they cost about one-third as much as personal interviews, which have, on average, a response rate of only 10%. The following are some phone survey guidelines:

- At the beginning of the conversation, your interviewer should confirm the name of the respondent if calling a home, or give the appropriate name to the switchboard operator if calling a business.
- Pauses should be avoided, as respondent interest can quickly drop.
- Make sure that a follow-up call is possible if additional information is required.
- Make sure that interviewers do not divulge details about the poll until the respondent is reached.

As mentioned, phone interviews are cost-effective, but speed is another big advantage. Some of the more experienced interviewers can get through up to 10 interviews an hour (speed for speed's sake is not the goal of any of these surveys), but 5–6 per hour is more typical. Phone interviews also allow you to cover a wide geographical range relatively inexpensively.

10.8.2.3 Personal Interviews

There are two main types of personal interviews:

1. *Group survey.* Used mostly by big businesses, group interviews can be useful as brainstorming tools resulting in product modifications and new product ideas. They also give you insight into buying preferences and purchasing decisions among certain populations.
2. *Depth interview.* One-on-one interviews where the interviewer is guided by a small checklist and basic common sense. Depth interviews are either focused or nondirective. Nondirective interviews encourage respondents to address certain topics with minimal questioning. The respondent, in essence, leads the interview. The focused interview, on the other hand, is based on a preset checklist. The choice and timing of questions, however, is left to the interviewer, depending on how the interview goes.

When considering which type of survey to use, keep the following cost factors in mind:

- *Mail.* Most of the costs here concern the printing of questionnaires, envelopes, postage, the cover letter, the time taken in the analysis and presentation, the cost of researcher time, and any incentives used.

- *Telephone.* The main costs here are the interviewer's fee, phone charges, preparation of the questionnaire, the cost of researcher time, and the analysis and presentation of the results of the questioning.
- *Personal interviews.* Costs include the printing of questionnaires and prompt cards if needed, the incentives used, the interviewer's fee and expenses, the cost of researcher time, and analysis and presentation.
- *Group discussions.* Your main costs here are the interviewer's fees and expenses in recruiting and assembling the groups, the fee for renting the conference room or other facility, researcher time, any incentives used, analysis and presentation, and the cost of recording media such as tapes, if any are used.

10.9 Competitive Intelligence

The Society of Competitive Intelligence Professionals (SCIP) defines competitive intelligence as "the process of ethically collecting, analyzing and disseminating accurate, relevant, specific, timely, foresighted and actionable intelligence regarding the implications of the business environment, competitors and the organization itself."

Competitive intelligence (CI) is the selection, collection, interpretation, and distribution of publicly held information that is strategically important to a firm. A substantial amount of this information is publicly accessible via the World Wide Web, periodic company Securities and Exchange Commission filings, the patent literature, company promotional campaigns, and so forth.

The knowledge-intensive world is ruled by hypercompetition. Hypercompetition is rapid and dynamic competition characterized by unsustainable advantage. It is the condition of rapid escalation of competition based on price–quality positioning, competition to protect or invade established product or geographic markets, and competition based on vast scientific knowledge, deep pockets, and the creation of even deeper-pocketed alliances.[20]

The knowledge base for managing in this hypercompetitive environment is called competitive intelligence. CI is a process that provides you insights into what might happen in the near future. This process requires that we go from data to information to intelligence. Here is a basic example:

Data → Prices for our products have dropped by 5%.

Information → New offshore facilities enjoy significantly lower labor costs.

Intelligence → Our key competitor is about to acquire a facility in China that will ….

The differences between data, information, and intelligence can be subtle, but very real:

> Data → Unconnected pieces of information: Nice to know, but so what!
>
> Information → Increased knowledge derived by understanding the relationships of data: Interesting, but how does it relate to what I do? The knowledge-intensive business world is driven by hypercompetition.
>
> Intelligence → Organizing the information to fully appreciate the implications and impact on the organization: Oh really, then we better do something!

A formalized CI program should

- Anticipate changes in the marketplace
- Anticipate actions of competitors
- Discover new or potential competitors
- Learn from the successes and failures of others
- Increase the range and quality of acquisition targets
- Learn about new technologies, products, and processes that affect your business
- Learn about political, legislative, or regulatory changes that can affect your business
- Enter new businesses
- Look at your own business practices with an open mind
- Help implement the latest management tools

10.9.1 Competitive Intelligence Is a Top Management Function

CI is not for everyone. In fact, most companies do not use CI. Despite the fact that most executives rely on the flow of information for decision making, only a handful of companies have a fully functional, integrated CI process in place. Why is that? Perhaps the most important reason is attitudinal: the way executives think about CI.[21] Have you ever heard some of comments listed below? Or perhaps you have said them yourself!

- CI is spying; it is unethical. I don't want any part of it.
- It was not part of my school curriculum. It must not be important.
- CI is a cost center. We do not have a budget for it.
- How do I quantify CI's cost–benefit ratio?
- Nothing happens in this industry that I don't know already.

- If I don't know it, is it not worth knowing.
- We tried it before, and it didn't work.
- I am too busy to review all this garbage.

CI requires authorization by the highest echelons of management. CI is a top management function. It can provide vital analysis of competitor capabilities, plans, intentions, and limitations. It spotlights industry structure and trends. It may also reveal political, economic, and social forces affecting your company.

The CI life cycle is iterative, consisting of four major functions: (1) planning and direction, (2) information collection, (3) analysis and forecast, and finally, (4) information and dissemination, as shown in Figure 10.3.

CI is particularly useful in industries with long development and approval cycles, such as the pharmaceutical and biotechnology industries. These industries are faced with long R&D times—sometimes 10–15 years for innovative drugs—coupled with uncertain and hugely expensive clinical trials. This allows continual tracking of a drug's progress by competitors through the public Food and Drug Administration (FDA) approval process.

Thus, pharmaceutical and biotechnology companies utilize CI during the years of drug development to help determine if a new drug development should be continued or dropped. Likewise, it allows companies to monitor

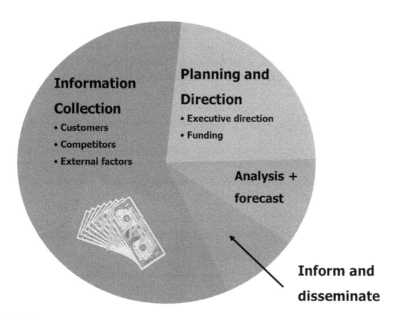

FIGURE 10.3
The competitive intelligence life cycle.

competitor's activities and decide whether to initiate their own drug development for a specific indication.

10.9.2 Competitive Intelligence Should Be Actionable

CI differs from data and information since it requires some form of analysis. The purpose of this analysis is to derive some meaning from the piles of data and information that bury everyone. By going through analysis and filtering, we can refine it enough so that someone can act on it and understand their options, giving them an opportunity to make forward-looking decisions.

Note that *information* is factual. It is numbers, statistics, bits of data, and interesting stories that seem important. *Intelligence*, on the other hand, is an *actionable* list of data that has been analyzed, filtered, and distilled. This is what we call intelligence know-how.

Thus, when you present CI to your staff, they should draw a conclusion and make an important decision quickly. Therefore, CI should put conclusions and recommendations up front with supporting research behind the analysis. CI should not simply present the facts, declaring what we found, but instead make a statement, saying this is what we believe is about to happen.

CI involves the use of public sources to develop data on your competition, competitors, and the market environment. It can then transform that data into actionable policies (intelligence). In this context, "public" means all the information you can legally and ethically identify, obtain, locate, deduce, and access.[22]

CI is also known by several other names: competitor intelligence, business intelligence, strategic intelligence, marketing intelligence, competitive technical intelligence, technology intelligence, and technical intelligence, depending on what specific information is being targeted.[23]

The development of CI usually proceeds in a five-phase predetermined cycle, as seen below.

1. *Establish your needs.* Clearly identify the information needed on the competition

    or the competitive environment.

2. *Collect data.* Assemble raw data, using legal and ethical means, from public sources.

3. *Analyze the data.* Convert data into useful information.

4. *Communicate intelligence.* Convey the finished intelligence to the decision makers for their use.

5. *Actionable intelligence.* Provide strategic direction to decision makers in a timely manner.

These five phases are visually summarized in Figure 10.4.

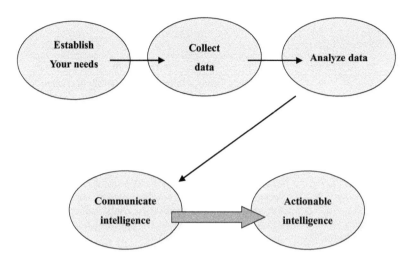

FIGURE 10.4
Five-phase intelligence cycle.

10.9.3 Thou Shall Not Steal Your Competitor's Secrets

According to *Moneywatch*'s Hodges,[24] there is nothing unethical about CI. Most of the time, it simply involves gathering together pieces of a puzzle that are available to anyone—if they have the time and the determination to find them.

But because the search can be tedious, it is tempting to look for shortcuts to get the needed information, especially when time is tight. When that happens, legal and ethical lines may be crossed. Table 10.2 lists some of the most common tactics that may get you into trouble.

Modern CI is often divided four different, but overlapping, types: (1) strategic, (2) competitor, (3) tactical, and (4) technical.

10.9.4 What Is Strategic Intelligence?

Strategic intelligence is CI supporting strategic, as distinguished from tactical, decision making. This means providing higher-level intelligence on the competitive, economic regulatory, and political environment in which you firm operates now and in which it will operate in the future.

Strategic intelligence typically is used by senior managers and executives who make and then execute overall corporate strategy. Its most common applications are in the development of the following:

- Long-term (3- to 5-year) strategic plans
- Capital investment plans

TABLE 10.2

Competitive Intelligence Tactics to Avoid

Tactics	Description
Pretext	Approaching a source under a false identity or deceptive pretense
Dumpster mining (diving)	Surreptitiously gathering discarded key documents through garbage or empty raw material pails in dumpsters
Confidential disclosure agreement (CDA), NDA bypassing	Encouraging a source to violate terms of a noncompete or nondisclosure agreement (NDA) they signed with their employer
Acquiring trade secrets	Finding the proprietary advantage to a competitor's success, specifically when it is a closely guarded secret, such as stealing formulas or software proprietary codes
Paying sources for proprietary information	Giving cash to someone who can tell you what you want to know about a competitor
Enticement recruitment	Deliberately targeting a competitor's key employees for the purpose of obtaining trade secrets
Computer hacking	Penetrating a competitor's computer systems to gain access to proprietary information on pricing, business plans, customer lists, etc.
Wiretapping tactics	Electronically eavesdropping into a competitor's communications

- Political risk assessments
- Merger and acquisition, joint venture, and corporate alliance policies and plans
- Research and development planning

Strategic intelligence usually focuses on the overall strategic environment. A firm's direct competitive environment and its direct competitors are, of course, included in that focus. It should also include its indirect competitors. In addition, strategic intelligence should develop CI on the long-run changes caused by, as well as affecting, all of the forces driving industry competition, including

- Suppliers
- Customers
- Substitute products or services
- Potential competitors

You conduct strategic CI analysis when you must focus on many critical factors, such as technology trends, regulatory developments, and even political risks, that in turn effect these forces.

Strategic intelligence's focus is primarily on the future. The time horizon of interest typically runs 5 years into the future.

- In terms of an interest in the past, you will be collecting and analyzing data so that your firm can evaluate the actual success (or failure) of its own strategies and of those of your competitors. This, in turn, permits you to better weigh options for the future. You are looking to the past to learn what may happen in the future.

- With respect to the future, you are seeking a view of your firm's total environment: competitive, regulatory, and political. As with radar, you are looking for warnings of impending problems and alerts to upcoming opportunities—always in time to take appropriate action.

10.9.4.1 Competitor Intelligence

Competitor intelligence focuses on your direct competitors and their capabilities, current activities, plans, and intentions. Competitor intelligence is most often used by strategic planning operations and by operating managers within strategic business units (SBUs). It may also be useful to product managers, as well as to those involved with product development, new business development, and mergers and acquisitions.

Competitor intelligence usually focuses on key business questions, such as

- Who are our competitors right now?
- Who are our potential competitors?
- How do our competitors see themselves? How do they see us?
- What are the track records of the key people at our competitors? What are their personalities? What is the environment in their own company? What difference do these people make in terms of our ability to predict how these competitors will react to our competitive strategy?
- How and where are our competitors marketing their products or services? What new directions will they probably take?
- What markets or geographic areas will (or will not) be tapped by our competitors in the future?
- How have our competitors responded to the short- and long-term trends in our industry in the past? How are they likely to respond to them in the future?
- What patents or innovative technology have our competitors or potential competitors recently obtained or developed? What do those changes and innovations mean to us?
- What are our competitors' overall plans and goals for the next 1–2 years in the markets where they currently compete with us? What are their plans and goals for their other firms, and how will those affect the way they run their business competing with us?

10.9.4.2 Market Intelligence

Market intelligence is focused on the very current activities in the marketplace. You can look it as it as the qualitative side of the quantitative data research you have conducted in many retail markets. The primary beneficiaries of market intelligence are usually the marketing department, market research, and the sales force. To a lesser degree, market intelligence serves those in market planning by providing retrospective data on the success and failure of their own sales efforts.

Market intelligence's focus is on sales, pricing, payment and financing terms, promotions being offered, and their effectiveness. Market intelligence's time horizon typically runs from 3–6 months back to no more than 6 months in the future. Some of the time, however, the horizon is actually measured in terms of weeks, or even days, rather than months.

10.9.4.3 Technical Intelligence

Technical intelligence permits you to identify and exploit opportunities resulting from technical and scientific changes as well as to identify and respond to threats from such changes. Technical intelligence is particularly useful if you are involved with your firm's research and development activities. Using basic CI techniques, those practicing technical intelligence now often can determine the following:

- Competitors' current manufacturing methods and processes
- A competitor's access to, use of, and dependence on outside technology, as well as its need for new technology
- Key patents and proprietary technology being used by, being developed by, or being acquired by competitors
- Types and levels of research and development conducted by competitors, as well as estimates of their current and future expenditures for research and development
- The size and capabilities of competitors' research staff

10.9.4.4 Business Intelligence

Business intelligence is a particularly difficult term to define. At one time, this term was used by some CI professionals to describe CI in a very broad way, and to describe only intelligence provided in support of corporate strategy by others. Now its use seems to have been fully co-opted by those involved with data management and data warehousing. There, it can refer to

- The software used to manage vast amounts of data
- The process of managing that data, also called data mining
- The output of either of the first two

In any case, virtually all of the reported applications and successes of business intelligence deal with processes that are internally oriented, from process control to logistics, and from sales forecasting to quality control. The most that can be said of its relationship to intelligence is that data mining and related techniques are useful tools for some early analysis and sorting tasks that would be impossible for human (intelligence) analysts.

10.9.5 Ten Commandments of Competitive Intelligence

In 1988, Fuld and Company[25] published its "Ten Commandments of Legal and Ethical Intelligence Gathering":

1. Thou shall not lie when representing thyself.
2. Thou shall observe thy company's legal guidelines.
3. Thou shall not tape record a conversation.
4. Thou shall not bribe.
5. Thou shall not plant eavesdropping devices.
6. Thou shall not mislead anyone in an interview.
7. Thou shall neither obtain nor give price information to thy competitor.
8. Thou shall not swap misinformation.
9. Thou shall not steal a trade secret.
10. Thou shall not knowingly press someone if it may jeopardize that person's job or reputation.

Notes

1. Heasman, L. Modern marketing principles: Building a better toolbox. http://www.moderndaymarketing.co.uk/SpecialReportWebOpt.pdf.
2. Heasman, L. Modern marketing principles: Building a better toolbox. http://www.moderndaymarketing.co.uk/SpecialReportWebOpt.pdf
3. Gummesson, E. and Polese, F. (2009). B2B is not an island! *Journal of Business & Industrial Marketing*, 24(5), 337–350.
4. Market research. https://en.wikipedia.org/wiki/Market_research.
5. Welsh, J. A. and White, J. F. (1981). A small business is not a little big business. *Harvard Business Review*, 50(4), 9172. https://hbr.org/1981/07/a-small-business-is-not-a-little-big-business/ar/4.
6. Churchill, N. C., and Lewis, V. L. (1983) Growing concerns: topics of particular interest to owners and managers of smaller businesses. *Harvard Business Review*, Edited by David E. Gumpert, May http://my.liuc.it/MatSup/2002/E88760/Churchil%20&%20Lewis%20complete%20model.pdf

7. Bean-Mellinger, B. (2018). The difference between marketing, advertising, public relations & sales promotion. http://smallbusiness.chron.com/difference-between-marketing-advertising-public-relations-sales-promotion-22873.html.

8. Wynne, R. (2014). The real difference between PR and advertising. *Forbes*, July 8. http://www.forbes.com/sites/robertwynne/2014/07/08/the-real-difference-between-pr-and-advertising-credibility/.

9. Drucker, P. F. (1974). *Management: Tasks, Responsibilities, Practices*. Sydney: Harper & Row (p. 864).

10. Marketing effectiveness. https://en.wikipedia.org/wiki/Marketing_effectiveness.

11. Entrepreneur staff. Conducting market research. http://www.entrepreneur.com/article/217388.

12. Inc. staff. Conducting online market research: Tips and tools. http://www.inc.com/guides/biz_online/online-market-research.html.

13. Staff of Entrepreneur Media. *Start Your Own Business*, 6th ed. https://bookstore.entrepreneur.com/product/start-your-own-business-6th-edition/.

14. Margolies, J. and Gerrigan, P. (2008). *Guerrilla Marketing for Dummies*. Hoboken, NJ: Wiley.

15. Levinson, J. C. (1933). *Guerrilla Marketing*. New York: Houghton Mifflin Company.

16. Hutter, K. and Hoffmann, S. (2011). Guerrilla marketing: The nature of the concept and propositions for further research. *Asian Journal of Marketing*, 5(2), 39–54.

17. Chazin, S. The secrets of Apple's retail success. http://www.marketingapple.com/Apple_Retail_Success.pdf.

18. How to create a successful marketing plan. http://www.entrepreneur.com/article/43018.

19. Researching your market. http://www.entrepreneur.com/article/43024.

20. Hypercompetition. http://en.wikipedia.org/wiki/Hypercompetition.

21. Kahaner, L. (1996). *Competitive Intelligence*. Rockefeller Center, NY: Touchstone Books.

22. McGonagle, J. J. and Vella, C. M. (2002). *Bottom Line Competitive Intelligence*. Westport, CT: Quorum Books.

23. McGonagle, J.J., and Vella, C.M. (2012). What is competitive intelligence and why should you care about it? In *Proactive Intelligence*. London: Springer.

24. Hodges, J. (2007). Thou shall not steal thy competitor's secrets. *Moneywatch*, March 28. http://www.cbsnews.com/news/thou-shalt-not-steal-thy-competitors-secrets.

25. Fuld, L. M. The new competitor intelligence: The complete resource for finding, analyzing, and using information about your competitors. http://cdn2.hubspot.net/hub/17073/file-13332891-pdf/resource-center/fuld-and-company-new-competitor-intelligence-excerpt.pdf.

Section IV

Classical Initial Decisions

11

Strategic Planning for Startups

Plans are nothing. Planning is everything.
—**Dwight D. Eisenhower**

11.1 Introduction

Why do some companies succeed while others fail? In the fast-evolving world of the Internet, for example, how is it that companies such as Yahoo, Amazon.com, eBay, Facebook, and Google have managed to attract millions of customers, while most others have gone bankrupt?

This chapter demonstrates that startups that develop and pursue a well-designed *strategic planning* policy display superior performance compared with their rivals. In this context, a *strategy* is a set of actions that founders take to increase their startup's performance relative to rivals. If a startup's strategy does result in superior performance, it is said to have a *competitive advantage*.

Thus, strategic planning is a tool for organizing the present on the basis of the projections of the desired future. That is, a strategic plan is a road map to lead an organization from where it is now to where it would like to be in 5 or 10 years.

It is necessary to have a strategic plan for your chapter or division. In order to develop a comprehensive plan for your chapter or division that includes both long-range and strategic elements, we suggest the methods and mechanisms outlined in this manual.

Your plan must be

- Simple to follow.
- Written logically and purposefully.
- Clear to everyone.
- Based on the real current situation.
- Given enough time to settle. It should not be rushed.

Over the past few decades, you may have witnessed an explosion in the use of management tools and techniques—everything from Six Sigma to benchmarking. Keeping up with the latest and greatest, as well as deciding which tools to put to work, is a key part of every leader's job. But it's tough to pick the winners from the losers.

As new management tools appear every year, others seem to drop off the radar screen. Unfortunately, there is no official scorekeeper for management tools. Thus, choosing and using "fad management" tools can become a risky and potentially expensive gamble, leaving many business leaders stymied and confused.[1]

In 1993, Bain & Co., a leading management consulting company, launched a multiyear research project to get the facts about management tools and trends. The objective of the study was to provide managers with information to identify and integrate tools that improve bottom-line results as well as understand their strategic challenges and priorities.

Bain systematically assembled a database that now includes nearly 8000 businesses from more than 70 countries in North America, Europe, Asia, Africa, the Middle East, and Latin America. The *Bain & Company's 2005 Management Tools* survey received responses from a broad range of international executives. To qualify for inclusion in the study, a tool had to be relevant to senior management, topical (as evidenced by coverage in the business press), and measurable. Bain focused on the most discussed management tools, as shown in Table 11.1.

Would you like to know the surprising results? Out of all the management tools surveyed, 79% of respondents preferred strategic planning, followed closely by customer relationship management (CRM) at 75%. In fact, strategic planning is a long-time favorite tool, having been used by more than half of companies in every survey since Bain started this project. Not

TABLE 11.1

Most Frequently Discussed Management Tools

1. Activity-based management	13. Mass customization
2. Balanced scorecard	14. Mission and vision statements
3. Benchmarking	15. Offshoring
4. Business process reengineering	16. Open-market innovation
5. Change management programs	17. Outsourcing
6. Core competencies	18. Price optimization models
7. Customer relationship management (CRM)	19. Radio frequency identification (RFID)
8. Customer segmentation	20. Scenario and contingency planning
9. Economic value–added analysis	21. Six sigma
10. Growth strategies	22. Strategic alliances
11. Knowledge management	23. Strategic planning
12. Loyalty management	24. Supply chain management
	25. Total quality management

Modified from: Rigby, D. (2005). Management tools and trends 2005. Bain and Company report.

TABLE 11.2

Top Five Management Tools Ranked by Usage Rate

Management Tool Name	Usage (%)
Strategic management	79
Customer relationship management	75
Benchmarking	73
Outsourcing	73
Customer segmentation	72

Modified from: Rigby, D. (2005). Management tools and trends 2005. Bain and Company report.

surprisingly, the most popular tools are the ones that create the highest returns and results-oriented ratings.[2] See Table 11.2 for more details.

11.2 Strategic Planning for Startups

Strategic planning is the process used by an organization to visualize its desired future and develop the necessary steps and operations to achieve those aims. It directs managers to determine how they will be expected to behave. In order to determine the direction of the organization, it is necessary to understand its current position and the possible avenues through which it can pursue a particular course of action. Generally, strategic planning deals with at least one of three key questions:[3]

1. What do we do?
2. For whom do we do it?
3. How do we excel?

The key components of strategic planning include an understanding of the firm's vision, mission, values, and strategies. (Often, a *vision statement* and a *mission statement* will encapsulate the vision and mission.)[4]

- **Vision:** Outlines what the organization wants to be or how it wants the world in which it operates to be (an "idealized" view of the world). It is a long-term view and concentrates on the future. It can be emotive and is a source of inspiration. For example, a charity working with chronic disease patients might have a vision statement that reads, "A world without disease."
- **Mission:** Defines the fundamental purpose of an organization or an enterprise, succinctly describing why it exists and what it does to achieve its vision. For example, the charity might have

a mission statement as "providing jobs for the homeless and unemployed."

- **Values:** Beliefs that are shared among the stakeholders of an organization. Values drive an organization's culture and priorities and provide a framework in which decisions are made. For example, "Knowledge and skills are the keys to success" or "Give a man bread and feed him for a day, but teach him to farm and feed him for life." These example maxims may set the priorities of self-sufficiency over shelter.

- **Strategy:** Strategy, narrowly defined, means "the art of the general"— a combination of the ends (goals) for which the firm is striving and the means (policies) by which it is seeking to get there. A strategy is sometimes called a *road map*, which is the path chosen to plow toward your end vision. The most important part of implementing the strategy is ensuring the company is going in the right direction—that is, toward the end vision.

Unlike operational planning, which stresses how to get things done, and long-range planning, which primarily focuses on translating goals and objectives into current budgets and work programs, strategic planning is concerned with identifying barriers and issues to overcome. Managers are more likely to act on the assumption that current trends will continue into the future (steady state management), while entrepreneurs need to anticipate new trends and possible surprises that represent both opportunities and threats.

11.2.1 Competitive Advantage and Superior Performance

Superior performance is typically thought of in terms of one company's profitability relative to that of other companies in the same or a similar kind of business or industry.[5] The profitability of a company is measured by the return earned on the capital invested in the enterprise.[6] The return on invested capital is defined as profit over the capital invested in the firm (profit / capital invested). By *profit*, we mean earnings after tax. By *capital*, we mean the sum of money invested in the startup—that is, stockholders' equity plus debt owed to creditors.

This working capital is used to buy the resources a company needs to produce and sell products. A company that uses its resources efficiently makes a positive return on invested capital. The more efficient a company is, the higher are its profitability and return on invested capital. And your startup's profitability—your return on invested capital—will be determined by your strategic planning.

A company is said to have a *competitive advantage* over its rivals when its profitability is greater than the average profitability for all firms in its

TABLE 11.3

"Advantage" Definitions

Competitive Advantage	The advantage over rivals achieved when a company's profitability is greater than the average profitability of all firms in its industry
Sustained Competitive Advantage	The competitive advantage achieved when a company is able to maintain above-average profitability for a number of years
Superior Performance	Your company's profitability relative to that of other companies in the same or a similar kind of business or industry

industry. The greater the extent to which a company's profitability exceeds the average profitability for its industry, the greater is its competitive advantage. A company is said to have a *sustained competitive advantage* when it is able to maintain above-average profitability for a number of years, and *superior performance* is profitability relative to the industry, as summarized in Table 11.3.

It must be clearly understood that in addition to its strategies, a company's performance is also determined by the specific characteristics of the industry in which the company competes. Different industries are characterized by different competitive conditions. In some industries, demand is growing rapidly, while in others it is contracting. Some might have excess capacity and persistent price wars, others strong demand and rising prices. In some, technological change might be revolutionizing competition.

Others might be characterized by a lack of technological change. In some industries, high profitability among incumbent companies might induce new companies to enter the industry, and these new entrants might depress prices and profits in the industry. In other industries, new entry might be difficult, and periods of high profitability might persist for a considerable time. Thus, the average profitability is higher in some industries and lower in others because competitive conditions vary greatly from industry to industry.[7]

In general, knowledge-intensive industries are characterized by rapid technological change and wildly fluctuating markets, with above-average return for investors.

11.3 Strategic Planning Process

It is relatively easy to perform your strategic planning process when your competition fits the ideal research qualifications: for example, a U.S.-owned, non-diversified, publicly traded company in a large industry with full-time analysts (*visible companies*). However, very little information is available from your usual sources about privately held firms, small divisions of large

TABLE 11.4

Seven-Step Formal Strategic Planning Model

Step	Characteristics
1	Select the corporate mission and major corporate goals.
2	Perform value chain analysis.
3	Undertake value proposition analysis.
4	Complete SWOT analysis.
5	Recognize the growth stages of your organization.
6	Ensure strategies are consistent with mission/vision statements.
7	Implement the strategies.

companies, or foreign-owned enterprises (*opaque companies*). For the latter you will need a formal, rational planning process.

A formal, rational planning process is a useful starting point for our journey into the world of strategy. Table 11.4 presents a typical formal strategic planning model for a strategic planning process.

11.4 Your Value Chain Analysis

The term *value chain* was first used by Michael Porter in "Competitive Advantage: Creating and Sustaining Superior Performance" (1985).[8] A value chain analysis describes the activities that an organization must undertake and links them to its competitive strength and position.

The value chain concept revolves around the notion that an organization is more than just an agglomeration of machinery, equipment, facilities, technology, and human resources. Only when these support activities are aligned with *primary activities* will customers be persuaded to buy its products or services. The combination of all these factors becomes the source of competitive advantage. This is illustrated in Figure 11.1.

Notice the important distinction between *primary* and *support activities*. Primary activities are those directly involved with the creation or delivery of your product or service. Support activities help to improve the effectiveness or efficiency of the operation. *Profit margin* is the ability of the organization to successfully deliver a product/service at a price that is higher than the combined costs of all the activities in the value chain. The numerical difference between price and cost is your profit margin.

You should perform your competitive advantage analysis within your value chain by

- Analyzing which costs are related to every single activity
- Determining the optimal price of your product/service to your customer

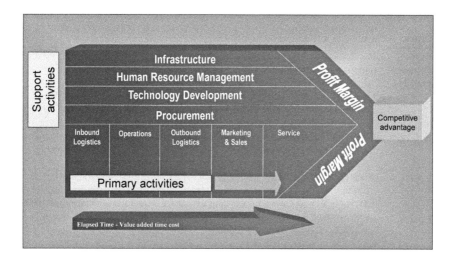

Modified after Porter 1985

FIGURE 11.1
Porter's value chain—The total value of an organization is greater than its component parts.

- Identifying potential cost advantages you may have over your competitors
- Analyzing how your product/service potentially adds value (lower cost, higher performance, user-friendly, just-in-time delivery, etc.) to your customer's value chain

11.4.1 Value Chain Concept

When a company enters and competes in any industry, it must perform a number of discrete but interconnected value-creating activities. Examples are engineering and designing, producing and marketing, warehousing and shipping, and servicing and supporting.

These activities are connected with the activities of suppliers, internally with marketing channels, and ultimately to the end users. Linked together, they must include a markup, which is also called a *profit margin*, over the cost of performing these value-creating activities. Porter separated all these services into primary and support activities, as summarized in Table 11.5.

11.4.2 Value Chain Interlocking Characteristics

According to Jonathan Aberman of Amplifier Ventures, a successful value chain analysis (otherwise known as "how you make money") requires a number of interlocking characteristics:[9]

TABLE 11.5

Business Activities in Value Chain Analysis

Primary Business Activities	**Purchasing** includes activities, costs, and assets related to buying the inputs and supplies, and inbound logistics such as receiving, storing, and distributing.
	Operations include activities, costs, and assets associated with converting inputs into final product form, such as production, assembly, packaging, equipment maintenance, and quality assurance.
	Outbound logistics include activities, costs, and assets dealing with physically distributing the product to buyers such as warehousing, order processing, order picking, packing, shipping, and delivery vehicle operations.
	Marketing and sales are related to sales force efforts, advertising and promotion, market research and planning, and dealer/distributor support.
	Service is associated with providing assistance to buyers, such as installation, spare parts delivery, maintenance and repair, technical assistance, buyer inquiries, and handling complaints.
Support Activities	**Research, technology, and systems development** includes all activities, costs, and assets related to product R&D, process R&D, equipment design, databasing, and computerized support systems.
	Human resource management includes all activities, costs, and assets associated with the recruitment, hiring, training, development, and compensation of all types of personnel and development of knowledge-based skills.
	General administration relates to general management, accounting and finance, legal and regulatory affairs, safety and security, management information systems, and all other overhead functions.

1. A clear and compelling value chain proposition that will cause customers to demand your product/service

2. An ability to compete on price (by being more efficient) or an ability to demand a price premium, when compared with competitors

3. An ability to understand your competitive advantage (the combination of 1 and 2), and systematically apply it

11.4.2.1 Understand Your Competitive Position

Startup owners exuberantly exclaim, "My business has no competition." Baloney. Every business has competition; even if a business has a truly novel approach to solving a problem—the current "gold standard" for solving that problem—it has competition. Even an anti-gravity machine has competition; it's called walking. The fundamental issue for competition is whether what you have innovated is special enough to cause customers to abandon their current choices.

11.4.2.2 Understand the Dynamics of the Market You Wish to Enter

It is essential for all entrepreneurs to understand the *industry* in which their businesses will operate. An industry is the environment within which similarly viewed businesses compete for resources and customers. For example, social media startups is an "industry." Businesses in an industry have to understand the dynamics between buyers and sellers of resources within their industry. If there is more power on the part of sellers of resources, then the amount of profit available for industry participants is less. If there is more power on the part of sellers, then there is more profit available for industry participants.

11.4.2.3 Clearly Understand Your Value Chain

A business is nothing more than a series of transactions where resources are acquired and combined into a product or service that is sold to customers. At each point of the value chain there is a wrestling match over profit. No one provides resources at less than their marginal cost—or as my grandfather used to say, "No one gives you something for nothing." However, the more power you have in each negotiation, the more of the profit you will be able to obtain at each part of the value chain. A value chain without the ability to create scarcity for consumers, or uniqueness on the part of the buyer of resources, is unlikely to be very profitable. In other words, if you have scarcity to the customer, you have value; and if you are important to the vendor of resources, you have value. Otherwise, your value chain is diminished.

11.4.2.4 Appreciate the Presence of Dominant Players in Your Industry

Dominant players in an industry have much greater ability to control their value chain. Moreover, they have the ability to interfere with your value chain, if they chose to. For example, when Apple changed its economic terms for revenue from sales in the App Store, it could do so because of its dominance. But, for the startup, it takes away a portion of its expected profits. Or, when Google decided to make GPS a commodity by giving it away in Android, it took away a big part of the value chain for Garmin. Entrepreneurs who say, "I will compete with the big guys well, because they are slow" miss the point. The presence of dominant players affects your value chain, even if they do not notice you. And, if they do notice you, you better have a plan.

11.4.2.5 Appreciate How to Legally Protect Uniqueness

There is a trend to suggest that software patents are a bad thing. However, the larger issue is that every business that is successful must create scarcity around some part of its value chain. If you are not unique and not substitutable in some way, then you will not be particularly profitable or successful. Intellectual property is a state of mind, as much as it is a legal tool. In other words, think about what makes your business unique at all times, and then use legal means (patents, copyrights, trademark, trade secrets) and business means (business model, customer service, data, profiles) to protect your uniqueness.

11.4.2.6 Have a Road Map for Growth in Your Industry

Growth does not occur by accident, it occurs through successful exploitation of a competitive advantage through a replicable business model. If entrepreneurs do not have a plan that is specific to their industry's dynamics, they are likely to fail.

11.4.2.7 Do Not Analogize a Microclimate for a Weather Pattern

If you have experienced coming into a valley on a sunny day and suddenly feeling the temperature drop and the air become damp, then you have experienced a microclimate. Entrepreneurs often have initial success in a business that is marketed to a small number of customers in a limited geographic location. The dynamics of an industry sometimes do not apply to a small corner. That does not mean that the larger trends and issues do not apply, or will not apply, as the business grows. A successful road map does not analogize to a microclimate; it plans for the national weather.

11.4.2.8 Understand that Only High Growth and Profitability Rewards Equity Investors

Because equity owners get the residual of a business, after everyone else gets paid, a business needs to grow to be of interest. What entrepreneurs do not appreciate is how much a business has to grow to be interesting to an equity investor. Very, very, very few businesses are suitable for equity investment by investors.

11.4.2.9 If You Want to Create a Big Business, Start in a New Industry

It is a proven truth that it is easier to be unique and capture a value chain if you create a new industry or get in early on a new industry. It is an interesting question whether Internet software is still a new industry, for example. That is something that bears some further consideration.

All in all, my thinking on this is that the best thing about being an entrepreneur is autonomy. Entrepreneurs should always have the freedom to conceive and start the business that they want to run. However, in a world where resources are scarce, entrepreneurs who think through their value chain are more likely to succeed.

11.5 Your Value Proposition: Killing Two Stones with One Bird

A *value proposition* is a promise of worth to be delivered and a belief from the customer that profit will be experienced. A value proposition can apply

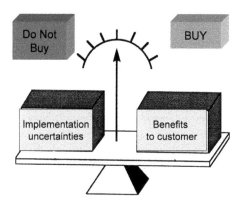

Value = (Seriousness of problem + benefits) − (cost of solution + risks)
Value = (Benefits) − (Implementation uncertainties)

FIGURE 11.2
Value equation—How much "value" (benefits) are you delivering to your costumers?

to an entire organization, or parts thereof, or customer accounts, or products or services. Creating a value proposition is a part of business strategy.[10] Developing a value proposition is based on a review and analysis of the benefits, costs, and value that an organization can deliver to its customers, prospective customers, and other constituent groups within and outside the organization. It is also a positioning of value, where value = benefits − uncertainty (including economic risk).[11]

Why should anyone buy anything from you? What do you have to offer? New products are "new" and therefore untested; generally, they cannot attract customers. The value proposition is best quantified by the value equation shown in Figure 11.2.

11.5.1 Your Value Proposition as a Marketing Tool

A value proposition can assist in a startup's marketing strategy and may guide a business to target a particular market segment. For example, "AnyFirm Co. can provide benefits a, b, and c because of competencies x, y, and z." Whether for a product, a service, or a company as a whole, this formulation can allow a startup to determine whether its core competencies align with the business segment it plans to target.

For example, AnyFirm Co. has the value proposition of increasing its market share and growing revenue by providing

1. Superior customer service
2. Product differentiation
3. Operational efficiency

TABLE 11.6

Value Proposition Identities

Meaning	Investopedia Comments
Core Competencies The main strengths or strategic advantages of a business. Core competencies are the combination of pooled knowledge and technical capacities that allow a business to be competitive in the marketplace. Theoretically, a core competency should allow a company to expand into new end markets as well as provide a significant benefit to customers. It should also be hard for competitors to replicate.	A business just starting out will try to first identify and then focus on its core competencies, allowing it to establish a footprint while gaining a solid reputation and brand recognition. Using, and later leveraging, core competencies usually provides the best chance for a company's continued growth and survival, as these factors are what differentiate the company from competitors. The term *core competency* is relatively new. It originated in a 1990 *Harvard Business Review* article. In it, the authors suggest that business functions not enhanced by core competencies should be outsourced if economically feasible.
Barriers to Entry The existence of high startup costs or other obstacles that prevent new competitors from easily entering an industry or area of business. Barriers to entry benefit existing companies already operating in an industry because they protect an established company's revenues and profits from being whittled away by new competitors.	Barriers to entry can exist as a result of government intervention (industry regulation, legislative limitations on new firms, special tax benefits to existing firms, etc.), or they can occur naturally within the business world. Some naturally occurring barriers to entry could be technological patents or patents on business processes, a strong brand identity, strong customer loyalty, or high customer switching costs
Market Segmentation A marketing term referring to the aggregating of prospective buyers into groups (segments) that have common needs and will respond similarly to a marketing action.	For example, a pharmaceutical company might have distinct market segments for cardiovascular diseases or cancer treatments. As distinct groups, patients will respond to very different announcements.

Table 11.6 summarizes the three identities a startup may use in its preliminary value proposition.

11.5.2 Compelling Value Propositions

In order to attract their customers, entrepreneurs need to develop a compelling value proposition. As shown in Figure 11.3, a customer would be persuaded to buy your new product/service if (1) the benefits outweigh his costs/risks, and (2) it solves a major, serious problem. Figure 11.3 presents a step-wise process for establishing your value proposition.

Examples of compelling value propositions (also called *company slogans*) include the following:

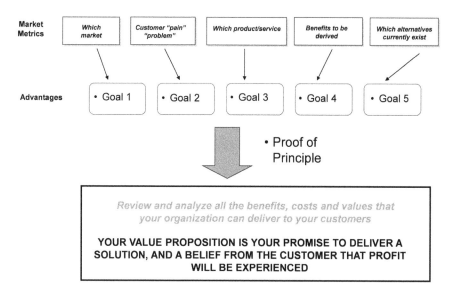

FIGURE 11.3
Value proposition—How compelling is your product/service to your customers?.

Coke	The pause that refreshes.
FedEx	The world on time.
E.F. Hutton	When E.F. Hutton speaks, people listen.
American Express	Don't leave home without it.
Lexus	The passionate pursuit of perfection.
IBM	Global solutions for a small planet.
Apple	The power to be your best.
DeBeers	A diamond is forever.
Visa	It is everywhere you want it to be.
Intel	Intel inside.
AT&T	Reach out and touch someone.
BMW	The ultimate driving machine.
FOX	Fair and balanced.
CNN	The most trusted name in news.
Clairol	Only her hairdresser knows for sure.

11.6 SWOT Analysis

A SWOT analysis is a strategic planning tool used to evaluate the *strengths, weaknesses, opportunities*, and *threats* involved in a project or in a business venture. It involves specifying the objective of the business venture or project and identifying the internal and external factors that are favorable and unfavorable to achieving that objective. The technique is credited to Albert Humphrey,[12] who led a research project at Stanford University in the 1960s and 1970s using data from Fortune 500 companies.

- **Strengths:** Attributes of the organization helpful to achieving the objective
- **Weaknesses:** Attributes of the organization harmful to achieving the objective
- **Opportunities:** *External* conditions helpful to achieving the objective
- **Threats:** *External* conditions harmful to achieving the objective

A generic SWOT analysis is presented in Figure 11.4.
Your SWOT analysis should be conducted as follows:

- **STEP 1:** The present: List all your current strengths and weaknesses.
- **STEP 2:** The future: List all future opportunities and strengths.
- **STEP 3:** Your action plan: Address all four areas individually.

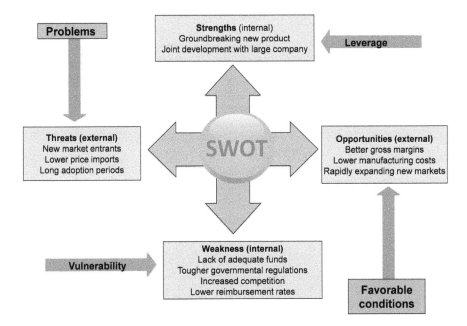

FIGURE 11.4
Generic SWOT analysis—A SWOT analysis is a powerful strategic planning tool to help you evaluate your competitive position vis-à-vis your intended objectives.

- **STEP 4:** Develop an operational plan, complete with specific tasks and dates of completion.

11.6.1 SWOT Example

The aim of any SWOT analysis is to identify the key internal and external factors that are important to achieving your objectives. SWOT analysis groups key pieces of information into two main categories:

1. **Internal factors:** The *strengths* and *weaknesses* internal to the organization.
2. **External factors:** The *opportunities* and *threats* presented by the external environment.

The internal factors may be viewed as strengths or weaknesses depending on their impact on the organization's objectives. What may represent strengths with respect to one objective may be weaknesses for another objective. The factors may include personnel, finance, manufacturing capabilities, and so on. The external factors may include macroeconomic matters, technological change, legislation, and sociocultural changes, as well as changes in the marketplace or competitive position.

For SWOT results to be meaningful, you have to be brutally honest about your business. Remember, you will only be kidding yourself. Table 11.7 presents an example of what a SWOT matrix may look in a generic startup.

Next, understanding each of the relevant issues you have identified, draw up an action plan, listing what you can do to

TABLE 11.7

SWOT Matrix of a Generic Startup

	Potential Issues
Strengths	Strong market position; niche market; successful advertising campaign; effective management procedures; regular financial monitoring; well-trained staff; location of premises; good market research; suitable pricing policy; reliable suppliers
Weaknesses	Accounts not paying on time; cash flow problems; underpricing; not enough customers; sporadic business; skills shortage; lack of adequate publicity; publicity not reaching right clients; poor market information; working too many hours
Opportunities	New funding streams; new clients; market expansion; free business support; free training; Internet marketing and sales; attending exhibitions; networking; publications; social media exposure
Threats	Strong competitors with better features; general economic decline leading to clients reprioritizing spending; new competitor in market; product/service no longer "trendy"; new legislation requiring investment; new regulatory demands

- Reduce or eliminate weaknesses, making some into strengths
- Build on your strong points
- Forestall avoidable threats
- Take advantage of the opportunities arising

Prioritize the tasks you have set for yourself, set a time schedule, and start putting your plan into action! And be sure to empower your staff to accomplish your goals.

11.7 Recognizing Growth Stages

Small business success doesn't just happen. Some fairly predictable but not very orderly (chaotic) stages characterize its evolution. Most entrepreneurs caught up in the day-to-day goings-on in a business don't recognize these stages until they've passed, though. Time to open your eyes. The following sections describe the three stages of business evolution.

11.7.1 The Startup Years

The startup years are the years when survival motivates your thoughts and actions. Everything that happens within the business is dominated by you; words such as delegation, team, and consensus are generally not yet part of the business's vocabulary. These are the hands-on years. For some owners, they're the most enjoyable years of the business; for all owners, they're an integral part of the learning process.

The work during this time is exceptionally hard—often the physically and emotionally draining kind of hard. The hours are long and sometimes tedious, but by the end of the day, you can see, touch, and feel the progress you've made. The gratification is instantaneous. The duration of this first stage can vary greatly. Some businesses may fly through the startup stage in less than a year, but most spend anywhere from 1 to 3 years growing out of the stage. Others, oftentimes those in the more competitive niches, spend as many as 5 or more years in the startup stage.

You'll know you've graduated from the startup stage when profitability and orderliness become a dependable part of your business. The hectic days of worrying about survival are replaced by the logical, orderly days of planning for success.

11.7.2 The Growth Years

The growth years are the years when your business achieves some sense of order, stability, and profitability. Your evolving business has survived the

mistakes, confusion, and chaos of the startup years, and now optimism, cama-
raderie, and cooperation should play an important role in the organization.

Key employees surface, efficient administrative systems and controls
become part of the business's daily operating procedures, and the need to
depend on you for everything disappears.

The business of doing business remains fun for most small-business owners in this stage, because increasing sales translates into increasing profits—
every small-business owner's dream. The balance sheet puts some flesh on
its scraggly bones as you generate cash as a result of profitability. You learn
to delegate many of those unpleasant tasks that you performed in the past.

Survival is no longer your primary motivator. At last, the daily choices that
you make can be dictated by lifestyle goals instead of by survival. We have
further good news: This stage can last a long time if the growth is gradual
and remains under control, and if you manage the business and its expanding population of employees properly. More than likely, however, this stage
will last anywhere from a few years to 6 or 7 years or so before the next stage
raises its ugly head.

11.7.3 The Transition Years

The third stage, the transition years, can also be called the *restructuring stage* or
the *diversification stage*. This is the stage when something basic to the success
of the growth years has changed or gone wrong. As a result, in order for the
business to survive, a strategic change in direction, or transition, is required.

Many factors can bring about the transition period, but the following are
the most common:

- **Relentless growth:** This is because relentless sales growth requires
  relentless improvement in the business's employees, systems, procedures, and infrastructure, and many businesses simply can't keep
  up with such pressures.
- **Shrinkage of sales and the disappearance of profits, or even prolonged periods of stagnation:** This is the opposite of growth. The
  causes for this shrinkage or stagnation can come from anywhere
  and everywhere, and they often include such uncontrollable factors as new competitors, a changing economy, new technology, and
  changes in consumer demand.

11.8 How to Think Like an Executive

You decided to start your own company because you are a specialist in some
technical field. Your technical expertise allowed you to innovate a new product that you want to commercialize a soon as possible.

You were the acknowledged specialist as a researcher-inventor. Surprisingly, as an owner you must now become the great generalist. Being a generalist means knowing your specialty but also knowing (and appreciating) about all the other specialties needed to build a successful company. Now you must think like an executive, not a specialist, researcher, or inventor.

11.8.1 The Great Irony

There is only one generalist job in a startup, and that is the job of the owner-inventor. But there is no generalist path that gets you there. Ironically, it takes a specialist path to prepare you for the generalist's top job (i.e., the executive).

First, you must be a specialist in some advanced technical field, such as medical science, pharmacology, engineering, life sciences, computer science, telecommunications, and the like. As an owner-inventor you must be able to become an orchestra conductor, not just a great instrument player, and still perform a brilliant job in your specialty. This is graphically depicted in Figure 11.5.

11.8.2 Your Team Depends on You

Your team members want to know the mission, vision, direction, and status of the company on a periodic basis. And that can only come from the communications ability of the owner-inventor. As top dog, you must be the ultimate communicator, coach, counselor, pacifier, and arbiter, particularly during conflicts, as shown in Figure 11.6.

The Great Irony

FIGURE 11.5
You, as the greatest generalist.

Team

Customers/investors

FIGURE 11.6
You, the great communicator.

Each team member wants to know how they fit into the overall organizational structure and what their future will be as the organization grows. You must provide the tools, resources, and empowerment to your team to allow them to do their specialized jobs.

11.8.3 Sole Proprietorship or Partnership?

Sole ownership is always the least conflictive and most popular of the options for starting a company, assuming that you have access to the necessary funds to launch your business, industry knowledge, and energy to make a go of the business by yourself. Sure, the leverage and financial benefits that partners and shareholders bring to the table can be worth their weight in potential opportunities, but decision making in shared ownership situations requires consensus, and consensus can take a lot of time. Besides, consensus doesn't always represent your own personal best interests, and when your name is on the dotted line, your personal best interests should be at or near the top of the reasons for making decisions.

11.8.3.1 Being the Sole Owner

Being the sole owner has the following advantages:

- It's generally easier, quicker, and less expensive. No lawyers are required to write partnership agreements and assist in determining answers to all the questions that partnership agreements require.
- The profits (or losses) are totally yours.
- You have no need to seek consensus. Your way is the only way.

- You don't waste time catering to the often-aggravating demands of shareholders, minority or otherwise. There's no possibility of shareholder lawsuits.

Being the sole owner also has the following disadvantages:

- You have no one to share the risk with you.
- Your limited skills will have to make do until you can hire someone with complementary skills.
- Single ownership can be lonely. Many times, you'll wish you had someone with whom to share the problems and stress. You may be able to do this with trusted, senior employees. Of course, if you have good friends and/or a strong marriage partner, these people can be a source of much-needed support.

Still confused as to whether you want to go it alone or share ownership? Answer the following questions to help with the decision.

11.8.3.2 Partnership?

Do you absolutely, positively need a partner? To provide cash? Knowledge? If you do, that settles the issue; if you don't, continue with the following questions:

- Are you capable of working with partners or shareholders? Will you have a problem sharing the decisions and the profits as well as the risks?
- Does your business fit the multiple ownership profile? In other words, does this business have room for two partners, and is it a business that has the growth potential to support two partners? Will a partner have an important role in the organization? Would his or her complementary skills enhance the business's chance for success?
- What are the legal requirements of multiple ownership? Can you live within these legal parameters?
- What do you have in common with other business owners who have opted for multiple ownership? Where do you see conflicts? Ask your banker, accountant, or attorney for the names of other business owners who have opted for multiple ownership. Interview those owners. Get their feedback on the list of pluses and minuses.
- What's the likelihood of finding a partner with complementary skills and a personality compatible with yours? This ability depends on how wired into the business community you are and the line of work you're going into. If you have a lot of business contacts and know exactly what you want, finding a partner may be easy. More typically, it isn't.

If you opt for multiple ownership, you'll live with the decision for a long, long time. If you elect sole ownership at the start, however, you can always seek partners later if you feel that you need them for the business success that you desire.

Partners make sense when they can bring capital to the business along with complementary management skills. Unfortunately, partners also present the opportunity for turmoil, and, especially in the early stages of a business's growth, turmoil takes time, burns energy, and costs money—all of which most small-business founders lack.

A partnership in the right hands will outperform a sole proprietorship in the right hands, any day. Having *minority shareholders* (any and all shareholders who collectively own less than 50%) can also make sense, especially after the business is out of the blocks and has accumulated value.

However, minority shareholders can be a pain; they have legal rights that often run counter to the wishes of the majority. Because majority shareholders are ceded the right to make the final decisions, courts have determined that minority shareholders must have an avenue of appeal. Thus, minority shareholders, particularly in our litigious society, sometimes look to the courts whenever they feel their rights of ownership are being violated. Unfortunately, shareholder suits are a sign of the times.

Occasionally, especially where venture capital financing is involved, the founder of the business may find himself or herself working for majority shareholders. Fortunately, this situation rarely occurs because the typical small-business founder has already proven that taking orders from others is not exactly one of his or her inherent strengths. We've found that, on the infrequent occasions when this situation does occur, more often than not the founder of the company is the first one to get the boot when the going gets tough, as the chief financiers step in to protect their investment. That's why we strongly recommend that you find a way to retain majority control.

11.8.3.3 *Getting a Business Partner*

Here's a fact that not everyone knows: According to studies, partnerships outperform sole proprietorships by a wide margin. We're not talking rocket science here; this statement is nothing more than a simple fact of life: two heads are better than one!

Sometimes, one plus one equals significantly more than two if the partners can blend their skills and talents. In other words, synergy. (Google, Apple, and Hewlett-Packard are examples of companies that began as partnerships.)

So, why may a partnership make sense to you? Here are some reasons.

Although you're probably aware of your own strengths, your human nature lets you more easily overlook your weaknesses. Ask those who know you well—family, friends, and current or previous co-workers—what complementary skills you should seek in a business partner. Consider the following advantages:

- **Additional capital:** Two savings accounts are better than one.
- **Greater problem-solving capacity:** Two heads are better than one.
- **More flexibility:** One partner goes on vacation or gets sick, the other one minds the store.
- **Ease of formation:** Legally speaking, partnerships are easier and less expensive to form than corporations.
- **Less risk:** Profits aren't the only thing partnerships share.

How do you find a partner (or partners)? The same way you locate a key employee, a consultant, or a mentor. Clearly identify your need (in this case, the skills you're looking for) and then network your available resources.

When forming a partnership, you're beginning what you hope will be a long-term relationship—a relationship that oftentimes rivals a marriage in terms of complexity. If you're smart, you can determine a way to test the chemistry of the partnership before you get too far involved and cannot get out.

Want to hear a business partner joke? Here is one for you.[13]

A very successful businessman had a meeting with his new son-in-law. "I love my daughter, and now I welcome you into the family," said the man. "To show you how much we care for you, I'm making you a 50:50 partner in my business. All you have to do is go to the factory every day and learn the operations."

The son-in-law interrupted: "I hate factories. I can't stand the noise."

"I see," replied the father-in-law. "Well, then you'll work in the office and take charge of some of the operations."

"I hate office work," said the son-on-law. "I can't stand being stuck behind a desk all day."

"Wait a minute," said the father-in-law. "I just made you a half-owner of a highly profitable corporation, but you don't like factories and won't work in a office. What am I going to do with you?"

"Easy," said the young man. "Buy me out!"

11.9 Competitive Intelligence

The Society of Competitive Intelligence Professionals (SCIP) defines *competitive intelligence* (CI) as "the process of ethically collecting, analyzing and disseminating accurate, relevant, specific, timely, foresighted and actionable intelligence regarding the implications of the business environment, competitors and the organization itself."

CI is the selection, collection, interpretation, and distribution of publicly held information that is strategically important to a firm. A substantial amount of this information is publicly accessible via the World Wide Web, periodic company SEC filings, the patent literature, company promotional campaigns, and so on.

The knowledge-intensive world is ruled by hyper-competition. Hyper-competition is rapid and dynamic competition characterized by unsustainable advantage. It is the condition of rapid escalation of competition based on price–quality positioning, competition to protect or invade established product or geographic markets, and competition based on vast scientific knowledge, deep pockets, and the creation of even deeper-pocketed alliances.[14]

CI is the knowledge base for managing in this hyper-competitive environment. CI is a process that provides you insights into what might happen in the near future. This process requires that we go from data to information to intelligence. The following is a basic example.

Data	Prices for our products have dropped by 5%.
Information	New offshore facilities enjoy significantly lower labor costs.
Intelligence	Our key competitor is about to acquire a facility in China that will....

The practical differences between data, information, and intelligence can be subtle, but very real, as follows:

Data	Unconnected pieces of information: "Nice to know, but so what!"
Information	Increased knowledge derived by understanding the relationships of data: "Interesting, but how does it relate to what I do!" The knowledge-intensive business world is driven by hyper-competition.
Intelligence	Organizing the information to fully appreciate the implications and impact on the organization: "Oh really, then we better do something!"

Thus, a formalized CI program should

- Anticipate changes in the marketplace
- Anticipate actions of competitors
- Discover new or potential competitors
- Learn from the successes and failures of others
- Increase the range and quality of acquisition targets
- Learn about new technologies, products, and processes that affect your business
- Learn about political, legislative, or regulatory changes that can affect your business
- Enter new businesses
- Look at your own business practices with an open mind
- Help implement the latest management tools

11.9.1 Intelligence Should Be Actionable

Intelligence differs from data and information, since it requires some form of analysis.

The purpose of this analysis is to derive some meaning from the piles of data and information that bury everyone. By going through analysis and filtering, we can refine it enough so that someone can act on it and understand their options, giving them an opportunity to make forward-looking decisions.

When we present "intelligence" to people, they can draw a conclusion and make an important decision quickly. Therefore, CI should put conclusions and recommendations up front with supporting research behind the analysis. CI should not simply present the facts, declaring what has been found, but instead make a statement, saying this is what is likely about to happen.

CI involves the use of public sources to develop data on your competition, competitors, and the market environment. It can then transform that data into actionable policies (intelligence). In this context, *public* means all the information you can legally and ethically identify, obtain, locate, deduce, and access.[15]

CI is also known by several other names: competitor intelligence, business intelligence, strategic intelligence, marketing intelligence, competitive technical intelligence, technology intelligence, and technical intelligence, depending on what specific information is being targeted.[16]

The development of CI usually proceeds in a six-phase predetermined cycle, as follows:

1. **Establish needs:** Clearly identify the information needed on the competition
2. or the competitive environment.
3. **Collect data:** Assemble raw data, using legal and ethical means, from public sources.
4. **Analyze data:** Covert data into useful information.
5. **Communicate intelligence:** Convey the finished intelligence to the decision maker(s) for their use.
6. **Actionable intelligence:** Provide strategic direction to decision maker(s) in a timely manner.

These phases are visually summarized in Figure 11.7.

11.9.2 Thou Shall Not Steal Your Competitors Secrets

According to Moneywatch's Hodges,[17] there is nothing unethical about CI. Most of the time, it simply involves gathering together pieces of a puzzle

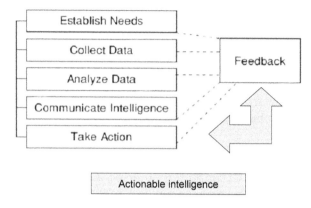

FIGURE 11.7
Traditional intelligence cycle.

that are available to anyone—if they have the time and the determination to find them.

But because the search can be tedious, it is tempting to look for shortcuts to get the necessary information, especially when time is tight. When that happens, legal and ethical lines may be crossed. Table 11.8 lists some of the most common tactics that may get you into trouble.

TABLE 11.8

Competitive Intelligence Tactics to Avoid

Tactics	Description
Pretext	Approaching a source under false identity or deceptive pretense
Dumpster mining (diving)	Surreptitiously gathering discarded key documents through garbage or empty raw material pails on dumpsters
Bypassing employer agreements	Encouraging a source to violate the terms of a confidential disclosure agreement (CDA), non-compete agreement (NCA), or non-disclosure agreement (NDA) they have signed with their employer
Acquiring trade secrets	Finding the proprietary advantage to a competitor's success, specifically when it's a closely guarded secret, such as stealing formulas or software proprietary code
Paying sources for proprietary information	Giving cash to someone who can tell you what you want to know about a competitor
Enticement recruitment	Deliberately targeting competitor's key employees with the purpose of obtaining trade secrets
Computer hacking	Penetrating competitor's computer systems to gain access to proprietary information on pricing, business plans, customer lists, etc.
Wiretapping offices	Electronic eavesdropping on conversations

11.9.3 Business Intelligence Types

According to McGonagle and Vella,[18] modern CI is divided into four different but overlapping types: (1) strategic, (2) competitor, (3) tactical, and (4) technical. We have added business and counterintelligence to the list. This is summarized in Table 11.9.

Figure 11.8 summarizes the various types of intelligence activities likely to be undertaken by a business organization.

11.9.3.1 Strategic Intelligence

Strategic intelligence is CI supporting strategic, as distinguished from tactical, decision making. This means providing higher-level intelligence on the

TABLE 11.9

Types of Modern Competitive Intelligence

Strategic Intelligence	Emphasizes the relationship between the intelligence function and strategic decision making.
Competitor Intelligence	• Industry experts/analysts • Industry publications • Trade shows/conferences • Advertisements/PR • University research centers • Financial • Court documents/patents • Suppliers/customers • Newspapers/business wire • "Help wanted" ads • Reverse engineering
Tactical Intelligence	Functional units such as sales and marketing need and request tactical information to assist in business development and customer problem solving. Tactical intelligence is present-oriented. This level of intelligence provides organizational decision makers with the information necessary to monitor changes in the company's current environment and proactively helps them search for new opportunities. Tactical intelligence is real time in nature and provides analysis of immediate competitive conditions.
Business Intelligence	Incorporates the monitoring of a wide array of developments across an organization's external environment, which includes customers, competitors, suppliers, and economic issues, as well as technical and regulatory changes.
Technical Intelligence	Monitors R&D issues Reduces risky decision making Broadens awareness of competitive situation Identifies business alternatives Increases warning time in chemical/pharmaceuticals industry
Counterintelligence	Protects intelligence collection activities and protects plans, programs, and projects from competitors Hiring security specialists Training employees not to give away sensitive information

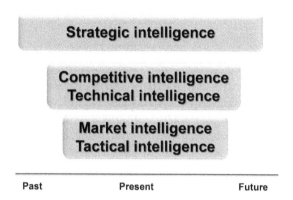

Scope of intelligence activities

Strategic intelligence

Competitive intelligence
Technical intelligence

Market intelligence
Tactical intelligence

| Past | Present | Future |

FIGURE 11.8
Competitive intelligence is composed of strategic, competitive, technical, market, and tactical activities.

competitive, economic, regulatory, and political environment in which your firm operates now and in which it expects to operate in the future.

Strategic intelligence is typically used by senior managers and executives who make and then execute overall corporate strategy, as depicted in Figure 11.9.

Strategic intelligence's most common applications are in the development of the following five activities:

1. Long-term (3–5 year) strategic plans
2. Capital investment plans

Whose Job Is It?

Project Managers

Top Execs

Project Managers

Planning & Finance Analysts

Group Managers

Independent Consultants

FIGURE 11.9
Competitive intelligence is the "job" of just about anybody in a position of leadership.

3. Political risk assessments

4. Merger and acquisition, joint venture, and corporate alliance policies and plans

5. Research and development planning

Strategic intelligence usually focuses on the overall strategic environment. A firm's direct competitive environment and its direct competitors are, of course, included in that focus. It should also include its indirect competitors. In addition, strategic intelligence should develop CI on the long-term changes caused by, as well as affecting, all of the forces driving industry competition, including

- Suppliers
- Customers
- Substitute products or service
- Potential competitors

You conduct strategic CI analysis when you must focus on many critical factors, such as technology trends, regulatory developments, and even political risks that, in turn, affect these forces. Strategic intelligence's focus is less on the present than it is on the past and is primarily the future. The time horizon of interest typically runs from 2 years in the past to 5 or even 10 years in the future.

- In terms of an interest in the past, you will be collecting and analyzing data so that your firm can evaluate the actual success (or failure) of its own strategies and of those of your competitors. This in turn permits you better to weigh options for the future. You are looking to the past to learn what may happen in the future.

- With respect to the future, you are seeking a view of your firm's total environment: competitive, regulatory, and political. As with radar, you are looking for warnings of impending problems, and alerts to upcoming opportunities—always in time to take the necessary action.

However, in most companies, there is tremendous organizational resistance to accept the value of CI. It is not a traditional function taught in business schools. Most top managers act under the delusion that they know everything there is to know about their technology or market. Figure 11.10 lists some of the common problems associated with CI.

11.9.3.2 Competitor Intelligence

Competitor intelligence is most often used by strategic planning operations or by operating managers within strategic business units (SBUs). It may also

Common problems associated with accepting "competitive intelligence"

- Top managers do not value intelligence
- Top managers consider intelligence a luxury
- Inability to incorporate into corporate strategy
- Managers believe *"I know my industry!"*
- Unskilled people try to perform intelligence
- Managers hoard information
- The function does not meet the "real" needs and concerns of decision makers
- Intelligence is seldom used by top decision makers

FIGURE 11.10
Competitive intelligence has a bad reputation in business.

be useful to product managers, as well as to those involved with product development, new business development, and mergers and acquisitions.

Figure 11.11 summarizes the most useful information derived from competitor intelligence.

Competitor intelligence usually helps you answer a wide variety of key business questions, including the following:

- Who are our competitors right now?
- Who are our potential competitors?

Useful competitor information

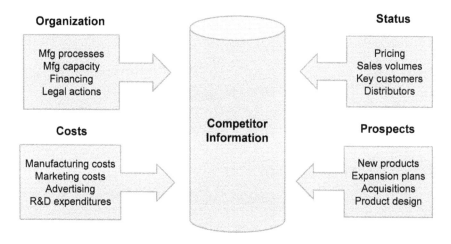

FIGURE 11.11
The many legitimate uses of competitor information.

- How do our competitors see themselves? How do they see us?
- What are the track records of the key people at our competitors? What are their personalities? What is the environment in their own company? What difference do these people make in terms of our ability to predict how these competitors will react to our competitive strategy?
- How and where are our competitors marketing their products/services? What, new directions will they probably take?
- What markets or geographic areas will (or won't) be tapped by our competitors in the future?
- How have our competitors responded to the short- and long-term trends in our industry in the past? How are they likely to respond to them in the future?
- What patents or innovative technology have our competitors or potential competitors recently obtained or developed? What do those changes and innovations mean to us?
- What are our competitors' overall plans and goals for the next 1–2 years in the markets where they currently compete with us? What are their plans/goals and how will those affect the way they conduct their business?
- Competitor intelligence's time horizon typically runs from 6–12 months in the past to 1–2 years in the future.

It is most frequently used to decipher competitor profiles and industry trends, followed by scenario development and SWOT analyses, as shown in Figure 11.12.

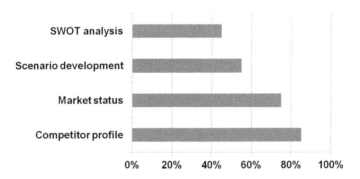

FIGURE 11.12
The four main tools of competitive intelligence.

11.9.3.3 Technical Intelligence

Technical intelligence is particularly useful if you are involved with your firm's research and development activities. Using basic CI techniques, those practicing technical intelligence now often can determine the following:

- Competitors' current manufacturing methods and processes.
- A competitor's access, use, and dependence on outside technology, as well as their need for new technology.
- Key patents and proprietary technology being used by, being developed by, or being acquired by, competitors.
- Types and levels of research and development conducted by competitors, as well as estimates of their current and future expenditures for research and development.
- Size and capabilities of competitors' research staff.

11.9.3.4 Tactical Intelligence

Effective CI organizations maintain strong links with the sales and marketing functions not only to provide CI to those functions but also to gather intelligence. The sales function of an organization often provides a rich pool of information because it is a primary interface with the firm's competitive market (e.g., customers, competitors, suppliers, and distributors). This interface allows for the continuous collection of "human" competitive information.

The continuous use of CI from primary sources provides an organization with dynamic stocks of knowledge as opposed to more filtered, static public and secondary sources. CI is crucially important in providing marketing with timely information regarding market dynamics, as shown in Figure 11.13.

11.9.4 Business Intelligence

Business intelligence is a particularly difficult term to deal with. At one time, this term was actually used by some CI professionals to describe CI in a very broad way, and to describe only intelligence provided in support of corporate strategy by others. Now its use seems to have been fully co-opted by those involved with data management and data warehousing. There, it can refer to

- The software used to manage vast amounts of data
- The process of managing that data, also called *data mining*
- The output of either of the first two

In summary, virtually all of the reported applications and successes of business intelligence deal with processes that are internally oriented, from process control to logistics, and from sales forecasting to quality control. The most that can be said of it its relationship to intelligence is that data mining

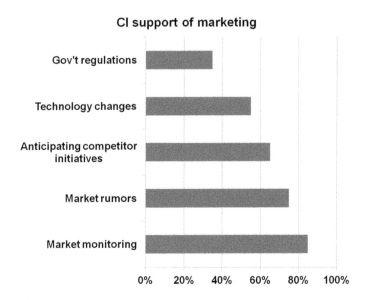

FIGURE 11.13
Effective marketing is heavily dependent on competitive intelligence.

and related techniques are useful tools for some early analysis and sorting tasks that would be impossibly tedious for human analysts.

11.9.5 Counterintelligence

Knowledge has emerged as the most strategically significant intangible asset of modern firms.[19] Thus, the need to protect the firm's knowledge from theft or the prying eyes of competitors is of critical importance.

According to estimates by Ocean Tomo,[20] on average, 84% of company value consists of intangible assets, as shown in Figure 11.14.

Traditional protective mechanisms are now inadequate in the electronic age. Business counterintelligence appears to mitigate many of the new threats. As such, business counterintelligence includes all the activities undertaken to limit the ability of competitors to gather actionable information about your company.[21]

Not long ago, traditional "corporate espionage" was dangerous. It required the corporate spy to betray coworkers, clandestinely collect company documents, load and mark dead drops, and operate under the constant risk of exposure and arrest. Yet corporate espionage, like so many activities, has moved into the realm of cyberspace. In cyberspace, many companies are left working in the modern equivalent of the Wild West, an unregulated frontier where the crown jewels of the corporation—trade secrets and intellectual property—are hijacked every day, often without the victim's knowledge. In turn, companies often find themselves competing with the very developments and technologies the companies pioneered.

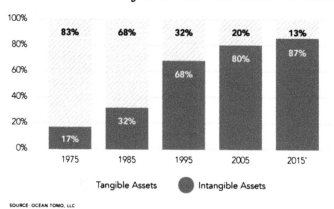

COMPONENTS *of* S&P 500 MARKET VALUE

SOURCE: OCEAN TOMO, LLC

FIGURE 11.14
Intangible assets represent the lion's share of enterprise the S&P 500 market value.

Companies must have aggressive security programs to protect their intellectual property, trade secrets, business processes, strategic goals, and the integrity of their brands. An effective CI program will ensure that your company has identified its most vulnerable assets, understands the threats to those assets, has discovered the vulnerabilities that might make your company susceptible to exploitation, and has taken the appropriate steps to mitigate risks.

11.9.5.1 Counterintelligence and Security

Counterintelligence and security are distinct but complementary disciplines, and it is important for organizations contemplating the establishment of a CI program to understand the difference.

- Every corporation needs an effective physical security capability that ensures employees, facilities, and information systems are protected. Security, at its root, is defensive.
- Counterintelligence is both defensive and proactive, and it incorporates unique analysis and investigation activities designed to anticipate, counter, and prevent a competitor's actions, protecting company resources and innovation.[22]

Counterintelligence and security are established in a sequential program, as follows:

Step One: Conducting a Counterintelligence Risk Assessment (Table 11.10)

Step Two: Laying the Groundwork for a Corporate CI Program

The risk assessment will provide a better understanding of the scope and nature of the threats to your company's most important assets. At this point,

TABLE 11.10

Conducting a Counterintelligence Risk Assessment

While companies will need to tailor CI risk assessments to their unique circumstances, all assessments require three important actions:	
1. Identifying and Prioritizing Assets	You should identify and prioritize its most critical assets, to include people, groups, relationships, instruments, installations, processes, and supplies. The loss or compromise of these assets would be the most damaging to your organization, could result in substantial economic losses.
2. Determining Threats	Your company will need to assess the capabilities, intentions, and opportunities of competitors to exploit or damage company assets or information. You also should determine whether there are any gaps in a competitor's knowledge of the company or if your company is working on a particular technology or product that they may be trying to acquire.
3. Assessing Vulnerabilities	Finally, your company will need to assess the inherent susceptibility of its procedures, facilities, information systems, equipment, or policies to a breach. You will need to determine how a competitor, including a malicious insider, would attempt to gain access to your critical assets. When assessing vulnerabilities, a company should consider the physical location of its assets and who has access to them, including both employees and outsiders.

a number of initial activities should be considered for building an effective CI program. To prepare for implementation, your company should

- Assign or hire a program manager who is dedicated to the CI program and has direct access to the CEO or senior partners so that CI and security issues can be addressed expeditiously, discreetly, and with appropriate authority.
- Establish that the CI program will have a centralized management structure but will support the entire corporation, regardless of location.
- Take steps to begin or continue strengthening strong relationships among the company's security, information assurance (IA), general counsel, and human resources (HR) departments; these relationships are critical to effective CI.
- Ask your company's legal counsel to provide clear guidance on the new program's potential activities.

Step Three: Identifying the Capabilities Needed

As progress continues on laying the groundwork, your company should begin identifying the CI capabilities needed for an effective CI program that is focused on protecting your company's assets, brand, and intellectual property. The risk assessment will be an important guide during this step. CI capabilities are essential to identifying and countering insider and cyber threats, which represent the two most challenging threats to U.S. corporate assets.

The following are primary capabilities that should be considered when determining the size and scope of the CI program your company requires.

Threat Awareness and Training	New employee orientations and continual refresher training can equip the workforce with the skills needed to understand who your company's adversaries are, identify threats, and follow reporting procedures for suspicious activities. A highly trained and aware workforce is key to the early detection of potential threats. Companies should utilize a CI-specific non-disclosure agreement before divulging their threat and vulnerabilities.
Analysis, Reporting, and Response	An analysis, reporting, and response capability can integrate resources and information from across relevant corporate elements (CI, security, IA, HR, general counsel) and provide assessments and warning on data that may be indicative of a threat.
Suspicious Activity Reporting	Defining, training the workforce, and developing reporting policies on suspicious activities that are deemed inappropriate or potentially threatening could provide an effective "early warning system" for potential threats.
CI Audit	A CI audit capability would enable your company to monitor user activity on corporate IT systems. This would help to identify anomalous behavior, deter the theft or unauthorized use of company information, and protect the company from network intrusions.

Step Four: Implementing Your Corporate CI Program

Once the risk has been assessed, the groundwork laid, and the required CI capabilities identified, your company can begin the implementation of a CI program. Although the investment needed to build an effective program will use company resources that might otherwise be dedicated to product development, marketing, and other priorities, it is important to remember that a properly designed program that is tailored to your company's unique security needs and that protects your critical corporate assets can more than justify the costs.

11.9.6 Ten Commandments of Competitive Intelligence

In 1988, Fuld and Company[23] published its "Ten Commandments of Legal and Ethical Intelligence Gathering," as follows:

1. Thou shall not lie when representing thyself.
2. Thou shall observe thy company's legal guidelines.
3. Thou shall not tape record a conversation.
4. Thou shall not bribe.
5. Thou shall not plant eavesdropping devices.
6. Thou shall not mislead anyone in an interview.

7. Thou shall neither obtain nor give price information to thy competitor.

8. Thou shall not swap misinformation.

9. Thou shall not steal a trade secret.

10. Thou shall not knowingly press someone if it may jeopardize that person's job or reputation.[24]

11.10 Strategy versus Tactics

As this chapter has emphasized, strategic planning is a crucial part of setting an organizational blueprint of action that's mid- to long-term in duration and is designed to help your company achieve its broad mission. Thus, if your company's mission is to be number one in its market by 2020, the strategies you develop should form a plan of action for getting your company to achieve that goal.

The traditional view is that *strategies* are long-term goals set by top management, while *tactics* are the steps followed by middle management to achieve those goals. In a startup, however, the boundaries between strategies and tactics are blurred. In a startup, middle managers are frequently asked to help establish organizational goals, for the following three reasons:

1. Goals simplify guidelines and provide a clear management focus.

2. Goals motivate the entire team to achieve greatness.

3. Goals provide an unambiguous basis for measuring achievement and performance.

11.10.1 Strategic Goals

According to Allen and Economy,[25] examples of strategic goals are

- Growth
- Raising capital
- Reducing employee turnover
- New product development

11.10.2 Tactical Goals

Examples of tactical goals are

- Reaching customers
- Providing incentives for employees
- Raising capital

Allen and Economy summarize strategy and tactics as follows:

> The metaphor most commonly used to describe tactics is that tactics are
> to the battle what strategy is to the war. Strategy is the big picture, and
> tactics are the steps taken to achieve the strategy. Where strategy gener-
> ally is concerned with resources, market environment, and the mission
> of the company, tactics usually deal more with people and actions. In
> essence, tactics are about execution.

Notes

1. Olsen, E. (2007). *Strategic Planning for Dummies*. Hoboken, NJ: Wiley.
2. Rigby, D. (2005). Management tools and trends 2005. Bain and Company report. http://www.bain.com/management_tools/Management_Tools_and_Trends_2005.pdf.
3. Renger, R., and Titcomb, A. (2002). A three step approach to teaching logic models. *American Journal of Evaluation*, 23(4), 493–503.
4. Wikipedia. (2018). Strategic planning. https://en.wikipedia.org/wiki/Strategic_planning.
5. Hill, W.L, and Jones, G.R. *Essentials of Strategic Management*, 3rd Edition. Mason, OH: Cengage. http://www.foxebook.net/essentials-of-strategic-management-3rd-edition.
6. Copeland, T., Koller, T., and Murrin, J. (1996). *Valuation: Measuring and Managing the Value of Companies*. New York: Wiley.
7. Rumelt, R.P. (1991). How much does industry matter? *Strategic Management Journal*, 12: 167–185.
8. Porter, M.E. (1985). *Competitive Advantage: Creating and Sustaining Superior Performance*. New York: The Free Press.
9. Aberman, J. (2011). Should entrepreneurs be required to work hard? Amplifier Ventures blog. November 30. http://www.amplifierventures.com/2011/11.
10. Wikipedia. (2018). Value proposition. http://en.wikipedia.org/wiki/Value_proposition.
11. Kaplan, R.S., and Norton, D.P. (2004). *Strategy Maps: Converting Intangible Assets into Tangible Outcomes*. Boston, MA: Harvard Business Press.
12. Humphrey, A. (2005). SWOT analysis for management consulting. *SRI Alumni Newsletter*, December (SRI International).
13. Not Boring. (2018). Business partners. http://www.notboring.com/jokes/work/5.htm.
14. Wikipedia. (2018). Hypercompetition. http://en.wikipedia.org/wiki/Hypercompetition.
15. McGonagle, J.J., and Vella, C.M. (2002). *Bottom Line Competitive Intelligence*. Westport, CT: Quorum Books.
16. McGonagle, J.J. and Vella, C.M. (2012). What is competitive intelligence and why should you care about it? In *Proactive Intelligence*. London: Springer.

17. Hodges, J. (2007). Thou shall not steal your competitors secrets. *Moneywatch*, March 28. http://www.cbsnews.com/news/thou-shalt-not-steal-thy-competitors-secrets.
18. McGonagle, J.J. and Vella, C.M. (2012). What is competitive intelligence and why should you care about it? In *Proactive Intelligence*. London: Springer.
19. Zack, M.H. (1999). Competing on knowledge. In *Handbook of Business Strategy*, pp. 81–88. New York: Faulkner & Gray. http://providersedge.com/docs/km_articles/Competing_on_Knowledge.pdf.
20. Oceon Tomo. (2015). Annual study of intangible asset market value from Ocean Tomo, LLC. http://www.oceantomo.com/2015/03/04/2015-intangible-asset-market-value-study.
21. WhatIs.com. (2015). Business counterintelligence (business CI). http://whatis.techtarget.com/definition/business-counterintelligence-business-CI.
22. Office of the National Counterintelligence Executive. Protecting key assets: A corporate counterintelligence guide. https://www.ncsc.gov/publications/reports/fecie_all/ProtectingKeyAssets_CorporateCIGuide.pdf.
23. Fuld, L.M. (1995). *The New Competitor Intelligence*. New York: Wiley.
24. Fuld and Company. (1999). Competing on knowledge. In *Handbook of Business Strategy*, pp. 81–88. New York: Faulkner & Gray.
25. Allen, K., and Economy, P. (2000). *The Complete MBA for Dummies*, pp. 66–67. New York: Wiley.

12

Product–Market Fit

12.1 Introduction

Building an innovative product is key to entrepreneurship, and that process is predictable. Entrepreneurship is chaotic and unpredictable, and this chapter will bring some method to the madness.

You have an idea for an innovative product, but answer the following questions:

- Who will buy it? Who is your target customer?
- How large is your target market? Is it large enough?
- How do you design and build your product? How do you scale up?
- How long before you can start selling? Are there barriers to entry?

The key step in the *innovation process* is the *product–market fit* (PMF) concept. PMF is the degree to which a product satisfies a strong market demand. PMF is now identified as the Golden Rule to building a successful venture in which the company meets early adopters, gathers feedback, and gauges interest in its product(s).[1]

The PMF concept was developed and named by Andy Rachleff (co-founder of Benchmark Capital). The core of Rachleff's idea for PMF was based on his analysis of the investing style of the pioneering venture capitalist and Sequoia founder Don Valentine.

Rachleff famously quipped, "When a great team meets a lousy market, market wins. When a lousy team meets a great market, market wins. When a great team meets a great market, something special happens."[2] Further, "If you address a market that really wants your product—if the dogs are eating the dog food—then you can screw up almost everything in the company and you will succeed. Conversely, if you're really good at execution but the dogs don't want to eat the dog food, you have no chance of winning."

In 2007, Marc Andreessen wrote a seminal article entitled "The Only Thing that Matters." According to Andreessen, "Product/market fit means being in a good market with a product that can satisfy that market."[3]

Andreessen emphasizes that *market matters most*: "You can obviously screw up a great market—and that has been done, and not infrequently—but assuming the team is baseline competent and the product is fundamentally acceptable, a great market will tend to equal success and a poor market will tend to equal failure." That's why time spent building a business around the product alone is pointless: "Best case, it's going to be a zombie. … In a terrible market, you can have the best product in the world and an absolutely killer team, and it doesn't matter–you're going to fail. You'll break your pick for years trying to find customers who don't exist for your marvelous product, and your wonderful team will eventually get demoralized and quit, and your startup will die." The converse is also true. You can have an OK team and a buggy and incomplete product but if the market is great and you are the best product available success can happen both suddenly and quickly. That success won't last unless those products are fixed, but at least the business has the beginnings of something wonderful.

12.2 An Elusive Concept

The PMF concept has undergone modifications from its humble beginnings. Table 12.1 lists some of the most popular definitions.

Fortunately, the PMF concept can be sequentially applied by startups in their initial stages by following the Aulet method (Table 12.2).[4]

TABLE 12.1

Definitions of Product–Market Fit

Marc Andreessen	"Product/market fit means being in a good market with a product that can satisfy that market."
	Many people interpret PMF as creating a so-called minimum viable product that addresses and solves a problem or need that exists.
Sean Ellis	PMF is a precondition for effectively scaling marketing for a company in his startup marketing pyramid.
Steve Blank	Referred to the concept of PMF as a step in between customer validation (step 2 in his book *The Four Steps to the Epiphany*) and customer creation.

TABLE 12.2

Simplified Aulet Method

Market Segmentation	Who is your customer?
Beachhead Market	Making your first sale.
Quantify Value Proposition	Benefits to the customer.
Pricing Framework	How will you make a profit?
Sales Forecast	Cost of customer acquisition (COCA).
Show Dogs Will Eat the Dog Food	Does your customer like the product offering?

12.3 Product–Market Fit in the Real World

"TurboTax Deluxe searches more than 350 tax deductions and credits so you get maximum refund, guaranteed." That is the slogan adopted by Turbo Tax to promote its software product. And it works: TurboTax controlled 65% of the do-it-yourself market for tax software, according to UBS analysts.

TurboTax is an American tax preparation software package developed by Michael A. Chipman of Chipsoft in the mid-1980s. The Intuit Corporation acquired Chipsoft, based in San Diego, in 1993. Chipsoft, now known as the Intuit Consumer Tax Group, is still based in San Diego, having moved into a new office complex in 2007. Intuit is headquartered in Mountain View, California.[5]

Intuit (the parent company of TurboTax) had revenue of $4.2 billion in the fiscal year ended July 31, 2015, with approximately 7700 employees in major offices in the United States, Canada, India, the United Kingdom, Singapore, and Australia.

Figure 12.1, is a graphical representation of the PMF used by TurboTax to become the market leader in the tax software business segment.

TurboTax is one of the most popular income tax preparation software packages in the United States, along with its main competitors, Jackson Hewitt, H&R Block at Home, TaxSlayer, and TaxAct.

**Product-Market fit
Turbo Tax example**

FIGURE 12.1
Turbo Tax software filled an important market need (simplified tax filing).

There are a number of different versions, including TurboTax Deluxe, TurboTax Premier, and so on. TurboTax is available for both federal and state income tax returns. The software is designed to guide users through their tax returns step by step. The TurboTax software provides taxpayers additional support for their self-prepared returns by offering Audit Defense from TaxResources, Inc.

Typically, TurboTax federal software is released late in the year and the state software is released mid-January to mid-February. TurboTax normally releases its new versions as soon as the IRS completes revisions to the forms and approves the TurboTax versions, usually late in the tax year. The process is similar for states that collect income taxes.

Intuit creates business and financial management solutions that help simplify the business of life for small businesses, consumers, and accounting professionals. With flagship products and services that include QuickBooks and TurboTax, Intuit helps customers solve important business and financial management problems such as running a small business, paying bills, and filing income taxes. ProSeries and Lacerte are Intuit's leading tax preparation offerings for professional accountants.

12.3.1 TurboTax's "Secret Sauce"

What propelled TurboTax to the top of its market category? TurboTax improved tax preparation for the average taxpayer so profoundly, nobody could imagine going back to the old ways. TurboTax simplified their product line, moving from the desktop to the Internet and mobile devices to provide more value, as depicted in Figure 12.2.

The 2016, Intuit Form 10K states the following:[6]

- *Our Growth Strategy*: Based on our assessment of key technology and demographic trends—an increasingly borderless world, the prevalence of mobile devices, and the scalability of the cloud—we see significant opportunities to drive future growth by continuing to solve the unmet needs of consumers, small businesses, and accounting professionals. Our evolving growth strategy includes three key elements:
- *Focus on the product—we call it "Delivering awesome product experiences."* Computing devices are moving to the palm of our hands in the form of tablets and smart phones. Our TurboTax solutions, for example, let customers prepare and file their entire tax returns online, via tablet, mobile phone or desktop computer. We also believe that a key factor in growing our customer base is delivering an amazing first-use experience so our customers can get the value they expect from our offerings as quickly and easily as possible.
- *Creating network effect platforms—we call it "Enabling the contributions of others."* We expect to solve problems faster and more

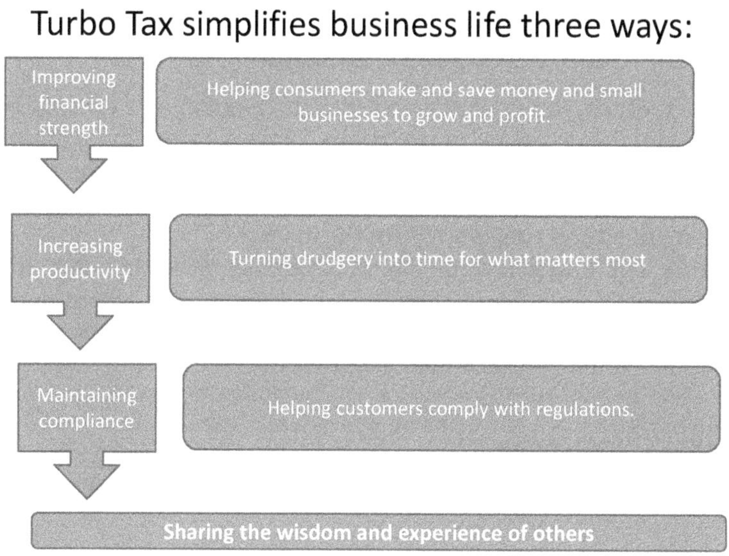

Turbo Tax simplifies business life three ways:

Improving financial strength	Helping consumers make and save money and small businesses to grow and profit.
Increasing productivity	Turning drudgery into time for what matters most
Maintaining compliance	Helping customers comply with regulations.

Sharing the wisdom and experience of others

FIGURE 12.2
Consumers able to file taxes, and get maximum refunds, like professionals.

efficiently for our growing customer base by moving to more open platforms with application programming interfaces that enable the contributions of end users and third-party developers. One example of this is QuickBooks Online, which allows small business customers all over the world to localize, configure, and add value to the offering.

- *Leveraging our data for our customers' benefit—we call it "Using data to create delight."* Our customers generate valuable data that we seek to appropriately use to deliver better products and breakthrough benefits by eliminating the need to enter data, helping them make better decisions, and improving transactions and interactions.

This strategy recognizes the emergence and influence of the digital generation, the increasing relevance of social networks, and customers' growing reliance on the Internet, mobile devices and information-based technology to manage important financial tasks. It also acknowledges the potential of new market opportunities around the world. The result is a global market that is shifting from traditional services that are paper-based, human-produced, and brick-and-mortar bound, to one where people understand, demand, and embrace the benefits of connected services.

We continue to make significant progress in this environment. Connected services (total service and other revenue) generated $3.0 billion or 73% of our total revenue in fiscal 2015, compared with about 50% of our total revenue seven years ago.

12.4 eBay's Product–Market Fit Example

eBay is the most successful *first mover* into the E-commerce entrant. It revolutionized social *buy and sell* transactions, bypassing the brick-and-mortar middlemen stores. eBay pioneered the popularity of the online auction by selling everything from antiques to automobiles. It is estimated to host 90% of online auctions and controls 85% of the market

eBay was the brainchild of Pierre Omidyar, who in 1995 founded AuctionWeb with the idea of providing an Internet site where person-to-person trading could take place. Buyers and sellers rushed to the site, and by 1997, AuctionWeb had become eBay (Figure 12.3).

12.4.1 eBay's "Secret Sauce"

eBay's distinguishing characteristics can be summarized as follows:

- Auction-based online sales of products (and sometimes services) where users try to outbid one another by placing a higher maximum amount; Dutch and reverse-auction style also recently available in some regions

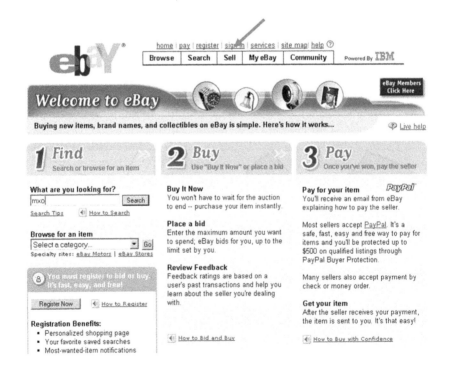

FIGURE 12.3
eBay quickly became the industry standard.

- Transaction fees for listing (regardless of whether item sells or not) and additional fees for premium auction features (i.e., extra photos, Buy It Now, Feature It!, etc.) or premium seller memberships

The e-commerce (selling online) PMF was achieved with the following customer sequence:

- Select a category
- Write a title
- Item specifics
- Item description
- Add pictures
- Pricing and duration
- Item location
- Payment and shipping information
- Communicate with the buyer
- Receive payment
- Ship item to the buyer
- Request buyer feedback

Figure 12.4 is a graphical representation of the PMF used by eBay to become the market leader in the online selling business segment.

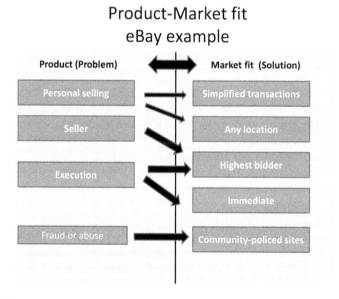

FIGURE 12.4
Purchasing products online made ridiculously simple.

eBay Inc. is a global commerce leader, which includes our Marketplace, StubHub and Classifieds platforms.[7] Collectively, we connect millions of buyers and sellers around the world. The technologies and services that power our platforms are designed to enable sellers worldwide to organize and offer their inventory for sale, and buyers to find and purchase it, virtually anytime and anywhere. Our Marketplace platforms include our online marketplace located at www.ebay.com, its localized counterparts and the eBay mobile apps. We believe that these are among the world's largest and most vibrant marketplaces for discovering great value and unique selection. Our StubHub platforms include our online ticket platform located at www.stubhub.com, its localized counterparts, the StubHub mobile apps and Ticketbis.

These platforms connect fans with their favorite sporting events, shows and artists and enable them to buy and sell tens of thousands of tickets whenever they want. Our Classifieds platforms include a collection of brands such as mobile.de, Kijiji, Gumtree, Marktplaats, eBay Kleinanzeigen and others. Offering online classifieds in more than 1,500 cities around the world, these platforms help people find whatever they are looking for in their local communities.

Our platforms are accessible through a traditional online experience (e.g., desktop and laptop computers), from mobile devices (e.g., smartphones and tablets) and by API (platform access for third-party software developers). Our multi-screen approach offers downloadable, easy-to-use applications for iOS and Android mobile devices that allow access to ebay.com and some of our other websites and vertical shopping experiences. In addition, our platform is increasingly based on open source technologies that provide industry-standard ways for software developers and merchants to access our application programming interfaces, or APIs, to develop software and solutions for commerce.

Offerings. Delivering the best choice, the most relevance and the most powerful selling platform Our objective is to drive the best choice, the most relevance and the most powerful selling platform for our buyers and sellers. We continue to focus on customizing our buying and selling experiences to make it easier for users to list, find and buy items by offering formats dedicated to specific products or categories. On our Marketplace platforms, we have built specialized experiences such as eBay Deals, which offers a variety of products in multiple categories at discounted prices with free shipping. Other experiences include Fashion, Motors and Electronics.

One of the changes we are making to our Marketplace platform is the shift to better understand, organize and leverage the inventory on eBay. This initiative, which we call structured data, will allow us to expand new experiences to more traffic and drive data quality. As one of the world's largest ticket marketplaces, StubHub connects people through inspiring live experiences. Event-goers can find more than 10 million live sports, music, theater and other events in more than 40 countries on our StubHub platforms, and can browse, buy and sell anytime, anywhere through desktop and mobile devices.

As a world leader in online classifieds, eBay's Classifieds platforms are designed to help people list their products and services generally for free, find whatever they are looking for in their local communities and trade at a local level. eBay Classifieds Group's 11 global brands offer both horizontal and vertical experiences, such as motors, real estate and jobs.

Business model and pricing. Our business model and pricing are designed so that our business is successful primarily when our sellers are successful. We partner, but do not compete with, our sellers to enable their success on eBay's platforms. Our eBay Top Rated Seller program rewards qualifying sellers with fee discounts and improved search standing for qualifying listings if they are able to maintain excellent customer service ratings and meet specified criteria for shipping and returns. We believe that sellers who fulfill these standards help promote our goal of maintaining an online marketplace that is safe and hassle-free.

eBay Money Back Guarantee covers most items purchased on our websites in a number of countries, including the United States, the United Kingdom, Germany and Australia, through a qualifying payment method and protects most buyers with respect to items that are not received or are received but not as described in the listing. Some purchases, including some vehicles, are not covered. eBay Money Back Guarantee provides coverage for the purchase price of the item, plus original shipping costs, for a limited period of time from the original date of transaction, and includes a streamlined interface to help buyers and sellers navigate the process.

The size and scale of our platforms are designed to enable our buyers and sellers to leverage economies of scale and capital investment, for example in sales and marketing, mobile, customer acquisition and customer service.

Providing value to buyers and sellers. We believe that our sellers offer some of the best value and deals available for a number of consumer products. In the United States, the United Kingdom and Germany, the majority of transactions included free shipping during 2016. We have developed a number of features on our Marketplace platforms in the areas of trust and safety (including our Seller Performance Standards, eBay Top Rated Seller program, eBay Money Back Guarantee, Verified Rights Owner Program and Feedback Forum), customer support and value-added tools and services, as well as loyalty programs (for both buyers and sellers). These features are designed to build trust and make users more comfortable buying and selling with unknown partners and completing transactions online or through mobile devices, as well as rewarding our top sellers for their loyalty.

For sellers in particular, in 2016 we implemented a number of changes to our seller policies to primarily help small- and medium-sized sellers be more successful on our platforms and better reward sellers who provide exceptional service to eBay buyers. These changes included providing more objective standards; giving sellers the ability to customize how they manage returns based on their specific business needs; and launching the Seller Hub, which puts a seller's listing and marketing tools in one central place (Table 12.3).

TABLE 12.3

Choice to Buyers and Sellers

Sellers	Can choose to list their products and services through fixed-price listings or an auction-style format. The fixed-price format on eBay allows buyers and sellers to close transactions at a predetermined price set by the seller. Sellers also are able to signal that they would be willing to close the transaction at a lower price through the Best Offer feature. Additionally, our auction-style format allows a seller to select a minimum price for opening bids.
Sellers	Can list items that are new, refurbished and used, and common and rare on our Marketplace platforms.
Buyers	Can search for and purchase items that are new, refurbished and used, and common and rare on our Marketplace platforms.
Buyers	Can have items shipped to them through shipping options offered by the seller and selected by the buyer on our Marketplace platforms. For certain items purchased from certain retailers, buyers can pick up items they purchased online or through mobile devices in one of the retailer's physical stores (which we refer to as *in-store pickup*).

12.5 The Social Media Phenomenon

There was a time when consumers searching for product ratings, reliability reports and expert insights relied on publications such as consumer reports. Suppose a consumer is interested in learning about self-driving cars, where microsecond management can mean the difference between a safe journey and a dangerous one. The new consumer is now likely to rely on social media for their purchase decision.

What is social media? Social media refers to computer-mediated technologies that facilitate the creation and sharing of information, ideas, and careers. Social media uses the "wisdom of crowds" to connect information in a collaborative manner. Social media can take many different forms, including Internet forums, message boards, weblogs, wikis, podcasts, pictures, and videos, and other forms of expression via virtual communities and networks.[8]

The meaning of the term *social media* is derived from two words. *Media* generally refers to advertising and the communication of ideas or information through publications/channels. *Social* implies the free interaction of individuals within a group or community. Taken together, *social media* refers to all communication/publication platforms that are generated and sustained by the interpersonal interaction of individuals through the specific medium or tool.

A phenomenon of social media is the extraordinary power it confers to the consumer. The consumer need not rely on classical advertisements or the supplier. The *age of information* came in 1990 with the advent of the Amazon and Google. We are now in the *age of the consumer*, where a simple click opens the universe to the savvy consumer, as shown in Figure 12.5.

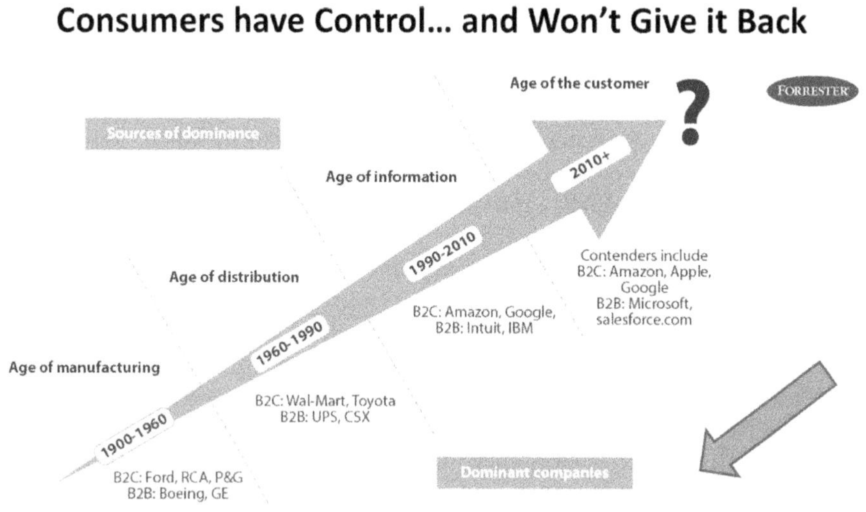

Consumers have Control... and Won't Give it Back

FIGURE 12.5
The Internet gives consumers unprecedented purchasing control.

Social media uses Web-based technologies, desktop computers, and mobile technologies (e.g., smartphones and tablets) to create highly interactive platforms through which individuals, communities, and organizations can share, co-create, discuss, and modify user-generated content or premade content posted online. They introduce substantial and pervasive changes to communication between businesses, organizations, communities, and individuals.

Businesses have new social media strategies, all information is easily accessible, customers are more engaged, and the power of word of mouth can make or break a business in just few days. Something that did not exist last year, people are taking for granted this year. That is the speed of social media.

According to a report by Markets and Markets,[9] the global social media analytics market is expected to grow from $1.60 billion in 2015 to $40 billion by 2020, at a compound annual growth rate (CAGR) of 27.6% from 2015 to 2020. The social media analytics market is growing rapidly because of the transition from traditional *business intelligence* (BI) techniques to advanced analytics techniques and the massive surge in the number of social media users.

12.5.1 Defining Social Media Academically

Kaplan and Haenlein[10] define social media as "a group of online, Internet-based applications that build on the ideological and technological foundations of Web 2.0, and that allow the creation and exchange of user-generated content." The term *social media* encompasses digital social networking sites, collaborative services, blogs, content hosting sites, and virtual communities. In this context, *online* or *digital* refers to the electronic posting of information using computers, smart phones, and so on. *Web 2.0* refers to those resources in which self-created content by users is posted for unlimited public dissemination by means of media-sharing platforms.

Social media creates highly interactive platforms through which individuals and communities share, co-create, discuss, and modify user-generated content.[11] It introduces substantial and pervasive changes to communication between organizations, communities, and individuals.

Social media differs from traditional/industrial media in many aspects such as reach, frequency, usability, immediacy, permanence, and quality.[12,13] For content contributors, the benefits of participating in social media have gone beyond simply social sharing to building reputations and bringing in career opportunities and monetary income.[14]

In 2016, Merriam-Webster defined social media as "forms of electronic communication (such as Web sites) through which people create online communities to share information, ideas, personal messages, etc." The term *social media* is usually used to describe social networking sites such as those described in Table 12.4.

Social media technologies take many different forms, including blogs, business networks, enterprise social networks, forums, microblogs, photo sharing, products/services review, social bookmarking, social gaming, social networks, video sharing, and virtual worlds. The development of social media started off with simple platforms such as sixdegrees.com. Unlike instant messaging clients such as ICQ and AOL's AIM or chat clients such as IRC, iChat, or Chat Television, sixdegrees.com was the first online business that was created for real people, using their real names.

However, the first social networks were short-lived because their users lost interest. The Social Network Revolution has led to the rise of networking sites. Research shows that audiences spend 22% of their time on social

TABLE 12.4

Popular Social Networking Sites

Facebook	Online social networking site that allows users to create their personal profiles, share photos and videos, and communicate with other users
Twitter	Internet service that allows users to post "tweets" for their followers to see updates in real time
LinkedIn	Networking website for the business community that allows users to create professional profiles, post resumes, and communicate with other professionals and jobseekers
Pinterest	Online community that allows users to display photos of items found on the Web by "pinning" them and sharing ideas with others
Snapchat	App for mobile devices that allows users to send and share photos of themselves doing their daily activities

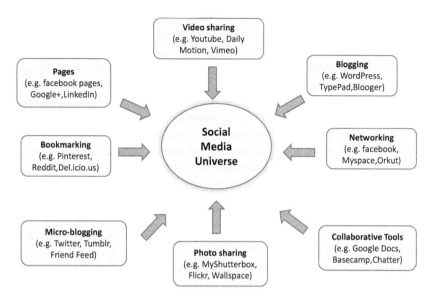

Social media is a broad term used to describe all the different online technology tools that enable users to communicate effortlessly via the Internet through sharing information and resources.

FIGURE 12.6
Social media at a glance.

networking sites, thus proving how popular social media platforms have become. This increase is because of smartphones, which are now in the daily lives of most humans.

There are many different types of social media. Figure 12.6 highlights some popular types and corresponding examples.

12.5.2 Social Media History

The era of social media started when Abelson[15] founded Open Diary, the first online blogging[16] community. In 1979, Tom Truscott and Jim Ellis from Duke University created Usenet,[17] a worldwide discussion system that allowed Internet users to post public messages. Usenet was conceived and publicly established in 1980 at the University of North Carolina at Chapel Hill and Duke University,[18] over a decade before the World Wide Web was developed and the general public received access to the Internet, making it one of the oldest computer network communications systems still in widespread use.

The term *weblog* was first used at the same time and truncated as *blog* a year later when one blogger jokingly transformed the noun *weblog* into the sentence "We blog." The growing availability of high-speed Internet access further added to the popularity of the concept, leading to the creation of social networking sites such as MySpace (2003) and Facebook (2004).

What is Social Media?

Social media are the various forms of user generated content
and the collection of websites and applications that enable
people to interact and share information online

- Social networking sites (*Facebook, Twitter, Myspace*)
- Blogs (*Wordpress*)
- Video sharing sites (*YouTube*)
- Photo sharing sites (*Flickr*)
- Crowdsourcing (*Wikipedia*)
- User reviews (*Amazon, Yelp*)
- Streaming sites (*Ustream*)
- Social bookmarking (*Digg, del.icio.us*)

FIGURE 12.7
Social media definition.

After the invention of blogging, social media began to explode in popularity. Sites such as MySpace and LinkedIn gained prominence in the early 2000s, and sites such as Photobucket and Flickr facilitated online photo sharing. YouTube came out in 2005, creating an entirely new way for people to communicate and share with each other across great distances.[19]

By 2006, Facebook and Twitter had both become available to users throughout the world. These sites remain some of the most popular social networks on the Internet. Other sites such as Tumblr, Spotify, Foursquare, and Pinterest began popping up to fill specific social networking niches.

These developments, in turn, coined the term *social media* and contributed to the prominence it has today. The most recent addition to this glamorous grouping has been so-called virtual worlds—that is, computer-based simulated environments inhabited by three-dimensional avatars. Perhaps the best-known virtual world is that of Linden Lab's Second Life.[20] Figure 12.7 summarizes social media.

12.5.3 Business Potential

Some major vendors that offer social media analytics solutions and services globally are the SAS Institute, IBM Corporation, Oracle Corporation, Adobe Systems, Salesforce.com, GoodData, HootSuite Media, Tableau Software, NetBase Solutions (all based in the United States), and SAP SE (Germany). These vendors have adopted different types of organic and inorganic growth strategies, such as new product launches, partnerships and collaborations, and mergers and acquisitions, to expand their offerings in the social media analytics market.

Although social media accessed via desktop computers offers a variety of opportunities for companies in a wide range of business sectors, mobile social media, which users are accessing "on the go" via tablet computer or smartphone, can take advantage of the location- and time-sensitive awareness of users. Mobile social media tools can be used for marketing research, communication, sales promotions/discounts, and relationship development/loyalty programs, according to Andreas Kaplan.[21]

- **Marketing research:** Mobile social media applications offer data about offline consumer movements at a level of detail heretofore limited to online companies. Any firm can know the exact time at which a customer entered one of its outlets, as well as know the social media comments made during the visit.

- **Communication:** Mobile social media communication takes two forms: company-to-consumer (in which a company may establish a connection to a consumer based on its location and provide reviews about locations nearby) and user-generated content. For example, McDonald's offered $5 and $10 gift cards to 100 users randomly selected among those checking in at one of its restaurants. This promotion increased check-ins by 33% (from 2146 to 2865), resulted in over 50 articles and blog posts, and prompted several hundred word-of-mouth customers plus consumer blogs.

- **Sales promotions and discounts:** Although customers have had to use printed coupons in the past, mobile social media allows companies to tailor promotions to specific users at specific times.

- **Relationship development and loyalty programs:** In order to increase long-term relationships with customers, companies can develop loyalty programs that allow customers who check in via social media regularly at a location to earn discounts or perks. For example, American Eagle Outfitters remunerates such customers with a tiered 10%, 15%, or 20% discount on their total purchase.

- **e-Commerce:** Social media sites are increasingly implementing marketing-friendly strategies, creating platforms that are mutually beneficial for users, businesses, and the networks themselves. The user who posts her or his comments about a company's product or service benefits because they are able to share their views with their online friends and acquaintances. The company benefits because it obtains insight (positive or negative) about how their product or service is viewed by consumers. Mobile social media applications such as Amazon and Pinterest have started to influence an upward trend in the popularity and accessibility of e-commerce or online purchases.

e-Commerce businesses may refer to social media as consumer-generated media (CGM). A common thread running through all definitions of social media is a blending of technology and social interaction for the co-creation of value for the business or organization that is using it. People obtain valuable information, education, news, and other data from electronic and print media. Social media is distinct from industrial or traditional media such as newspapers, magazines, television, and film as they are comparatively inexpensive and accessible (at least once a person has already acquired Internet access and a computer).

Social media enables anyone (even private individuals) to publish or access information. Industrial media generally requires significant resources to publish information, as in most cases the articles go through many revisions before being published. This process adds to the cost and the resulting market price. Originally, social media was only used by individuals, but now it is used by businesses, charities, and also in government and politics.

One characteristic shared by both social and industrial media is the ability to reach small or large audiences; for example, a blog post or a television show may reach no people or millions of people. Some of the attributes that help describe the differences between social and industrial media are as follows:

1. **Quality:** In industrial (traditional) publishing—mediated by a publisher—the typical range of quality is substantially narrower (skewing to the high-quality side) than in niche, unmediated markets such as user-generated social media posts. The main challenge posed by content in social media sites is the fact that the distribution of quality has high variance: from very high-quality items to low-quality, sometimes even abusive or inappropriate content.

2. **Reach:** Both industrial and social media technologies provide scale and are capable of reaching a global audience. Industrial media, however, typically uses a centralized framework for organization, production, and dissemination, whereas social media is by its very nature more decentralized, less hierarchical, and distinguished by multiple points of production and utility.

3. **Frequency:** The number of times users access a type of media per day. Heavy social media users, such as young people, check their social media account numerous times throughout the day.

4. **Accessibility:** The means of production for industrial media are typically government or corporate (privately owned); social media tools are generally available to the public at little or no cost, or they are supported by advertising revenue. While social media tools are available to anyone with access to the Internet and a computer or mobile device, due to the digital divide, the poorest segment of the population lacks access. Low-income people may have more access to traditional media (TV, radio, etc.), as an inexpensive TV and aerial or radio costs much less than an inexpensive computer or mobile device. Moreover, in many regions, TV or radio owners can tune in to free over-the-air programming; computer or mobile device owners need Internet access to go on social media sites.

5. **Usability:** Industrial media production typically requires specialized skills and training. For example, in the 1970s, to record a pop song, an aspiring singer would have to rent time in an expensive professional recording studio and hire an audio engineer. Conversely, most social media activities, such as posting a video of oneself singing a song require only modest reinterpretation of existing skills (assuming a person understands Web 2.0 technologies); in theory, anyone with access to the Internet can operate the means of social media production and post digital pictures, videos, or text online.

6. **Immediacy:** The time lag between communications produced by industrial media can be long (days, weeks, or even months, by the time the content has been reviewed by various editors and fact-checkers) compared with social media (which can be capable of virtually instantaneous responses). The immediacy of social media can be seen as a strength, in that it enables regular people to instantly communicate their opinions and information. At the same time, the immediacy of social media can also be seen as a weakness, as the lack of fact-checking and editorial "gatekeepers" facilitates the circulation of hoaxes and fake news.

7. **Permanence:** Industrial media, once created, cannot be altered (e.g., once a magazine article or paper book is printed and distributed, changes cannot be made to that same article in that print run), whereas social media posts can be altered almost instantaneously, when the user decides to edit their post or due to comments from other readers.

Community media constitutes a hybrid of industrial and social media. Though community owned, some community radio, TV, and newspapers are run by professionals and some by amateurs. They use both social and industrial media frameworks. Social media has also been recognized for the way it has changed how public relations professionals conduct their jobs. They have provided an open arena where people are free to exchange ideas on companies, brands, and products. Social media provides an environment where users and PR professionals can converse and where PR professionals can promote their brand and improve their company's image by listening and responding to what the public is saying about their product.

12.5.4 Business Performance

Social media has a strong influence on business activities and business performance. There are four channels by which social media resources are transformed into business performance capabilities.

1. **Social capital** represents the extent to which social media affects firms' and organizations' relationships with society and the degree to which their use of social media increases corporate social performance capabilities.

2. **Revealed preferences** represents the extent to which social media exposes customers' likings (e.g., "likes" and followers) and increases a firm's financial capabilities (e.g., stock price, revenue, profit), or for nonprofits, increases their donations, volunteerism rate, and so on.

3. **Social marketing** represents the extent to which social marketing resources (e.g., online conversations, sharing links, online presence, sending text messages) are used to increase a firm's financial capabilities (e.g., sales, acquiring new customers) or a nonprofit's voluntary sector goals.

4. **Social corporate networking** refers to the informal ties and linkages of corporate/organizational staff with other people from their field or industry, clients, customers, and other members of the public, which were formed through social networks. Social corporate networking can increase operational performance capabilities in many ways, as sales staff can find new clients; marketing staff can learn about client/customer needs and demand; and management can learn about the public perceptions of their strategy or approach.

There are four tools or approaches that engage experts, customers, suppliers, and employees in the development of products and services using social media. Companies and other organizations can use these tools and approaches to improve their business capacity and performance.

1. **Customer relationship management** (CRM) is an approach to managing a company's interaction with current and potential future customers that tries to analyze data about customers' history with a company and to improve business relationships with customers, specifically focusing on customer retention and ultimately driving sales growth. One important aspect of the CRM approach is the systems of CRM that compile data from a range of different communication channels, including a company's website, telephone, e-mail, live chat, marketing materials, and social media. Through the CRM approach and the systems used to facilitate CRM, businesses learn more about their target audiences and how to best cater to their needs. However, adopting the CRM approach may also occasionally lead to favoritism within an audience of consumers, resulting in dissatisfaction among customers and defeating the purpose of CRM.

2. **Innovation** can be defined simply as a "new idea, device, or method" or as the application of better solutions that meet new requirements, unarticulated needs, or existing market needs. This is accomplished through more effective products, processes, services, technologies, or business models that are readily available to markets, governments,

and society. The term *innovation* can be defined as something original and more effective—and, as a consequence, new—that "breaks into" the market or society. It is related to, but not the same as, invention. Innovation is often manifested via the engineering process. Innovation is generally considered to be the result of a process that brings together various novel ideas in a way that they affect society. In industrial economics, innovations are created and found empirically from services to meet the growing consumer demand.

3. **Training** in social media techniques, tactics, and unwritten rules may not be needed for "digital natives," such as workers who are already comfortable and experienced with using social media. However, for workers who are not familiar with social media, formal or informal training may be needed. Brand management and engagement is done differently on social media platforms than over traditional advertising formats such as TV and radio ads. To give just one example, with traditional ads, customers cannot respond to the advertisement. However, if an organization makes a major gaffe or politically incorrect statement on social media, customers and other regular citizens can immediately post comments about the advertisement.

4. **Knowledge management** could be done in traditional small businesses such as coffeehouses and ice cream parlors just by using the owner-proprietor's own memory of his key customers, their preferences, and their client service expectations. However, with the shift to national or even multinational e-commerce businesses that operate online, companies are generating far more data on transactions for a single person or even a team to grasp only in their memory. As such, 2010-era global e-commerce firms typically use a range of digital tools to track, monitor, and analyze the huge streams of data their businesses are generating, a process called *data mining*.

12.5.5 Most Popular Services in 2017

The following is a list of the leading social networks based on the number of active user accounts as of April 2017.

- Facebook: 1,968,000,000 users
- WhatsApp: 1,200,000,000 users
- YouTube: 1,000,000,000 users
- Facebook Messenger: 1,000,000,000 users
- WeChat: 889,000,000 users
- QQ: 868,000,000 users

- Instagram: 600,000,000 users
- QZone: 595,000,000 users
- Tumblr: 550,000,000 users
- Twitter: 319,000,000 users
- Sina Weibo: 313,000,000 users
- Baidu Tieba: 300,000,000 users
- Snapchat: 300,000,000 users
- Skype: 300,000,000 users
- Viber: 260,000,000 users
- Line: 220,000,000 users
- Pinterest 150,000,000 users

12.6 Social Media Marketing

According to Neti,[22] there are two benefits of social media that are important to businesses.

1. Cost reduction by decreasing staff time
2. Increased probability of revenue generation

Social media marketing (SMM) consists of the attempt to use social media to persuade consumers that products and/or services are worthwhile. SMM is marketing using online communities, social networks, blog marketing, and more. Thus, social media enables companies to

- Share their expertise and knowledge (awareness)
- Tap into the wisdom of their consumers (perception, judgment)
- Enable customers to help customers (referrals, reputation)
- Engage prospects through customer evangelism (word of mouth)

Significantly different from conventional marketing strategies, SMM offers three distinct advantages:

1. It provides a window to marketers to not only present products/ services to customers but also listen to customers' grievances and suggestions.

2. It makes it easy for marketers to identify various peer groups or influencers among various groups, who in turn can become brand evangelists and help in the organic growth of a brand.
3. All this is done at negligible cost (compared with conventional customer outreach programs) as most of the social networking sites are free.

SMM is most effective in the following areas:

- Generating consumer exposure to businesses
- Increasing traffic/subscribers
- Building new business partnerships
- Increasing search engine rankings
- Generating immediate qualified leads
- Selling more products and services
- Reducing overall marketing expenses

According to Ramos,[23] in this "age of the customer," businesses that succeed will focus strategy, energy, and budget on processes that enhance knowledge of and engagement with customers—and prioritize investment in customer relationships over maintaining traditional competitive barriers, as shown in Figure 12.8.

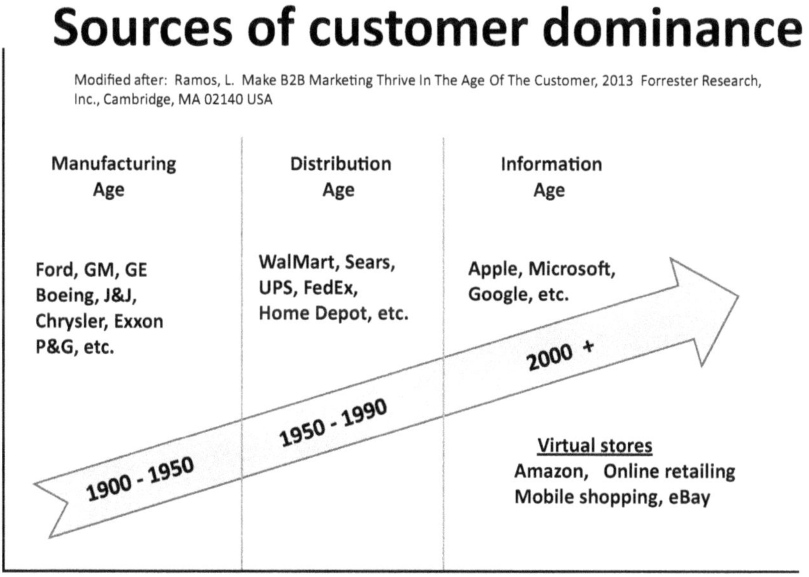

Sources of customer dominance

Modified after: Ramos, L. Make B2B Marketing Thrive In The Age Of The Customer, 2013 Forrester Research, Inc., Cambridge, MA 02140 USA

Manufacturing Age	Distribution Age	Information Age
Ford, GM, GE Boeing, J&J, Chrysler, Exxon P&G, etc.	WalMart, Sears, UPS, FedEx, Home Depot, etc.	Apple, Microsoft, Google, etc.

1900 - 1950 1950 - 1990 2000 +

Virtual stores
Amazon, Online retailing
Mobile shopping, eBay

FIGURE 12.8
Customers can make purchasing decisions anytime, anywhere, and for all budgets.

12.6.1 Social Media Influencers

The advent of social media has created a new specialty: that of the *influencers*—that is, *social media influencers*, everyday people who have an outsized influence on their peers by virtue of how much content they share online and who can help to achieve an organization's marketing and business needs. This is because one influencer can reach a few buyers, who in turn can influence many other buyers, as shown schematically in Figure 12.9.

12.6.2 Types of Social Media Influencers

According to Singh, when you think about social influence in the context of your marketing objectives, you must separate social influencers online into three types: referent, expert, and positional (Table 12.5).[24]

As a marketer seeking to deploy social influence marketing techniques, the first question to answer is this: Which social influencers sway your consumers as they make purchasing decisions about your product? After you identify those social influencers, you can determine the best ways to market to them. Any major brand affinity or purchasing decision has referent, expert, and positional social influencers all playing distinct and important

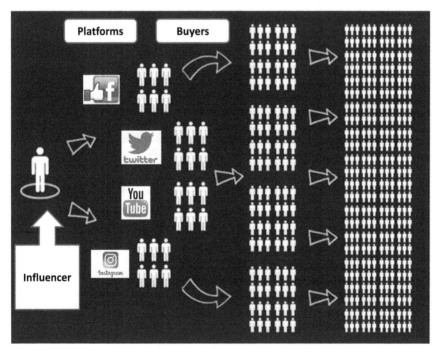

FIGURE 12.9
How social media creates "going viral" messaging.

TABLE 12.5

Social Media Online Influencers

Referent Influencers	A referent influencer is someone who participates on the social platforms. These users are typically in a consumer's social graph and influence brand affinity and purchasing decisions through consumer reviews, by updating their own status and Twitter feeds and by commenting on blogs and forums. In some cases, the social influencers know the consumers personally.
Expert Influencers	A consumer who is mulling over a high-consideration purchase might also consult an expert influencer. An expert influencer is an authority on the product that the consumer is considering purchasing. Also called key influencers, they typically have their own blogs, huge Twitter followings, and rarely know their audiences personally.
Positional Influencers	A positional influencer is closest to both the purchasing decision and to the consumer. Sometimes called peer influencers, they are typically family members or part of the consumer's inner circle. They influence purchasing decisions most directly at the point of purchase and have to live with the results of their family member's or friend's decision as well.

roles. Which one is most important may vary slightly based on the purchase, but the fact remains that you need to account for these three distinct types of social influencers in your marketing campaigns. If you're a marketer trying to positively affect a purchasing decision, you must market not just to the consumer but also to these influencers.

12.6.2.1 Referent Influencers

Because the consumers know and trust their referent influencers, they feel confident that their advisers are also careful and punctilious. As they're people they trust, they value their advice and guidance over most other people. Referent influencers influence purchasing decision more than anyone else at the consideration phase of the marketing funnel, according to "Fluent," the social influence marketing report from Razorfish.[25]

For example, if you decide to make a high-consideration purchase, such as a car, you might start by going online and discussing different cars with a few friends in a discussion forum or on a social network. And then that weekend, you might meet those friends over coffee and carry on that discussion in person. This influence is considered *referent influence* because these friends sway you by the strength of their charisma and interpersonal skills, and they have this sway because you respect them.

12.6.2.2 Expert Influencers

A consumer who's mulling over a high-consideration purchase might also consult an *expert influencer.* An expert influencer is an authority on the product that the consumer is considering purchasing. Also called *key influencers,* they typically have their own blogs and huge Twitter followings, and rarely know their audiences personally.

When considering buying a car, suppose you do not rely just on friends for advice but also visit some car review websites. On these websites, experts rate, rank, and pass judgment on cars. They're the expert social influencers—people who you may not know personally but are recognized as authorities in a certain field. Their influence is derived from the skills or expertise that they—or broadly speaking, their organization—possess based on training.

12.6.2.3 Positional Influencers

A *positional influencer* is closest to both the purchasing decision and to the consumer. Sometimes called *peer influencers*, they are typically family members or part of the consumer's inner circle. They influence purchasing decisions most directly at the point of purchase and have to live with the results of their family member's or friend's decision as well.

Now, you know that you cannot make a high-consideration purchase such as buying a car without discussing it with your partner.

Invariably, you both will drive the car and sit in it as much as each other. It is as much your partner's purchase as it is yours. His or her opinion matters more than anyone else's in this case. Your partner is closest to the purchasing decision and to the consumer and therefore has the most social influence.

12.6.2.4 Types of Influencers

The *Influencer Handbook*[26] categorizes five types of social media *expert influencers*, as shown in Table 12.6.

How much a person is influenced depends on multiple factors. The product itself is the most important one. When buying *low-consideration purchases* (those with a small amount of risk), people rarely seek influence, nor are they easily influenced by others. Buying toothpaste, for example, is a low-consideration purchase because each product may not be that different from the next one, and they are all fairly inexpensive.[27]

On the other hand, buying a new car is typically a *high-consideration purchase* (a purchase that includes a large risk). The price of the car, the maintenance costs, and its reputation for safety all contribute to making it a high-consideration purchase. Social influence plays a much bigger role in car purchases than in toothpaste decisions.

Social influence matters with every purchase, but it matters more with high-consideration purchases than with low-consideration ones. Most consumers realize that when making high-consideration purchases, they can make better and more confident purchasing decisions when they take into account the advice and experience of others who have made those decisions before them. That is how influence works.

TABLE 12.6

Types of Influencers

Category	Identification	Channels of Influence
Formal position of authority	Political/government	Laws and regulations
Opinion Leaders	Leaders/staff	Decision and spending
Decision makers	Business leaders	authority
C-suite		Top-down directives
Individuals or institutions cognized	Academics/scientists	Academic journals
as subject matter experts, advocates,	Industry analysts	Traditional media
and mavens	NGO leaders	New media
Critics; analysts	Consumer activists	Social media
Media elite	Journalists	Traditional media
Columnists	Commentators	New media
Politicos	Talk show hosts	Social media
Cultural elite	Celebrities	Traditional media
Trendsetters	Designers	New media
Fashionistas	Artists	New styles/products
Tastemakers	Musicians	Social media
Creators		
Socially connected	Neighborhood	Personal relationships
Personal relationships	leaders	E-mail lists
E-mail lists	Members of	Social gatherings
Social gatherings	community groups	Websites
Websites	Online networkers	Social media
Social media	Business networkers	

12.6.3 Immutable Laws of Internet Branding

In 2000, the father and daughter Ries team[28] published *The 11 Immutable Laws of Internet Branding*. While *so* much has changed in the practice of online business branding since then, many of their laws are relevant and helpful to growing your business online (Table 12.7).

12.7 Venture Capital and Social Media Nexus

Magnusdottir and Johnson[29] identified seven factors most relevant in a venture capitalist's assessment of social media startup companies. These factors are summarized in Table 12.8.

The following describes each factor in the seven-factor model in greater detail.

1. **Scalability:** Venture capitalists will want to invest in solutions for significantly large target markets. Scalable infrastructure supports the possibility to enlarge the customer base by expanding into new

TABLE 12.7

Ries and Ries 11 Immutable Laws of Internet Branding

1. The Law of Either/Or	View the Internet as an entirely new business, not just another communicating medium.
2. The Law of Interactivity	Internet branding must be interactive and engaging to the customer for best results.
3. The Law of the Common Name	Common names such as Business.com make poor brands.
4. The Law of the Proper Name	Proper names work best. Ries and Ries suggest that the best names will follow most of these eight principles: (1) short, (2) simple, (3) suggestive of the category, (4) unique, (5) alliterative, (6) speakable, (7) shocking, and (8) personalized.
5. The Law of Singularity	The Internet demands a single, unique brand.
6. The Law of Advertising	Advertising on the Internet will eclipse all other forms of advertising.
7. The Law of Globalism	All Web-based businesses are automatically global businesses.
8. The Law of Time	The brand that is first into the prospect's mind—not necessarily the first into the marketplace—develops an insurmountable competitive advantage.
9. The Law of Vanity	Stay focused. Keep your original brand and instead launch a new brand if possible.
10. The Law of Divergence	Online brands built on "You can get it all done here at this single site" are going against the laws of branding and are bound to fail.
11. The Law of Transformation	The Internet has already transformed all aspects of our lives.

customer segments or new geographical regions. So that the company can grow quickly and manage the scale necessary to maximize the size of its market opportunity, there must be high internal consistency between the company's key resources, key activities, and key partners, who should fit well together and reinforce each other.

2. **Uniqueness:** Something in your company's value proposition is new or distinctive in ways that are valued by customers. Venture capitalists prefer to invest in first-of-a-kind ideas that have proprietary features that distinguish them from competitors and give them competitive advantage in their market segment.

3. **Loyalty:** Customers stay loyal because they love the product or service offered or because it is difficult or painful to leave or switch. The company has efficiently segmented its customer base and provided each segment with appropriate customer relationships that meet the needs and wants of customers. Companies that are able to execute this well are favored by venture capitalists.

4. **Profitability:** Financial viability is in place as your company is generating revenues, or is expected to be generating future revenues,

TABLE 12.8

Seven Factors Relevant to Venture Capital Financing of Social Media Startups

Factors	Weight	Framework	References
1. Scalability	25%	Scalability, market fit	Hamel, G. (2000). *Leading the Revolution*. Boston, MA: Harvard Business School Press.
2. Uniqueness	20%	Novelty	Morris, M., Schindehutte, M., Richardson, J., & Allen, J. (2006). Is the business model a useful strategic concept? Conceptual, theoretical, empirical insights. *Journal of Small Business Strategy*, 17(1): 27–50.
3. Loyalty	15%	Lock-in, complementarities	Amit, R., & Zott, C. (2001). Value creation in e-business. *Strategic Management Journal*, 22: 493–520.
4. Profitability	15%	Financial viability	McOsker, G. (2015). Financial viability, social mission, and homeboy industries. Irish Impact blog. https://irishimpact.net/2015/07/28/financial-viability-and-the-social-mission-homeboy-industries.
5. Sustainability	10%	Profitability, efficiency, plausibility	Taneja, S., & Tooms, L. (2015). Putting a face on small businesses: Visibility, viability and sustainability. The impact of social media on small business marketing. Texas A&M University. http://www.tourbillonalliance.com/wp-content/uploads/2015/01/Social-Networking-Abstract.pdf.
6. Mobility	10%	Adaptability	Grusky, D.B. & Cumberworth, E. (2010). A national protocol for measuring intergenerational mobility. Workshop on Advancing Social Science Theory: The Importance of Common Metrics. Washington, DC: National Academy of Science.
7. Inimitability	5%	Patentability, robustness	Quinn, G., & Brachmann, (2014). S. Facebook and Twitter: Patent strategies for social media. IPWatchdog. http://www.ipwatchdog.com/2014/02/14/facebook-and-twitter-patent-strategies-for-social-media/id=48004.

that are greater than your costs. Venture capital investment is dependent on the company's ability to exceed financial indicators.

5. **Sustainability:** Your company is efficient as it offers customers products and services that are cheaper, faster, of better quality, and on average simpler. Moreover, the company is built on a strong foundation, and forecasts for the future are plausible and well supported with reliable data. Consequently, the company has a promising operational strategy in place that shows the specific steps it will take to achieve a successful exit for the venture capital. Thus, venture capitalists perceive your company as sustainable.

6. **Mobility:** Your company is flexible as it its business model can be adapted if required due to changes in its environment, such as technological advances. That includes the possibility of increasing business productivity by reaching out to customers through different channels from those originally intended. Venture capitalists desire to invest in a proven and verifiable technology that makes this possible.

7. **Inimitability:** Infrastructure is difficult to imitate, because of resources, activities, partnerships, patents, and reputation. This motivates venture capital investments as the company is robust and able to fend off threats. Consequently, there are high barriers of entry into the given market segment.

12.8 Social Media and Startups

Why should startups engage in social media? Because you fish where the fish congregate. The challenges to startups and social media according to Christos[30] are summarized in Table 12.9.

Prior to the advent of social media platforms, startup companies faced a number of tough marketing decisions. They had to determine product features and quality, establish technical services, set the price, determine the distribution channels, decide how much to spend on marketing, and decide how to divide their resources among advertising, sales force, and other promotional tools. It used to take a long time to establish a company, start a marketing campaign, and this marketing cost would always be high.[31]

However, over the past few years, an interesting transformation has occurred in the business world. Social media has become less of an optional marketing opportunity and more of a priority. Platforms such as Facebook and Twitter have become integral parts of brand awareness, content

TABLE 12.9

Challenges to Startups and Social Media

Startups Want to Gain	Traction (a market beachhead)
	Sales
	Leads
	Revenues
	Immediate income
Your Customers Want	Relationships
	Benefits not features
	Unbiased information
	Entertainment
Your Decision	Meet customers
	Create relationships
	Do business
	Social media attracting the right audience
	Build relationships
	Turn those relationships into conversions and sales
SMM Plan	WHAT is your business about?
	WHO is your target audience?
	WHERE is your target audience on social media?
	HOW to connect/engage with the target audience?
	WHAT to post/tweet/share?
Startup/Business Post?	Share your WHY
	Talk about your team
	Show off your product/MVP
	Post about relevant events
	Share your milestones
	Talk about the community
	Share industry news

distribution, lead generation, and customer acquisition strategies for businesses. This is especially true for startups working with marketing on a limited budget, with limited time, and using grassroots campaigns. However, despite its importance, very few startups and new ventures understand how to maximize the potential of social media.[32]

12.8.1 Marketing on a Limited Budget

There is an incredible burden on startups to maximize marketing dollars without compromising quality. On the one hand, you are told you will not succeed unless consumers know your products and services exist. On the other hand, you do not have a large budget, and a "proper" launch campaign can doom you financially from the start. However, somewhere in the middle there is a sweet spot that should allow you to reach a large audience with a conservative budget.

Over the years, that sweet spot has changed, but the concept has remained the same. Word-of-mouth marketing has always been a startup's best chance of success when working with a limited budget. Thankfully, the Internet has significantly accelerated the pace at which word-of-mouth marketing takes place. Specifically, social media has made it possible for small startup businesses to reach millions of consumers with the click of a button.

Clearly, social media has a solid foundation and is poised for continued long-term growth. The question startups should be left asking is, "How can we maximize our potential with social media?" Start with a social media strategy. As an entrepreneur, you understand the value of strategizing and planning. That's exactly what you need to do before proceeding any further. Even before selecting which channels you'll use, you'll need a detailed strategy that will drive your focus and keep you on track.

Your first step is to decide what type of brand fits your company. For best results, align your social media approach with your company culture. Does your company prefer a straightforward, classic approach, or do you take more of an easygoing, relaxed feel? Whichever defines your company, that's the approach you should take when building your social media strategy.

Determine your primary goals. While many large, established corporations use social media to facilitate growth in all areas of business, a startup should focus on one or two of the following:

- **Brand awareness:** Every startup uses social media as a channel for driving brand awareness. It happens organically as you post content, engage with users, and promote your brand.

- **Content distribution:** Many brands and businesses use social media as a content distribution and dissemination platform. If your content is engaging and unique enough, it is possible that others will share your posts and advertise your brand for you.

- **Lead generation:** Ideally, your social media profiles will be lead generators that drive traffic to your website or blog. This requires a long-term investment and results usually cannot be seen for many months.

- **Customer acquisition:** Finally, the best-case scenario is that your social media profiles raise brand awareness, your content generates leads, and leads turn into customers. If you can use social media as a customer acquisition tool, you have maximized its value.

12.8.2 Choosing Your Social Media Platforms

Depending on your strategy, approach, and goals, you should be able to determine which social media platforms are right for your startup. Currently, there are six major social media platforms potentially of value to startups like yours.

1. Facebook	By far the largest social media platform on the Internet, Facebook boasts more than 700 million active monthly users. If you're looking to reach the masses, this is the best place to start. It's also the most credible platform. Any healthy and established business has a Facebook page, and a lack of one is a warning sign to potential customers.
2. Twitter	Research shows that 68% of Twitter users are more likely to make a purchase from the brands they follow. If content distribution and one-on-one customer engagement is important to you, Twitter should be a key part of your social media strategy.
3. LinkedIn	For B2B startups and companies looking to find business partners, LinkedIn is extremely valuable. It's a more professional Facebook and serves the purpose of facilitating global networking.
4. YouTube	If brand awareness is your primary goal, YouTube can be your best friend. This platform gives you the opportunity to distribute engaging videos to millions of eager users. By investing in high-quality videos that are intriguing and engaging, you can begin to facilitate conversation and effectively cross-market your brand by sharing content on other platforms.
5. Google	While a late addition to the social media game, Google has quickly established itself as the second largest network, with more than 350 million active monthly users. As a rule of thumb, it's a good idea for businesses to support anything that Google does or encourages.
6. Pinterest	Pinterest is of supreme value for many businesses. It is the fastest-growing social media platform and is particularly conducive to startups with physical products.

12.8.3 General Business Tips for Social Media

While each business is unique and your specific strategy will determine how to best proceed for optimal results, here are a few general tips that apply to just about any startup using social media.

- **Build a community:** For long-term growth and success, the best thing you can do is build an online community of ambassadors that give your startup additional exposure and promote brand awareness. While this won't happen overnight, a prolonged investment over many months and years will pay off.

- **Listen instead of talking:** The biggest mistake you can make on social media is spending all of your time talking. Your focus should be on listening to your followers and garnering valuable feedback. When used correctly, social media platforms such as Facebook and Twitter essentially serve as ongoing focus groups for your startup.

- **Try new things:** Do not copy what everyone else is doing. It's OK to experiment and try new things. As long as what you're doing does not compromise your brand's integrity, give it a shot!

- **Unlock the power of social media**: As an entrepreneur, it can be challenging to work with limited resources and capabilities.

Thankfully, tools such as social media, when properly used, are capable of promoting your brand at very little financial cost. Learn to use social media and discover the key to driving word-of-mouth marketing and brand awareness.

12.9 Pharma and Social Media

It wasn't long ago that pharma brands tended to avoid social media. The strict regulation of the industry's advertising communication acted as a motivator for the industry to be cautious with social content, yet increasing numbers of brands are taking to social media anyway.[33]

The industry now realizes that even if it ignores social media, its customers will not. Other industries have led the way on social media, perhaps resulting in consumers developing expectations around social media responsiveness. People know that if they have a bad experience with a brand they need only @mention them on Twitter and, often, someone from the company will get in touch to resolve the issue. Consumers expect this as well from prescription pharmaceuticals.

You could say pharma has a disease called social anxiety. In fact, of the 50 largest drug makers worldwide, only half even dabble in social media. Only 10 use all three of the oldest, biggest social sites—Facebook, Twitter, and YouTube—according to a study by the IMS Institute for Healthcare Informatics,[34] and within that small group, few are actually interacting with patients and the public,[35] as shown in Figure 12.10.

The IMS report provides examples of metrics that reflect the scope and scale of the new digital healthcare landscape, which include the following:

- Social networking sites have grown from 8% of all adults online in 2005 up to 72% of U.S. adults online in May 2013.[36]
- When making clinical decisions, physicians spend twice as much time using online resources compared with print.[37]
- In 2009, 70% of Canadians turned to the Internet for health-related information, and 92% of those used the search engine Google, rather than a health portal, to gather this information.[38]
- Facebook is reported as the fourth most popular source of health information in the United Kingdom.
- Physicians on average spend 3 hours per week watching online videos for professional purposes and cite Medscape and YouTube followed by pharmaceutical company websites as the most important sources of video.

Physicians use the Internet and social media to research pharmaceutical, biotech and medical devices.
Modified after 30 Facts & Statistics On Social Media And Healthcare
https://getreferralmd.com/2017/01/30-facts-statistics-on-social-media-and-healthcare/

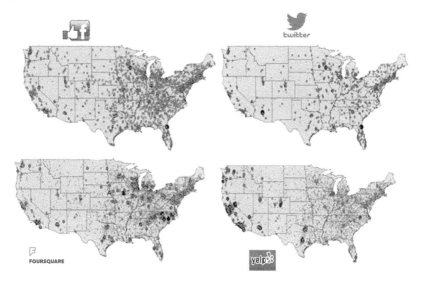

FIGURE 12.10
Physicians' use of the Internet and social media.

- In the United States, interest in specific diseases receives the greatest amount of attention in social media relating to health care, followed by lifestyle changes, health insurance details, and safety information.[39]
- Sites such as WebMD and AskDrWiki are regarded as expert sites designed to allow patients to ask questions and get answers from medical professionals.

12.9.1 Screen to Script

The synergy between the pharmaceutical industry, pharma products, and consumers is now firmly established. Rather than their physicians, consumers are increasingly relying on social media to decipher side effects, the best products for chronic diseases, and drug pricing, as depicted in Figure 12.11.[40]

The top 10 pharmaceutical companies in social media are as follows (in alphabetical order):

- AstraZeneca
- Bayer
- Boehringer Ingelheim

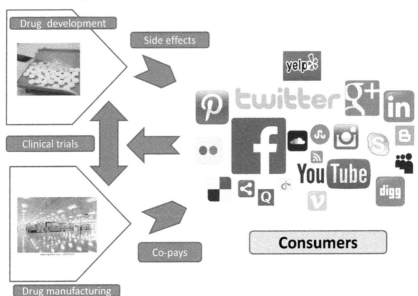

FIGURE 12.11
Medical practice in the Internet age.

- GlaxoSmithKline
- Johnson & Johnson
- Merck & Co.
- Novartis
- Novo Nordisk
- Pfizer
- UCB

12.9.2 FDA Guidance on Internet/Social Media Platforms

In 2014, the FDA issued "Guidance for Industry Internet/Social Media Platforms with Character Space Limitations: Presenting Risk and Benefit Information for Prescription Drugs and Medical Devices." The draft guidance was intended to describe the FDA's current thinking about how manufacturers, packers, and distributors of prescription human and animal drugs and medical devices for human use that choose to present benefit information should present both benefit and risk information within the advertising and promotional labeling (sometimes collectively referred to in this guidance document as *promotion*) of FDA-regulated medical products on electronic/digital platforms that are associated with character space limitations—specifically on the Internet and through social media or other technological venues (*Internet/social media*).

Examples of Internet/social media platforms with character space limitations include online microblog messaging (e.g., messages on Twitter or "tweets," which are currently limited to 140 character spaces per tweet) and online paid searches (e.g., "sponsored links" on search engines such as Google and Yahoo, which have limited character spaces as well as other platform-imposed considerations). The draft guidance presented considerations to illustrate the FDA's thinking on 30 factors that are relevant to the communication of benefit and risk information on Internet/social media platforms with character space limitations.

12.9.3 FD&C Act on Advertisements

The FD&C Act does not define what constitutes an *advertisement*, but FDA regulations provide several examples, including "advertisements in published journals, magazines, other periodicals, and newspapers, and advertisements broadcast through media such as radio, television, and telephone communication systems" (21 CFR 202.1(l)(1)).

Under the FD&C Act and the FDA's implementing regulations, promotional labeling for drugs and devices and advertisements for prescription drugs and restricted devices misbrand the product if they make representations about the use of a firm's product without disclosing certain information about the product's risk (FD&C Act Sections 502(a)(n)(q)(r), 201(n); 21 CFR 1.21(a); 21 CFR 201.1). When using Internet/social media platforms with character space limitations for product promotion, firms should consider the following provisions:

- Any promotional labeling for a drug or device must be truthful and non-misleading (FD&C 82 Act Sections 502(a), 201(n)).

- Any promotional labeling that makes claims about a firm's prescription drug or prescription device must include certain information, such as the indicated use of the product and the risks associated with use of the product (21 CFR 201.100(d), 201.105(d) and 801.109(d)).

- Pursuant to Section 502(c) for drugs and devices, information required to appear on the label or labeling must be placed prominently thereon with such conspicuousness and in such terms as to render it likely to be read and understood by the ordinary individual under customary conditions of purchase and use.

- Any advertising that makes representations about the use of a firm's prescription drug must include certain risk information (FD&C Act Section 502(n); 21 CFR 202.1). Similarly, Section 502(r) of the FD&C Act requires a "brief statement of intended uses" and relevant risk information in restricted-device advertising. Section 502(q) of the

FD&C Act provides that restricted-device advertising that "is false or misleading in any particular" misbrands the device. Note that "reminder" promotion, which calls attention to the name of a product but does not make any representations or suggestions about the product, is exempt from many of these labeling and advertising disclosure requirements (21 CFR 200.200, 201.100(f), 101 201.105(d)(2), 202.1(e)(2)(i), 801.109(d)).

- Prescription drug advertisements must present a fair balance between information relating to risk and information relating to benefit (21 CFR 202.1(e)(5)(ii)). In addition, risk information must be presented with a prominence and readability reasonably comparable to claims about drug benefits (21 CFR 202.1(e)(7)(viii)).

- Furthermore, for prescription drug advertisements to be truthful and non-misleading, they must contain risk information in each part, as necessary, to qualify any representations and/or suggestions made in that part about the drug. The risk information may be concise if supplemented by a prominent reference to the presence and location elsewhere in the advertisement of a more complete discussion (21 CFR 202.1(e)(3)(i)).

- In addition, Section 201(n) of the FD&C Act provides that in determining whether a drug or device is misbranded because its labeling or advertising is misleading, it must be considered whether the labeling or advertising fails to reveal facts that are material with respect to possible consequences of the use of the product as represented in the labeling or advertising or under conditions of use that are customary or usual.

Risk information should be comparable in content and prominence to benefit claims within the product promotion (i.e., a balanced presentation). Achieving a balanced presentation requires firms to carefully consider the desired benefit claims and risk profiles for their products when choosing a promotional platform. FDA acknowledges that Internet/social media platforms associated with character space limitations may pose challenges for firms in providing a balanced presentation of both risks and benefits of medical products.

12.10 Physicians in the Social Media Environment

With the creation and use of information online and the widespread use of social media platforms, physicians are increasingly required to consider how best to protect patient interests and apply principles of professionalism to new settings.[41]

User-created content and communications on Web-based applications, such as networking sites, media-sharing sites, or blog platforms, have dramatically increased in popularity over the past several years, but there has been little policy or guidance on the best practices to inform standards for the professional conduct of physicians in the digital environment.

According to a policy statement by the American College of Physicians,[42] areas of specific concern include the use of such media for nonclinical purposes, implications for confidentiality, the use of social media in patient education, and how all of this affects the public's trust in physicians, as patient–physician interactions extend into the digital environment.

Innovations often bring benefits, but the rapid introduction of technology sometimes outpaces existing policies, laws, and guidelines. The policy statement provides a framework for analyzing medical ethics and professionalism issues in online postings and interactions, including the use of electronic resources for clinical or direct patient care involving patient information outside of the electronic health record and the nonclinical or personal use of these media.

It presents the implications of online activities for patients, physicians, the profession, and society and contains recommendations that address online communication with patients, the use of social media sites to gather and share information about patients, physician-produced blogs, physician posting of personal information that patients can access, and communications among colleagues about patient care, as seen in Table 12.10.

As new technologies and practices, such as social networking, are embraced, it is paramount to maintain the privacy and confidentiality of patient information, demonstrate respect for patients, ensure trust in physicians and in the medical profession, and establish appropriate boundaries.[43] To protect patients and the public and promote quality health care, it is critical to strike the proper balance to harness opportunities while being aware of inherent challenges in using technology.

12.11 Summary

Social media are online platforms that allow people to form a community to create and share content to communicate and to build relationships.[44,45,46,47] Text, picture, audio, and/or video are used depending on the type of social media platform.[48] Social media can be classified as social networks, blogs, wikis, podcasts, forums, virtual game worlds, and content communities.[49,50]

However, of all the social media platforms, Facebook is by far the most commonly used, with 67% of online users using it in the United States.[51] Internet users spend about 7 hours more per month on average on Facebook

TABLE 12.10

Online Physician Activities: Benefits and Pitfalls

Activity	Benefits	Pitfalls
Communications with patients using e-mail, text, and instant messaging	Greater accessibility Immediate answers to non-urgent issues	Confidentiality concerns Replacement of face-to-face or telephone interaction Ambiguity or misinterpretation of digital interactions
Use of social media sites to gather information about patients	Observe and counsel patients on risk-taking or health-averse behaviors Intervene in an emergency	Sensitivity to source of information Threaten trust in patient–physician relationship
Use of online educational resources and related information with patients	Encourage patient empowerment through self-education Supplement resource-poor environments	Non-peer-reviewed materials may provide inaccurate information Scam "patient" sites that misrepresent therapies and outcomes
Physician-produced blogs, microblogs, and physician posting of comments by others	Advocacy and public health enhancement Introduction of physician's "voice" into such conversations	Negative online content, (e.g., "venting" or "ranting") that disparages patients and colleagues
Physician posting personal information on public social media sites	Networking and communications	Blurring of professional and personal boundaries Impact on representation of the individual and the profession
Physician use of digital venues (e.g., text and Web) for communicating with colleagues about patient care	Ease of communication with colleagues	Confidentiality concerns Unsecured networks and accessibility of protected health information

Source: Position paper, American College of Physicians, 2013.

than they do on Google, Yahoo, YouTube, Microsoft, Wikipedia, and Amazon combined.[52]

Social media is used not only as a platform to make connections and share user-generated content but also to evaluate products, make recommendations on purchases, and link current purchases to future purchases through status updates and twitter feeds.[53] The following statistics present a clearer view of the extent and influence of social media.

- Consumers generally search for information on social media before making a purchase decision.
- Marketers search consumers' social media behavior to better understand their product brand image and to identify potential new customers.[54]

TABLE 12.11

Sources of Consumer Information from Social Media

Internal	From the knowledge a consumer already has of the product, its features, and its benefits.
External	Marketer-dominated or personal and interpersonal information (advertising, reseller information, trade groups, product demonstrations).

- Marketers use social media to influence consumer purchase decisions through (1) electronic word of mouth[55,56] or (2) *word-of-mouse* marketing[57,58] (a new version of the older term *word of mouth* that applies to the digital era; people passing along messages about a company or product on digital forums).
- Social media offers worldwide reach since it is accessible by the general public.

For the consumer, these new media present the opportunity not only to receive and transmit communications to and from marketers but also to communicate directly with other consumers. Therefore, in addition to finding out about a particular product through a company website, the views of other consumers are available through Internet chat rooms, discussion newsgroups, and through websites free from marketer control.

When faced with risk or uncertainty in a buying situation, consumers seek information from a variety of sources.[59] Murray[60] and Schmidt and Spreng[61] broadly classified these information sources as shown in Table 12.11.

As we see from the preceding discussion, social media must be an integral part of a well-planned PMF strategy. Consumer perceptions are initially forged in the cauldron of the Internet. Marketers must insure that initial consumer perceptions are in line with the company's own information and values.

Notes

1. https://en.wikipedia.org/wiki/Product/market_fit.
2. http://caps.fool.com/Blogs/the-pmarca-guide-to-startups/410455.
3. Andreesen, M. (2007). EE204: Business Management for Electrical Engineers and Computer Scientists. Stanford University. http://web.stanford.edu/class/ee204/ProductMarketFit.
4. Aulet, W. How will entrepreneurship change? Martin Trust Center for MIT Entrepreneurship. http://ilp.mit.edu/images/conferences/2014/machine/presentations/Aulet.2014.2MA.pdf.
5. https://en.wikipedia.org/wiki/TurboTax.
6. https://www.bizpedia.xyz/d/intuit-inc/filings/16236241.

7. https://www.marketing91.com/market-follower-strategies/
8. https://en.wikipedia.org/wiki/Social_media.
9. http://www.marketsandmarkets.com/PressReleases/social-media-analytics. asp.
10. Kaplan A., and Haenlein, M. (2010). Users of the world, unite! The challenges and opportunities of Social Media. *Business Horizons*, 53(1): 59–68.
11. Kietzmann, J., Hermkens, K., Mccarthy, I., and Silvestre, B. (2011). Social media? Get serious! Understanding the functional building blocks of social media. *Business Horizons*, 54(3): 241–251.
12. Agichtein, E., Castillo, C., Donato, D., Gionis, A., and Mishne, G. (2008). Finding high-quality content in social media. 183–194.
13. The Social Media Guys. *The Complete Guide to Social Media*. 2010.
14. Tang, Q., Gu, B., and Whinston, A. (2012). Content contribution in social media: The case of YouTube. 4476–4485.
15. Macnamara, J. (2010). *The 21st Century Media (R)Evolution: Emergent Communication Practices*, p. 48. New York: Peter Lang.
16. Richmond, S. (2009). What is a blog? How the technology shapes the medium. *Telegraph* (London), January 22.
17. https://en.wikipedia.org/wiki/Usenet.
18. Lueg, C., and Fisher, D. (2003). *From Usenet to CoWebs: Interacting with Social Information Spaces*. Springer.
19. https://smallbiztrends.com/2013/05/the-complete-history-of-social-media-infographic.html.
20. Kaplan, A.M., and Haenlein, M. (2009). The fairyland of Second Life: About virtual social worlds and how to use them. *Business Horizons*, 52(6), 563–572.
21. https://en.wikipedia.org/wiki/Andreas_Kaplan.
22. Neti, S. (2011). Social media and its role in marketing. *International Journal of Enterprise Computing and Business Systems*, 1(2).
23. http://sterliteusa.com/wp-content/uploads/2014/02/Bridgeline-Forrester-Make-B2B-Marketing-Thrive-in-the-Age-of-the-Customer.pdf.
24. Singh, S. (2010). *Social Media Marketing for Dummies*, p. 10–11. John Wiley: Mississuaga, ON. http://www.pdfdrive.net/social-media-marketing-for-dummies-e74369.html.
25. http://www.socialmediatoday.com/content/fluent-razorfish-social-influence-marketing-report.
26. WOMMA (Word of Mouth Marketing Association). (2015). *Influencer Handbook*. Womma, Chicago, IL. http://painepublishing.com/wp-content/uploads/2015/06/Influencer-Handbook-v4-2.pdf.
27. Singh, S. (2010). *Social Media Marketing for Dummies*, p. 10. John Wiley: Mississuaga, ON. http://www.pdfdrive.net/social-media-marketing-for-dummies-e74369.html.
28. Ries, A., and Ries, L. (2000). *The 11 Immutable Laws of Internet Branding*. Collins. https://www.goodreads.com/book/show/33450.The_11_Immutable_Laws_of_Internet_Branding.
29. Magnusdottir, K.Y., and Johnson, O.P. (2012). Venture capital investments in social media. Master's thesis, Copenhagen Business School, Denmark.http://studenttheses.cbs.dk/bitstream/handle/10417/3607/katrin_yr_magnusdottir_og_olafur_pall_johnson.pdf?sequence=1.

30. Christos, M. (2016). Harness the power of social media for your startup.http://www.hamagbicro.hr/wp-content/uploads/2016/02/Presentation-Croatia-Social-media-for-startups.pdf.

31. Akula, S.C. (2015). The influence of social media platforms for startups. *Journal of Mass Communication and Journalism*, 5: 264.

32. Edwards, S. (2015). A social media guide for startups and entrepreneurs: How startups can leverage the power of social media. *Inc.* https://www.inc.com/samuel-edwards/a-social-media-guide-for-startups-and-entrepreneurs.html.

33. https://econsultancy.com/blog/67993-why-pharma-marketers-are-increasingly-turning-to-social-media.

34. Aitken, M., and Altmann, T. (2014). Engaging patients through social media: Is healthcare ready for empowered and digitally demanding patients? IMS Institute for Healthcare Informatics, Parsippany, NJ. http://magazine.imshealth.it/wp-content/uploads/2015/09/IIHI_Social_Media_Report.pdf.

35. Staton, T. (2014). The top 10 pharma companies in social media. Fierce Pharma. http://www.fiercepharma.com/special-report/top-15-pharma-companies-by-2014-revenue.

36. Manhattan Research. New study shows 72% of European online consumers are social health users. http://manhattanresearch.com/News-and-Events/Press-Releases/european-social-health-users.

37. Google. *Screen to Script: The Doctor's Digital Path to Treatment.* 2012.

38. Law, M. (2012). Online drug information in Canada. Pharmaceutical Advertising Advisory Board.

39. Fox, S., and Duggan, M. (2013). Health online 2013. Pew Research Center. http://pewinternet.org/Reports/2013/Health-online.aspx.

40. Bottom left image available through Creative Commons license, attribution to Vetter03.

41. Farnan, J.M., Paro, J.A., Higa, J.T., Reddy, S.T., Humphrey, H.J., and Arora, V.M. (2009). Commentary: The relationship status of digital media and professionalism: It's complicated. *Academic Medicine* 84: 1479–1481.

42. Farnan, J.M., Sulmasy, L.S., Worster, B.K., Chaudhry, H.J., Rhyne, J.A., and Arora, V.M., for the American College of Physicians Ethics, Professionalism and Human Rights Committee; the American College of Physicians Council of Associates; and the Federation of State Medical Boards Special Committee on Ethics and Professionalism. Online medical professionalism: Patient and public relationships. Policy statement from the American College of Physicians and the Federation of State Medical Boards. http://annals.org/pdfaccess.ashx?url=/data/journals/aim/926759.

43. Thompson, L.A., Dawson, K., Ferdig, R., Black, E.W., Boyer, J., Coutts, J., et al. (2008). The intersection of online social networking with medical professionalism. *Journal of General Internal Medicine*, 23: 954–957.

44. Raghupathi, V., and Fogel, J. (2015). The impact of opinion leadership on purchases through social networking websites. *Journal of Theoretical and Applied Electronic Commerce Research*, 10(3): 18–29.

45. Hennig-Thurau, T., Malthouse, E.C., Friege, C., Gensler, S., Lobschat, L., Rangaswamy, A., and Skiera, B. (2010). The impact of new media on customer relationships. *Journal of Service Research*, 13(3): 311–330.

46. Libai, B., Bolton, R., Bugel, M., de Ruyter, K., Gotz., O. Risselada, H., and Stephen, A. (2010). Customer to customer interactions: Broadening the scope of word of mouth research. *Journal of Service Research*, 13(3): 267–282.
47. Mohammadian, M., and Mohammadreza, M. (2012). Identify the success factors of social media (marketing perspective). *International Business and Management*, 4(2): 58–66.
48. Safko, I., and Brake, D. (2009). *The Social Media Bible*. Hoboken, NJ: John Wiley.
49. Heinonen, K. (2011). Consumer activity in social media: Managerial approaches to consumers' social media behavior. *Journal of Consumer Behavior*, 10(6): 356–364.
50. Kaplan, A.M., and Haenlein, M. (2010). Users of the world, unite! The challenges and opportunities of social media. *Business Horizons*, 53(1): 59–68.
51. Duggen, M., and Brenner, J. (2013). The demographics of social media users: 2012. Pew Research Center, February. http://pewinternet.org/Reports/2013/Social-media-users.aspx.
52. Nielsen. (2012). State of the media: The social media report 2012. Nielsen, April. http://www.nielsen.com/us/en/reports/2012/state-of-the-media-the-social-media-report-2012.html.
53. Forbes, L.P., and Vespoli, E.M. (2013). Does social media influence consumer buying behavior? An investigation of recommendations and purchases. *Journal of Business and Economics Research*, 11(2): 107–111.
54. Heinonen, K. (2011). Consumer activity in social media: Managerial approaches to consumers' social media behavior. *Journal of Consumer Behavior*, 10(6): 356–364.
55. Cheung, M.Y., Luo, C., Sia, C.L., and Chen, H. (2009). Credibility of electronic word-of-mouth: Informational and normative determinants of on-line consumer recommendations. *International Journal of Electronic Commerce*, 13(4): 9–38.
56. Hennig-Thurau, T., Gwinner, K., Walsh, G., and Gremler, D. (2004). Electronic word-of-mouth via consumer-opinion platforms: What motivates consumers to articulate themselves on the internet? *Journal of Interactive Marketing*, 18(1): 38–52.
57. https://www.techopedia.com/definition/31780/word-of-mouse.
58. Martin, D., and Lomax, W. Word-of-mouse vs word-of-mouth: The effects of the Internet on consumer's pre-purchase information-search activities. Kingston Business School.http://eprints.kingston.ac.uk.
59. Cox, D.F. (1967). *Risk Taking and Information Handling in Consumer Behavior*. Boston, MA: Harvard University Press.
60. Murray, K.B. (1991). A test of services marketing theory: Consumer informatio-nacquisition activities. *Journal of Marketing*, 55(January): 10–25.
61. Schmidt, J.B., and Spreng, R.A. (1996). A proposed model of external consumer information search. *Academy of Marketing Science Journal*, 24(3): 246.

13

Growth Strategies

13.1 Introduction

Recombinant DNA, the desktop computer revolution, the Internet, mobile telephony, and social networking are examples of areas where dramatic changes have occurred in the lives of billions of people and still occurs in all parts of the world. In each of these areas, startups have been a key stimulus to the discovery, development, and commercialization of the innovative product.

If only half of high-tech startups survive more than 5 years and only one-third make it to 10, what's the one thing you could do to ensure your company is sustainable? The answer is to create a growth strategy for your business, according to Rob Biederman,[1] co-founder and CEO of HourlyNerd.

A growth strategy involves more than simply envisioning long-term success. If you do not have a tangible plan, you're actually *losing* business—or you're increasing the chance of losing business to competitors. The key with any growth strategy is to be deliberate. Establish the rate-limiting step in your growth and pour as much fuel on the fire as possible. But for this to be beneficial, Biederman advises the adoption of the following seven steps:

1. **Establish a value proposition:** For your business to sustain long-term growth, you must understand what sets it apart from the competition. Identify why customers come to *you* for a product or service. What makes you relevant, differentiated, and credible? Use your answer to explain to other consumers why they should do business with you.

   For example, some companies compete on *authority*; Whole Foods Market is the *definitive* place to buy healthy, organic foods. Others, such as Walmart, compete on price. Ascertain what special benefit only *you* can provide and forget everything else. If you stray from this proposition, you will only run the risk of devaluing your business.

2. **Identify your ideal customer:** You got into business to solve a problem for a certain audience. Who is that audience? Is that audience

your ideal customer? If not, who are you serving? Nail down your ideal customer and revert back to this audience as you adjust the business to stimulate growth.

3. **Define your key indicators:** Changes must be measurable. If you're unable to measure a change, you have no way of knowing whether it's effective. Identify which key indicators affect the growth of your business and then dedicate time and money to those areas. Also, A/B test properly; making changes over time and comparing historical and current results isn't valid.

4. **Verify your revenue streams:** What are your current revenue streams? What revenue streams could you add to make your business more profitable? Once you identify the potential for new revenue streams, ask yourself if they're sustainable in the long run. Some great ideas or cool products don't necessarily have revenue streams attached. Be careful to isolate and understand the difference.

5. **Look to your competition:** No matter your industry, your competition is likely excelling at something that your company is struggling with. Look toward similar businesses that are growing in new, unique ways to inform your growth strategy. Don't be afraid to ask for advice. Ask yourself why your competitors have made alternate choices. Are they wrong? Or are your businesses positioned differently? The assumption that you're smarter is rarely correct.

6. **Focus on your strengths:** Sometimes, focusing on your strengths— rather than trying to improve your weaknesses—can help you establish growth strategies. Reorient the playing field to suit your strengths, and build on them to grow your business.

7. **Invest in talent:** Your employees have direct contact with your customers, so you need to hire people who are motivated and inspired by your company's value proposition. Be cheap with office furniture, marketing budgets, and holiday parties. Hire few employees but pay them appropriately. The best will usually remain if you need to cut back their compensation during a slow period.

Developing a growth strategy is not a one-size-fits-all process. In fact, due to changing market conditions, making strategic decisions based on someone else's successes would be foolish. That is not to say that you cannot learn from another company, but blindly implementing a cookie-cutter plan won't create sustainable growth.

You need to adapt your plan to smooth out your business's inefficiencies, refine its strengths, and better suit your customers, who could be completely different from those in a vague, one-size-fits-all strategy.

Your company's data should lend itself to all your strategic decisions. Specifically, you can use the data from your key indicators and revenue streams to create a personalized growth plan. That way, you will better understand your business and your customers' nuances, which will naturally lead to growth.

A one-size-fits-all strategy implies vague indicators. But a specific plan is a successful plan. When you tailor your growth strategy to *your* business and customers, you will keep your customers happy and fulfill their wants and needs, which will keep them coming back.

13.2 Steps to the Epiphany

In 2006, Steve Blank[2] published a seminal book entitled *The Four Steps to the Epiphany*.

The book catered to a specific audience: entrepreneurs looking to launch and wannabe entrepreneurs at the stage of making business plans or marketing plans. Within this audience, Blank's book was meant for the tech world. So if you belong to this audience, the book is almost a textbook-level must read. Blank offers some profound insight when he stresses the importance of customer development, alongside product development.

The book focuses on reverse engineering, where you are asked to refine your product based on the needs and expectations of the targeted customer base, gathered from interacting with said audience. Blank emphasizes on how this little step is often missed by startups and leads to their failure. The book has some amazing examples, making them into a great learning experience by offering a postmortem of sorts for startups that failed, as follows:

- **Volkswagen Phaeton:** Volkswagen took all of Toyota's lessons in launching its high-end Lexus brand and ignored them. Cost to date: $500 million.

- **Kodak's Photo CD:** Kodak offered film camera customers the ability to put their pictures on a compact disc and view them on their TVs. It was 10 years ahead of its time and marketed to customers who were not ready. A viable early adopter market in corporate marketing departments was ignored. Cost: $150 million.

- **Segway:** Thought their market was everyone in the world who walked and confused world-class public relations with customers with checkbooks. Still searching for their real markets. Cost to date: $200 million.

- **Apple's Newton:** They were right about the personal digital assistant market but 5 years too soon. Yet they spent like they were in an existing market. Cost: $100 million.

- **Jaguar X-Type:** Created a Ford-type, low-end product and slapped the Jag name on it, alienating their high-end customers. Cost: $200 million.
- **Webvan:** Groceries on demand: the killer app of the Internet. The company spent money like a drunken sailor. Even in the Internet Bubble, costs and infrastructure grew faster than the customer base. Loss: $800 million.
- **Sony's MiniDisc players:** A smaller version of the CD wildly popular in Japan. The United States isn't Japan. Cost: $500 million after the first 10 years of marketing.
- **R.J. Reynolds' Premier and Eclipse smokeless cigarettes:** Understood what the general public (non-smokers) wanted but did not understand that their customers didn't care. Cost: $450 million.
- **Motorola's Iridium:** A satellite-based phone system. Engineering triumph and built to support a customer base of millions. No one asked the customer if they wanted it. Cost: $5 billion. Yes, *billion*. Satellites are awfully expensive.

In contrast, the methods advocated in the book are easily explained and understood, but they run counter to the way most companies operate. There aren't many managers around who are willing to reject the conventional wisdom that guides most firms in their quest to take new products to market.

Those managers and entrepreneurs who do follow this different path find that there are eager customers for their products. A few who did it right in their recent, very successful product launches include the following:

- **Procter & Gamble's Swiffer:** A swiveling, disposable mop on a stick. Sophisticated planning and consumer research resulted in an initial $2.1 billion market in 2003.
- **Toyota's Prius:** They found a profitable niche for their electric hybrid car. As a classic disruptive innovation, sales will grow and Toyota will continue to eat the existing U.S. car companies for lunch. In its first 5 years, sales grew to $5 billion. By 2015, hybrids could make up 35% of the U.S. car market.
- **General Mills's Yoplait GoGurt:** Yogurt in a tube. The goal was to keep their yogurt consumer base of toddlers and little kids for as long as possible. Research led to the tube packaging, making yogurt easier to consume on the go.

13.3 Growth Strategies for New Ventures

According to a 2001 report for the U.S. World Economic Forum,[3] not all companies consistently have a single growth strategy in their early years. Nor

TABLE 13.1

Growth Strategies for New Ventures

1. Disruptive Technology Ventures	A. Creating disruptive technology ventures B. Building disruptive technology ventures C. Riding disruptive technology ventures
2. New Product in New Category Ventures	A. Innovative design B. New business models C. New distribution channels D. Disintermediation plays E. Execution excellence plays
3. New Product in Existing Category Ventures	A. Innovative design B. New business models C. New distribution channels D. Disintermediation plays E. Execution excellence plays
4. Redesign of Business Value Chain Ventures	A. Faster, cheaper, better B. Redesign of value chain delivery C. Introduction of new value chains
5. Discovery and Research Knowledge Ventures	A. Fundamental research and discovery (e.g., new drugs) B. Exploration and discovery (e.g., minimally invasive devices) C. University-based technology transfers
6. Rollup (Aggregation) of Existing Players' Ventures	A. Strategic alliances B. Mergers and acquisitions C. Outsourcing
7. Governmental/Regulatory/Political Change Ventures	A. Gaining regulatory approvals B. Selling to governments C. Patent protection
8. Idea Transfer or Transplant Ventures	A. Exporting existing ideas to new geographies or new sectors (e.g., eBay clones, Amazon clones) B. Entering underserved markets

is there always clarity going forward on which of these growth strategies best describes an individual company at any point in time. However, the fundamental characteristics of each of the following growth strategies and the differences among them provide important insights into the diversity of opportunities for early-stage company growth (Table 13.1).

13.3.1 Growth and Chaos Are Twins

Chaos is a state of utter confusion in which chance is supreme—a total lack of organization or order. In a high-growth startup, chaos is inevitable. Every task becomes a moving target. Written policies are not in place. Teams do not understand the reasoning behind decisions, thus sending employees mixed messages. It feels like every day starts with a new mission statement. This constant shifting makes running startups chaotic, unfocused, and unpredictable.

Patricia J. Hutchins[4] lists the following varieties of workplace chaos:

> Not being able to finish one project before being given another ... too many people to support ... lack of communication ... constant interruptions ... self-imposed versus real expectations ... loss of control over work ... poor time management ... too many priorities ... lack of organizational skills ... too many bosses ... no downtime ... no precise job description ... not knowing what is expected of you ... harder not smarter ... office politics ... too much to do and too little time or too few people to do it ... lack of direction ... procrastination ... immediate demands ... no enthusiasm ... E-mail demanding immediate attention ... mental overload ... scheduling multiple people for multiple meetings ... bringing personal problems to work ... critical coworker ... inability to focus ... inability to say no ... equipment failures ... traffic ... inconsistent workload.

Chaos means that strategies go wildly astray. It is often associated with missed deadlines, understaffing, runaway costs, and similar situations generally considered negative. Under these circumstances, *chaos* describes a situation where the strategic goals are unachievable, and therefore the outcomes become random, unpredictable, and undesirable.[5]

But what if the goals of a strategy are achievable? What if a small deviation from the plan or regulation leads to very different outcomes?[6] This behavior is called *deterministic chaos*.[7] Without management's involvement, deterministic chaos can produce arbitrary outcomes—some very positive, some very negative.

An organization practices deterministic chaos when it encourages "thinking out of the box" and implements these new ideas rapidly, such as Google's "chaos by design" strategy. If management does a good job prioritizing ideas for implementation, the overall outcome can be positive.

Google's "chaos by design" strategy is clearly working. According to Lashinsky:

> Spend just a few minutes on Google's sprawling campus in Mountain View, Calif., and you will feel it right away: This is a company thriving on the edge of chaos. The 1.3-million-square-foot headquarters is a mélange of two-story buildings full of festive cafeterias (yes, they're all free), crammed conference rooms, and hallway bull sessions, all of it surrounded by sandy volleyball courts, youngsters whizzing by on motorized scooters, and—there's no better way to put this—an anything-goes spirit. It's a place where failure coexists with triumph, and ideas bubble up from lightly supervised engineers, none of whom worry too much about their projects ever making money.[8]

13.4 Managing Chaos

Chaos leadership requires steady nerves and clarity. The following are ways to manage chaos (an oxymoron?) in a startup environment.

- **Be open to change:** Change will be your only constant and will be part of your daily existence as leader. As founder, "how" you achieve your vision will change many times until it fits the needs of the marketplace.
- **Cut your losses quickly:** Do not get bogged down in "sunk costs." If you focus on the past, you cannot move forward. Learn the lessons and move on, making necessary adjustments. And importantly, keep your team fully informed of the changes.
- **Lead the change for the team:** Change is difficult, but you must lead. Acknowledge all the hard work done and build an irrefutable case for change.
- **Celebrate little successes:** Nothing succeeds like success. Give your team a pat on the back and publicly recognize team members that succeeded in their tasks. Rome was not built in a day.
- **Embrace change as fun:** If you wanted a predictable path, you did not want a startup. Change gives you the freedom to create, innovate, and build something big from nothing.

13.5 Szycher's Law of Decreased Productivity

Paradoxically, in any given project, the productivity of your team is *indirectly* proportional to the square number of people assigned to that project, as depicted in Equation 13.1.

$$P = 1/(n-1)^2$$

(13.1)

where:
   P = productivity (time to finish the task)
   n = additional number of people in project (not including yourself)

Each worker must be trained in the technology, the goals of the effort, the overall strategy, and the plan of work. This training cannot be partitioned, so this part of the added effort is geometrically inverse to the number of workers.

This is particularly true if each part of the task must be separately coordinated with each other part; productivity decreases as $1/(n-1)^2$. Thus, three additional workers require four times as much development time as the original team, four additional workers require nine times as much development time as the original team, and so on. Moreover, if there need to be conferences among three, four, or more workers to resolve things jointly, productivity decreases even further.

Simply stated, Szycher's Law of Decreased Productivity states that adding incremental manpower to an ongoing project paradoxically delays the project.

13.6 Founder's Dilemmas

Most entrepreneurs want to make lot of money *and* run the show. But Wasserman[9] revealed that it is tough to do both. If you do not figure out which matters most to you, you could end up being neither rich nor in control. (Wasserman is associate professor and Tukman Faculty Fellow at Harvard Business School. His HBS class, Founder's Dilemmas, was named one of the top entrepreneurship classes in the county by *Inc.* magazine. He focused his research on early founders' decisions, particularly those that can trigger startup dissolution.)[10]

Consider the following: To make a lot of money from a new venture, you need financial resources to capitalize on the opportunities before you. That means attracting investors, which requires relinquishing control as you give away equity and as investors alter your board's membership. To remain in charge of your business, you have to keep more equity. But that means fewer financial resources to fuel your venture.

So, according to Wasserman, you must choose between money and power. Begin by articulating your primary motivation for starting a business. Then understand the trade-offs associated with that goal. As your venture unfolds, you will make choices that support—rather than jeopardize—your dreams.

At every step in their venture's life, entrepreneurs face a choice between making money and controlling their businesses. And each choice comes with a trade-off. Startup founders who give up more equity to attract co-founders, key executives, and investors build more valuable companies than those who part with less equity. And the founder ends up with a more valuable slice of the pie.

On the other hand, to attract investors and executives, you have to cede control of most decision making. And once you're no longer in control, your job as CEO is at risk. Conversely, to retain control of your new business, you may need to bootstrap the venture—using your own capital instead of taking money from investors. You'll have less financial fuel to increase your company's value, as summarized in Table 13.2.

13.6.1 Anticipating and Avoiding Pitfalls

Table 13.3 is a quick but comprehensive summary of *The Founder's Dilemmas: Anticipating and Avoiding the Pitfalls That Can Sink a Startup*, released in 2013 by Princeton University Press.[11]

TABLE 13.2

Are You Motivated by Wealth or Power?

If you want to get rich (motivated by wealth)	• You need broader skills—such as creating formal processes and developing specialized roles—to continue building your company than you did to start it. This stretches most founders' abilities beyond their limits, and investors may force you to step down. • Investors dole out money in stages. At each stage, they add their own people to your board, gradually threatening your control. • Recognize when the top job has stretched beyond your capabilities, and hire a new CEO yourself. • Work with your board to develop post-succession roles for yourself. • Be open to pursuing ideas that require external financing.
If you want to run the company (motivated by power)	• Restrict yourself to businesses where you already have the skills and contacts you need. • Focus on a business in which large amounts of capital aren't required to get your venture off the ground and flying. • Consider waiting until late in your career before setting up shop for a new venture. That will give you time to develop the broader skills you'll need as your business grows and to accumulate some savings for bootstrapping.

13.7 Do You Need a Co-Founder?

Undoubtedly, your most important initial decision will be the first person you hire. Is a co-founder your first hire? You may need a co-founder for two reasons:

1. **Technical and moral support:** In entrepreneurship, every problem is existential. So you will need backup, a "safety net."

2. **Statistics:** These predict that solo founders fail more often. Therefore, most investors simply will refuse to invest in a solo founder (unless the startup is already successful).

A common challenge faced by every entrepreneur is that they do not have the bandwidth, interest, or skills to do everything that is required to build their startup alone. Of course, you can outsource part of the work or hire employees, but that approach means more time and money to manage the work, which you do not have. The best answer is to find a co-founder with complementary skills.[12]

Two heads are better than one in a startup. Both need to share the passion, long-term opportunities, and risk, rather than just getting paid to do a job, win or lose. Investors worry about a single entrepreneur being overloaded,

TABLE 13.3

Summary: The Founder's Dilemmas: Anticipating and Avoiding the Pitfalls that Can Sink a Startup

Relationships.	You're taking the leap and starting a company. But do you go solo or bring in cofounders? If you plan for co-founders, what skills will they have and where will they come from? The basics for facing this first dilemma.
Know your capital.	Do you have the necessary human, social, and financial capital to get the startup off the ground? If not, you may need cofounders who have the technical expertise, sales background, or social connections that you lack. The most successful solo founders are those with significant expertise in multiple business and technical functions, a hearty financial cushion, and valuable industry connections in the relevant field.
Don't flock together.	Birds of a feather flock together, and so do founders. If your founding team is too similar in background, age, and experience, you're likely to have overlapping skills and role confusion, which can cause tension. Creating a more diverse team gives you access to a wider network and those skills that you originally craved for your team in the first place
Avoid temptation.	As much as the siren calls you to found with best friends and family, don't give in. As much as they may share the intangible qualities and values of the startup, they are highly likely to cause trouble (e.g., when the board asks you to fire your brother). There's data to back this up; don't lose your loved ones for the sake of the startup, because you'll likely lose both.
	Above all, make your expectations clear for the founding team. There will undoubtedly be "elephants in the room" you need to address. Address them. Bring in an objective outside voice if necessary. Some founding teams, including those with friends and family, make disaster plans ahead of time to soften arguments and exits.
Roles.	You chose to have a founding team and picked the very best people to complement your weaknesses in human, social, and financial capital. Now it's time to determine the workflow
Yes, you need a CEO.	As fluid and dynamic as initial roles can be, you will still need someone to carry the CEO title. And you need to think really carefully about who that person is. One way to make the call is to assess who brings the most to the table: who is most invested in the startup? The original idea person is not automatically the most committed on the team, although most startups will naturally gravitate to crowning the idea person chief.
Differentiate.	Tension among founders grows from overlapping skill sets and responsibilities—when you envision a better product design, but you're actually tasked with distribution. Creating a clear division of labor will help accountability and creativity to flourish. But heed this warning: assigning roles and titles prematurely can feed inflexibility and *title inertia*, when the title of the member no longer matches the individual's skill set. Successful founding teams balance strict divisions of labor and collective work styles.
Determine how you'll make decisions.	Founding teams can lean toward egalitarian decision-making models (unanimous votes, equal say in every decision) or hierarchy. Don't fall into a power structure: decide which one you want and which pole fits with your business model, and let others know how it works. This will be critical, especially once you start to hire others without founder status.

(Continued)

TABLE 13.3 (CONTINUED)

Summary: The Founder's Dilemmas: Anticipating and Avoiding the Pitfalls that Can Sink a Startup

	Overall, founders need to recognize there will be conflict among your founding team. Any good team doing a great task will face disagreement regardless of how much rapport and camaraderie you have in the bank. Make a plan for how you'll settle disputes and think through the political implications of the titles you give; changing these decisions later on in the process is painful and sometimes impossible.
Rewards.	You've chosen your team and have slogged through roles, but perhaps the hardest set of dilemmas revolve around a technical black hole: equity. Choosing when to spell out equity shares, how to apportion them, and when to revisit the split may be the most delicate set of questions you face.
Address rewards after relationships and roles.	Do not spell out equity until you know who is committed to your team and their contribution. Many founding teams early on determine an equal split of equity, only to find out that one member can't continue with the team or has a significantly smaller role than expected.
It's okay to care about money.	Some members of your founding team will be motivated by decision-making power and control, and perhaps a lasting seat on the board. Others will care more about their equity stake and increasing the value of the company as quickly as possible. Having significant equity stakes available for new hires can sweeten the deal for an experienced hand to join your team.
Vesting has its place.	It is not always a sign of mistrust if you include vesting in the equity agreement. Dynamic forms of equity arrangements can account for unexpected loss of a team member, a dispute, or the ever-changing market. If the timing is right, put the agreement in writing to keep communication clear and avoid further disputes.
	Any way you slice it, equity splits are dangerous but necessary. Decide too early, and the agreement won't reflect the reality of the company. Decide too late, and you might lose valuable employees and founding team members. Acknowledge that rewards are a common source of conflict, and the least tense agreements will be aligned with the aforementioned knowledge of relationships and roles.
Wealth and control.	Wasserman posits that there are two main motivations for founders: wealth and control. It helps to know which camp you're in, and will help you clarify decisions about new hires, boards, and when you will need to exit the startup.
	Control-motivated founders need to assess carefully their solicitation and acceptance of money from family and friends, angel investors, and venture capitalists. They should expect to grow the company slowly in order to maintain control, whether that be control of product, hiring, or outside cash flow.
	Wealth-motivated founders should realize that the ultimate goal is the increased value of the company, and that may mean losing control of the board, attracting top-flight hires with excellent experience (and corresponding equity loss), and eventually helping the board find your replacement.
Could I do both?	Most founders, optimistic as they are, will assume that they can be the next Bill Gates or Mark Zuckerberg– the CEOs who have become both *king* (control) and *rich* (wealth). Wasserman makes a clear point that the reason that Gates and Zuckerberg are so unique is because they are both king and rich. It is an incredibly unlikely outcome, and any founder needs to be ready to pick which outcome they truly want to achieve

TABLE 13.4

Your "Perfect Fit" Co-Founder

Write a *complementary job description* for your ideal partner.	Objectively analyze your own business strengths and weaknesses, and write down what partner skills and experiences would best complement yours. Seek input from seasoned investors and peers.
Attend local university entrepreneur activities.	University professors and student leaders always have a list of top entrepreneurs, alums, or staff members who are just waiting to find the perfect match for their own interests, skills, and entrepreneurial ideas to change the world.
Look for a partner with complementary background.	You will save a lot of arguments if you and your co-founder have different and complementary skill sets.
Jointly define and agree on major milestones and key metrics for the startup.	This process is the ultimate test of a true shared vision and working style. Building a startup is chaotic and unpredictable work, and people get busy, so now is the time to jointly commit. If you cannot work as a team now, it probably will not happen at all in the future. Save yourself the future aggravation.
Negotiate and document roles early, including who is the boss.	Memorialize your agreement. There can be only one CEO.

disabled, or led astray, with no balancing and supporting partner. So your challenge is how to find that elusive perfect-fit partner.

Oftentimes, a startup entrepreneur has a good business idea but doesn't know how to build the product. Or the entrepreneur has deep technology skills but is lacking in business skills. In many cases, these entrepreneurs should be on the hunt for co-founders to help them build their businesses. The problem is, they often do not know how to start the process or where best to look. While every founder has distinctive needs for a co-founder, Table 13.4 suggests five steps common to all technology-intensive startups.

To ensure the success of your startup, finding the right co-founder is one of the most important first decisions that a founder entrepreneur needs to do. There are so many challenges in a startup that no founder should attempt it alone. Great teams persevere, and success breeds success.

13.8 The Great Dilemma: Equity Distribution

According to the law firm Figeroux and Associates,[13] one of the toughest decisions that startup founders have to make is how to allocate or split the equity among co-founders. The easy answer of splitting it equally among all co-founders, since there is minimal value at that point, is usually *the worst possible answer* and often results in the failure of the startup later on due to an obvious inequity.

Another common "failure to start" situation I see is one where the "idea person" insists that the idea is 90% of the value (and 90% of the equity). In the real world, however, the "idea" is a very small part of the overall equation. A startup is all about "execution," meaning the equity should be allocated based on the value that each partner brings to the table.

13.8.1 Dividing Equity among Founders

Objectively, each founder should receive equity for the contribution they individually bring to the table. Founders may contribute in many ways. Some bring capital. Some bring patents or product ideas. Some bring knowledge, experience, and competence that have been acquired through a consistent track record of successful projects accomplished in various areas. Some bring business and investor network connections.

How then can you quantify what the founders bring to the table? L. Frank Demmler,[14] an associate professor of entrepreneurship at the Donald H. Jones Center for Entrepreneurship at the Tepper School of Business at Carnegie Mellon University, invented an interesting way to divide equity among founders in a way that is both logical and fair: the Founders' Pie Calculator.

Demmler's calculator provides a way to quantify five elements of the decision-making process. The concept behind the Founders' Pie Calculator is to assign a numerical weight for each of these five elements and then assign a value to each founder on a scale of 0 to 10. Then you take the weight and multiple it by the founders' scores to come up with the weighted score. From there you can get the percentage of equity.

13.8.2 Demmler's Factors

Let's revisit the factors that should be considered.

Idea	The company wouldn't exist if it weren't for the original idea, and that is certainly worth something, *but* there's a lot of truth in the saying "A successful business is 1% inspiration, and 99% perspiration."
Business Plan Preparation	The development of an initial business plan is a surprisingly difficult and time-consuming effort. To pull together and organize all the thoughts of the founding team—filling in the blanks, identifying and reconciling the differences, and producing a document that captures the essence of the business and helps persuade banks, investors, board members, and others to support the company—is a mammoth undertaking, as anyone who has done it will attest. Again, the plan is a necessary element of starting the business, *but* execution against the plan is where the real value lies.

Domain Expertise	To what degree do you and your partners have meaningful experience in the business of your business? Knowing the industry, having relevant experience, and having a Rolodex full of accessible contacts can greatly improve the company's probability of success and speed up its growth rate. Otherwise, it will take longer to get commercial traction, and you'll have to pay for these assets, usually by hiring someone and including equity in their compensation package.
Commitment and Risk	You've probably heard the old saying "A chicken is involved with breakfast, but a pig is committed." Similarly, the founders who join the company full time and are committed to making it a success are much more valuable than founders who are going to sit on the sideline and be cheerleaders. In addition, the opportunity cost for those who join the company instead of pursuing a career is not trivial.
Responsibilities	Who is going to do what? Who is going to go stay up at night when you can't make tomorrow's payroll? Where does the buck stop?

13.8.3 Hypothetical Example

Let us look at a hypothetical example. Assume that we have a high-tech startup spinning out of a university with four members in the founding team.[15]

- The inventor who is recognized as the technology leader in his domain
- The "business guy" who is bringing business and industry knowledge to the company
- The technologist who has been the inventor's "right-hand man"
- The research team member who happened to be at the right place at the right time but has not and will not contribute much to the technology or the company

From this hypothetical example, the Founders' Pie Calculator would determine the allocation of the founding team's equity in the startup as follows.

This sheet has values entered to demonstrate the output. You can use this sheet to calculate your own values by replacing the numbers in the Absolute Scores table. If these were all first-time entrepreneurs, it is likely that they would each get 25% of the company's stock, because it's "fair." Is that right? Let us take a look at what the Founders' Pie Calculator says.

		Absolute Scores (1–10)			
	Weight	Founder 1	Founder 2	Founder 3	Founder 4
Idea	7	10	3	3	0
Business Plan	2	3	8	1	0
Domain Expertise	5	6	4	6	4
Commitment and Risk	7	0	7	0	0
Responsibilities	6	0	6	0	0

	Weighted Scores (1–10)				
	Founder 1	Founder 2	Founder 3	Founder 4	
Idea	70	21	21	0	
Business Plan	6	16	2	0	
Domain Expertise	30	20	30	20	
Commitment and Risk	0	49	0	0	
Responsibilities	0	36	0	0	
Total Points	106	142	53	20	321
% of Total	33.0%	44.2%	16.5%	6.2%	100.0%

Notes

1. Biederman, R. (2015). 7 key steps to a growth strategy that works immediately. *Entrepreneur*, January 29. https://www.entrepreneur.com/article/240853.
2. Blank, S.G. *The Four Steps to the Epiphany: Successful Strategies for Products that Win*, 3rd Edition. Lulu.com.
3. World Economic Forum. (2011). Global entrepreneurship and the successful growth strategies of early-stage companies. Report. https://www.weforum. org/reports/global-entrepreneurship-and-successful-growth-strategies-early-stage-companies.
4. Hutchins. P.J. (2002). Managing workplace chaos. American Management Association. https://www.scribd.com/presentation/334802186/Managing-Work place-Chaos.
5. Hubler, A., Foster, G., and Phelps, K. (2007). Managing chaos: Thinking out of the box. *Complexity*, 12: 10–13.
6. Wheeler, D. J. (1999). *Understanding Variation: The Key to Managing Chaos*, 2nd Edition. Knoxville, TN: SPC Press.
7. Schuster, H.G. (1987). *Deterministic Chaos*, 2nd Edition. Weinheim, Germany: Wiley.
8. Lashinsky, A. (2006). Chaos by design The inside story of disorder, disarray, and uncertainty at Google. And why it's all part of the plan. *Fortune*, October 2, p. 154. http://archive.fortune.com/magazines/fortune/fortune_archive/2006/10/02/8387489/index.htm.
9. Wasserman, N. (2008). The founder's dilemma. *Harvard Business Review*, February.https://hbr.org/2008/02/the-founders-dilemma.
10. May, A. (2013). A book in 5 minutes: "The Founder's Dilemmas" by Noam Wasserman. Tech.co, October 14. http://tech.co/founders-dilemmas-noam-wasserman-2013-10.
11. May, A. (2013). A book in 5 minutes: "The Founder's Dilemmas" by Noam Wasserman. Tech.co, October 14. http://tech.co/founders-dilemmas-noam-wasserman-2013-10.
12. Zwilling, M. (2015). 10 Steps to finding the right co-founder. *Entrepreneur*, March 27. https://www.entrepreneur.com/article/244259.

13. http://falaw.us/How%20to%20Divide%20Equity%20Among%20Startup%20 Founders.pdf.
14. Demmler, F. (2018). The Founder's Pie Calculator. http://www.andrew.cmu. edu/user/fd0n/35%20Founders%27%20Pie%20Calculator.htm.
15. https://www.innovationworks.org/toolkit/wp-content/uploads/2009/09/ founders-pie-calculator-final.xls.

14

Business Law 101

Everything is legal, until you ask a lawyer.

Disclaimer: This chapter is designed to provide general information in regard to the subject matter and may not reflect the most current legal or financial developments, verdicts, or settlements. This information is made available with the understanding that the chapter does not constitute the rendering of legal advice or other professional services. If legal advice is required, such professional services should be sought.

14.1 Introduction

Founder-entrepreneurs must know accounting although they are not accountants; they must know advertising and promotion although they are not marketing experts. Likewise, they must know fundamental business law although they are not attorneys. This chapter will introduce some of the basic law concepts all entrepreneurs must know to stay out of legal trouble.

Black's Law Dictionary defines law as "a body of rules of action or conduct prescribed by a controlling authority, and having binding legal force that must be obeyed and followed by citizens subject to sanctions or legal consequences."

The entrepreneur must realize that the "law" is not necessarily based on logic or common sense. The applicable law is generally based on *precedent*—that is, deciding cases on the basis of prior written decisions. In relying on those prior decisions, the judge will reason that since a current case is pretty much like a prior case, it ought to be decided the same way. This is essentially reasoning by analogy. Thus the use of precedent[1] in common-law cases came into being, and the doctrine of *stare decisis*[2] became accepted in all English-speaking lands.

This chapter is not meant to replace consultation with a lawyer. On the contrary, because of the complexities of the business laws, rules, and regulations, it is advisable to "partner" with a knowledgeable attorney. Table 14.1 lists the four most important functions your attorney can provide.

TABLE 14.1

The Four Most Important Functions of Attorneys for Startups

1. Counsel, advisor	Assist in preparing all required legal documentation
2. Referral source	To venture capital firms, bankers, private investors, and regulatory agencies
3. Supporter	By preparing and negotiating agreements and by making sure you understand what you are signing
4. Confidant	Your trusted source under attorney–client privilege

Your small-business lawyer will help you navigate the process of incorporation and represent your small business during legal negotiations. Perhaps the lawyer will agree to be paid in installments tied to specific milestones. Mark Suster, a small-business lawyer, blogs that lawyers should be selected based on three criteria: they should be local, the right size, and startup focused.[3]

However, be aware there is also a downside to small-business lawyers. The Walker Corporate Law Group listed their "Top 10 Reasons Why Entrepreneurs Hate Lawyers"[4] as follows:

- 10: "Because they don't communicate clearly or concisely"
- 9: "Because they don't keep me informed"
- 8: "Because they are constantly over-lawyering"
- 7: "Because they have poor listening skills"
- 6: "Because inexperienced lawyers are doing most of the work"
- 5: "Because they spend too much time on insignificant issues"
- 4: "Because they don't genuinely care about me or my matter"
- 3: "Because their fees are through the roof"
- 2: "Because they are unresponsive"
- 1: "Because they are deal-killers"

14.2 Naming Your Baby (The Legal Way)

You are now the parent of a new baby, and like all parents you need to name your company and the products it will offer. Corporations conduct their business activities under their "true" legal name—that is, the name that identifies a company for legal, administrative, and other official purposes. As you will see, this is no easy task. Large and small companies alike have made embarrassing and costly mistakes.

Your optimal company name will depend on two factors: (1) How much *gravitas* your company requires for customer acquisition. Gravitas, in this context, is the perception of your company's connectedness, funding, and relevance in its intended market(s). (2) Whether you are business to business (B2B) or business to customer (B2C). Since many B2C businesses depend on advertising, their potential to go "viral," perception, and social discovery for customer sales, carefully consider how you intend to acquire customers and then determine the importance of *name equity* in your customer acquisition strategies.[5]

14.2.1 Bad Company Names

(1) An Egyptian airline, Misair, was very unpopular with the French, since the name, when pronounced in French, meant "misery." (2) The AMF Corporation had to change its name because AMF is the official acronym of the Australian Military Forces. (3) Sew What, Hair Foyer, and Outerware Outhouse are other examples of poorly chosen company names.

14.2.2 Bad Product Names

(1) The pharmaceutical giant Abbott Labs named its blockbuster anti-arthritis drug Humira, which the company marketing department insists should be pronounced "hu-MARE-ah." (2) General Motors had problems in Latin America when it introduced the Chevrolet Nova. Literally translated in Latin, *nova* means "new star," but in Spanish it sounds like *no va*, meaning "does not go." (3) Yves St. Laurent faced a storm of criticism in China when it named its new fragrance Opium, an illegal drug.

14.3 Types of Law Related to Business

Business law dictates how to form, run, buy, manage, sell, or close any type of business. Law pervades every aspect of business to prevent confusion and ensure predictability. For instance, no game—be it baseball, football, or hockey—can be played without rules; knowledge of the law is vitally important for business leaders. But ignorance of the law is no defense, as will be discussed.

Ignorantia juris non excusat or *Ignorantia legis neminem excusat* (Latin for "Ignorance of the law excuses not" and "Ignorance of the law excuses no one," respectively) is a legal principle holding that a person who is unaware of a law may not escape liability for violating that law merely because one was unaware of its content.[6] The rationale behind the doctrine is that if ignorance of the law were a legal defense, a person charged with criminal offenses or a subject of a civil lawsuit would merely claim that he or she was unaware of the law in question to avoid liability, even if that were not really the case.

Thus, the law imputes knowledge of all laws to all persons within the jurisdiction, no matter how transiently. Even though it would be impossible, even for practicing attorneys, to be aware of every law in operation in every aspect of a state's activities, this is the price paid to ensure that willful blindness cannot become the basis of exculpation. Thus, it is a well-settled principle that persons engaged in commerce, such as running a nuclear power plant, will learn the laws necessary to engage in that activity. If they do not, they cannot protest if they break the law and incur a liability.

The doctrine assumes that the law in question has been properly promulgated—published and distributed, for example, by being printed in a government gazette, made available over the Internet, or printed in volumes available for sale to the public at affordable prices. In the ancient phrase of Gratian, *Leges instituuntur cum promulgantur* (Laws are instituted when they are promulgated).[7] A law can only bind when it is reasonably possible for those to whom it applies to acquire the necessary knowledge, even if actual knowledge of the law is absent for a particular individual. A secret law is no law at all.

Therefore, an entrepreneur must be familiar with the many types of law that will affect the business. Table 14.2 lists the most important laws that impact the business community concerning trade industry and commerce.

14.3.1 Legal Structure

Once you have selected your company's name, it is time (in conjunction with your lawyer) to select the firm's legal structure. Each structure has specific advantages and disadvantages, so your circumstances will dictate which legal structure(s) are available, and which choice might be optimal for your vision and mission. Your choices are shown in Figure 14.1.

Before we discuss the relative strengths and disadvantages of different corporate structures, Table 14.3 reviews the legal terminology associated with various types of entities.

14.4 Choosing Your Business Form

One of the first decisions that will need to be made by a startup enterprise is to choose a form of business organization. In order to make such a determination, an entrepreneur will need to focus on the likely capital structure of the organization (i.e., who are the likely or targeted equity owners of the business) and the exit strategy. The following is a general description of the advantages and disadvantages of the three major business entities. There are at least five legally recognized forms of business organizations:

1. **Sole proprietorship:** Easy to make, unlimited liability
2. **General partnership:** Easy to make, unlimited liability

TABLE 14.2

Important Definitions

Contract law	Delineates rules on agreements to buy and sell items or services. A contract is a legally binding agreement made between two or more persons, enforceable by the courts.
Property law	Specifies the rights and obligations that a person (or corporation) has when they buy, sell, or rent homes and land (called *real property* or *realty*) and objects (also called *personal property*).
Intellectual property (IP)	Rights people have over things they create, such as art, music, and literature. This is called *copyright*. It also protects inventions, by a type of law called *patent*. It also covers the rights people have to the names of their company or a distinctive mark or logo. This is called a *trademark*.
Trust law (business law)	Rules for money placed into an investment, such as pension funds that people save up for their retirement. It involves many different types of law, including administrative and property law.
Tort law	Wrongs between persons, used to make claims for compensation (repayment) when someone hurts them or hurts their property.
Criminal law	Used by the government to prevent people from breaking laws and punish people who do break them.
Constitutional law	Deals with the important rights of the government and its relationship with the people. It primarily involves the interpretation of a constitution, including the *separation of powers* of the different branches of government.
Corporations, partnership laws	Corporate law deals with firms that are incorporated or registered under the corporate or company law of a sovereign state or their subnational states. The four defining characteristics of the modern corporation are 1. Separate legal personality of the corporation (access to tort and contract law in a manner similar to a person) 2. Limited liability of the shareholders (A shareholder's personal liability is limited to the value of their shares in the corporation.) 3. Shares (If the corporation is a public company, the shares are traded on a stock exchange.) 4. Delegated management (The Board of Directors delegates the day-to-day management of the company to executives.)
Regulatory laws	Involves regulations and the operation of the administrative agencies, such as the FDA, EPA, etc.
International law	Rules on how countries can act in areas such as trade, the environment, or healthcare delivery.
Consumer protection law	Group of laws and organizations designed to ensure the rights of consumers, as well as fair trade, competition, and accurate information in the marketplace. The laws are designed to prevent the businesses that engage in fraud or specified unfair practices from gaining an advantage over competitors.
Employment law	Covers how to hire and fire, benefits, medical insurance, and employee taxes.

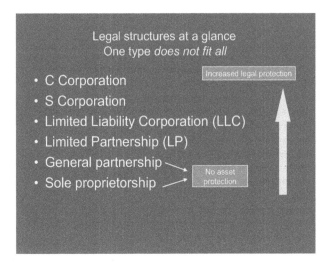

FIGURE 14.1
U.S. business entities and their respective legal protection to owners.

3. **Limited partnership:** Regulated formation, different levels of liability

4. **S and C corporations:** Regulated formation, liability limited to investment

5. **Limited liability company:** Regulated formation, liability limited to investment

A number of considerations factor into the decision as to which business entity is best suited for your startup company. Some of these factors include (1) business size, (2) capital requirements, (3) tolerance of personal risk, (4) taxes, (5) corporate governance and control, (6) plans for growth, (7) your leadership style, and (8) your exit strategy.

Each legal form has advantages and disadvantages. For example, while it is simple to set up and operate a sole proprietorship, the owner will be subject to unlimited personal liability for the business. On the other hand,

TABLE 14.3

Legal Terminology of Corporations

Term	C and S Corps	LLCs	LPs and GPs
Owner	Shareholder	Member	General or limited partner
Executive management	Board chairman, CEO, CFO	Managers	General or limited partners
Incorporated in a state	Articles of incorporation	Articles of incorporation	Certificate of limited or general partnership
Governance documents	Bylaws	Operating agreement	LP & GP agreement

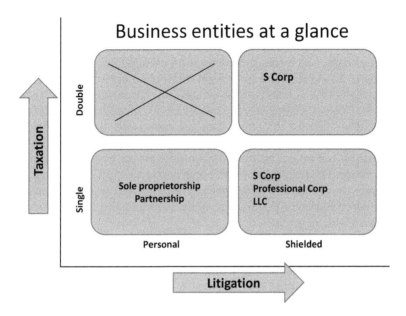

FIGURE 14.2
Advantages of business entities.

the administration of a corporation can be cumbersome and corporate earnings can be subject to *double taxation*. However, the owners of a corporation typically have limited liability and shares that are saleable and transferable.

In this section, we will provide an overview of the various forms of business organizations and highlight the potential advantages and disadvantages for your business, as summarized in Figure 14.2.

As a business owner, you should match a legal structure to your business having considered five key factors, as follows:

1. Taxation (taxes on profits paid through personal taxes or through corporation)
2. Liability and risk (harm to a person, torts, strict product liability)
3. Management (decision-making authority, corporate governance)
4. Continuity and transferability (how the business persists and how it is sold)
5. Expense and formality (cost, legal responsibilities, degree of complexity)

14.4.1 Sole Proprietorship

The sole proprietorship is the simplest form of a business entity; that is, "You are on your own." In a sole proprietorship, ownership is limited generally to a single individual. There is no legal distinction between the person and the business entity. A sole proprietor can hire employees or contractors to work in the business; however, the owner alone is legally responsible for all aspects of the business, meaning they are personally liable for the obligations of the business.

The entity is not taxed, as the profits and losses are passed through to the sole proprietor. The proprietor contributes whatever capital is needed to start and operate the business. The owner is in direct control of all elements and is legally accountable for the finances of the business; this may include debts, loans, losses, and so on.[8]

It is a "sole" proprietorship, in contrast with a partnership (which has at least two owners). A sole proprietor may use a trade name or business name other than their legal name. They may have to legally trademark their business name. If a sole proprietor wishes to run the business under a name different from his or her own, the owner must file a Certificate of Assumed Name in the county clerk's office. The certificate is sometimes called a Certificate of Conducting Business as a Sole Proprietor. This entire process is referred to as a *doing business as* (DBA) filing.

If you are dissatisfied with this kind of exposure, you should consider a more complex entity and consider allowing additional owners to join the business or to manage and mitigate the personal risk of the owner. Sole proprietorships are easy to set up. Generally speaking, all that is legally required is a license to do business, a notice filed with local or state government, and an application for the proper tax identification numbers.

14.4.2 Liability of Sole Proprietorships

The greatest downside to the simplicity of a sole proprietorship is the unlimited financial and legal exposure of the owner. Because the owner and the business are legally indistinguishable, a sole proprietor has unlimited personal liability for the business; the debts of the business are the debts of the owner, and conversely, the debts of the owner are the debts of the business.

Moreover, because an owner's personal assets may be available to satisfy the debts of the sole proprietorship, a legal judgment against a sole proprietorship could be financially devastating. Any entrepreneur thinking about forming a sole proprietorship should perform due diligence to determine if any insurance is available to alleviate the risks associated with running a sole proprietorship.

Creditors may ask for personal loan guarantees, and the owner will be responsible for these loan amounts even if the sole proprietorship is dissolved as a business. If the business is found liable for causing harm, loss, or injury to an individual, such as someone being injured by a faulty product sold by the company, then all of his personal financial assets are at risk when compensating the victim.

14.4.3 Capital Contributions

A sole proprietorship's growth potential is limited by the availability of capital. The growth of a sole proprietorship depends entirely on the resources available to the sole proprietor and the ability of the business to generate sales to support growth.

Practically speaking, most capital originates from the proprietor's own resources or loans that can be secured from banks or third parties. It can be very difficult for a sole proprietorship to raise additional capital, because the sole proprietor remains personally liable for all the debts of the sole proprietorship, regardless of how large and sophisticated the business becomes.

14.4.4 Taxation Issues

A sole proprietorship is a *pass-through* entity: taxation of the business is accomplished by passing the business's income and expenses through the owner's personal tax return. In addition, your business may be subject to other taxes from the city or county in which the sole proprietor resides, such as a city income tax. An entrepreneur should consult a tax accountant, as needed, to determine what federal, state, and local taxes may apply to the sole proprietorship.

14.4.5 Management Structure

The sole proprietor manages the business. The owner may decide to employ others to fulfill business requirements, but the final decisions rest with the owner. The business owner does not have to answer to anyone regarding decisions about business operations. They only need to keep business operations safe and legal and run a business that is profitable enough to meet its financial obligations and goals.[9]

Decision making in a sole proprietorship is ultimately the responsibility of the sole owner. Although a shrewd sole proprietor may hire consultants with knowledge and experience who can help make sound decisions, in the end it is the owner's decision whether to implement any of the suggestions that advisers make. A sole proprietor can authorize employees to make certain types of decisions, typically those with limited scope such as making inventory purchases, equipment maintenance, and so on.

Table 14.4 summarizes the salient features of a sole partnership.

TABLE 14.4

Salient Features of a Sole Partnership

Ownership	One owner
Personal Liability	Unlimited personal liability for the owner.
Taxation Issues	Entity is not taxed, as the profits and losses are passed through to the sole proprietor.
Documents Needed for Formation	Doing business as (DBA).
Capital Contributions	Sole proprietor contributes whatever capital needed.

14.5 General Partnerships

A general partnership is a business with multiple owners, where each owner contributes resources, time, and effort to accomplish common business objectives. It allows interested individuals to combine their talents and come together as partners. Business ventures with more than one principal may choose to begin as a general partnership because it is relatively easy to administer. As the business grows, it is possible to evolve into a different form of business. However, due to the financial exposure of *joint and several liability*,[10] in a general partnership model, general partnerships are not commonly chosen as the business model for technology ventures.

14.5.1. Formation, Ownership Transfer, Dissolution, and Termination

As with the sole proprietorship, a general partnership typically does not require formal formation documents. As a practical matter, the terms governing the partnership should put into a written document signed by the parties and not simply left as a verbal agreement between individuals.

Written documentation allows for clarity when depicting partner rights and responsibilities. A discussion of partnership agreements follows.

- If a trade name is adopted for the business, it is necessary to file a DBA in each county or municipality in which the general partnership will do business with a Certificate of Assumed Name.
- Barring any agreement to the contrary, partnerships are dissolved when one or both of the partners dies or otherwise withdraws from the partnership. Partnerships can also terminate in a period stipulated by agreement.
- In the event that a partnership agreement can be reached, that agreement may give a partner rights to buy or sell his or her interest in the partnership. The dissolution of a partnership occurs when one of the partners leaves the business. This happens generally when a partner resigns, dies, or is permanently disabled, and can also occur if the

other partners expel a partner from the business. The business continues to operate after the dissolution but only for a limited period of time. The outgoing partner may negotiate a settlement with the other partners that details the division of the firm's assets between the owners. Dissolutions generally go to court if the partners cannot agree on how to split the firm's assets and liabilities.[11]

- Under state and federal laws, the termination of a partnership occurs when it ceases operations. Additionally, the IRS regards a partnership as having been terminated if more than 50% of its assets are sold or disbursed within a 12-month period. Therefore, partnership terminations are easily distinguished from dissolutions because the partnership remains active during the dissolution process. It could take several years for the partners of a major firm to reach an agreement on the dissolution of the business, but all activities of the partnership cease upon termination.

14.5.2 Liability of General Partnerships

Each partner is an agent of the general partnership, meaning that each partner has the ability to act on behalf of the general partnership and has unlimited personal liability with respect to the partnership. This form of liability is known as *joint and several* liability, meaning each partner is both jointly liable with the other partners and individually liable if another partner's assets cannot satisfy the judgment.

This creates a situation where each partner may have to contribute personal assets to pay damages that result from decisions or actions that other partners make with respect to the partnership. For this reason, general partnerships are not usually selected as a business entity for technology enterprises. A corporation or *limited liability company* (LLC) may act as a general partner, thus limiting an individual owner's liability—provided that the proper formalities are maintained.

14.5.3 Management and Ownership

Because there are multiple principals or partners involved, management of a general partnership is more complicated than a sole proprietorship. Each partner may have different interests and demands, bring different skills to the business, and have different expectations. General partners have the ability to define the obligations and benefits for each partner in a written partnership agreement. Such an agreement can prevent conflicts before they arise and provide a way to address the issues.

Absent a partnership agreement, and regardless of the contributions that each partner makes, each partner is likely to have: (1) an equal share in the management of the general partnership, (2) the ability to bind the general partnership in contract, and (3) the right to share in the profits and losses in equal proportion to other partners.

As mentioned, however, terms and conditions governing the partnership may be set out in an agreement, thereby limiting conflicts and formalizing management. Partnership agreements can be fairly general, addressing only the most basic provisions of the partnership and laying out the basic processes for running the business. Alternatively, they can be detailed documents, addressing very specific issues and focusing on the partners' needs, their contributions, the distribution of profits and debts, and the elements of termination.

A typical partnership agreement will usually address

- Percentages of ownership
- Distributions and distribution plans
- Buyout provisions
- Alternative dispute resolution, in case there is a disagreement
- Continuation of the business following the withdrawal of a partner
- Business administration (titles, hours, benefits, etc.)
- Bankruptcy and partnership dissolution

Regardless of whether a formal partnership agreement exists, partners stand in a fiduciary relationship[12] with respect to all matters affecting the partnership. A fiduciary duty is the most protective duty owed to one another in the legal community. It requires partners to act with loyalty, good faith, fairness, and honesty in their dealings with the partnership. Partners are essentially expected to put the interests of the partnership ahead of their own personal interests and avoid real or perceived conflicts of interest.

Specifically, partners must not appropriate opportunities that are within the scope of the partnership's business for their private benefit without the consent of the other partners. This obligation, known as the *opportunity doctrine*,[13] often referenced in the corporate context, is important because it prohibits partners from diverting business opportunities for their own gain, particularly in the instance where a general partner is also a partner in other businesses. A partner who violates his or her fiduciary duties may have to account for/repay all the money gained.

The corporate opportunity doctrine is the legal principle providing that directors, officers, and controlling shareholders of a corporation must not take for themselves any business opportunity that could benefit the corporation. The corporate opportunity doctrine is one application of the fiduciary duty of loyalty.[14]

14.5.4 Growth Potential

Because there are additional individuals involved, the growth potential for a general partnership is greater than that of a sole proprietorship. However, some of the same limitations exist for partnerships: it can be difficult to buy or sell an interest in the partnership, financing may require that owners personally guarantee a loan, and it may be difficult to minimize personal liability for the owners of the business.

14.5.5 Taxation Issues

As with a sole proprietorship, a general partnership is not taxed as a separate entity. It is a pass-through entity. Profits and losses are ascribed in proportion to the ownership percentage of each partner. This avoids double taxation. Nonetheless, a general partnership must obtain a Taxpayer Identification Number and file an informational tax return every year for federal taxes. In addition, it may be subject to other taxes from the state, city, or county in which the partnership does business.

14.5.6 Summary Advantages and Disadvantages

Because each of the partners has unlimited personal liability, a general partnership is the single most dangerous form for conducting business. Not only is a partner liable for contracts entered into by other partners, each partner is also liable for the other partners' negligence. For example, when two or more physicians or other professionals practice together as a partnership, each partner is liable for the negligence or malpractice of any other partner.[15]

Table 14.5 summarizes the salient features of a general partnership.

Because of the joint and several liabilities of general partners, the level of business risk is increased dramatically by this form of business organization. Since most of these risks are effectively eliminated with an LLC, the general partnership seems to be a legal relic. It is now used primarily in situations where state law does not permit physicians and other professionals to use an LLC to conduct business. Figure 14.3 summarizes the most important advantages and disadvantages of a general partnership.

TABLE 14.5

Salient Features of a General Partnership

Ownership	Unlimited number of general partners allowed.
Personal Liability	Unlimited personal liability of the general partners for the obligations of the business.
Taxation Issues	Entity not taxed, as the profits and losses are passed through to the general partners.
Documents Needed for Formation	General partnership agreement; local filings if partnership is formed.
Management of the Business	General partners have equal management rights, unless they agree otherwise.
Capital Contributions	General partners typically contribute money or services to the partnership, and receive an interest in profits and losses.

- Owned by two or more people
- Examples
  - Law firms
  - Medical practices
  - Public accountants
- Advantages
  - Relatively easy to start
  - Easier to obtain capital than in a sole proprietorship
  - Partners share skills and talents
  - Partners share risks
- Disadvantages
  - Partnership agreement is needed to start
  - Partners might not get along well
  - Partners must share profits
  - Partnership must be reorganized if one partner quits
  - Partners share unlimited liability—all partners share the responsibility of a bad decision made by one partner (including debts)

FIGURE 14.3
General partnership characteristics.

14.6 Limited Partnerships

A *limited partnership* (LP) is defined as a partnership formed by two or more persons under the laws of a state and having one or more general partners and one or more limited partners, under the Uniform Limited Partnership Act (ULPA),[16] Section 102(11). It is a hybrid form, since it shares some aspects of partnerships and some of corporations. Corporations encompass the benefits of limited liability, while partnerships enjoy the benefit of limited taxation.

This type of structure tends to be attractive in business situations that focus on a single or limited-term project, such as making a movie or developing a blockbuster software program; it is also widely used by private equity firms.

In general, the rules of general partnerships also apply to LPs. The fundamental difference is that in an LP, there are two classes of partners: general partners, who have unlimited liability for the actions of the partnership, and limited partners, whose liability is limited to their capital contribution to the partnership—the amount of capital invested in the partnership. A second significant difference is that the limited partners do not have fiduciary duties to the partnership; general partners generally shoulder the burden of fiduciary duties. And as with general partnerships, a corporation may act as either a general partner or a limited partner.

14.6.1 Formation, Transfer of Ownership, and Dissolution

An LP must file a Certificate of Limited Partnership with the corresponding Department of State, Division of Corporations, and, in some states, in each municipality or county in which they will do business within 120 days of filing. The publication must appear weekly in two newspapers in the county for six successive weeks detailing the LP.

An LP allows an investor to put capital into a partnership in exchange for a proportional share of the profits without being subject to the liabilities that a general partner may be subjected. A limited partner is only liable for their actual investment; their personal assets are protected. Because of this, a limited partner cannot write checks or sign contracts on behalf of the partnership and usually is not involved in the management of the business or its operations. If a limited partner is more involved in the company's activities, they may be deemed as a general partner by law.

An LP, if it chooses, may also become a limited liability partnership (LLP). In an LLP, there is no general partner and the limited partners have a right to manage the business directly and are not responsible for the misconduct of the other partners. Not all states allow LLPs, and in some states, they are only permitted for lawyers, accountants, or architects.

- **Transfer:** A limited partner's interest is a security that can be transferred, or assigned, to a third party, but general and limited partners generally have the right to refuse the transfer. This is to protect the original partnership interests. The Certificate of Limited Partnership may grant any assignee the right to become a limited partner without the consent of other members of the partnership.

- **Dissolution:** Unless a partnership agreement says otherwise, a general partner can dissolve an LP in the same manner as a general partnership. A limited partner may only seek judicial dissolution, which is more limiting than a general partner's dissolution powers. Because limited partners are not managers, they can leave the partnership without dissolving the entity. In many states, after the partnership is dissolved and the partnership has finished winding up business, the partnership must file a Certificate of Cancellation.

14.6.2 Liability of Limited Partnerships

An LP has at least one general partner and at least one limited partner. The general partner has the same role as in a general partnership: controlling the company's day-to-day operations and being personally liable for business debts, as follows:[17]

- **Limited partners do not play an active role in the business.** The limited partners (most LPs have more than one limited partner) contribute financially to the business (e.g., a limited partner might invest $100,000 in a real estate partnership) but have minimal control over business decisions or operations and normally cannot bind the partnership to business deals.

- **Limited partners are not personally liable.** In return for giving up management power, limited partners are generally protected from personal liability. This means that a limited partner can't be forced to pay off business debts or claims with personal assets. A limited partner, however, can lose his or her financial investment in the business.

- **Limited partners face slightly different tax rules.** For income tax purposes, LPs are generally treated like general partnerships, with all partners individually reporting and paying taxes on their share of the profits each year. Limited partners, as a rule, do not have to pay self-employment taxes because they are not active in the business; their share of partnership income is not considered "earned income" for the purposes of self-employment tax.

Note: Limited partners need to understand that they can become *personally liable* if they do not adhere to their passive role. If a limited partner starts taking an active role in the business, that partner's liability can become unlimited. If a creditor can prove that a limited partner engaged in acts that led the creditor to believe that he or she was a general partner, that partner can be held fully and personally liable for the creditor's claims.

14.6.3 Management and Ownership

An LP is distinctly different from a general partnership. Limited partners have no voice in how the business is managed. The management of an LP business may or may not have officers and a Board of Directors. The level of management structure depends on the size and purpose of the LP.[18]

The LP structure allows a company to be run like more like a corporation, with limited partner units trading on the stock exchanges. A publicly traded LP will have officers and a Board of Directors for the general partner. A completely separate publicly traded company that is a corporation or another LP may own the general partner interests of a publicly traded LP. You will know if a stock is a partnership if it has "Partners" in the name or "LP" at the end of the name instead of "Inc." or "Corp."

You can organize a small business as an LP, using the partnership as a way to bring in investors without giving up any control of how your business is run. As the general partner of a closely held LP, you can decide if your business needs a Board of Directors or other officers besides yourself. It is possible to just be the general partner yourself, or you can have multiple general partners who run the business together while the limited partners just receive a portion of the profits.

14.6.4 Growth Potential

The growth of an LP is theoretically unlimited. It is primarily dependent on the partners' ability to attract investors to the partnership in order to reach financial goals.

14.6.5 Taxation Issues

The main tax advantage of an LP is that it is a flow-through entity; all profits and losses flow directly to the individual limited partners. The business itself pays no taxes on its income. Limited partners receive income in the form of distributions. Part of the distribution may be taxed as ordinary income, part may be treated as capital gains, and part may not be taxed at all if it is a return on invested capital.

However, because the limited partners do not participate directly in the business, the income from an LP is considered passive income, and the losses can only be used to offset other passive income until the investor's interest in the partnership is terminated—after which, losses can be used to offset other types of income

14.6.6 Summary of Advantages and Disadvantages

An LP is a creature of statute: it requires filing a certificate with the state because it confers on some of its members the marvel of limited liability. It is an investment device composed of one or more general partners and one or more limited partners; limited partners may leave with 6 months' notice and are entitled to an appropriate payout.

General partners in an LP are liable in the same way as partners in a general partnership; limited partners' liability is limited to the loss of their investment, unless they exercise so much control of the firm as to become general partners. The general partner is paid, and the general and limited partners split profit as per the agreement or, if none, in proportion to their capital contributions.

The firm is usually taxed like a general partnership: it is a conduit for the partners' incomes. The firm is dissolved at the end of its term, upon an event specified in the agreement, or in several other circumstances, but it may have indefinite existence. Table 14.6 lists the salient features of an LP.

TABLE 14.6

Salient Features of a Limited Partnership

Formation	Limited partnership certificate; limited partnership agreement.
Ownership	Unlimited number of general and limited partners allowed.
Personal Liability	Unlimited personal liability of the general partners for the obligations of the business. Limited partners generally have no personal liability.
Taxation Issues	Entity not taxed, as the profits and losses are passed through to the general and limited partners.
Management of the Business	The general partner manages the business, subject to any limitations of the limited partnership agreement.
Capital Contributions	The general and limited partners typically contribute money or services to the partnership and receive an interest in profits and losses.

14.7 Limited Liability Company

An LLC is an incorporated organization of one or more persons or entities established in accordance with applicable state laws and whose members may actively participate in the organization without being personally liable for the debts, obligations, or liabilities of the organization.

LLCs gained sweeping popularity in the late twentieth century because they combine the best aspects of partnerships and the best aspects of corporations: an LLC allows all its owners (members) insulation from personal liability and pass-through (conduit) taxation. The first efforts to form LLCs were opposed by IRS rulings that the business form was too much like a corporation to escape corporate tax complications. Continued industry pressure by advocates of the LLC concept and flexibility by the IRS solved those problems in interesting and creative ways.

Corporations have six characteristics: (1) associates, (2) an objective to carry on a business and divide the gains, (3) continuity of life, (4) centralized management, (5) limited liability, and (6) free transferability of interests. Partnerships also have the first two corporate characteristics; under IRS rulings, if an LLC is *not* to be considered a corporation for tax purposes, it must lack at least one-half of the remaining four characteristics of a corporation: an LLC, then, must lack two of these corporate characteristics (otherwise it will be considered a corporation): (1) limited liability, (2) centralized management, (3) continuity of life, or (4) free transferability of interests.

But limited liability is essential, and centralized management is necessary for passive investors who do not want to be involved in decision making, so pass-through taxation usually hinges on whether an LLC has continuity of life and free transferability of accounts. Thus, it is extremely important that LLC promoters avoid these two corporate characteristics.

14.7.1 Formation and Capitalization

An LLC is created according to the statute of the state in which it is formed. It is required that LLC members file a Certificate of Organization with the secretary of state, and the name must indicate that it is an LLC.

Partnerships and LPs may convert to LLCs; the partners' previous liability under the other organizational forms is not affected, but going forward, limited liability is provided. The members' operating agreement spells out how the business will be run; it is subordinate to state and federal law. Unless otherwise agreed, the operating agreement can be amended only by unanimous vote. The LLC is an entity. Foreign LLCs must register with the secretary of state before doing business in a "foreign" state, or they cannot sue in state courts.

Capitalization of an LLC is like a partnership: members contribute capital to the firm according to their agreement. As in a partnership, the LLC property is not specific to any member, but each has a personal property interest in general. Contributions may be in the form of cash, property, or services rendered, or a promise to render them in the future.

14.7.2 Liability

Generally speaking, there is no personal liability of the members for the obligations of the business. The great accomplishment of the LLC is to provide limited liability for all its members: no general partner has exposure to liability. Members are not liable to third parties for contracts made by the firm or for torts committed in the scope of business (but a person is always liable for his or her own torts, of course), regardless of the owner's level of participation—unlike an LP, where the general partner is liable. Third parties' only recourse is restricted against the firm's property.[19]

Unless the operating agreement provides otherwise, members and managers of the LLC are generally not liable to the firm or its members except for acts or omissions constituting gross negligence, intentional misconduct, or knowing violations of the law. Members and managers, though, must account to the firm for any personal profit or benefit derived from activities not consented to by a majority of disinterested members or managers from the conduct of the firm's business or member's or managers use of firm property, which is the same as in partnership law.

14.7.3 Management and Ownership

The LLC operating agreement may provide for either a member-managed LLC or a manager-managed (centralized) LLC. If it is the former, all members have actual and apparent authority to bind the LLC to contracts on its behalf, as in a partnership, and all members' votes have equal weight unless otherwise agreed. Member-managers have a duty of care and a fiduciary duty, although the parameters of those duties vary from state to state. If the firm is manager managed, only managers have the authority to bind the firm; the managers have the duty of care and fiduciary duty, but the non-manager members usually do not.

Most statutes provide that any extraordinary firm decisions be voted on by all members (e.g., amending the agreement, admitting new members, selling all assets prior to dissolution, merging with another entity). Members can make their own rules without the structural requirements (e.g., voting rights, notice, quorum, approval of major decisions) imposed under state corporate law.

Distributions are allocated among owners of an LLC according to the operating agreement; managing partners may be paid for their services. Absent an agreement, distributions are allocated among members in proportion to the values of contributions made by them or required to be made by them. Upon a member's dissociation that does not cause dissolution, a dissociating member has the right to distribution as provided in the agreement, or—if there is no agreement—the right to receive the fair value of the member's interest within a reasonable time after dissociation. No distributions are allowed if making them would cause the LLC to become insolvent.

14.7.4 Growth Potential

Compared with corporations, the LLC is not a good form if the owners expect to have multiple investors or to raise money from the public. The typical LLC has relatively few members (six or seven at most), several of whom usually are engaged in running the firm. Raising public capital is best performed under a corporate structure.

The LLC type is best suited for the "lifestyle" entrepreneur, who is comfortable with "making a good living" but does not aspire to become a large, publicly held company.

14.7.5 Taxation Issues

Assuming the LLC is properly formed so that it is not too much like a corporation, it will—upon its members' election—be treated like a partnership for tax purposes. If the firm has a centralized manager system, it gets a check in its "corporate-like" box, so it will need to make sure there are enough non-corporate-like attributes to make up for this one. If it looks too much like a corporation, it will be taxed like a corporation.

14.7.6 Summary Advantages and Disadvantages

The LLC has become the entity of choice for many entrepreneurs.. It is created by state authority, which issues the Certificate of Organization upon application. It is controlled either by managers or by members, it affords its members limited liability, and it is taxed like a partnership. But these happy results are obtained only if the firm lacks enough corporate attributes to escape being labeled as a corporation.

To avoid too much "corporateness," the firm's certificate usually limits its continuity of life and the free transferability of interest. The ongoing game is to finesse these limits: to make them as non-constraining as possible, to get right up to the line to preserve continuity, and to make the interest as freely transferable as possible.

14.8 S Corporation

A corporation is a legal person that can be created under state law and is thus a legal fiction. As a "person," a corporation has certain rights and obligations, including the right to do business in its own name and the obligation to pay taxes. Some laws use the words *natural persons*, referring only to individual human beings, but with few exceptions, corporations have many of the rights and obligations as individuals.

An *S corporation* (also referred to as an *S corp*) is a special type of corporation created through an IRS tax election. An eligible domestic corporation can avoid double taxation (once to the corporation and again to the shareholders) by electing to be treated as an S corp.[20]

An S corp is a corporation with the Subchapter S designation from the IRS. What makes the S corp different from a traditional corporation (C corporation or C corp) is that profits and losses can pass through to your personal tax return. Consequently, the business is not taxed itself. Only the shareholders are taxed.

A corporation must meet certain conditions to be eligible for a subchapter S election. First, the corporation must have no more than 75 shareholders. In calculating the 75 shareholder limit, a husband and wife count as one shareholder. Also, only the following entities may be shareholders: individuals, estates, certain trusts, certain partnerships, tax-exempt charitable organizations, and other S corps (but only if they are the sole shareholders).

There is an important caveat, however: any shareholder who works for the company must pay him or herself "reasonable compensation." Basically, the shareholder must be paid fair market value, or the IRS may reclassify any additional corporate earnings as "wages."

14.8.1 Formation and Capitalization

The term *S corporation* means a "small business corporation" that has made an election under Section 1362(a). In order to be taxed as an S corp, a corporation must meet the following four requirements:

- Has no more than 100 shareholders
- Has shareholders who are all individuals (exceptions are made for various tax exempt organizations, estates, and trusts)
- Has no non-resident aliens as shareholders
- Has only one class of stock

An LLC is eligible to be taxed as an S corp under the check-the-box regulations at Section 301.7701-2. The procedure is twofold: The LLC first elects to be taxed as a corporation, at which point it becomes a "corporation" for tax purposes; then it makes a second S corp election under Section 1362(a).[21]

To file as an S corp, you must first file as a corporation. After you are considered a corporation, all shareholders must sign and file Form 2553 to elect your corporation to become an S corp. Once your business is registered, you must obtain business licenses and permits. Regulations vary by industry, state, and locality.

There is always the possibility of requesting S Corp status for your LLC. Your attorney can advise you on the advantages and disadvantages. You will have to make a special election with the IRS to have the LLC taxed as an S Corp using Form 2553. And you must file before the first 2 months and 15 days from the beginning of the tax year in which the election is to take effect.

An S Corp designation allows a business to have an independent life, separate from its shareholders. If a shareholder leaves the company or sells his or her shares, the S Corp can continue doing business relatively undisturbed. Maintaining the business as a distinct corporate entity defines clear lines between the shareholders and the business that improve the protection of the shareholders.

14.8.2 Liability

An S corp operates as a partnership or LLC in that income and expenses are "passed through" to individual owners' tax returns, thus avoiding the double tax of C corps. Yet an S corp protects personal assets from debts and claims against the company, a protection shared by all corporations and LLCs. Only shareholders' actual investments are at risk. But that protection is limited and can even be lost without proper accounting.

14.8.3 Management and Ownership

The Board of Directors is the controlling body of a corporation that makes major corporate decisions and elects the officers. It usually meets just once a year. In most states, a corporation can have one director (who can also hold all offices and own all the stock). In a small corporation, the officers are appointed by the Board of Directors to run the day-to-day operations of the corporation. Commonly, and by law in many states, a corporation will have at least three officers: a president, a treasurer or chief financial officer, and a secretary. Officers do not necessarily have to be shareholders or directors.[22]

Shareholders must be U.S. citizens or residents (not non-resident aliens) and must be natural persons, so corporations and partnerships are ineligible shareholders. However, certain trusts, estates, and tax-exempt corporations, notably 501(c)(3) corporations, are permitted to be shareholders. An S corp may be a shareholder in another, subsidiary S corp if the first S corp owns 100% of the stock of the subsidiary corporation, and an election is made to treat the subsidiary corporation as a *qualified subchapter S subsidiary* (QSub). After the election is made, the subsidiary corporation is not treated as a separate corporation for tax purposes, and all "assets, liabilities, and items of income, deduction, and credit" of the QSub are treated as belonging to the parent S corp.

An S corp may only have one class of stock. A single class of stock means that all outstanding shares of stock confer "identical rights to distribution and liquidation proceeds"; that is, profits and losses are allocated to shareholders proportionately to each one's interest in the business (Section 1.1361-1(l)(1) of the Code of Federal Regulations (26 CFR)). Differences in voting rights are disregarded, which means that an S corp may have voting and non-voting stock.

14.8.4 Growth Potential

In general, all corporations have the legal right to sell shares to (1) generate capital, (2) limit liability, and (3) provide for a perpetual existence, allowing for significant growth and the ability to take on projects that have higher costs and longer payback periods.

An S Corp may sell shares to the public, but this ability to raise capital is constrained by some tax and ownership issues, since not all states tax S Corps in an identical fashion (see the following section on taxation issues). Up to 75 shareholders are allowed; only one basic class of stock is allowed.

14.8.5 Taxation Issues

The LLC remains an LLC from a legal standpoint, but for tax purposes it's treated as an S corp. All states do not tax S corps equally. Most recognize them similarly to the federal government and tax the shareholders accordingly. However, some states (e.g., Massachusetts) tax S Corps on profits above a specified limit. Other states don't recognize the S Corp election and treat the business as a C Corp, with all the tax ramifications. Some states (e.g., New York and New Jersey) tax both the S Corp's profits and the shareholder's proportional shares of the profits.

Your S Corp must file Form 2553 to elect S corp status within 2 months and 15 days after the beginning of the tax year or any time before the tax year for the status to be in effect.

- **Tax Savings:** One of the best features of the S Corp is the tax savings for you and your business. While members of an LLC are subject to employment tax on the entire net income of the business, only the wages of the S corp shareholder who is an employee are subject to employment tax. The remaining income is paid to the owner as a *distribution*, which is taxed at a lower rate, if at all.
- **Business Expense Tax Credits:** Some expenses that shareholder-employees incur can be written off as business expenses. Nevertheless, if such an employee owns 2% or more shares, then benefits such as health and life insurance are deemed taxable income.

14.8.6 Summary Advantages and Disadvantages

S corps also have certain advantages with respect to exit strategies. Unlike C corps, because S corps are generally only subject to one level of tax, the taxable sale of an S corp can generally be structured in a tax-efficient manner that delivers a stepped-up basis to the buyer with only one level of tax imposed on the seller.

The IPO of an S corp can generally be accomplished with minimal restructuring. The primary disadvantage of an S corp is its limited flexibility with respect to its capital structure. Among other requirements, the S corp can have only one class of stock and no more than 75 shareholders. Subject to certain limited exceptions, its shareholders must be individuals, which prevents many potential investors from being shareholders in an S corp, including most institutional investors and venture capitalists.

The advantages of an S corp often outweigh any perceived disadvantages. The S corp structure can be especially beneficial when it comes time to transfer ownership or discontinue the business. These advantages are typically unavailable to sole proprietorships and general partnerships. Advantages include the following:[23]

- **Protected assets:** An S corp protects the personal assets of its shareholders. Absent an express personal guarantee, a shareholder is not personally responsible for the business debts and liabilities of the corporation. Creditors cannot pursue the personal assets (house, bank accounts, etc.) of the shareholders to pay business debts. In a sole proprietorship or general partnership, owners and the business are legally considered the same—leaving personal assets vulnerable.

- **Pass-through taxation:** An S corp does not pay federal taxes at the corporate level. Most, but not all, states follow the federal rules. Any business income or loss is "passed through" to shareholders who report it on their personal income tax returns. This means that business losses can offset other income on the shareholders' tax returns. This can be extremely helpful in the startup phase of a new business.

- **Tax-favorable characterization of income:** S corp shareholders can be employees of the business and draw salaries as employees. They can also receive dividends from the corporation, as well as other distributions that are tax free to the extent of their investment in the corporation. A *reasonable* characterization of distributions as salary or dividends can help the owner-operator reduce self-employment tax liability, while still generating business expense and wages paid deductions for the corporation.

- **Straightforward transfer of ownership:** Interests in an S corp can be freely transferred without triggering adverse tax consequences. (In a partnership or an LLC, the transfer of more than a 50% interest can trigger the termination of the entity.) The S corp does not need to make adjustments to the property basis or comply with complicated accounting rules when an ownership interest is transferred.

- **Heightened credibility:** Operating as an S corp may help a new business establish credibility with potential customers, employees, vendors, and partners because they see the owners have made a formal commitment to their business.

An S corp may have some potential disadvantages, as follows:

- **Stricter operational processes:** As a separate structure, S Corps require scheduled director and shareholder meetings, minutes from those meetings, adoptions of and updates to bylaws, stock transfers, and records maintenance.
- **Shareholder compensation requirements:** A shareholder must receive reasonable compensation. The IRS takes notice of shareholder red flags such as low-salary/high-distribution combinations and may reclassify your distributions as wages. You could pay a higher employment tax because of an audit with these results.
- **Formation and ongoing expenses:** To operate as an S corp, it is necessary to first incorporate the business by filing articles of incorporation with your desired state of incorporation, obtain a registered agent for your company, and pay the appropriate fees. Many states also impose ongoing fees, such as annual report and/or franchise tax fees. Although these fees are usually not expensive and can be deducted as a cost of doing business, they are expenses that a sole proprietor or general partnership will not incur.
- **Tax qualification obligations:** Mistakes regarding the various election, consent, notification, stock ownership, and filing requirements can accidentally result in the termination of S corp status. Although this is relatively rare and can usually be remedied easily, it is still an issue that is not a factor with other business forms.
- **Stock ownership restrictions:** An S corp can have only one class of stock, although it can have both voting and non-voting shares. Therefore, there can't be different classes of investors who are entitled to different dividends or distribution rights. Also, there cannot be more than 100 shareholders. Foreign ownership is prohibited, as is ownership by certain types of trusts and other entities.
- **Closer IRS scrutiny:** Because amounts distributed to a shareholder can be dividends or salary, the IRS scrutinizes payments to make sure the characterization conforms to reality. As a result, wages may

be recharacterized as dividends, costing the corporation a deduction for compensation paid. Conversely, dividends may be recharacterized as wages, which subjects the corporation to employment tax liability.

- **Less flexibility in allocating income and loss:** Because of the one-class-of-stock restriction, an S corp cannot easily allocate losses or income to specific shareholders. Allocation of income and loss is governed by stock ownership, unlike a partnership or LLC, where the allocation can be set in the operating agreement. Also, the necessary accumulated adjustment account can be cumbersome to maintain, requiring input from an accounting professional.

14.9 C Corporations

Any corporation is strictly defined as a legal entity that is *immortal*; that is, a corporation does not terminate upon the owner's death. Corporations can enter into and dissolve contracts, incur debts, sue or be sued, own property, and sell property, as any individual may do. Corporation owners themselves have limited liability. While an individual may own all the shares in a corporation, that owner is not personally responsible for the corporation.

With this limited liability, investors cannot lose more money than the amount they have invested in the corporation. Owners are not personally responsible for the debts and obligations of the corporation in the event these are not fulfilled. In other words, if a company with limited liability is sued, then the plaintiffs are suing the company itself, not its owners or investors.

C corps are one of the oldest forms of business entity in the country and one of the most common. As a result, some businesses may instinctively form as C corps without really considering the pros and cons as applied to their business model. It is important to note that C corps operate under state law. As a result, some issues regarding regulation will vary.[24]

C corps are subject to double taxation. The corporation is subject to income tax on its revenue, and shareholders are subject to income tax on any distribution made by the corporation to them, which includes shareholders' dividend-based income. As a result of this tax treatment, the owners of a corporation pay a higher tax rate with respect to the income earned and distributed by the corporation than they would for other sources of income. For small businesses, this high tax burden can be an unpleasant outcome.

14.9.1 Formation and Capitalization

Only after the articles of incorporation are filed and accepted by your state does the corporation acquire legal existence. Once incorporated, the board of directors meets for the first time, followed by at least one annual meeting per year. The board of directors appoints officers who conduct the business of the corporation. C Corps are formed by a six-step procedure:

1. Choose a legal name and reserve it, if the secretary of state in your state does that sort of thing (not all do). You may acquire a legal name by obtaining and retaining a trade name.
2. Draft and file your articles of incorporation with your secretary of state.
3. Issue stock certificates to the initial shareholders.
4. Apply for a business license and other certificates specific to your industry.
5. File Form SS-4 or apply online at the Internal Revenue Service website to obtain an employer identification number (EIN).
6. Apply for any other ID numbers required by state and local government agencies. Requirements vary from one jurisdiction to another, but generally your business most likely will be required to pay unemployment, disability, and other payroll taxes; you will need tax ID numbers for those accounts in addition to your EIN.

Capitalization of a C Corp is accomplished by the issuance and sale of shares. Corporate shares can be sold by the corporation or otherwise transferred by agreement, including the purchase and sale of shares in public markets. Shares can also be transferred by the shareholders to other individuals or institutions. The transfer of shares may be subject to state and federal securities laws and regulations, which can make such a transfer of shares complex and more difficult than selling other assets.

14.9.2 Liability

Generally there is no personal liability of the shareholders for the obligations of the corporation. A corporation shields owners from the debts and liabilities of the business, so long as the business is run as a true corporation. Shareholders may make agreements among themselves to pledge their own assets to protect investments in case the business fails, but this is strictly an agreement between individual shareholders and not a corporate characteristic.

It is very difficult for a creditor to pierce through the corporation to pursue the assets of individual shareholders. Even if there is only one shareholder, his or her personal assets are not available to the creditors of the corporation. This is known as the *corporate veil*.

There are, however, two limits to the protection that the corporate entity provides: criminal limits and piercing the corporate veil. The managers and officers of a corporation are not shielded from criminal repercussions if they break the law in their corporate capacity, even if the illegal activity is performed to benefit the business. For example, an officer of a corporation who commits criminal fraud can be prosecuted as an individual even if the officer's fraudulent actions were on behalf of the corporation.

14.9.3 Management and Ownership

The Board of Directors has overall strategic responsibility, and officers have day-to-day responsibilities. Regarding ownership, an unlimited number of shareholders is allowed, and there are no limits regarding stock classes.

Corporations can have complex ownership structures. Where there is institutional outside investment, it is common to have different classes of stock with different rights and privileges within the same corporation. Typically, this occurs because investors insist on the creation of a class of stock that carries with it the right to approve certain decisions, such as the payment of dividends or the composition of a Board of Directors. In other cases, the stock may carry certain preferential rights, such as the right to receive dividends, the right to purchase additional shares in future financing, or the right not to have the value of an investment diluted.

The power and rights of a corporation's owners, managers, and board members are defined and memorialized in the bylaws of the corporation. The bylaws are created during the organizational meeting and must be adopted by the shareholders. Bylaws are important because they express the rules for a business, provide comprehensive guidelines for business protocol, set forth the exact duties for the company's Board of Directors, and solidify the voting scheme for director nomination and election.

14.9.4 Growth Potential

One of the primary advantages of starting a C corp is that it allows for many owners. If you plan on starting a large corporation with thousands of shareholders, this is the route to take.

The C corp is the method of choice for publicly traded companies. Another advantage for C corps is the lower tax rate on the first $75,000 of business income. This means that even if you have a small business, the C corp can be beneficial.

Most of the largest businesses in the world are corporations (or their foreign equivalents). The combination of the ability to sell shares to generate capital, to limit liability, and to provide for a perpetual existence allows for significant growth and the ability to take on projects that have higher costs and longer payback periods.

14.9.5 Taxation Issues

One of the primary disadvantages of the C corp is double taxation. With this type of business entity, you have to pay taxes at the corporate level, and then, once the profits are distributed to shareholders, they must pay taxes on the money they receive as well. This maximizes the amount of money that goes to the government. Another drawback of using a C corp is that it requires a great deal of formality. You must have shareholder meetings, a Board of Directors and corporate minutes.

14.9.6 Summary of Advantages and Disadvantages

The primary advantages of a C corp are that they have very flexible capital structures and investors are very familiar with them. C corps also offer certain exit strategy advantages. If the exit strategy is a sale of the business, C corps can participate in tax-free reorganizations. If the exit strategy is an IPO, no significant structural changes will need to be made to consummate the IPO.

A C corp generally has three parties sharing power and control: directors, officers, and shareholders. Directors are the managers of the corporation, and officers control the day-to-day decisions and work more closely with the employees. The shareholders are the owners of the corporation, but they have little decision-making authority. The C Corp exists in perpetuity, and the ownership is transferred by the sale or inheritance of stock.

The corporation itself has certain powers. While a corporation is not the same as a natural person (e.g., a corporation cannot be put in prison), it is allowed to conduct certain activities and has been granted certain rights and privileges. Table 14.7 lists some advantages and disadvantages of C corps.

14.10 Summary of Advantages and Disadvantages of Business Types

	S Corp	C Corp	Partnership	LLP	LLC
Limited liability	Liable for money or property paid into S Corp	Liable for money or property paid into C Corp	Unlimited; not liable for negligence of other partners	Not liable for negligence of other partners	Protected, unless provided otherwise
Participation in management	No restrictions	No restrictions	Restricted to preserve limited liability	No restrictions	Only managers have authority
Legal formalities	Articles of incorporation; annual reports	Articles of incorporation; annual reports	Partnership agreement; annual reports	Partnership agreement; annual reports	Articles of incorporation; annual report
Transferability	Restrictions as imposed by securities laws	Restrictions as imposed by securities laws	Restrictions as imposed by securities laws; partners by approval of other partners	Restrictions as imposed by securities laws; partners by approval of other partners	Restrictions as imposed by state laws
Continuity of life	Perpetual	Perpetual	Dissolved upon death or withdrawal of partner	Dissolved upon death or withdrawal of partner	Dissolved upon death or withdrawal of partner
Ownership	Eligibility requirements	No restrictions	Individual to serve as general partner	No restrictions	No restrictions
Number of owners	1–100	No restrictions	At least two	At least two	At least two
Classes of ownership	One	Multiple	Multiple	Multiple	Multiple

TABLE 14.7

Advantages and Disadvantages of C Corporations

Advantages	Disadvantages
• Limited personal liability for shareholders	• Requires separate tax returns
• Easy to transfer ownership/add investors	• Net income may be double taxed
• Perpetual continuity presumed	• More costly to set up and maintain
• Unlimited number of shareholders	• Subjected to great SEC scrutiny
• Limitless ability to expand	

14.11 Business and Strict Liability Law

Criminal laws are of interest to all businesses, especially since companies may inadvertently break criminal laws. A criminal case involves a governmental decision—whether state or federal—to prosecute a defendant for violating federal laws. The law establishes a minimum penalty and does so especially in the area of criminal laws; if a criminal law is broken, the defendant can lose their freedom (go to jail) or their life (if you are convicted of a capital offense).

In a civil action, the defendant will not be sent to prison; in the worst case, they can lose property (usually money or other assets). Some of the basic differences between civil law and criminal law[25] cases are illustrated in Table 14.8.[26]

Implanted medical devices, such as pacemakers, hip replacements, analgesic pumps, coronary stents, and artificial hearts have revolutionized the way medicine is practiced. Countless Americans have had medical devices implanted directly into their bodies with miraculous results unimagined just a few decades ago. But if these devices fail, manufacturers may be held liable for civil and/or criminal liability.

14.11.1 "Defective" Ethical Drugs or Medical Devices

Product liability claims resulting from defective ethical drugs medical devices are based on all of the following, as described in Table 14.9.[27]

According to Section 2307.74 of the Ohio Revised Code on product liability, a product is defective in manufacture or construction, if,

- when it left the control of its manufacturer:
- It deviated in a material way from the design specifications, formula, or performance standards of the manufacturer.
- It deviated from otherwise identical units manufactured to the same design specifications, formula, or performance standards.

TABLE 14.8

Differences between Civil and Criminal Cases

	Civil Cases	Criminal Cases
Parties	• Plaintiff brings case • Defendant must answer or lose by default	• Prosecutor brings case • Defendant may remain silent
Proof	• Preponderance of evidence • Simple majority (51% sure)	• Beyond a reasonable doubt • Super majority (67% certain)
Reason	• To settle disputes, usually between private parties	• To maintain order in society • To punish the most blameworthy • To deter serious wrongdoing
Remedies	• Money damages (legal remedy) • Injunctions (equitable remedy) • Specific performance (equity)	• Fines, jail, and forfeitures

Please note that a product may be defective in manufacture or construction as described in this section, even though its manufacturer exercised all possible care in its manufacture or construction.

According to Section 2307.75, a product is defective in design or formulation as follows:

A. Subject to divisions (D), (E), and (F) of this section, a product is defective in design or formulation if, at the time it left the control of its manufacturer, the foreseeable risks associated with its design or formulation as determined pursuant to division (B) of this section exceeded the benefits associated with that design or formulation as determined pursuant to division (C) of this section.

B. The foreseeable risks associated with the design or formulation of a product shall be determined by considering factors including, but not limited to, the following:

TABLE 14.9

Ohio Product Liability Act Revised Code, Section 2307.73: Liability of Manufacturer

Product "defective" in:	Summary
Manufacture or construction Section 2307.74	Improperly manufactured or otherwise damaged
Design or formulation Section 2307.75	Properly manufactured but have an unreasonably dangerous design that result in injury
Inadequate warning or instruction Section 2307.76	Confusing or insufficient "Instructions for Use"
Did not conform to a representation made by its manufacturer Section 2307.77	Warrantees and guarantees of merchantability

Source: Ohio Revised Code, Title [23] XXIII Courts, Common Pleas, Chapter 2307: Civil Actions. http://codes.ohio.gov/orc/2307.73.

1. The nature and magnitude of the risks of harm associated with that design or formulation in light of the intended and reasonably foreseeable uses, modifications, or alterations of the product;

2. The likely awareness of product users, whether based on warnings, general knowledge, or otherwise, of those risks of harm;

3. The likelihood that that design or formulation would cause harm in light of the intended and reasonably foreseeable uses, modifications, or alterations of the product;

4. The extent to which that design or formulation conformed to any applicable public or private product standard that was in effect when the product left the control of its manufacturer;

5. The extent to which that design or formulation is more dangerous than a reasonably prudent consumer would expect when used in an intended or reasonably foreseeable manner.

C. The benefits associated with the design or formulation of a product shall be determined by considering factors including, but not limited to, the following:

1. The intended or actual utility of the product, including any performance or safety advantages associated with that design or formulation;

2. The technical and economic feasibility, when the product left the control of its manufacturer, of using an alternative design or formulation;

3. The nature and magnitude of any foreseeable risks associated with an alternative design or formulation.

D. An ethical drug or ethical medical device is not defective in design or formulation because some aspect of it is unavoidably unsafe, if the manufacturer of the ethical drug or ethical medical device provides adequate warning and instruction under Section 2307.76 of the Revised Code concerning that unavoidably unsafe aspect.

E. A product is not defective in design or formulation if the harm for which the claimant seeks to recover compensatory damages was caused by an inherent characteristic of the product, which is a generic aspect of the product that cannot be eliminated without substantially compromising the product's usefulness or desirability and which is recognized by the ordinary person with the ordinary knowledge common to the community.

F. A product is not defective in design or formulation if, at the time the product left the control of its manufacturer, a practical and technically feasible alternative design or formulation was not available that would have prevented the harm for which the claimant seeks to recover compensatory damages without substantially impairing the usefulness or intended purpose of the product.

According to Section 2307.76, a product is defective due to inadequate warning or instruction as follows:

A. Subject to divisions (B) and (C) of this section, a product is defective due to inadequate warning or instruction if either of the following applies:

   1. It is defective due to inadequate warning or instruction at the time of marketing if, when it left the control of its manufacturer, both of the following applied:

      a. The manufacturer knew or, in the exercise of reasonable care, should have known about a risk that is associated with the product and that allegedly caused harm for which the claimant seeks to recover compensatory damages;

      b. The manufacturer failed to provide the warning or instruction that a manufacturer exercising reasonable care would have provided concerning that risk, in light of the likelihood that the product would cause harm of the type for which the claimant seeks to recover compensatory damages and in light of the likely seriousness of that harm.

   2. It is defective due to inadequate post-marketing warning or instruction if, at a relevant time after it left the control of its manufacturer, both of the following applied:

      a. The manufacturer knew or, in the exercise of reasonable care, should have known about a risk that is associated with the product and that allegedly caused harm for which the claimant seeks to recover compensatory damages;

      b. The manufacturer failed to provide the post-marketing warning or instruction that a manufacturer exercising reasonable care would have provided concerning that risk, in light of the likelihood that the product would cause harm of the type for which the claimant seeks to recover compensatory damages and in light of the likely seriousness of that harm.

B. A product is not defective due to lack of warning or instruction or inadequate warning or instruction as a result of the failure of its manufacturer to warn or instruct about an open and obvious risk or a risk that is a matter of common knowledge.

C. An ethical drug is not defective due to inadequate warning or instruction if its manufacturer provides otherwise adequate warning and instruction to the physician or other legally authorized person who prescribes or dispenses that ethical drug for a claimant in question and if the federal food and drug administration has not provided that warning or instruction relative to that ethical drug is to be given directly to the ultimate user of it.

According to Section 2307.77, a product does not conform to the representation made by manufacturer as follows:

- A product is defective if it did not conform, when it left the control of its manufacturer, to a representation made by that manufacturer. A product may be defective because it did not conform to a representation even though its manufacturer did not act fraudulently, recklessly, or negligently in making the representation.

14.11.2 Product Liability Litigation (Mass Tort)

When ethical drugs or medical devices are judged "defective" due to a defect, hundreds of people can suffer from the same type of injuries. For this reason, lawsuits against ethical drugs and medical device manufacturers are frequent in a type of lawsuit called a *mass tort*.

A mass tort happens when a number of cases are brought together in a single court and evidence is shared between the cases. Mass torts are often confused with class action lawsuits, but they are actually very different. In class action suits, a large number of plaintiffs are all given the same judgment, in mass torts each case is still valued individually.[28]

Since the late 1980s, product liability litigation has exploded in the United States. Product liability mass torts have amounted to billions of dollars in compensatory, exemplary, and/or punitive charges. The huge liability attached to implantable devices has forced even large raw materials suppliers to abandon the industry.

Furthermore, the price of those raw materials that remain in the marketplace has escalated. In 1995, companies that make catheters, heart valves, and other devices reported that silicone prices skyrocketed to $100/lb. from $6/lb.[29]

While raw material suppliers have strong defenses to the product liability claims of medical device consumers, the cost of a legal defense itself can be daunting. It is those costs, and the associated embarrassment of being dragged into court, that have in large part driven the decision of many suppliers to withdraw from the medical implants market.[30]

For these reasons, medical device manufacturers, (as well as pharmaceutical producers) must fully understand the legal nuances involved in litigation, such as torts and criminal law, as they affect strict liability claims, as discussed in subsequent paragraphs.

14.11.3 Tort Law: A Primer

A *tort*, in common-law jurisdictions, is a civil wrong that unfairly causes someone else to suffer loss or harm, resulting in legal liability for the person who commits the tortious act, called a *tortfeasor*. The word is derived from the Old French and Anglo-French *tort* (injury), which is derived from the medieval Latin *tortum*.

Although crimes may be torts, the cause of a legal action is not necessarily a crime, as the harm may be due to negligence that does not amount to criminal negligence. The victim of the harm can recover their loss as damages in a lawsuit.[31] Tort law is different from criminal law in that (1) torts may result from negligent as well as intentional or criminal actions, and (2) tort lawsuits have a lower burden of proof, such as a *preponderance of evidence* rather than *beyond a reasonable doubt*.

Generally defined, tort law encompasses civil wrongs where one person's conduct causes injury to another in violation of a duty imposed by law.[32] The principles of tort law developed within the common-law tradition, evolving through state court judicial decisions. In the context of product liability, tort law encompasses (a) negligence, based on fault, and (b) strict liability, which is premised on no-fault principles.[33] It is generally agreed that tort law has three major functions:[34]

1. To compensate plaintiffs by awarding compensatory damages. These damages can include economic losses such as medical expenses or lost wages, and non-economic losses such as pain and suffering. This is tort law's response to individuals.

2. Medical devices should be distinguished from other consumer products for the purposes of policy reform. Medical devices present unique issues, and their special nature has led to the passage of medical device legislation. Drugs and devices are the only consumer products subject to intense scrutiny through federal agencies such as the Food and Drug Administration (FDA).

3. Medical devices are an integral part of the healthcare system, which provides essential services to the American public. All policies that directly or indirectly affect medical devices must acknowledge their impact on the healthcare system as a whole. For example, if product liability suits raise the costs of particular products, this result must be evaluated against the public's demands for widespread access to advanced medical technology and the real cost constraints that the government and third-party payers face.

In summary, business or economic torts typically involve commercial transactions and include tortious interference with trade or contract, fraud, injurious falsehood, and negligent misrepresentation. Negligent misrepresentation torts are distinct from contractual cases involving misrepresentation in that there is no privity of contract; these torts are likely to involve pure economic loss that has been less commonly recoverable in tort. One criterion for determining whether economic loss is recoverable is the *foreseeability* doctrine.[35]

14.11.4 Criminal Law: A Primer

Most crimes require an element called *mens rea*, which is Latin for "guilty mind." In other words, what the defendant *intended* to do when the offense (crime) was committed. The mens rea principle allows the criminal justice system to differentiate between a crime committed by someone who did not intentionally plan to commit a criminal offense and someone who deliberately and purposefully plotted to commit a crime.[36]

Intentionally harmful behavior is often a criminal offense, but unintentionally harmful behavior is classified into two basic forms: (1) a *mistake in fact* and (2) a *mistake of law*, as follows:

1. **Mistake in fact** means that although the behavior fits the definition of a crime in an objective sense, the defendant was acting on mistaken knowledge. For example, a person could objectively be selling a pharmaceutical product, but the product was not approved for that indication. As a result, that person lacks the necessary mens rea necessary under a drug law, because he never intended to sell an *illegal* drug. (In this case, and illegal drug is one being used in an unapproved indication.)

2. **Mistake of law**, however, will never save the defendant from criminal liability. "Ignorance of the law is no excuse," and that is exactly how the case will be adjudicated. Using the preceding example, a mistake of law would be if the seller knew he was selling an illegal drug but honestly did not know the indications for use did not cover a specific condition, unlike mistake in fact, in which ignorance would not relieve criminal liability. Allowing ignorance of the law would discourage people from learning the law and undermine the effectiveness of the legal system.

14.11.5 Strict Liability Cases in the Life Science Industry

Most of the examples we will analyze in this chapter are civil cases. However, both pharmaceutical producers and medical device manufacturers are liable for strict both civil and criminal prosecutions. For example, in 2012, GlaxoSmithKline[37] was assessed at a total of $3 billion, as depicted in Table 14.10.

In 2013, global healthcare giant Johnson & Johnson (J&J) and its subsidiaries paid more than $2.2 billion to resolve criminal and civil liability arising from allegations relating to the prescription drugs Risperdal®, Invega®, and Natrecor®, including promotion for uses not approved as safe and effective by the FDA and the payment of kickbacks to physicians and to the nation's

TABLE 14.10

Civil and Criminal Charges GlaxoSmithKline

Criminal ($1 billion)	Off-label promotion, failure to disclose safety data
Civil ($2 billion)	Making false and misleading statements concerning the safety of the drug Avandia, and paying kickbacks to physicians

largest long-term care pharmacy provider. The global resolution is one of the largest healthcare fraud settlements in U.S. history, including criminal fines and forfeiture totaling $485 million and civil settlements with the federal government and states totaling $1.72 billion.[38]

Civil and criminal legal claims against the pharmaceutical industry have varied widely over the past two decades,[39] including Medicare and Medicaid fraud, off-label promotion, and inadequate manufacturing practices.[40,41] With respect to off-label promotion, specifically, a federal court recognized off-label promotion as a violation of the False Claims Act for the first time in Franklin v. Parke-Davis, for off-label usage,[42] leading to a $430 million settlement.[43]

14.11.5.1 Strict Liability Cases Involving Medical Devices

Strict liability for implantable medical devices typically starts with the manufacturer, from failure to report adverse events,[44] to off-label marketing,[45] to providing financial inducements/kickbacks. These products can include cardiac and orthopedic devices as well as neuroprosthetics (neural prosthetics), medical robots, and microchip implants.[46] This is illustrated in Figure 14.4.

The liability equation

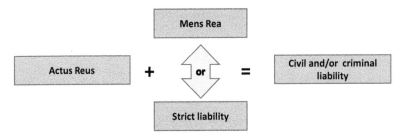

Implantable medical devices are subject to strict liability rules. That is, no *mens rea* is necessary to assess liability damages.

A company involved in a strict liability suit can be held liable if the product is "defective," even if the company was NOT negligent in their actions.

FIGURE 14.4
The strict liability conundrum.

The failure to report adverse events to the FDA as required by law may be a violation of the False Claims Act. Medical equipment fraud can also include manufacturing equipment and devices that deviate from the product's premarket approval (PMA), or 510-K, or that are made in violation of good manufacturing practices (GMP). A number of medical device companies have manufacturing plants overseas. They may then establish an import and/or sales office in the form of a wholly owned subsidiary to distribute the medical equipment to customers in the United States.

Medical device fraud also occurs when companies align themselves with physicians in a variety of kickback schemes. These relationships could include hiring physicians as "consultants" to help in the designing, testing, or developing of new products. These arrangements can violate the anti-kickback statute, particularly if it takes into account the volume or value of referrals or business on existing products.

It can also be a violation of the False Claims Act to use studies/trials in violation of the anti-kickback statute to get physicians to use more of and/ or exclusively use their products. For example, St. Jude Medical, Inc. settled and paid $16 million as the result of whistleblower allegations that it violated the anti-kickback statute when it used post-market studies as vehicles to pay participating physicians kickbacks to implant St. Jude pacemakers and implantable cardiac defibrillators (ICDs.)

Post-market studies are intended to assess the clinical performance of a medical device or drug after that device or drug has been approved by the FDA. Registries are collections of data maintained by a device manufacturer concerning its products that have been sold and implanted in patients.[47]

The St Jude case: In a famous case, the United States contended that St. Jude, used three post-market studies and a device registry as vehicles to pay participating physicians kickbacks to induce them to implant St. Jude pacemakers and defibrillators. Although St. Jude collected data and information from participating physicians, it was alleged that the company knowingly and intentionally used the studies and registry as a means of increasing its device sales by paying certain physicians to select St. Jude pacemakers and implantable cardioverter defibrillator for their patients. In each case, St. Jude paid each participating physician a fee that ranged up to $2000 per patient. The United States alleged that St. Jude solicited physicians for the studies in order to retain their business and/or convert their business from a competitor's product.

14.12 Business Contracts

According to the Restatement (Second) of Contracts, Section 1, "A contract is a promise or a set of promises for the breach of which the law gives a remedy, or the performance of which the law in some way recognizes as a duty."

Similarly, the Uniform Commercial Code, Section 1-201(11), states, "'Contract' means the total legal obligation that results from the parties' agreement as affected by this Act and any other applicable rules of law." A shorthand definition is "A contract is a legally enforceable promise."

The purpose of a business contract is to establish an agreement between the parties fixing the rights and responsibilities in accordance with the terms of the agreement. The courts may not create or interpret a contract; the courts will enforce the terms of a valid contract.

According to Richard Posner, contract law performs three significant economic functions:[48]

1. It helps maintain incentives to individuals to exchange goods and services efficiently.
2. It reduces the costs of economic transactions because its very existence means that the parties need not go to the trouble of negotiating a variety of rules and terms already spelled out.
3. The law of contracts alerts the parties to trouble spots that have arisen in the past, thus making it easier to plan the transactions more intelligently and avoid potential pitfalls.

A contract arises when the parties agree that there is an agreement. Formation of a contract generally requires an offer, acceptance, consideration, and a mutual intent to be bound. Each party to a contract must have capacity to enter the agreement. Minors, intoxicated persons, and those under a mental affliction may have insufficient capacity to enter a contract. Some types of contracts may require formalities, such as a memorialization in writing,[49] as seen in Table 14.11.

As we can see, the main function of a contract is a set of promises or a single promise that is enforceable by law. The offer is the first step in the promise process because it represents the terms outlined in the agreement. The person who makes the offer is called the *offeror* and the person the offer is made to is called the *offeree*.

TABLE 14.11

Contract Law Basics

	Elements
1. Offer	• Commitment to enter into contract • Clearly communicated • Objectives and circumstances • Terms and duration
2. Acceptance	• Terms in compliance with offer • Unilateral or bilateral • Agreed under no compulsion
3. Consideration	• Bargain-for-exchange • Legal value
4. Mutual Intent	• Meeting of the minds, or *consensus ad idem*

The following three requirements determine whether something is a valid offer.

1. **Requirement 1:** There must be some current intent to contract on the part of the offeror that is shown by an objective indication.
2. **Requirement 2:** The alleged offer terms must be definite and specific.
3. **Requirement 3:** The alleged offer must be communicated to the offeree in some suitable form or fashion.

The other component of the agreement is the *acceptance*. An acceptance is "a manifestation of assent to the terms of the offer made by the offeree in the manner invited or required by the offer."[50] The following are three factors that the court will consider to determine whether the offeree has accepted the offer and formed a contract.

- **Factor 1:** Whether the offeree wanted to enter into a contract with the offeror
- **Factor 2:** Whether the terms proposed by the offeror were accepted by the offeree
- **Factor 3:** Whether the offeree let the offeror know that they accept the terms

The most important aspect of the acceptance component is that the offeree must intend to do business with the offeror. There are many ways that one can agree to the terms of an agreement or contract. There are three ways to accept the terms of an agreement or contract.

1. Accepting the terms verbally or by way of verbal agreement and handshake
2. Accepting the terms by way of sending notice in the mail (*mailbox rule*)
3. Acceptance by shipment

14.12.1 Boilerplate Provisions

The term *boilerplate* refers to standardized language in contracts. Although often grouped together, boilerplate provisions do not have much in common with one another except that they don't fit anywhere else in the agreement. For that reason, they are usually dumped at the end of the agreement under a title such as "Miscellaneous," "General," or "Standard."[51]

Even though boilerplate is buried in the back of the agreement, these provisions are important. They affect how disputes are resolved and how a court enforces the contract. The effect of boilerplate is most often noticed when it is omitted from a contract in case of litigation. Table 14.12 lists some common boilerplate provisions and their meanings.

TABLE 14.12

Boilerplate Contract Provisions

Arbitration	Any disputes about the contract must be resolved through arbitration proceedings, not in a lawsuit.
Assignments	Affects the ability of the parties to sell or transfer their rights or responsibilities under the agreement to another party.
Announcements	This establishes the manner in which the parties can make certain public disclosures, such as statements about a forthcoming merger, acquisition, or joint business venture.
Attachments	This guarantees that all pertinent attachments and exhibits will be included as part of the final agreement.
Counterparts	This sets forth the right of the parties to execute (sign) copies of the agreement without everyone being present in one place at one time to sign the pages.
Costs and Attorneys' Fees	In the event of a legal dispute, the losing party pays the winning party's court costs.
Choice of Law	In the event of a dispute, a choice of law provision determines which state's legal rules will be applied in the lawsuit.
Confidentiality	This guarantees that the parties will not disclose certain information. May also be covered by a confidentiality agreement.
Escrow	This clause allows a party to place trade secrets, payments, or other information into a special account that will be opened only under certain conditions.
Force Majeure (also Referred to as "Acts of God")	This clause establishes that the agreement will be suspended in the event of unforeseen circumstances (e.g., earthquakes, hurricanes, floods, labor strikes, and so on).
Headings	This clause provides that the headings used throughout the agreement have no special significance.
Jury Trial Waivers	This establishes that if there is a court battle over the contract, the parties agree to have the dispute heard by the judge and to give up their right to a jury trial.
Jurisdiction	In the event of a dispute, a jurisdiction clause determines where (in which state and county) the lawsuit must be filed. It goes with "choice of law."
Indemnity	In an indemnity provision, one party guarantees that it will cover the costs of certain disputes brought by third parties (i.e., people who are not parties to the agreement).
Integration	An integration clause states that the written contract represents the final agreement of the parties. Often, it explicitly states the any prior agreement or discussions of the agreement are replaced by the written contract and that any further modification to the contract must be in writing and mutually agreed.
Limitations on Damages	This sets a cap or otherwise limits the types of monetary damages that may be awarded in a contract dispute.
Notice	This describes how each party must provide notices to the other (e.g., to amend or terminate the agreement).

(Continued)

TABLE 14.12 (CONTINUED)

Boilerplate Contract Provisions

Relationships	This prevents either party from falsely claiming any special business relationship with the other (e.g., by stating that the parties are partners or that one is the other's employee).
Severability	This permits a court to sever an invalid provision while still keeping the rest of the agreement intact and enforceable.
Waiver	This clause permits the parties to forego the right to sue for breach of a particular provision of the agreement without giving up any future claims regarding the same provision.
Warranties	Commercial promises or assurances made by each party regarding various contract obligations.

14.12.2 Contract Types

Contracts are pervasive in business. Businesses typically draft and sign a staggering amount of contracts with customers, suppliers, partners, investors, and other stakeholders. Sometimes they are simple, but frequently they are legally complex. Before you sign on the dotted line, make sure you fully understand the terms and conditions. It is often a good idea to consult with your attorney, who can help you make the best decision.[52]

Table 14.13 lists some of the most common business contracts encountered by businesses in the conduct of their affairs.

14.13 Bankruptcy Laws

No entrepreneur starts an enterprise with bankruptcy in the strategic vision. The reasons for bankruptcy are many. In some cases, the bankruptcy process provides an opportunity to "turn back the clock" and reorganize the enterprise for a more economically feasible future. In other cases, bankruptcy is a way to "put to sleep" a failing enterprise and distribute its remaining assets to its creditors.

Pan Am, Standard Oil, Montgomery Wards, Woolworth's, and Circuit City all went bankrupt. These formerly great companies were once giants of American business. Today, they exist only in people's memories. Changing consumer tastes, evolving technology, globalization, and bad business decisions meant the end of these once iconic brands.

Whatever the case, the United States has a legal process that defines the steps that an enterprise and its creditors must take once an entity has filed for bankruptcy. Bankruptcy laws protect all parties in a structured, orderly, and predictable manner.

TABLE 14.13

Most Common Business Contracts

Contracts	Description
Sales Related	
Bill of sale	Ownership transfer of goods between merchants
Purchase order	Official offer made by the buyer
Warrantee	Conditions or actions that may void a contract
Limited warranty	Warrantee limited to specific parts
Employment Related	
Employment agreement	Contract for employment, including length of contract, salary, responsibilities, authority, title, etc.
Employee non-compete agreement	Agreement not to work for a direct competitor for a specified amount of time following termination or voluntary departure
Independent contractor	Unlike an employee, an independent freelance contractor that does not work regularly for an employer but works as and when required, during which time they may be subject to laws of agency
Consulting agreement	Tasks, responsibilities, and compensation for expert advice
Distributor agreement	Defines relationship with companies that sell to retailers
Sales representative agreement	Defines commissions, geographical area. and incentives
Confidentiality agreement	Agreement not to disclose certain information or trade secrets to third parties
Stock purchase agreement	Agreement to sell a certain amount of stock to an individual, typically as an employment incentive
Termination agreements	Conditions formally ending the employment relationship
General Business Contracts	
Advertising agency agreement	Establishes the scope of duties performed by the agency, duration payment terms, and copyrights
Assignment of contract	Agreement to transfer benefits and obligations of a contract from one party to another
Franchise agreement	Relationship between franchisor and franchisee, such as advertising, use of brand, employee training, general support, etc.
Indemnity agreement	Agreement to transfer risk from one party to another
Settlement agreement	Agreement to terminate a lawsuit in exchange for mutual concessions
Agreement to sell business	Documents the terms of selling an existing business
Joint venture agreement	Obligations, goals, and financial contributions of all parties in a joint venture
Business Leases	
Real property lease	Contract to lease office, manufacturing, or retail estate between landlord and lessee
Equipment lease	Agreement between a party who owns the equipment rents to another party for a fixed rate and time

The term *bankruptcy* goes back to the Roman Empire. In those days, a vendor who did not pay his debts had his table, or bench, broken and was put out of business. *Bankus* is the Latin term for "bench," while *ruptus* means "broken." The term is also partially derived from Italian *banca rotta*, meaning "broken bank," which stems from the custom of breaking a moneychanger's bench or counter to signify his insolvency.[53]

14.13.1 Legal Foundations

Bankruptcy law in the United States was initially passed in 1898 and was last amended by the Bankruptcy Abuse Prevention and Consumer Protection Act of 2005, under Title 11 of the United States Code (referred to as the Bankruptcy Code).[54] Bankruptcy is thus a legal procedure for dealing with the debt problems of individuals and businesses—specifically, a case filed under one of the chapters of Title 11. There are six types of bankruptcy filings under the Bankruptcy Code. They are listed in Table 14.14, with a brief description of the circumstances when such a filing may be appropriate.

In this section, we will focus on the two most common types of bankruptcies—namely, Chapter 7 and Chapter 11 filings, as outlined in Figure 14.5.

TABLE 14.14

Types of Bankruptcy Filings

Type	Corresponding Filer	Description
Chapter 7	Businesses/individuals (In reality, it is often the creditors who file for Chapter 7 bankruptcy.)	Provides for the orderly final liquidation of the total assets of the debtor for the settlement of some or all of its liabilities to its creditors
Chapter 9	Municipalities	Provides protection to a municipality from its creditors while it renegotiates a plan to adjust its debts
Chapter 11	Businesses and individuals	Allows for the reorganization of the business and a "fresh start," most likely with modified, and generally reduced, liabilities and continues to operate
Chapter 12	Individuals	Provides for the adjustment of debts of a family farmer with regular income
Chapter 13	Individuals	Provides for the adjustment of debts of an individual with regular income
Chapter 15	Ancillary and other cross-border cases	Allows for cross-border insolvency cases to be governed on a uniform and coordinated basis

U.S. Bankruptcy System

Firms that are unable to make required
payments to their creditors can file:

(1) Chapter 7 which leads to the liquidation of the firm's
assets in the settlement of the creditors' claims, or

(2) Chapter 11 which allows the firm to restructure its
debt and equity claims and continue to operate during the
reorganization plan

In reality, it is most often the creditors who file
for Chapter 7 bankruptcy

FIGURE 14.5
Bankruptcy laws.

14.13.2 Chapter 11 Reorganizations

An entity that files for Chapter 11 protection is attempting to continue its
business without the full burden of debt that existed prior to the proceeding.
This is truly a "fresh start," as shown in Figure 14.6, to save the business.
However, not all enterprises that enter a Chapter 11 bankruptcy eventually
exit as newly reorganized entities; as the legal case progresses, a planned
reorganization frequently develops into the court-approved sale of some or
all of the enterprise's assets or a liquidation of the assets of the enterprise.[55]

A Chapter 11 proceeding revolves around the debtor. On behalf of the
debtor, the entity that seeks to be reorganized will emerge from the process
either (1) with greatly improved chances for its continued existence, arising
generally from satisfactory payment arrangements with creditors, or (2) with
its assets liquidated for the complete or partial satisfaction of its obligations.
The underlying considerations for the debtor's continued existence involves
determining whether it is likely that the emerging entity can continue to
operate without the need for further financial reorganization. A trustee
may be appointed by the court to oversee all the ongoing business and legal
aspects of the reorganized entity.

Fresh Start

- The primary purpose of federal bankruptcy
  law is to discharge the debtor from
  burdensome debts.
- The debtor can try to reorganize and save the
  business
- The law gives debtors a "fresh start" by
  freeing them from legal responsibility for past
  debts.

FIGURE 14.6
Reorganization from bankruptcy.

14.13.2.1 DIP Procedures

In cases where a trustee is not appointed, the senior debtor may become a *debtor-in-possession* (DIP) following the filing of the petition for bankruptcy. This term refers to a debtor that will continue to manage the business and, if necessary, initiate the liquidation process, albeit supervised by the court, during the bankruptcy proceedings.

The DIP has certain fiduciary duties, as set forth in the Bankruptcy Code and Federal Rules of Bankruptcy Procedure, including accounting for property (arising due to examinations of records by the office of the United States Trustee, as a representative of the bankruptcy court). The DIP also has many of the powers and duties of a trustee, including the right, with the court's approval, to engage attorneys, accountants, appraisers, auctioneers, or other professionals to assist during its bankruptcy case.

14.13.2.2 Classification of Creditors

Confusion abounds concerning the classification and characterization of creditor claims.[56] For convenience, some of the more common classifications are shown in Table 14.15.

The determination of the different classes of creditors is significant, as is the process of collecting and evaluating claims. No payments can be made to a subordinate class unless the prior class has been paid in full or otherwise settled in an equitable manner as determined by the court. This is known as the *absolute priority doctrine*.

Note: The *equity holders* hold the equity in the debtor at the time of its bankruptcy filing. While the equity holders may have a residual claim to the assets of the debtor, their interests are usually eliminated during bankruptcy proceedings.

Legal counsel, accountants, and other *advisors* are critical to the debtor during the bankruptcy process. As the bankruptcy plays out in the court system, counsel will advise its client as to proper process and assist in the negotiations between the debtor and the other various parties of interest.

In addition, accountants are often engaged to assist the debtor with its preparation of the monthly financial reports and the various accounting and valuation challenges that occur prior to, during, and upon emergence from the bankruptcy proceedings.

Tax advisors are often involved in assisting the debtor with contemplation of certain bankruptcy-specific income tax planning considerations, including the tax treatment of debt extinguishment and the post-emergence use of existing tax attributes.

Advisors that specialize in restructurings and other areas of the bankruptcy process often play a critical role in helping the debtor navigate the process. In many cases, a chief restructuring officer is retained to work alongside management and assist in the development and execution of the

TABLE 14.15

Classification and Characterization of Creditor Claims

Classification	Characterization
Secured claim	Obligations scheduled by the debtor or for which a proof of claim has been filed by the creditors are deemed secured, USC §101 (50) to which a creditor has a duly perfected security interests. Common examples are a mortgage on real estate and a security interest held by a bank in equipment, inventory, and receivables of a company to which the bank has lent money.
Priority claim	This characterization of a claim, pursuant to applicable provisions of the Bankruptcy Code, including 11 USC §507, assists in establishing *priority* payment is paid first from the available assets of the debtor. Among the priority obligations are taxes, employee wages, certain benefits, and governmental obligations. In individual bankruptcies, sums owing to a former spouse for alimony, maintenance, and child support also enjoy a priority.
Unsecured claims Non-priority claims	Creditor obligations that are not subject to priority payment under the applicable Bankruptcy Code provision. These most often are the unsecured debt.
Administrative expenses	These debts are most often construed as expenses, which accrue during the pendency of the bankruptcy proceeding. A typical expense is a quarterly fee paid to the office of the United States Trustee. Other debts, if they are ordinary vendor expenses, usually are paid at the time the debt is incurred. If they are professional fees, these administrative expenses must receive bankruptcy court approval prior to payment. Administrative expenses are paid before any other priority claim.
General unsecured claims	These obligations include creditor obligations, which are typically incurred pre-petition and which are paid ratably from available assets. Thus, this debt most frequently makes up the bulk of the debt incurred.
Post-petition claims	This is another name for the debts of a bankruptcy debtor incurred subsequent to the filing of the bankruptcy petition. This description is most often relevant when the timing of the incurring of the debt determines whether it is paid in full or partially and when the debtor is obligated to pay. Taxes and other debts incurred post-petition are usually expected to be paid in the ordinary course of business.
Pre-petition claim	This is another name for the debt incurred by a bankruptcy debtor prior to the filing of the bankruptcy petition. These debts, unless deemed priority obligations, are paid in a Chapter 11 pursuant to the terms of a plan or in a Chapter 7 context, from available assets, if any.

entity's reorganization strategy. These professionals must be approved by the court prior to performing work for the debtor.

14.13.2.3 Disclosure Statement

After filing the plan with the court and with court approval of its contents, the proponents of the plan will seek its acceptance by a vote of the creditors. The information given to those entitled to vote on the plan is contained in one of several documents referred to as the *disclosure statement*. The disclosure statement is usually prepared by the debtor and cannot be distributed until the court approves it as well as the adequacy of the reorganization plan. The Bankruptcy Code does not contain specific disclosure requirements for the disclosure statement, but the document is generally expected to include sufficient information to enable creditors to make an informed judgment about the fairness and appropriateness of the plan.

The disclosure statement usually includes the following:

- Information about the history of the company and the causes of its financial difficulty
- Historical financial information, including the financial statements for at least the year before the petition was filed and the financial statements for the period the company has been in Chapter 11
- A summary of the plan of reorganization
- Prospective financial statement information, including cash projections that will be used to calculate the reorganization value of the debtor
- A pro forma balance sheet based on the reorganization value of the company, showing the expected financial structure when it emerges from Chapter 11
- An estimated range of the reorganization value as calculated by the debtor, and related disclosures and support for the valuations
- A summary of the debtor's proposed exit financing vehicles, including the key terms and provisions, amended credit facilities, and, if applicable, equity rights offerings
- Information about the current and future management of the company, including the makeup of the Board of Directors
- A statement showing the amount creditors would be expected to receive if the company was liquidated rather than reorganized— known as the *best interest test*
- A summary of the key points from the business plan that describes the future operations of the debtor

Following a solicitation period, during which the reorganization plan is distributed to the various parties for their review, each impaired class will vote independently, as a class, to accept or reject the plan. Acceptance of the plan by a class of claim holders has occurred if it is approved by

- At least two-thirds in dollar amount of allowed claims in the class
- More than one-half in number of the class members

Since equity holders generally receive little, if any, value in the reorganization plan, they are often deemed to reject the plan and no vote is necessary.

Similarly, impaired creditors who will not receive any consideration under the plan are deemed to reject it. In contrast, unimpaired classes are deemed to accept the reorganization plan and its appropriateness.

14.13.2.4 Chapter 11 Timeline

Although every bankruptcy case will have its own unique timeline, some key dates are set by statute and are reasonably predictable. The timeline in Table 14.16 provides some general guidance as to how a common reorganization case under Chapter 11 might move through the process. However, prepackaged and prearranged bankruptcies operate on a more compressed timeline, given the anticipated approval by the creditors.

TABLE 14.16

Timeline for a Typical Chapter 11 Reorganization Plan

Prior to Petition	A company should engage professional advisors to assist with the various filing and other legal requirements that will need to be met throughout the bankruptcy process if it determines that a bankruptcy filing is its best course of action.
	Certain payments and transfers made in the period prior to the petition date may be considered preferential transfers that would be subject to claw-back provisions.
Petition Date	The date the petition for bankruptcy is filed with the court.
Within 45 Days after Petition Date	During this time, in most cases, the initial meeting of creditors will take place. This is known as a *341 meeting*, named after the applicable section of the Bankruptcy Code.[57]
Bar Date	The date set by the court by which all creditors that have claims against the debtor have to file information to support the validity of their claims. If the debtor has included the claims in its initial schedules as a valid obligation, the creditors need not file additional information unless the creditor believes the debtor's information is inaccurate. Multiple bar dates may be assigned for different classes of claims.
120 Days after Petition Date	Unless extended by the court, the debtor's plan of reorganization and disclosure statement must be filed by this date.
180 Days after Petition Date	If the debtor's plan has not been confirmed by this date (after considering any extensions for filing the plan of reorganization), its creditors, trustees, or other parties of interest can file competing plans.
Solicitation and Voting	The debtor's plan of reorganization is distributed to creditors and others, and each class of creditors votes to accept or reject the plan.
Confirmation Date	The date the court approves the plan of reorganization.
Effective Date	The date, on or after the confirmation date, that the reorganization plan becomes effective and all material conditions for emergence have been satisfied.

14.14 Chapter 7 Liquidation

Chapter 7 of the Bankruptcy Code is titled "Liquidation." Chapter 7 is what most people understand when they use the word *bankruptcy*. Liquidation means that an enterprise may have financial debts so significant that it does not expect a court to be able to affirm its future feasibility as a going concern[58] (i.e., a company's ability to make enough money to stay afloat or avoid bankruptcy).

A Chapter 7 petition is typically begun by the debtor filing a voluntary petition in bankruptcy. Under certain circumstances, a number of creditors of an entity qualified to be a debtor under the Bankruptcy Code may file an involuntary petition against that entity.

Upon the filing of a petition under Chapter 7 of the Bankruptcy Code, the court assigns an independent trustee to manage the business and the process of liquidation. The Chapter 7 independent trustee takes immediate control over the debtor's assets and is entitled to all of the debtor's non-exempt assets vested in the trustee for the duration of the case. The debtor's non-exempt assets are referred to as the *bankruptcy estate*.[59]

This is significantly different from a petition under Chapter 11, where the debtor generally retains at least some of the rights to control its own assets. The trustee will usually discontinue the enterprise's operations to conserve its remaining resources and sell its assets to the highest bidder using the proceeds of sale for the benefit of the creditors.

The trustee will usually decide to abandon assets with little or no value. Furthermore, the trustee may abandon or allow a holder of a secured claim, such as a bank, to foreclose on collateral that is part of the bankruptcy estate in those cases in which the value of the collateral is less than, or equal to, the amount of the secured claim. Finally, if there is any non-exempt asset in the debtor's estate that still has value after deducting any security interest in said asset, the trustee will liquidate it and apply the proceeds to various debts and expenses pursuant to the priority established by the Bankruptcy Code.

Once all the priority expenses have been paid (e.g., the cost of administration and certain taxes), the amount left over, if anything, will be distributed to general unsecured creditors on a pro-rata basis. The amount so distributed is referred to as a *dividend*.

14.14.1 Creditor and Debt Classification

Secured creditors generally will seek a return of their collateral or its value. Administrative claims are usually paid first, and any remaining proceeds are paid to the remaining creditors according to the provisions of the Bankruptcy Code. Upon completion of the process, the debtor receives a discharge from its prepetition debts.

Debts are divided into two classes: secured debts and unsecured debts. A secured debt is one where the debtor has pledged certain property as security for payment, such as with a mortgage or auto loan. An unsecured debt is not connected with any particular property, such as credit card debt and medical bills.[60]

Debts are also divided into dischargeable debts (which are eliminated by bankruptcy) and non-dischargeable debts (which are still owed after bankruptcy). Most consumer debts are dischargeable. However, during Chapter 7 proceedings, the court may deny a discharge if you[61]

- Do not provide requested tax documents
- Transfer or hide property in order to defraud or hinder your creditors
- Destroy or hide books or records
- Commit perjury or other fraudulent acts in connection with your bankruptcy case
- Cannot account for lost assets
- Violate a court order
- Have previously filed a bankruptcy case and were granted a discharge, within certain time frames, depending on the type of bankruptcy filed

Following the filing of the petition and schedules, the next important duty for the debtor is to appear for examination at a meeting of creditors.[62] When the bankruptcy petition is filed, the Bankruptcy Court Clerk's Office will send to all creditors listed in the schedules a notice of the date, time, and place where the meeting of creditors will be held. This meeting is held between 20 and 40 days after the filing.

The meeting of creditors is held in Chapter 7, Chapter 13, and Chapter 11 cases. In a Chapter 7 case, the trustee presides over the meeting. The Chapter 7 trustee is assigned to each case by the bankruptcy court and is chosen from a standing panel of Chapter 7 trustees. The majority of Chapter 7 trustees are attorneys who also have private practices. Although they are chosen for the panel by the U.S. Trustee's Office, they are not government employees.

In a Chapter 11 case, an attorney or agent from the U.S. Trustee's Office presides over the meeting of creditors. The purpose of this meeting is to give creditors and the presiding officer an opportunity to question the debtor regarding his or her property, conduct, and any other matter that affects the bankruptcy estate. The debtor's petition will be reviewed and questions may arise regarding the information set forth therein.

An important duty of the debtor is to cooperate fully with any appointed trustee in the performance of his or her duties.[63] This duty of cooperation includes providing the trustee with any requested documents and records and surrendering all non-exempt property to the trustee. Failure to cooperate

Bankruptcies at a glance

Chapter 7	Chapter 11
• Trustee is appointed	• Fresh start
• Trustee liquidates estate	• Debtor remains in possession of company and management (Debtor-in-Possession)
• Trustee powers also include avoidance actions (e.g., preference, fraudulent transfer actions)	• Designed to preserve "going concern value" of business.
• Prompt liquidation of assets and distribution of proceeds to creditors under court supervision	• Reorganized company (if not liquidated) emerges after court accepts the Chapter 11 Plan
• No restructuring obligations	• Provides a forum for negotiation with creditors
• Prescribed payment distribution	
• Entity ceases to exist	• Company may re-emerge stronger and leaner

FIGURE 14.7
Main differences between chapter 7 and chapter 11 rules.

with the trustee and appear at the meeting of creditors can result in dismissal of the case and denial of a discharge.[64]

Figure 14.7 summarizes the important characteristics of business bankruptcies.

14.15.2 Procedural Steps in Chapter 7 Bankruptcy

1. **Pre-bankruptcy credit counseling:** Chapter 7 bankruptcy filers must get credit counseling from an approved agency within the 6 months prior to the bankruptcy filing.

2. **Bankruptcy petition:** You must file a packet of forms consisting of the bankruptcy petition, schedules (which contain detailed information about your finances), and other forms (which calculate your income and expenses, let the court know which property you claim as exempt, and inform the court of various other information).

3. **Automatic stay:** Once you file your bankruptcy petition, the automatic stay goes into effect. The automatic stay prohibits almost all of your creditors from continuing collection actions against you.

4. **The bankruptcy trustee:** The court assigns a bankruptcy trustee to administer your case. The trustee will try to maximize assets in the bankruptcy estate to distribute to your unsecured creditors, look for inaccuracies in your paperwork, and check for any possible fraud.

5. **The meeting of creditors:** You must attend the meeting of creditors (341 hearing). This is not a court hearing but a meeting run by your bankruptcy trustee. The trustee will ask you questions about your

petition and finances. Creditors may, but often don't, appear and ask questions.

6. **Eligibility for Chapter 7:** The court decides if you are eligible for Chapter 7. One reason that the court might deny eligibility is that you didn't pass the means test.

7. **Your property:** If your property is exempt, you keep it. If you have some non-exempt property, the trustee must decide what to do: seize and sell it to repay your creditors or abandon it. Even if your property is not exempt, all is not lost.

8. **Secured debts:** You must decide what to do about your secured debts—those debts for which you pledged property as collateral, such as a mortgage or a car loan. Typically you can surrender (give back) the property, redeem (pay for) the property, reaffirm the loan, or do nothing and keep paying the debt.

9. **Financial management course:** Before you get your discharge, you must take a debtor's education course. This is in addition to the credit counseling you received before you filed for bankruptcy (see Step 1).

10. **Your discharge:** Somewhere between 3 and 6 months after you file for bankruptcy, the court will generally grant your bankruptcy discharge. When this happens, the automatic stay ends.

11. **Case closed:** After the court grants your discharge, it will close your case—usually a few days or weeks later.

Most Chapter 7 bankruptcy cases take about 4 to 6 months to complete. Chapter 7 filers rarely go to court, although the process does require one mandatory non-court appearance before the trustee. The case ends with a discharge of most or all of the filer's debt.[65]

Notes

1. A prior judicial decision that is either binding (from the same state) or persuasive (from another state), and as such provides a rule useful in making a decision in the case at hand.

2. Latin for "let the decision stand." By keeping within the rule of a prior judicial decision (of a similar case), a court follows precedent by letting the prior decision govern the result in the case at hand.

3. Suster, M. (2010). How to work with lawyers at a startup. https://bothsidesofthe table.com/how-to-work-with-lawyers-at-a-startup-cf4f15feb8d3

4. Walker, S.E. (2010). Top 10 reasons why entrepreneurs hate lawyers. Venture Hacks, January 14. http://venturehacks.com/articles/hate-lawyers.

5. http://thenextweb.com/entrepreneur/2012/04/22/before-naming-your-startup-read-this.

6. https://en.wikipedia.org/wiki/Ignorantia_juris_non_excusat.

7. Decretum Gratiani, Distinctio 4, dictum post c.3.

8. https://en.wikipedia.org/wiki/Sole_proprietorship.

9. http://yourbusiness.azcentral.com/organizational-structure-sole-proprietorship-6011.html.

10. A designation of liability by which members of a group are either individually or mutually responsible to a party in whose favor a judgment has been awarded.The Free Dictionary (2018). Joint and several liability. http://legal-dictionary.thefreedictionary.com/Joint+and+several+liability.

11. Claran, J. (2018). Dissolution vs. termination of partnership. Chron. http://smallbusiness.chron.com/dissolution-vs-termination-partnership-31021.html.

12. Where one person places complete confidence in another in regard to a particular transaction or one's general affairs or business relationships.The Free Dictionary (2018). Fiduciary relationship. http://legal-dictionary.thefreedictionary.com/fiduciary+relationship.

13. The corporate opportunity doctrine is the legal principle providing that directors, officers, and controlling shareholders of a corporation must not take for themselves any business opportunity that could benefit the corporation. The corporate opportunity doctrine is one application of the fiduciary duty of loyalty. https://en.wikipedia.org/wiki/Corporate_opportunity.

14. https://en.wikipedia.org/wiki/Corporate_opportunity.

15. http://www.rjmintz.com/family-limited-partnership/partnership-types/general-partnerships.

16. https://en.wikipedia.org/wiki/Uniform_Limited_Partnership_Act.

17. Pakroo, P. (2018). Limited partnerships and limited liability partnerships: The partnerships that limit personal liability for business debts. Nolo. http://www.nolo.com/legal-encyclopedia/limited-partnerships-limited-liability-partnerships-29748.html.

18. http://smallbusiness.chron.com/limited-partnership-directors-officers-63801.html.

19. Puleo v. Topel. 856 N.E.2d 1152 (2006), 306 III. Dec. 57.

20. https://www.sba.gov/starting-business/choose-your-business-structure/s-corporation.

21. https://en.m.wikipedia.org/wiki/S_corporation.

22. https://www.legalzoom.com/knowledge/corporation/topic/choosing-the-best-type-of-corporation-s-corporation-or-c-corporation.

23. http://www.bizfilings.com/learn/s-corporation-advantages-and-disadvantages.aspx.

24. Cromwell, J. (2018). What are the benefits & disadvantages of a C corp? Legalzoom. http://info.legalzoom.com/benefits-disadvantages-c-corp-22998.html.

25. That body of law in any nation state that defines offenses against society as a whole, punishable by fines, forfeitures, or imprisonment.

26. *The Legal Environment and Business Law: Executive MBA Edition* (v. 1.0). http://2012books.lardbucket.org/attribution.html?utm_source=header. https://creativecommons.org/licenses/by-nc-sa/3.0.

27. Michon, K., Types of defective product claims involving medical devices. Nolo. http://www.nolo.com/legal-encyclopedia/product-liability-claims-medical-devices-29684.html.
28. http://www.wattsguerra.com/mass-torts/defective-medical-device-mass-torts.
29. Weinstein, R., and Olmos, D.R. (1995). The product liability morass: Complications set in, big suppliers pulling out of medical market, *Los Angeles Times*, May 6, at D1.
30. http://www.khlaw.com/showpublication.aspx?Show=726.
31. https://en.wikipedia.org/wiki/Tort.
32. Kionka, E.J. (1977). *Torts: Injuries to Persons and Property*. St. Paul, MN.: West Publishing.
33. http://www.gosale.com/549872/prosser-and-keeton-on-the-law.
34. Foote, S.B. Product liability and medical device regulation: Proposal for reform. https://www.ncbi.nlm.nih.gov/books/NBK218294.
35. ABA (2012). Section of Litigation, Corporate Counsel CLE Seminar, February 16–19. When can a breach of contract be a tort and what difference does it make? http://www.americanbar.org/content/dam/aba/administrative/litigation/materials/2012_cccle_materials/12_tort.authcheckdam.pdf.
36. Find Law (2018). Mens rea: A defendant's mental state. http://criminal.findlaw.com/criminal-law-basics/mens-rea-a-defendant-s-mental-state.html.
37. U.S. Department of Justice. (2012). GlaxoSmithKline to plead guilty and pay $3 billion to resolve fraud allegations and failure to report safety data. justice.gov, 2 July. https://www.justice.gov/opa/pr/glaxosmithkline-plead-guilty-and-pay-3-billion-resolve-fraud-allegations-and-failure-report.
38. https://www.justice.gov/opa/pr/johnson-johnson-pay-more-22-billion-resolve-criminal-and-civil-investigations.
39. https://en.wikipedia.org/wiki/List_of_largest_pharmaceutical_settlements.
40. Almashat, S., et al. (2010). Rapidly increasing criminal and civil monetary penalties against the pharmaceutical industry: 1991–2010. Public Citizen's Health Research Group report, December 16.
41. Thomas, K., and Schmidt, M.S. (2012). Glaxo agrees to pay $3 billion in fraud settlement. *New York Times*, 2 July.
42. U.S. District Court, MA (2003). U.S. ex rel. Franklin v. Parke-Davis, Div. of Warner-Lambert Co., Civil action no. 96-11651-PBS, WL 22048255, at *1, August 22.
43. Lavoie, D. (2007). Drug whistleblower collects $24M. CBS News, 5 December.
44. False Claims Act liabilities include failure to disclose adverse events to the FDA; failure to report that changes to the design, manufacture, or labeling have been made that are associated with medical device reporting requirements; and hiding the results and conclusions of internal clinical investigations that adversely impact the known safety and effectiveness profile of the device.
45. The FDA prohibits companies from marketing medical devices for uses that the federal agency has not approved. Off-label promotion comes in two forms: marketing a device that has not received FDA approval and promoting an approved device for an unapproved use.
46. Medical equipment fraud. http://www.whistleblowerfirm.com/medical-equipment-fraud.
47. Minnesota-based St. Jude Medical pays U.S. $16 million to settle claims that company paid kickbacks to physicians. https://www.justice.gov/opa/pr/minnesota-based-st-jude-medical-pays-us-16-million-settle-claims-company-paid-kickbacks.

48. Posner, R.A.(2011). *Economic Analysis of the Law*. New York: Aspen.
49. https://en.wikipedia.org/wiki/Contract.
50. Restatement (Second) of Contracts §50(1) (1981).
51. http://www.nolo.com/legal-encyclopedia/common-boilerplate-provisions-contracts-32654.html.
52. http://smallbusiness.findlaw.com/business-contracts-forms/common-business-contracts.html.
53. https://en.wikipedia.org/wiki/Bankruptcy.
54. https://www.utb.uscourts.gov/title-11-united-states-bankruptcy-code.
55. PricewaterhouseCoopers International (2014). https://www.pwc.com/us/en/cfodirect/assets/pdf/accounting_guides/pwc_guide_bankruptcies_and__liquidations_2014_.pdf. It should be noted that the Bankruptcy Code provides for different rules for a so-called small-business debtor that has debt totaling less than approximately $2.5 million.
56. Kerwin, R.J., and Shea, R.J. Bankruptcy manual. Tarlow, Breed, Hart, Murphy and Rodgers, P.C. http://www.tbhr-law.com/newsviews/TBHMR BankruptcyManual.pdf.
57. 11 U.S. Code §341 of the Bankruptcy Code directs the U.S. Trustee to convene and preside at a meeting of creditors within a reasonable time after the bankruptcy filing. This meeting is formally called the *meeting of creditors* but oftentimes referred to as the *341 meeting*. This is not a hearing conducted at the courthouse; rather, this is a meeting with the trustee, the debtors, and the creditors conducted at a location determined by the U.S. Trustee. The trustee may ask the debtors questions regarding information contained in the required documents for the bankruptcy case. Creditors may also attend the meeting and ask questions, but are not required to do so.
58. http://www.investopedia.com/terms/g/goingconcern.asp.
59. 11 U.S. Code §541: Property of the estate.
60. https://www.legalzoom.com/articles/filing-chapter-7-bankruptcy-basic-steps.
61. http://www.nolo.com/legal-encyclopedia/nondischargeable-debts-chapter-7-bankruptcy.html.
62. 11 U.S. Code §341(a).
63. 11 U.S. Code §521(3).
64. 11 U.S. Code §727(a).
65. Michon, K. (2018). Steps in a Chapter 7 bankruptcy case. All Law. http://www.alllaw.com/articles/nolo/bankruptcy/steps-chapter-7-case.html.

15

If You Cannot Innovate, Copy

> Things that make Apple products great are not always
> their own creation.

15.1 Introduction

The great Apple co-founder Steve Jobs famously quoted Pablo Picasso in a documentary. "Good artists copy, great artists steal," he proudly said.

For the generation that saw the late innovator bickering with Google, HTC Corporation (a Taiwanese electronics company), and others for patent rights in his final few years, it may come as a surprise that he actually endorsed the plagiarism of technology earlier in his career. Of course, it was advantageous to Apple at that time.

Then, there was this other quote: "We [Apple] have always been shameless about stealing great ideas," Jobs once admitted arrogantly, suggesting that it is acceptable to appropriate art and technology if the (legal) theft results in a better end product than your competitors'.

But then he came up with a contingent of the slick, attractive iPods and iPads that changed his entire philosophy on creativity and art. The products were an immediate marketing hit throughout the world, sending Apple into an unsurpassed stratospheric market capitalization.

But once an established Apple got a taste of its own medicine, Jobs made a 180° turn on the subject. After Google launched Android, he had this to say: "I'm going to destroy Android, because it's a stolen product. I'm willing to go thermonuclear war on this."

And on a similar feud with HTC, he added, "We can sit by and watch competitors steal our patented inventions, or we can do something about it. We've decided to do something about it. We think competition is healthy, but competitors should create their own original technology, not steal ours."

Since then, patent infringement lawsuits have proliferated in the smartphone world.

15.2 Nothing Is *Completely* Original

Despite all the branding differences, Apple iCloud, Microsoft SkyDrive, Google Cloud Storage, and Dropbox are continually imitating one another. And who can argue that smartphone manufacturers aren't copying each other?[1]

In the high-tech business, it seems immaterial whether the ideas are copied or not, provided that the process is lawful. We can thank the highly successful and equally controversial Samwer brothers at Rocket Internet for leading the way and showing what the rest of the world has to offer in terms of "reproduction" of existing business models' capabilities.

Rocket Internet SE is a German Internet company headquartered in Berlin. The company builds online startups and owns shareholdings in various models of Internet retail businesses. The company model is known as a startup studio or a venture builder.[2]

It provides office space to new companies at its headquarters in Berlin, with IT support, marketing services, and access to investors. As of 2016, Rocket Internet had more than 28,000 employees across its worldwide network of companies, which consists of over 100 entities active in 110 countries.

15.2.1 Rocket Internet's "Copycat" Strategy

While there is no denying that they reproduce existing business models, they also have an uncanny ability to execute in unknown markets in the most perfect way. Every good entrepreneur will tell you that ideas are worthless and execution is everything. It certainly holds true for venture builders, and the Samwer brothers are the undisputed kings in that category at the global level.[3]

From its low-key offices near the center of the city, Rocket Internet has turned the usual business model for technology companies on its head, compiling a team of high-flying finance and management specialists and arming them with the money and expertise they need to mimic (copy) already successful Internet companies—applying these proven ideas in other countries, often in emerging markets.[4]

Since starting in 2007, Rocket has backed about 75 startups in more than 50 countries that now generate more than $3 billion in annual revenue and employ about 25,000 people. This business model stands in sharp contrast with the ethos that dominates Silicon Valley, where originality is perceived as the main currency for successful startups. It also has raised questions over whether Europe's tech sector, where Rocket is a major player, can ever foster the same level of innovation that has led to a conveyor belt of successful American tech giants, like Oracle, Google, and Facebook.

But Rocket is not without controversy. The company has been criticized for its copycat strategy of founding startups that replicate the business models of other established, successful companies.

In 2011, 20 of the then 130 employees left Rocket Internet at the same time. According to media coverage at the time, the reason for this string of layoffs was "bad quality of new products" and a "gruff manner" toward employees in the course of Rocket Internet's expansion into a "large corporation." The former Rocket Internet managers subsequently went on to found the incubator Project A Ventures with help from the Otto Group.

Questions have also been raised around Rocket's support of multiple competing companies in a particular business sector. Rocket Internet's original backing of both Take Eat Easy and Delivery Hero was questioned when Take Eat Easy was forced into liquidation in July 2016.

15.2.2 Rocket's 2016 Annual Report

The annual report stated,[5]

> Our company will celebrate its 10th anniversary this year. We are still a very young company, yet proud of our achievements over the last decade. We have created and supported some of the largest Internet companies in Europe and in emerging markets and continue to focus on our core competency of building and investing in new Internet-based business models. We have the necessary capital and financial flexibility to continue to execute on the core of our strategy.
>
> In 2016, Rocket Internet continued to make progress on the execution of its strategy. In particular, we focused on reducing the complexity at the group level, as well as at the individual company level and continued to show steady improvements across our selected companies. Furthermore, we continued to identify new and attractive online business models and companies.
>
> Our business model remains unchanged. We build and invest in great Internet companies around the globe and support our companies with operational expertise and capital over their development lifecycle, thereby enabling entrepreneurship and providing our shareholders with a diversified exposure to the global Internet sector.
>
> Rocket Internet's know-how to scale businesses distinguishes it from competitors. Recently founded companies greatly benefit from having access to this know-how and experience, giving them a competitive advantage: they benefit from strong network effects, our technological, functional and regional expertise, strategic partnerships and in-house knowledge sharing. These benefits taken together enhance a company's probability of success.
>
> Our functional experts support companies in key areas such as systems engineering, product design and online marketing. This enables companies to develop a market leading presence in a shorter period of time and with best-in-class functional know-how. As they mature, companies continue to turn to Rocket Internet for support on special projects to cover temporary high demand or specialist know-how.
>
> Rocket Internet's global network helps companies achieve economies of scale and synergies. Our people in target markets worldwide have

deep local expertise (e.g. operations and logistics), thus reducing marginal costs for building new companies.

We have established strategic partnerships that offer extensive financial, operational and strategic support to our network of companies. In addition, framework agreements with leading global technology firms provide our companies with competitively priced leading technology and services.

Through incubation, investment and growth, Rocket Internet supports companies in the Internet sector worldwide and provides investors with a diversified exposure to the global Internet sector.

15.3 Great Artists Steal!

Many people think that they are not truly thinking creatively unless they come up with *something* that is wholly original. This is absolutely not the case, according to Connolly of Creative Thinking Hub.[6] You see, it turns out that all truly great artists steal, as Picasso is credited with saying.

Did Pablo Picasso actually say that? Whether Picasso did indeed say that is open to some debate, but it is an extremely valuable insight for anyone interested in developing their ability to think creatively. So, what does Picasso's saying actually mean and what can we learn from it? Picasso was probably referring to the fact that good artists and great artists work very differently:

- A *good artist* will see another artist's style and then try and emulate that style as closely as they can.
- A *great artist* will select elements from another artist's work and incorporate it into their own unique mix of influences. Being better than the original is better than being the first loser.

A good artist simply copies another person's art. A great artist selectively takes (steals) elements from multiple sources and then creatively combines their influences to create something that is uniquely their own.

Some well-known business examples include the following:

- Apple did not create tablet computing. Toshiba and other companies had manufactured tablet devices almost a decade earlier. What Apple's iPad team did was take the concept of tablet computing and build it into something that worked extremely well, was wafer thin, and looked great.
- Google was not the first company to create a search engine. In fact, Google was late to the game. What Google did was take the concept of search engines and apply a super-simple interface to it, with a

unique program that consistently delivered very good search results. They created a unique-looking product that worked extremely well.

- When George Lucas created *Star Wars*, he fused the best of science fiction with old-time stories of the battle between good and evil.

15.3.1 Creative Thinking and Original Thought

Connolly continues:

> Many people assume they are not creative, because they set the bar impossibly high for themselves. They are happy to regard Apple, Google and George Lucas as creative, yet they feel that unless they come up with something wholly original, they themselves are not creative. The reality is that even if you believe you have had a wholly unique thought, someone in a robe probably had the same idea, 3 thousand years earlier.
>
> Give yourself the creative freedom to pull influences in from your whole life experience and forge them into your own; answers, paintings, ideas, dance moves, marketing, designs, stories, lyrics, sculptures, blog posts, products, food dishes, services, melodies—Anything!
>
> You will be amazed what you can create, when you learn to steal like an artist.

15.4 Don't Innovate, Imitate!

"What is the quickest way to startup success in the high-tech business? One is to think of a great innovation. Another is to copy someone else's great innovation. That is a lot easier than coming up with your own. And it is often a shorter, surer path to your first million—or billion," according to Devaney and Stein.[7]

"Just ask the Samwer brothers," as we have seen. "The founders of the Berlin-based imitator incubator Rocket Internet, they have cloned dozens of successful Internet companies, from eBay to Facebook. And all three of them are billionaires."

But could the growing acceptance of the Rocket business model also be due to the fact that people in the tech industry are finally admitting in public that imitation is good business?

"In the tech startup world, people tend to equate entrepreneurial activity with innovation, and that's the wrong assumption," according to Shenkar, a professor of management and human resources at Ohio State University, who wrote the book on the business of clones: *Copycats: How Smart Companies Use Imitation to Gain a Strategic Edge*. "There's a long history of successful startups that are built on imitation, not innovation." The following paragraphs describe Shenkar's unconventional pronouncements.

15.5 Clones and Copycats in the Digital World

Devaney and Stein also point out that Facebook is a copycat. Apple is another. We should recognize Mark Zuckerberg and Steve Jobs as great imitators, Shenkar said. Zuckerberg didn't invent social networking. Friendster launched in 2002, MySpace and LinkedIn in 2003. Facebook didn't come along until 2004. Similarly, Jobs cobbled together the Macintosh user interface circa 1984 out of ideas and technology he first encountered at Xerox PARC in 1979. Shankar doesn't count these imitations against the two men. Rather, he celebrates their seminal work in duplication.

"We have this reverence for innovation, but imitation is often the key to success," Shenkar explained. "Imitation was critical to human evolution, and today imitation is more critical than ever—because it's much cheaper and more feasible than previously. Business is the only discipline that's 50 years behind, in that it looks at imitation as a dumb thing that's done by people who can't innovate. In all other academic fields there is a belief that imitation is an intelligent capability. But in business we're still stuck on this religion of innovation."

Partly that's because innovation is hard, and the business world exalts high achievers. But imitation isn't easy, Shenkar said. You have to know how to do it, which is why some imitators fail and others, like the Samwers, succeed so well. Their hit rate is around 50%. Their neatest trick: copying successful companies, then selling the knockoffs to the originals. They sold their Groupon clone to Groupon. Recently they sold their version of Care.com to Care.com.

And imitation does not work only in the Internet world, Shenkar pointed out. It's easier there, yes, but copycatting has long been common in all sorts of industries. RC introduced the original diet cola, Diet Rite, in 1958, but it was flattened by imitations from Coke and Pepsi. European discount airline Ryanair was in a downward spiral until management flew off to Texas to learn from Southwest how to properly run a cut-rate carrier. Now Ryanair is profitable. Hertz and Enterprise are currently in the process of ripping off Zipcar.

When imitators execute well, they usually succeed better than the first movers, because they study the errors of the innovators and learn from them, as Facebook learned from the mistakes of MySpace.

"Every study that has looked at this issue has found support for the imitators," Shenkar continues. "And even those that found a modest advantage for the pioneers invariably found that the effect is getting smaller over time. So even if there is an advantage for innovators, it's getting smaller not larger, despite our worship of innovators. On balance, the research supports the imitators and we're moving more and more into an imitator age."

Imitators often outperform innovators, as shown in Table 15.1.

TABLE 15.1

Imitators That Have Come to Dominate Their Markets

Pioneers	Imitators
Blackberry smartphone	Apple iPhone 6
Rio PMP300 digital audio player	iPod
White Castle hamburgers	McDonald's, Burger King, Wendy's
Korvette discount stores	Walmart, Kohl's
Diners Club	American Express, Visa, Mastercard
de Havilland Comet jet airplane	Boeing 707
Chrysler minivan	Ford, General Motors, Toyota

15.5.1 How to Be a Successful Imitator

In their book summary of *Copycats*,[8] the International Achievement Institute state on page 6:

> There are six capabilities which must be developed and mastered in order to succeed as an imitator. These six essential capabilities are intertwined—they build and amplify each other.
>
> The six capabilities are:
>
> **1. Identify people who value imitation**
>
> To be a good imitator, you have to build a culture and mind-set which values imitation as much as innovation. You need people who are comfortable and enthused about applying "Not Invented Here" ideas and concepts. You must have the humility to acknowledge other people and other organizations are capable of coming up with good ideas. Good imitators are curious, flexible and engagingly open-minded. Look for people who are outcome focused more than anything else.
>
> **2. Find the right model to imitate**
>
> People have a natural tendency to try and imitate:
>
> - Their industry peers with which they are most familiar.
> - Other comparable companies which have a profile of success.
> - Processes which seem to produce highly favorable outcomes.
>
> Those tendencies are well and good but they can also be self-limiting to a degree. Instead of looking only at what can be termed "the usual suspects," you should get into the habit of searching globally for potential imitation models. Systematically look beyond your industry confines for firms which are doing noteworthy things. Look at obvious innovators and clear-cut imitators in a number of industries for raw material to work with. And don't forget the smaller players—they have a way of being the most innovative of all in order to survive.

3. Scan and filter for opportunities

Conduct regular, systematic searches for fresh ideas. Train everyone on how to spot the most promising targets for imitation.

To make that judgment call, your spotters will need to be technologically savvy enough to grasp the idea opportunities which come before them. Reverse engineering means to take a product or service and break it down into its components. You need people who can do "forward engineering"—who can visualize how an imitation would potentially fit into an existing or future product, process or business model. One way to do this is to offer to swap employees so practices worth imitating could be understood in more depth. Another option would be to give your people discretionary time they can use to study outside ideas that interest them. Come up with workable ways to get better at forward engineering.

4. Put imitation in its proper context

To imitate effectively, you have to understand the context within which the other firm's ideas work. Don't think of other companies as a black box where inputs go in one end and mysteriously come out the other end as polished and refined products.

Understand how the environment impacts on what they do. Figure out what adjustments will be needed to make an idea from another setting work for you. Capture all of the various intricacies involved and be prepared to make the changes which will be required to make the idea fit your company.

5. Understand what's beneath the surface

Never fall into the trap of settling for quick, knee-jerk superficial answers to complex problems. To become a good imitator, you have to appreciate and deal with complexity. If you're combining two different business models to come up with a hybrid third option, address all the contradictions which will be involved. By all means note the outcomes but focus on the means and processes required to generate those outcomes. Decipher cause-and-effect by understanding the capabilities, processes and culture required. Know what the various components contribute to the system as a whole.

6. Be able to implement what you want

Creative ideas are interesting but invention doesn't have an impact until it is implemented. Similarly, imitation won't amount to much unless you can execute. Come up with an implementation plan which takes into account the capabilities of your own organization and resources. Put together interdisciplinary teams so you cover all your bases when it comes to getting the right things happening.

In addition to these six essential capabilities, imitators also have to be able to overcome the various imitation defenses which innovators will erect wherever possible. The usual repertoire of imitation defenses are:

- An innovator might attempt to make it difficult for an outsider to decipher their product, service or business model. They might limit or restrict information to cause ambiguity.

- An innovator might have in place an elaborate network of relationships which the imitator would not be able to access. This might make putting together a supply chain difficult.

- It might be hard for a customer to switch from the innovator's product to the imitator's product.

- The innovator might signal to the market they have demonstrable superiority which cannot be cloned. Or alternatively the innovator might build production overcapacity in an attempt to scare off potential imitators.

- The innovator might have specialized manufacturing assets, exclusive supply sources and dedicated distribution channels which would not be available to the imitator.

- The innovator might have an established brand which is well known in its market. To overcome this, an imitator might use private label sales, the acquisition of a smaller brand, tie-ins with other established entities or the offer of a superior warranty. Imitators have to find ways to overcome all of these deterrents in order to prosper. Viable strategies exist for all of these defenses.

Good imitators not only figure out ways to overcome these defenses but at the same time they also use the defenses themselves to prevent or delay the arrival of others who want to imitate them.

15.6 Smartphone Patent Wars

A *smartphone* is a mobile personal computer with an advanced mobile operating system with features useful for mobile or handheld use. Smartphones, which are typically pocket sized (as opposed to tablets, which are much larger in measurement), have the ability to place and receive voice and video calls and create and receive text messages, and have personal digital assistants (such as Siri, Google Assistant, Alexa, Cortana, or Bixby), an event calendar, a media player, video games, GPS navigation, a digital camera, and a digital video camera. Smartphones can access the Internet through cellular or Wi-Fi and can run a variety of third-party software components ("apps" from places like Google Play Store or Apple App Store). They typically have a color display with a graphical user interface that covers more than 76% of the front surface. The display is almost always a touchscreen and sometimes additionally a touch-enabled keyboard like the Priv/Passport BlackBerrys, which enables the user to use a virtual keyboard to type words and numbers and press onscreen icons to activate app features.[9]

There is no clear and universally accepted definition of the smartphone marketplace. Because smartphones are at the boundaries of computing, telephony, and telecommunications

services, the lines between smartphones, mobile phones, and notebook computers have become blurred through the introduction of tablets and tablet–phone hybrids. In order to narrow the scope of the study to exclude non-phone tablet devices and other types of phone devices, this study focuses on handheld computing devices that (1) have the ability to make phone calls over cellular networks and (2) can transfer data and run applications over mobile computing networks.[10] For our purposes, we will define a smartphone as "mobile phones that use the Google Android, Apple iOS, RIM Blackberry, Microsoft, and other similar platforms."

The smartphone industry today is characterized by a thicket of patents and an ongoing business battle by every major smartphone manufacturer in which patents are used as leverage against competitors to secure or increase their respective market shares while slowing competitors' progress.[11] According to patent attorney Bui,[12] the conflict is part of the larger "patent wars" between technology and software multinational corporations based in the United States, Canada, Europe, Japan, Korea, Taiwan, and China. The companies involved include Apple, HTC, Microsoft, Motorola Mobility, Nokia, Research in Motion (RIM), and Samsung.

Attorney Bui continued:

> The current smartphone wars started in the late 2000s in part because of a long-running feud between Apple, the world's largest technology company by market capitalization, and Google regarding Google's competing Android mobile operating system (OS) and Android phones when Google jumped into the smartphone market while former Google CEO Eric Schmidt was on Apple's Board of Director from 2006–2009, and in part because of the success of Google Android as the dominant operating system (OS) in the global smartphone market relative to Apple's own operating system (iOS).
>
> The late Steve Jobs, co-founder and former chairman and CEO of Apple, referred to Google's Android phone concept as a "stolen product." In the Steven Jobs biography by Walter Issacson, Jobs promised "thermonuclear war" against what he saw as Android's systematic copying of Apple features.[13]
>
> However, Apple has not attacked Google head on; rather, Apple fired off a series of lawsuits against Google-Android partners and smartphone manufacturers in part because these smartphone manufacturers actually generate revenue and profit from those Android phones whereas Google gives the Android operating system (OS) away for free and generates revenue only indirectly through mobile advertising. For example, in March 2010, Apple first sued Google-Android partner HTC for patent infringement of iPhone's features including iOS user interface, underlying architecture and hardware in the U.S. District Court for the District of Delaware and the International Trade Commission (ITC).[14]

The conflict with HTC mushroomed into 10 different lawsuits in various jurisdictions in the United States, United Kingdom and Germany, and eventually settled in November 2012. Similarly, in October 2010, Apple also filed lawsuits against Motorola Mobility over six multi-touch OS patents that make up much of the signature touch-screen inventions of the iPhones.

In April 2011, Apple then sued Google leading Android partner, Samsung for patent infringement of user interface and design features of iPhones and iPads in the U.S. District Court for the Northern District of California. However, unlike HTC, Samsung is the world's largest technology company by revenues from 2009 to 2012, and also the world's largest maker of smartphones supporting Google Android as the primary operating system (OS). Samsung is also no stranger to patent lawsuits and innovation, having one of the largest patent portfolios in the United States and the World. The legal battle between Apple and Samsung is particularly intriguing because Apple and Samsung have worked closely together for many years. Samsung has been one of Apple's largest suppliers of components such as memory chips and components for all Apple's products including iPhones and iPads, and Apple one of Samsung's biggest customers. Nevertheless, this symbiotic relationship between Apple and Samsung has not deterred either company from competing head-on in the smartphone market, together winning ½ of the global market share and 90% of the profit for smartphones and tablets, and now using patents as weapons to gain market share and draw product differentiations. The legal dispute between Apple and Samsung has mushroomed into 50 different lawsuits in 10 different countries, including four in the United States, 12 in Germany, one in the United Kingdom, two each in France, Italy, the Netherlands, South Korea, and Australia, and three in Spain.

On August 24, 2012, Apple won a $1.049 billion patent-infringement verdict in a jury trial against Samsung in the United States District Court for the Northern District of California. The jury found that Samsung had infringed on all three Apple's user interface patents (U.S. Patent No. 7,469,481, known as "Bounce-Back-Effect" patent; U.S. Patent No. 7,844,915, known as "On-Screen Navigation" patent; U.S. Patent No. 7,864,163, known as "Tap-To-Zoom" patent), and three out of four design patents that Apple had asserted. The jury rejected Samsung's defense that these patents were invalid. In addition, the jury found that Samsung willful infringed five of these patents. The jury also denied all of Samsung's infringement counterclaims.

15.7 Legal Consequences of Imitators

While the big boys are busy imitating each other, there is a bewildering amount of litigation among them. Below is an excellent example of one such case, litigated between Apple and Samsung.[15]

United States Court of Appeals, Federal Circuit.

APPLE INC., Plaintiff—Appellant, v. SAMSUNG ELECTRONICS CO., LTD., Samsung Electronics America, Inc., and Samsung Telecommunications America, LLC, Defendants—Appellees.

No. 2013–1129.

Decided: November 18, 2013

Before PROST, BRYSON, and O'MALLEY, Circuit Judges. William F. Lee, Wilmer Cutler Pickering Hale and Dorr LLP, of Boston, MA, argued for plaintiff-appellant. With him on the brief were Mark C. Fleming, Joseph J. Mueller and Lauren B. Fletcher; and Jonathan G. Cedarbaum, of WA, DC. Of counsel on the brief were Michael A. Jacobs, Rachel Krevans, Erik J. Olson, Richard S.J. Hung and Grant L. Kim, Morrison & Foerster LLP, of San Francisco, CA of counsel were Andrew J. Danford, Wilmer Cutler Pickering Hale and Dorr LLP, of Boston, MA; Mark D. Selwyn, of Palo Alto, CA; and Rachel Weiner, of WA, DC. Kathleen M. Sullivan, Quinn Emanuel Urquhart & Sullivan, LLP, of New York, New York, argued for defendants-appellees. With her on the brief were William B. Adams; and Kevin A. Smith, of San Francisco, CA of counsel were John B. Quinn, of Los Angeles, CA and Derek Shaffer, of WA, DC. Patrick J. Flinn, Alston and Bird LLP, of Atlanta, GA, for amici curiae Nokia Corporation, et al. With him on the brief was Keith E. Broyles. Kevin X. McGann, White & Case LLP, of New York, New York, for amici curiae Google, Inc., et al. With him on the brief were Christopher J. Glancy, and Warren S. Heit, of Palo Alto, CA.

Apple Inc. appeals from an order of the U.S. District Court for the Northern District of California denying Apple's request for a permanent injunction against Samsung Electronics Company, Ltd., Samsung Electronics America, Inc., and Samsung Telecommunications America, LLC (collectively, "Samsung"). See Apple Inc. v. Samsung Elecs. Co., 909 F.Supp.2d 1147 (N.D.Cal.2012) ("Injunction Order"). Apple sought to enjoin Samsung's infringement of several of Apple's design and utility patents, as well as Samsung's dilution of Apple's iPhone trade dress. We affirm the denial of injunctive relief with respect to Apple's design patents and trade dress. However, we vacate the denial of injunctive relief with respect to Apple's utility patents and remand for further proceedings.

Background

A. Proceedings Below

Apple sued Samsung in April 2011, alleging infringement of several Apple patents and dilution of Apple's trade dress. Samsung filed counterclaims, alleging infringement of several of its own patents. The case was tried to a jury beginning on July 30, 2012, and on August 24, 2012, the jury returned a verdict substantially in Apple's favor. The jury found that twenty-six Samsung smartphones and tablets infringed one or more of six Apple patents. The jury also found that six Samsung smartphones diluted Apple's registered iPhone trade dress and unregistered iPhone 3G trade dress. In addition, the jury rejected Samsung's infringement counterclaims and awarded Apple more than $1 billion in damages. The district court later set aside a portion of the damages award for certain products and scheduled a partial new trial on damages, but it affirmed the jury's liability findings.

After trial, Apple moved for a permanent injunction to enjoin Samsung from importing or selling any of its twenty-six infringing smartphones and tablets[1] "or any other product not more than colorably different from an Infringing Product as to a feature or design found to infringe." Injunction Order, 909 F.Supp.2d at 1149. Apple also sought to enjoin Samsung from selling any of its six smartphones found to dilute Apple's trade dress.[2]

On December 17, 2012, the district court denied Apple's request for a permanent injunction. See id. at 1149–50. Apple appealed, and we have jurisdiction under 28 U.S.C. §§ 1292(c)(1) and 1295(a)(1).

B. Prior Appeals

This court has previously issued two opinions in appeals involving these particular parties and the issue of injunctive relief.[3] In Apple Inc. v. Samsung Electronics Co., 678 F.3d 1314 (Fed.Cir.2012), referred to here as Apple I, we resolved an appeal in this case arising from the district court's denial of a preliminary injunction with respect to four Apple patents, including three patents that are at issue in the current appeal. We affirmed the district court's denial of injunctive relief with respect to those three patents but vacated the denial of injunctive relief with respect to the fourth patent on the ground that the patent was likely not invalid. See id. at 1333. On remand, the district court entered a preliminary injunction against Samsung's Galaxy Tab 10.1 tablet, but the injunction was lifted after the jury found the Tab 10.1 not to infringe.

In Apple Inc. v. Samsung Electronics Co., 695 F.3d 1370 (Fed.Cir.2012), referred to here as Apple II, we resolved an appeal in a separate case that Apple filed in 2012, involving different patents but some of the same products. In Apple II, we reversed the district court's grant of a preliminary injunction against Samsung's Galaxy Nexus smartphone. See id. at 1372.

There is some overlap between the issues raised in Apple I and Apple II and the present appeal. However, whereas in our prior opinions we addressed Apple's requests for preliminary injunctive relief, in the present appeal we are asked to address Apple's request for permanent injunctive relief.

C. Apple's Patents and Trade Dress

Apple is seeking a permanent injunction against Samsung's infringement of six patents—three design patents and three utility patents. The design patents are U.S. Design Patent Nos. 618,677 ("D'677 patent"), 593,087 ("D'087 patent"), and 604,305 ("D'305 patent"). We previously discussed the D'677 and D'087 patents in Apple I, where we explained:

Both patents claim a minimalist design for a rectangular smartphone consisting of a large rectangular display occupying most of the phone's front face. The corners of the phone are rounded. Aside from a rectangular speaker slot above the display and a circular button below the display claimed in several figures of the patent, the design contains no ornamentation. The D'087 patent claims a bezel surrounding the perimeter of the phone's front face and extending from the front of the phone partway down the phone's side. The parts of the side beyond the bezel, as well as the phone's back, are disclaimed, as indicated by the use of broken lines in the patent figures. The D'677 patent does not claim a bezel but instead shows a black, highly polished, reflective surface over the entire front face of the phone. The D'677 patent disclaims the sides and back of the device.

The D'305 patent claims the ornamental design of the iPhone's graphical user interface, including the arrangement of rows of square icons with rounded corners.

The three utility patents at issue in this appeal are U.S. Patent Nos. 7,469,381 ("'381 patent"), 7,844,915 ("'915 patent"), and 7,864,163 ("'163 patent"). We discussed the '381 patent in Apple I. As we explained there:

[T]he '381 patent claims a software feature known as the "bounce-back" feature, which is found on Apple's smartphones and tablets, such as the iPhone and the iPad. The bounce-back feature is activated when the user is scrolling through a document displayed on the device. If the user attempts to scroll past the end of the document, an area beyond the edge of the document is displayed to indicate that the user has reached the document's end. Once the user input ceases (i.e., when the user lifts up the finger that is used for scrolling), the previously visible part of the document "bounces back" into view.

Apple I, 678 F.3d at 1318.

The '915 patent claims a type of "multi-touch display" functionality, which allows a touchscreen device to distinguish between single-touch commands for scrolling through documents and multi-touch gestures for manipulating a document, such as a two-fingered "pinch-to-zoom" gesture.

The '163 patent claims a "double-tap-to-zoom" functionality, which allows a touchscreen device to enlarge and center the text of an electronic document when a user taps twice on a portion of the document, and in response to a second user gesture on another portion of the document, recenters the screen over that portion of the document.

Apple is also seeking a permanent injunction against Samsung's dilution of its registered iPhone trade dress and its unregistered iPhone 3G trade dress. These two trade dresses protect the overall visual impression of the non-functional elements of the iPhone's front face, including: (i) a rectangular product with four evenly rounded corners; (ii) a flat clear surface covering the front of the product; (iii) the appearance of a metallic bezel around the flat clear surface; (iv) a display screen under the clear surface; (v) under the clear surface, substantial black borders above and below the display screen and narrower black borders on either side of the screen; (vi) when the device is on, a row of small dots on the display screen; (vii) when the device is on, a matrix of colorful square icons with evenly rounded corners within the display screen; and (viii) when the device is on, a bottom dock of colorful square icons with evenly rounded corners set off from the other icons on the display, which does not change as other pages of the user interface are viewed.

Discussion

In accordance with the principles of equity, a plaintiff seeking a permanent injunction "must demonstrate: (1) that it has suffered an irreparable injury; (2) that remedies available at law, such as monetary damages, are inadequate to compensate for that injury; (3) that, considering the balance of hardships between the plaintiff and defendant, a remedy in equity is warranted; and (4) that the public interest would not be disserved by a permanent injunction." eBay Inc. v. MercExchange, L.L.C., 547 U.S. 388, 391 (2006). The Supreme Court has cautioned that "[a]n injunction is a drastic and extraordinary remedy, which should not be granted as a matter of course." Monsanto Co. v. Geertson Seed Farms, 130 S.Ct. 2743, 2761 (2010) (citing Weinberger v. Romero–Barcelo, 456 U.S. 305, 311–12 (1982)). Rather, "[i]f a less drastic remedy [is] sufficient to redress [a plaintiff's] injury, no recourse to the additional and extraordinary relief of an injunction [is] warranted." Id.

"The decision to grant or deny permanent injunctive relief is an act of equitable discretion by the district court, reviewable on appeal for abuse of discretion." eBay, 547 U.S. at 391. "We may find an abuse of discretion on a showing that the court made a clear error of judgment in weighing relevant factors or exercised its discretion based upon an error of law or clearly erroneous factual findings." Innogenetics, N.V. v. Abbott Labs., 512 F.3d 1363, 1379 (Fed.Cir.2008) (internal quotation marks omitted). "To the extent the court's decision is based upon an issue of law, we review that issue de novo." Sanofi–Synthelabo v. Apotex, Inc., 470 F.3d 1368, 1374 (Fed.Cir.2006).

On appeal, Apple challenges the district court's denial of its request for a permanent injunction against Samsung's infringement of its patents and dilution of its trade dress. We first address the denial of an injunction against

Samsung's patent infringement, followed by the denial of an injunction against Samsung's trade dress dilution.

A. Apple's Request to Enjoin Samsung's Patent Infringement

The district court analyzed the four principles of equity enumerated in eBay and then, weighing the factors, concluded that they did not support the issuance of an injunction against Samsung's infringement of Apple's patents. We find no reason to dislodge the district court's conclusion that Apple failed to demonstrate irreparable harm from Samsung's infringement of its design patents. Accordingly, we affirm the denial of injunctive relief with respect to those patents. However, with respect to Apple's utility patents, we conclude that the district court abused its discretion in its analysis and consequently remand for further proceedings. As discussed below, we reach our conclusion by applying the eBay factors.

1. Irreparable Harm

The district court found that the irreparable harm factor weighed in favor of Samsung. The court began by acknowledging our precedent establishing that there is no presumption of irreparable harm upon a finding of patent infringement. Robert Bosch LLC v. Pylon Mfg. Corp., 659 F.3d 1142, 1148 (Fed. Cir.2011). The court also cited our statement in Apple II that "to satisfy the irreparable harm factor in a patent infringement suit, a patentee must establish both of the following requirements: 1) that absent an injunction, it will suffer irreparable harm, and 2) that a sufficiently strong causal nexus relates the alleged harm to the alleged infringement." Apple II, 695 F.3d at 1374.

The district court then turned to Apple's claim that it has suffered three types of irreparable harm as a result of Samsung's patent infringement: (1) lost market share; (2) lost downstream and future sales; and (3) injury to Apple's "ecosystem." As an initial matter, the court found that "Apple and Samsung are direct competitors" that "compete for first-time smartphone buyers." Injunction Order, 909 F.Supp.2d at 1151. Regarding market share, Apple introduced unrefuted evidence that Samsung's market share had grown substantially from 2010 to 2012, and that Samsung had an explicit strategy to increase its market share at Apple's expense. Based on this evidence, the court found that "Apple has continued to lose market share to Samsung," which it recognized "can support a finding of irreparable harm." Id. at 1152. As for downstream sales, Apple introduced evidence regarding network compatibility and brand loyalty, from which the court concluded that "there were potentially long-term implications of an initial purchase, in the form of lost future sales of both future phone models and tag-along products like apps, desktop computers, laptops, and iPods." Id. Accordingly, the court found that "Apple has suffered some irreparable harm in the form of loss of downstream sales." Id. Finally, with respect to harm to Apple's ecosystem, the court concluded that any such harm would be included in lost downstream sales. These findings are not disputed on appeal.

After making its initial findings that Apple has suffered harm as a result of Samsung's sales of smartphones and tablets, the district court considered whether Apple could demonstrate a causal nexus between that harm and Samsung's patent infringement. As will be discussed in more detail below, the district court concluded that Apple's evidence did not establish the requisite nexus for either its design patents or its utility patents. As a result, the court concluded that the irreparable harm factor did not support entry of an injunction.

On appeal, Apple challenges the district court's irreparable harm analysis on two main grounds. First, Apple argues that the court erroneously adopted a causal nexus requirement in the permanent injunction context. Second, Apple argues, in the alternative, that it satisfied any reasonable causal nexus requirement with respect to both the design patents and the utility patents.

We begin with Apple's challenge to the causal nexus requirement. As in the preliminary injunction context, "[w]e hold that the district court was correct to require a showing of some causal nexus between Samsung's infringement and the alleged harm to Apple as part of the showing of irreparable harm." Apple I, 678 F.3d at 1324. In Apple I, we explained the reasoning behind the causal nexus requirement as follows:

To show irreparable harm, it is necessary to show that the infringement caused harm in the first place. Sales lost to an infringing product cannot irreparably harm a patentee if consumers buy that product for reasons other than the patented feature. If the patented feature does not drive the demand for the product, sales would be lost even if the offending feature were absent from the accused product. Thus, a likelihood of irreparable harm cannot be shown if sales would be lost regardless of the infringing conduct.

Id. Similarly, in Apple II, we explained:

[I]t may very well be that the accused product would sell almost as well without incorporating the patented feature. And in that case, even if the competitive injury that results from selling the accused device is substantial, the harm that flows from the alleged infringement (the only harm that should count) is not. Thus, the causal nexus inquiry is indeed part of the irreparable harm calculus: it informs whether the patentee's allegations of irreparable harm are pertinent to the injunctive relief analysis, or whether the patentee seeks to leverage its patent for competitive gain beyond that which the inventive contribution and value of the patent warrant.

Apple II, 695 F.3d at 1374–75.

The reasoning in Apple I and Apple II reflects general tort principles of causation and applies equally to the preliminary and permanent injunction contexts. Indeed, as the district court noted, we cited a permanent injunction case in Apple I to support the requirement of a causal nexus in the preliminary injunction context. See Apple I, 678 F.3d at 1324 (citing Voda v. Cordis Corp., 536 F.3d 1311 (Fed.Cir.2008)). Moreover, the Supreme Court has explained that "[t]he standard for a preliminary injunction is essentially the same as for a permanent injunction with the exception that the plaintiff must show a likelihood of success on the merits rather than actual success." Amoco Prod. Co. v. Vill. of Gambell, AK, 480 U.S. 531, 546 (1987); see also eBay, 547 U.S. at 391 (citing Amoco, a preliminary injunction case, in support of the four-factor test for permanent injunctive relief). These considerations counsel us to treat the irreparable harm factor the same in both the preliminary and permanent injunction contexts.

Apple makes several arguments why it believes there should be no causal nexus requirement in the permanent injunction context.[4] First, Apple argues that the causal nexus requirement is an "unprecedented fifth requirement" beyond the traditional four factors for obtaining injunctive relief. Apple Br. 49. This assertion, however, is based on a misunderstanding of the causal nexus requirement. In Apple II, we explained that "the causal nexus inquiry is part of the irreparable harm calculus," and that "although the irreparable harm and the causal nexus inquiries may be separated for the ease of analysis, they are inextricably related concepts." Apple II, 695 F.3d at 1374–75. Put another way, the causal nexus requirement is simply a way of distinguishing between irreparable harm caused by patent infringement and irreparable harm caused by otherwise lawful competition—e.g., "sales [that] would be lost even if the offending feature were absent from the accused product." Apple I, 678 F.3d at 1324. The former type of harm may weigh in favor of an injunction, whereas the latter does not.

Apple also argues that the district court's application of the causal nexus requirement conflicts with this court's post-eBay rulings on permanent injunctions in cases such as Bosch, 659 F.3d 1142; Broadcom Corp. v. Qualcomm Inc., 543 F.3d 683 (Fed.Cir.2008); Acumed LLC v. Stryker Corp., 551 F.3d 1323 (Fed.Cir.2008); Presidio Components, Inc. v. American Technical Ceramics Corp., 702 F.3d 1351 (Fed.Cir.2012); and Douglas Dynamics, LLC v. Buyers Products Co., 717 F.3d 1336 (Fed.Cir.2013).[5] According to Apple, these cases demonstrate that there is no causal nexus requirement in the permanent injunction context because they upheld (or, in some cases, even reversed the denial of) permanent injunctive relief without discussing any causal nexus requirement.

Apple's reliance on those cases is misplaced. For one thing, there is no indication that any of the infringers in those cases challenged the existence of a causal nexus between their infringement and the patentees' alleged harm, so this court did not have occasion to address the issue. Moreover, some of the cases involved relatively simple products—at least in the sense that they had a small number of features when compared to the complex, multi-featured smartphones and tablets at issue in this case. Those products included windshield wiper blades (Bosch), orthopedic nails used to treat fractures of the upper arm bone (Acumed), and broadband capacitors used in electrical systems (Presidio). In those cases, the impact that the infringing features had on demand for the products may never have been in doubt. Apple contends that this "understanding of the causal nexus requirement would make the standard for injunctive relief turn on a determination whether the products involved are 'simple' or 'complex.'" Apple Reply Br. 6. Contrary to Apple's suggestion, however, the causal nexus requirement applies regardless of the complexity of the products. It just may be more easily satisfied (indeed, perhaps even conceded) for relatively "simple" products.

The cases cited by Apple are distinguishable on other grounds as well. For example, in Douglas Dynamics, this court found that the evidence showed the patentee had suffered irreparable "erosion in reputation and brand distinction" as a result of the defendant's infringement—a type of harm not asserted by Apple. Douglas Dynamics, 717 F.3d at 1344. And in Broadcom, the evidence at trial showed that the market for baseband chips was very different from the consumer goods market in which Apple and Samsung compete. Specifically, as the district court in Broadcom explained:

The market for baseband chips is unlike the typical market for consumer goods where competitors compete for each consumer sale, and the competition is instantaneous and on-going Competition for sales is not on a unit-by-unit basis, but rather competition is characterized by competing for "design wins" for the development and production of cell phones which will embody the proposed chip.

543 F.3d at 702; accord Broadcom Corp. v. Emulex Corp., 732 F.3d 1325, 1337 (Fed.Cir.2013) (affirming district court's finding of irreparable harm in part because "Emulex and Broadcom were competitors in a 'design wins' market, which is fundamentally different from the market in Apple" and "the undisputed evidence at trial linked the claimed invention of the '150 patent to the success of the products incorporating it"). Accordingly, we reject Apple's contention that the causal nexus requirement conflicts with this court's post-eBay permanent injunction cases.

Apple also argues that there are significant differences between preliminary and permanent injunctions that make the causal nexus unjustified and unnecessary for permanent injunctions. We disagree. For example, Apple argues that whereas a preliminary injunction is an "extraordinary remedy never awarded as of right," "the liability determination—provided in this case by a jury verdict that Samsung infringed numerous valid Apple patents—is a finding that the plaintiff has a 'property right granting the plaintiff the right to exclude' the defendant from practicing the patent." Apple Br. 51–52 (quoting Bosch, 549 F.3d at 1149 (alterations omitted)). However, as the Supreme Court made clear in eBay, "the creation of a right is distinct from the provision of remedies for violations of that right." 547 U.S. at 392. The fact that the jury's infringement verdict established Apple's "right[s] secured by [its] patents" does not necessarily say anything about the appropriate remedy other than that a court "may grant [an] injunction[ ] in accordance with the principles of equity." 35 U.S.C. § 283 (emphasis added).

In addition, Apple argues that the concern that gave rise to the causal nexus requirement in the preliminary injunction context can be eliminated in the permanent injunction context through delayed enforcement of an injunction. In Apple II, we stated that the causal nexus requirement "informs whether the patentee's allegations of irreparable harm are pertinent to the injunctive relief analysis, or whether the patentee seeks to leverage its patent for competitive gain beyond that which the inventive contribution and value of the patent warrant." Apple II, 695 F.3d at 1375 (emphasis added). Apple asserts that in situations where it would be inequitable to require immediate compliance with a permanent injunction, a district court can exercise its discretion to delay enforcement of the injunction until the defendant has time to design around the patent. According to Apple, this delayed enforcement would prevent the patentee from leveraging its patent beyond its inventive contribution. We agree with Apple that a delayed injunction may be more likely to prevent only infringing features rather than the sale of entire products, because the defendant would have time to implement a noninfringing alternative. For that reason, a delay in enforcement may make an injunction more equitable and, thus, more justifiable in any given case. However, it is unclear why such delayed enforcement would not also be available in the preliminary injunction context. More fundamentally, the purpose of the causal nexus requirement is to show that the patentee is irreparably harmed by the infringement. Without such a showing, it is reasonable to conclude that a patentee will suffer the same harm with or without an injunction, thus undermining the need for injunctive relief in the first place.

Finally, Apple argues that the causal nexus requirement is a bright-line rule that is inconsistent with eBay's rejection of categorical rules in the injunction context. Apple proposes that because no single equitable factor in the injunction analysis is dispositive, "[a] strong showing of irreparable harm should offset comparatively weak evidence of causal nexus, and vice-versa." Apple Br. 60. Like Apple's first argument, this argument seems to be premised on the mistaken notion that the causal nexus is a separate factor from irreparable harm. As we have explained, however, the causal nexus requirement is part of the irreparable harm factor. Without a showing of causal nexus, there is no relevant irreparable harm. In other words, there cannot be one without the other. Therefore, it would be illogical to say that a weak showing of causal nexus could be offset by a strong showing of irreparable harm.

Accordingly, we reject Apple's arguments and confirm that the district court was correct to require a showing of some causal nexus between Samsung's infringing conduct and Apple's alleged harm. That said, we agree with Apple that certain of the standards arguably articulated by the district court go too far.

First, the district court appears to have required Apple to show that one of the patented features is the sole reason consumers purchased Samsung's products. This is reflected in certain statements in the district court's opinion indicating, for example, that Apple must "show that consumers buy the infringing product specifically because it is equipped with the patented feature," or must provide "evidence that consumers will buy a Samsung phone instead of an Apple phone because it contains [the infringing] feature." Injunction Order, 909 F.Supp.2d at 1154, 1156. To the extent these statements reflect the view that Apple was necessarily required to show that a patented feature is the sole reason for consumers' purchases, the court erred.

It is true that Apple must "show that the infringing feature drives consumer demand for the accused product." Apple II, 695 F.3d at 1375. It is also true that this inquiry should focus on the importance of the claimed invention in the context of the accused product, and not just the importance, in general, of features of the same type as the claimed invention. See id. at 1376 ("To establish a sufficiently strong causal nexus, Apple must show that consumers buy the Galaxy Nexus because it is equipped with the apparatus claimed in the ' 604 patent—not because it can search in general, and not even because it has unified search."). However, these principles do not mean Apple must show that a patented feature is the one and only reason for consumer demand. Consumer preferences are too complex—and the principles of equity are too flexible—for that to be the correct standard. Indeed, such a rigid standard could, in practice, amount to a categorical rule barring injunctive relief in most cases involving multi-function products, in contravention of eBay. See eBay, 547 U.S. at 393 (rejecting "expansive principles suggesting that injunctive relief could not issue in a broad swath of cases").

Thus, rather than show that a patented feature is the exclusive reason for consumer demand, Apple must show some connection between the patented feature and demand for Samsung's products. There might be a variety of ways to make this required showing, for example, with evidence that a patented feature is one of several features that cause consumers to make their purchasing decisions. It might also be shown with evidence that the inclusion of a patented feature makes a product significantly more desirable. Conversely, it might be shown with evidence that the absence of a patented feature would make a product significantly less desirable.

To illustrate these points, it may be helpful to return to an example discussed in Apple II. There, we explained that a battery does not necessarily drive demand for a laptop computer simply because its removal would render the laptop ineffective as a portable computer. See Apple II, 695 F.3d at 1376. That is because consumers often do not choose a laptop based on its battery, and presumably at this point, no inventor has a patent covering all laptop batteries. Nevertheless, it is indisputable that the ability to carry around a computer without having to plug it in is one of the reasons people buy laptops. Thus, if the first person to invent a laptop battery had obtained a patent covering all laptop batteries, then it would be reasonable to say that the patented invention was a driver of demand for laptops. And if a particular patented laptop battery lasts significantly longer than any other battery on the market, then the replacement of that battery with a noninfringing battery might make a laptop less desirable. In that case, it might be reasonable to conclude that the patented battery is a driver of consumer demand for the laptop.

The second principle on which we disagree with the district court is its wholesale rejection of Apple's attempt to aggregate patents for purposes of analyzing irreparable harm. Specifically, the district court stated:

Apple has not analyzed its alleged harm on a patent-by-patent basis, but rather has argued for harm from each group of intellectual property rights: design patents, utility patents, and trade dress. Apple has also argued that the combined harm from the patents and trade dress combined justifies an injunction. However, Apple has identified no law supporting its position that an injunction could issue on a finding of harm caused by Samsung in the aggregate. Rather, injunctions are authorized by statute for specific acts of infringement and dilution.

Injunction Order, 909 F.Supp.2d at 1153.

While it is true that this court analyzed causal nexus on a patent-by-patent basis in Apple I, we did not mean to foreclose viewing patents in the aggregate. Rather, we believe there may be circumstances where it is logical and equitable to view patents in the aggregate. For example, it may make sense to view patents in the aggregate where they all relate to the same technology or where they combine to make a product significantly more valuable. To hold otherwise could lead to perverse situations such as a patentee being unable to obtain an injunction against the infringement of multiple patents covering different—but when combined, all—aspects of the same technology, even though the technology as a whole drives demand for the infringing product. We leave it to the district court, however, to address this issue in the first instance on remand.

With these principles in mind, we turn to Apple's alternative argument that even if some showing of a causal nexus is required, it made such a showing. We begin with Apple's design patents and conclude with its utility patents.

a. Apple's Design Patents

At the district court, Apple attempted to show a causal nexus for its design patents with evidence of the importance of smartphone design. For instance, Apple contended that its design patents "cover the iPhone's most prominent design elements," and it "presented significant evidence that design, as a general matter, is important in consumer choice" of smartphones. Id. at 1154. Apple also introduced evidence of quotations from Samsung consumer surveys and from an industry review praising specific elements of both Apple's and Samsung's phone designs, including some elements of Apple's patented designs. See id.

The district court found Apple's evidence inadequate. With respect to the evidence that design is important in consumer choice, the court noted that "the design of the phones includes elements of all three design patents, as well as a whole host of unprotectable, unpatented features," and that Apple had "ma[de] no attempt to prove that any more specific element of the iPhone's design, let alone one covered by one of Apple's design patents, actually drives consumer demand." Id. The court concluded that "even if design was clearly a driving factor," and "[e]ven if the Court accepted as true Apple's contentions that the patents cover the most central design features, it would not establish that any specific patented design is an important driver of consumer demand." Id. In other words, the court found this evidence too "general" to establish a nexus. Id.

With respect to Apple's evidence in the form of quotations, the district court found that they "refer[red] to such isolated characteristics as glossiness, reinforced glass, black color, metal edges, and reflective screen," some of which (e.g., glossiness) are not even incorporated into the patented designs. Id. The court concluded that "[n]one of the consumer quotations considers more than one characteristic or discusses the way the characteristics are combined into a complete, patentable design." Id. In addition, the court stated that "even if these quotations did specifically reference the precise designs covered by Apple's patents, they do not begin to prove that those particular features drive consumer demand in any more than an anecdotal way." Id. In sum, the court concluded that "while Apple has presented evidence that design, as a general matter, is important to consumers more broadly, Apple simply has not established a sufficient causal nexus between infringement of its design patents and irreparable harm." Id. at 1154–55.

On appeal, Apple contends that its evidence shows that its patented designs drive consumer demand. The district court correctly noted, however, that evidence showing the importance of a general feature of the type covered by a patent is typically insufficient to establish a causal nexus. The district court was also correct that isolated, anecdotal statements about single design elements do not establish that Apple's broader patented designs are drivers of consumer demand. Having reviewed the evidence cited by Apple, we find no abuse of discretion in the court's conclusion that Apple failed to establish a causal nexus.[6]

Apple contends that the district court's opinion conflicts with Apple I, in which we affirmed the district court's conclusion that Apple had established the requisite nexus for one of its design patents based on evidence showing that "design mattered to customers in making tablet purchases." Apple I, 678 F.3d at 1328 (emphasis added). However, as Samsung notes, we also relied on "[t]he fact that Apple had claimed all views of the patented device." Id. Moreover, we are reviewing the district court for an abuse of discretion. While we might not reverse the entry of an injunction based on this evidence, under that deferential standard of review, we cannot say that the district court abused its discretion when it found that Apple failed to demonstrate a causal nexus between Samsung's infringement of its design patents and Apple's lost market share and downstream sales.

b. Apple's Utility Patents

After rejecting Apple's evidence of a causal nexus with respect to its design patents, the district court addressed Apple's utility patents. Apple attempted to prove causal nexus for these patents with "three types of evidence: (1) documents and testimony showing the importance of ease of use as a factor in phone choice; (2) evidence that Samsung deliberately copied the patented features; and (3) a conjoint survey performed by Apple's expert, Dr. Hauser." Injunction Order, 909 F.Supp.2d at 1155. Dr. Hauser's survey purported to show the "price premium" that Samsung customers would pay for smartphones and tablets with Apple's patented features. J.A. 30488. In particular, the survey showed that Samsung consumers were willing to pay $39 more for a smartphone and $45 more for a tablet that included the '915 patent's claimed feature and $100 more for a smartphone and $90 more for a tablet that included all three utility patents' claimed features. See id.

The district court again found Apple's evidence inadequate. With respect to Apple's evidence concerning the importance of ease of use, the court concluded that—like Apple's evidence on the importance of design—the evidence was "simply too general." Injunction Order, 909 F.Supp.2d at 1155. As for the evidence of copying by Samsung, the court concluded that "Samsung's impressions of what might lure customers, while relevant, are not dispositive," and that although such evidence "may offer some limited support for Apple's theory, it does not establish that those features actually drove demand." Id. at 1156. Finally, the court rejected Dr. Hauser's survey evidence for failing to "measure willingness to pay for products" as opposed to features, and for failing to "address the relationship between demand for a feature and demand for a complex product incorporating that feature and many other features." Id.

On appeal, Apple cites surveys "identify[ing] Apple's easy-to-use user interface as critical to the success of Apple's products," consumer reviews praising Apple's "multi-touch user interface," and "unrebutted testimony at trial" describing ease of use as among the reasons for the success of the iPhone. Apple Br. 64–65. However, this evidence simply shows that ease of use, in general, is important to the iPhone. It does not prove that Samsung's incorporation of the patented features influenced demand for its products. See Apple II, 695 F.3d at 1376. The district court was thus correct in concluding that Apple's evidence of ease of use, although relevant, was too general, standing alone, to establish a causal nexus.

With respect to copying, Apple cites evidence purportedly showing that "Samsung and its consultants praised Apple's patented 'pinch-to-zoom,' 'double-tap-to-zoom,' and 'bounce-back' features, and recommended that Samsung copy them in order to compete with Apple." Apple Br. 64. But as we explained in Apple I, although "evidence that Samsung's employees believed it to be important to incorporate the patented feature into Samsung's products is certainly relevant to the issue of nexus between the patent and market harm, it is not dispositive." Apple I, 678 F.3d at 1327–28. Thus, as the district court properly recognized, Apple's evidence of copying by Samsung may be relevant, but it is insufficient by itself to establish the requisite causal nexus.

The district court did err, however, in its treatment of Dr. Hauser's survey evidence. Dr. Hauser's survey purports to show that consumers would be willing to pay fairly significant price premiums for the features claimed in Apple's utility patents. In rejecting Dr. Hauser's survey evidence, the district court stated that "evidence of the price premium over the base price Samsung consumers are willing to pay for the patented features is not the same as evidence that consumers will buy a Samsung phone instead of an Apple phone because it contains the feature." Id. (emphasis added) (internal quotation marks omitted). As we have already discussed above, however, a showing of causal nexus does not require this level of proof. Rather, there may be a variety of ways to show that a feature drives demand, including with evidence that a feature significantly increases the desirability of a product incorporating that feature. Moreover, we see no reason why, as a general matter of economics, evidence that a patented feature significantly increases the price of a product cannot be used to show that the feature drives demand for the product. This is not to suggest that consumers' willingness to pay a nominal amount for an infringing feature will establish a causal nexus. For example, consumers' willingness to pay an additional $10 for an infringing cup holder in a $20,000 car does not demonstrate that the cup holder drives demand for the car. The question becomes one of degree, to be evaluated by the district court. Here, the district court never reached that inquiry because it viewed Dr. Hauser's survey evidence as irrelevant. That was an abuse of discretion.

As an alternative ground for affirmance, Samsung argues that there are other methodological flaws with Dr. Hauser's survey. However, the district court did not base its decision on any such alleged flaws, and we believe it is more appropriate for the district court to address these arguments in the first instance. For these reasons, we vacate the district court's determination that Apple failed to show a causal nexus with respect to its utility patents and remand for further proceedings.

In conclusion, we find no abuse of discretion in the district court's determination that Apple failed to demonstrate irreparable harm as a result of Samsung's infringement of its design patents. As a result, we affirm the court's denial of a permanent injunction with respect to the design patents, and we will not address those patents in our discussion of the remaining permanent injunction factors.

With respect to Apple's utility patents, however, additional analysis is required. We therefore vacate that portion of the district court's irreparable harm findings and remand for further proceedings. On remand, the court must assess whether Apple's other evidence, including its ease-of-use evidence and evidence of copying, in combination with Dr. Hauser's survey evidence, suffices to establish irreparable injury. We will now address the remaining injunction factors as they relate to Apple's utility patents.

2. Inadequacy of Legal Remedies

This factor requires a patentee to demonstrate that "remedies available at law, such as monetary damages, are inadequate to compensate" the patentee for the irreparable harm it has suffered. eBay, 547 U.S. at 391. At the district court, Apple argued that its lost downstream sales could not be calculated to a reasonable certainty, and thus money damages could not provide full compensation for the harm it suffered. The district court seemed to agree. In particular, the court found that "Apple has likely suffered, and will continue to suffer, the loss of some downstream sales," which "does provide some evidence that Apple may not be fully compensated by the [jury's] damages award." Injunction Order, 909 F.Supp.2d at 1160; see also Apple I, 678 F.3d at 1337 ("Because the loss of customers and the loss of future downstream purchases are difficult to quantify, these considerations support a finding that monetary damages would be insufficient to compensate Apple.").

Nevertheless, the court determined that this factor favored Samsung based on Apple's past licensing behavior and Samsung's undisputed ability to pay any monetary judgment. With respect to Apple's licensing history, the court noted that Apple has licensed the asserted utility patents to other manufacturers (including licensing the '381 patent to Nokia, the '915 and '163 patents to IBM, and the '381, '915, and '163 patents to HTC), suggesting that these patents are not "priceless." Injunction Order, 909 F.Supp.2d at 1160. In addition, the court noted that Apple offered to license "some of [its] patents" to Samsung, suggesting that Samsung is not "off limits" as a licensing partner. Id. (citing October 2010 Apple presentation describing licensing offer to Samsung). As a result, the court rejected Apple's argument that it would not have licensed the patents-in-suit to Samsung "for use in iPhone knockoffs." Id. The court concluded:

In sum, the difficulty in calculating the cost of lost downstream sales does suggest that money damages may not provide a full compensation for every element of Apple's loss, but Apple's licensing activity makes clear that these patents and trade dresses are not priceless, and there is no suggestion that Samsung will be unable to pay the monetary judgment against it. Accordingly, the Court finds that this factor favors Samsung.

Apple argues on appeal that the district court erred in several respects. First, Apple submits that regardless of whether its patents are "priceless" or "off limits," money damages are inadequate in this case due to the difficulty of quantifying the damages attributable to the market share and downstream sales it has lost as a result of Samsung's infringing conduct. Second, Apple asserts that the district court's analysis is contrary to eBay, where the Supreme Court rejected a rule that a patentee's willingness to license its patents could suffice by itself to demonstrate a lack of irreparable harm. Third, Apple contends that it would not have licensed the asserted patents to Samsung for use in competing products, and that the district court clearly erred in finding that Apple's past licensing practices suggested otherwise. In support of this last point, Apple identifies several factors that it believes distinguish its prior licenses from its current injunction request.

We agree with Apple that the district court erred in its analysis of this factor. As an initial matter, we note that one of the two reasons the district court found this factor to weigh in favor of Samsung was Samsung's ability to pay any monetary judgment. However, unlike an infringer's inability to pay a judgment, which may demonstrate the inadequacy of damages, see Bosch, 659 F.3d at 1155–56, a defendant's ability to pay a judgment does not defeat a claim that an award of damages would be an inadequate remedy. Rather, a defendant's ability to pay merely indicates that a court should look to other considerations to determine whether a damages award will adequately compensate the patentee for the harm caused by continuing infringement. Cf. Roper Corp. v. Litton Sys., Inc., 757 F.2d 1266, 1269 n. 2 (Fed.Cir.1985) (rejecting the view that an alleged infringer's "ability to compensate" ends the court's inquiry).

We therefore turn to the district court's other reason for finding that this factor weighed in favor of Samsung—Apple's past licensing behavior. We have previously explained that:

While the fact that a patentee has previously chosen to license the patent may indicate that a reasonable royalty does compensate for an infringement, that is but one factor for the district court to consider. The fact of the grant of previous licenses, the identity of the past licensees, the experience in the market since the licenses were granted, and the identity of the new infringer all may affect the district court's discretionary decision concerning whether a reasonable royalty from an infringer constitutes damages adequate to compensate for the infringement.

Acumed, 551 F.3d at 1328. Consistent with Acumed, we find no error in the district court's decision to consider evidence of Apple's past licensing behavior. However, the court erred by ending its analysis upon concluding that the asserted patents are not "priceless" and that Samsung is not "off limits" as a licensing partner. While perhaps relevant, these findings, by themselves, do not fully answer the question at hand—i.e., whether monetary damages will adequately compensate Apple for Samsung's infringement of the particular patents at issue in this lawsuit. Rather, they merely show that Apple is willing to license the asserted utility patents in some circumstances, and that Apple is willing to license some patents to Samsung.

The district court's exclusive focus on whether Apple's patents are "priceless" and whether Samsung is "off limits" led it to disregard Apple's evidence that Samsung's use of these patents is different. Apple points to numerous factors that the district court failed to consider in determining the relevance of Apple's past licensing behavior. For example, Apple notes that IBM is not a competitor in the smartphone market, and that the license was entered into five years before Apple launched the iPhone. Apple further notes that it entered into the HTC and Nokia agreements to settle pending litigation. In addition, the Nokia agreement was a "provisional license" for a limited "standstill" period, J.A. 4076 ¶ 6, and the HTC agreement excluded HTC products that were "clones" of Apple's products, J.A. 4792 ¶ 5.1, 4811. Moreover, although the evidence shows that Apple offered Samsung a license to some of its patents, Apple is adamant that it never offered to license the asserted patents to Samsung, its primary competitor.[7] We agree with Apple that these factors are relevant to whether monetary damages will adequately compensate Apple for Samsung's infringement of the asserted patents, and the district court erred by failing to consider them. Indeed, the district court's focus on Apple's past licensing practices, without exploring any relevant differences from the current situation, hints at a categorical rule that Apple's willingness to license its patents precludes the issuance of an injunction. "To the extent that the District Court adopted such a categorical rule, its analysis cannot be squared with the principles of equity adopted by Congress." eBay, 547 U.S. at 393; see also Acumed, 551 F.3d at 1328 ("A plaintiff's past willingness to license its patent is not sufficient per se to establish lack of irreparable harm if a new infringer were licensed.").

In sum, the district court abused its discretion by failing to properly analyze whether damages would adequately compensate Apple for Samsung's infringement of these patents. Accordingly, we vacate the district court's finding with respect to this factor and remand for further consideration. Of course, if, on remand, Apple cannot demonstrate that demand for Samsung's products is driven by the infringing features, then Apple's reliance on lost market share and downstream sales to demonstrate the inadequacy of damages will be substantially undermined.

3. Balance of Hardships

The balance of hardships factor "assesses the relative effect of granting or denying an injunction on the parties." i4i Ltd. P'ship v. Microsoft Corp., 598 F.3d 831, 862 (Fed.Cir.2010). The district court found that neither party would be particularly harmed by either outcome and that this factor was therefore neutral. With respect to Apple, the court noted that "Apple's only argument" on this issue was that "Samsung's conduct was willful," which the court rejected as an appropriate rationale because "[a]n injunction may not be used as a punishment." Injunction Order, 909 F.Supp.2d at 1161. As for Samsung, the district court noted Samsung's representation that it had already stopped selling twenty-three of the twenty-six infringing products and had begun to implement design-arounds for the remaining three products. The court concluded that "[h]aving made this argument in the hopes of establishing that Apple cannot be harmed, Samsung cannot now turn around and claim that Samsung will be burdened by an injunction that prevents sale of these same products." Id. The court also rejected Samsung's argument that an injunction would disrupt its relationships with carriers and customers, noting that "Samsung has not explained how an injunction would cause the asserted disruptions" and that "[h]arm to consumers is more appropriately considered under the fourth factor." Id.

On appeal, each party argues that this factor weighs in its favor. Apple argues that Samsung would not be harmed by an injunction if, as Samsung claims, it has designed around Apple's patents, but that, absent an injunction,

Apple would be harmed by the risk of Samsung's continued infringement. According to Apple, "an injunction is essential to providing Apple the swift relief needed to combat any future infringement by Samsung through products not more than colorably different from those already found to infringe." Apple Br. 42. Samsung responds that Apple would not benefit from an injunction because Samsung is no longer selling the accused products, but that "Samsung and others would be harmed" by an injunction because it would "create fear, doubt and uncertainty in the market as to what other products Apple might later claim are covered by its sweeping injunction." Samsung Br. 45.

In essence, each party asks us to reweigh the various factors that go into the balance of hardships. However, we discern no clear error of judgment or error of law in the district court's analysis. Therefore, we conclude that the district court did not abuse its discretion in determining that this factor was neutral.

4. Public Interest

This factor requires a plaintiff to demonstrate that "the public interest would not be disserved by a permanent injunction." eBay, 547 U.S. at 391. In analyzing this factor, the district court agreed with Apple that "the public interest does favor the enforcement of patent rights to promote the 'encouragement of investment-based risk.' "Injunction Order, 909 F.Supp.2d at 1162 (quoting Sanofi–Synthelabo, 470 F.3d at 1383). The court also rejected Samsung's argument that an injunction would be disruptive to suppliers, retailers, carriers, and customers because Samsung claimed to have stopped manufacturing or selling any infringing phones. In addition, the court rejected Samsung's argument that an injunction would cause great harm to the public, concluding that "[c]onsumers will have substantial choice of products, even if an injunction were to issue." Id. On the other hand, the court found that an injunction was less likely to be in the public interest because "the injunction Apple has sought is extremely broad, and would prevent the sale of 26 specific products, as well as other potential future products incorporating the protected features." Id. In addition, the court found that "[t]he public interest does not support removing phones from the market when the infringing components constitute such limited parts of complex, multi-featured products." Id. at 1163. Ultimately, the court concluded that this factor weighed in favor of Samsung because "while the public interest does favor the protection of patent rights, it would not be in the public interest to deprive consumers of phones that infringe limited non-core features, or to risk disruption to consumers without clear legal authority." Id.

Apple argues on appeal that an injunction would promote the public interest in patent enforcement against a direct competitor. However, the public's interest in enforcing patent rights must also be weighed with other aspects of the public interest. See ActiveVideo, 694 F.3d at 1341 ("Although enforcing the right to exclude serves the public interest, the public interest factor requires consideration of other aspects of the public interest."). Here, the district court properly recognized the public's interest in enforcing patent rights but determined that it was outweighed by other considerations.

Apple criticizes the district court for relying on the breadth of its requested injunction as a reason to deny injunctive relief. Apple argues that—consistent with this court's injunction precedent—it properly requested an injunction limited to the infringing products and products not more than colorably different. See Int'l Rectifier Corp. v. IXYS Corp., 383 F.3d 1312, 1317 (Fed. Cir.2004) (endorsing an injunction against "infringement of the patent by the devices adjudged to infringe and infringement by devices no more than colorably different therefrom"). According to Apple, it was improper for the district court to focus on the number of products that would be affected by an injunction. See Apple Br. 45 ("Samsung cannot avoid an injunction simply because its infringement involved many products."). If this is what the court meant when it found Apple's requested injunction contrary to the public's interest in the enforcement of patent rights, we would agree with Apple that the trial court's analysis was flawed.

We have a different take on the district court's discussion of the breadth of the requested injunction, however. We believe the district court's overarching concern was not that a large number of products would be enjoined, but rather that entire products would be enjoined based on "limited non-core features." Injunction Order, 909 F.Supp.2d at 1163. This is reflected in, for example, the district court's explanation that "[t]hough the phones do contain infringing features, they contain a far greater number of non-infringing features to which consumers would no longer have access if this Court were to issue an injunction." Id. We see no problem with the district court's decision, in determining whether an injunction would disserve the public interest, to consider the scope of Apple's requested injunction relative to the scope of the patented features and the prospect that an injunction would have the effect of depriving the public of access to a large number of non-infringing features. See eBay, 547 U.S. at 396–97 (Kennedy, J., concurring) ("When the patented invention is but a small component of the product the companies seek to produce and the threat of an injunction is employed simply for undue leverage in negotiations, an injunction may not serve the public interest."). Accordingly, Apple has failed to show that the district court abused its discretion in concluding that the public interest weighs against the grant of an injunction.[8]

* * *

In conclusion, we find that the district court abused its discretion in analyzing Apple's evidence of irreparable harm and the inadequacy of legal remedies. We therefore remand the case to the district court to reconsider, consistent with this opinion, Apple's request for a permanent injunction against Samsung's infringement of its three utility patents.

B. Apple's Request to Enjoin Samsung's Trade Dress Dilution

Finally, we address Apple's request for an injunction against Samsung's dilution of Apple's iPhone trade dress. The Federal Trademark Dilution Act ("FTDA") provides:

Subject to the principles of equity, the owner of a famous mark that is distinctive, inherently or through acquired distinctiveness, shall be entitled to an injunction against another person who, at any time after the owner's mark has become famous, commences use of a mark or trade name in commerce that is likely to cause dilution by blurring or dilution by tarnishment of the famous mark, regardless of the presence or absence of actual or likely confusion, of competition, or of actual economic injury.

15 U.S.C. § 1125(c)(1). According to Ninth Circuit precedent:

[I]njunctive relief is available under the Federal Trademark Dilution Act if a plaintiff can establish that (1) its mark is famous; (2) the defendant is making commercial use of the mark in commerce; (3) the defendant's use began after the plaintiff's mark became famous; and (4) the defendant's use presents a likelihood of dilution of the distinctive value of the mark.

Perfumebay.com Inc. v. eBay Inc., 506 F.3d 1165, 1180 (9th Cir.2007) (internal quotation marks omitted).

As mentioned before, the jury found that six Samsung smartphones diluted Apple's trade dress. Based on this finding, the district court concluded that Apple had established the necessary irreparable harm for an injunction under the FTDA.[9] Nevertheless, the court denied Apple's request for an injunction because Samsung represented—and Apple did not dispute—that none of the products found to dilute Apple's trade dress were "still on the market in any form." Injunction Order, 909 F.Supp.2d at 1158. The court noted the absence of any Ninth Circuit cases discussing the propriety of an injunction under the FTDA where there is no allegation of continuing dilution. The court further noted that the Ninth Circuit's FTDA injunction test seems to focus on ongoing diluting behavior because it requires that the defendant "is making commercial use" of a mark. The district court concluded that under the circumstances, there was no need to issue an injunction. See id. at 1159 ("Here, there is no ongoing diluting behavior to enjoin, and Apple cannot credibly claim to suffer any significant hardship in the absence of a trade dress injunction."); see also id. at 1163 ("Regarding trade dress dilution, the case for an injunction is especially weak, because there are no diluting products still available, even without an injunction.").

On appeal, Apple argues that the district court erroneously viewed ongoing diluting behavior as a prerequisite for obtaining injunctive relief under the FTDA. Apple notes the "settled" principle that "an action for an injunction does not become moot merely because the conduct complained of has terminated, if there is a possibility of recurrence, since otherwise the defendants would be free to return to [their] old ways." Allee v. Medrano, 416 U.S. 802, 810–11 (1974) (internal quotation marks omitted). Apple also points out that at least two district courts have issued injunctions despite the defendant's voluntary cessation of diluting conduct. See Gucci Am., Inc. v. Guess?, Inc., 868 F.Supp.2d 207, 223–24 (S.D.N.Y.2012); OBH, Inc. v. Spotlight Magazine, Inc., 86 F.Supp.2d 176, 178 (W.D.N.Y.2000).

Ninth Circuit precedent indicates that ongoing diluting behavior is not necessary to obtain an injunction under the FTDA. See Polo Fashions, Inc. v. Dick Bruhn, Inc., 793 F.2d 1132 (9th Cir.1986) (recognizing that there is no requirement to prove ongoing trademark infringement to obtain an injunction). To the extent that the district court interpreted Ninth Circuit precedent differently, that interpretation was mistaken; the cessation of diluting activity does not bar entry of an injunction in all cases. However, it does not follow that a court commits legal error if, in conducting an injunction analysis, it considers a defendant's voluntary cessation of diluting behavior as a reason to deny injunctive relief. Indeed, Ninth Circuit precedent indicates the opposite. For example, in Volkswagenwerk Aktiengesellschaft v. Church, 411 F.2d 350 (9th Cir.1969), the Ninth Circuit affirmed a district court's denial of an injunction against trademark infringement because there was "little or no evidence in the record casting doubt on [the defendant's] good faith abandonment of this infringement, or indicating that it will be resumed." Id. at 352. Polo Fashions is not to the contrary. In that case, the Ninth Circuit reversed a district court's "refus[al] to grant an injunction because the plaintiffs had not introduced any specific evidence to demonstrate that the defendants would infringe in the future." Polo Fashions, 793 F.2d at 1135 (emphasis added). The problem in Polo Fashions was that the district court placed the burden on the wrong party—requiring the plaintiff to show that the defendants would likely infringe the plaintiff's trademark again, instead of requiring the defendants to show that they would not infringe. Even in that case, the Ninth Circuit recognized that a plaintiff might properly be denied injunctive relief based on a defendant's voluntary cessation of trademark infringement if "'the reform of the defendant [is] irrefutably demonstrated and total.'" Id. at 1135 (quoting 2 J. Thomas McCarthy, McCarthy on Trademarks and Unfair Competition § 30:6, at 471 (2d ed.1984)).

Here, the undisputed evidence shows that Samsung has stopped selling the products found to dilute Apple's trade dress, and there is no evidence suggesting that Samsung will resume selling them. Under these circumstances, we cannot say that the district court abused its discretion in denying Apple's request for an injunction. Therefore, we affirm the district court's denial of an injunction against Samsung's trade dress dilution.[10]

Conclusion

For the foregoing reasons, we affirm the district court's denial of Apple's request for a permanent injunction with respect to its design patents and trade dress. However, we vacate the district court's denial of Apple's request for a permanent injunction with respect to its utility patents and remand for further proceedings.

AFFIRMED IN PART, VACATED IN PART, AND REMANDED

Costs

Each party shall bear its own costs.

FOOTNOTES

1. The twenty-six products found to infringe Apple's patents are Samsung's Captivate, Continuum, Droid Charge, Epic 4G, Exhibit 4G, Fascinate, Galaxy Ace, Galaxy Prevail, Galaxy S, Galaxy S 4G, Galaxy S II (AT & T), Galaxy S II (i9000), Galaxy Tab, Galaxy Tab 10.1 (Wi-fi), Gem, Indulge, Infuse, Mesmerize, Nexus S 4G, Replenish, Vibrant, Galaxy S II (T–Mobile), Transform, Galaxy S Showcase, Galaxy S II (Epic 4G Touch), and Galaxy S II (Skyrocket).

2. The six products found to dilute Apple's trade dress are Samsung's Galaxy S 4G, Galaxy S Showcase, Fascinate, Mesmerize, Vibrant, and Galaxy S (i9000).

3. In addition, we recently issued an opinion in another appeal in this case regarding requests by Apple and Samsung to seal certain confidential information. See Apple Inc. v. Samsung Elecs. Co., 727 F.3d 1214 (Fed.Cir.2013).

4. Some of Apple's arguments against the causal nexus requirement are really criticisms of how the district court applied the requirement in this case. We address the court's fact-specific application of the causal nexus requirement later in our opinion.

5. Apple also cites Edwards Lifesciences AG v. CoreValve, Inc., 699 F.3d 1305 (Fed.Cir.2012), for the proposition that "[a]bsent adverse equitable considerations, the winner of a judgment of validity and infringement may normally expect to regain the exclusivity that was lost with the infringement." Id. at 1314. While Apple seeks to rely on this statement to suggest that there is a presumption in favor of injunctions, that is not what the Edwards court said, and it is not the law. The Edwards court expressly noted that the right of an injunction as a remedy to "regain exclusivity" is subject to "equitable considerations." And we have recognized that, in eBay, the Supreme Court "jettisoned the presumption[of irreparable harm" and "abolishe[d] our general rule that an injunction normally will issue when a patent is found to have been valid and infringed." Bosch, 659 F.3d at 1149.

6. In the previous section, we concluded that the district court arguably articulated two erroneous legal principles—i.e., that a patented

feature must be the sole driver of demand to establish a causal nexus between Samsung's infringement and Apple's harm, and that irreparable harm must always be analyzed on a patent-by-patent basis. Nevertheless, having reviewed the district court's discussion of irreparable harm and the evidence cited by Apple, we are satisfied that these erroneous principles did not affect the court's analysis with respect to Apple's design patents. Therefore, we can affirm the district court's conclusion on irreparable harm with respect to the design patents, notwithstanding the errors identified above.

7. The parties dispute the scope of Apple's October 2010 licensing offer to Samsung. Samsung claims that Apple's offer included the asserted patents and trade dress. Apple strenuously objects to this assertion, citing the testimony of its director of patents and licensing, who testified that Apple was "very clear" that any license would not include "Apple's user experience patents," which include the patents-in-suit. J.A. 22013–22014 (2013:9–2104:6). We cannot tell if the district court reached a conclusion on this issue. Instead, it merely noted that Apple offered Samsung a license to "some of [its] patents." Injunction Order, 909 F.Supp.2d at 1160. The answer may be quite relevant to the injunction analysis. See ActiveVideo Networks, Inc. v. Verizon Commc'ns, Inc., 694 F.3d 1312, 1339–40 (Fed.Cir.2012) (finding clear error in the district court's determination that money damages would not provide adequate compensation based in part on the patentee's attempts to license the asserted patents to the defendant). Thus, before relying on Apple's licensing offer as evidence of the adequacy of damages, the court should have resolved whether Apple's offer included the asserted patents and trade dress.

8. If, on remand, the district court modifies its conclusion with regard to irreparable harm, it can determine whether such modification requires any reevaluation of the public interest factor.

9. The district court interpreted the FTDA as permitting injunctive relief without any additional showing of irreparable harm beyond the harm of dilution itself. This interpretation was premised on the language in § 1125(c)(1) authorizing injunctions "regardless of the presence or absence of actual or likely confusion, of competition, or of actual economic injury." On appeal, Samsung challenges the district court's interpretation of the statute, arguing that the principles of equity require a showing of irreparable harm beyond the harm of dilution. Because we affirm the district court's denial of injunctive relief on other grounds, we need not reach this issue.

10. Apple also challenges the district court's finding that "there is some evidence that Apple has not always insisted on the exclusive use of its trade dress." Injunction Order, 909 F.Supp.2d at 1160. The court based this finding on testimony from Apple's director of patents and

licensing, Boris Teksler, who identified Apple's trade dress as part of Apple's "unique user experience IP." Id. (citing J.A. 21956 (1956:9–12)). But as Apple correctly notes, the portions of Mr. Teksler's testimony cited by the district court indicate only that Apple has licensed some of the patents included in Apple's "unique user experience IP." See J.A. 21957 (1957:3–5) ("Q. Has Apple ever licensed any of the patents within this category? A. Certainly over time we have "(emphasis added)). The cited testimony says nothing about licensing trade dress. Nevertheless, we believe it is clear from the district court's opinion that the decision to deny injunctive relief was based on Samsung's cessation of its diluting conduct. See Injunction Order, 909 F.Supp.2d at 1159, 1163. Thus, we conclude that any erroneous findings with respect to whether Apple has licensed its trade dress did not materially affect the court's decision.

PROST, Circuit Judge.

15.8 Ten Commandments of Imitation

1. Never reinvent the wheel.
2. Put buzz into your imitation.
3. Be open about legally copying competitors.
4. Expand your gene pool for ideas.
5. Be aware of your environment lens.
6. Avoid oversimplifications.
7. Remember timing is not everything.
8. Build more value into your imitations.
9. Be both offensive and defensive.
10. Get started immediately, if not sooner.

Notes

1. Ekekwe, N. (2012). When you cannot innovate copy. *Harvard Business Review*, May 24.https://hbr.org/2012/05/when-you-cant-innovate-copy.
2. Rocket Internet. https://en.wikipedia.org/wiki/Rocket_Internet.
3. Diallo, A. (2015). How 'venture builders' are changing the startup model. https://venturebeat.com/2015/01/18/how-venture-builders-are-changing-the-startup-model/.

4. Scott, M. (2014). Copycat business model generates genuine global success for start-up incubator. *New York Times*, February 27. https://www.nytimes.com/2014/02/28/technology/copycat-business-model-generates-genuine-global-success-for-start-up-incubator.html?_r=0.

5. Rocket Internet Annual Report (2016). https://www.rocket-internet.com/sites/default/files/investors/Rocket%20Internet_Annual%20Report%202016_English.pdf.

6. Connolly, J. Great artists steal!http://www.creativethinkinghub.com/creative-thinking-and-stealing-like-an-artist/.

7. Devaney, T. and Stein, T. (2012). Don't innovate, imitate.http://readwrite.com/2012/08/14/dont-innovate-imitate/.

8. Shenkar, O. (2010). *Copycats: How Smart Companies Use Imitation to Gain a Strategic Edge*. Cambridge, MA: Harvard Business Review Press. http://www.bizbriefings.com/Samples/IntlAchieve%20---%20Copycats.PDF.

9. Smartphone. https://en.wikipedia.org/wiki/Smartphone.

10. The impact of the acquisition and use of patents on the smartphone industry. (2012). WIPO. http://www.wipo.int/export/sites/www/ip-competition/en/studies/clip_study.pdf.

11. Carrier, M. A. (2012). A roadmap to the smartphone patent wars and FRAND licensing. *CPI Antitrust Chronicle*, April 2012. http:papers.ssrn.com/sol3/papers.cfm?abstract_id=2050743.

12. Bui, J. H. Apple vs. Samsung: Smartphone patent war, practical implications and repercussions of Samsung verdict within the smartphone industry. http://www.buigarcia.com/docs/Apple%20v%20Samsung.pdf.

13. *Steve Jobs* is the authorized biography of Steve Jobs, written by Walter Isaacson. The book was released on October 24, 2011, by Simon & Schuster in the United States.

14. http://scholar.google.com/scholar_case?case=12312555522065197626.

15. *Apple Inc. v. Samsung Electronics Co. Ltd LLC*, [2013] 2013–1129 (United States Court of Appeals, Federal Circuit.). Available from https://caselaw.findlaw.com/us-federal-circuit/1649900.html.

16

Corporate Governance Guidelines

16.1 Introduction

According to Investopedia,[1] corporate governance is the system of rules, practices, and processes by which a company is directed and controlled. Corporate governance essentially involves balancing the interests of a company's many stakeholders, such as shareholders, management, customers, suppliers, financiers, government, and the community. Since corporate governance also provides the framework for attaining a company's objectives, it encompasses practically every sphere of management, from action plans and internal controls to performance measurement and corporate disclosure. In short, corporate governance is the system by which companies are directed and controlled.

Good corporate governance consists of [2]

- Contracts between the Board of Directors and all stakeholders for the distribution of authority, responsibility, and rewards
- Procedures for handling conflicting interests between management and stakeholders
- Procedures for supervision, management, and control of information to serve as a system for proper checks and balances

Good corporate governance is not an end in itself. It is a means to create market confidence and business integrity, which in turn is essential for companies that need access to equity capital for long-term investment. Access to equity capital is particularly important for future-oriented entrepreneurial high-growth companies and to balance any increase in leveraging.

16.2 Principles of Corporate Governance

Rights of shareholders: The corporate governance framework should protect shareholders and facilitate their rights in the company. Companies should generate investment returns for the risk capital put up by the shareholders.

Equitable treatment of shareholders: All shareholders should be treated equitably (fairly), including those who constitute a minority and individual shareholders. Shareholders should have redress when their rights are contravened or when an individual shareholder or group of shareholders is dominated by the majority.

Stakeholders: The corporate governance framework should recognize the legal rights of stakeholders and facilitate cooperation with them in order to create wealth, employment, and sustainable enterprises.

Disclosure and transparency: Companies should make relevant, timely disclosures on matters affecting financial performance, management, and ownership of the business.

Board of directors: The Board of Directors should set the direction of the company and monitor management in order that the company will achieve its objectives. The corporate governance framework should underpin the board's accountability to the company and its members.

16.2.1 Agency Problem

The agency problem is a conflict of interest inherent in any relationship where one party is expected to act in another's best interests. In the corporate world, the agency problem usually refers to a conflict of interest between a company's management and the company's stockholders. The manager, acting as the agent for the shareholders, or principals, is supposed to make decisions that will maximize shareholder wealth even though it is in the manager's best interest to maximize his own wealth.[3]

Most of the attention given to corporate governance is directed toward public companies whose securities are traded in capital markets. The reason for this is that such organizations have hundreds or even thousands of shareholders whose wealth and income can be enhanced or compromised by the decisions of senior management. This is often referred to as the "agency problem."

Potential and existing shareholders make investment decisions based on information that is historical and subjective, usually with little knowledge of the direction that the company will take in the future. They therefore place trust in those who make decisions to achieve the right balance between return and risk, to put appropriate systems of control in place, to provide timely and accurate information, to manage risk wisely, and to act ethically at all times.

The agency problem becomes most evident when companies fail. In order to make profits, it is necessary to take risks, and sometimes risks that are taken with the best intentions—and are supported by the most robust business plans—result in loss or even the bankruptcy of the company. Sometimes corporate failure is brought about by inappropriate behaviors of directors and other senior managers.

16.3 Board of Directors

Effective corporate governance requires a clear understanding of the respective roles of the board, management, and shareholders; their relationships with each other; and their relationships with other corporate stakeholders.

The *Board of Directors* has the vital role of overseeing the company's management and business strategies to achieve long-term value creation. Selecting a well-qualified chief executive officer (CEO) to lead the company, monitoring and evaluating the CEO's performance, and overseeing the CEO succession planning process are some of the most important functions of the board.

The board delegates to the CEO—and through the CEO to other senior management—the authority and responsibility for operating the company's business.[4]

Effective directors are diligent monitors, but not managers, of business operations. They exercise vigorous and diligent oversight of a company's affairs, including key areas such as strategy and risk, but they do not manage—or micromanage—the company's business by performing or duplicating the tasks of the CEO and senior management team. The distinction between oversight and management is not always precise, and some situations (such as a crisis) may require greater board involvement in operational matters. In addition, in some areas (such as the relationship with the outside auditor and executive compensation) the board has a direct role instead of an oversight role.

The Board of Directors is the primary direct stakeholder influencing corporate governance. Directors are elected by shareholders or appointed by other board members, and they represent shareholders of the company. The board is tasked with making important decisions, such as corporate officer appointments, executive compensation, and dividend policy. In some instances, board obligations stretch beyond financial optimization, when shareholder resolutions call for certain social or environmental concerns to be prioritized.[5]

The role of the Board of Directors can thus be summarized as

- Defining the primary purpose of the company
- Defining the values by which the company will perform its daily duties
- Identifying the stakeholders relevant to the company
- Developing a successful strategy combining the above factors
- Ensuring implementation of the strategy
- Ensuring maximal wealth formation for shareholders

Lastly, the board's oversight function encompasses a number of responsibilities, as illustrated in Figure 16.1.

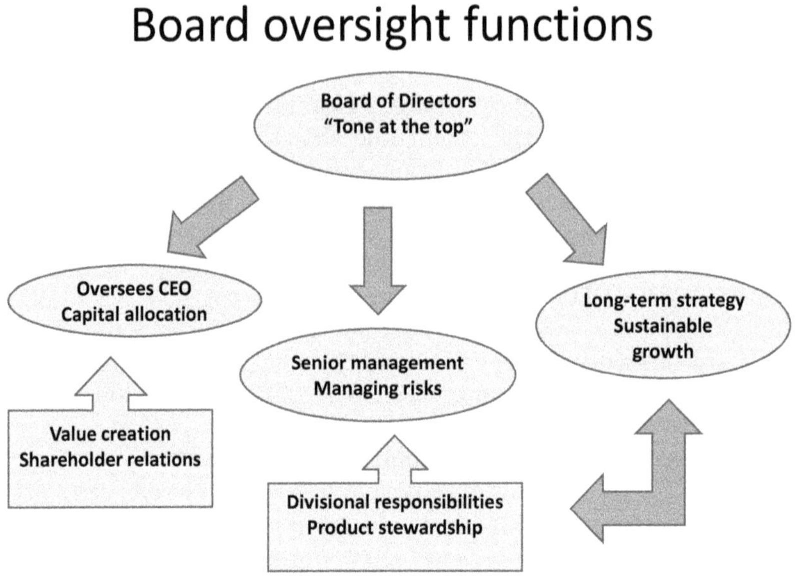

Board oversight functions

FIGURE 16.1
The Board of Directors.

Selecting the CEO. The board selects and oversees the performance of the company's CEO and oversees the CEO succession planning process.

Setting the "tone at the top." The board should set a tone at the top that demonstrates the company's commitment to integrity and legal compliance. This tone lays the groundwork for a corporate culture that is communicated to personnel at all levels of the organization.

Approving corporate strategy and monitoring the implementation of strategic plans. The board should have meaningful input into the company's long-term strategy from development through execution, should approve the company's strategic plans, and should regularly evaluate implementation of the plans that are designed to create long-term value. The board should understand the risks inherent in the company's strategic plans and how those risks are being managed.

Setting the company's risk tolerance, reviewing and understanding the major risks, and overseeing the risk management processes. The board oversees the process for identifying and managing the significant risks facing the company. The board and senior management should agree on the company's risk appetite, and the board should be comfortable that the strategic plans are consistent with it. The board should establish a structure for overseeing risk, delegating responsibility to committees, and overseeing the designation of senior management responsible for risk management.

Focusing on the integrity and clarity of the company's financial reporting and other disclosures about corporate performance. The board should be satisfied that the company's financial statements accurately present its financial condition and results of operations, that other disclosures about the company's performance convey meaningful information about past results as well as future plans, and that the company's internal controls and procedures have been designed to detect and deter fraudulent activity.

Allocating capital. The board should have meaningful input and decision-making authority over the company's capital allocation process and strategy to find the right balance between short-term and long-term economic returns for its shareholders.

Reviewing, understanding, and overseeing annual operating plans and budgets. The board oversees the annual operating plans and reviews annual budgets presented by management. The board monitors implementation of the annual plans and assesses whether they are responsive to changing conditions.

Reviewing the company's plans for business resiliency. As part of its risk oversight function, the board periodically reviews management's plans to address business resiliency, including such items as business continuity, physical security, cybersecurity, and crisis management.

Nominating directors and committee members, and overseeing effective corporate governance. The board, under the leadership of its nominating or corporate governance committee, nominates directors and committee members and oversees the structure, composition (including independence and diversity), succession planning, practices, and evaluation of the board and its committees.

Overseeing the compliance program. The board, under the leadership of appropriate committees, oversees the company's compliance program and remains informed about any significant compliance issues that may arise.

16.3.1 Inside and Independent Members

Boards are often composed of inside and independent members. Insiders are major shareholders, founders, and executives. Independent directors do not share the ties of the insiders, but they are chosen because of their experience in managing or directing other large companies. Independent members are often considered helpful for governance, because they dilute the concentration of power and help align shareholder interest with those of the insiders.

The Board of Directors is made up of executive directors and nonexecutive directors.

Executive directors are full-time employees of the company and therefore have two relationships and sets of duties. They work for the company in a senior capacity, usually concerned with policy matters or functional business areas of major strategic importance. Large companies tend to have executive directors responsible for finance, manufacturing, marketing, regulatory, and so on.

Executive directors are usually recruited by the Board of Directors. They are the highest earners in the company, with remuneration packages made up partly of basic pay and fringe benefits and partly of performance-related pay. Most large companies now engage their executive directors under fixed-term contracts, often rolling over every 24 months.

The CEO and the chief financial officer are nearly always executive directors.

Nonexecutive directors (NEDs) are not employees of the company and are not involved in its day-to-day running. They usually have full-time jobs elsewhere, or may sometimes be prominent individuals from public life. The NEDs usually receive a fixed stipend for their services and are engaged under a service contract (engagement contract, similar to that used to hire an independent consultant).

NEDs should provide a balancing influence and help to minimize conflicts of interest. Their role may be summarized as

- Contributing to the strategic plan
- Scrutinizing the performance of the executive directors
- Providing an external perspective on risk management
- Dealing with personnel issues, such as the future board composition, and resolution of conflicts

The majority of NEDs should be independent. Factors to be considered in assessing their independence include their business, financial, and other commitments; other shareholdings and directorships; and involvement in businesses connected to the company. However, holding shares in the company does not necessarily compromise independence.

NEDs should have high ethical standards and act with integrity and probity. They should support the executive team and monitor its conduct, demonstrating a willingness to listen, question, debate, and challenge management whenever necessary.

16.4 Key Corporate Actors

The *chair of the board* (COB) is the most powerful member on the Board of Directors, who provides leadership to the firm's officers and executives. The COB ensures that the firm's duties to shareholders are being fulfilled by acting as a link between the board and upper management.[6]

The chair of the company is the leader of the Board of Directors. It is the chair's responsibility to ensure that the board operates efficiently and effectively, getting the best out of all of its members. The chair should, for example, promote regular attendance and full involvement in discussions. The chair decides the scope or agenda of each meeting and is responsible for time management of board meetings, ensuring that all matters are discussed fully, but without spending limitless time on individual agenda items as described by *Robert's Rules of Order*. In most companies the chairman is a NED.

The COB supports and sustains the directions of the organization and provides governance leadership and strategic fundraising support. Specific responsibilities of leadership, governance, and oversight typically include

- Being a trusted advisor to the CEO as he or she develops and implements the organization's strategic plan
- Developing and managing relationships and communicating with funders, partners, and other stakeholders
- As a board member, approving the annual budget, audit reports, and material business decisions; being informed of, and meeting all, legal and fiduciary responsibilities
- Reviewing outcomes and metrics created by evaluating their impact, and regularly measuring the board's performance and effectiveness in using those metrics
- Coordinating an annual performance evaluation of the CEO
- Assisting the CEO and nominating committee in recruiting board members
- Periodically consulting with board members on their roles and helping them assess their performance
- Planning, presiding over, and facilitating board and committee meetings; partnering with the CEO to ensure that board resolutions are carried out
- Acting as an ambassador for the organization
- Ensuring that the commitment to a diverse board and staff reflects the communities served

Fundraising (If Applicable)

- In collaboration with the CEO, generating substantial annual revenue and fostering the overall financial health
- Ensuring that 100% of board members make an annual contribution that is commensurate with their capacity
- Identifying, qualifying, cultivating, soliciting, and stewarding major individual donor, corporate, and/or foundation gifts

The *CEO* is the leader of the executive team and is responsible for the day-to-day management of the organization. As such, this individual is nearly always an executive director. As well as attending board meetings as a director, the CEO will usually chair the management committee or executive committee. While most companies have monthly board meetings, it is common for management or executive committee meetings to be held weekly.

The *secretary* is the chief administrative officer of the company. The secretary provides the agenda and supporting papers for board meetings, and often for executive committee meetings also. He or she takes minutes of meetings and provides advice on procedural matters, such as terms of reference. The secretary usually has responsibilities for liaison with shareholders and the government registration body. As such, the notice of general meetings will be signed by the secretary on behalf of the Board of Directors. The secretary may be a member of the Board of Directors, though some smaller companies use this position as a means of involving a high-potential individual at the board level prior to being appointed as a director.

The *management team*, led by the CEO, is responsible for setting, managing, and executing the strategies of the company, including but not limited to running the operations of the company under the oversight of the board and keeping the board informed of the status of the company's operations.

Management's responsibilities include strategic planning, risk management, and financial reporting. An effective management team runs the company with a focus on executing the company's strategy over a meaningful time horizon while avoiding any undue emphasis on short-term metrics, which is the purview of middle management.

16.4.1 Segregation of Responsibilities

According to Sarbanes–Oxley, it is advisable that the CEO should not hold the position of chairman, as the activities of each role are quite distinct from one another.

The secretary should also not be the chairman of the company. As the secretary has a key role in liaising with the government registration body, having the same person occupying both roles could compromise the flow of information between this body and the Board of Directors.

16.5 An Effective Governance Team

The Sarbanes–Oxley Act of 2002 is generally considered the first major corporate governance legislative measure in the United States. Also known as the Public Company Accounting Reform and Investor Protection Act and the Corporate and Auditing Accountability and Responsibility Act (in the

Senate and House of Representatives, respectively), the legislation is also known informally as Sarbanes–Oxley, Sarbox, or SOX. The act is named after its proponents: Senator Paul Sarbanes and Representative Michael G. Oxley.

16.5.1 Standing Committees

The term *standing committee* refers to any committee that is a permanent feature within the management structure of an organization. In the context of corporate governance, it refers to committees made up of members of the board with specified sets of duties. The three committees most often chosen by public companies are the audit committee, the compensation committee, and the nomination committee.

16.5.2 Audit Committee

This committee should be made up of independent NEDs, with at least one individual having expertise in financial management. It is responsible for

- Oversight of internal controls; approval of financial statements and other significant documents prior to agreement by the full board
- Liaison with external auditors
- High-level compliance matters
- Reporting to the shareholders

Sometimes the committee may carry out investigations and deal with matters reported by whistle-blowers.

A summary of audit committee responsibilities is shown in Figure 16.2.

16.5.3 Compensation Committee

This committee decides on the compensation of executive directors and sometimes other senior executives. It is responsible for formulating a written remuneration policy that should have the aim of attracting and retaining appropriate talent, and for deciding the forms that remuneration should take. This committee should also be made up entirely of independent NEDs, consistent with the principle that executives should not be in a position to decide their own remuneration.

It is generally recognized that executive remuneration packages should be structured in a manner that will motivate them to achieve the long-term objectives of the company. Therefore, the compensation committee has to offer a competitive basic salary and fringe benefits (these attract and retain people of the right caliber), combined with performance-related rewards such as bonuses linked to medium- and long-term targets, shares, share

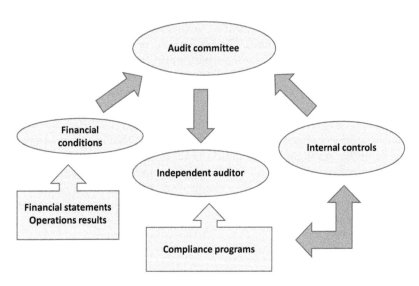

FIGURE 16.2
Audit committee and its responsibilities.

options, and eventual retirement benefits (often subject to minimum length of service requirements).

16.5.4 Nomination Committee

A nomination committee is a committee that acts under the corporate governance area of an organization. A nomination committee is focused on evaluating the Board of Directors of its respective firm and on examining the skills and characteristics that are needed in board candidates.

16.6 A Model Corporate Governance Policy (Johnson & Johnson)[7]

16.6.1 Principles of Corporate Governance

Johnson & Johnson is governed by the values set forth in Our Credo, created by General Robert Wood Johnson in 1943. These values have guided us for many years and will continue to set the tone of integrity for the entire Company. All of us at Johnson & Johnson, the employees, officers and Directors, are committed to the ethical principles embodied in Our Credo.

Our Credo values extend to our corporate governance. In fact, over sixty years ago, General Johnson recognized our responsibility to four groups of stakeholders—our customers, our employees, our communities and our shareholders. These Principles of Corporate Governance build on the foundation of Our Credo.

We believe that good corporate governance results from sound processes that ensure that our Directors are well supported by accurate and timely information, sufficient time and resources and unrestricted access to management. The business judgment of the Board must be exercised independently and in the long-term interests of our shareholders.

We also believe that ethics and integrity cannot be legislated or mandated by directive or policy. So while we adopt these Principles of Corporate Governance, we reaffirm our belief that the ethical character, integrity and values of our Directors and senior management remain the most important safeguards of corporate governance at Johnson & Johnson.

1. Duties and Responsibilities of the Company and the Board of Directors

Responsibilities of the Board. All Directors are elected annually by the shareholders as their representatives in providing oversight of the operation of the Company. The Directors select, oversee and monitor the performance of the senior management team, which is charged with the day-to-day conduct of the Company's business. The fundamental responsibility of the Directors is to exercise their business judgment on matters of critical and long-term significance to the Company in furtherance of what they reasonably believe to be in the best interest of the Company, and therefore its shareholders.

Board Meetings. Directors are expected to attend Board meetings and meetings of the Committees on which they serve, to spend the time needed and to meet as frequently as necessary to properly discharge their responsibilities. Meetings should include presentations by management and, when appropriate, outside advisors or consultants, as well as sufficient time for full and open discussion.

Written Materials. Written materials that are important to the Board's understanding of the agenda items to be discussed at a Board or Committee meeting should be distributed to the Directors sufficiently in advance of the meeting to allow the Directors the opportunity to prepare. Directors are expected to review these materials thoroughly in advance of the meeting.

Agenda for Board Meetings. The Chairman of the Board, with participation by the Lead Director, will set the agenda for Board meetings with the understanding that certain items necessary for appropriate Board oversight will be brought to the Board periodically for review, discussion and decision making. The Lead Director will review, and ultimately approve, the agenda for each Board meeting in advance of the meeting and may request changes as he or she deems appropriate in order to ensure that the interests and requirements of the independent Directors are appropriately addressed. Any Director may request that an item be included on any meeting agenda.

Executive Sessions of Independent Directors. The independent Directors will meet in regular executive sessions without any non-independent Directors or members of management present at least four times each year. The Lead Director will chair these executive sessions. In addition, the independent Directors will hold private meetings with the Chairman and Chief Executive Officer on a regular basis.

Chairman of the Board. On an annual basis, the Board will select a member of the Board to serve as Chairman of the Board of Directors to act in accordance with the By-Laws of the Company. The Chairman shall preside at all meetings of shareholders and all Board meetings. The Chairman will perform such other functions as the Board may direct.

Lead Director. On an annual basis, the independent Directors will select an independent member of the Board to serve as Lead Director. The Lead Director will chair executive sessions of the independent Directors and function as the Board may direct. The current duties and responsibilities of the Lead Director, as approved by the Board, are set forth in the attached Annex A.

Conflicts of Interest. Every employee and Director has a duty to avoid business, financial or other direct or indirect interests or relationships which conflict with the interests of the Company or which may affect his or her loyalty to the Company. Each Director must deal at arm's length with the Company and should disclose to the Chairman, a Vice Chairman or the Lead Director any conflict or any appearance of a conflict of interest. Any activity which even appears to present such a conflict must be avoided or terminated, unless after appropriate disclosure and discussion, it is determined that the activity is not harmful to the Company or otherwise improper.

Other Board Seats. A Director should engage in discussion with the Chairman prior to accepting an invitation to serve on an additional public company board. A Director who serves as a chief executive officer (or similar position) should not serve on more than two public company boards (including the Johnson & Johnson board and his or her own board). Other Directors should not serve on more than five public company boards (including the Johnson & Johnson board).

2. Director Qualifications

Independence. It is our goal that at least two-thirds of our Directors should be "independent," not only as that term may be defined legally or mandated by the New York Stock Exchange, but also without the appearance of any conflict in serving as a Director. To be considered independent under these Principles, the Board must determine that a Director does not have any direct or indirect material relationship with the Company (other than in his or her capacity as a Director). We have established guidelines to assist in determining whether a Director has a direct or indirect material relationship. These guidelines are attached to these Principles as Annex B.

General Criteria for Nomination to the Board. Attached to these Principles as Annex C are the General Criteria for Nomination to the Board which has been adopted by the Nominating & Corporate Governance Committee.

These General Criteria set the traits, abilities and experience that the Board looks for in determining candidates for election to the Board. Board appointments will be made on merit, in the context of the qualifications which the Board as a whole requires to be effective, including diversity.

Term Limits. We do not believe that our Directors should be subject to term limits. Due to the complexity of the businesses of the Company, we value the increasing insight which a Director is able to develop over a period of time. We believe that a lengthy tenure on our Board provides an increasing contribution to the Board and is therefore in the interests of our shareholders. However, renomination to the Board is based on an assessment of each Director's performance and contribution and is not automatic.

Resignation. Directors should offer their resignation in the event of any significant change in their personal circumstances, including a change in their principal job responsibilities. (Also see Annex D for the Director Resignation Policy for Incumbent Directors in Uncontested Elections.)

3. Rights of the Board of Directors

As the elected representatives of the shareholders, the Directors are entitled to certain rights that enable them to fulfill their responsibilities more effectively, including the following:

Access to Officers and Employees. Directors have full and free access to officers and employees of the Company. The Directors will use their judgment to ensure that any such contact is not disruptive to the business operations of the Company and will, to the extent not inappropriate, inform the Chief Executive Officer of any significant communication between a Director and an officer or employee of the Company.

Compensation. Non-Employee Directors should be compensated for their time dedicated to and other contributions on behalf of the Company. The Compensation & Benefits Committee will annually review and approve or suggest changes to the compensation of Directors. In fulfilling this responsibility, the members of the Compensation & Benefits Committee should take into consideration the following factors, among others: compensation should fairly pay Directors for the responsibilities and duties undertaken in serving as a director of a company of the size and complexity of the Company; compensation should align the Directors' interests with the long-term interests of shareholders; and Non-Employee Director compensation should be targeted to be consistent with the compensation philosophy applicable to senior management of the Company. Furthermore, Director's fees (which include all fees, share awards, stock options and other consideration given to Directors in their capacity as Directors) are the only compensation that members of the Audit Committee may receive from the Company. Directors who are employees of the Company should receive no additional compensation for their services as Directors.

Outside Advisors. The Board and each Committee has the authority to engage independent legal, financial or other advisors as it may deem necessary, without consulting or obtaining the approval of any officer of the Company in advance, but each Committee will notify the Chairman and the Lead Director of any such action. Management of the Company will cooperate with any such engagement and will ensure that the Company provides adequate funding.

4. Rights of the Shareholders

Our shareholders are also entitled to certain rights, many of which are mandated by the Securities and Exchange Commission, the New York Stock Exchange and Federal and state laws and regulations. In addition to those rights, we recognize the following rights of our shareholders:

Management of the Company. Management of the Company must be ethical, strive to uphold the highest standards of business practice and act in the long-term interests of the Company and its shareholders.

Annual Election of Directors. All Directors are elected annually by the shareholders. We do not have staggered terms or elect Directors for longer periods. Any vacancies on the Board may be filled or new Directors appointed by the Board between Annual Meetings of Shareholders, but any such appointment will only remain in effect until the next Annual Meeting of Shareholders, when any such appointee will be presented to the shareholders for election.

Access to the CEO at Annual Meetings. Subject to reasonable constraints of time and topics and the rules of order, shareholders are allowed to direct comments to or ask questions of the Chief Executive Officer during the Annual Meeting of Shareholders.

Communication with Directors. Shareholders, employees and others may contact any of our Directors (including our Lead Director) by writing to them c/o Johnson & Johnson, One Johnson & Johnson Plaza, Room WH 2133, New Brunswick, NJ 08933 USA. Employees, and others, who wish to contact the Board (or any member of the Audit Committee) to report any complaint or concern with respect to accounting, internal accounting controls, auditing matters or corporate governance may do so anonymously by using that address. Shareholders, employees and others may also contact any of the directors by sending an e-mail to LeadDirector@its.jnj.com. General comments to the Company (including complaints or questions about a product) should be sent to https://secure-www.jnj.com/wps/wcm/jsp/contactUs.jsp.

5. Election of Directors

The Directors are elected each year by the shareholders at the Annual Meeting of Shareholders. The Board proposes a slate of nominees to the shareholders for election to the Board. The Board also determines the number of Directors on the Board provided that there are at least 9 and not more than 18 Directors. Any vacancies on the Board may be filled or new Directors appointed by the Board between Annual Meetings of Shareholders, but any such appointment will only remain in effect until the next Annual Meeting, when any such appointee would be presented to the shareholders for election. Shareholders may propose nominees for consideration by the Nominating &

Corporate Governance Committee by submitting the names and supporting information to: Office of the Corporate Secretary, Johnson & Johnson, One Johnson & Johnson Plaza, New Brunswick, NJ 08933.

6. Board Committees

Committee Structure. It is the general policy of the Company that all major decisions be considered by the Board as a whole. As a consequence, the committee structure of the Board is limited to those committees which public companies are required to establish and those committees which focus on areas of critical importance to the Company, like science and technology, and utilize the specific talents and expertise of certain members of the Board. Currently, the Board has the following committees: Audit Committee, Compensation & Benefits Committee, Nominating & Corporate Governance Committee, Regulatory, Compliance & Government Affairs Committee, Science, Technology & Sustainability Committee and Finance Committee. The Board may, from time to time, eliminate committees or establish or maintain additional committees, as it deems necessary or appropriate.

Committee Members. The members and chairmen of these committees are appointed annually by the Board, upon recommendation of the Nominating & Corporate Governance Committee. The Audit Committee, Compensation & Benefits Committee, Nominating & Corporate Governance Committee, Regulatory, Compliance & Government Affairs Committee and Science, Technology & Sustainability Committee are comprised of independent Directors only.

Committee Meetings. The Chairman of each Committee, in consultation with the other Committee members and management, will develop the agendas for and determine the frequency and length of the Committee meetings. Each Committee will meet in executive sessions from time to time, as required or as requested by any member; provided that the Audit Committee, Compensation & Benefits Committee, Nominating & Corporate Governance Committee, Regulatory, Compliance & Government Affairs Committee and Science, Technology & Sustainability Committee will each hold at least one executive session each year without members of management present.

Committee Charters. The Audit Committee, Compensation & Benefits Committee and Nominating & Corporate Governance Committee, Regulatory, Compliance & Government Affairs Committee and Science, Technology & Sustainability Committee will each have its own charter, which will be adopted, and may be amended, by the Board.

7. Annual Performance Evaluations

The Board and each of the Audit Committee, Compensation & Benefits Committee, Nominating & Corporate Governance Committee, Regulatory, Compliance & Government Affairs Committee and Science, Technology & Sustainability Committee will conduct an annual self-evaluation. These self-evaluations are intended to facilitate an examination and discussion by the entire Board and each Committee of its effectiveness as a group in fulfilling its Charter requirements and other responsibilities, its performance as measured against these Principles and areas for improvement. The Nominating & Corporate Governance Committee will propose the format for each annual self-evaluation.

8. Director Orientation

The Company has a comprehensive orientation program for all new Non-Employee Directors. All new Directors receive extensive written materials and meet in one-on-one sessions with members of senior management to discuss the Company's business segments, strategic plans, financial statements, significant financial, accounting and legal issues, compliance programs and business conduct policies. All Directors can receive periodic updates throughout their tenure.

9. Executive Performance Evaluations and Succession Planning

Executive Committee Performance Evaluations. The independent Directors will conduct an annual review of the performance of the Chief Executive Officer. The Chairman, the Compensation & Benefits Committee and the Lead Director will also provide input to the CEO on the performance of the other Executive Committee members.

Succession Planning. In light of the critical importance of executive leadership to the success of the Company, the Board will also work with senior management to ensure that effective plans are in place for management succession. As part of this process, the Chief Executive Officer will review periodically the succession plan for Executive Committee members and other critical positions with the Nominating & Corporate Governance Committee, which has oversight of the succession planning process for senior management. In addition, the Chief Executive Officer will report at least annually to the full Board on succession planning. The Board will evaluate potential successors to the Chief Executive Officer and any Vice Chairman, and certain other senior management positions.

10. Stock Ownership Guidelines

To further align the interests of the Company's Directors and senior management with shareholders, the Board has established minimum share ownership guidelines that apply to all Non-Employee Directors and designated members of senior management. Each Non-Employee Director is required to retain the shares issued upon the Director's election to the Board (if applicable) and to own Company shares or share units equal in value to three times his or her annual retainer. The Chief Executive Officer is required to own share or share units equal in value to six times his or her annual salary, and each Executive Committee member is required to own share or share units equal to three times his or her annual salary. Other executives may become subject to these guidelines as may be determined by the Board.

The Nominating and Corporate Governance Committee of the Board will develop and review from time to time the Share Ownership Guidelines to implement the principles set forth above, and will recommend any proposed changes to those Guidelines to the Board of Directors for approval.

11. Periodic Review of These Principles

These Principles will be reviewed annually by the Nominating & Corporate Governance Committee and may be amended by the Board from time to time.

Approved: January 17, 2017

ANNEX A

Duties and Responsibilities of the Independent Lead Director of the Board of Directors of Johnson & Johnson

Board Agendas and Schedules	• Approves information sent to the Board and determines timeliness of information flow from management. • Periodically provides feedback on quality and quantity of information flow from management. • Participates in setting, and ultimately approves, the agenda for each Board meeting. • Approves meeting schedules to assure that there is sufficient time for discussion of all agenda items. • With the Chair/CEO, determines who attends Board meetings, including management and outside advisors.
Committee Agendas and Schedules	• Reviews in advance the schedule of committee meetings. • Monitors flow of information from Committee Chairs to the full Board. *Board Executive Sessions* • Has the authority to call meetings and Executive Sessions of the Independent Directors. • Presides at all meetings of the Board at which the Chair/CEO is not present, including Executive Sessions of the Independent Directors.
Communicating with Management	• After each Executive Session of the Independent Directors, communicates with the Chair/CEO to provide feedback and also to effectuate the decisions and recommendations of the Independent Directors. • Acts as liaison between the Independent Directors and the Chair/CEO and management on a regular basis and when special circumstances exist or communication out of the ordinary course is necessary.
Communicating with Stakeholders	• As necessary, meets with major shareholders or other external parties, after discussions with the Chair/CEO. • Is regularly apprised of inquiries from shareholders and involved in correspondence responding to these inquiries. • Under the Board's guidelines for handling shareholder and employee communications to the Board, is advised promptly of any communications directed to the Board or any member of the Board that allege misconduct on the part of company management, or raise legal, ethical or compliance concerns about company policies or practices.

Chair and CEO Performance Evaluations	• Leads the annual performance evaluation of the Chair/CEO, distinguishing as necessary between performance as Chair and performance as CEO.
Board Performance Evaluation	• Leads the annual performance evaluation of the Board.
New Board Member Recruiting	• Interviews Board candidates, as appropriate.
CEO Succession	• Leads the CEO succession process.
Crisis Management	• Plays an increased role in crisis management oversight, as appropriate.
Limits on Leadership Positions of Other Boards	• May only serve as chair, lead or presiding director, or similar role, or as CEO or similar role at another public company if approved by the full Board upon recommendation from the Nominating & Corporate Governance Committee.

ANNEX B

Standards of Independence for Board of Directors of Johnson & Johnson

As contemplated under the Rules of the New York Stock Exchange, the Board of Directors of Johnson & Johnson (the "Company") has adopted these Standards of Independence in order to assist it in making determinations of independence.

1. *No Material Relationships with the Company.* No Director qualifies as "independent" unless the Board of Directors affirmatively determines that the Director has no material relationship with Johnson & Johnson (other than in his or her capacity as a Director). In making such determinations, the Board will broadly consider all relevant facts and circumstances. In particular, when assessing the materiality of a Director's relationship with the Company, the Board should consider the issue not merely from the standpoint of the Director, but also from that of persons or organizations with which the Director has an affiliation.

2. *Business Relationships.* The New York Stock Exchange has identified specific relationships that automatically preclude a Director from being considered independent. Pursuant to the requirements of the New York Stock Exchange:

   a. A Director who is an employee, or whose immediate family member is an executive officer, of Johnson & Johnson is not independent until three years after the end of such employment relationship;

   b. A Director who receives, or whose immediate family member receives, more than $120,000 during any 12-month period in direct compensation from Johnson & Johnson, other than Director and committee fees and pension or other forms of deferred compensation for prior service (provided such compensation is not contingent in any way on continued service), is not independent until three years after he or she ceases to have received more than $120,000 during any such 12-month period in compensation (provided that this paragraph (B) (ii) shall not include compensation received by an immediate family member for service as an employee of the Company, unless such immediate family member serves as an executive officer);

c. A Director who is currently employed by or a Partner of, or whose immediate family member is currently a Partner of, the internal or external auditor of Johnson & Johnson is not "independent." A Director whose immediate family member is currently employed by the internal or external auditor of Johnson & Johnson and who personally works on the Company's audit is not "independent." A Director who has been, or who has an immediate family member who has been, a Partner or employee of such internal or external auditor and personally worked on the Company's audit is not "independent" until three years after the completion of the audit;

d. A Director who is employed, or whose immediate family member is employed, as an executive officer of another company where any of Johnson & Johnson's present executive officers at the same time serve or served on that company's compensation committee is not "independent" until three years after the end of such service or the employment relationship; and

e. A Director who is an employee, or whose immediate family member is an executive officer, of a company that makes payments to, or receives payments from, Johnson & Johnson for property or services in an amount which, in any single fiscal year, exceeds the greater of $1,000,000, or two percent (2%) of such other company's consolidated gross revenues, is not "independent" until three years after falling below such threshold.

3. *Charitable Relationships.*

a. The Board recognizes that the relationship between the Company and a charitable (i.e., tax exempt) organization of which a Director serves as an executive officer, director or trustee could be deemed to be a material relationship. For purposes of these Standards of Independence, such a relationship will not be considered a "material relationship" if the Company's contributions to any such organization in each of the past three fiscal years are equal to or less than two percent (2%) (or $1,000,000, if greater) of that organization's consolidated gross revenues. (The amount of any "match" of Director or employee charitable contributions will not be included in calculating the amount of the Company's contributions for this purpose.)

b. For charitable relationships that do not fall within the guidelines in paragraph (C)(i) above, the determination as to whether a Director has a material relationship with the Company, and therefore may not be independent, will be made in good faith by the other Directors who satisfy all of these Standards of Independence. For example, if a Director is an officer of a charitable foundation that receives greater than two percent (2%) of its revenues from Johnson & Johnson, the other independent Directors could determine, after considering all of the relevant circumstances, that such relationship was nonetheless not material, and that the Director could therefore be considered independent. If the independent Directors so determine that any such charitable relationship is not material and would not otherwise impair the Director's independence or judgment, then the Company will disclose in its next proxy statement the basis for such determination.

4. *Other Relationships.* In addition to the business and charitable relationships described in paragraphs (B) and (C) above, the Board should consider any other relationships between each Director and the Company, including:

a. If the Director provides banking, consulting, legal, accounting or similar services to the Company;

b. If the Director is a partner or shareholder with an ownership interest of 5% or more of any organization that provides such services to or otherwise has a significant relationship with the Company; and

c. If a similar relationship exists between the Company and an immediate family member of the Director.

Any such relationship will not be deemed a material relationship if such relationship is at arm's length, does not conflict with the interests of the Company and would not impair the Director's independence or judgment.

5. *Definitions.* As used in these Standards of Independence, the terms "Company" and "Johnson & Johnson" will be deemed to include Johnson & Johnson and any subsidiaries in a consolidated group with Johnson & Johnson, except that an "executive officer" of Johnson & Johnson shall be deemed to refer only to an individual who is an executive officer of Johnson & Johnson, the parent company; the

term "immediate family member" of a Director will mean his or her spouse, parents, children, siblings, mother- and father-in-law, sons- and daughters-in-law, brothers- and sisters-in-law and anyone (other than domestic employees) who share such Director's home, but does not include adult stepchildren who do not share a stepparent's home or the in-laws of such stepchildren.

ANNEX C

General Criteria for Nomination to the Board of Directors of Johnson & Johnson

1. Directors should be of the highest ethical character and share the values of Johnson & Johnson as reflected in the Credo.
2. Directors should have reputations, both personal and professional, consistent with the image and reputation of Johnson & Johnson.
3. Directors should be highly accomplished in their respective fields, with superior credentials and recognition.
4. In selecting Directors, the Board should generally seek active and former chief executive officers of public companies and leaders of major complex organizations, including scientific, government, educational and other nonprofit institutions.
5. At the same time, in recognition of the fact that the foundation of the Company is in medical science and technology, the Board should also seek some Directors who are widely recognized as leaders in the fields of medicine or the biological sciences, including those who have received the most prestigious awards and honors in their field.
6. Each Director should have relevant expertise and experience, and be able to offer advice and guidance to the Chief Executive Officer based on that expertise and experience.
7. All outside Directors on the Board should be and remain "independent," not only as that term may be legally defined in SEC and New York Stock Exchange rules and regulations, but also without the appearance of any conflict in serving as a Director. In addition, Directors should be independent of any particular constituency and be able to represent all shareholders of the Company.
8. Each Director should have the ability to exercise sound business judgment.
9. Directors should be selected so that the Board of Directors is a diverse body, with diversity reflecting differences in skills, regional

and industry experience, background, race, ethnicity, gender and other unique characteristics. Accordingly, the Board is committed to seeking out highly qualified women and minority candidates as well as candidates with diverse backgrounds, skills and experiences as part of the search process for each Director.

10. The Board also reconfirms the mandatory retirement age of 72.

ANNEX D

Director Resignation Policy for Incumbent Directors in Uncontested Elections

Under the Company's By-Laws and in accordance with New Jersey law, a Director's term extends until his or her successor is duly elected and qualified, or until he or she resigns or is removed from office, with cause, by a majority vote of shareholders entitled to vote. Thus, an incumbent Director who fails to receive the required vote for re-election at the Company's Annual Meeting of Shareholders would continue serving as a Director (sometimes referred to as a "holdover" director), generally until the next meeting of shareholders.

In order to address the situation where an incumbent member of the Company's Board of Directors receives more votes "against" his or her re-election than votes "for" his or her re-election (hereinafter referred to as a "Majority Against Vote") in an uncontested election of Directors, the Board has adopted a policy whereby such incumbent Director receiving a Majority Against Vote must promptly tender an offer of his or her resignation following certification of the shareholder vote.

The Nominating & Corporate Governance Committee will consider and recommend to the Board whether to accept the resignation offer. Following the recommendation of the Nominating & Corporate Governance Committee, the independent members of the Board will decide the action to take with respect to the offer of resignation within 90 days following certification of the shareholder vote.

The Nominating & Corporate Governance Committee and Board of Directors will evaluate any such tendered resignation in the best interests of the Company and its shareholders. When deciding the action to take, the Board could accept or turn down the offer of resignation or decide to pursue additional actions such as the following:

- allow the incumbent Director to remain on the Board but not be nominated for re-election to the Board at the next election of Directors;

- defer acceptance of the resignation until such vacancy can be filled by the Board of Directors in accordance with the Company's By-Laws with a replacement Director with certain necessary qualifications held by the subject incumbent Director (for example, audit committee financial expertise); or
- defer acceptance of the resignation if the incumbent Director can cure the underlying cause of the Majority Against Vote within a specified period of time (for example, if the withheld votes were due to another board directorship, by resigning from that other board).

The Board's decision will be disclosed in a Form 8-K furnished by the Company to the SEC within four business days of the decision. If the Board has decided to turn down the tendered resignation, or to pursue any additional action (as described above or otherwise), then the Form 8-K will fully disclose the Board's reasons for doing so.

Any incumbent Director who offers his or her resignation pursuant to this provision will not participate in any discussions with or actions by either the Nominating & Corporate Governance Committee or the Board of Directors with respect to accepting or turning down his or her own resignation offer, but will otherwise continue to serve as a Director during this period. However, if enough members of the Nominating & Corporate Governance Committee receive a Majority Against Vote in the same uncontested election, so that a quorum of the Nominating & Corporate Governance Committee cannot be attained, then the other independent Directors who received a greater number of votes "for" than "against" in that election will be asked to consider and decide whether to accept the resignation offer of each incumbent Director who received a Majority Against Vote. If only three or fewer independent Directors did not receive a Majority Against Vote in the same election, then all independent Directors may participate in any discussions or actions with respect to accepting or turning down the resignation offers (except that no Director will vote to accept or turn down his or her own resignation offer).

For purposes of this Policy, an "uncontested election" will be any election of Directors where the number of nominees for election is less than or equal to the number of Directors to be elected.

Notes

1. Corporate governance. http://www.investopedia.com/terms/c/corporategovernance.asp.
2. Corporate governance. http://www.businessdictionary.com/definition/corporate-governance.html.

3. Agency problem. http://www.investopedia.com/terms/a/agencyproblem.asp.
4. Business Roundtable. (2016). Principles of corporate governance. https://businessroundtable.org/sites/default/files/Principles-of-Corporate-Governance-2016.pdf.
5. ACCA. (2012). Corporate governance: The board of directors and standing committees. http://www.accaglobal.com/content/dam/acca/global/PDF-students/2012s/sa_oct12-f1fab_governance.pdf.
6. Chair of the board (COB). http://www.investopedia.com/terms/c/chair-of-the-board.asp#ixzz4iskWecrQ.
7. Johnson & Johnson Principles of Corporate Governance. Available from http://www.investor.jnj.com/_document/2018-principles-of-corporate-governance?id=00000161-a078-d89d-ad75-befa96510000.

Section V

Exit Strategies, AKA Harvesting

17

Knowledge-Intensive Industries

17.1 Introduction

Knowledge work can be differentiated from other traditional forms of work by its emphasis on "nonroutine" problem solving that requires a combination of convergent, divergent, and creative thinking.[1]

A knowledge-intensive (KI) job, firm, or industry is one where the workers need (1) a higher education, (2) highly focused skills, and (3) specialized experience in order to work effectively.[2] In this chapter, we define knowledge economy as production and services based on KI activities that contribute to an accelerated pace of technical and scientific advance, as well as rapid obsolescence. The key component of a knowledge economy is a greater reliance on intellectual capabilities than on physical inputs or natural resources.[3]

The commercial knowledge and technology-intensive (KTI) industries play a big role in the U.S. economy. The larger component of KTI industries—the KI services industries—employed 18 million workers and produced 22% of the U.S. gross domestic product (GDP) in 2012. The smaller component—the high-technology (HT) manufacturing industries—employed 2 million workers and produced 2% of the GDP in 2012. Although smaller than KI services industries, HT manufacturing industries have a greater concentration of workers in science and engineering occupations and perform a larger proportion of U.S. research and development (R&D). Both KI services industries and HT manufacturing industries pay substantially higher wages than the private-sector average.[4]

Three KI services industries (business, finance, and information) and six HT manufacturing industries (aircraft; communications; computers and office machinery; pharmaceuticals; semiconductors; and testing, measuring, and control instruments) are classified by the Organisation for Economic and Cooperation and Development.[5]

Since the 1960s, the cutting edge of the economy in developed countries has become driven by technologies based on knowledge and information production and dissemination. These new technologies, which expanded with the proliferation of personal computers, and then surged dramatically with the widespread use of e-mail and the Internet, are changing the nature of work and the economy.

The key components of a knowledge economy include a greater reliance on intellectual capabilities than on physical inputs or natural resources, combined with efforts to integrate improvements in every stage of the production process, from the R&D laboratory to the factory floor to the interface with customers. These changes are reflected in the increasing relative share of the GDP that is attributable to "intangible" capital.[6]

A KI organization refers to an organization where knowledge has more importance than other inputs[7] (i.e., in contrast to labor-intensive or capital-intensive). Although there is no clear or unambiguous definition of *knowledge-intensive work* or *knowledge work*, it is possible to identify some salient characteristics that are often related to these terms.[8]

The salient characteristics of KI work can be synthesized into six different categories. These categories are labeled (1) content of knowledge work, (2) complexity of the work, (3) knowledge and skills required, (4) autonomy versus control, (5) collective knowledge systems, and (6) learning orientation. The borders between individual categories are blurry, and often the categories overlap, as enumerated in Table 17.1.

TABLE 17.1

Categories of Knowledge-Intensive Work

Salient Categories	Characteristics and Authors
Content of knowledge work	KI work is the acquisition, creation, packaging, and/or application of knowledge[35] with knowledge workers *enriching* the input information,[36] working *from* knowledge, *with* knowledge,[37] *for* knowledge, while emphasizing that *outcomes* are important, and *quality* instead of quantity is imperative.[38]
Complexity of the work	Unstructured with an inherent conflict between "knowing" as part of the work experience and "knowledge" as an economic commodity,[39] ambiguity-intensive,[40] often requires tacit knowledge,[41] is nonrepetitive and nonroutine,[42,43] varies in terms of complexity over time and task.[44]
Knowledge and skills required	KI work requires a high level of skills and expertise[45] where scientific and technical knowledge and skills are required, and these must be acquired through formal education.[46] Knowledge workers manipulate and coordinate symbols and concepts, and their skills may become rapidly obsolete.[47]
Autonomy over work	Knowledge workers demand autonomy over the work they perform,[48,49] and they may even tend to resist standard operating procedures.[50]
Collective knowledge systems	Working with knowledge is an individual activity, where most of the organizational knowledge is inside the worker's head.[51,52] Nonetheless, collective knowledge still plays a fundamental role in KI work.[53,54] Collectivity offers a platform for joint interaction, which in turn leads to collective development and learning.[55]
Learning orientation	Continual learning is considered a fundamental element of KI work. The content of KI work itself offers learning opportunities for knowledge workers. Ambiguities, uncertainties, and contradictions provide opportunities for individual and collective team development and learning. Knowledge workers need to adapt to new situations and cope with uncertainty, ambiguity,[56] flexibility, interdisciplinary coordination, and rapid learning.[57]

17.2 Knowledge Workers

Peter Drucker coined the term *knowledge workers* in 1959. He said knowledge workers believe they are paid to be effective, not to work nine-to-five, and that smart businesses will "strip away everything that gets in the knowledge workers' way." Those that succeed will attract the best performers, securing "the single biggest factor for competitive advantage in the next 25 years."

A characteristic of knowledge workers is that you cannot lead knowledge workers by merely telling them what to do. You must treat them with respect and dignity and provide opportunities that they would not be able to have on their own. To lead knowledge workers effectively and unlock their true potential, you need to define the following:

- What knowledge work professionals do
- How they do it best
- What drives them to do it

Currently, the term *knowledge* has become an all-embracing term that encompasses all the "fascination and enchantment" of contemporary organizations, making them successful; an elusive, yet pervasive "asset" that remains unseen, residing only in the individual's intellect and drive to succeed.

Organizations are encouraged to become knowing organizations,[9] knowledge companies,[10,11] knowledge-based businesses,[12] knowledge-based organizations,[13] knowledge-creating companies,[14] or learning organizations.[15] It is the "alchemy of competence," as expressed by Thomas Durand.[16]

17.3 Early-Stage Innovation

In the field of economics, fewer relationships are more broadly supported by both theory and empirical evidence than the relationship between technological innovation and long-term growth.[17] Yet prior to the mid-1980s, economists undertook little detailed study of the process by which ideas are transformed into new goods and services, or how new industries and sectors of economic activity arise. Innovations are one of the least analyzed parts of economics, in spite of the verifiable fact that they have contributed more to per capita economic growth than any other factor.[18]

According to a 2002 report from the prestigious National Institute of Standards and Technology (NIST),[19] technological innovation is critical to long-term economic growth. Most technological innovation consists of incremental change in existing industries. As the pace of technical advance quickens and product cycles compress, established corporations have strong incentives to seek opportunities for such incremental technological change.

However, incremental technical change alone is not adequate to ensure sustained growth and economic security. Sustained growth can occur only with the continuous introduction of truly new goods and services—radical technological innovations that disrupt markets and create new industries.

The capacity to turn science-based inventions into commercially viable innovations is critical to radical technological innovation. As economist Martin Weitzman[20] noted, "The ultimate limits to growth may lie not as much in our ability to generate new ideas, so much as in our ability to process an abundance of potentially new seed ideas into usable forms." Understanding the invention-to-innovation transition is essential in the formulation of both public policies and private business strategies designed to convert the nation's research assets more efficiently into economic assets.

NIST uses *invention* as shorthand for a commercially promising product or service idea, based on new science or technology that is protectable (though not necessarily by patents or copyrights). By *innovation* we mean the successful entry of a new science or technology-based product into a particular market. By early-stage technology development (ESTD) we mean the technical and business activities that transform a commercially promising invention into a business plan that can attract enough investment to enter a market successfully, and through that investment become a successful innovation.

17.4 Transitioning from Invention to Innovation in Universities

Most of the federal investment into R&D supports basic scientific research carried out in university-affiliated research laboratories. While such investment may lead to science-based inventions and other new product ideas, it is primarily intended to support basic research with potential to generate fundamental advances in knowledge. In contrast, most venture capital and corporate investment into R&D exploits science-based inventions that have already been translated into new products and services, with specifications and costs matching well-defined market opportunities.

The basic science and technology research enterprise of the United States—sources of funding, performing institutions, researcher incentives and motivations—is reasonably well understood by academics and policymakers alike. Similarly, corporate motivations, governance, finance, strategy, and competitive advantage have been much studied and are relatively well understood. But the process by which a technical idea of possible commercial value is converted into one or more commercially successful products—the transition from invention to innovation—is highly complex, poorly documented, and little studied.

- What is the distribution of funding for ESTD across different institutional categories? How do government programs compare with private sources in terms of magnitude?
- What kinds of difficulties do firms face when attempting to find funding for early-stage, high-risk R&D projects? To what extent are such difficulties due to structural barriers or market failures?

17.5 Conditions for Success

NIST found that conditions for success in science-based, HT innovation are strongly concentrated in a few geographical regions, indicating the importance in the process of innovator–investor proximity and networks of supporting people and institutions.

If ESTD investments from all sources are distributed as nonuniformly as venture capital investments, then they are concentrated in a few states and a few industries. This would be expected, for our research results suggest that angel investments are even more locally focused than venture capital. Furthermore, theory suggests that the quality of social capital in the locality where inventions are being exploited is an important determinant of success. Where the social capital is strongly supportive, in places like Route 128 in Boston or Silicon Valley near San Francisco, one might expect not only strong venture capital and angel investments but also a concentration of federal support for ESTD and industry-supported HT ventures.

Since angel investors make the vast majority of their investments close to home, ESTD activities, particularly those of smaller firms, are likely to be concentrated in regions with active communities of tech-savvy angels.

17.5.1 Role of State Governments in Early-Stage Funding

State governments, while providing a relatively small portion of total ESTD funding, play a critical role in establishing regional environments that help bridge the gap from invention to innovation. State governments facilitate university–industry partnerships, leverage federal academic research funds by providing both general and targeted grants, build a technically educated workforce through support of public colleges and universities, and ease regulatory burdens to create a more fertile ground for technology startups. While Route 128 and Silicon Valley arose with little local- or state-level political support (in part because they had developed the needed networks, stimulated by defense funding, in the 1950s), a number of states have created many of the environmental features needed for successful innovation. Research Triangle Park in North Carolina, for example, was conceived and initiated by Governor Luther Hodges.

These geographical concentrations create additional challenges to champions of ESTD projects located outside of favored geographical or market spaces. Such challenges may be of considerable importance to public policy. The implications for public policy will depend heavily on whether the federal government attempts to compensate for such tendencies toward concentration or chooses instead to accept them as reflecting the flow of resources to geographical and market areas in which expected economic returns are highest. In subsequent work, we will further explore the causes and implications of inter-regional and inter-industry differences in funding for ESTD projects.

17.6 Knowledge and Technology-Intensive Industries

Knowledge-based and technology-intensive industries are based on technological innovation. *Technological innovation* is the successful implementation of a technical idea new to the institution creating it. The essence of knowledge and technology-based innovation is the systematic and successful use of science to create new forms of economic activity. Technology-based innovation thus represents a subset of all innovation but has the potential to create entire new industries.[21]

Figure 17.1 summarizes what a typical knowledge and technology-based firm looks like.

The theoretical distinction between radical technology innovation and incremental product enhancement is based on the extent of novelty in the science or technology being used in the product, where technical risk is greater than market risk.[22] Of course, the most radical technology-based innovations are often accompanied by unique capabilities that allow new markets to be created, thus introducing high levels of both market and technical risks.

17.6.1 Technology-Based Innovations

Technology-based innovations are also common to certain business models. Thus, a company that defines its business by specializing in a specific area of technology, which addresses many markets, can expect to introduce many technology-based innovations.[23] In contrast, a company that defines itself narrowly by its market or its products will be less able to specialize in an area of science or engineering and is less likely to produce radical, knowledge or technology-based innovations on its own.

It is important to definition the stage of development of a technology, although any division of the innovation process into temporal stages is

- Radical technology and innovation
  - Product requirements and specifications
  - Manufacturing sequence
  - Value creation model
  - Develop enabling technologies; build prototype
- Value proposition
  - Market requirements; product differentiation
  - Revenue stream; profitability profile
- Personnel
  - Technical skills
  - Attract talent
  - Devotion to project
  - Financial incentives
- Funding mechanisms
  - Founders, Angels, VCs
  - Government grants and contracts
  - Beta sites, clinical trials, proof-of-principle

FIGURE 17.1
Characteristics of knowledge/technology firms.

bound to be arbitrary and imperfect. One distinction that has often been employed by practitioners is that between "proof of principle" and "reduction to practice," as summarized in Table 17.2.

17.7 Knowledge Workers

The term *knowledge worker* was originally coined by Peter Drucker in 1959.[24] Knowledge workers include leaders, designers, researchers, architects,

TABLE 17.2

Proof of Principle versus Reduction to Practice

Proof of principle	Means that a project team has demonstrated its ability, within a research setting, to meet a well-defined technological challenge: to show in a laboratory setting that a model of a possible commercial product, process, or service can demonstrate the function that, if produced in quantity at low enough cost and high enough reliability, could meet an identified market opportunity. It involves the successful application of basic scientific and engineering principles to the solution of a specific problem.
Reduction to practice	Means that a working model of a product has been developed in the context of well-defined and unchanging specifications, using processes not unlike those that would be required for scaled-up production. Product design and production processes can be defined that have sufficient windows for variability to validate the expectation that a reliable product can be made through a high-yield, stable process.

TABLE 17.3

Knowledge Workers' Characteristics

Knowledge workers represent a new category of workers and are growing significantly,	Nearly 40% of the labor force in advanced industries are classified as knowledge workers.
They are the most expensive type of worker that companies employ,	Knowledge workers enjoy great mobility and demand "pleasant and stimulating" working facilities.
They are essential to the growth and stability of many enterprises.	Many are dissatisfied, since they are managed by obsolete management methods, better suited to assembly-line manufacturing.
They demand to be consulted on matters relating to their jobs and performance.	The traditional command-and-control managerial structure does not work well with knowledge workers.
The know their value to the organization.	Generally, they do not share their knowledge with coworkers.
They work less structured hours.	They cannot simply schedule 8 creative hours and then punch the clock.
It is impossible to tell if they are "working."	Only when there is a tangible result can you measure or value what has been accomplished.
The resist micromanagement.	Work does not fit into predictable boxes and arrows. They cannot be managed the traditional way.

software designers, engineers, consultants, financial analysts, scientists, academics, and lawyers. Even then, he saw the emergence of new forms of organization that relied on the creativity, ingenuity, and competence of a new breed of workers: knowledge workers who would "think" for a living (as opposed to "do" for a living).

Knowledge workers create the innovations and strategies that keep their firms competitive and the economy healthy. Yet, companies continue to manage this new breed of employee with techniques designed for the Industrial Age. As this critical sector of the workforce continues to increase in size and importance, that is a mistake that could cost companies their future. According to Thomas Davenport,[25] knowledge workers are vastly different from other types of workers in their motivations, attitudes, and need for autonomy—and they require different management techniques to improve their performance and productivity.

Davenport provides the following definition: "Knowledge workers have high degrees of expertise, education, or experience, and the primary purpose of their jobs involves the creation, distribution, or application of knowledge." In short, *they think for a living*. Knowledge workers are a breed apart, as described in Table 17.3.

17.7.1 Knowledge Worker Spectrum

Andrew Hawson in "The Six Factors of Knowledge Worker Productivity: Six Factors That Can Change Your Organization,"[26] described a "knowledge worker spectrum," as depicted in Figure 17.2.

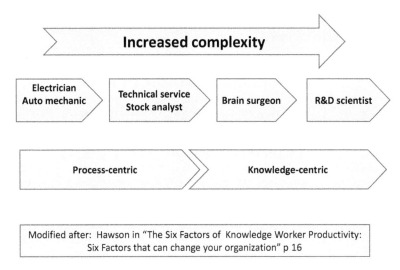

FIGURE 17.2
Knowledge worker spectrum.

Hawson explains that on the left-hand end of the spectrum, roles have much less dependency on knowledge and a greater dependency on adherence to well-defined processes. These might include delivery drivers, checkout clerks in a supermarket, or call center agents. On the right-hand side of the spectrum, we have the knowledge workers, such as researchers, development staff, designers, engineers, and biostatisticians.

Between these two ends of the spectrum there are, of course, many roles with differing levels of knowledge content. The surgeon may be "routinely" performing brain surgery or replacing hip joints where a high level of knowledge is needed but where, by and large, the process is the same time after time. But the surgeon's knowledge becomes critical when something is nonstandard or goes wrong, in order to save the life of the patient.

In a knowledge organization, workers are constantly making personal choices (consciously or subconsciously) on how much to contribute their ideas, energy, and cognitive resources to the endeavors of their organization. Creating the conditions under which people choose to contribute their best knowledge and energy to each other and the larger organization becomes critical.

17.7.2 Six Knowledge Worker Productivity Factors

Based on the above considerations, Hawson identified six factors that impact knowledge worker productivity, as shown in Table 17.4.

TABLE 17.4

Hawson's Six Knowledge Worker Productivity Factors

Factor 1—Social cohesion	The first and most highly correlated factor is social cohesion: a shared liking or team attraction that includes bonds of friendship, caring, closeness, and enjoyment of each other's company.
Factor 2—Perceived supervisory support	Workers need to feel that the person to whom they report is positively supporting them in achieving their endeavors and their own professional development.
Factor 3—Information sharing and the transactive memory system	How teams pool and access their knowledge and expertise, which positively affects decision making and team processes. This leads to the idea of a team transactive memory system (TMS), which can be thought of as a collective memory in a collective mind—enabling a team to think and act together.
Factor 4—Vision and goal clarity	The extent to which team members have a common understanding of objectives and display high commitment to those team goals. For this reason, "vision" at the team level is also referred to as goal clarity.
Factor 5—External communication	The ability of teams to span boundaries (team and organizational) to seek information and resources from others.
Factor 6—Trust	The firm belief in the reliability, truth, or ability of others. It is created by the expectation that the actions of other people will be to one's benefit or at least not detrimental to them.

17.8 Knowledge Management

Knowledge is a changing system with interactions among experience, skills, facts, relationships, values, thinking processes, and meanings.[27] It consists of two dimensions, explicit and tacit, as shown in Table 17.5.

Knowledge workers work with both dimensions of knowledge. Explicit knowledge is usually present in the form of data in some information system; tacit knowledge is linked to its human holder or holders. Organizations

TABLE 17.5

The Two Dimensions of Knowledge

Explicit knowledge	Expressed in formal and systematic language and can be shared in the form of data, scientific formulas, specifications, and manuals. Explicit knowledge and intuition are created by mental models, experience, abilities, skills, etc. It is deeply rooted in action, procedures, routines, commitments, ideas, values, and emotions. It is difficult to share and communicate.
Tacit knowledge	The tacit dimension of knowledge is highly personal and difficult to discover and formalize. Nonverbalized, unarticulated knowledge. Tacit knowledge is know-how and learning embedded within the minds of the people in an organization. It involves perceptions, insights, experiences, and craftsmanship. Managing tacit knowledge means managing people.

do not usually have a problem organizing work with explicit knowledge. Information and communications technology and modern information systems offer many solutions on how to adjust work with explicit knowledge to the needs of knowledge workers of individual organizations. Explicit knowledge is packaged, easily codified, communicable, and transferable.

Tacit (implied, not stated) knowledge is more problematic. KI organizations tend to underestimate its significance and do not create the environment necessary for knowledge sharing.[28] Tacit knowledge is personal, context specific, difficult to formalize, and difficult to communicate.

Tacit knowledge can be described as experience that is embedded in an individual, such as perspective and inferential knowledge. It includes insights, hunches, intuitions, and skills that are highly personal and difficult to formalize, and as a result are hard to communicate or share with others. It can only be "learned" by close association over an extended period of time.[29]

According to Mládková,[30] the specifics of knowledge workers can be explained by the difference between knowledge and nonknowledge work. Knowledge work differs from nonknowledge work in many parameters.

The major raw materials for knowledge work are not material elements but knowledge. Contrary to nonknowledge work, the most important part of knowledge work happens in the heads of employees even though the final result of their work has a manual character. Table 17.6 lists the most significant differences between knowledge and nonknowledge work.

17.8.1 Knowledge Management Architecture

According to Jerry Honeycutt,[31] knowledge management depends on the interactions of four basic processes: development of knowledge, distribution

TABLE 17.6

Differences between Nonknowledge and Knowledge Work

Characteristics	Nonknowledge Work	Knowledge Work
Raw materials	Physical elements	Knowledge
Work process	Obvious, open, timely	Hidden, concealed
Work visibility	High, subject to counting	Low, cerebral
Results	Direct, immediate	Delayed, intellectual
Knowledge	Within the organization	In worker's head
Power	Positional, titles, structural	Based on worker's ability and contributions
Response to crises	Position and tasks	Individual evaluation and action
Standards	Organizational or professional	Individualized
Performance measures	Standards based	Individual accomplishment
Control	Organizational	Diffused
Worker's role	Tool, cog in the machinery	Independent agent

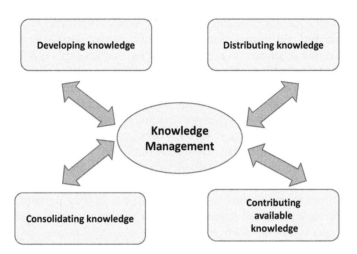

FIGURE 17.3
The four basic operations of knowledge.

of knowledge, knowledge consolidation, and contribution of available knowledge. The organization structure can significantly affect the pace of knowledge sharing by the four basic operations on knowledge that can be found in any KI organization, as depicted in Figure 17.3.

1. *Developing knowledge*: In today's global competition, it is necessary to develop new knowledge based on creative ideas, analysis of failure, daily experience, and work in the R&D department. Corporate memories can support these processes by recording failures and successes. It is necessary to give more explicit recognition to tacit knowledge and related human aspects, such as ideas, values, or emotions, for developing a richer conceptualization of knowledge management

2. *Consolidating knowledge*: Knowledge must be safeguarded against loss due to different causes, such as retirement, transfer, and death. Consolidation of knowledge is supported by corporate memories and knowledge transfer programs. The knowledge thus stored must be available at the right time and at the right place.

3. *Distributing knowledge*: Knowledge must be actively distributed to those who can make use of it. The turnaround speed of knowledge is crucial for the competitiveness of companies. To distribute the knowledge, implement new, flexible technologies and systems that support and enable communities of practice, informal and semi-informal networks of internal employees and external individuals based on shared concerns and interests.

4. *Combining available knowledge*: An organization can only perform at its best if all available knowledge areas are combined in its new products.

17.8.2 Motivating Knowledge Workers

Few companies can say that their employees are not their most valuable assets; knowledge management can help every company take better care of its employees. With an effective knowledge management solution, companies can better motivate their employees, better reward them, and align their skills with corporate needs.[32]

Effective knowledge management solutions deliver training, track employees' skills and competencies, remove barriers to productivity, provide current company information, manage benefits, help supervisors staff their departments, and simplify expense reimbursement. Dynamic market conditions can catch companies without valuable skills sets across its employees. For example, knowledge management systems can identify skills gaps as well as provide mechanisms for closing those gaps.

Knowledge management can help companies save significant sums of money by enabling them to improve employee management. Key areas, in which knowledge management is most effective, include the following:[33]

1. Training helps keep knowledge workers and employees sharp: It can take many forms, including multimedia, online handbooks, and manuals.

2. Skill alignment ensures that the right people are working on the right projects at the right time: Knowledge management enables companies to find experts that are available for a particular job.

3. Benefits management is a natural target for any knowledge management system: Companies can simplify paper-based systems, reduce human resources costs, provide corporate information to employees, and more.

4. Bigger companies can benefit most from better staffing management: Using knowledge management, those companies can keep track of head count and reorganize more quickly.

5. Performance reviews are more efficient when moved from manual processes to a knowledge management system: As a result, reviews are completed on time and supervisors can better manage their budgeting processes.

6. Expense reimbursement is best done on an Internet: Companies can significantly reduce the cost and turnaround time for reimbursing employees for out-of-pocket expenses, improving morale and productivity.

17.9 Knowledge-Intensive Companies' Characterization

As defined by Alvesson,[34] knowledge-intensive companies, as opposed to labor-intensive or capital-intensive companies, are characterized by the following factors:

- Significant incidents of problem solving and nonstandardized production.
- Creativity on the part of the practitioner and the organizational environment.
- Heavy reliance on individuals (and less dependence on capital) and a high degree of independence on the part of the practitioners.
- High educational levels and a high degree of professionalism on the part of most employees.
- Traditional concrete (material) assets are not a central factor. The critical elements are in the mind of employees and in networks, customer relationships, manuals, and systems for supplying services.
- Heavy dependence on the loyalty of key personnel and—this is the other side of the picture—considerable vulnerability when personnel leave the company.

Consequently, the potential loss of key personnel leads to the fear that the organization could lose their competitive edge, which was dependent on the knowledge acquired and developed by these employees. This is particularly crucial for small business entities, which traditionally rely heavily on particular individuals and lack the recruiting capacity of large organizations.

Notes

1. Reinhardt, W., Schmidt, B., Sloep, P. and Drachsler, H. (2011). Knowledge worker roles and actions—Results of two empirical studies. *Knowledge and Process Management*, 18(3), 150–174.
2. Rylander, A. and Peppard, J. What really is a knowledge-intensive firm? (Re) framing research in the "knowledge economy." https://pdfs.semanticscholar. org/0e9c/8690f581e687c0aa8160ebaeed3fe98e146d.pdf.
3. Powell, W. W. and Snellman, K. (2004). The knowledge economy. *Annual Review of Sociology*, 30, 199–220.
4. Hill, D. (2014). U.S. knowledge-intensive services industries employ 18 million and pay high wages. NSF 15-300. Arlington, VA: National Science Foundation, National Center for Science and Engineering Statistics.

5. National Science Board (NSB). (2014). Science and engineering indicators 2014. NSB 14-01. Arlington, VA: National Science Foundation. http://www.nsf.gov/statistics/seind14/.

6. Abramovitz, M. and David, P. A. (1996). Technological change and the rise of intangible investments. The U.S. economy's growth-path in the twentieth century. In *Employment and Growth in the Knowledge-Based Economy*. Paris: OECD (pp. 35–60).

7. Starbuck, W. H. (1992). Learning by knowledge intensive firms. *Journal of Management Studies*, 29(6), 713–740.

8. Mäki, E. (2008). Exploring and exploiting knowledge research on knowledge processes in knowledge-intensive organizations. Helsinki University of Technology Department of Industrial Engineering and Management Doctoral Dissertation Series.

9. Choo, C. W. (1998). *The Knowing Organization: How Organizations Use Information to Construct Meaning, Create Knowledge, and Make Decisions*. New York: Oxford University Press.

10. Stewart, T. A. (1997). *Intellectual Capital*. New York: Doubleday.

11. Sveiby, K. E. (1997). *The New Organizational Wealth*. San Francisco: Berrett-Koehler Publishers.

12. Davis, S. and Botkin, J. (1994). The coming of knowledge based business. *Harvard Business Review*, September–October, 165–170.

13. Leonard-Barton, D. (1995). *Wellsprings of Knowledge: Building and Sustaining the Sources of Innovation*. Boston: Harvard Business School Press.

14. Nonaka, I. and Takeuchi, H. (1995). *The Knowledge Creating Company*. New York: Oxford University Press.

15. Senge, P. (1994). *The Fifth Discipline: The Art and Practice of the Learning Organization*. New York: Currency/Doubleday.

16. Durand, T. (1998). The alchemy of competence. In G. Hamel, C. K. Prahalad, H. Thomas and D. O'Neal (Eds.), *Strategic Flexibility: Managing in a Turbulent Environment*. Chichester, UK: John Wiley & Sons (pp. 303–330).

17. Jones, C. J. and Williams, J. C. (1998). Measuring the social return to R&D. *Quarterly Journal of Economics*, 113, 1119–1153.

18. Ulku, H. R&D, innovation, and economic growth: an empirical analysis. https://www.imf.org/external/pubs/ft/wp/2004/wp04185.pdf.

19. National Institute of Standards and Technology. (2002). Between invention: An analysis of funding for early-stage and innovation technology development. NIST GCR 02-841.

20. Weitzman, M. L. (1998). Recombinant growth. *Quarterly Journal of Economics*, 113, 333–360.

21. Nelson, R. (Ed.). (1993). *National Innovation Systems: A Comparative Analysis*. Oxford: Oxford University Press.

22. Auerswald, P. E., Kauffman, S., Lobo, J. and Shell, K. (2000). The production recipes approach to modeling technological innovation: An application to learning by doing. *Journal of Economic Dynamics and Control*, 24. https://papers.ssrn.com/sol3/papers.cfm?abstract_id=1461801.

23. Branscomb, L. M., Kodama, F. and Florida, R. L. (Eds.). (1999). *Industrializing Knowledge: University-Industry Links in Japan and the United States*. Cambridge MA: MIT Press.

24. Drucker, P. F. (1959). *The Landmarks of Tomorrow*. New York: Harper & Row.

25. Davenport, T. H. (2005). Thinking for a Living: How to Get Better Performances and Results from Knowledge Workers. Cambridge, MA: Harvard Business School Press.
26. Hawson, A. The six factors of knowledge worker productivity: Six factors that can change your organization. http://www.allsteeloffice.com/SynergyDocuments/SixFactorsOfKnowledgeWorkerProductivity.pdf.
27. Veber, J. (2000). [*Management, Basics, Prosperity, Globalization.*] Praha: Management Press.
28. Cavusgil, T. S., Calantone, R. J. and Zhao, Y. (2003). Tacit knowledge transfer and firm innovation capability. *Journal of Business & Industrial Marketing*, 18(1), 6–12.
29. Nunes, M. B., Annansingh, F. and Eaglestone, B. (2005). Knowledge management issues inknowledge-intensive SMEs. www.emeraldinsight.com/0022-0418.htm.
30. Mládková, L. Knowledge management for knowledge workers. *The Electronic Journal of Knowledge Management*, 9(3), 248–258. Available from http://ejkm.com/issue/download.html?idArticle=296.
31. Honeycutt, J. (2002). *Knowledge Management Strategies.* Redmond, WA: Microsoft Press.
32. Tripathi, K. P. (2010). *International Journal of Computer Applications*, 12(7).
33. Drucker, P. (1999). *Management Challenges for the 21st Century.* New York: HarperCollins.
34. Alvesson, M. (1995). *Management of Knowledge-Intensive Companies.* Berlin: Walter de Gruyter.
35. Davenport, T., Jarvenpaa, S. and Beers, M. (1996). Improving knowledge work process. *Sloan Management Review*, 37(4), 53–65.
36. Hayman, A. and Elliman, T. (2000). Human elements in information system design for knowledge workers. *International Journal of Information Management*, 20, 297–309.
37. Scarbrough, H. (1999). Knowledge as work: Conflicts in the management of knowledge workers. *Technology Analysis & Strategic Management*, 11(1), 5–16.
38. Kelloway, E. and Barling, J. (2000). Knowledge work as organizational behavior. *International Journal of Management Reviews*, 2(3), 287–304.
39. Scarbrough, H. (1999). Knowledge as work: Conflicts in the management of knowledge workers. *Technology Analysis & Strategic Management*, 11(1), 5–16.
40. Alvesson, M. (2001). Knowledge work: Ambiguity, image and identity. *Human Relations*, 54(7), 863–886.
41. Donaldson, L. (2001). Reflections on knowledge and knowledge-intensive firms. *Human Relations*, 54(7), 955–963.
42. Pyöriä, P. (2005). The concept of knowledge work revisited. *Journal of Knowledge Management*, 9(3), 116–127.
43. Hayman, A. and Elliman, T. (2000). Human elements in information system design for knowledge workers. *International Journal of Information Management*, 20, 297–309.
44. Drucker, P. (1999). Knowledge workers productivity: The biggest challenge. *California Management Review*, 41(2), 79–94.
45. Davenport, T., Jarvenpaa, S. and Beers, M. (1996). Improving knowledge work process. *Sloan Management Review*, 37(4), 53–65.

46. Hayman, A. and Elliman, T. (2000). Human elements in information system design for knowledge workers. *International Journal of Information Management*, 20, 297–309.

47. Despres, C. and Hiltrop, J.-M. (1995). Human resource management in the knowledge age: Current practice and perspectives on the future. *Employee Relations*, 17(1), 9–23.

48. Hayman, A. and Elliman, T. (2000). Human elements in information system design for knowledge workers. *International Journal of Information Management*, 20, 297–309.

49. Robertson, M. and Swan, J. (2003). 'Control—What control?' Culture and ambiguity within a knowledge intensive firm. *Journal of Management Studies*, 40(4), 831–858.

50. Davenport, T., Jarvenpaa, S. and Beers, M. (1996). Improving knowledge work process. *Sloan Management Review*, 37(4), 53–65.

51. Alavi, M. and Leidner, D. (2001). Review: Knowledge management and knowledge management systems: Conceptual foundations and research issues. *MIS Quarterly*, 25(1), 107–136.

52. Tsoukas, H. and Vladimirou, E. (2001). What is organizational knowledge? *Journal of Management Studies*, 38(7), 973–993.

53. McInerney, C. (2002). Knowledge management and the dynamic nature of knowledge. *Journal of the American Society for Information Science and Technology*, 53(12), 1009–1018.

54. Styhre, A. (2002). The knowledge-intensive company and the economy of sharing: Rethinking utility and knowledge management. *Knowledge and Process Management*, 9(4), 228–236.

55. Blackler, F., Reed, M. and Whitaker, A. (1993). Editorial introduction: Knowledge workers and contemporary organizations. *Journal of Management Studies*, 30(6), 851–862.

56. Alvesson, M. (2001). Knowledge work: Ambiguity, image and identity. *Human Relations*, 54(7), 863–886.

57. Pyöriä, P. (2005). The concept of knowledge work revisited. *Journal of Knowledge Management*, 9(3), 116–127.

18

Getting Your Company Ready for an Exit

18.1 Introduction

Selling your private business as an exit strategy is one of the most complex financial transactions that face successful entrepreneurs. It is much simpler to sell an exchange-listed company, since the market has established an enterprise value.

As an entrepreneur, the clearer you are about your objectives, the easier it will be to create the right strategy. Are you looking to sell the business completely, or would you like to maintain some level of ownership? Do you want certain employees to remain or become shareholders of the business after your departure? Your objectives will ultimately guide the sale process.[1]

Businesses are not sold overnight; these are complex transactions that are influenced by multiple variables. To maximize your value, it is critical to plan carefully before entering into any sale process. Even if you think you are many years away from selling, planning now can ensure that you can take full advantage of future opportunities.

Are you ready to hang up the "for sale" sign? The question then becomes, how do I sell my business for the biggest profit? It is a tough question to answer, because a business is a complicated item. If you are selling your car, you make sure it is clean and running smoothly. If you are selling a house, you make sure it has some curb appeal and no major damages.

But your private business? What should you do in order to maximize profit from selling your business?[2]

18.1.1 Know the Value Range of Your Business

You want to sell your business for the highest *profit*. Obviously. But you are not going to fool anyone. If your business is worth small potatoes, then no buyer in their right mind is going to overpay. You must to be realistic about your business's valuation.

And here is where you enter the bean-counting realm of business appraisers and valuators. A competent valuator will be able to determine how much your business is worth and determine a realistic price range.

Be prepared for a professional appraisal. Prospective buyers will either ask for one or order one, so you might as well have one to show them. You will gain credibility by doing so.

Importantly, you will know personally if you are in a good position to sell. If the prospect of selling looks financially abysmal, you can either lower your expectations or take some time to get your business into better condition.

18.1.2 Choose the Right Time to Sell

In real estate, it is location, location, and location. In selling your business, it is timing, timing, and timing.

When is your magical "right moment" for selling? It is when your company is performing at its best. A business that is firing on all cylinders is enormously appealing to investors. The better the business is doing at making money, the higher the price can you demand.

Experienced business buyers know that there is going to be a learning curve as they acquire a new business. Investors realize that there will be some slowdown as management changes hands. If you can prove that the business is operating like a well-oiled moneymaking machine, you will be able to sell at a good price.

But you must take into consideration market conditions as well. Is your industry in a bubble? Are interest rates low or high? Is the industry expanding rapidly? The economic status of your industry segment is another critical factor in the timing of the sale.

18.2 Entrepreneurial Exit Definitions

Common to most exit definitions is the idea of reward for earlier investment in the venture, the nature of these rewards being both financial and nonfinancial, and the distinction of an ownership and a management dimension throughout the exit process.[3] Whereas the shareholding can in some cases be reduced rapidly, entrepreneurs are often linked to the future management of their businesses, primarily to ensure transition, integration, and the achievement of predefined milestones in the further development of the company.

For our purpose, the term *exit* will be clearly delineated from the term *failure*, a situation where the entrepreneur has no other option but to discontinue the firm and declare bankruptcy.[4] Watson and Everett distinguish four types of failure: discontinuance of a business for any reason, bankruptcy or loss to creditors, disposed of to prevent further losses, and failing to "make a go of it."[5]

Petty, J. W. (1997). Harvesting. In W. D. Bygrave (Ed.), *The Portable MBA in Entrepreneurship*. New York: Wiley (pp. 71–94).	"Harvesting an entrepreneurial firm is the approach taken by the owners and investors to realize terminal after-tax cash flows on their investment."
Bygrave, W. D. (1993). Towards a theory of entrepreneurship. *Journal of Business Venturing*, 8(3), 183–195. Bygrave, W. D. (1997). *The Portable MBA in Entrepreneurship*, 2nd ed. New York: Wiley.	"Exit is the final piece necessary in creating the ultimate value to all the participants in the venture, especially the owners, and employees."
Bygrave, W. D. (1997). *The Portable MBA in Entrepreneurship*, 2nd ed. New York: Wiley. Bygrave, W. D. and Hofer, C. W. (1991). Theorizing about entrepreneurship. *Entrepreneurship Theory & Practice*, 16(2), 13–22.	"The harvest is the owners' and investors' strategy for achieving the terminal after-tax cash flows on their investment. It does not necessarily mean that the entrepreneur will leave the company; it merely defines how she will extract some or all of the cash flows from the investment to be used for other purposes. Nor should it totally disregard the personal and non-financial aspects of the transaction."
Sonnefeld, J. (1988). *The Hero's Farewell*. New York: Oxford University Press.	"Entrepreneurial exit can also be viewed as part of the universal organizational problem of leadership succession, where a 'clash between an organization's goals and a leader's personal goals' occurs."

18.3 Exiting Your Business Is a Process, Not an Event

According to Phil Thompson,[6] business lawyer, there are eight rules that must be followed to ensure a successful process:

Rule 1: Do not try to sell your business yourself.

Rule 2: Have a clear understanding of why you are selling your business.

Rule 3: Have a realistic understanding of what it is you have to sell and how valuable it really is.

Rule 4: Have a good understanding of why someone would want to buy your business.

Rule 5: Get your house in order.

Rule 6: Plan to sell a business opportunity, not a pile of assets or a set of financial statements.

Rule 7: Plan to have multiple, enthusiastic buyers for your business.

Rule 8: Do not get attached to a particular price for your business; plan to let the market give you the best idea of what your business is worth.

18.4 Site Visits: Your Opportunity to Shine

Thompson further recommends that you assemble all the expressions of interest and review them with your team. Identify the most promising interested parties, using your characteristics of the ideal buyer and the expressions of interest. The most promising parties may not be those indicating the highest valuation. Knowledgeable buyers will entice you into discussions with a value they have no intention of maintaining.

Do not give anyone an exclusive option at this point, even though most buyers will tell you they do not want to participate in an "auction." Serious buyers will stay in the hunt for your business even if you tell them there are other interested buyers.

Arrange a series of introduction meetings with the most promising interested parties, including site visits to your business and more detailed presentations on your business opportunity. Ask them to present their business background, financing capability, and overall intentions.

Ask the selected parties to submit nonbinding term sheets or letters of intent by a fixed deadline, assuming they are interested in proceeding to the next step. Offer to sign a "lockup" provision with them if their preliminary offer is your first choice to negotiate and finalize.

Even at this stage, you do not have to set an asking price for your business. Let the market give you a better idea of what your business is worth.

When people ask you what you want for your business, tell them you want a fair purchase price and good deal overall, you know there is more to a good deal than price, and you are as interested in finding the right buyer as in getting the right price. Let them know you have ideas of value, which you will happily share with them if you get to the negotiation stage, but that you want your buyers to take the first crack at putting something down on paper.

Be willing to discuss all deal factors in general terms, but let it be known that you have an open mind and that everything is up for discussion to get the best deal overall with the right buyer.

18.5 10 Crucial Steps Required to Get Ready

Below are the 10 crucial steps you should take to ensure that your business is ready for an exit, as described by *Entrepreneur* magazine.[7]

18.5.1 Get a Business Valuation

One of the first things you should do is obtain a realistic idea of what your business is worth from an objective, outside source. A professional valuation will give you a basis for gauging buyer offers and will give you an idea of what you can expect to net from the sale. It will also tell you your business's market position, financial situation, strengths, and weaknesses (which you can hopefully correct prior to putting it on the market).

Valuations can be obtained from a number of sources, ranging from local accounting firms to regional business brokers and investment banking firms. As a rule, you should make sure the company performing your valuation has access to the most current national data regarding privately held transactions in your industry. Experience in selling firms of your type is obviously helpful as well.

18.5.2 Get Your Books in Order

Buyers evaluating your business generally require at least 3 years' worth of financial information. The more formal your statements (accountant reviewed or prepared vs. internally generated statements), the better the impression you will make—and the easier the due diligence for a buyer. Tax returns may suffice.

18.5.3 Understand the True Profitability of Your Business

Most privately held businesses claim a variety of nonoperational expenses. Make sure you have supporting documentation for these expenses. For example, your business may be paying for your personal automobile lease.

In addition, there may be infrequent expenses you have incurred during the past 3 years that should be excluded in a buyer's analysis of recurring cash flow. There may be moving expenses if you have moved to a larger facility or unusual legal expenses.

18.5.4 Consult Your Financial Advisor

It is wise to speak to your tax advisor for help in planning your financial future. Understanding your personal and corporate tax situation may also help you recognize your options with regard to deal structure.

18.5.5 Make a Good First Impression

Will a buyer visiting your shop for the first time see order or chaos? Buyers look for companies that show well, as an orderly shop is often indicative of an orderly management team and backroom operations.

18.5.6 Organize Your Legal Paperwork

Review your incorporation papers, permits, licensing agreements, leases, customer and vendor contracts, and so forth. Make sure you have them readily available, current, and in order.

18.5.7 Consider Management Succession

If you are absolutely vital to your business, who will a buyer be able to turn to for help running the business after you leave? You should have a succession plan in place before going to market.

18.5.8 Know Your Reason for Selling

Buyers are always curious as to why a seller wants to exit a business. (If it is so great, why are you leaving?) Be prepared to articulate your reasons.

18.5.9 Get Your Advisory Team in Place

Start interviewing attorneys and accountants who are proficient in mergers and acquisitions. Strongly consider hiring an intermediary, either a business broker or an investment banker, to represent you and help you through the selling process.

18.5.10 Keep Your Eye on the Target

Do not let your business performance decline because you are too focused on the sale of your business. This will only give buyers additional negotiating power to lower their offers.

18.6 Embarking on Your Journey

Ernst & Young recommends the following points to consider before you embark on your journey:[8]

Determining what it's worth	Although many factors determine the value of your company, at the end of the day, your business is worth what another party is willing to pay for it. Factors typically considered include current rates of return in the marketplace, growth rates, industry outlook, your organization's management structure, your business's financial and operational strength, and competitive advantages of your products or services.
Marketing your company to buyers	Every business has a story. Telling that story in a compelling way will act as a valuable sales tool and help you successfully sell your company. By strategically marketing your company's opportunities and strengths, you'll attract more interest and earn a higher value from the sale.

	To do this, focus on your company's history and reputation, highlighting your technological know-how, possession of key intellectual property and ability to realize potential synergies. Vocalizing strong customer and vendor relations and key product or service advantages won't hurt either, but a strong future outlook will be the key to producing higher-than-average returns.
Do your due diligence	A potential buyer will want to perform an extensive investigation into your company before any transaction occurs. You need to be prepared before contemplating a sale. In particular, you should ensure that all your financial and legal information is organized, analyze trends your company has seen in the past five years, and determine what information can be shared to help the buyer make an informed decision. A buyer may also want to review operations to help develop plans and identify operational issues.
Figuring out the appropriate type of sale	There are many options available to you when selling your company. Among the common types of transactions are asset sales and share sales. Although it's a more complex transaction, an asset sale offers more flexibility to the vendor and purchaser than a share sale. However, a share sale can give the seller a lower tax rate on the transaction and the option of transferring all liabilities to the buyer. But if you're going with an asset sale, be aware of possible double taxation at the corporate and shareholder levels, and a higher asking price.
	If neither of these options appeals to you, then there is another transaction option available: a hybrid sale. Hybrid sales offer more comfort through security for the buyer and continuity for the seller. Even if a sale is not in your short- or medium-term plans, structuring from the outset to facilitate a future business sale can make the end game a lot easier and less costly. When you've entered the marketing process, it's too late for many strategies.
Considering potential buyers	Organizations acquire businesses for several different reasons. A strategic buyer is looking for a business to establish or realize synergies, while a financial buyer may or may not have investments in your industry. The strategic buyer is looking to grow and capitalize by integrating other businesses, while the financial buyer acquires a company because the business (or industry) is attractive and profitable. Other purchasers include diversified groups and private individuals.
	Regardless of your choice, there will be benefits and downsides with any type of buyer, so you need to decide what you want out of the sale before you make an informed choice.
Reviewing the process	Selling a business is a lot of work. To begin, you must first select a process, either a targeted or a broad auction. You then begin building a list of potential buyers to approach during the sales process.
	Then your focus turns to marketing to draw in and approach interested buyers. When a potential buyer submits a letter of intent, it's then time to perform due diligence and solicit offers before closing the sale.
Working with an advisor	It's difficult to market your business if you don't have a clear plan. That's where an advisor can step in, to help you weigh the many options available and find one that is ideal for you.
	Bringing valuable benefits and insights to the table, your advisor can guide you through the selling process and help you determine the right approach to effectively market your business and identify potential buyers. Efficient and experienced advisors can also help you facilitate diligence, negotiate offers, assist with closing and aid with legalities.

Notes

1. Thinking about selling your business? Consider this your roadmap. HarrisWilliams&Co. https://www.pnc.com/content/dam/pnc-ideas/articles/hw_how_to_sell_updated_august_2015.pdf.
2. Patel, N. (2015). 4 ways to get your business ready to sell. *Forbes*, October 22. https://www.forbes.com/sites/neilpatel/2015/10/22/4-methods-to-sell-your-business-for-a-huge-profit/#63575b43100b.
3. Crijns, H. and Ooghe, H. (1997). *Processes in Ownership and Management in Growing Medium-Sized Entrepreneurial Studies*. Wellesley, MA: Frontiers of Entrepreneurship Research.
4. Sten, J. (1998). Exit—Success or failure? Paper presented at 43rd ICSB World Conference, Singapore.
5. Watson, J. and Everett, J. E. (1996). Do small retailers have high failure rates? Evidence from Australian retailers. *Journal of Small Business Management*, 34(4), 45–62.
6. Thompson, P. Selling your business: Ten steps and eight rules for getting the best possible deal. www.thompsonlaw.ca.
7. Preparing to sell your business. https://www.entrepreneur.com/article/40302#.
8. Selling your business? What you need to know before letting go. EY PDF © 2013 Ernst & Young LLP. A member firm of Ernst & Young Global Limited. 1122956 ED 0114 EY. http://www.ey.com/Publication/vwLUAssets/EY-Selling-yourbusiness/$FILE/EY-Sellingyour-business.pdf,.

19

Exit Strategies (Harvesting Options)

An exit occurs when an entrepreneur is financially rewarded for all of
the creativity, hard work, investment, and risk put into the startup.

19.1 Introduction

Even before you started your entrepreneurial venture, you strategized *how
you personally intended to exit*. An *exit strategy* is the way in which a venture
capitalist or business owner intends to use to monetize an investment. An
exit strategy is also called a *liquidity event*.

Planning an exit strategy is one of the most misunderstood considerations
of a business strategy, yet the exit strategy plays a crucial role in determining
the strategic direction. Founders must have a definitive exit strategy before
approaching investors, clearly reflected in their business plan. An entrepreneur's exit is both a career choice as well as a liquidation of a financial
investment.[1]

This is euphemistically called *harvesting*. Harvesting is the term used
to describe a major monetizing event from the business you created by
taking the company public, selling it, merging with a larger company,
out-licensing the technology, and so on. Waking up one day as a mul-
timillionaire and exiting your "baby" is a life-changing event. Are you
prepared?

Keep in mind that the term *harvest* refers to an event where the venture
continues while the entrepreneur exits as both manager and major investor.
Figure 19.1 summarizes some of the common strategies envisioned by founders prior to approaching potential investors.

19.2 "Bountiful Harvest"

Bygrave and Timmons[2] help introduce this topic: "Just like farmers, venture
capitalists seed, tend, and feed portfolio companies in the hopes of reaping

Harvesting your business

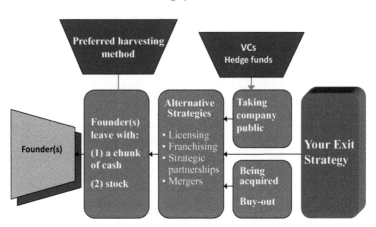

FIGURE 19.1
How do you personally intend to exit?

a bountiful harvest." Founder-owners and investors know that harvesting an entrepreneurial venture is the preferred approach taken by the owners and investors to realize terminal after-tax cash flows on their investment. It defines how they will extract (monetize) some or all of the economic value from their investment.[3]

Just because an entrepreneurial team can build a successful business does not mean they can become rich from it. Investors who provide equity financing to high-risk ventures need to know how and when they are likely to realize a return on their investments before they commit any funds. They invest not for eternity but on average for 3 to 7 years, after which they expect to make a profit that reflects the scale of the risk they have taken on in making their investment. An exit should be seen as a critical milestone that focuses on the monetization of their investment. It is at this critical stage in the entrepreneurial life cycle that the capital gains (or losses) occur; in other words, there is a harvest (or an exit) from the investment.

Your exit strategy is crucial because it helps you define your ultimate success in business. When entrepreneurs have not thought through an exit strategy, it may be an indicator that they are not focused on the eventual transition of the venture. There is a saying among venture capitalists: "It's easy to get into an investment, but how do we get out?" And investors do not want an exit strategy to be difficult or bloody. In essence, having a harvest goal and a strategy to achieve it is indeed what separates successful entrepreneurs from the rest of the pack.

19.3 Making Your Business Marketable

Business owners considering selling their business should consider ways of making their businesses *marketable*. Some of the considerations include

- **Current and future profitability:** Purchasers need to feel confident in the ability of the business to continue to be profitable in the future. Evidence of predictable and stable cash flows and revenues will greatly encourage potential buyers.
- **Growth potential:** Provide evidence that the business operates in a growth market and can continue to operate profitably in the future.
- **Strong brand and customer loyalty:** A loyal customer base will be very appealing to buyers, particularly in the medical and high-tech industries.

19.4 Typical Exit Strategies

Common to all exit strategies is the concept of a large financial reward for an earlier risky investment in the venture. However, every exit strategy has advantages and disadvantages. Table 19.1 highlights both and may provide you with some considerations you have not thought of before. These exit strategies can take a business to its next stage. As your business transitions to the next stage, you may end your involvement or remain with the business in a new role.

19.5 Selling to Your Senior Team (MBO)

When it comes time for the owner to sell the business, the natural thought is to "sell to the highest bidder." This is often done as a part of the "auction" process. Sometimes this makes sense, but other times it does not. The advantages of selling to the highest bidder include a potential higher valuation. However, disadvantages may include your company's financials and customer lists becoming available to many interested suitors and maybe even your competitors.[4]

Selling to the highest bidder generally involves "going public." But going public as an exit strategy is a big endeavor. Your company has to be big enough

TABLE 19.1

Exit Strategies Available to the Founder-Entrepreneur

Types of Exit Strategies (Harvesting)	Description	Advantages	Disadvantages
Merger with another company	A joining together of two previously separate corporations. A true merger in the legal sense occurs when both businesses dissolve and move their assets and liabilities into a newly created entity.	Sellers may receive cash and/or stock, the resources of both companies are combined, and some of the management may remain in place.	New owners or executives may have different philosophies or ways of doing business. Original staff may have less control, and integrating the two cultures may be difficult.
Acquisition by another company	An acquisition occurs when one entity takes ownership of another entity's stock, equity interests, or assets.	Sellers receive cash or stock for the sale, and the management contract is negotiable for the owner to stay on during transition.	Fit is not always appropriate for the business or employees, and the corporate identity or brand may diminish.
Sale to senior team (MBO)	Company is sold to senior management, where all the assets are sold.	Sellers may receive cash immediately or over time. Often business milestones (incentives) are attached to additional cash.	May be difficult to find the right buyer at the right price and changes in ownership may be difficult for employees.
Franchise of the company	The business concept is replicated and the company expands locally, regionally, nationally, or internationally.	Franchisor receives cash for each franchise, current corporate management is maintained, and the enterprise sees an opportunity for large-scale growth.	Process may be difficult and time-consuming, and the business concept may not be appropriate for franchising. Finding suitable location(s) may be complicated.
Employee stock ownership plan (ESOP)	An ESOP is an employee–owner program that provides a company's workforce with an ownership interest in the company. Employees receive shares or stock of the company over time.	Key employees are rewarded for their contributions, receive incentives for staying with the company for a number of years, and share in the profits of the company they have helped to grow.	Owner can borrow funds from the plan as a loan to the company; employees may lose their shares if they leave the company; and if the value of the company or company stock decreases, the employees share in the burden.

(Continued)

TABLE 19.1 (CONTINUED)

Exit Strategies Available to the Founder-Entrepreneur

Types of Exit Strategies (Harvesting)	Description	Advantages	Disadvantages
Initial public offering (IPO)	An IPO is the first sale of stock by a private company to the public. IPOs are often smaller, younger companies seeking capital to expand their business.	Shares convert to cash for investors, major shareholders control the company, and investors see potentially high returns.	Company needs high growth to generate earnings and investors' interest, process is costly, and the outcome is uncertain.

to justify all the additional regulatory requirements under Sarbanes–Oxley. An *initial public offering* (IPO) as an exit strategy is complex, time-consuming, and phenomenally expensive for a small company.

Is there a better way? As a possible exit strategy, owner-entrepreneurs may consider their senior team as potential buyers of their business. The technical term for this transaction is a *management buyout* (MBO). There are several advantages to selling to your management team as a real exit option, and not a last resort, as listed in Table 19.2.

19.5.1 Your Senior Team as Ideal Successors

The classic MBO is a transaction where the owner of a company sells some or all of the shares in that company to a new company that has been set up by the senior management team, paid for by the senior management team,

TABLE 19.2

Advantages of an MBO to Selling Owner(s)

Rewarding those that made it all possible	By selling to your management, you are rewarding the people who helped make you successful.
Selling to an informed and motivated buyer	Your senior team intimately *know* the business and growth opportunities better than anyone. They are likely to pay a reasonable price because they are confident in their knowledge of the company and their ability to execute growth strategies.
Accelerated due diligence	The due diligence phase is typically faster and less intrusive when selling to the management. Senior management is already familiar with the ins and outs/ups and downs of your company. Selling to an outsider will most likely take significantly longer to close a transaction relative to selling to the management team.
Not exposing your competitive advantages to outsiders	If you try to sell your business to an outsider, you may have several potential suitors digging through significant financial and operational details, as they obviously need to know what they are buying.

private equity investors, and a bank. Around 15% of private exits have some MBO element.

It is increasingly common for the seller to retain an interest in the company in the form of debt that is repaid by the company over time. This is called an *earn-out* or *vendor financing* and, in extreme cases, it is vendor financed (i.e., the seller is prepared to transfer ownership of the company but only receives payment if and when the company is in a position to pay back the debt). In these circumstances, a seller will typically require security or other rights of priority to ensure payment is made.

According to business lawyer Phil Thompson,[5] your senior team may be your ideal successors because

- They know the company as well or better than you.
- They respect and trust you, otherwise they should not be working for you.
- They already have a lot "invested" in the business emotionally and career-wise.
- Since maximizing price requires purchasers who are comfortable with the risks of the company at the time of sale, your senior managers represent excellent potential buyers.
- They know the risks and opportunities associated with the business and should be comfortable with their ability to manage them.
- Your other stakeholders—customers, suppliers, employees, and lenders—will probably be familiar and comfortable with your senior managers.
- You have a chance to prepare them to take over the business.
- They are more likely to permit you to leave lines of communication and tentacles of control in the business than a true third-party purchaser.
- You can often phase things over time and keep control of the business until the right moment.
- Management buyouts are usually earn-out based with lots of vendor take-back financing, two factors that usually result in a higher valuation for the business.

Figure 19.2 presents the classical funding mechanism for an MBO.

An MBO can represent a solution to those owners who have a successful company but don't have a succession plan in place. It goes without saying that without a vendor who is prepared to sell, there is no deal; however, many vendors do not take the time to seriously consider all of their liquidity options.[6]

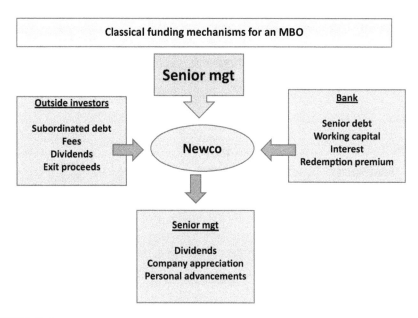

FIGURE 19.2
Classical funding mechanisms for an MBO.

In some instances, a buyout may be the vendor's best option due to the nature of the business and the lack of succession options. Those vendors who are in a position to pursue multiple options (Figure 19.3) should consider the elements of a buyout and the main reasons for pursuing it.

The selling owner-entrepreneur (vendor) may have the following motivations:

- The vendor may pursue a buyout because you want to compensate management with an equity stake in the future growth prospects of the company. From this point of view, the vendor crystallizes his investment in the company while rewarding the core management team that helped her generate the return.

- Selling to management significantly decreases the risk of exposing confidential information. As an owner, it can be unnerving to proceed with a sale process with a third party due to the overwhelmingly sensitive nature of the company's operations. A buyout represents an opportunity for the vendor to sell a controlling interest in the company without having to provide confidential information to a strategic purchaser (i.e., a competitor).

- Management represents a sophisticated buyer who is already well educated on the operations of the business; therefore, the timeline of the sale process may be shortened and the risk of not closing may be less compared with selling to a strategic purchaser.

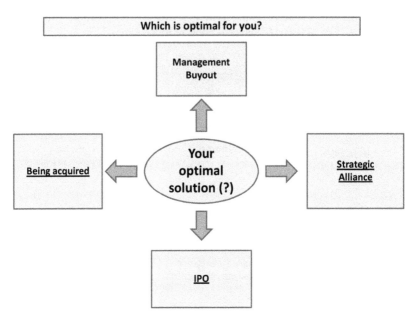

FIGURE 19.3
Which is best for you?

- Management may not continue with the business if a third-party transaction takes place. In this situation, the vendor may be forced to pursue a buyout or be handcuffed.
- The cyclical nature and niche aspects of the business may not be understood by an external party, therefore a buyout may represent the best option for the vendor.
- It is important to understand that the key to a successful MBO is entering the process for the right reasons. If value is the highest priority for a vendor, an MBO may not be preferable as the management team will not have access to the same amount of capital as a strategic purchaser would. These and other motivations are key to understanding what a successful buyout looks like.

19.5.2 Biggest Senior MBO Mistakes

According to the MBO Group,[7] MBOs present significant opportunities for business owners, financial sponsors, and entrepreneurial management. For the business owner it is often a chance to exit, retire, and unlock their wealth in the business.

From the perspective of the buyout management, MBOs provide an opportunity to gain direct equity ownership of the business and maintain an entrepreneurial environment. And an MBO is likely to be the best way for the senior team to build significant personal wealth.

But pursuing an MBO is extremely demanding. The pressures on managers, colleagues, family, and friends can be severe. And this is just to complete the deal. Once you've bought your company, the difficulties and challenges are unlikely to abate. The risks can be significant, even for a well-managed and successful business. Managers can largely reduce the stress by understanding the lessons learned by managers and advisors who have been through the process before them.

The MBO Group identifies the following biggest mistakes made by the senior team:

1. **Not having a leader and confusing *ownership* and *employment*:**

   The senior team might all invest the same amount of money, so some might think that everyone has an equal say in running the business.

   This won't work. It is absolutely essential to understand that each member is an employee first and a shareholder second. No organization can operate without a leader; someone has to have the final say and make the tough decisions. While MBO companies typically have better corporate cultures than non-MBOs, they still require the presence a strong capable leader.

   Once the MBO is completed, individuals will feel better about expressing their views on the business, but there still needs to be one boss! And being a shareholder does not change this. Being a shareholder means that members benefit from the success of the business and the efforts of the new team; it does not mean that each member has an equal say on how the business is going to be managed.

2. **Getting greedy: The wrong mix of financing:**

   There are various sources of financing that may be available to complete your deal—banks, term lenders, subordinated debt providers, private equity, vendor financing—all of which have different costs and attributes. Banks are the cheapest form of financing, but they have strict rules, while private equity is very expensive but also more patient.

   You may well be tempted to go for the cheapest financing and the one that allows members to keep the most equity. This may not be the best approach. Why? Because the financing that you get to buy your company must also allow you to grow the company and weather the bumps along the road that you will inevitably experience.

   Once the team runs some financial "what if" scenarios, it may be decided that, for the long-term success, it would be better having a smaller piece of a much more successful and stable pie. This means financing the MBO with more equity-type money and less bank debt.

3. **Not understanding your financial partners:**

   Each of the sources of financing noted has their unique rules of engagement, and it's very important that you understand these rules. Banks are not your equity partners, and bringing on a private equity investor is very different from what banks expect.

   Obviously, all financial partners need to be treated with openness, honesty, and full disclosure. But one of the keys to successfully growing the buyout business is to understand what each of your financial partners will and will not do.

4. **Not spending enough time on the shareholders agreement:**

   There is probably not a more critical document for you and your managers in the MBO than the shareholders agreement, and it can also be one of the most difficult to craft properly.

   A well-drafted shareholders agreement has to address all those difficult "what if" questions, such as what happens if someone gets sick, dies, or is fired (with or without cause), and what are the issues going forward that require a majority consent from the shareholders.

   How a shareholder exits the business and how, and at what value, they sell their shares is a key topic that needs to be spelled out in the shareholders agreement. While many of these topics can result in fairly emotional discussions, getting these important issues on the table before closing the deal will avoid massive headaches and disruption down the road. Don't kid yourselves; these issues will arise, so take care of them up front.

5. **Not being candid and honest about key issues:**

   The best candidate for an MBO is a business (or business unit) that can assume debt and is stagnating because management is being prevented from unlocking upside revenue opportunities by the current owners.

   In order to unlock the revenue potential, the MBO plan often calls for increased investment in product development, new equipment, staff training, marketing, and in the case of *carve-outs* of non-strategic assets, a new accounting system. The management must operate as a team that can adapt to the new environment and unlock the upside revenue and accomplish other key objectives. If there are fault lines within management, they will be exposed. The sooner these issues are dealt with candidly and honestly, the greater the chances of success of the MBO.

6. **Deal fever: Taking your eyes off the ball:**

   The MBO process is seldom straightforward or smooth. Negotiations often get derailed. Managers are tempted to focus more on the deal than the business, and if the business results start to deteriorate, it can scare off financial backers or raise the suspicion of the business's owner-seller that management is deliberately impacting the results to help build the case to lower the price.

Provided that the management team is well advised, it is usually possible to ensure that management is not exposed, or "left holding the baby," if the deal fails to complete. One of the key benefits of dealing with a good advisor is that they ensure that you are not swamped by trying to do a deal, allowing you to remain focused on your company's operations.

7. **Not anticipating potential "deal-breaker" issues:**

Some of the surprises that arise during an MBO that threaten to derail the process include

- Landlords who are not willing to let the seller off the hook on leases
- Unexpected deal costs (including legal fees) that make it difficult to close the deal with the arranged financing
- Financial backers changing the terms of their deal once they have completed their due diligence
- An inability of your financial partners to agree on the terms of how they will deal with each other (covered in an inter-lender agreement)
- Managers getting cold feet and opting out of the MBO

An experienced advisor will have seen most of these issues before and will take steps to address them early in the process so as to minimize their risk to the deal.

8. **Not making the tough decisions:**

Once the MBO is completed, the fate of the venture, to a large degree, rests in the hands of the new management. Management will be faced with difficult decisions that need to be made in order to successfully grow the business.

These decisions are made even more difficult if they involve managers who have participated in the MBO. Sometimes downsizing is required. Sometimes (more often than you would think) someone on your MBO team figures that, now that they are an owner, the rules don't apply to them anymore. Most leaders who are faced with these tough decisions and who delay in making them end up regretting not taking action sooner. And while it's hard to fire someone who helped you buy the company, you owe it to your other partners to make the right decisions and move on.

9. **Not appreciating that you are in it for the long haul:**

Most MBO companies do better than their non-MBO peers. It's not surprising to see companies excel post MBO (studies have actually tracked this phenomenon). And as owners, you and your team may be keen to start seeing a return on your invested capital.

Since you have probably taken on a significant amount of debt to finance your MBO, it's important that your "financial" focus be on paying down this debt as quickly as possible.

You need to go into an MBO with your eyes open; most of your financial partners expect to be paid out before you see any money (and while most bankers will consider allowing dividends at year-end, its best to assume that they will say no). A good rule of thumb is that you should consider your money locked in for at least 5 years, assuming that you remain with the company. Provisions obviously need to be made to allow you to get your money out should you end up leaving the company.

10. **Not having an advisor:**

Advisors and financial backers can help make or break a deal. For a manager, an MBO is a life-changing experience and so it is important to pick an advisor that your managers can really trust, who will take the time to "educate" you on the risks of what potentially awaits you, and who will not just discuss the upside.

An MBO advisor, like a golf pro, can help with selecting the right financial backers to get the MBO done while management focuses on running the business. There is no shortage of accountants, legal firms, bankers, and private equity firms that have an appetite for a good deal. However, it is important for the management team to feel very comfortable with their advisors and backers; it is a bumpy ride, and the managers may not be able to grasp all the ramifications as the process unfolds!

19.5.3 Typical Timetable and Process

Each MBO is different. Some can have a gestation period of several years, particularly if new MBO team members need to be recruited and become proven before the MBO team can initiate the process. It can be a difficult first step for a potential MBO team to raise the idea with owners and vice versa. Generally, it makes sense for the MBO team to have at least expressions of interest from funders before raising it, and getting to this stage can take some time.[8]

Once an MBO team is together and the underlying company is a viable target, the process typically lasts 6 to 9 months. Each of the following stages is usually required.

- Appointment of lead adviser and lawyers to management team
- Approach to seller (now or once funding is in place in principle)

- Agreement of outline terms with seller
- Preparation of information memorandum by lead adviser
- Discussions with outside investors and bank backers
- Selection of outside investors and bank
- Agreement of detailed heads of agreement with seller, outside investors, and bank
- Commencement of due diligence
- Preparation of investment agreements and share purchase agreements
- Due diligence/disclosure process
- Agreement of MBO team contracts and share options
- Completion

19.5.4 How Does an MBO Work?

The investment firm Zachary Scott provides the following example.[9]

Consider Acme Enterprises, a hypothetical company having $22 million of revenue and earning before interest, tax, depreciation, and amortization (EBITDA) of $3.3 million. A reasonable, perhaps even a bit conservative, enterprise value (outstanding debt + value of equity) would be $18.2 million, which represents a 5.5× multiple of EBITDA. After accounting for transaction expenses, a total of $18.9 million would be required to fund the Acme Enterprises buyout.

In today's aggressive credit markets, it should be possible to borrow senior debt equal to 3.0× EBITDA and another 1.5× of mezzanine debt. Equity of $3.9 million is required to fill out the capital structure. In this example, the financial investor (private equity firm) kicks in $3.3 million and management pulls together $600,000 of equity.

In order to fully compensate the mezzanine lender, it would be granted a 16% equity position (typically nominal-cost warrants), leaving 84% of the equity value for the owners. Assuming that 10% of the equity is carved out for management as an incentive after the cash investors' capital is returned, the financial investors and management would split the incremental value created on an 84.6% and 15.4% basis, respectively.

If management's vision of Acme Enterprises' future performance (7% compound annual growth and 15% EBITDA margin) comes to fruition, at the end of five years, Acme would be generating EBITDA of $4.6 million on revenue of $30.9 million. Assuming that there is a liquidity event at that point, and the business is valued on the same multiple (5.5×) as it was purchased, the company would be worth $25.5 million, as total enterprise value grew by $6.6 million over five years. More importantly, the equity share of the value pie expanded from $3.6 million to $17.6 million as the company's cash flow was allocated to paying down the senior debt. Results are pretty attractive—the mezzanine lender earns a 20% return based on the 12% coupon and the implied value of the warrants; the cash investors triple their investment to earn a 29% annual return, and management earns an additional $1.1 million from the incentive shares for an all-in return of almost 40%. This was a successful deal because the key elements—purchase price, performance expectations, and capital structure—were aligned, all having been considered in the design of the transaction from the outset. Interestingly, this outcome creates an opportunity for managers to now own a controlling interest in the company by rolling their gains and re-leveraging the company to take out the investors.

19.6 Strategic Alliances

> You have to break eggs to make omelets.

Strategic alliances represent a way for aggressive companies to pursue growth by broadening product lines, penetrating new markets, and stabilizing cyclical businesses despite limited resources.

A strategic alliance is an agreement between two or more parties to pursue a set of agreed-on objectives while still remaining independent organizations. This form of cooperation lies between M&A and organic growth.[10] But it is the exchange of managerial talent, resources, capabilities, and possibly an equity investment that elevates the alliance beyond a mere contractual agreement. The three main characteristics of strategic alliances are as follows:

1. Multifaceted, goal-oriented, long-term partnerships between two companies.
2. Both risks and rewards are shared.
3. Typically lead to long-term strategic relationships.

19.6.1 The "Big Question"

Before embarking on any strategic alliance quest, management must answer the "big question":

Do we create organic sales growth versus sales growth through acquisitions? The firm can grow organically (by internal investment) or inorganically (by strategic alliances—i.e., *cooperative ventures, joint ventures* (JV), *joint ownership,* or *mergers and acquisitions* [M&A]). One theoretical way of approaching the

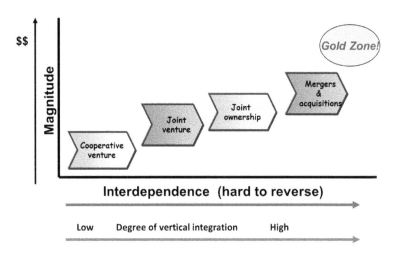

FIGURE 19.4
Continuum of strategic alliance options.

"big question" is to look at the continuum of strategic partnerships interdependence, as shown in Figure 19.4.

When two or more companies combine to participate in a project, it is a cooperative venture. This participation can be in the form of sharing financial or technical resources for mutual benefit.

A JV creates a separate entity in which both firms invest. The JV agreement specifies investment rights, operational responsibilities, voting control, exit alternatives, and generally the allocation of risks and rewards. The entity could be a division or an entirely new business established for the venture.

In a *joint ownership* alliance, the parties agree to long-term licensing agreements, co-marketing agreements, co-development agreements, joint purchasing agreements, and/or long-term supply or toll agreements, with each party owning 50% of the intellectual property plus other non-tangible assets.

Lastly, M&A is a general term used to refer to the consolidation of two independent companies to form an entirely new company, while an acquisition is the purchase of one company by another in which no new company is formed.

19.6.2 Drivers of M&A Activities

> You name the price. I'll name the terms.

M&A activities display a unique set of *drivers*, summarized in Table 19.3.

TABLE 19.3

M&A Strategic Drivers

Push Factors
- Technology
- Increased regulation

Pull Factors
- Use of equity as currency
- Greater liquidity

Vertical Integration
- Global presence
- Entry into developing economies

Historically, M&A presents management with the following hard-to-resist list of opportunities:

- Geographic expansion
- Market leadership position
- Broadened intellectual property portfolio
- Becoming a larger company
- Manufacturing and distribution synergies
- Immediate increase in infrastructure
- Broader product offering

Every M&A transaction has it own set of unique reasons for combining the two companies. From management's standpoint, the underlying principle behind an M&A transaction is deceptively simple: $2+2=5$. The value of the acquirer is $2 billion and the value of the acquired is $2 billion, but when we merge the two companies, the market values the new entity at $5 billion. This is classical *synergy*.

In addition to perceived synergies, there are real strategic drivers to M&A activities. Figure 19.5 summarizes the strategic picture.

19.6.3 Advantages of Strategic Alliances

Traditionally, inorganic growth can be achieved by the judicious use of strategic alliances. Strategic alliances are multifaceted, goal-oriented, long-term partnerships between two companies. In a strategic alliance, both risks and rewards are shared and typically lead to long-term strategic benefits for both partners, as follows:

- Adding value to products
- Improving market access
- Strengthening operations

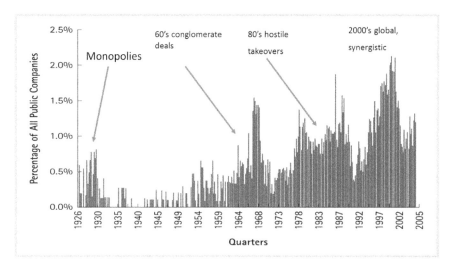

FIGURE 19.5
M&A historically occur in waves.

- Adding technological strength
- Enhancing strategic growth
- Enhancing organizational skills
- Building financial strength

In addition, strategic alliances display other benefits, such as those seen in Figure 19.6.

19.6.4 Pitfalls of Strategic Alliances

Buying all or part of a business is one of the most complex strategic moves a company can make. Despite the number and size of headline-making deals in the popular press, research indicates that success rate of strategic alliances is very low. Short-term stock price results can be summarized as shown in Table 19.4.[11]

Of course the pitfalls of strategic alliances are legendary. In general, alliance conflict emanates from six core areas, as shown in Figure 19.7.

According to alliance guru Ed Rigsbee,[12] conflict doesn't have to be a roadblock to a successful alliance if you and your partnering alliance members are willing to resolve the conflict at the core level, in a timely manner. In fact, the resolved conflict can lead to a stronger relationship through improved communication. Unfortunately, conflict that is left unresolved will lead to fatal flaws that will erode the relationship. Some of the more common areas of conflict in alliance relationships are accessibility, culture clashes,

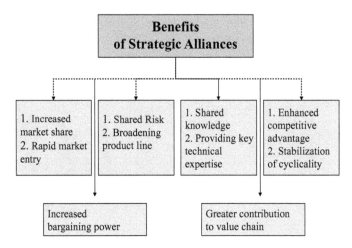

FIGURE 19.6
Strategic alliances and their benefits.

hidden agendas, management tenure, poor communications, and unrealistic expectations.

19.6.4.1 Example of a Partnering Pitfall (TIMEX)

Rigsbee selected Timex, who forfeited $60 million in lost revenue and learned about the challenges of partnering overseas. You could say it took a licking and kept on ticking. After 18 months of frustration, Timex wanted out of the partnership it created in India. It all started a decade ago when it was illegal to export watches into India. Timex wanted into the market and proceeded to select a local watchmaker as its partner. Unfortunately, Timex should have spent more time on due diligence and asked around a bit more about the partner-to-be. Timex assumed it could dominate the relationship and have the Indian manufacturer carry out its manufacturing needs on cue.

Was Timex surprised? The head of Timex's joint venture in India, Robert Werner, was quoted in a *Los Angeles Times* article as stating, "Until its Indian joint venture, Timex had been accustomed to owning companies outright, and its problems in India were a learning experience for many at Timex." He

TABLE 19.4

M&A by the Numbers

Short-term stock price	Seller's price increases, whereas buyer's stock price decreases.
Premium over pre-merger price = 38%	Announcement price reaction: Target = +16% Acquirer = −1%
Long-term performance	Over 80% lost market value in the first 2 years post transaction.

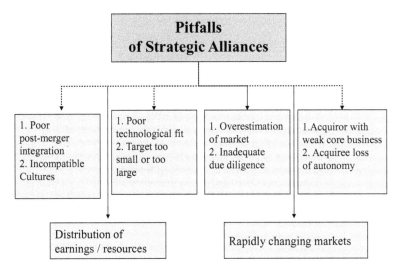

FIGURE 19.7
The six major pitfalls of strategic alliances.

said it took Timex 6 months of negotiations and an undisclosed settlement before the company could rid itself of the partner.

Today, Timex is happily partnered with Indian watchmaker Titan Industries, a subsidiary of Tata Group, one of the largest corporations in India. The Timex–Tata joint venture went to market in late 1992 and in its first year sold 400,000 watches. Two years later, annual sales leaped to 1.9 million watches.

Once you get back in the action, you can go after small wins to reestablish your confidence to take risks in pursuit of an even larger prize. The key is to not wait for all to be perfect before you commence. It's okay to subscribe to the idea of "ready, shoot, aim," but take the time to adjust your aim after you begin. Be like a commercial airline pilot and course correct regularly. Keep your future focus on the partnering journey. Keep it improving. Be decisive, and show the qualities of a leader in your industry. You will be rewarded.

19.6.4.2 Partnering Pitfalls Description

Finally, Rigsbee identified the pitfalls described in Table 19.5.

19.7 Mergers and Acquisitions

M&A is an aspect of corporate strategy, corporate finance, and management dealing with the buying, selling, dividing, and combining of different

TABLE 19.5

Partnering Pitfalls

Pitfalls	Description
Values based	In looking at the issue of values, partners of an alliance will frequently have core values that are conflicting. This is especially a problem with issues such as trust and integrity. Corporate culture clashes, employee turf protection, and resistance of certain employees to new ideas can wreak havoc on your efforts to maintain a prosperous alliance. When one of the alliance partners does not completely embrace the principles of partnering, big challenges occur. This can include top-level executives or even supervisory and functional employees in departments, divisions, or regions within a partnering organization. As an example, DuPont believes that if a contractor is looking just to maximize his profits, on just one job, then partnering with that contractor is not for DuPont because they know there will be problems in the relationship. There is the situation where you might lose control of a technology or best practice to an alliance partner who later becomes a competitor. Staples and Office Depot were going to merge, but it did not work out. A problem for Office Depot was that Staples learned of an Office Depot best practice during the merger talks. Office Depot was delivering COD to small businesses in the northeast and getting most of the business. After the failed merger, Staples duplicated Office Depot's practice and took away Office Depot's competitive advantage in the area.
Goals based	In situations where a customer is the driving force behind a partnering arrangement, you can be left holding the bag. Be sure to examine each partnering proposal in the context of your company's overall business strategy. This challenge was recently apparent to IBM, and it discontinued its alliance with Somerset PowerPC and Motorola in producing microprocessors for Apple. When sitting down at the partnering table, a partner might find the relationship seat uncomfortable. It could be that your partner has a different level of emotional and physical comfort, or sometimes it is simply a change in corporate strategy or a restructuring that leads away from a partner's product and/or technology, causing the partners distress. It is important that you know the short- and long-term goals of your alliance partner. When you try to partner with a potential or current customer and have them renege on the promise of purchasing from you, the disloyalty challenges that can occur can be wasteful. Be cautious, as there is also the possibility of your partner being unethical and attempting to capture your technology or trade secrets. This is a difficult area from which to protect yourself, but if you do your due diligence, your chances for success increase.
Facts based	Relinquishing some control with the expectation of greater shared returns can be a difficult waiting game. Additionally, your resources can get pulled in too many directions based on collective alliance decisions. Be certain you can spare the resources you devote to your alliance. Otherwise, you may put the success of your entire operation in harm's way.

(Continued)

TABLE 19.5 (CONTINUED)

Partnering Pitfalls

Pitfalls	Description
	The lack of third-party cooperation can be a true relationship problem. All the primary members of a partnering agreement will have to "give a little" for your agreement to work. Worse yet is your partner receiving unfavorable or harmful media coverage. This is because you are usually pulled into the picture and believed guilty by association. Real or perceived, image and reputation are critical to any company's success.
	Be careful in global alliances. Contracts with an overseas market, for instance, often take a long time to finalize. By the time you get going in the technology industries, your competition may have already gotten started. If you are already behind and you have developed an alliance with a partner organization that is weak and bleeding, they will only bring you down faster and harder.
Procedures based	It is easy to underestimate how much time, energy, and resources will be necessary to commit to your new alliance. Then, not having access to your alliance partner's employees is an important issue. The closer the planned relationship between the two companies, the greater the importance of the linkages between them. You might find yourself in a situation of a small company partnering with a large company. A challenge in working together will be that the representatives, usually top executives, of the small company can make decisions on the spot. Unfortunately, the employees of the giant must take a proposal up the chain of command. This sometimes slows progress to a snail's pace.
	Culture clash is a frequent partnering challenge. The failed alliance of IBM and Apple is a typical example. The heralded fall 1991 announcement promising cooperation eventually spawned Taligent Technology and Kaleida Labs. Unfortunately, the two could not coexist, so the alliances eventually gave way to a quiet winter 1995–1996 breakup.
Misinformation based	You could easily be guilty of underestimating the complexity of coordinating and integrating corporate resources, and overestimating your partner's abilities to achieve the end result. Self-doubt and not believing you have the skills and tools to create an alliance can crop up here.
	Eventually, partnering success depends on management's abilities, skills, commitment, aspirations, and passions in assembling the pieces of the puzzle. When unequal dependence in a relationship occurs, the partner with the least dependence could be less likely to compromise and put energy into the relationship.
	Meanings assigned to words by different cultures can cause serious problems. In one culture quick delivery could mean a day, and in another it could mean a month. This opens the can of worms often referred to as *unrealistic expectations* of a partner's capabilities. The areas commonly include technology, research, production skills, marketing might, and financial backing.
	The unexpected inefficiencies or poor management practices of a partner can be the demise of a well-intended alliance plan. Also at risk is the area of developing an alliance with multiple partners who later become rivals to one another. This puts a serious strain on the integrity of the remaining alliance.

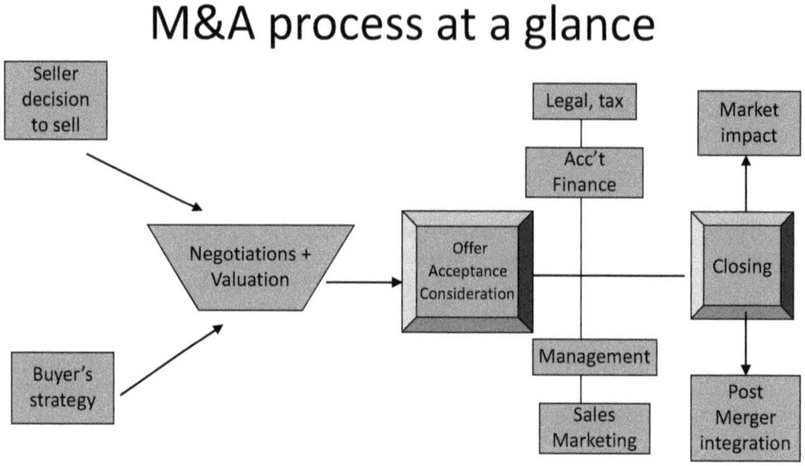

M&A process at a glance

FIGURE 19.8
Merger and acquisitions process.

companies and similar entities that can help an enterprise grow rapidly in its sector or location of origin, or in a new field or new location, without creating a subsidiary or child entity or using a joint venture,[13] as depicted in Figure 19.8.

Big companies stink at innovation but are good at M&A of smaller entities. Most established companies spend more money acquiring startups than on R&D. For example, Cisco also prefers to "buy rather than build." According to Basil Peters,[14] fund manager for Fundamental Technologies II, "It is also a great time to sell a business because large companies are sitting on loads of cash. This situation presents a problem for company management because shareholders want them to either invest the capital to create growth or distribute it to the shareholders as dividends. Distributing cash is considered an admission of defeat for tech company management because it shows they don't have any ideas about how to invest cash to increase shareholder value."

There has also been a remarkable growth in private equity buyout funds in the past few years. These funds are similar to what used to be called *merchant banks* years ago. These funds often buy companies for cash, operate them for a few years, make them highly profitable, and then resell them, usually for a significant gain.

Often, private equity funds will purchase a number of companies in an industry and increase their value by consolidating and realizing operating synergies and efficiencies. These funds are very active acquirers of companies in the under-$30 million range.

It is logical that the optimum strategy for tech startups today is to design the company and its corporate DNA so that everyone is aligned around the idea of a company acquisition in the under-$30 million range. The good news is that these exits can often be completed in just a few years from startup.

Founding a tech startup has a much higher probability of success than swinging for the fences and hoping for a big homerun NASDAQ initial public offering. This exit strategy was nicely summarized in "The New Homerun" by Tom Stein[15] in *Mergers & Acquisitions Magazine*, when he said, "Startups must be content with hitting singles or doubles, that is, a buyout of [less than] $50 million."

19.7.1 Merger Definition

Theoretically, a *merger* happens when two firms agree to go forward as a single new company rather than remain separately owned and operated. This kind of action is more precisely referred to as a *merger of equals*. In practice, however, actual mergers of equals don't happen very often. Usually, one company will buy another and, as part of the deal's terms, simply allow the acquired firm to proclaim that the action is a merger of equals, even if it is technically an acquisition.

19.7.2 Acquisition Definition

Practically speaking, an *acquisition* is the process through which one company completely takes over the controlling interest of another company. Such controlling interest may be 100%, or nearly 100%, of the assets or ownership equity of the acquired entity. An acquisition usually refers to a purchase of a smaller firm by a larger one.

There are two sets of stockholders affected by a merger or acquisition: those of the firm being acquired and those of the firm doing the acquiring.

19.7.3 Challenges of M&A

There are many examples of successful M&A (and many more failures). The most spectacular M&A failure of all time was the acquisition of Time Warner by AOL. In January 2000, AOL merged with Time Warner in a deal valued at a stunning $350 billion. It was then, and is now, the largest merger (and eventual de-merger) in U.S. business history.

Due to the larger market capitalization of AOL, they would own 55% of the new company, while Time Warner shareholders owned only 45%, so in actual practice AOL had acquired Time Warner, even though AOL had far fewer assets and revenues.[16]

What was the perception of the average stockholder when AOL offered such a large premium over market price to purchase Time Warner? The average AOL stockholder wondered whether the acquisition was being made in their interest or in the interest of management. Some important lessons have been learned from the AOL–Time Warner failure. The following four criteria have been offered as success principles for M&A/strategic alliances:[17]

- Compatible strategy and culture
- No overpayment
- Comparable contribution
- Compatible strengths
- No conflict of interest

So what is an M&A success and what is an M&A failure? Is it a matter of luck, perception, or timing? The author recommends a quantitative measure, based on return on invested capital (ROIC) and weighted average cost of capital (WACC), as shown in Table 19.6.

19.7.4 Enduring Questions

Prior to consummation of the transaction, the buyer and the seller find themselves in an adversarial position. Table 19.7 lists the 10 most frequently asked

TABLE 19.6

Quantization of M&A Success or Failure

Success	Failure
ROIC < WACC	ROIC > WACC
where:	
ROIC = earnings before interest and taxes/(invested capital equity + long term liabilities)	
WACC = sum of after-tax debt and equity × their respective % of capital structure	

TABLE 19.7

Ten Most Frequently Asked Questions

Seller	Buyer
Why is their offering price so low?	Why is their asking price so high?
Are they bottom fishing?	Are they serious about selling?
Is it OK for us to shop around?	This should be a no-shop negotiation.
Why are they interested in us?	What do we really know about them?
Do we really need money now?	What will they do with our money?
Is this transaction for cash or shares?	What are their future financial demands?
Who should be part of our negotiation team?	Are we really negotiating with the decision makers?
How much independence do we retain post transaction?	How do we integrate them into our winning culture?
Could we do better on our own?	Do we really need them?
What happens if the deal collapses? How vulnerable do we remain?	What if we find deal-killers during due diligence?
What happens if our CEO is run over by the mythical train during negotiations?	How indispensable is their CEO? Do they have a succession strategy?

questions in buying or selling a business. Paradoxically, although the questions look similar, the answers are not (Table 19.7).

19.7.5 M&A Best Practices

There are two schools of thought regarding M&A transactions. Practitioners of the first school argue that transactions are accomplished by the hubris of the two respective executives, with details negotiated later by the respective company specialists. The second school of thought recognizes the intricacies of the transaction and develops a mutually acceptable systematic methodology, thus increasing the likelihood of long-term success.

The establishment of a formal methodology for analyzing a potential M&A transactions is the difference between an amateur and an experienced buyer. Table 19.8 presents a summary of best practices to be followed.

19.7.6 Definitive Agreement

At closing, a *definitive agreement* is reached. In contrast to the *letter of intent*, which is non-binding, the final agreement is definite; that is, it describes all the necessary details relevant to consummating the deal and is a legally binding contract, subject to preconditions, such as shareholder approval.

The definitive agreement is a risk management device focused only on the completion of the transaction and contains a number of elements in common, including the following:

1. **Parties to the deal:** Specifies the players and their roles.
2. **Recitals:** Specifies what the parties wish to accomplish, and is easily identified by clauses that begin with "Whereas."
3. **Definition of terms:** Mutually agreed understanding of the terminology contained in the agreement.
4. **Description of transaction:** Purchase or sale of assets or equity, or merger. Describes exactly what is to be exchanged, by whom, and when.
5. **Representations and warranties:** Enumerates mechanisms by which the two sides disclose information about each other. A *representation* is a statement of fact; a *warranty* is a commitment that a fact is or will be true. Together, *reps and warranties* present a snapshot of the target and buyer at the time of the transaction.
6. **Covenants:** The management of risks that may arise as a result of the behavior of the parties between signing the agreement and closing the transaction. (Closing is not considered finalized until funds have been transferred.) *Covenants* are mutual promises—forward-looking commitments. They are affirmative ("We promise to do this")

TABLE 19.8

Best Practices for M&A Negotiations

Common Mistakes	Common Solutions
Unrealistic timetables and expectations	Select an acquisitions team experienced in cost–benefit time allocation.
Inexperienced M&A negotiation team	Establish an acquisitions team with defined responsibilities and authority.
Lack of structured transaction process	Clearly define team member roles. Be prepared to "walk away" from a bad deal.
Disproportionate time spent on minor issues	Focus on outcomes, not activities. Set "drop dead" dates.
Incomplete or irrelevant information	Obtain corroborating data.
Inadequate or nonexistent due diligence	Engage industry experts.
Inadequate sensitivity analysis	Perform financial and commercial sensitivity analyses. Set minimums.
Overlooking integration issues	Thoroughly assess the impact of "culture clashes." Can value be created?
Poor negotiating techniques	Pre-plan negotiation strategies, tactics, and strategic objectives.
Naive and inexperienced negotiators	Decide on deal-breakers ahead of time.
No meeting transcriptions or minutes	Include a "secretary" as note-taker.
Communications failures	Debrief other party on issues discussed and agreements reached.
Long time to reach a term sheet agreement (Deals have a life. A lengthy negotiation for a term sheet is an early warning sign of impending impasse.)	This is the most significant document in the early stages. It should list price, form of payment, deal structure, and management issues. The letter of intent will follow the overall principles contained in the term sheet.
Overreliance on a letter of intent by seller (It is merely "an agreement to agree.")	Understanding that a letter of intent is a non-binding agreement. While it is crucially important, an agreement to agree is not an agreement.

or negative ("We promise not to do that"). Breach of covenants can usually trigger litigation for damages.

7. **Conditions to closing:** List of conditions that each side must fulfill in order to close. Failure of one party to meet the conditions permits the other party to terminate the deal without recourse.

8. **Termination:** This section outlines the conditions under which one party will allow the other party to exit from the agreement without penalty.

9. **Indemnifications:** Damage payments in the event of losses discovered after closing has occurred or even breach of provisions in the agreement.

Notes

1. Wennberg K., et al. (2009). Reconceptualizing entrepreneurial exit: Divergent exit routes and their drivers. *Journal of Business Venturing*, 25(4): 361–375. doi:10.1016/j.jbusvent.2009.01.001.
2. Bygrave, W.D., and Timmons, J. (1999). Venture capital at the crossroads. University of Illinois at Urbana–Champaign's Academy for Entrepreneurial Leadership. http://ssm.com/abstract=1496172.
3. Price, R.W. (2014). Why is an exit strategy important for entrepreneurs? Global Entrepreneurial Institute, June 19. https://news.gcase.org/2014/06/19/why-is-an-exit-strategy-important-for-entrepreneurs-2.
4. Harnett, M. (2018). Have you considered a management buy out? Exit Promise. http://exitpromise.com/considering-a-management-buy-out.
5. Thompson, P. (2006). Management buyouts: Selling out to senior management. https://bcphysio.org/sites/default/files/file_attachments/resource/Article-Management-Buyouts-Selling-to-Senior-Management-Phil-Thompson.pdf.
6. Deloitte Private (2018). Anatomy of a management buy-out: Common ailments and remedies when considering a private company buy-out.https://www2.deloitte.com/content/dam/Deloitte/ca/Documents/deloitte-private/ca-en-14-2672t-anatomy-of-a-management-buy-out-aoda.PDF.
7. MBO Group (2014). 10 biggest mistakes of management buyouts.http://www.thembogroup.com/management_buyouts/management_buyouts_biggest_mistakes.html.
8. Michelmores (2018). Management buy-out guide: More than just lawyers. http://docplayer.net/13700990-Management-buy-out-guide-more-than-just-lawyers.html.
9. Newsome, M. (2006). Anatomy of a management buyout. Zachary Scott, July 15. http://www.zacharyscott.com/blog/blog/uncategorized/anatomy-of-a-management-buyout.
10. Wikipedia (2018). Mergers and acquisitions. http://en.wikipedia.org/wiki/Mergers_and_acquisitions.
11. Andrade, G., Mitchell, M., and Stafford, E. (2001). New evidence and perspectives on mergers. *Journal of Economic Perspectives*, 15(2): 103–120.
12. Rigsbee, E. (2016). Alliance pitfalls that challenge your strategic alliance success. Rigsbee Research, September 27. http://rigsbee.com/the-pitfalls-to-successful-strategic-alliances-3032-words.
13. Wikipedia (2018). Mergers and acquisitions. http://en.wikipedia.org/wiki/Mergers_and_acquisitions.
14. Peters, B. (2009). Early exits. MeteorBytes Data Management Corp. http://www.Early-Exits.com.
15. Stein, T. (2008). The new homerun: M&A instead of R&D and IPO's, *Mergers & Acquisitions Magazine: The Dealmaker's Journal*, 43(1): 32–36.
16. Time Warner (2000). America Online and Time Warner will merge to create world's first internet-age media and communications company. Time Warner corporate homepage, October 1.
17. Houghton, J.R. (1990). Corning cultivates joint ventures that endure. *Planning Review* 18(5): 15–17.

20

Alternative Exits: Selling Patents and Software

Disclaimer: The information provided in this chapter is informational only. The reader is advised to seek competent legal and/or financial counsel.

20.1 Introduction

The decision to sell your company (i.e., exit or harvest) can be highly emotional. After all, you have spent many years building a successful business. So it can be difficult to step away and let someone else take over. And there are many details you should be aware of before going ahead. If you are considering selling your business, then planning will be essential for your successful exit.

Entrepreneurs may choose to sell their business for a variety of reasons, but a prepared seller should have a legitimate, marketable reason for selling the business. Potential buyers will always ask about the seller's motivation for exiting. A reasonable and logical answer removes uncertainty in the mind of the buyer and ultimately makes the business more attractive.

Table 20.1 enumerates some common internal and external motivations for selling.[1]

Exiting your business is a daunting exercise even when the owners are well prepared. Given the endless number of stumbling blocks on the path to a successful sale, it is critical that a seller engages appropriate advisers early on in the pre-sale process. A potential buyer is likely to have a team of professionals assisting throughout the process as well.

Traditionally, businesses engage an adviser such as an investment banker or a broker to assist in the marketing and negotiation of the sale. Investment bankers and competent brokers have assisted in the sale of many businesses and can add value through their network of potential buyers, knowledge of comparable transactions, and experienced negotiation tactics, among other areas.

Advisors typically require clients to sign an *engagement letter*, creating a contractual arrangement between the seller and the advisor. The three general components of an engagement letter include:

1. **A description of the services provided:** The description may be comprehensive and include an identification of prospects purchasers, the creation of selling memorandum and marketing documents,

TABLE 20.1

Motivations for Selling

Internal	External
Recent success, leading to relatively high valuation (i.e., successful completion of a pivotal clinical trial)	A motivated buyer has expressed interest
Key employees desire to purchase the business	Onerous new governmental regulations
Founder's readiness to relinquish power in exchange for ready cash	Market shift requiring large additional investment

         assistance in the negotiation of the sales agreement and related agreements (employment, non-compete, etc.), and guidelines for conducting due diligence.

  2. **How the advisor will be paid:** The broker's compensation is typically a percentage of the total payment, ranging from 10% on smaller deals to 1% on deals in the tens of millions. All fees should be negotiated upfront.

  3. **The length or *term* of the agreement:** Typically, the term is 12–24 months and may include a *tail* payment, whereby the broker will still receive some payment if a sale is consummated prior to the end of a specified period of time (i.e., during the tail). The tail clause prevents the seller from abandoning the broker once a deal appears imminent.

20.2 Is Your Business Saleable?

When you voluntarily sell your business (as an exit strategy), a buyer should pay to acquire not only the physical assets of your business—the assets listed on your balance sheet—but also the *goodwill* of your business, including the worth of such intangible assets as your business name, reputation, clientele, systems, and marketplace advantage.[2]

    Although many factors determine the value of your company, at the end of the day, your business is worth what another party is willing to pay for it. Factors typically considered include current rates of return in the marketplace, growth rates, industry outlook, your organization's management structure, your business's financial and operational strength, and the competitive advantages of your products or services.

    The optimal way to harvest the value of business goodwill is through a business sale. Thus, the decision to sell rather than to liquidate rests on a determination of whether the goodwill of your business—the value of your business beyond its physical assets—is of high enough value to attract interest and encourage a purchase decision by an appropriate buyer.

20.3 What Are Your Personal Motivations?

The *BizBuySell Guide to Selling Your Small Business* will help you focus on what's motivating your exit decision and how your motivation affects the timing and approach for exiting your business. Table 20.2 lists some of the motivations behind exit plans. Use the left column to check the factors that are influencing your desire to sell your business, then use the right column to check the urgency of your situation.

As you consider the preceding questions, realize that your perceived need for an immediate exit often correlates with a lower sale price, for several reasons:

- If your business sale timing is immediate, you eliminate the opportunity to strengthen the attractiveness of your offering prior to a sale listing.

- If pressing financial needs force an immediate sale and payoff, you preclude your ability to offer *seller financing*, which typically supports a higher selling price.

- If you want or need to make a very prompt departure from your business, you shorten or eliminate the possibility of a transition period, which likely forces a lower offer from buyers.

20.4 Performing Your Pre-Sale Due Diligence

Due diligence is the preliminary process through which a potential acquirer evaluates a target company or its assets for an acquisition. The theory behind due diligence holds that performing this type of investigation contributes significantly

TABLE 20.2

Personal Motivations behind Your Decision to Exit

Exit Plan Motivation (Check All that Apply)	Timing (Check to Indicate Your Urgency)
Your business would benefit from increased investment and energy you don't feel able to provide.	Immediate/□Flexible
All your net worth is tied up in your business and you want to sell in order to diversify.	Immediate/□Flexible
Your business could use leadership by a professional chief executive.	Immediate/□Flexible
Your senior team is ready to buy your business (management buyout).	Immediate/□Flexible
You are ready to retire.	Immediate/□Flexible
Acqui-hire (selling your company mainly for its talent rather than its product, the current "rage" of Silicon Valley).	Immediate/□Flexible

to informed decision making by enhancing the amount and quality of information available to decision makers and by ensuring that this information is systematically used to deliberate in a reflexive manner on the decision at hand and all its costs, benefits, and risks.[34] According to Ernst & Young, a potential buyer will want to perform an extensive investigation into your company before any transaction occurs. You need to be prepared before contemplating a sale.[5]

In particular, you should ensure that all financial and legal information is organized, analyze trends your company has experienced in the past 5 years, and determine what information can be shared to help the buyer make an informed decision. A buyer may also want to review operations to help develop plans and identify operational issues.[6]

20.4.1 Selecting the Appropriate Type of Sale

There are many options available to you when selling your company. Among the common types of transactions are asset sales and share sales. Although it is a more complex transaction, an asset sale offers more flexibility to the vendor and purchaser than a share sale. However, a share sale can give the seller a lower tax rate on the transaction and the option of transferring all liabilities to the buyer. But if you are going with an asset sale, be aware of possible double taxation at the corporate and shareholder levels and a higher asking price.

Asset purchases are common in technology transactions where the buyer is most interested in particular intellectual property (IP) rights but does not want to acquire liabilities or other contractual relationships. Asset purchases and equity purchases are each taxed differently, and the most beneficial structure for tax purposes is highly situation dependent. One hybrid form often employed for tax purposes is a triangular merger, where the target company merges with a shell company wholly owned by the buyer, thus becoming a subsidiary of the buyer. In a *forward triangular merger*, the buyer causes the target company to merge into the subsidiary; a *reverse triangular merger* is similar except that the subsidiary merges into the target company

20.4.2 Considering Potential Buyers

Organizations acquire small businesses for several different reasons. You need to decide, up front, whether you will be seeking strategic or financial buyers, as shown in Table 20.3.

Regardless of your initial choice, there will be benefits and downsides with any type of buyer, so you need to decide what you want out of the sale before you make an informed choice.

20.4.3 Reviewing the Process

Selling a business is a lot of work. To begin, you must first select a process: either a targeted or a broad auction. You then begin building a list of potential buyers to approach during the sales process.

TABLE 20.3

Strategic Buyers versus Financial Buyers

Strategic Buyers	Financial Buyers
A strategic buyer is looking for a business to establish or realize synergies.	Financial buyers may or may not have investments in your industry.
The strategic buyer is looking to grow and capitalize by integrating other businesses.	Financial buyers acquire a company because the business (or industry) is attractive and profitable.

Then your focus turns to marketing to attract and approach interested buyers. When a potential buyer submits a letter of intent, it is time to perform due diligence and solicit offers before closing the sale.

20.4.4 Marketing Your Company to Buyers

Every business has a story. Telling that story in a compelling way will act as a valuable sales tool and help you successfully sell your company. By strategically marketing your company's opportunities and strengths, you'll attract more interest and earn a higher value from the sale.

To accomplish this task, focus on your company's history and reputation, highlighting your technological know-how, possession of key IP, and ability to realize potential synergies. Vocalizing strong customer and vendor relations and key product or service advantages is good practice, but a strong financial outlook will be the key to producing higher-than-average returns.

Whether you're selling your business on your own or through a broker, you'll need to be ready to present a thorough written overview of your business and why it's a good purchase prospect.[7]

Some experts call this document a *selling memo*. Others call it a *confidential description book* or an *offering memo*.

- If your business is small, uncomplicated, and likely to sell for under $1 million, you can probably reduce the selling memo to a terms sheet that presents little more than a business description, financial information, and presentation of price and terms.

- If your business is large, and if its assets, products, and systems are complicated, your selling memo will likely run considerably longer in order to adequately explain your offering and its higher price.

20.5 Selling Your Patent as an Exit Strategy

According to Tynax,[8] the technology exchange website, your patent gives you the right to *exclude* others from practicing your unique invention. It provides the right to ask the court to force infringers to pay a reasonable royalty and/or issue an injunction preventing future infringement. So, the marketability and value of the patent depends on its infringement status.

Please notice that this description of a patent focuses on legal issues and does not include mention of the strength or maturity of the underlying technology. This is because the technology is a different asset to the patent, although the two can be related. When you are selling the patent, you're not selling a right to use your technology, but you are *selling the right to prevent others from developing technologies using the patented invention.* Understanding this point can help eliminate much confusion surrounding the possible sale of your patents.

By buying your patent, the buyer acquires the right to assert the patent against infringers. Of course, if the buyer is an infringer itself, acquisition of the patent removes the possibility of the buyer being sued for infringement.

Technically, as the patent right is *purely exclusionary,* the patent buyer is not acquiring a right to use the invention itself, as use of this invention may actually involve infringement of another patent. Imagine that the patent covered the design of a bicycle, but each of the components of the bicycle—the wheels, gears, brakes, and so on—were all subject to separate patents held by others.

20.5.1 Motivations of Patent Buyers

The motivations of patent buyers vary, and they acquire for a variety of purposes. However, as a patent is merely a right to exclude others and enforce in court, buyers can be broadly categorized as either assertive or defensive. An assertive buyer acquires patents to enforce against infringers with the view of winning licensing royalties or an injunction preventing future production or distribution of infringing products. A defensive buyer acquires patents they can use in a countersuit if they are accused of infringement by another patent holder and find themselves defending a lawsuit. So, both assertive and defensive buyers acquire patents that they can assert against infringers in court. The difference is merely when and how the lawsuit is triggered.

Assertive buyers generally hire armies of lawyers to file lawsuits and negotiate licensing transactions with infringers. Organizations that assert patents as their primary business activity and don't make or market their own products have attracted the unfortunate label of *patent trolls.* However, there are many forms of organizations that assert patents and this activity has been part of the business landscape in the United States for decades.

In response to ongoing litigation, defensive buyers are often operating companies that make and/or sell products in the U.S. market. Large product-oriented corporations with deep pockets are the most likely target of the patent asserters, and hence, are the most active buyers for defensive purposes. Defensive buyers are grouping together and forming patent pools. Patent pools involve several corporations pooling funds to acquire patents that are then licensed to the members of the consortium.

Whether these pools are primarily defensive or assertive is not yet clear; they are probably both. The stimulus for joining forces was probably the result of costly defensive litigation, but with growing stockpiles of patents, it is inevitable that the pools see compelling opportunities to assert the patents for profit. Patent pools certainly acquire patents to take them off the market, and out of the hands of assertive buyers, but they likely acquire patents that they can assert themselves.

Assertive buyers, defensive buyers, and patent pools form the vast bulk of the demand for patents today. Of the three, patent pools are the most active, defensive buyers second, and assertive buyers a distant third in terms of the number of patents acquired.

20.5.2 What Is Your Patent Worth?

Patents are worth what the buyers are willing to pay. But some patents are worth more because they deal in a hot *active sector*. Currently, the most active sectors for patent sales are high-tech sectors that have seen a good deal of infringement litigation in the past. Buying activity is currently taking place in areas such as wireless communications, telephony, flash memory, semi-conductors, e-commerce, the Internet, software applications, and medical devices/biopharmaceuticals.

Many patent holders are misled by unrealistic valuation calculations and their expectations in terms of pricing are unreasonably high. As with any commodity or asset, the value is driven by what a ready and willing buyer is prepared to pay. Some websites and valuation firms unscrupulously prey on inventors and sell valuation reports that appear very appealing but are not driven by actual buying activity.

The valuation in Table 20.4 reflects actual buying activity seen by brokers in the United States and worldwide, including the thousands of listings syndicated on the Tynax exchange. The valuations reflect the sale of a large proportion of the patents sold in the marketplace during the last 12 months. These prices apply to issued U.S. patents.

20.5.3 How Are Pending Continuations and Divisional Applications Valued?

Pending patent applications are generally too speculative to justify any value as the patent or some of the claims may never be approved by the patent office. Buyers are usually not interested in acquiring individual pending applications until the claims are allowed and the patent is subsequently issued.

An issued patent can spawn children in the form of continuation and divisional applications. As these applications are not yet allowed by the patent examiners, they are somewhat speculative; however, they can add value to the patent. If an issued U.S. patent is sold together with pending continuation and divisional children applications, this can increase the value of the issued patent by 10%–25%.

TABLE 20.4

Patent Valuation Ranges, According to Tynax

Group A Patent Value: $0.00	Patents that are expired or otherwise found invalid have no value. As roughly half of litigated patents are found to be invalid by the court, a large number of issued patents fall into this category.
Group B Patent Value: $10,000–$30,000 per Patent	Valid U.S. patents that do not have particularly broad claims are not in a particularly large market, have no licensees, and have not been litigated.
Group C Patent Value: $30,000–$100,000 per Patent	If the patents have broad claims or the market is particularly large and growing, then the price of unlitigated patents can increase toward the six-figure range
Group D Patent Value: $100,000–$500,000 per Patent	Where multiple competing buyers bid to acquire a patent with strong claims for application in a large growing market, the price can rise to several hundred thousand dollars.
Group E Patent Value: $500,000–$1,000,000 per Patent	Generally, the patents that sell for the mid to high six-figure range are those that have been litigated and won, and where there are known infringers. The price is justified by the potential royalty stream from such infringers.
Group F Patent Value: $1 million+ per Patent	A patent that has been successfully litigated and is battle tested with identified Fortune 500 infringers can sometimes bring a price in excess of $1 million.
Group G Industry Standard	A very small number of industry-standard patents sell for low to medium seven-figure sums. These prices are generally justified by the huge strategic advantage such a patent offers the owner, together with the long-term potential royalty stream from infringers/licensees. Industry-standard patents can be found in many high-tech sectors, especially pharmaceuticals and medical/biotech areas.

Often, a continuation involves broadening the claims of the parent, so buyers are highly reluctant to acquire parents without continuations, and these are almost always bundled together in the sale. However, divisional applications are somewhat different from the parent, involving different inventions, so they can sometimes be sold separately from the parent patent.

20.5.4 Setting an Asking Price

Patent buyers are wary of sellers with unrealistic pricing expectations. The process of evaluating a patent is time-consuming and expensive for the buyer and many are reluctant to undertake this work if they suspect they will be unable to reach a mutually agreeable price with the seller.

Many buyers, certainly many of the most active, experienced buyers, refuse to evaluate and consider a patent until they have assurance that the seller's pricing expectations are reasonable. Of course, they expect some negotiation on price, but a patent with an unjustified multimillion dollar price tag will not be taken seriously by buyers.

The purpose of setting the asking price is to grab attention of the buyer and set their expectations. As previously discussed, setting an unrealistic price will make your patent difficult, if not impossible, to sell.

Sellers should discuss pricing with their patent brokers, but the pricing should be within the preceding framework. If you believe your patent is in group F, then provide evidence of prior litigation and claims charts showing ongoing infringement. Of course, setting an asking price a little higher than you are ultimately prepared to accept will provide you with some room for negotiation.

20.5.5 Why Do Buyers Ask for Representations and Warranties?

When the buyer is asked to rely on statements or assurances made by the seller, the buyer is likely to ask for representations and warranties from the seller that the information is accurate.

This places a liability on the seller if the information is subsequently found to be inaccurate.

The most likely scenario where representations and warranties are important is where the seller is unable to provide copies of all relevant assignments. The assignment documents effectively provide proof of ownership of the patents. If these important papers cannot be provided by the seller, the buyer will often request a representation and warranty from the seller that the seller does indeed own the title to the patents that are being sold. This is less than ideal for the buyer, as often the only recourse the buyer has if it is found that they have paid the seller for patents they didn't own is a refund of the purchase price, and this is often insufficient to fully compensate the loss incurred by the buyer.

If you are concerned about liability, you may be able to negotiate the elimination of representations and warranties if you provide the buyer with copies of all the assignments and strong evidence that you own a clean title to the patents being sold.

20.5.6 Do You Need a Lawyer to Sell a Patent?

It is highly advisable. A patent sale involves intricate paperwork that must be customized for each transaction. The best way of protecting your interests is to have a lawyer with experience in these transactions represent you. Your lawyer can structure the transaction in a way that minimizes your liability exposure.

The buyer lawyer will draft a *patent purchase agreement* (PPA), otherwise known as the *patent acquisition agreement* (PAA). This is generally drawn up by the buyer and includes the following provisions:

- Identification of the patents and assets being sold
- Purchase price and payment details
- License back for seller, where negotiated

- Assignment (transfer) of the patent rights on closing
- Representations and warranties that the seller owns the patents being sold
- Representations and warranties that the information provided by the seller is accurate
- Confidentiality agreement

20.5.7 Example of a Patent Purchase Agreement

The following is an example of a patent purchase agreement between companies in Hong Kong and Malaysia:[9]

PATENT PURCHASE AGREEMENT

This PATENT PURCHASE AGREEMENT ("**Agreement**"), effective as of June 27, 2011 (the "**Effective Date**"), is made and entered into by and between Sunway Technology Development Limited, having its principal place of business at Room 2103, Futura Plaza, 111 How Ming Street, Kwun Tong, Hong Kong ("**Seller**"), and Info-Accent Sdn Bhd, having its principal place of business at A-1-5 Jaya One, 72A Jalan Universiti, 46200 Petaling Jaya, Selangor, Malaysia ("**Purchaser**"). Seller and Purchaser may hereinafter be referred to collectively as the "**Parties**" and individually as a "**Party**" when convenient.

RECITALS

WHEREAS, Seller is the owner of the entire right, title, and interest of a certain invention entitled "DATA COMMUNICATIONS BETWEEN SHORT-RANGE ENABLED WIRELESS DEVICES OVER NETWORKS AND PROXIMITY MARKETING TO SUCH DEVICES" for which a patent application has been filed with the United States Patent and Trademark Office on June 30, 2008.

WHEREAS, Purchaser entered into an exclusive Marketing, Distribution and License Agreement (the "License Agreement") with VyseTech Asia Sdn Bhd on April 8, 2010 and paid a one-time license fee of Ringgit Malaysia One Million Six Hundred Thousand (approximately $500,000).

WHEREAS, Seller has received notification on April 18, 2011 from the United States Patent and Trademark Office that the application has been examined and allowed for issuance as a patent.

WHEREAS, this Agreement specifically does not transfer any ownership interest in and to the continuation patent application or inventions and Seller specifically retains the entire right, title, and interest in and to the continuation patent application and to any continuations, divisions, continuations-in-part, reissues, and reexaminations associated with the continuation patent application.

WHEREAS, Purchaser is desirous of acquiring said entire right, title, and interest of Seller in and to the patent application.

WHEREAS, the Parties now desire to enter into this Agreement.

NOW, THEREFORE, IN consideration of the terms and provisions contained herein and other good and valuable consideration, the receipt, adequacy, and sufficiency of which are hereby acknowledged, the Parties agree as follows:

1. DEFINITIONS

For the purpose of this Agreement, the following terms, whether in singular or in plural form, when used with a capital initial letter shall have the respective meanings as follows.

1.1 **"Action"** means an assertion made or a proceeding filed by a Person or one of its affiliates.

1.2 **"Assigned Patent"** means the issued patent and patent applications listed in Exhibit A hereto.

1.3 **"Person"** means any natural person, corporation, company, partnership, association, sole proprietorship, trust, joint venture, nonprofit entity, institute, governmental authority, trust association, or other form of entity not specifically listed herein including, without limitation, Seller or any of its affiliates, or Purchaser or any of its affiliates.

2. PURCHASE AND SALE OF PATENT

2.1 **Purchase and Sale of Patent.** Effective as of the Closing Date and subject to the fulfillment of the Parties' obligations set forth in Sections 3.2 and 3.3, Seller hereby sells, assigns, transfers, and sets over unto Purchaser its entire right, title, and interest in and to all of the Assigned Patent, including all past, present, and future causes of actions and claims for damages derived by reason of patent infringement thereof for Purchaser's own use and for the use of its assigns, successors, and legal representatives, to the full end of the term of each of the Assigned Patent. To evidence the assignment of the Assigned Patent, Seller shall execute a patent assignment document ("**Patent Assignment**") for the Assigned Patent. Notwithstanding the foregoing assignment, in the event that the Closing is not con-summated within sixty (60) calendar days from the Effective Date, Seller shall have the right, in its sole discretion, to termi-nate this Agreement including all obligations of Seller and all rights of Purchaser set forth in this Agreement.

2.2   **Purchase Price.** Purchaser hereby agrees to pay to Seller, pursu-ant to the terms set forth in Section 3.2, the non-refundable sum of Three Million Five Hundred Thousand United States Dollars (US$3,500,000) (the **"Purchase Price"**). Notwithstanding the foregoing, Seller hereby agrees to receive net payment of Three Million United States Dollars (US$3,000,000) after setting off a sum of Five Hundred Thousand United States Dollars (US$500,000) previously paid by Purchaser to VyseTech Asia Sdn Bhd as a one-time license fee. The Purchase Price shall be fully settled by Purchaser within sixty (60) calendar days from the Effective Date.

3. CLOSING AND DELIVERY

3.1   **The Closing.** The transaction shall be consummated at A-1-5 Jaya One, 72A Jalan Universiti, 46200 Petaling Jaya, Selangor, Malaysia on June 30, 2011 (the **"Closing Date"**).

3.2   **Seller Deliverables.** At the closing, Seller shall deliver to Purchaser a duly executed Patent Assignment.

3.3   **Purchaser Deliverables.** At the closing, Purchaser shall deliver or cause to be delivered to Seller or its affiliate the Purchase Price by wire transfer or any other mode(s) of payment as may be mutually agreed between the parties.

4. TRANSFER OF PATENT

4.1   **Patent Assignment.** Effective as of the Closing Date, Seller hereby sells, assigns, transfers, and conveys to Purchaser all rights, title, and interest it has in and to the Assigned Patent and all inventions and discoveries described therein and all rights of Seller to collect royalties under such Patent.

4.2   **Assignment of Causes of Action.** Effective as of the Closing Date, Seller hereby sells, assigns, transfers, and conveys to Purchaser all right, title, and interest it has in and to all causes of action and enforcement rights, whether currently pending, filed, or otherwise, for the Assigned Patent and all inventions and discoveries described therein, including without limitation all rights to pursue damages, injunctive relief, and other remedies for past, current, and future infringement of the Assigned Patent as of the Effective Date.

5. ADDITIONAL OBLIGATIONS

5.1   **Further Assurances.** Seller agrees to cooperate with Purchaser in the obtaining and sustaining of any and all such Letters Patent and in confirming Purchaser's exclusive ownership of the invention(s). At the reasonable request of Purchaser and without demanding further consideration from Purchaser, Seller agrees to execute and deliver such other instruments and do and perform such other acts and things as may be reasonably necessary for effecting completely the consummation of the transfer of ownership in and to the Assigned Patent as contemplated hereby, including without limitation execution, acknowledgment and recordation of other such papers, as necessary or desirable for fully perfecting and conveying unto Purchaser the benefit of the transfer of ownership in and to the Assigned Patent as contemplated hereby.

5.2   **Further Assistance.** Subject to the terms and conditions hereof, Seller agrees, upon the reasonable request of Purchaser, to do all things necessary, proper, or advisable, including without limitation the execution, acknowledgment, and recordation of specific assignments, oaths, declarations, and other documents on a country-by-country basis, to assist Purchaser in obtaining, perfecting, sustaining, and/or enforcing the patent rights. Such assistance may also include providing prompt production of pertinent facts and documents, giving of testimony, execution of petitions, oaths, powers of attorney, specifications, declarations, or other papers, and other assistance reasonably necessary for filing patent applications, complying with any duty of disclosure, and conducting prosecution, reexamination, reissue, interference or other priority proceedings, opposition proceedings, cancellation proceedings, public use proceedings, infringement, or other court actions and the like with respect to the Assigned Patent. Seller's agreement to render any of the foregoing assistance is subject to Purchaser's payment of all reasonable expenses of Seller incurred in connection therewith and the availability of Seller's personnel.

5.3   **Payment of Fees.** Seller shall pay any maintenance fees, annuities, and the like due on the Assigned Patent for a period of sixty (60) calendar days following the Effective Date.

6. REPRESENTATIONS AND WARRANTIES

Seller hereby warrants to Purchaser as follows:

6.1 **No Assignment.** Seller warrants that (i) no assignment of the invention(s), application, or patent therefor has been made to a party other than Purchaser and (ii) there is no obligation to make any assignment of the invention(s), application, or any patent therefor to any party other than Purchaser.

6.2 **Title and Contest.** Seller has good and marketable title to the Assigned Patent, including without limitation all rights, title, and interest in the Assigned Patent to sue for infringement thereof. The Assigned Patent is free and clear of all liens, mortgages, security interests or other encumbrances, and restrictions on transfer. There are no actions, suits, claims, or proceedings threatened, pending or in progress on the part of any named inventor of the Patent relating in any way to the Assigned Patent and Seller has not received notice of (and Seller is not aware of any facts or circumstances that could reasonably be expected to give rise to) any other actions, suits, investigations, claims, or proceedings threatened, pending, or in progress relating in any way to the Patent. There are no existing contracts, agreements, options, commitments, proposals, bids, offers, or rights with, to, or in any Person to acquire the Assigned Patent.

6.3 **Restrictions on Rights.** Purchaser will not be subject to any covenant not to sue or similar restrictions on its enforcement or enjoyment of the Assigned Patent as a result of the transaction contemplated in this Agreement, or any prior transaction related to the Assigned Patent.

6.4 **Payment of Fees Due.** Seller has paid all fees due on the Assigned Patent to the United States Patent and Trademark Office as of the Effective Date of this Agreement.

7. MISCELLANEOUS

7.1 **No Representation or Warranty.** SELLER MAKES NO REPRESENTATIONS OR WARRANTIES WHATSOEVER THAT THE PATENT COVERED BY THIS AGREEMENT ARE EITHER VALID OR ARE INFRINGED BY ANY OTHER PARTIES.

7.2 **Limitation on Consequential Damages.** EXCEPT IN THE CASE OF FRAUD BY SELLER, NEITHER PARTY SHALL BE LIABLE TO THE OTHER FOR LOSS OF PROFITS, OR ANY OTHER INDIRECT OR SPECIAL, CONSEQUENTIAL, PUNITIVE OR INCIDENTAL DAMAGES, HOWEVER CAUSED, EVEN IF

ADVISED OF THE POSSIBILITY OF SUCH DAMAGE. THE PARTIES ACKNOWLEDGE THAT THESE LIMITATIONS ON POTENTIAL LIABILITIES WERE AN ESSENTIAL ELEMENT IN SETTING CONSIDERATION UNDER THIS AGREEMENT.

7.3 **Limitation of Liability.** EXCEPT IN THE CASE OF FRAUD BY SELLER, IN NO EVENT SHALL EITHER PARTY'S TOTAL LIABILITY UNDER THIS AGREEMENT EXCEED THE PURCHASE PRICE. THE PARTIES ACKNOWLEDGE THAT THESE LIMITATIONS ON POTENTIAL LIABILITIES WERE AN ESSENTIAL ELEMENT IN SETTING CONSIDERATION UNDER THIS AGREEMENT.

7.4 **Confidentiality of Terms.** The parties hereto shall keep the terms and existence of this Agreement and the identities of the parties hereto confidential and shall not now or hereafter divulge any of this information to any third party except: (a) with the prior written consent of the other party, such consent shall not be unreasonably withheld; (b) as otherwise may be required by law or legal process, including in confidence to financial advisors in their capacity of advising a party in such matters; (c) during the course of litigation, so long as the disclosure of such terms and conditions are restricted in the same manner as is the confidential information of other litigating parties; or (d) in confidence to its legal counsel, accountants, banks, and financing sources and their advisors solely in connection with complying with financial transactions; provided that, in (b) through (d), (i) the disclosing party shall use all legitimate and legal means available to minimize the disclosure to third parties, including without limitation seeking a confidential treatment request or protective order whenever appropriate or available; and (ii), other than disclosures pursuant to subsection (d), the disclosing party shall provide the other party with at least ten (10) business days prior written notice of such disclosure.

7.5 **Governing Law.** This Agreement shall be governed and construed in accordance with the laws of Hong Kong.

7.6 **Severability.** If any provision of this Agreement shall be held invalid or unenforceable, such invalidity or unenforceability shall attach only to such provision and shall not in any manner affect or render invalid or unenforceable any other severable provision of this Agreement, and this Agreement shall be carried out as if any such invalid or unenforceable provisions were not contained herein.

7.7 **Indemnification.** Each party to this Agreement, shall indemnify and hold harmless each other party at all times after the date of this Agreement against and in respect of any liability, damage or deficiency, all actions, suits, proceedings, demands, assessments, judgments, costs and expenses including attorney's fees incident to any of the foregoing, resulting from any misrepresentations, breach of covenant or warranty or non-fulfillment of any agreement on the part of such party under this Agreement or from any misrepresentation in or omission from any certificate furnished or to be furnished to a party hereunder. Subject to the terms of this Agreement, the defaulting party shall reimburse the other party or parties on demand, for any reasonable payment made by said parties at any time after the Closing, in respect of any liability or claim to which the foregoing indemnity relates, if such payment is made after reasonable notice to the other party to defend or satisfy the same and such party failed to defend or satisfy the same.

7.8 **Entire Agreement; Waiver of Breach.** This Agreement constitutes the entire agreement between the parties and supersedes any prior agreement or understanding among them in respect of the subject matter hereof, and there are no other agreements, written or oral, nor may the Agreement be modified except in writing and executed by all of the parties hereto; and no waiver of any breach or condition of this Agreement shall be deemed to have occurred unless such waiver is in writing, signed by the party against whom enforcement is sought, and no waiver shall be claimed to be a waiver of any subsequent breach or condition of a like or different nature.

IN WITNESS WHEREOF, the parties have executed this Agreement the day and year first above written.

SUNWAY TECHNOLOGY DEVELOPMENT LIMITED

INFO-ACCENT SDN BHD

/s/Rohaya Rahim

/s/Chong Aik Fun

Name: Rohaya Rahim

Name: Chong Aik Fun

Title: Chief Operating Officer

20.6 What Is Your Software Worth?

No matter how skilled or innovative your software programs are, you need to find customers in order to sell your programs as an exit strategy. Understand how to sell software, whether it's selling some already-made software to those who want it or finding a niche market with a software need that you can fill.

Selling software presents a unique set of challenges. An issue, not dealt with in the literature of valuing intangibles, is that software is continually being upgraded.

Software creators believe that although what they produce is highly valuable, they are rarely called on to quantify its benefits. One reason may be that much investment in software engineering has been motivated by military and governmental applications, where benefits are hard to quantify.

In many other fields, the creators have a substantial awareness of the market value of their innovative products. Architects are aware of the cost for houses they build; a potter will know the price for the dishes, as will a manufacturer of computers. These innovators deal with tangible products and have a firm appreciation for costs. But since software, once written, is easy to replicate at a negligible incremental cost, each subsequent improvement may be sold for much more than its development cost.

For our purposes, we can define software as computer programs, procedures, associated documentation, and data pertaining to the operation of a computer system.

20.6.1 Software as Intangible Asset

Proprietary software is part of an organization's intangible assets, as described in Figure 20.1.

Figure 20.1 shows that IP rights are a subset of intangible assets, which in turn are a subset of an enterprise's total asset base. The characteristics of your software's intangible property compared with tangible assets are:

- Software value is not diminished by use and can be used simultaneously by many parties.
- There is no linear relationship between the cost of software development and its market value.
- Software may be licensed on a standalone basis or as part of a business combination.
- Royalties may be part of a royalty agreement.

According to Gio Wiederhold,[10] the value of your software is based on the following IP principles.

IP rule: *The value of the intellectual property is the income it generates over time.*

That rule is the basis for any IP valuation: estimating future income and calculating current value.[11]

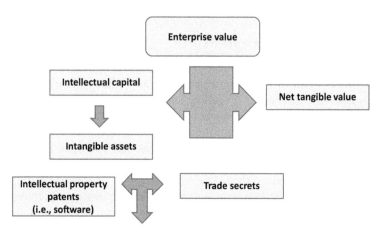

FIGURE 20.1
Intellectual property rights.

Wiederhold continues: to value the IP inherent in software, one must estimate how much income the software will bring in during its future life, which in turn requires estimating its life. We distinguish now between software producers and software users. In the United States, software sold to users amounted to about $120 billion in the year 2000, about half for prepackaged software and the other half for custom software. Another $128 billion was invested by companies for internal software development, both for new software and maintenance.[12]

20.6.2 Software Idiosyncrasies

What is income for one segment of industry is an investment for another segment, but in the end there should be an economic benefit gained from the use of all that software. According to Wiederhold, in valuing your software you must keep the following points in mind.

If the software you produced is sold to others	The expected income depends on the sales revenue, the product of the amount of software sales, and its price. We assess the software from the viewpoint of the seller. When a new version of a software product has been prepared and is ready for sale, sales of the prior version will rapidly diminish. Since the costs of copying and packaging software are very low, there is no benefit in continuing to sell the old software, a characteristic particular to intangible property. Software is different even from other intangibles: while a book written and printed 2 years ago can be profitably sold for, say, 80% of its new price, selling a prior version of software at an 80% price makes no sense for the seller. Supporting old versions of software to keep some existing customer creates a net loss for the seller, while being out of sync creates inefficiencies for the customer. Furthermore, the new version, if adequately debugged, should be substantially better than the prior version. For the purchaser, a deal on

obsolete software is likely to create expenses in adaptation and integration. Sometimes an old version of software has to be supported to keep some existing customer who cannot or will not update, but that support creates a net loss for the seller and being a year or so out of sync with one's peers creates inefficiencies for the customer. Since a new version of the software product includes much of the code and all of the functionality of the prior version, IP from the prior version continues to contribute to that new version. Disasters have occurred when new versions did not replicate all prior functionalities [Splosky:04]. Fundamental parts of software can easily live 10–15 years and hence continue to contribute to the generation of revenue.

For companies that use software

The valuation must be based in its contribution to the income of the company. In early days, one could compare a company's operation prior to using software and subsequent to installation, and assess the benefits of software based on the difference [Batelle:73]. The value would be based on an increase of productivity—that is, how many more goods were produced and how much production *costs of the goods sold* (CoGS) were reduced. For consulting companies, productivity is in terms of services, and the capability and cost of the workforce has an equivalent role. The improvements brought about by automation, after considering its cost, provide a measure of income attributable to software for that year. Future years would bring in similar or higher benefits, as the organizations adjusted to new tasks and workflow.

Today, it is rare that a broad set of new software applications will be installed within an ongoing company. More commonly, upgraded versions of existing software will be obtained, or some poorly served aspect of the company will be automated. At times, a major subsystem will be substituted [TamaiT:927]. Major substitutions were rare after the Y2K bulge, when fear of serious operational problems motivated much scrapping of obsolete software. Comparing a business that has adopted a significant improvement (e.g., online ordering) to a similar business that has not yet converted can provide input to assess the benefits that are due to the additional software. However, finding comparables is hard, and invariably adjustments will be needed before incomes can be compared. In large integrated companies it becomes impossible to relate income directly to software applications. Many resources are employed to generate income. There are routine operational costs as well as *intellectual property–generating expenses* (IGEs), such as software development and maintenance, advertising for new products and corporate recognition, investments in quality control, and the like. An approach that remains is based on a belief that the management of a company is efficient in the allocation of its resources [Samuelson:83].

Revenue and gross profit

In business financial reporting, the revenue realized is immediately reduced by the cost of the goods sold. Here is where software and other IP differ from tangible products. The effort to make the first unit of a product is a major cost in both cases, but tangible goods incur a manufacturing cost for each successive unit, while for software and many other intangibles the manufacturing cost is negligible. If software distribution is over the Internet, there are no direct incremental costs for each sale.

Revenue and gross profit, the revenue after the CoGS, become similar, and common financial indicators such as gross margin (gross profit/revenue) are close to one and essentially meaningless. One cannot base investment decisions on income margins that are, say, 98.5% versus 97.2% of sales. These ratios obviously do not represent reality over any period of time. We make a suggestion about this problem in the conclusion.

If we were to amortize initial research and development costs, as well as ongoing maintenance costs, over each unit of product and include them in the CoGS, then those margins could become more meaningful. However, without predicting future sales, the initial costs cannot be allocated to units of products. In IP assessments, those prior costs are ignored. Once the value of the software beyond today has been determined, then one can decide whether those earlier investments were worthwhile.

Since we only assess here the value of existing software, we ignore its initial research and development cost. We also ignore its negligible manufacturing cost. Now the income per unit is equal to the revenue (i.e., the price it fetches and the sales volume).

However, there will be ongoing costs to keep the software viable for sales. That distinction is recognized by accounting rules: costs prior to showing that the software is feasible are to be expensed; development costs beyond that point are to be capitalized [SmithP:00]. No mention is made of maintenance costs, which would be more properly accounted for as CoGS, since they sustain the ongoing viability of the product.

The next section addresses the issues that occur because maintained software is so slithery. Software keeps changing while one tries to understand and measure it. If software were stable, it would act like a tangible product with low manufacturing costs: "Hardware is petrified software" [Panetta:89].

Sustaining software

Before we can proceed from the income generated by software to the valuation of its IP, we must consider what happens to software over the time that it generates income.

It is here where software differs crucially from other intangible goods. Books and music recordings remain invariant during their life, but little software beyond basic mathematical libraries is stable [ReillyS:98].

Methods used to depreciate tangibles as well as intangibles over fixed lifetimes are based on the assumption that the goods being valued lose value over time. Such depreciation schedules are based on wear, or the loss of value due to obsolescence, or changes in customer preferences. However, well-maintained software, in active use, does not wear out and is likely to gain value [Spolsky:04].

All substantial business software must be sustained through ongoing maintenance to remain functional. What maintenance provides was stated many years ago by Barry Boehm [Boehm:81, p.533]: "The majority of software costs are incurred during the period after the developed software is accepted. These costs are primarily due to software maintenance, which here refers both to the activities to preserve the software's existing functionality and performance, and activities to increase its functionality and improve its performance throughout the life-cycle."

Ongoing maintenance generates IP beyond the initial IP, and its contribution will have to be deducted in the valuation. In order to be able to quantify that deduction, we summarize a prior business analysis [Wiederhold:03].

Successful software products have many versions, long lifetimes, and correspondingly high maintenance cost ratios over their lifetime. Software lifetimes before complete product (not version) substitution is needed are 10–15 years and are likely to increase [SmithP:00] [Wiederhold:95]. Version frequency is determined by the rate of changes needed and the tolerance of users to dealing with upgrades. In our example, we will assume a steady rate of 18 months, although when software is new, versions may be issued more frequently, while the rate reduces later in its life.

> The maintenance costs of such enterprise software amount to 60%–90% of total costs [Pigoski:97]. Military software is at the low end of the maintenance cost range, but that seems to be because users of military software can't complain much, and most of the feedback they generate is ignored. The effect is that military software is poorly maintained and requires periodic wholesale substitution [Hendler:02].

20.6.3 Continual Improvements

Your ability to successfully sell your software as an exit strategy is directly related to your ability to provide assurances that your product is capable of meeting (or surpassing) the following software quality factors:

- **Verifiability** refers to design and programming features that enable efficient verification of the design and programming. Refer to commitment to documentation and programming guidelines.
- **Expandability** refers to future efforts that will be needed to improve service or add new applications in order to improve usability.
- **Safety** means to eliminate risky conditions as a result of errors in process control software.
- **Manageability** refers to the administrative tools that support software modification during the software development and maintenance periods.
- **Survivability** refers to the stability of service.

We recommend the following continual improvements:

1. **Bug fixing** or **corrective maintenance** is essential to keep customers. In practice, most required bug fixing is performed early in the post-delivery cycle; if it is not successfully performed, the product will not be accepted in the marketplace and hence will not have any significant life. There is substantial literature on the benefits of having high-quality software to enable reuse, a form of long life, but those analyses document cost avoidance rather than income.

2. **Adaptive maintenance** is needed to satisfy externally mandated constraints. Adaptations allow the software to deal with new hardware, operating systems, networks, browser updates, as well as other software used in the customers' environment. Governmental regulations may also require adaptations, new taxation rules affect financial programs, accounting standards are upgraded periodically, and so on. All such changes must be complied with if the software is to remain useful. Within a business, new mergers and acquisitions force changes in information systems, and new medical technologies affect healthcare software.

3. **Perfective maintenance** includes improvements as performance upgrades, assuring scalability as demands grow, keeping interfaces smooth and consistent with industry developments, and being able to fully exploit features of interoperating software by other vendors, as databases, Web services, schedulers, and the like. Perfecting makes existing software work better. In that process, the functionality is upgraded, but not to the extent that truly new products are created. Perfection may be less urgent, but keeps the customer happy and loyal [Basili:90]. Military software, rarely perfected, wastes much user effort, and hence rates low on a benefit–cost scale. Bug fixing, for software that is accepted in the market, eventually reduces to less than 10% of the maintenance effort. Adaptation consumes 15%–50% of the maintenance costs. The effort needed varies with the number of interfaces that have to be maintained. Ongoing perfection is known to require about half of the maintenance costs in the long term. Marketing staff often tout the results of perfective maintenance as being novel and innovative, even when base functionality does not change. The effectiveness of maintenance is greatly hindered by poor design and lack of adequate documentation. A simple mathematical model promotes the use of a common architecture for interacting applications to lower maintenance costs. Well-designed systems will be improved more rapidly, and hence, paradoxically, consume more maintenance. But those systems will also have a longer life. There are several related aspects that motivate a supplier to maintain a product at a high level. With every version, the product will be better and will be easier to sell. If a maintenance fee is charged, ongoing maintenance is expected and essential to keeping costumers; then those fees contribute a stable income. It is easier to keep an old customer than to gain a new one. Good maintenance has a high value to the customer and can generate substantial revenue. Maintenance fees contribute in time as much revenue as new sale licenses.

20.6.4 How Did Microsoft Do It?

Many consider Bill Gates a tech nerd who got lucky. But he is one of the few CEOs of a major company who not only understands the technology but also understands business.

It's hard to see a mention of Steve Jobs without the worlds "changed the world" or "changing an industry." And let us give him his due as one of the greatest entrepreneurs in history, an amazing entrepreneur and visionary who left many "dents" in the universe. And he did change many industries, such as music, film, and yes, personal computing.[13]

But in terms of sheer impact on the world? Microsoft wins, hands down.

Microsoft gave the world two things:

1. Microsoft was the first real software company.
2. Microsoft did put a PC on every desk and in every home.

At the end of the day, it's that last part that matters. By shifting the value in computing to software, Microsoft commoditized computing hardware and made computing accessible to the masses. If this isn't one of the most significant events in history, nothing is. Microsoft, being a software company, built an operating system platform that let thousands of others innovate, which, along with Moore's Law, made PCs cheaper and more valuable every year, which meant more and more people could get access to them, in a vicious circle.

Being the first big, viable software company also meant Microsoft cleared the way for thousands of other software innovators, when it was in no way obvious at the start that a company could be viable making just software.

The hardware may have been ugly and the software clunky, but a big reason why Windows is buggy is because of Microsoft's amazing 20 year commitment to backward compatibility, which makes PC software a cohesive environment, a tremendous service to users and the world, for which it gets no credit.

Table 20.5 lists the seven basic principles that according to Cusumano and Selby account for Microsoft's amazing success.[14]

20.7 Legal Documentation

The documentation of an any business sale transaction typically begins with a letter of intent. The letter of intent generally does not bind the parties to commit to a transaction but may bind the parties to confidentiality and exclusivity obligations so that the transaction can be considered through a due diligence process involving lawyers, accountants, tax advisors, and other professionals, as well as business people from both sides.[15,16]

TABLE 20.5

Seven Basic Principles for Microsoft

1. **Managing the company:** Finding smart people who know the technology and business
2. **Managing creative people with technical skills:** Organizing small teams of specialists
3. **Competing with products and standards:** Pioneering and orchestrating evolving mass markets
4. **Defining products and development processes:** Focusing creativity by evolving features
5. **Developing and shipping products:** Doing everything in parallel and constantly synchronizing (the basic development model)
6. **Building a learning organization:** Feedback and sharing through self-criticism
7. **Attacking the future with new technology**

After due diligence is completed, the parties may proceed to draw up a definitive agreement, known as a *merger agreement, share purchase agreement,* or *asset purchase agreement,* depending on the structure of the transaction. Such contracts are typically 80–100 pages long and focus on six key types of terms:[17]

1. **Conditions**, which must be satisfied before there is an obligation to complete the transaction. Conditions typically include matters such as regulatory approvals and the lack of any materially adverse change in the target's business.

2. **Representations and warranties** by the seller with regard to the company, which are claimed to be true at both the time of signing and the time of closing. Sellers often attempt to craft their representations and warranties with knowledge qualifiers, dictating the level of knowledge applicable and which seller parties' knowledge is relevant.[18] Some agreements provide that if the representations and warranties by the seller prove to be false, the buyer may claim a refund of part of the purchase price, as is common in transactions involving privately held companies (although in most acquisition agreements involving public company targets, the representations and warranties of the seller do not survive the closing). Representations regarding a target company's net working capital are a common source of post-closing disputes.

3. **Covenants**, which govern the conduct of the parties, both before the closing (e.g., covenants that restrict the operations of the business between signing and closing) and after the closing (e.g., covenants regarding future income tax filings and tax liability or post-closing restrictions agreed to by the buyer and seller parties).

4. **Termination rights**, which may be triggered by a breach of contract, a failure to satisfy certain conditions or the passage of a certain period of time without consummating the transaction, and fees and damages payable in case of a termination for certain events (also known as *breakup fees*).

5. **Provisions** relating to obtaining required shareholder approvals under state law and related SEC filings required under federal law, if applicable, and terms related to the mechanics of the legal transactions to be consummated at closing—for example, the determination and allocation of the purchase price and post-closing adjustments (e.g., adjustments after the final determination of working capital at closing or earn-out payments payable to the sellers), repayment of outstanding debt, and the treatment of outstanding shares, options and other equity interests.

6. **An indemnification provision**, which provides that an indemnitor will indemnify, defend, and hold harmless the indemnitee(s)

TABLE 20.6

Benefits of the Sale to the Owners

Consideration	Advantages	Disadvantages
All-cash transaction	• Deal considered concluded • No further obligations by either party	• Difficult to find an all-cash buyer for a business • Lump-sum payout may push seller into a higher tax bracket • Typically equates to lower selling price
Stock *If the buyer is a publicly traded business, it may pay for the selling company with stock.*	• Receiving stock in the buying entity may avoid all immediate taxes • Share in future gains (or losses) of the consolidated business	• Most transactions require a 6-month or 1-year holding period (blackout) • Selling the stock in public market may be restricted
Third-party financing *A lender provides a percentage of the purchase price of the business after conducting its own investigation into the business and potential buyer.*	• Expanded list of potential buyers • The third party providing the loan will conduct its own due diligence on the buyer, serving as validation	• Bank loans can require extensive qualification process • Deal likely delayed to allow third party to conduct its own due diligence on the seller
Earn-out payments *The seller "earns" a percentage of the purchase price based on the business meeting specified financial performance targets.*	• Similar to seller financing, earn-out payments demonstrate the seller's faith in the business' ability to generate future profits • Spreads taxable sale income over multiple years • May be used to bridge gap when buyer and seller cannot agree on value of the business	• Payments are usually determined by accounting calculations that put both selling and buying parties at risk • Seller may need to stay involved to ensure business meets the specified performance targets
Seller financing *The seller finances a portion of the purchase price with a secured promissory note to be paid down with interest over time. Often the loan will have a "balloon" payment due 3–5 years after the sale with the expectation that the buyer will be able to refinance the loan with a bank at that time*	• Demonstrates confidence in the business' ability to generate future profit • Greatly expand the number of potential buyers to include those that need financing beyond what third party can provide • May avoid higher tax rates by spreading the proceeds over multiple years • The promissory note may yield interest to the seller	• Seller takes on the significant risk that buyer doesn't pay interest or principal on the promissory note • Upon default of note secured by business' assets, seller may end up as owner of the business again

Source: Modified from Tracey, D.K. (2015). Guide to selling a small business. North Carolina Small Business and Technology Development Center. http://www.sbtdc.org/pdf/selling-small-biz.pdf.

for losses incurred by the indemnitees as a result of the indemnitor's breach of its contractual obligations in the purchase agreement.

Post-closing adjustments may still occur to certain provisions of the purchase agreement, including the purchase price. These adjustments are subject to enforceability issues in certain situations. Alternatively, certain transactions use the "locked box" approach, where the purchase price is fixed at signing and based on the seller's equity value at a pre-signing date and an interest charge.

20.8 Closing the Deal

Closing is the technical term that describes when the buyer delivers and the seller receives the agreed payment, whether it be a bank check, wire transfer, stock certificate, or other valuable consideration. In a small-business sale, the signing of the sales agreement and closing are typically performed simultaneously. The closing may take place in person (all parties and advisers are physically present at a single location) or virtually (signed documents are e-mailed and payment is transferred electronically). It is not until the actual closing that the owners of the selling business realize the benefit of the sale, as summarized in Table 20.6.

Notes

1. Tracey, D.K. (2015). Guide to selling a small business. North Carolina Small Business and Technology Development Center. http://www.sbtdc.org/pdf/selling-small-biz.pdf.
2. Schenck, B.F. (2015). *The BizBuySell Guide to Selling Your Small Business*, 3rd Edition. BizBuySell. http://www.bizbuysell.com/seller/guide/selling-a-business.
3. Harvey, M.G., and Lusch, R.F. (1995). Expanding the nature and scope of due diligence. *Journal of Business Venturing*, 10, 5–21.
4. Gillman (2002). The link between valuations and due diligence. *Academy of Accounting and Financial Studies Journal*.
5. Ernst and Young (2013). Selling your business? What you need to know before letting go.
6. Chapman, C.E. (2006). *Conducting Due Diligence*. New York: Practicing Law Institute.
7. Handelsman, M. (2012). Selling your business? Get your buyer's attention. *Inc.*, May 16. https://www.inc.com/mike-handelsman/selling-your-business-preparing-an-effective-selling-memo.html.

8. Tynax. Guide to selling your patent. http://tynax.com/PDFDocs/Guide_To_Selling_Your_Patent.pdf.
9. https://www.sec.gov/Archives/edgar/data/1424822/000146970911000199/ex101patentpurchaseagreement.htm.
10. Wiederhold, G. (2007). What is your software worth? Stanford University, April. http://infolab.stanford.edu/pub/gio/2006/worth40.pdf.
11. Smith, G., and Parr, R. (2000). *Valuation of Intellectual Property and Intangible Assets*, 3rd Edition. Hoboken, NJ: Wiley.
12. Hand, J., and Lev, B. (eds) (2003). *Intangible Assets: Values, Measures. and Risks*. Oxford, UK: Oxford University Press.
13. Gobry, P.E. (2011). Yes, Microsoft did change the world more than Apple. *Business Insider*, September 8. http://www.businessinsider.com/yes-microsoft-did-change-the-world-more-than-apple-2011-9.
14. Cusumano, M.A., and Selby, R.W. (1998). *Microsoft Secrets: How the World's Most Powerful Software Company Creates Technology, Shapes Markets and Manages People*. New York: Touchstone.
15. McKenna Long and Aldridge. Mergers & acquisitions quick reference guide.
16. Wikipedia. (2018). Mergers and acquisitions. https://en.wikipedia.org/wiki/Mergers_and_acquisitions.
17. Barusch, R. (2010). WSJ M&A 101: A guide to merger agreements. *Wall Street Journal*, Deal Journal, November 9.
18. Avery, D,. and Crossley, K. (2014). Use of knowledge qualifiers for representations and warranties. *Transaction Advisors*, December. ISSN 2329-9134.

21

IPO Your Ultimate Exit Strategy I

"An exit (harvest) occurs when an entrepreneur gets
financially rewarded for all of the creativity, hard
work, investment and risk put into the startup."

21.1 Introduction

In their book, *Venture Capital at the Crossroads*, Bygrave and Timmons[1] help
introduce the "harvest" concept as: "Just like farmers, venture capitalists
seed, tend, and feed portfolio companies in the hopes of reaping a bountiful harvest." Founder/owners and investors know that harvesting an
entrepreneurial venture is the approach taken by the owners and investors
to realize terminal after-tax cash flows on their investment. It defines how
they will extract (monetize) some or all of the economic value from their
investment.[2]

However, just because an entrepreneurial team can build a successful
business does not mean they can become rich from it. Investors who provide
equity financing to high-risk ventures need to know how and when they
are likely to realize a return on their investments before they commit any
funds. They invest not for eternity but on average for three to seven years,
after which they expect to make a profit that reflects the scale of the risk they
have taken on in making their investment. An exit should be seen as a critical
milestone that focuses on the monetization of their investment. It is at this
critical stage in the entrepreneurial life cycle that the capital gains (or losses)
occur, or, in other words, that there is a harvest (or exit) from the investment.

Your exit strategy is crucial because it helps you define your ultimate success in business. When entrepreneurs have not thought through an exit
strategy, it may be an indicator that they are not focused on the eventual
transition of the venture. There is a saying among venture capitalists, "It's
easy to get into an investment, but how do we get out?" And investors do not
want an exit strategy to be difficult or bloody. In essence, having a harvest
goal and a strategy to achieve it is indeed what separates successful entrepreneurs from the rest of the pack.

Table 21.1 lists applicable definitions of exits and harvesting:

TABLE 21.1

Exit and Harvesting Definitions

An exit is the final piece necessary in creating the ultimate value to all the participants in the venture, especially the owners, and employees	Bygrave, W.D. (1997). *The Portable MBA in Entrepreneurship*, 2nd Ed., Wiley, New York, p. 416.
Entrepreneurial exit can also be viewed as part of the universal organizational problem of leadership succession, where a "clash between an organization's goals and a leader's personal goals" occurs	Sonnefeld, J. (1988). *The Hero's Farewell*, Oxford University Press, New York.
Harvesting an entrepreneurial firm is the approach taken by the owners and investors to realize terminal after-tax cash flows on their investment	Petty, J.W. (1997a). Harvesting, in Bygrave, W.D. (Ed.), *The Portable MBA in Entrepreneurship*, Wiley, New York, pp. 71–94.
The harvest is the owners' and investors' strategy for achieving the terminal after-tax cash flows on their investment. It does not necessarily mean that the entrepreneur will leave the company; it merely defines how she will extract some or all of the cash flows from the investment to be used for other purposes. Nor should it totally disregard the personal and non-financial aspects of the transaction	Bygrave, W.D. (1997). *The Portable MBA in Entrepreneurship*, 2nd Ed., Wiley, New York, p. 416. Bygrave, W.D. (1993). Towards a theory of entrepreneurship, *Journal of Business Venturing*, Vol. 8 (1993), No. 3, pp. 255–280

Note: For our purposes, the terms exit or harvest are clearly differentiated from the term failure, or bankruptcy, a situation where the entrepreneur has no other option but to discontinue the firm. In their review of past research, Watson and Everett[3] plainly distinguish four types of failure: (1) discontinuance of a business for any reason, (2) bankruptcy or loss to creditors, (3) disposed of to prevent further losses, and (4) failing to "make a go of it."

21.2 Making Your Business "IPO Ready"

Business owners considering selling their business should consider ways of making their businesses "marketable." Some of the considerations include:

- *Current and future profitability*: Purchasers need to feel confident in the ability of the business to continue to be profitable in the future. Evidence of predictable and stable cash flows and revenues will greatly encourage potential buyers.
- *Growth potential*: Provide evidence that the business operates in a growth market and can continue to operate profitably in the future.
- *Strong brand and customer loyalty*: A loyal customer base will be very appealing to buyers, particularly in the medical and high-tech industries.

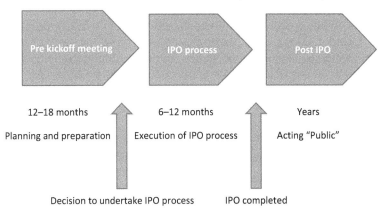

FIGURE 21.1
Time from planning to IPO.

But beware: an initial public offering (IPO) is a not a sprint; it is a marathon that will consume a huge proportion of upper management's time and energy, as seen in Figure 21.1.

21.3 Going Public via an IPO

An IPO is the traditional ultimate exit strategy of many entrepreneurs. It means that your startup has matured into a full-fledged company, ready to be listed on one of the stock exchanges. Going public is a monumental success for you and your team.

An initial public offering is the realization of a dream for entrepreneurs, executives, board members and stockholders, a singular achievement that demonstrates their success in building a strong business and creating value for owners, employees, and customers.

"Going public" is the process of offering securities—generally common stock—of a privately owned company for sale to the general public. The first time these securities are offered is referred to as an initial public offering, or IPO. It will forever change how your company goes about doing business. A public company has access to more, and often deeper, sources of capital than a private company.

An IPO in which a company sells its unissued securities and receives all the proceeds in the form of additional capital is called a primary offering. A securities sale in which securities held by the owners of the company are sold, and from which the owners receive the proceeds, is called a secondary offering. IPOs are almost always primary offerings, but may include the sale of shares held by the present shareholders.[4] You may be one of the "selling shareholders" listed in the offering document.

By virtue of being one of the selling shareholders, you may monetize some of your founder shares, thus "exiting" or "harvesting" at the IPO stage. Or, you may decide to keep all your shares if you feel that there is tremendous upside to the share price if the company executes the promises made in the offering document.

You may decide to go public for any of the following reasons:

- To provide liquidity for you and your founding team
- For private and personal reasons
- To access capital for quick expansion
- To acquire other companies with publicly traded stock as the currency
- To attract and retain talented employees
- To diversify and reduce investor holdings
- To enhance your company's reputation

21.4 Practical Considerations

There are a number of practical considerations you should evaluate when contemplating an IPO, including restrictions on publicity before and during the offering; selection of underwriters; disclosure of related party transactions; disclosure of executive compensation; prohibition on loans to directors and officers; structure of the board and board committees; adequacy of disclosure practices and procedures; ethics and conduct codes and procedures; accounting and corporate law matters; listing on a stock exchange; and compliance with the lengthy U.S. Securities and Exchange Commission (SEC) registration process.[5]

Be aware that an initial public offering requires a great deal of effort, cost and management focus. The preparation and execution of an IPO require the company, working closely with legal counsel, auditors, and underwriters, to identify, analyze and resolve a myriad of legal, accounting and business issues. The criteria an IPO candidate should use to evaluate readiness include:

- The ability of your current management team and Board of Directors to transition into a public company, readiness to reorganize Board of Directors

- The company's profitability, growth prospects, financial condition and results of operations
- The company's visibility and predictability of future financial results;
- The strength of the company's intellectual property portfolio and key commercial arrangements
- The company's competitors and competitive position, and the status of the company's competitive barriers to entry
- Risk factors relevant to the company, its industry, and the public markets generally;
- The status of the public markets and market conditions for the particular company's industry
- Legal, accounting and regulatory compliance obligations of public companies, including extensive initial and ongoing SEC and national securities exchange filings and disclosure requirements, corporate governance, disclosure controls and internal controls over financial reporting
- Investor relations demands, including the need to build and preserve credibility with analysts, the financial press, regulators, institutional stockholders and other players in the capital markets
- Complexities involved in changing a company's corporate and capital structure, or taking other actions that require stockholder approval, once the company is public

Generally, a company that outpaces the industry average in growth will have a better chance of attracting prospective IPO investors than one with marginal or inconsistent growth. Investment bankers want the offering that they underwrite to be successful. Therefore, they look for companies that can fulfill tried and true criteria to boost the chances for a successful offering and good performance in the aftermarket, such as an experienced management team coupled with an innovative product offering, preferably one with a defensible competitive advantage.

21.5 Are You Ready to Take the Plunge?

Owners begin to think about going public when the funding required to meet the demands of its business begins to exceed the company's ability to raise additional capital through other channels at attractive terms. But simply needing capital does not always mean that going public is the right, or even possible, answer. There are a number of questions it should ask itself before deciding to take the plunge and go public. Some of the questions and answers are found in Table 21.2:

TABLE 21.2

Are You Ready to Go Public?

Have you reached the point at which prospects for a strong sales and earnings growth trend in the future are secured?	Successful IPOs sustain an increasing annual sales and earnings growth rate over a period of time
Do your products serve both your customers and investing public?	Established companies can rely on historical sales data, while the early-stage company must use market research projections and demonstrated product superiority. An early-stage company may qualify as an IPO candidate due to the uniqueness of its product offering
Are you prepared to file timely financial statements with the Securities and Exchange Commission ("SEC")?	Public companies need to file financial statements on a quarterly and annual basis with the SEC, with prescribed data requirements and required adherence to rigorous GAAP standards. These financial statements are due relatively soon after each period end, so there is increased time pressure on reporting compared to that of a privately held company
Is your leadership capable and committed?	In any public offering, the quality of the leadership team is a key factor. It is vital to ensure that the Board of Directors, as well as management, has the right blend of experience and skills to run a public company
Are you Sarbanes–Oxley compliant?	The passage of the Sarbanes–Oxley Act of 2002 raised the bar on internal controls. This legislation, among other things, requires CEOs and CFOs to sign and attest to financial statements
Are you prepared to undertake substantial initial costs? Do the expected benefits outweigh the costs of going public?	Raising equity capital in the public markets entails substantial costs, such as underwriting and other advisors' fees and expenses. However, the answer as to whether the benefits outweigh the cost cannot be realistically known until several years after an IPO
Choosing an appropriate stock market	Each stock market has specific entry requirements, such as earnings history, shareholders' equity, market capitalization, number of expected shareholders, and corporate governance. A company must choose the market that is right for its stock
Is the market timing right?	The appetite for initial public offerings can vary dramatically, depending on overall market strength, the market's opinion of IPOs, industry economic conditions, technological changes, etc. Stock market volatility is one of the most unpredictable aspects of going public and it makes timing the IPO key in achieving the best possible result
Are you prepared for restrictions on insider sales?	Stock sales by insiders are usually limited. Most underwriters require that a company's existing shareholders enter into contractual agreements to refrain from selling their stock during a specified time following the IPO, typically 180 days. This is called the "lock-up" period

(Continued)

TABLE 21.2 (CONTINUED)

Are You Ready to Go Public?

Ongoing expenses will be large	Public companies are required to report and certify financial information on a quarterly and annual basis. There will be ongoing expenses related to these changes, such as the expense of independent auditors. Administrative and investor relations costs include those related to quarterly reports, proxy materials, annual reports, transfer agents, and public relations
Loss of control	If more than 50% of a company's shares are sold to the public, the original owners will lose control of the company. Some companies attempt to structure their offerings so that after an initial offering the founders still have control
Constant pressure for quarterly performance	In a private company, the business owner is free to operate independently. However, once the company becomes publicly owned, the owner acquires many shareholders and is accountable to all of them. Shareholders demand steady growth in areas such as sales, profits, market share, and product innovation. Thus, in a publicly held company, management is under constant pressure to balance short-term demands for growth with strategies that achieve long-term goals
New board of directors	Sarbanes–Oxley requires that a majority of the members of a Board of Directors be from outside the company and independent. At least one board member must have a financial background either as a CPA or CFO. One member must chair the audit committee, and outside directors must meet in executive session
Risk of personal liability	Management and directors are personally liable for financial reporting
Abort costs	There is a possibility of a failed attempt to go public and the attendant costs of an aborted IPO
Being and acting public	The process of transforming the company to operate as a public company on an ongoing basis; Investor/media relations

21.6 IPO Exit for Venture Capital or Private Equity

Venture capital (VC) or private equity funds look at IPO exits differently than owner-entrepreneurs. Venture capital or private equity funds have multiple factors to consider when analyzing an exit strategy. A fund will need to consider, among other things, the strategy for liquidating its position; the time it will take to fully liquidate; the aggregate price it will receive for its investment when selling over time at prevailing market prices; the multiple it would receive in a public offering compared to a private sale; the fund's continued ability (or inability) to control the company; ongoing disclosure, including disclosure of affiliated relationships and transactions; and the heightened scrutiny of compliance with fiduciary duties by fund representatives on the board.[6]

For funds, ultimately, it may be more difficult to exit a significant investment through the public offering process than a private sale, and the fund will have less control and more disclosure requirements. However, often the public will pay a higher price than a private buyer for a company with strong growth potential.

One way to approach the IPO exit decision is to first determine whether to gain liquidity through an IPO exit strategy or through a sale of the company. If through an IPO, then determine a post-IPO liquidity strategy—secondary sales to the public; distribution to fund investors; or private sales or a sale of the company following the IPO. Analysis of your post-IPO liquidity strategy, and related issues, may affect your threshold exit decision.

While many funds may want to exit an investment through a straightforward sale process to gain immediate liquidity, funds face situations where an exit is ripe, but a typical sales process may not appear to yield significant or timely demand for the company. One strategy to stimulate demand is to begin or even complete an IPO while still seeking a private sale. A strategic buyer may become more interested in a company if, in a competitive situation, it believes the company will gain resources or momentum through the public offering process. Regardless of whether the company is a competitor, a buyout will become more expensive and difficult after the target is public.

21.7 Recent IPOs by Funds

Seventy-seven venture-backed IPOs raised $9.4 billion in 2015, marking a 40% decline in dollars raised compared to 2014, according to the exit poll report by Thomson Reuters and the National Venture Capital Association (NVCA). For the fourth quarter, 16 venture-backed IPOs raised $2.2 billion, an 18% increase compared to the total dollars raised during the previous three-month period and up slightly compared to the number of offerings listed during the third quarter of 2015.

Ninety-one venture-backed mergers and acquisitions (M&A) deals were reported in the fourth quarter, 26 of which had an aggregate deal value of $3.6 billion, decreasing 48% compared to the third quarter of this year. For full-year 2015, 372 M&A transactions were reported, with 84 deals combining for a disclosed value of $16.3 billion, the slowest full-year period for venture-backed M&A since 2009.[7]

The year 2016 saw the lowest pace of IPOs since 2009. Venture managers continue to take advantage of strategic acquirers hungry to purchase growth rather than build organically, with two VC-backed companies valued at over $1 billion. According to the PitchBook 2016 report, the IPO activity is shown in Figure 21.2.

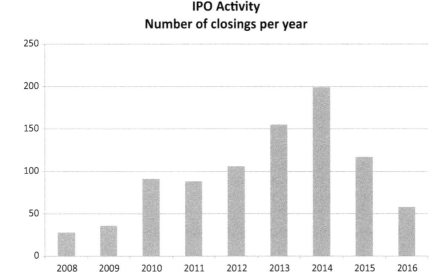

FIGURE 21.2
IPOs are heavily dependent on overall market health.

On the other hand, successful companies may decide to undergo a private sale to a strategic buyer. For example, Android was sold to Google in July 2005 for a reported $50 million.[8] Typical of Google's acquisition strategy, the search giant quietly bought the wireless start-up. Android operated quietly itself. Little was published on the company's website, or in the press. But it was the next-generation operation of Andy Rubin, who previously founded mobile-device maker Danger. Android made software, or operating systems, for wireless devices that are location-sensitive or personalized for the owner.[9] After the private sale, Andy Rubin remained with Google.

Alternatively, going public as an IPO can be seen as an alternative to a private sale, so it can effectively serve as another bidder in an exit process. If a sale is not completed and the company goes public, the company may increase its visibility and essentially market itself through public disclosure of its business, strategies and financial results. In some cases, a "two-step" sale—partial liquidity through an IPO at a short-term market peak, followed by a negotiated sale of control—could extract total higher value for a fund than a straight sale or complete liquidity through secondary sales to the public.

21.8 Your New "Publicly Listed Company" Board of Directors

In order to comply with listing regulations and Sarbanes–Oxley requirements, you may have to reshuffle your Board of Directors. After stewarding your startup through the tumultuous years of survival and growth, you will be forced to vacate your original loyal board members in favor of a new batch of independent directors arbitrarily selected by your venture capital investors.

It will also be quite likely that you will be asked to step down as board chairman, in favor of a well-connected (hopefully) venture capitalist, who will be expected to "take the company to new heights." It is equally likely that a new chief executive officer (CEO) will be named, prior to going public.

It will be explained to you that founder-technologists are ill-equipped to run public companies. A professional CEO will be better suited to navigate the financial and managerial complexities faced by public companies. A new set of business skills is required to ensure success. If in spite of this, you are still determined to go public, please read on!

21.8.1 Corporate Governance and the Boardroom

The ultimate responsibility for the oversight of a company's business and affairs rests squarely with the Board of Directors. The board monitors financial reporting, public disclosure announcements, and oversees internal controls and compliance with laws. In addition to making choices about strategic focus and significant policies, the directors set the strategic and ethical tone of the business.

An important question is the optimal board size. There is no "optimal" board size—it, of course, depends on many factors, such as the needs of the business and the talents and skills of the individual members—and the board size should be tailored accordingly. Nevertheless, as a company prepares for an IPO, there is usually some anxiety regarding whether its board has the right size and composition for the rigors of public company life. Pre-IPO companies often find themselves agonizing over how to attract qualified new board members and puzzling over what the appropriate kind of compensation would be for an individual agreeing to help administer a soon-to-be-public corporation.

According to Investopedia,[10] there is no universal agreement on the optimum size of a Board of Directors. A large number of members represent a challenge in terms of using them effectively and/or having any kind of meaningful individual participation. A study by corporate libraries found the median board size is nine members, while most boards range from 3 to 31 members. Many consultants[11] propose an odd number such as five, while academic researchers think the statistically-derived ideal size is seven for best decision-making purposes.[12]

In addition, there are two critical board committees that must be made up of independent members:

- The compensation committee
- The audit committee

The minimum number of members for each committee is three. This means that a minimum of six board members are needed so that no one is on more than one committee. Having members doing double duty may compromise the important wall between audit and compensation, which helps avoid any conflicts of interest. Members serving on a number of other boards may not devote adequate time to their responsibilities.

The seventh member is the chairperson of the board. It's the responsibility of the chairperson to make sure the board is functioning properly and the CEO is fulfilling his duty and following the directives of the board. According to this view, a conflict of interest is created if the CEO is also the chairperson of the board.

To staff any additional committees, such as nominating or governance, additional people may be necessary. However, having more than nine members may make the board too big to function effectively.

21.8.2 Independent Directors

Public exchanges in the United States require that a majority of a public company's directors be "independent" within a relatively short period of time following the company's proposed initial public offering. However, if possible, it is better if the majority of the board is independent at the time of the IPO, because investors may focus on this aspect of a company's governance at the time of the offering.

An "independent director" is an individual who can exercise judgment as a director independent of the influence of company management. An independent director will be free from business, family or personal relationships that might interfere with the director's independence. Many institutional investors suggest that a "substantial" majority of a company's directors be independent.

A company should determine whether current outside board members meet the definition of "independent" under the applicable rules and identify any new needs regarding board composition. If the company desires to add additional independent board members, it should begin the process of identifying and recruiting them several months in advance of the public offering, or as soon as practicable. Any agreement with a new director may have to be disclosed in the IPO prospectus.

Exchanges establish a number of relationships that will disqualify a director from being independent. For example, each of the following may disqualify a director under exchange independence standards:

- Previous employment relationships
- Receipt of compensation over $100,000 (other than for board service)
- Certain relationships with the company's auditor;
- Significant business relationships between the listed company and another entity where the director serves as an executive officer

- Significant stockholder
- Certain interlocking directorships

21.9 The Securities and Exchange Commission

The SEC is charged with ensuring a fair and orderly playing field for public companies and their investors. It has the authority to pursue civil and criminal prosecution against those who breach established procedures. As a public company executive, you will live with the SEC for all your waking hours.

Liability may arise from material misstatements or omissions in a registration statement. If the SEC finds mistakes or requests clarification during the registration process, it can delay an IPO.

It is a company's duty to potential shareholders to constantly monitor the drafting of the registration statement. Companies should ensure that they completely understand all of its components and the assumptions behind those components. The outside professionals that companies hire to advise on your IPO are experienced business advisors. They help companies make the final decisions; they do not make decisions for companies.

The SEC's Division of Corporation Finance reviews the registration statement and ultimately allows or denies an issue to "go effective," that is, sell shares. Registrants generally are assigned to the SEC's Division of Corporation Finance's review branches on the basis of standard industrial classification codes. Teams of government attorneys and accountants and, in some cases, industry specialists or engineers, review each filing. The chain of review leads up to the director of the division and the issuance of a "comment letter."[13]

The SEC concerns itself with the thoroughness and clarity of the registration statement and the prospectus to ensure that these documents adequately inform potential investors. Keep in mind that the SEC only regulates the vehicle used to offer a security. It evaluates neither the company nor the quality of the security.

21.10 Your Managing Underwriter

Companies can go to market without an underwriter,[14] but the process is so complex and the know-how so specialized that it is rarely done. The complicated market issues that are arcane to most people are the stock-in-trade of underwriters, and it is in the best interest of a company's offering to take advantage of their expertise. The value added by an underwriter should be the assurance that an IPO will be properly managed and successfully marketed and supported, both before and after going public.

A principal, or managing, underwriter works with a company to develop the registration statement, coordinate the road show, underwrite certain risks and form a syndicate. This syndicate is composed of an underwriting group, which bears the risk of the underwriting, and the selling group. The selling group solicits interest from its retail and institutional clients, sells stock once an IPO goes effective, and provides after-market support. The share allotment each underwriter is committed to buy will be stipulated in the prospectus. Good managing underwriters and investment bankers have a highly developed sense of what sells (or doesn't sell) and for how much. They also have an instinct for timing an issue, and they are able to anticipate pitfalls and calculate risks. Underwriters and investment bankers contribute other skills and support, including:

- Experience in marketing, structuring the deal, and facilitating syndications with co-underwriters and brokers to create support for the stock after it is issued
- Knowledge of market conditions and various types of investors
- Experience in pricing stock so it will be attractive to the company but also attain a reasonable return for the investor
- The ability to help client companies with future offerings
- A research department with the scope to enable it to analyze the client company, its competitors, the market, and the economy as a whole

Generally speaking, underwriters come in three sizes: "major bracket" or "wirehouse" firms with well-known names, a middle-tier company comprising mostly regional firms, and local firms. Not surprisingly, the size and scope of a company and of its offering will, in part, determine the size of the underwriter it enlists for its IPO.

A good working relationship with an underwriter is critical, regardless of the size of the firm a company selects. Companies should trust their underwriters to provide all of the information they will need to execute an IPO successfully.

Of course, the professional relationship between a company and its underwriter is mutually beneficial. An underwriter earns money from an offering in a variety of ways. They include:

- The discount or commission. This averages around 7% but could be up to 10% for more difficult or smaller offerings and down to 5% for larger or simpler offerings in a competitive market
- The right to underwrite future offerings of the company's securities
- Non-accountable expense allowance. This standard practice allows underwriters to bill a company an amount that may not exceed 3% of gross proceeds

TABLE 21.3

Two Forms of Underwriting Commitments

Firm commitment	The underwriters pledge to buy all of the stock offered in the IPO and resell it to the public. This arrangement offers the company the most security because the owners know they will receive the full sales price of the issue
Under a best-efforts commitment	In which the underwriter uses his or her best efforts to sell the stock but is under no obligation to purchase the stock should all or part of the issue remain unsold

- Other compensation, such as warrants to purchase stock
- Overallotments[15]

While these items may seem to allow quite a few charges by an underwriter, maximum underwriters' compensation, both direct and indirect, are regulated and reviewed for fairness by the Financial Industry Regulatory Authority (FINRA).[16] Blue sky laws also require a review of underwriters' compensation by state examiners.

Generally, the underwriter's agreement can come in two basic forms as shown in Table 21.3.

There are variations on these two basic agreements. They include an "all-or-none" commitment, which is a modification of the "best-efforts" agreement. In this commitment, all of the stock must be sold by the underwriter or the entire issue is canceled (at considerable cost to the company). In a partial "all-or-none" agreement, the underwriter requires the sale of a specified portion of the issue (typically two-thirds) for the "best efforts" to remain in effect on the remainder of the issue.

21.11 Independent Auditors

As strategic and technical advisors, a company's independent auditors will play a key role throughout the registration process. Therefore, at the start of the IPO process, a company will need to ensure that it has selected an audit firm that is registered with the Public Company Accounting Oversight Board (PCAOB). The selection of an auditing firm should also be based on its:

- Experience with public company financial reporting
- Expertise in generally accepted accounting principles (GAAP) and the auditing standards of the PCAOB
- Reputation and experience with IPOs and other capital markets transactions

- Ability to continue to service the company appropriately through its growth and global expansion and its experience in the company's industry. Some of the specific services the independent auditor will provide include:
  - Strategic advice in the planning stage of the process to establish a realistic plan to enter the capital markets
  - Requisite technical expertise in U.S. GAAP and SEC requirements so it can advise a company on preparing the registration statement and obtaining SEC clearance
  - Guidance on the identification of potentially sensitive or problematic accounting issues (e.g., cheap stock considerations), financial disclosure issues, and the overall transparency of financial reporting
  - Audits of the financial statements (The process of auditing multiple years of financial statements and related disclosure requirements for public offerings can be extensive. An established relationship with an auditor who knows a company's business well, coupled with thorough preparation on the company's part, should enable it to complete the process faster and more effectively, which can be crucial to the success of the offering.)
  - A comfort letter to assist the underwriter in its due diligence efforts (This letter details certain procedures that the company's external auditor performed at the request of the underwriter, along with other representations the auditor made concerning the financial statements or other information contained in the prospectus.)
  - A full review of the prospectus and expert assistance in responding to the SEC comment letter process

The importance of engaging qualified, independent auditors long before the IPO cannot be overstated, particularly if a company has never had prior audited financial statements. The first audit of many young and expanding companies often discloses accounting and financial reporting problems that must be resolved before the registration statement can be filed.

Typically, large accounting firms are structured as full-service professional firms, offering services in various lines of business (e.g., audit, tax, consulting, and human resource advisory). A company's independent auditors, as well as individuals from these other lines of business, can play a valuable role as advisors in a variety of areas before, during, and after the going-public process.

Some of these roles include evaluating whether going public is the best alternative for a company, evaluating incentive compensation plans, addressing a company's accounting system needs and capabilities, reviewing the terms and conditions of acquisitions, and tax planning. A company may also consider consulting an accounting firm that can provide IPO and financial reporting advisory services.

21.12 The Going-Public Process

Your going-public process should follow an orderly and predictable timeline, if you have done your homework, as described in the preceding sections. The most successful IPOs are launched by those businesses that begin to operate as public companies well in advance of the actual IPO date.

A typical IPO execution process can take about 6–12 months. Advance preparation is a key success factor that allows for a smooth and efficient execution process. The following Table 21.4 outlines a typical execution timeline involving key participants in an IPO for the period leading up to and after an offering.

Once a company reaches a preliminary understanding with its underwriters, the IPO process starts in full force, and a "quiet period" begins during which a company is subject to SEC guidelines regarding the publication of information outside the prospectus. The opportunity to enhance awareness of a company, its name, products, and geographic markets will be limited since any publicity that creates a favorable attitude toward the company's securities could be considered illegal. However, the continuation of established, normal advertising and publicizing of information is acceptable.

This phase of the offering should start with a sense of urgency, because the clock is ticking. Companies will need to juggle four tasks in parallel timelines and keep business running as usual. These four tasks are:

1. The preparation of the preliminary prospectus
2. The investigation of the company's affairs for underwriter due diligence
3. The monitoring of market conditions for pricing purposes
4. The preparation of marketing materials for the road show

As previously mentioned, a company can generally expect it to take anywhere from six months to one year from the time the company decides to go public until the time it receives the proceeds from an offering. The actual length of this period depends on, among other things, the readiness of the company to go public, the availability of the information that must be disclosed in the registration statement, and market conditions.

TABLE 21.4

Master Execution Timeline

	6–12 Months before	Before Effective Date 20 Days	Before Effective Date 1–10 Days	Offering Day
Company	Quiet period begins; Hold an all-hands meeting; Execute a letter of intent. Ensure compliance with Regulation S-X[17]	Cooling-off period begins; Executives perform road show	Continue road show; Inform suppliers and customers	Execute underwriting agreement; Issue press release
Company legal counsel	Perform housekeeping of company records; Draft S-1; File with the SEC; File FINRA listing application	Answer SEC comments	Pricing amendment filed; Acceleration requested; File final registration statement	
Independent auditor	Complete audit of annual financial statements and review of interim financial statements; Review registration statement	Audit/review updated financial statements, if necessary; Respond to SEC comment letter	Deliver draft comfort letter[18]	Deliver final comfort letter
Investment Banker	Assess market; Make presentation to board; Continue due diligence	Distribute "red herring";[19] Orchestrate road show; Solicit expressions	Form syndicate; Place tombstone document into circulation	Execute underwriting agreement; Continue run of tombstone document
Investment banker's counsel	Begin due diligence; Prepare FINRA regulation filing; Undertake "Blue Sky" filings	Clear FINRA regulation comments	Continue due diligence	
Financial printer		Print preliminary registration statement/prospectus (red herring); Produce SEC & FINRA regulation filing packages		Print final registration statement/prospectus
SEC	Review preliminary registration statement; Issue comment letter			Declare offering effective
FINRA regulation	Review preliminary registration statement; Issue comment letter	Resolve comments		Declare no objections

21.13 Preparing Your S-1 Registration Statement

Preparing and filing your registration statement is a hugely complicated, time-consuming, technical process requiring substantial planning and coordination. It involves providing the all the information specified by the SEC form and complying with the applicable SEC rules in the most efficient manner possible. It requires a great deal of effort by the management team, lawyers, and independent accountants to position your company as accurately and positively as possible, while also disclosing any negative risk factors.

It is during the preparation process that a scheduled timetable for going public can take longer than expected, causing a delay in the anticipated filing date. It is therefore imperative that the entire team be thoroughly familiar with the registration statement requirements, be cognizant of the deadlines set, periodically assess the status of specific sections of the registration statement, and ensure that reviews of each section are timely.

The registration statement (Form S-1)[20] consists of two principal parts. Part I contains the essential facts regarding the business operations, financial condition, and management of the company that are required to be included in the prospectus, including the company's financial statements. Part II contains additional information that is not required to be included in the prospectus.

21.13.1 Part I—Information Required in the Prospectus (Summary)

This appears at the beginning of the prospectus and is basically a short summary describing the company, its business, the type of securities being offered, the amount of estimated proceeds, the intended use of the proceeds, and principal risk factors. It may also include certain summary financial information.

This section also includes the complete mailing address and the telephone number of the company's principal executive offices. Although not required, many companies include their website addresses in this section. The summary should not merely repeat the text of the prospectus but should provide a brief overview of the key aspects of the offering.

Risks associated with the business—Risk factors are those that are specific to the company and not to any other company or any offering. Risk factors that make an offering speculative or risky must be disclosed. These factors may include those that appear in the following list:

- Recent adverse developments or operating losses
- The need for additional financing in the near future
- The dilution to public investors
- Industry trends or business seasonality

- The existence of significant competition and competitor's names
- The company's dependence on a few customers, suppliers, or key members of management
- Information regarding significant contracts or licenses
- Impact of current or proposed legislation (e.g., communications, healthcare regulations)
- Technology changes that may impact the company in the future

Use of proceeds—A company must disclose and discuss the planned use of the proceeds from the offering. This section of the registration statement should be carefully drafted because the SEC requires reports on the actual disposition of the proceeds after the offering is completed. Because the actual use of proceeds may change between the filing date and the effective date as the company's plans change, it may be necessary to revise this section of the registration statement on the effective date. Typical uses might include debt reduction, acquisitions, capital purchases, research and development expenditures, and marketing expenses.

Dividend policy and restrictions—A company must disclose its current dividend policy, any anticipated changes to that policy, and any restrictions on the company's ability to pay dividends. For example, it is not uncommon for many new public companies not to pay dividends, but rather retain earnings to finance operations and the company's expansion. Restrictions might be based on debt, contractual agreements, or the regulatory environment in which a company operates.

Capitalization—Although not a specific requirement of Regulation S-K, the capital structure of a company both prior to the offering and after all securities offered are sold is usually presented in a tabular format.

Dilution—When there is a disparity between the IPO price and the net book value per share of tangible assets, dilution results. The effects of any material dilution on prospective investors must be disclosed; this is usually presented in a dilution table.

Underwriting and distribution of securities—Information must be provided about the price of the securities being offered, the members of the underwriting syndicate, the type of underwriting, and any relationship between a company and any of its underwriters.

Information about the company's business—A company must make extensive disclosures about its business. Among these are the items cited in the following list:

- A company's business plan, particularly if it has less than three years' operating results
- A description of principal segments, products, services, and markets for the company's products and services

- A description of its properties
- Information relating to foreign operations, if any
- Amount of research and development expenditures
- Regulations affecting the industry and company
- Pending or threatened legal proceedings
- Revenues, profits, assets, products and services, product development, major customers, order backlog, inventory, patents, suppliers, and the competitive position of each major industry and geographic segment of the company

Financial information—The SEC has specific and sometimes complex rules regarding the content and age of the financial statements that must be presented in a registration statement, and a company's accountants can be invaluable in helping it comply with these rules. In a Form S-1 registration statement, a company must generally present the items listed in the following:

- Audited balance sheets as of the end of the two most recent fiscal years
- Audited statements of income, cash flows, and changes in shareholders' equity for each of the past three fiscal years (Smaller companies may present such information for two years only.)
- Selected financial information (summarized from the balance sheets and income statements) for the past five fiscal years (Smaller companies are not required to present selected financial information.)
- Interim financial statements are required if the fiscal year-end financial statements are more than 134 days old, except for third-quarter financial statements, which are timely through the 45th day after the most recent fiscal year-end. After the 45th day, audited financial statements for the fiscal year must be included. Interim financial statements can be presented in a condensed format and generally are not audited. However, a review of the interim financial statements is typically performed by independent accountants

It should also be noted that:

- The latest audited financial statements cannot be more than one year and 45 days old at the date the registration statement becomes effective.
- Separate financial statements of businesses acquired or to be acquired should be listed.

The financial statement requirements range from one to three years depending on whether certain criteria are met.

- Insofar as practicable, the separate financial statements of significant equity investees of a registrant (except smaller reporting company registrants) shall be as of the same dates and the same periods as the audited consolidated financial statements. These financial statements only need to be audited for periods in which the equity investment is deemed to be significant (as defined by the SEC rules).
- Companies should report separate, standalone (unconsolidated) financial information in instances in which restrictions prevent its subsidiaries from freely transferring funds to the registrant.

Pro forma—Pro forma financial information includes financial statements or financial tables prepared as though certain transactions have already occurred. While the need for pro forma financial information most frequently occurs in connection with business combinations, the rule also applies to other events. For example, the use of proceeds from the IPO to repay outstanding debt obligations also necessitates the provision of pro forma financial information. There could be other events or transactions for which pro forma financial information may be required if the pro forma financial information would be material to investors, including situations in which:

- The registrant's financial statements are not indicative of the ongoing entity (e.g., tax or cost-sharing agreements will be eliminated)
- Dividends are declared by a registrant subsequent to the balance sheet date
- Redeemable preferred stock or debt converts to common stock at either the effective or closing date of an IPO
- Other changes in capitalization occur at or prior to the closing date of an IPO
- An issuer was formerly a subchapter S corporation, a partnership, or similar company

The basic guidelines for pro forma adjustments are as follows in Table 21.5:

- Balance Sheet: Pro forma presentation should be based on the latest historical balance sheet included in the filing. A pro forma balance sheet is not required if the transaction is already reflected in a historical balance sheet.
- Income Statement: Pro forma presentation should be based on the latest fiscal year and interim period included in the filing.

TABLE 21.5

Pro Forma Adjustments Guidelines

	Assumed Date of Transaction	Adjustments Are Directly Attributable to Transaction	Adjustments Are Factually Supported	Adjustments Are Expected to Have On-Going Impact
Balance sheet	Balance sheet date	Yes	Yes	No
Income statement	Beginning of earliest pro forma period presented	Yes	Yes	Yes

- Footnote disclosures on pro forma adjustments for the income statement and balance sheet may also be required.

Information about the company's officers, directors, and principal shareholders—Form S-1 requires a company to identify and describe the business experience of its executive officers and directors; the security holdings of directors and principal shareholders; transactions with and indebtedness of officers, directors, and principal shareholders; and the identity of transactions with, and compensation paid to, its promoters.

Executive compensation—The SEC requires extensive disclosures that are intended to ensure that investors and other parties receive clear, comprehensive, and transparent disclosures regarding executive and director compensation and related matters.

The executive compensation disclosures include:

- Expanded disclosure related to named executive officers including the principal executive officer (CEO) and principal financial officer (CFO)
- A compensation discussion and analysis (CD&A) section, which requires a disclosure of the roles of management and the compensation committee in making underlying compensation decisions and the methodologies and rationales used in establishing the type and amount of executive compensation
- A summary compensation table, accompanied by six supplemental tables, to disclose compensation components relating to salary, bonus, stock awards, option awards, non-equity incentive plan compensation, pensions, non-qualified deferred compensation, and all other compensation (including perquisites)
- Disclosure related to amounts payable to executive officers upon termination of employment, and, separately, upon a termination of employment following a change in corporate control

- Enhanced related-person disclosures, including disclosure of the policies for the review, approval, or ratification of transactions with related persons

Management Discussion and Analysis (MD&A)—In this section, management provides investors and users with information relevant to the assessment of the financial condition, results of operations, liquidity, and capital resources of the company, with particular emphasis on the company's prospects for the future. MD&A continues to be an area of focus for the SEC staff when reviewing registration statements. It inevitably results in comments (particularly the lack of forward-looking information required by each of the major sections of MD&A). It is therefore imperative that this section be carefully drafted. It must be written as objectively as possible, pointing out both favorable and unfavorable developments, and it should be written from the point of view of the company's management.

An MD&A statement includes:

- *Results of operations*: This is a comparison of the income statement amounts for each period presented and an explanation of the reasons for any material changes that should be incorporated. The MD&A should also discuss the reasons for any recent positive or negative trends, as well as the quality of the company's earnings. Any known trends or uncertainties that have had or are expected to have a material impact on the company and any changes in significant balance sheet items also should be analyzed and discussed.

- *Liquidity*: Any known trends or any known demands, commitments, events, or uncertainties that will result in or that are reasonably certain to result in the company's liquidity increasing or decreasing in any material way should be identified. Any course of action the company has taken or proposes to take to remedy any deficiencies should be indicated. Also, internal and external sources of liquidity should be identified and described, and any material unused sources of liquid assets should be briefly discussed.

- *Capital resources*: A description of the registrant's material commitments for capital expenditures, the general purpose of such commitments, and the anticipated source of funds needed to fulfill such commitments should be included in the MD&A. Any known material trends, favorable or unfavorable, in the company's capital resources should be divulged.

- *Disclosure about off-balance sheet arrangements, aggregate contractual obligations, and other matters*: This section should include, among other things, an explanation of off-balance sheet transactions and arrangements, including the company's relationships with unconsolidated entities or other persons that have or are reasonably likely to have a current or future material effect on financial condition, changes in financial condition, revenues or expenses, results of operations, liquidity, or capital resources.

- *Critical accounting policies and estimates*: This section should provide greater insight into the quality and variability of the company's financial condition and operating performance resulting from key accounting policies, assumptions, and estimates. It should supplement, not duplicate, the description of significant accounting policies in the notes to the financial statements and include quantitative and qualitative disclosures, a sensitivity analysis, and critical estimates by segment if necessary. This section continues to be an area of significant focus of comment from the SEC.
- *Other disclosures*: Other disclosures that are required in a registration statement include (but are not limited to):
    - Legal proceedings, if any
    - Interests of named experts and counsel
    - Certain relationships and related transactions

21.13.2 Part II—Information not Required in the Prospectus

This part includes disclosures regarding the expenses associated with the issuance and distribution of the securities, the indemnification of directors and officers acting for the company, any sales of unregistered securities within the last three years, undertaking representations made by the company acknowledging that it will keep the registration statement and prospectus current, various exhibits (such as certain material contracts entered into by the company, articles of incorporation and bylaws, and the underwriting agreement), and various financial statement schedules.

21.13.3 Sources of SEC Technical Requirements

The form and content of registration statements, including the requirements for most financial statements and other financial information to be included in the registration statement, are contained in the following SEC rules, regulations, and interpretations:

- Regulation S-X is the principal accounting regulation of the SEC. It specifies the financial statements to be included in filings with the SEC and provides rules and guidance on their form and content.
- Regulation S-K[21] contains the disclosure requirements for the non-financial statement portion of filings with the SEC (otherwise referred to as the "forepart" of the document).

- Financial Reporting Releases (FRRs) are designed to communicate the SEC's positions on accounting and auditing principles and practices. They are used to adopt, amend, or interpret rules and regulations relating to accounting and auditing issues or financial statement disclosures.

- Staff Accounting Bulletins (SABs) are the interpretations and practices followed by the SEC staff. Although they are not formally approved by the SEC commissioners, they are generally required to be followed by registrants.

- Industry guides are intended to assist registrants in the preparation of registration statements. They outline the policies and practices required by the SEC staff relative to specific industries. Industries covered by the guides include oil and gas, mining, banking, insurance, and real estate.

- Regulation S-T governs the preparation and submission of documents filed via the SEC's Electronic Data Gathering, Analysis, and Retrieval (EDGAR) system. Beginning in 1996, virtually all documents processed by the SEC, including filings by first-time issuers, must be submitted electronically via EDGAR. Copies of documents filed with the SEC using EDGAR may be obtained at the SEC's website: www.sec.gov. The general and specific instructions to the relevant form (S- 1, etc.) are also helpful.

21.13.4 Performing Due Diligence Procedures

Throughout the registration statement preparation process, the entire IPO team will perform necessary procedures to provide a reasonable ground for belief that, as of the effective date, the registration statement contains no significant untrue or misleading information and that no material information has been omitted. These procedures are referred to as due diligence and are performed primarily in response to the Securities Act of 1933 ("1933 Act"), which holds all parties participating in the registration liable for any material misstatements or omissions in the registration statement. Due diligence serves as the primary defense in any actions brought against the parties, other than the issuer, under this section of the 1933 Act.

Due diligence procedures entail a company's attorneys and underwriters reviewing a company and its management, including, but not limited to, visiting facility sites; reviewing significant agreements and contracts, financial statements, tax returns, Board of Directors' and shareholders' meeting minutes; and performing various analyses of the company and the industry in which it operates.

A company's attorneys and its underwriter's attorneys will also distribute questionnaires to the directors and officers, requesting them to review, verify, and comment on the information contained in the draft registration statement.

In addition, the directors and officers may be interviewed by the attorneys. "Keeping current" procedures are performed by the independent auditors to ascertain whether anything has occurred up to the effective date of the registration statement with respect to the company's financial position or operations that would have a material effect on the audited financial statements included in the registration statement.

Due diligence also encompasses reading the entire registration statement by all parties involved in its preparation to ensure that there are no material misstatements, omissions, or inconsistencies.

In addition, as part of their due diligence procedures, underwriters request comfort letters from a company's independent auditors with respect to information that appears in the registration statement outside of the financial statements and on events subsequent to the accountants' report date. It is common for underwriters to request comfort on as much information as possible. Auditing standards allow auditors to provide comfort on information that is derived from accounting records that are subject to the company's internal control over financial reporting. Generally, the more information the underwriters seek comfort on, the more expensive the process becomes. In light of this, and to avoid any misunderstandings and undue time delays, it is important that a company, the auditors, and underwriters agree, in the early stages of the registration process, on the information about which the auditors will be giving comfort.

Generally, two comfort letters are issued to the underwriters, one at the time the underwriting agreement is signed (generally the pricing date), and one (an updated letter or "bring-down letter") at the closing date. After the registration statement is filed, (but before it becomes effective), the principal underwriter holds a due diligence meeting. The due diligence meeting is attended by the principal underwriter and often by members of the underwriting group, as well as by a company's principal officers and counsel, counsel for the underwriter, and the independent accountants. At this meeting, the members of the underwriting group are afforded the opportunity to exercise due diligence as to the proposed offering in that they may ask any questions concerning the company and its business, products, competitive position, recent developments in finance, marketing, operations, and future prospects.

21.13.5 Commencing the Selling Effort

No offering of securities, either orally or in writing, is permitted before the registration statement is initially filed with the SEC. These rules are very strict, and a company must be careful not to generate undue publicity about itself that could be construed as an attempt to stimulate interest in its securities.

After the initial filing, however, and concurrent with the preparation of the amended registration statement, SEC regulations do permit certain types of promotional activities within the brokerage community, such as those noted in the following.

21.13.6 The Preliminary Prospectus or "Red Herring"

The "red herring" preliminary prospectus is circulated during the waiting period to potential investors. It is commonly referred to as a red herring because the disclaimer, at one time, was required to be printed in red ink. A red herring preliminary prospectus may be sent to interested institutions or persons prior to the effective date of the registration statement. This preliminary prospectus is a key tool in the lead underwriter's ability to form an underwriting syndicate, made up of various brokerage companies that will distribute the stock. While in the past companies have occasionally printed and distributed the red herring prior to receipt of SEC comments, companies are now encouraged not to print the red herring until SEC comments have been received, reviewed, and incorporated into the draft prospectus.

SEC rules require that this prospectus substantially conforms to the requirements of the 1933 Act and that the cover page bears the caption "Preliminary Prospectus." Prior to the full implementation of EDGAR, this language was required to be printed in red ink (hence the term red herring). The following statement must be printed on the cover in type as large as that generally used in the body of the prospectus:

> *Information contained herein is subject to completion or amendment. A registration statement relating to these securities has been filed with the SEC. These securities may not be sold nor may offers to buy be accepted prior to the time the registration statement becomes effective. This prospectus shall not constitute an offer to sell or the solicitation of an offer to buy, nor shall there be any sale of these securities in any State in which such offer, solicitation, or sale would be unlawful prior to registration or qualification under the securities laws of any such State.*

SEC rules also stipulate that the preliminary prospectus may omit the offering price, underwriting discounts or commissions, discounts or commissions to dealers, amount of proceeds, or other matters dependent on the offering price.

21.13.7 Tombstone Ads

A "tombstone ad"—a promotional advertisement that is shaped like a cemetery tombstone (it is rectangular with black borders)—is simply an announcement (not an offer) of a new security for sale. It is the only advertisement allowed during the cooling-off period. Companies may place tombstone ads in various periodicals announcing the offering and its dollar amount, identifying certain members of the underwriting syndicate, and noting where and from whom a copy of the company's prospectus may be obtained. Tombstone ads are not intended to be a selling document; their main purpose is to assist in locating potential buyers who are sufficiently interested in the security being advertised to obtain a statutory prospectus.

Tombstone ads may be published once the registration statement has been filed; typically, they are not published until after the effective date of the registration statement.

21.13.8 Financial Analyst Meetings or "Road Shows"

For potential investors to learn about the company, an underwriter will arrange meetings, euphemistically called "road shows,"[22] with financial analysts, brokers, and potential institutional investors. These meetings are generally attended by the company's president and key management such as the chief financial officer and may take place in many different locations throughout the country or the world, if the company has an international offering. It is vital that the management team be well prepared for these meetings.

This cannot be emphasized enough. The company should not assume that the prospectus is able to "stand on its own"—a company should anticipate potential questions concerning specifics about its business and know the answers. The credibility projected by a management team in its presentation and its ability to respond to potential investors' and brokers' questions will be a major influence on the success of the offering.

The road shows represent a critical part of a company's selling efforts, since it is here that a management team promotes interest in the offering with the institutional investors. This can be a very grueling process, since the span of time can last up to two weeks with a number of presentations a day. In addition, a company cannot discount the fact that in an active market it becomes more difficult to pique institutional investors' interest if they are going through three to five "dog and pony" shows a day. Undoubtedly, underwriters will play a significant role in preparing you and your management team for these presentations.

Some companies have sought assistance from professional investor relations organizations. Although a company may have a good "story" to tell, these advisors can help tailor it to investors.

21.13.9 Negotiating and Signing the Price Amendment and the Underwriting Agreement

By the time the registration statement has been filed, a company and its underwriter have generally agreed on the securities—both in number of shares and dollar amount—to be sold. However, the (1) final price at which to offer the securities to the public, the (2) exact amount of the underwriter's discount, and the (3) net proceeds to the registrant have not yet been determined. The negotiation and final determination of these amounts depend on a number of factors, including the past and present performance of a company, current conditions in the securities markets, and indications of interest received during the road show.

For example, in establishing an offering price, the underwriters will look at a multiple of earnings or cash flow based upon that experienced by similar companies. These multiples may be applied to the company's most recent results of operations or projected future earnings based on the outlook of the company's growth curve. The underwriter will also examine the current stock market price of comparable companies and recommend a stock offering "pricing."[23]

Timing also plays as important a part as any other factor in determining the final offering price of the shares. Almost any company that went public during the dot-com boom would have done so at a higher offering price than in the economic crises that began in 2008. In addition to cyclical market factors, particular industries go through "hot" and "cold" periods. Unlike the private sale of stock, where negotiations can be in the form of face-to-face meetings, stock sold through the public market is often priced by market psychology.

Another consideration is the anticipated aftermarket share value. That is, after a period of trading, the stock should settle at an aftermarket share value, and, ideally, the offering price should reflect a discount from this aftermarket share value. In other words, the initial offering price should allow for a small appreciation of the price per share in the aftermarket immediately subsequent to the IPO. An offering at the high end of a range may not provide adequate investor return, resulting in a weak or depressed aftermarket, while pricing at the low end may result in a run-up immediately following the offering (thus lost opportunity for the company or selling shareholders).

Market perceptions of the risk inherent in a company's stock are sometimes related to the per-share price. That is, a company that offers its shares at a price of $15 may be perceived to be offering a more speculative stock, while a $50 stock price may not be so perceived. At the other end of the spectrum, an IPO price of $25 may be considered overpriced. In addition to the price, the number of shares offered should be sufficient to ensure broad distribution and liquidity.

Upon completion of negotiations with the underwriter—usually about the time the registration statement is ready to become effective and the road show is over—the underwriting agreement is signed by authorized representatives of a company and the underwriter. Also at this time, the final amendment to the registration statement is prepared, including (as applicable) the agreed-upon offering price, underwriter's discount or commission, and the net proceeds to the company.

This amendment is called the price amendment and is filed with the SEC. In an effort to simplify the filing requirements associated with the final pricing amendment, the SEC passed a rule allowing companies to omit information concerning the public offering price, price-related information, and the underwriting syndicate from a registration statement that is declared effective.

In such cases, the information omitted would either be included in the final prospectus and incorporated by reference into the registration statement or included in a post-effective amendment to the registration statement. If the staff of the SEC's Division of Corporation Finance has no important reservations with respect to the registration statement, a company and its underwriter will customarily request that the offering be declared effective immediately—referred to as requesting acceleration. If acceleration is granted, the underwriter may proceed with the sale of securities to the public.

21.14 Your New Life as a Public Company

The IPO is not the end of the story—it is only the beginning. Once listed, a company will be under far greater public scrutiny and will have a range of continuing obligations with which to comply. Any weakness in systems or failure to comply with regulations could cause management public embarrassment, reputational damage, and the potential for company and personal fines. The benefits of careful preparation and planning are realized within the first year of the IPO. Public companies are required to comply with a host of reporting and other requirements. The most significant change for many companies is the need to close and report publicly on their financial results on an accelerated timeline and to comply with Sarbanes–Oxley requirements. This is a process the company will need to be fully prepared to meet; the inability to meet these requirements will shake investor confidence or subject the company to a delisting. Throughout the IPO process, the company will need to be prepared to discuss their Sarbanes–Oxley readiness plan and must be sure that it can comply with these requirements.

Preparing for life as a public company should happen in parallel with the process the company undertakes for its IPO. The company should take stock of its processes and infrastructure so it can make any necessary changes in advance of the IPO date. Key questions to ask include:

- Do we have the ability to close our books accurately each quarter and report the results to the public in accordance with SEC guidelines? Do we currently have a repeatable monthly and quarterly close process?
- Does our finance department have the expertise with SEC accounting and reporting requirements to allow us to comply with regulations we did not need to consider before as a private company (e.g., stock compensation and segment reporting)?

- Does our planning and analysis function have the ability to accurately forecast our results to allow for more effective interaction with the investor community and to assist in the analysis of the current period results for reporting purposes?
- Are all our processes and controls adequately documented and tested to comply with our Sarbanes–Oxley requirements?
- Does our technology infrastructure adequately support our compliance efforts?
- Have we established an ethics and compliance process and communicated it throughout the organization?

This preparation process can often be lengthy, depending on the current maturity of a company's existing processes. It is vital that the company understand and address any gaps before going public. The magnitude of the required improvements will determine the number of resources required. Many companies have resource constraints during the going-public process, during which there is so much attention being paid to the initial filing documents and the marketing efforts.

21.14.1 Managing Reporting Requirements

Public companies are required by the SEC, under the Securities 1934 Act, and Sarbanes–Oxley to file certain periodic reports to keep the investing public informed. This requirement will continue as long as the investor and asset tests are met. As noted previously, preparing to meet these requirements should be a focus for a company as it creates its filings. Companies should discuss their obligations under the various regulations with their attorneys and accountants at the beginning to lay out the obligations and ensure they can be met.

Legal counsel should also be consulted to confirm the SEC requirements pertaining to the form, content, and timing of specific reports. A financial public relations firm can assist companies with furnishing annual reports to shareholders. Table 21.6 presents an overview of the basic SEC reporting requirements for public companies based on their designated filer status.

21.14.2 SEC-Designated Filer Status

The SEC designates companies into three categories of filers to determine filing deadlines for Forms 10-K and 10-Q, as identified in the Table 21.6. The SEC has also designated a "Smaller Reporting Company" filer option. The distinction among the different categories is based on the non-affiliated (i.e., excluding large institutional investors, directors, officers, etc.) market capitalization (also known as "public float") of companies as of the last business day of the company's most recently completed second quarter. Companies

TABLE 21.6

SEC Reporting Requirements

Form	Description	Due Date
Form 10-K	This is the annual report to shareholders (conforming to SEC specifications), and it discloses in detail information about the company's activities, risks, financial condition, and results of operations. It also contains the company's audited annual financial statement, which includes the external auditor's opinion of financial statements and Section 404 of Sarbanes–Oxley (only required from the second Form 10-K filed after going public)	Large accelerated filer—60 days after fiscal year-end • Accelerated filer—75 days after fiscal year-end • Non-accelerated filer—90 days after fiscal year-end • Newly public company—90 days after fiscal year-end
Form 10-Q	This is the quarterly report required for each of the first three-quarters of the fiscal year. It includes condensed financial data and information on significant events. In addition, SEC rules require that the interim financial information included in the quarterly report be subject to a review by an independent accountant prior to filing	Large accelerated filer—40 days after fiscal quarter end • Accelerated filer—40 days after fiscal quarter end • Non-accelerated filer—45 days after fiscal quarter end • Newly public company
Form 8-K	This is a report filed for significant events such as an acquisition or disposal of assets; a change in control; bankruptcy; a change in independent accountants; resignation of directors because of disagreement with the registrant; the entry into a material definitive agreement; creation of direct obligations or obligations under off-balance sheet arrangements; a commitment to a plan involving exit or disposal activities; asset impairments; and when a company concludes or is advised by its independent accountants that previously issued financial statements should no longer be relied on	Due within four business days of event
Proxy	This contains data furnished to shareholders so they can decide how to assign their statements proxies (votes)	Due dates vary

should discuss their categorization in detail with their counsel and accountants. However, the general guidelines for the categories are as follows:

> *Large accelerated filer*: A company whose market value of publicly floated equity is equal to or exceeds $700 million as of the last business day of the company's most recently completed second fiscal quarter
>
> *Accelerated filer*: A company whose market value of publicly floated equity is between $75 million and $700 million as of the last business day of the company's most recently completed second fiscal quarter

In addition to the market capitalization requirements, to be designated as a large accelerated filer or an accelerated filer, a company needs to meet the following conditions as of the end of its fiscal year:

- The company has been subject to SEC reporting requirements (specifically Section 13(a) or 15(d) of the 1934 Act) for a period of at least 12 calendar months
- The company has previously filed at least one annual report pursuant to Section 13(a) and 15(d)
- The company is not eligible to use the requirements for smaller reporting companies

Companies not meeting these definitions are considered non-accelerated filers. Note that companies will generally be considered non-accelerated filers in the first year of operation, as the requirements are calculated at the fiscal year-end, and a newly public company would generally not have filed an annual report for the prior year. Accelerated filer status must be considered at each year-end to determine whether the designated filer status has changed.

21.14.3 Smaller Reporting Companies

The SEC has created this designation to streamline and simplify the disclosure requirements. Companies qualify as smaller reporting companies if they:

- Have a common equity float of less than $75 million
- In the case of an initial registration statement, had a public float of less than $75 million as of a date within 30 days of the filing of the registration statement, calculated by multiplying the aggregate worldwide number of such shares held by non-affiliates plus the number of such shares included in the registration statement by the estimated public offering price of the shares

- Have annual revenues of $50 million or less during the most recently completed fiscal year for which audited financial statements are available
- This designation allows companies to qualify for disclosure requirements that are scaled to reflect the characteristics and needs of smaller companies and their investors and to make it easier and less costly for smaller companies to comply with disclosure requirements

Public companies are also required to provide annual reports to shareholders and to include those reports in financial information similar to what is in Form 10-K when soliciting proxies relating to annual shareholder meetings at which directors are to be elected.

The management of newly public companies is required to deliver a report that assesses the effectiveness of the company's internal control over financial reporting, pursuant to Section 302 of Sarbanes–Oxley, in the second annual report filed subsequent to the IPO. Section 404 of Sarbanes–Oxley also requires a company's independent registered public accounting firm to deliver an attestation report on the operating effectiveness of the company's internal control over financial reporting.

The independent accounting firm must also give its opinion of a company's audited financial statements as of the same date. A company must perform substantial work to implement the appropriate processes, document the system of internal control over key processes, assess their design, remediate any deficiencies identified, and test their operation.

These processes can be both costly and challenging. To meet the various reporting requirements imposed on them, public companies must maintain adequate financial staff, supported by legal counsel and knowledgeable independent accountants.

21.14.4 Timely Disclosure of Material Information

A public company must disclose all material information (unless there is a legitimate reason for not doing so), both favorable and unfavorable, as promptly as possible. Information that is generally considered material includes: significant financial transactions, new products or services, acquisitions or dispositions of assets, dividend changes, and top management or control changes.

The disclosure of such information should be made as soon as: (1) it is reasonably accurate, and (2) full details are available to the company. This information is usually disseminated by press releases; however, companies may decide to also send announcements directly to their shareholders. Generally, the need to disclose information should be discussed with legal counsel.

It should be noted that when a release or public announcement discloses material nonpublic information regarding a registrant's results of operations or financial condition, Item 2.02 requires that the release be identified and included as an exhibit to a Form 8-K filing within four business days. In addition, Regulation FD requires that when an issuer, or person acting on its behalf, discloses material nonpublic information to certain enumerated persons (in general, securities market professionals and holders of the issuer's securities who may well trade on the basis of the information), it must make public that information.

21.14.5 Safe Harbor Provisions

The Private Securities Litigation Reform Act of 1995 provides a safe harbor for forward-looking statements, such as forecasts, projections, and other similar disclosures in the MD&A. A safe harbor encourages registrants to disclose forward-looking information and protects them from investor lawsuits if the forward-looking information does not materialize. This protection does not extend to statements which, when issued, were known to be false. A safe harbor applies to any form of written communication (e.g., press releases, letters to shareholders), as well as oral communications (e.g., telephone calls, analyst' meetings) that contain forward-looking information.

It should be noted that the safe harbor provision is not applicable to historical financial statements, or to forward-looking statements included in IPO registration statements. However, the statutory safe harbor does not replace or alter the current judicial "bespeaks caution" doctrine, on which the safe-harbor rules were modeled. The bespeaks caution doctrine generally provides that, to the extent an offering statement (such as a prospectus) contains a forward-looking statement with sufficient cautionary language, an action brought about as a result of such a statement could be dismissed on those grounds.

To avail itself of the safe harbor provision, forward-looking information must be clearly identified as such by the company and must be accompanied by a cautionary statement identifying the risk factors that may prevent the realization of the forward-looking information. In meeting these criteria, two points should be noted:

- The forward-looking statements should be specifically identified. A general statement such as "certain information contained in this annual report is forward-looking..." does not clearly identify the forward-looking statements.
- Every risk factor need not be identified to gain protection under the safe harbor. "Boilerplate warnings," however, will not suffice as meaningful cautionary language.

The statutory safe harbor does not require a company to update a forward-looking statement. While companies are not legally required to update such information, materially changed circumstances may nonetheless have to be disclosed as dictated by MD&A disclosure requirements. From a business and investor relations standpoint, companies should consider updating such information.

A newly public company should ensure that, when disclosing forward-looking information in annual reports and press releases, the requirements for using the safe harbor provision are appropriately met. Legal counsel is invaluable in providing the necessary guidance. Such guidance is particularly essential when forward-looking information is communicated orally (e.g., in conference calls with analysts).

21.14.6 Restrictions of Trading on Nonpublic Information

Until important information is made public, SEC rules prohibit company insiders from personally trading the company's securities or passing this information onto others. Within the company, material information should be kept confidential. Persons privileged to this information must treat it as confidential until it is released to the public. In the past, violators of this rule have been dealt with harshly (fined or otherwise penalized).

21.14.7 Fiduciary Duties

Fiduciary laws require that transactions between a company and any of its officers, directors, or large shareholders be fair to the company. These laws apply to both privately and publicly held companies. However, since the officers and directors of a privately held company are usually its only shareholders, the ramifications of fiduciary laws are less than what they might be for a publicly held company.

Fiduciary laws must be carefully observed after a public offering due to the interests of the new shareholders. Whenever there is a potential conflict of interest between the company and its fiduciaries, management should obtain independent appraisals or bids and independent director approval (or even shareholder approval), depending on the nature and significance of the transaction.

21.15 Ongoing Costs

As mentioned previously, a further consequence of a company's being publicly held is the expense it entails. Significant costs and executive time is often incurred when periodic reports are prepared and then filed with the SEC. Board and shareholder meetings and communications may also be expensive.

Because of its responsibilities to the public shareholders, the Board of Directors and the audit committee are significantly more important in a public company. If the board was previously composed entirely of insiders, a number of outside directors would need to be added (which will likely result in incurring additional costs) to satisfy the New York Stock Exchange (NYSE) or the NASDAQ National Market listing requirements.

Table 21.7 shows a periodic reporting calendar for a first-time public registrant with fiscal year starting January 1st 20XX.

21.15.1 Prepare for Augmented Shareholder and Media Scrutiny

While shareholders encourage the alignment of executive and shareholder interests, they are actively monitoring pay practices for executives to ensure pay for performance. With "say on pay," advisory shareholder votes increasing at various companies, there is more scrutiny of pay practices for executives. Risk Metrics (formerly ISS) and other shareholder advisory groups have issued voting guidelines requiring that executive compensation aligns with the company's performance and shareholders' return. Questions may

TABLE 21.7

Periodic Reporting Requirements

6/30/XX	Fiscal Year 20XX Second Quarter End
7/17/XX	Effective Date of Registration Statement—Company becomes a reporting company
8/31/XX	Second Quarter Form 10-Q due (unless 6/30/XX financials are included and discussed in Registration Statement)
	A first-time registrant is required to file its first 10-Q by the later of: (i) 45 days after the effective date of the initial registration statement, or (ii) the date on which the Form 10-Q would have been otherwise due
9/30/XX	Fiscal Year 20XX Third Quarter End
11/15/XX	Third Quarter Form 10-Q due
12/31/XX	Fiscal Year 20XX Year-End
3/01/XX	Initiate Proxy search. Depending on timing of the meeting.
	Note: If a filing date falls on a Saturday, Sunday, or holiday, the document may be filed on the next business day (Rule 0–3(a)).
3/15/XX	File Preliminary Proxy Statement and form of Proxy with the SEC and FINRA, if necessary
3/31/XX	Fiscal Year 20XX Form 10-K due
3/31/XX	Fiscal Year 20XX First Quarter End
4/02/XX	Establish Record Date—Annual Meeting of Shareholders
4/16/XX	File Definitive Proxy Statement, form of Proxy, and Annual Report to Shareholders
4/16/XX	Mail Definitive Proxy, form of Proxy, and Annual Report to Shareholders
5/15/XX	First Quarter Form 10-Q due
5/30/XX	Annual Meeting of Shareholders; Management presentation of results
7/16/XX	Section 11(a) Earnings Statement available to security holders as soon as possible covering a period of at least 12 months beginning after the effective date of the Registration Statement

be raised as to both the reasonableness and competitive nature of the current total rewards program. Thus, a company should be prepared to justify pay strategy and practices.

21.15.2 Compensation Initiatives

Outlined in the following are planning and analysis initiatives that should be considered to ensure an appropriate compensation program:

- Review of competitive total-compensation levels and mix. Consider base salaries, annual bonuses, long-term incentives (primarily stock options for pre-IPO companies), perquisites, and benefits.
- Create a compensation structure that is aligned with competitive practices and based on real-time external research (not necessarily just on surveys that are out of date prior to publication). Consideration should be given to salary adjustments based on the value created by the incumbent—value based on performance, increased breadth of responsibilities, and success in helping teammates create value.
- Create an annual incentive plan that will: (1) assess performance measures driving shareholder value over the short and long-term, and (2) reward performance based on: minimum, target, and maximum performance; eligibility; form of payment; and timing of payment.
- Establish an independent board committee to: (1) oversee executive compensation (both from a strategic and regulatory standpoint), and (2) define the role played by the CEO and management in decision making.
- Depending on industry practices, establish executive employment contracts with change-in-control provisions for key contributors. It is difficult to anticipate what will happen after a public market is established. Make sure that key contributors can be retained under adverse circumstances and that they are taken care of in the event of a merger with another company.

However, the events that constitute a triggering change-in-control event should not be defined so broadly as to provide accelerated and unduly generous payouts to executives for an event that would not be considered "adverse." Shareholders are very sensitive about payouts deemed too generous, specifically severance exceeding three times an annual salary plus target bonuses, payouts upon single trigger, "voluntary for any reason" triggers, and excise tax gross-ups of any kind.

- Assess competitive boards of directors' compensation levels and programs. Directors of a public entity will anticipate remuneration commensurate with their time and efforts. They expect competitive retainers and fees. Many companies provide for cash compensation as well as restricted stock or stock options, sometimes fully vested to directors.

- Consider broad-based equity programs, such as all-employee stock options, restricted stock or restricted stock units, or an employee stock purchase plan.
- This is also a good time to assess the design and administration of employee benefit programs, including 401(k), profit sharing and other retirement plans, healthcare, and life and disability insurance.

21.15.3 Equity Grants

Equity-based compensation, stock options, and now increasingly restricted stock and restricted stock units have taken the primary role as a means of compensating valued employees without a cash outlay. A company may utilize equity as an integral part of a program to secure equity capital or to achieve widespread ownership of its stock among its employees. Equity packages are often calculated in terms of a percentage of ownership of the company as a means of strengthening the ownership mentality of its employees. Determining the appropriate equity vehicle is important. Often companies may choose to offer different equity incentives for different groups of employees. For example, companies may grant restricted stock at the executive and VP levels and grant stock options and/or restricted stock units more broadly. We are seeing migration from stock options to restricted stock units, especially when subject to performance vesting.

21.15.4 Equity Authorization

A key question for any company is, "How many shares should be allocated to the equity program?" Companies should consider the following factors before setting aside shares:

- Economic value of grants to employees
- Number of eligible employees
- Competitive industry practices
- Acceptable ownership dilution potential

The use of equity differs dramatically within each industry. Broad-based grant programs are prevalent in some industries. All companies should examine competitive total stock authorization as well as annual grant levels prior to finalizing a program.

21.15.5 Equity Grant Alternatives

Companies differ with respect to their industries and industry sectors, financial resources, stage of growth, form of ownership, culture, management, and philosophy. Due to these variations, there exist a number of long-term, incentive-type plans. The most common forms of compensation plans will utilize stock options, restricted stock, restricted stock units, or bonuses based on stock performance. There are several alternatives when granting equity including:

- Outright stock grants
- *Stock options*: Stock options entitle an employee to pay a purchase price to acquire company stock at any point in time after vesting. There are two types of stock options in the United States: incentive stock options, which provide for capital gains tax treatment at sale provided certain holding periods are met, and non-qualified stock options, which are taxed when the employee exercises and acquires the shares. For any privately held company's granting options, it is important to ensure that the exercise price is set at the fair market value of the shares on the date of grant as defined under Section 409A. This is most often done by securing an independent valuation of the stock price annually.
- *Restricted stock*: These grants are of actual stock. The stock is subject to restrictions on sale until vested by continued employment or the attainment of performance goals. Grants typically include dividend and voting rights.

These awards have become more prevalent for highly compensated individuals and often vest based on specific performance metrics instead of vesting over time.

- *Restricted stock units*: This is a promise to deliver stock in the future once restrictions are lifted. There is no grant of stock until the vesting conditions—time- or performance-based—are satisfied. At that time, the value of the shares delivered is subject to personal income tax. These awards have become more prevalent as a way to incentivize all employees.
- *Phantom stock*: Phantom stock entitles an employee to receive (at a future date in cash) any increase in stock value. It does, however, have adverse accounting implications that result in a charge to earnings as the underlying stock appreciates over time. It also does not allow for ultimate favorable capital tax treatment if the shares were actually being held.
- *Stock-for-stock exchange*: An equity plan may allow previously owned shares, rather than cash, to be accepted as payment for the exercise of stock options.

- *Performance units*: These are grants of dollar-denominated units whose value is contingent on performance against predetermined objectives over a multiyear period. Actual payouts may be in cash or stock.
- *Performance shares*: These are grants of actual shares of stock or stock units whose payment is contingent on performance against predetermined objectives over a multiyear period. They are the same as performance units, except that the unit value fluctuates with stock price changes and employee performance against objectives.
- *Deferred compensation arrangements*: These are arrangements whereby a company agrees to make cash or stock payments to an employee at a future date. These arrangements are now governed by Section 409A, which mandates very strict rules on the timing of election and the distributions of payouts. These agreements may be in the form of salary deferrals, profit-sharing plans, and deferred stock units, and they are sometimes funded by means of corporate-owned life insurance or split-dollar insurance in which the cash surrender value and death benefits are owned separately by the company and the individual.
- *Employee stock ownership plan*: This is a tax-qualified, defined contribution retirement plan that invests primarily in a company's common or convertible preferred stock. A company may either contribute cash or its stock to the plan; or, alternatively, the plan may borrow money to purchase the employer's stock. The stock is subsequently distributed to employees under the provisions of the plan.

Each of these plans has distinct advantages and disadvantages. When adopting any type of incentive vehicle, a company's primary criteria should be the program's ability to reinforce both the company's strategic business objectives and its supporting compensation philosophy.

21.16 The Board of Directors and the CEO

Effective corporate governance requires a clear understanding of the respective roles of the board, management, and shareholders; their relationships with each other; and their relationships with other corporate stakeholders, as shown in Figure 21.3.

The Board of Directors has the vital role of overseeing the company's management and business strategies to achieve long-term value creation. Selecting a well-qualified CEO to lead the company, monitoring and evaluating the CEO's performance, and overseeing the CEO succession planning process are some of the most important functions of the board.

Corporate governance

FIGURE 21.3
The three components of good corporate governance.

The board delegates to the CEO—and through the CEO to other senior management—the authority and responsibility for operating the company's day-to-day business. Effective directors are diligent monitors, but not managers, of business operations. They exercise vigorous and diligent oversight of a company's affairs, including key areas such as strategy and risk, but they do not manage—or micromanage—the company's business by performing or duplicating the tasks of the CEO and senior management team.

The distinction between oversight and management is not always precise, and some situations (such as a crisis) may require greater board involvement in operational matters. In addition, in some areas (such as the relationship with the outside auditor and executive compensation), the board has a direct role instead of an oversight role.

21.16.1 Management

Management, led by the CEO, is responsible for setting, managing and executing the strategies of the company, including, but not limited to, running the operations of the company under the oversight of the board and keeping the board informed of the status of the company's operations.

Management's responsibilities include strategic planning, risk management, and financial reporting. An effective management team runs the company with a focus on executing the company's strategy over a meaningful time horizon and avoids an undue emphasis on short-term metrics.

In summary, an effective management team should ideally run the company with a focus on executing the company's strategy over a meaningful time horizon and avoids an undue emphasis on short-term metrics, such as shareholder's quarterly earnings pressure.

21.16.2 Shareholders

Shareholders invest in a corporation by buying its stock and receive economic benefits in return. Shareholders are not involved in the day-to-day management of business operations, but they have the right to elect representatives (directors) and to receive information material to investment and voting decisions.

Shareholders should expect corporate boards and managers to act as long-term stewards of their investment in the corporation. They also should expect that the board and management will be responsive to issues and concerns that are of widespread interest to long-term shareholders and affect the company's long-term value. Corporations are for-profit enterprises that are designed to provide sustainable long-term value to all shareholders. Accordingly, shareholders should not expect to use the public companies in which they invest as platforms for the advancement of their personal agendas or for the promotion of general political or social causes.

Some shareholders may seek a voice in the company's strategic direction and decision making—areas that traditionally were squarely within the realm of the board and management.

Shareholders who seek this influence should recognize that this type of empowerment necessarily involves the assumption of a degree of responsibility for the goal of long-term value creation for the company and all of its shareholders.

Effective corporate governance requires dedicated focus on the part of directors, the CEO, and senior management to their own responsibilities and, together with the corporation's shareholders, to the shared goal of building long-term value.

21.17 Board Committees of a Public Company

The board has primary responsibility for overall corporate governance. Corporate governance is a mechanism through which boards and directors are able to direct, monitor, and supervise the conduct and operation of the corporation and its management in a manner that ensures appropriate levels of authority, accountability, stewardship, leadership, direction, and control.

Corporate law empowers boards to establish board committees and to delegate certain of their tasks to them. The committees and their responsibilities are generally set forth in the bylaws or established by board resolution; although they are increasingly outlined in a committee charter that is available to shareholders.[24]

The law codifies a common-law rule reflecting judicial acceptance and approval of board action through committees. Indeed, when the public corporation faces certain circumstances (such as a change of control or a corporate emergency), it may be appropriate for a board to establish a special committee to deal with the specific issue or problem.

This section discusses the major standing committees[25] that are required by law or stock exchange rules and that are differentiated by their specialized function. However, given the complexity of public companies and the changing business and financial environment in which they function, a public company may establish a board committee, such as an executive committee, to make decisions and to act on behalf of the board between meetings of the full board.

The power of the board to delegate matters to committees is limited, however. Corporate law generally establishes that certain matters cannot be delegated to committees (although a committee could make a recommendation on the matter). These restrictions generally refer to major corporate actions, where a resolution of the entire board is appropriate. Depending upon the state of the corporation's charter, they include any matter involving shareholder action, any amendment to the bylaws of the corporation, the filling of vacancies on the board, the alteration of a board resolution, the declaration of dividends, and the authorization of a reacquisition or an issuance of shares.

21.17.1 Committee Membership

Assignment of particular board members to committees is a matter for decision by the entire board, although a board committee might make a recommendation as to the assignment. Best practices guidelines provide that membership on a particular committee should depend upon the expertise of a director. For example, regarding the audit committee, Sarbanes–Oxley mandates that its members have a specialized financial background. In practice, the CEO has considerable influence on which directors sit on which committees. Increasingly, however, both the law and model codes of board behavior try to remove the CEO from this appointment role so that the CEO cannot unduly influence board monitoring of himself or other company executives.

According to The Business Roundtable:[26]

> Decisions about committee membership and chairs should be made by the full board based on recommendations from the corporate governance committee. Consideration should be given to whether periodic rotation of committee memberships and chairs would provide fresh perspectives and enhance directors' familiarity with different aspects of the corporation's business, consistent with applicable listing standards.

21.18 Corporate Governance Requirements

21.18.1 Preamble to the Corporate Governance Requirements

In addition to meeting the quantitative requirements in the Rule 5200, 5300, 5400, and 5500 Series, Companies applying to list and listed on Nasdaq must meet the qualitative requirements outlined in this Rule 5600 Series. These requirements include rules relating to a Company's Board of Directors, including audit committees and independent Director oversight of executive compensation and the director nomination process; code of conduct; shareholder meetings, including proxy solicitation and quorum; review of related party transactions; and shareholder approval, including voting rights. Exemptions to these rules, including phase-in schedules, are set forth in Rule 5615.[27]

Nasdaq maintains a website that provides guidance on the applicability of the corporate governance requirements by FAQs and published summaries of anonymous versions of previously issued staff interpretative letters. Companies are encouraged to contact Listing Qualifications to discuss any complex issues or transactions. Companies can also submit a request for a written interpretation pursuant to Rule 5602.

21.18.2 Written Interpretations of Nasdaq Listing Rules

(a) A Company listed on the Nasdaq Capital Market or the Nasdaq Global Market may request from Nasdaq a written interpretation of the Rules contained in the Rule 5000 through 5900 Series. In connection with such a request, the Company must submit to Nasdaq a non-refundable fee of $5,000. A response to such a request generally will be provided within four weeks from the date Nasdaq receives all information necessary to respond to the request.

(b) Notwithstanding paragraph (a), a Company may request a written interpretation of the Rules contained in the 5000 through 5900 Series by a specific date that is less than four weeks, but at least one week, after the date Nasdaq receives all information necessary to respond to the request. In connection with such a request for an expedited response, the Company must submit to Nasdaq a non-refundable fee of $15,000.

(c) An applicant to Nasdaq that has submitted the applicable entry fee under Rule 5910(a) or Rule 5920(a) will not also be required to submit a fee in connection with a request for a written interpretation involving the applicant's initial listing on Nasdaq. A listed Company that is subject to the All-Inclusive Annual Listing Fee described in IM-5910-1 or IM-5920-1 is not required to submit a fee in connection with a request for a written interpretation. In addition, a Company is not required to submit a fee in connection with a request for an exception from the Nasdaq shareholder approval rules pursuant to the financial viability exception as described in Rule 5635(f).

(d) The Nasdaq Board of Directors or its designee may, in its discretion, defer or waive all or any part of the written interpretation fee prescribed herein.

(e) Nasdaq shall publish on its website a summary of each interpretation within 90 days from the date such interpretation is issued.

(f) A Company is eligible to request a written interpretation from Nasdaq pursuant to paragraphs (a) or (b), subject to payment of the appropriate fee, if it has a class of securities that has been suspended or delisted from the Nasdaq Capital Market or the Nasdaq Global Market, but the suspension or delisting decision is under review pursuant to the Rule 5800 Series.

21.18.3 Board of Directors and Committees

(a) Definitions

(1) "Executive Officer" means those officers covered in Rule 16a-1(f) under the Act.

(2) "Independent Director" means a person other than an Executive Officer or employee of the Company or any other individual having a relationship which, in the opinion of the Company's Board of Directors, would interfere with the exercise of independent judgment in carrying out the responsibilities of a director. For purposes of this rule, "Family Member" means a person's spouse, parents, children, and siblings, whether by blood, marriage or adoption, or anyone residing in such person's home. The following persons shall not be considered independent:

(A) a director who is, or at any time during the past three years was, employed by the Company;

(B) a director who accepted or who has a Family Member who accepted any compensation from the Company in excess of $120,000 during any period of twelve consecutive months within the three years preceding the determination of independence, other than the following:

(i) compensation for board or board committee service;

(ii) compensation paid to a Family Member who is an employee (other than an Executive Officer) of the Company; or

(iii) benefits under a tax-qualified retirement plan, or non-discretionary compensation.

Provided, however, that in addition to the requirements contained in this paragraph (B), audit committee members are also subject to additional, more stringent requirements under Rule 5605(c)(2).

(C) a director who is a Family Member of an individual who is, or at any time during the past three years was, employed by the Company as an Executive Officer;

(D) a director who is, or has a Family Member who is, a partner in, or a controlling Shareholder or an Executive Officer of, any organization to which the Company made, or from which the Company received, payments for property or services in the current or any of the past three fiscal years that exceed 5% of the recipient's consolidated gross revenues for that year, or $200,000, whichever is more, other than the following:

    (i) payments arising solely from investments in the Company's securities; or

    (ii) payments under non-discretionary charitable contribution matching programs.

(E) a director of the Company who is, or has a Family Member who is, employed as an Executive Officer of another entity where at any time during the past three years any of the Executive Officers of the Company serve on the compensation committee of such other entity; or

(F) a director who is, or has a Family Member who is, a current partner of the Company's outside auditor, or was a partner or employee of the Company's outside auditor who worked on the Company's audit at any time during any of the past three years.

(G) in the case of an investment company, in lieu of paragraphs (A)-(F), a director who is an "interested person" of the Company as defined in Section 2(a)(19) of the Investment Company Act of 1940, other than in his or her capacity as a member of the Board of Directors or any board committee.

21.18.4 Definition of Independence—Rule 5605(a)(2)

It is important for investors to have confidence that individuals serving as Independent Directors do not have a relationship with the listed Company that would impair their independence. The board has a responsibility to make an affirmative determination that no such relationships exist through the application of Rule 5605(a)(2). Rule 5605(a)(2) also provides a list of certain relationships that preclude a board finding of independence. These objective measures provide transparency to investors and Companies, facilitate uniform application of the rules, and ease administration. Because Nasdaq does not believe that ownership of Company stock by itself would preclude a board finding of independence, it is not included in the aforementioned objective factors. It should be noted that there are additional, more stringent requirements that apply to directors serving on audit committees, as specified in Rule 5605(c).

The Rule's reference to the "Company" includes any parent or subsidiary of the Company. The term "parent or subsidiary" is intended to cover entities the Company controls and consolidates with the Company's financial statements as filed with the Commission (but not if the Company reflects such entity solely as an investment in its financial statements). The reference to Executive Officer means those officers covered in Rule 16a-1(f) under the Act. In the context of the definition of Family Member under Rule 5605(a)(2), the reference to marriage is intended to capture relationships specified in the Rule (parents, children, and siblings) that arise as a result of marriage, such as "in-law" relationships.

The three year look-back periods referenced in paragraphs (A), (C), (E) and (F) of the Rule commence on the date the relationship ceases. For example, a director employed by the Company is not independent until three years after such employment terminates.

For purposes of paragraph (A) of the Rule, employment by a director as an Executive Officer on an interim basis shall not disqualify that director from being considered independent following such employment, provided the interim employment did not last longer than one year. A director would not be considered independent while serving as an interim officer. Similarly, for purposes of paragraph (B) of the Rule, compensation received by a director for former service as an interim Executive Officer need not be considered as compensation in determining independence after such service, provided such interim employment did not last longer than one year. Nonetheless, the Company's Board of Directors still must consider whether such former employment and any compensation received would interfere with the director's exercise of independent judgment in carrying out the responsibilities of a director. In addition, if the director participated in the preparation of the Company's financial statements while serving as an interim Executive Officer, Rule 5605(c)(2)(A)(iii) would preclude service on the audit committee for three years.

Paragraph (B) of the Rule is generally intended to capture situations where a compensation is made directly to (or for the benefit of) the director or a Family Member of the director. For example, consulting or personal service contracts with a director or Family Member of the director would be analyzed under paragraph (B) of the Rule. In addition, political contributions to the campaign of a director or a Family Member of the director would be considered indirect compensation under paragraph (B). Non-preferential payments made in the ordinary course of providing business services (such as payments of interest or proceeds related to banking services or loans by a Company that is a financial institution or payment of claims on a policy by a Company that is an insurance company), payments arising solely from investments in the Company's securities and loans permitted under Section 13(k) of the Act will not preclude a finding of director independence as long as the payments are non-compensatory in nature. Depending on the circumstances, a loan or payment could be compensatory if, for example, it is not on terms generally available to the public.

Paragraph (D) of the Rule is generally intended to capture payments to an entity with which the director or Family Member of the director is affiliated by serving as a partner, controlling Shareholder or Executive Officer of such entity. Under exceptional circumstances, such as where a director has direct, significant business holdings, it may be appropriate to apply the corporate measurements in paragraph (D), rather than the individual measurements of paragraph (B). Issuers should contact Nasdaq if they wish to apply the Rule in this manner. The reference to a partner in paragraph (D) is not intended to include limited partners. It should be noted that the independence requirements of paragraph (D) of the Rule are broader than Rule 10A-3(e)(8) under the Act.

Under paragraph (D), a director who is, or who has a Family Member who is, an Executive Officer of a charitable organization may not be considered independent if the Company makes payments to the charity in excess of the greater of 5% of the charity's revenues or $200,000. However, Nasdaq encourages Companies to consider other situations where a director or their Family Member and the Company each have a relationship with the same charity when assessing director independence.

For purposes of determining whether a lawyer is eligible to serve on an audit committee, Rule 10A-3 under the Act generally provides that any partner in a law firm that receives payments from the issuer is ineligible to serve on that issuer's audit committee. In determining whether a director may be considered independent for purposes other than the audit committee, payments to a law firm would generally be considered under Rule 5605(a)(2), which looks to whether the payment exceeds the greater of 5% of the recipient's gross revenues or $200,000; however, if the firm is a sole proprietorship, Rule 5605(a)(2)(B), which looks to whether the payment exceeds $120,000, applies.

Paragraph (G) of the Rule provides a different measurement for independence for investment companies in order to harmonize with the Investment Company Act of 1940. In particular, in lieu of paragraphs (A)-(F), a director who is an "interested person" of the Company as defined in Section 2(a)(19) of the Investment Company Act of 1940, other than in his or her capacity as a member of the Board of Directors or any board committee, shall not be considered independent.

(b) Independent Directors

21.18.5 (1) Majority Independent Board

A majority of the Board of Directors must be comprised of Independent Directors as defined in Rule 5605(a)(2). The Company, other than a Foreign Private Issuer, must comply with the disclosure requirements set forth in Item 407(a) of Regulation S-K. A Foreign Private Issuer must disclose in its next annual report (e.g., Form 20-F or 40-F) those directors that the Board of Directors has determined to be independent under Rule 5605(a)(2).

(A) Cure Period for Majority Independent Board

If a Company fails to comply with this requirement due to one vacancy, or one director ceases to be independent due to circumstances beyond their reasonable control, the Company shall regain compliance with the requirement by the earlier of its next annual shareholders meeting or one year from the occurrence of the event that caused the failure to comply with this requirement; provided, however, that if the annual shareholders meeting occurs no later than 180 days following the event that caused the failure to comply with this requirement, the Company shall instead have 180 days from such event to regain compliance. A Company relying on this provision shall provide notice to Nasdaq immediately upon learning of the event or circumstance that caused the noncompliance.

Majority Independent Board. Independent Directors (as defined in Rule 5605(a)(2)) play an important role in assuring investor confidence. Through the exercise of independent judgment, they act on behalf of investors to maximize shareholder value in the Companies they oversee and guard against conflicts of interest. Requiring that the board be comprised of a majority of Independent Directors empowers such directors to carry out more effectively these responsibilities.

(2) Executive Sessions

Independent Directors must have regularly scheduled meetings at which only Independent Directors are present ("executive sessions").

Executive Sessions of Independent Directors

Regularly scheduled executive sessions encourage and enhance communication among Independent Directors. It is contemplated that executive sessions will occur at least twice a year, and perhaps more frequently, in conjunction with regularly scheduled board meetings.

(c) Audit Committee Requirements

21.18.6 (1) Audit Committee Charter

Each Company must certify that it has adopted a formal written audit committee charter and that the audit committee will review and reassess the adequacy of the formal written charter on an annual basis. The charter must specify:

(A) the scope of the audit committee's responsibilities, and how it carries out those responsibilities, including structure, processes, and membership requirements;

(B) the audit committee's responsibility for ensuring its receipt from the outside auditors of a formal written statement delineating all relationships between the auditor and the Company, actively engaging in a dialogue with the auditor with respect to any disclosed relationships or services that may impact the objectivity and independence of the auditor and for taking, or recommending that the full board take, appropriate action to oversee the independence of the outside auditor;

(C) the committee's purpose of overseeing the accounting and financial reporting processes of the Company and the audits of the financial statements of the Company; and

(D) the specific audit committee responsibilities and authority set forth in Rule 5605(c)(3).

Each Company is required to adopt a formal written charter that specifies the scope of its responsibilities and the means by which it carries out those responsibilities; the outside auditor's accountability to the audit committee; and the audit committee's responsibility to ensure the independence of the outside auditor. Consistent with this, the charter must specify all audit committee responsibilities set forth in Rule 10A-3(b)(2), (3), (4), and (5) under the Act. Rule 10A-3(b)(3)(ii) under the Act requires that each audit committee must establish procedures for the confidential, anonymous submission by employees of the listed Company of concerns regarding questionable accounting or auditing matters. The rights and responsibilities as articulated in the audit committee charter empower the audit committee and enhance its effectiveness in carrying out its responsibilities.

Rule 5605(c)(3) imposes additional requirements for investment company audit committees that must also be set forth in audit committee charters for these Companies.

21.18.7 (2) Audit Committee Composition

(A) Each Company must have, and certify that it has and will continue to have, an audit committee of at least three members, each of whom must: (i) be an Independent Director as defined under Rule 5605(a)(2); (ii) meet the criteria for independence set forth in Rule 10A-3(b)(1) under the Act (subject to the exemptions provided in Rule 10A-3(c) under the Act); (iii) not have participated in the preparation of the financial statements of the Company or any current subsidiary of the Company at any time during the past three years; and (iv) be able to read and understand fundamental financial statements, including a Company's balance sheet, income statement, and cash flow statement. Additionally, each Company must certify that it has, and will continue to have, at least one member of the audit committee who has past employment experience in finance or accounting, requisite professional certification in accounting, or any other comparable experience or background which results in the individual's financial sophistication, including being or having been a chief executive officer, chief financial officer, or other senior officer with financial oversight responsibilities.

(B) Non-Independent Director for Exceptional and Limited Circumstances

Notwithstanding paragraph (2)(A)(i), one director who: (i) is not an Independent Director as defined in Rule 5605(a)(2); (ii) meets the criteria set forth in Section 10A(m)(3) under the Act and the rules thereunder; and (iii) is not currently an Executive Officer or employee or a Family Member of an Executive Officer, may be appointed to the audit committee if the board, under exceptional and limited circumstances, determines that membership on the committee by the individual is required by the best interests of the Company and its Shareholders. A Company, other than a Foreign Private Issuer, that relies on this exception must comply with the disclosure requirements set forth in Item 407(d)(2) of Regulation S-K. A Foreign Private Issuer that relies on this exception must disclose in its next annual report (e.g., Form 20-F or 40-F) the nature of the relationship that makes the individual not independent and the reasons for the board's determination. A member appointed under this exception may not serve longer than two years and may not chair the audit committee.

IM-5605-4. Audit Committee Composition

Audit committees are required to have a minimum of three members and be comprised only of Independent Directors. In addition to satisfying the Independent Director requirements under Rule 5605(a)(2), audit committee members must meet the criteria for independence set forth in Rule 10A-3(b)(1) under the Act (subject to the exemptions provided in Rule 10A-3(c) under the Act): they must not accept any consulting, advisory, or other compensatory fee from the Company other than for board service, and they must not be an affiliated person of the Company. As described in Rule 10A-3(d)(1) and (2), a Company must disclose reliance on certain exceptions from Rule 10A-3 and disclose an assessment of whether, and if so, how, such reliance would materially adversely affect the ability of the audit committee to act independently and to satisfy the other requirements of Rule 10A-3. It is recommended also that a Company disclose in its annual proxy (or, if the Company does not file a proxy, in its Form 10-K or 20-F) if any director is deemed eligible to serve on the audit committee but falls outside the safe harbor provisions of Rule 10A-3(e)(1)(ii) under the Act. A director who qualifies as an audit committee financial expert under Item 407(d)(5)(ii) and (iii) of Regulation S-K is presumed to qualify as a financially sophisticated audit committee member under Rule 5605(c)(2)(A).

(3) Audit Committee Responsibilities and Authority

The audit committee must have the specific audit committee responsibilities and authority necessary to comply with Rule 10A-3(b)(2), (3), (4), and (5) under the Act (subject to the exemptions provided in Rule 10A-3(c) under the Act), concerning responsibilities relating to: (i) registered public accounting firms, (ii) complaints relating to accounting, internal accounting controls, or auditing matters, (iii) authority to engage advisers, and (iv) funding as determined by the audit committee. Audit committees for investment companies must also establish procedures for the confidential, anonymous submission of concerns regarding questionable accounting or auditing matters by employees of the investment adviser, administrator, principal underwriter, or any other provider of accounting related services for the investment company, as well as employees of the investment company.

IM-5605-5. The Audit Committee Responsibilities and Authority

Audit committees must have the specific audit committee responsibilities and authority necessary to comply with Rule 10A-3(b)(2), (3), (4) and (5) under the Act (subject to the exemptions provided in Rule 10A-3(c) under the Act), concerning responsibilities relating to registered public accounting firms; complaints relating to accounting; internal accounting controls or auditing matters; authority to engage advisers; and funding. Audit committees for investment companies must also establish procedures for the confidential, anonymous submission of concerns regarding questionable accounting or auditing matters by employees of the investment adviser, administrator, principal underwriter, or any other provider of accounting related services for the investment company, as well as employees of the investment company.

(4) Cure Periods for Audit Committee

(A) If a Company fails to comply with the audit committee composition requirement under Rule 10A-3(b)(1) under the Act and Rule 5605(c)(2)(A) because an audit committee member ceases to be independent for reasons outside the member's reasonable control, the audit committee member may remain on the audit committee until the earlier of its next annual shareholders meeting or one year from the occurrence of the event that caused the failure to comply with this requirement. A Company relying on this provision must provide notice to Nasdaq immediately upon learning of the event or circumstance that caused the noncompliance.

(B) If a Company fails to comply with the audit committee composition requirement under Rule 5605(c)(2)(A) due to one vacancy on the audit committee, and the cure period in paragraph (A) is not otherwise being relied upon for another member, the Company will have until the earlier of the next annual shareholders meeting or one year from the occurrence of the event that caused the failure to comply with this requirement; provided, however, that if the annual shareholders meeting occurs no later than 180 days following the event that caused the vacancy, the Company shall instead have 180 days from such event to regain compliance.

A Company relying on this provision must provide notice to Nasdaq immediately upon learning of the event or circumstance that caused the noncompliance.

(5) Exception

At any time when a Company has a class of common equity securities (or similar securities) that is listed on another national securities exchange or national securities association subject to the requirements of Rule 10A-3 under the Act, the listing of classes of securities of a direct or indirect consolidated subsidiary or an at least 50% beneficially owned subsidiary of the Company (except classes of equity securities, other than non-convertible, non-participating preferred securities, of such subsidiary) shall not be subject to the requirements of Rule 5605(c).

(d) Compensation Committee Requirements

The provisions of this Rule 5605(d) and IM-5605-6 are operative only subject to the effective dates outlined in Rule 5605(d)(6). During the transition period until a Company is required to comply with a particular provision, the Company must continue to comply with the corresponding provision, if any, of Rule 5605A(d) and IM-5605A-6.

(1) Compensation Committee Charter

Each Company must certify that it has adopted a formal written compensation committee charter and that the compensation committee will review and reassess the adequacy of the formal written charter on an annual basis. The charter must specify:

(A) the scope of the compensation committee's responsibilities, and how it carries out those responsibilities, including structure, processes, and membership requirements;

(B) the compensation committee's responsibility for determining, or recommending to the board for determination, the compensation of the chief executive officer and all other Executive Officers of the Company;

(C) that the chief executive officer may not be present during voting or deliberations on his or her compensation; and

(D) the specific compensation committee responsibilities and authority set forth in Rule 5605(d)(3).

(2) Compensation Committee Composition

(A) Each Company must have, and certify that it has and will continue to have, a compensation committee of at least two members. Each committee member must be an Independent Director as defined under Rule 5605(a)(2). In addition, in affirmatively determining the independence of any director who will serve on the compensation committee of a Board of Directors, the Board of Directors must consider all factors specifically relevant to determining whether a director has a relationship to the Company which is material to that director's ability to be independent from management in connection with the duties of a compensation committee member, including, but not limited to:

(i) the source of compensation of such director, including any consulting, advisory or other compensatory fee paid by the Company to such director; and

(ii) whether such director is affiliated with the Company, a subsidiary of the Company or an affiliate of a subsidiary of the Company.

(B) Non-Independent Committee Member under Exceptional and Limited Circumstances

Notwithstanding paragraph 5605(d)(2)(A), if the compensation committee is comprised of at least three members, one director who does not meet the requirements of paragraph 5605(d)(2)(A) and is not currently an Executive Officer or employee or a Family Member of an Executive Officer, may be appointed to the compensation committee if the board, under exceptional and limited circumstances, determines that such individual's membership on the committee is required by the best interests of the Company and its Shareholders. A Company that relies on this exception must disclose either on or through the Company's website or in the proxy statement for the next annual meeting subsequent to such determination (or, if the Company does not file a proxy, in its Form 10-K or 20-F), the nature of the relationship and the reasons for the determination. In addition, the Company must provide any disclosure required by Instruction 1 to Item 407(a) of Regulation S-K regarding its reliance on this exception. A member appointed under this exception may not serve longer than two years.

(3) Compensation Committee Responsibilities and Authority

As required by Rule 10C-1(b)(2), (3) and (4)(i)-(vi) under the Act, the compensation committee must have the following specific responsibilities and authority.

(A) The compensation committee may, in its sole discretion, retain or obtain the advice of a compensation consultant, legal counsel, or other adviser.

(B) The compensation committee shall be directly responsible for the appointment, compensation, and oversight of the work of any compensation consultant, legal counsel, and other adviser retained by the compensation committee.

(C) The Company must provide for appropriate funding, as determined by the compensation committee, for payment of reasonable compensation to a compensation consultant, legal counsel, or any other adviser retained by the compensation committee.

(D) The compensation committee may select, or receive advice from, a compensation consultant, legal counsel, or other adviser to the compensation committee, other than in-house legal counsel, only after taking into consideration the following factors:

    (i) the provision of other services to the Company by the person that employs the compensation consultant, legal counsel, or other adviser;

    (ii) the amount of fees received from the Company by the person that employs the compensation consultant, legal counsel or other adviser, as a percentage of the total revenue of the person that employs the compensation consultant, legal counsel, or other adviser;

    (iii) the policies and procedures of the person that employs the compensation consultant, legal counsel, or other adviser that are designed to prevent conflicts of interest;

    (iv) any business or personal relationship of the compensation consultant, legal counsel, or other adviser with a member of the compensation committee;

    (v) any stock of the Company owned by the compensation consultant, legal counsel, or other adviser; and

    (vi) any business or personal relationship of the compensation consultant, legal counsel, other adviser, or the person employing the adviser with an Executive Officer of the Company.

Nothing in this Rule shall be construed: (i) to require the compensation committee to implement or act consistently with the advice or recommendations of the compensation consultant, legal counsel, or other adviser to the compensation committee; or (ii) to affect the ability or obligation of a compensation committee to exercise its own judgment in fulfillment of the duties of the compensation committee.

The compensation committee is required to conduct the independence assessment outlined in this Rule with respect to any compensation consultant, legal counsel or other adviser that provides advice to the compensation committee, other than in-house legal counsel. However, nothing in this Rule requires a compensation consultant, legal counsel, or other compensation adviser to be independent, only that the compensation committee consider the enumerated independence factors before selecting, or receiving advice from, a compensation adviser. Compensation committees may select, or receive advice from, any compensation adviser they prefer, including ones that are not independent, after considering the six independence factors outlined previously.

For purposes of this Rule, the compensation committee is not required to conduct an independence assessment for a compensation adviser that acts in a role limited to the following activities for which no disclosure is required under Item 407(e)(3)(iii) of Regulation S-K: (a) consulting on any broad-based plan that does not discriminate in scope, terms, or operation, in favor of Executive Officers or directors of the Company, and that is available generally to all salaried employees; and/or (b) providing information that either is not customized for a particular issuer or that is customized based on parameters that are not developed by the adviser, and about which the adviser does not provide advice.

(4) Cure Period for Compensation Committee

If a Company fails to comply with the compensation committee composition requirement under Rule 5605(d)(2)(A) due to one vacancy, or one compensation committee member ceases to be independent due to circumstances beyond the member's reasonable control, the Company shall regain compliance with the requirement by the earlier of its next annual shareholders meeting or one year from the occurrence of the event that caused the failure to comply with this requirement; provided, however, that if the annual shareholders meeting occurs no later than 180 days following the event that caused the failure to comply with this requirement, the Company shall instead have 180 days from such event to regain compliance. A Company relying on this provision shall provide notice to Nasdaq immediately upon learning of the event or circumstance that caused the noncompliance.

(5) Smaller Reporting Companies

A Smaller Reporting Company, as defined in Rule 12b-2 under the Act, is not subject to the requirements of Rule 5605(d), except that a Smaller Reporting Company must have, and certify that it has and will continue to have, a compensation committee of at least two members, each of whom must be an Independent Director as defined under Rule 5605(a)(2). A Smaller Reporting Company may rely on the exception in Rule 5605(d)(2)(B) and the cure period in Rule 5605(d)(4). In addition, a Smaller Reporting Company must certify that it has adopted a formal written compensation committee charter or board resolution that specifies the content set forth in Rule 5605(d)(1)(A)-(C). A Smaller Reporting Company does not need to include in its formal written compensation committee charter or board resolution the specific compensation committee responsibilities and authority set forth in Rule 5605(d)(3).

(6) Effective Dates of Rule 5605(d) and IM-5605-6; Transition for Companies Listed On Nasdaq as of the Effective Dates

The provisions of Rule 5605(d)(3) shall be effective on July 1, 2013; to the extent a Company does not have a compensation committee in the period before the final implementation deadline applicable to it as outlined in the following paragraph, the provisions of Rule 5605(d)(3) shall apply to the Independent Directors who determine, or recommend to the board for determination, the compensation of the chief executive officer and all other Executive Officers of the Company. Companies should consider under state corporate law whether to grant the specific responsibilities and authority referenced in Rule 5605(d)(3) through a charter, resolution or other board action; however, Nasdaq requires only that a compensation committee, or Independent Directors acting in lieu of a compensation committee, have the responsibilities and authority referenced in Rule 5605(d)(3) on July 1, 2013. Companies must have a written compensation committee charter that includes, among others, the responsibilities and authority referenced in Rule 5605(d)(3) by the implementation deadline set forth in the following paragraph.

In order to allow Companies to make necessary adjustments in the course of their regular annual meeting schedule, Companies will have until the earlier of their first annual meeting after January 15, 2014, or October 31, 2014, to comply with the remaining provisions of Rule 5605(d) and IM-5605-6. A Company must certify to Nasdaq, no later than 30 days after the final implementation deadline applicable to it, that it has complied with Rule 5605(d). During the transition period, Companies that are not yet required to comply with a particular provision of revised Rule 5605(d) and IM-5605-6 must continue to comply with the corresponding provision, if any, of Rule 5605A(d) and IM-5605A-6.

Amended July 22, 2010 (SR-NASDAQ-2008-014); amended Jan. 11, 2013 (SR-NASDAQ-2012-109); amended Nov. 26, 2013 (SR-NASDAQ-2013-147), operative Dec. 26, 2013.

IM-5605-6. Independent Director Oversight of Executive Compensation

Independent oversight of executive officer compensation helps assure that appropriate incentives are in place, consistent with the board's responsibility to act in the best interests of the corporation. Compensation committees are required to have a minimum of two members and be comprised only of Independent Directors as defined under Rule 5605(a)(2).

In addition, Rule 5605(d)(2)(A) includes an additional independence test for compensation committee members. When considering the sources of a director's compensation for this purpose, the board should consider whether the director receives compensation from any person or entity that would impair the director's ability to make independent judgments about the Company's executive compensation. Similarly, when considering any affiliate relationship a director has with the Company, a subsidiary of the Company, or an affiliate of a subsidiary of the Company, in determining independence for purposes of compensation committee service, the board should consider whether the affiliate relationship places the director under the direct or indirect control of the Company or its senior management, or creates a direct relationship between the director and members of senior management, in each case of a nature that would impair the director's ability to make independent judgments about the Company's executive compensation. In that regard, while a board may conclude differently with respect to individual facts and circumstances, Nasdaq does not believe that ownership of Company stock by itself, or possession of a controlling interest through ownership of Company stock by itself, precludes a board finding that it is appropriate for a director to serve on the compensation committee. In fact, it may be appropriate for certain affiliates, such as representatives of significant stockholders, to serve on compensation committees since their interests are likely aligned with those of other stockholders in seeking an appropriate executive compensation program.

For purposes of the additional independence test for compensation committee members described in Rule 5605(d)(2)(A), any reference to the "Company" includes any parent or subsidiary of the Company. The term "parent or subsidiary" is intended to cover entities the Company controls and consolidates with the Company's financial statements as filed with the Commission (but not if the Company reflects such entity solely as an investment in its financial statements).

A Smaller Reporting Company must have a compensation committee with a minimum of two members. Each compensation committee member must be an Independent Director as defined under Rule 5605(a)(2). In addition, each Smaller Reporting Company must have a formal written compensation committee charter or board resolution that specifies the committee's responsibilities and authority set forth in Rule 5605(d)(1)(A)-(C). However, in recognition of the fact that Smaller Reporting Companies may have fewer resources than larger Companies, Smaller Reporting Companies are not required to adhere to the additional compensation committee eligibility requirements in Rule 5605(d)(2)(A), or to incorporate into their formal written compensation committee charter or board resolution the specific compensation committee responsibilities and authority set forth in Rule 5605(d)(3).

Adopted Mar. 12, 2009 (SR-NASDAQ-2009-018); amended Jan. 11, 2013 (SR-NASDAQ-2012-109); amended Nov. 26, 2013 (SR-NASDAQ-2013-147), operative Dec. 26, 2013.

(e) Independent Director Oversight of Director Nominations

    (1) Director nominees must either be selected, or recommended for the Board's selection, either by:

        (A) Independent Directors constituting a majority of the Board's Independent Directors in a vote in which only Independent Directors participate, or

> **(B)** a nominations committee comprised solely of Independent Directors.

(2) Each Company must certify that it has adopted a formal written charter or board resolution, as applicable, addressing the nominations process and such related matters as may be required under the federal securities laws.

(3) Non-Independent Committee Member under Exceptional and Limited Circumstances

> Notwithstanding paragraph 5605(e)(1)(B), if the nominations committee is comprised of at least three members, one director, who is not an Independent Director as defined in Rule 5605(a)(2) and is not currently an Executive Officer or employee or a Family Member of an Executive Officer, may be appointed to the nominations committee if the board, under exceptional and limited circumstances, determines that such individual's membership on the committee is required by the best interests of the Company and its Shareholders. A Company that relies on this exception must disclose either on or through the Company's website or in the proxy statement for next annual meeting subsequent to such determination (or, if the Company does not file a proxy, in its Form 10-K or 20-F), the nature of the relationship and the reasons for the determination. In addition, the Company must provide any disclosure required by Instruction 1 to Item 407(a) of Regulation S-K regarding its reliance on this exception. A member appointed under this exception may not serve longer than two years.

(4) Independent Director oversight of director nominations shall not apply in cases where the right to nominate a director legally belongs to a third party. However, this does not relieve a Company's obligation to comply with the committee composition requirements under Rules 5605(c), (d), and (e).

(5) This Rule 5605(e) is not applicable to a Company if the Company is subject to a binding obligation that requires a director nomination structure inconsistent with this rule and such obligation pre-dates the approval date of this rule.

Amended July 22, 2010 (SR-NASDAQ-2008-014); amended Jan. 11, 2013 (SR-NASDAQ-2012-109).

IM-5605-7. Independent Director Oversight of Director Nominations

Independent Director oversight of nominations enhances investor confidence in the selection of well-qualified director nominees, as well as independent nominees as required by the rules. This rule is also intended to provide flexibility for a Company to choose an appropriate board structure and reduce resource burdens, while ensuring that Independent Directors approve all nominations.

This rule does not apply in cases where the right to nominate a director legally belongs to a third party. For example, investors may negotiate the right to nominate directors in connection with an investment in the Company, holders of preferred stock may be permitted to nominate or appoint directors upon certain defaults, or the Company may be a party to a shareholder's agreement that allocates the right to nominate some directors. Because the right to nominate directors in these cases does not reside with the Company, Independent Director approval would not be required. This rule is not applicable if the Company is subject to a binding obligation that requires a director nomination structure inconsistent with the rule and such obligation pre-dates the approval date of this rule.

Adopted Mar. 12, 2009 (SR-NASDAQ-2009-018); amended Mar. 15, 2010 (SR-NASDAQ-2010-037), operative Apr. 14, 2010; amended June 9, 2011 (SR-NASDAQ-2011-082), operative July 9, 2011; amended July 19, 2012 (SR-NASDAQ-2012-062).

5605A. Sunsetting Provisions.

The provisions of this Rule 5605A shall apply until a Company is subject to the corresponding provisions of Rule 5605.

(a) Reserved.

(b) Reserved.

(c) Reserved.

(d) **Independent Director Oversight of Executive Officer Compensation**

    (1) Compensation of the chief executive officer of the Company must be determined, or recommended to the Board for determination, either by:

        (A) Independent Directors constituting a majority of the Board's Independent Directors in a vote in which only Independent Directors participate; or

        (B) a compensation committee comprised solely of Independent Directors.

    The chief executive officer may not be present during voting or deliberations.

    (2) Compensation of all other Executive Officers must be determined, or recommended to the Board for determination, either by:

        (A) Independent Directors constituting a majority of the Board's Independent Directors in a vote in which only Independent Directors participate; or

        (B) a compensation committee comprised solely of Independent Directors.

    (3) **Non-Independent Committee Member under Exceptional and Limited Circumstances**

Notwithstanding paragraphs 5605A(d)(1)(B) and 5605A(d)(2)(B), if the compensation committee is comprised of at least three members, one director who is not independent as defined in Rule 5605(a)(2) and is not currently an Executive Officer or employee or a Family Member of an Executive Officer, may be appointed to the compensation committee if the board, under exceptional and limited circumstances, determines that such individual's membership on the committee is required by the best interests of the Company and its Shareholders. A Company that relies on this exception must disclose either on or through the Company's website or in the proxy statement for the next annual meeting subsequent to such determination (or, if the Company does not file a proxy, in its Form 10-K or 20-F), the nature of the relationship and the reasons for the determination. In addition, the Company must provide any disclosure required by Instruction 1 to Item 407(a) of Regulation S-K regarding its reliance on this exception. A member appointed under this exception may not serve longer than two years.

Adopted Jan. 11, 2013 (SR-NASDAQ-2012-109).

IM-5605A-6. Independent Director Oversight of Executive Compensation

Independent director oversight of executive officer compensation helps assure that appropriate incentives are in place, consistent with the board's responsibility to maximize shareholder value. The rule is intended to provide flexibility for a Company to choose an appropriate board structure and to reduce resource burdens, while ensuring Independent Director control of compensation decisions.

Adopted Jan. 11, 2013 (SR-NASDAQ-2012-109).

5610. Code of Conduct

Each Company shall adopt a code of conduct applicable to all directors, officers, and employees, which shall be publicly available. A code of conduct satisfying this rule must comply with the definition of a "code of ethics" set out in Section 406(c) of the Sarbanes–Oxley Act of 2002 ("the Sarbanes–Oxley Act") and any regulations promulgated thereunder by the Commission. See 17 C.F.R. 228.406 and 17 C.F.R. 229.406. In addition, the code must provide for an enforcement mechanism. Any waivers of the code for directors or Executive Officers must be approved by the Board. Companies, other than Foreign Private Issuers, shall disclose such waivers within four business days by filing a current report on Form 8-K with the Commission or, in cases where a Form 8-K is not required, by distributing a press release. Foreign Private Issuers shall disclose such waivers either by distributing a press release or including disclosure in a Form 6-K or in the next Form 20-F or 40-F. Alternatively, a Company, including a Foreign Private Issuer, may disclose waivers on the Company's website in a manner that satisfies the requirements of Item 5.05(c) of Form 8-K.

IM-5610. Code of Conduct

Ethical behavior is required and expected of every corporate director, officer, and employee whether or not a formal code of conduct exists. The requirement of a publicly available code of conduct applicable to all directors, officers, and employees of a Company is intended to demonstrate to investors that the board and management of Nasdaq Companies have carefully considered the requirement of ethical dealing and have put in place a system to ensure that they become aware of and take prompt action against any questionable behavior. For Company personnel, a code of conduct with enforcement provisions provides assurance that reporting of questionable behavior is protected and encouraged, and fosters an atmosphere of self-awareness and prudent conduct.

Rule 5610 requires Companies to adopt a code of conduct complying with the definition of a "code of ethics" under Section 406(c) of the Sarbanes–Oxley Act of 2002 ("the Sarbanes–Oxley Act") and any regulations promulgated thereunder by the Commission. See 17 C.F.R. 228.406 and 17 C.F.R. 229.406. Thus, the code must include such standards as are reasonably necessary to promote the ethical handling of conflicts of interest, full and fair disclosure, and compliance with laws, rules and regulations, as specified by the Sarbanes–Oxley Act. However, the code of conduct required by Rule 5610 must apply to all directors, officers, and employees. Companies can satisfy this obligation by adopting one or more codes of conduct, such that all directors, officers and employees are subject to a code that satisfies the definition of a "code of ethics."

As the Sarbanes–Oxley Act recognizes, investors are harmed when the real or perceived private interest of a director, officer or employee is in conflict with the interests of the Company, as when the individual receives improper personal benefits as a result of his or her position with the Company, or when the individual has other duties, responsibilities, or obligations that run counter to his or her duty to the Company. Also, the disclosures a Company makes to the Commission are the essential source of information about the Company for regulators and investors—there can be no question about the duty to make them fairly, accurately and timely. Finally, illegal action must be dealt with swiftly and the violators reported to the appropriate authorities. Each code of conduct must require that any waiver of the code for Executive Officers or directors may be made only by the board and must be disclosed to Shareholders, along with the reasons for the waiver. All Companies, other than Foreign Private Issuers, must disclose such waivers within four business days by filing a current report on Form 8-K with the Commission, providing website disclosure that satisfies the requirements of Item 5.05(c) of Form 8-K, or, in cases where a Form 8-K is not required, by distributing a press release. Foreign Private Issuers must disclose such waivers either by providing website disclosure that satisfies the requirements of Item 5.05(c) of Form 8-K, by including disclosure in a Form 6-K or in the next Form 20-F or 40-F or by distributing a press release. This disclosure requirement provides investors the comfort that waivers are not granted except where they are truly necessary and warranted, and that they are limited and qualified so as to protect the Company and its Shareholders to the greatest extent possible.

Each code of conduct must also contain an enforcement mechanism that ensures prompt and consistent enforcement of the code, protection for persons reporting questionable behavior, clear and objective standards for compliance, and a fair process by which to determine violations.

5615. Exemptions from Certain Corporate Governance Requirements

This rule provides the exemptions from the corporate governance rules afforded to certain types of Companies, and sets forth the phase-in schedules for initial public offerings, Companies emerging from bankruptcy, Companies transferring from other markets and Companies ceasing to be Smaller Reporting Companies. This rule also describes the applicability of the corporate governance rules to Controlled Companies and sets forth the phase-in schedule afforded to Companies ceasing to be Controlled Companies. During the transition period before Companies are subject to revised Rule 5605(d) and IM-5605-6, a reference in this Rule 5615 to Rule 5605(d) or IM-5605-6 shall be deemed to refer to Rule 5605A(d) or IM-5605A-6.

(a) Exemptions to the Corporate Governance Requirements

(1) Asset-Backed Issuers and Other Passive Issuers

The following are exempt from the requirements relating to Majority Independent Board (Rule 5605(b)), Audit Committee (Rule 5605(c)), Compensation Committee (Rule 5605(d)), Director Nominations (Rule 5605(e)), the Controlled Company Exemption (Rule 5615(c)(2)), and Code of Conduct (Rule 5610):

(A) asset-backed issuers; and

(B) issuers, such as unit investment trusts, including Portfolio Depository Receipts, which are organized as trusts or other unincorporated associations that do not have a Board of Directors or persons acting in a similar capacity and whose activities are limited to passively owning or holding (as well as administering and distributing amounts in respect of) securities, rights, collateral or other assets on behalf of or for the benefit of the holders of the listed securities.

IM-5615-1. Asset-Backed Issuers and Other Passive Issuers

Because of their unique attributes, Rules 5605(b), 5605(c), 5605(d), 5605(e), and 5610 do not apply to asset-backed issuers and issuers, such as unit investment trusts, that are organized as trusts or other unincorporated associations that do not have a Board of Directors or persons acting in a similar capacity and whose activities are limited to passively owning or holding (as well as administering and distributing amounts in respect of) securities, rights, collateral, or other assets on behalf of or for the benefit of the holders of the listed securities. This is consistent with Nasdaq's traditional approach to such issuers.

Adopted Mar. 12, 2009 (SR-NASDAQ-2009-018).

(2) Cooperatives

Cooperative entities, such as agricultural cooperatives, that are structured to comply with relevant state law and federal tax law and that do not have a publicly traded class of common stock are exempt from Rules 5605(b), (d), (e), and 5615(c)(2). However, such entities must comply with all federal securities laws, including without limitation those rules required by Section 10A(m) of the Act and Rule 10A-3 thereunder.

IM-5615-2. Cooperatives

Certain member-owned cooperatives that list their preferred stock are required to have their common stock owned by their members. Because of their unique structure and the fact that they do not have a publicly traded class of common stock, such entities are exempt from Rule 5605(b), (d), and (e). This is consistent with Nasdaq's traditional approach to such Companies.

Adopted Mar. 12, 2009 (SR-NASDAQ-2009-018); amended Apr. 27, 2009 (SR-NASDAQ-2009-040).

(3) Foreign Private Issuers

(A) A Foreign Private Issuer may follow its home country practice in lieu of the requirements of the Rule 5600 Series, the requirement to disclose third party director and nominee compensation set forth in Rule 5250(b)(3), and the requirement to distribute annual and interim reports set forth in Rule 5250(d), provided, however, that such a Company shall: comply with the Notification of Noncompliance requirement (Rule 5625), the Voting Rights requirement (Rule 5640), have an audit committee that satisfies Rule 5605(c)(3), and ensure that such audit committee's members meet the independence requirement in Rule 5605(c)(2)(A)(ii). Except as provided in this paragraph, a Foreign Private Issuer must comply with the requirements of the Rule 5000 Series.

(B) Disclosure Requirements

(i) A Foreign Private Issuer that follows a home country practice in lieu of one or more of the Listing Rules shall disclose in its annual reports filed with the Commission each requirement that it does not follow and describe the home country practice followed by the Company in lieu of such requirements. Alternatively, a Foreign Private Issuer that is not required to file its annual report with the Commission on Form 20-F may make this disclosure only on its website. A Foreign Private Issuer that follows a home country practice in lieu of the requirement in Rule 5605(d)(2) to have an independent compensation committee must disclose in its annual reports filed with the Commission the reasons why it does not have such an independent committee.

(ii) A Foreign Private Issuer making its initial public offering or first U.S. listing on Nasdaq shall disclose in its registration statement or on its website each requirement that it does not follow and describe the home country practice followed by the Company in lieu of such requirements.

IM-5615-3. Foreign Private Issuers

A Foreign Private Issuer (as defined in Rule 5005) listed on Nasdaq may follow the practice in such Company's home country (as defined in General Instruction F of Form 20-F) in lieu of the provisions of the Rule 5600 Series, Rule 5250(b) (3), and Rule 5250(d), subject to several important exceptions. First, such an issuer shall comply with Rule 5625 (Notification of Noncompliance). Second, such a Company shall have an audit committee that satisfies Rule 5605(c)(3). Third, members of such audit committee shall meet the criteria for independence referenced in Rule 5605(c)(2)(A)(ii) (the criteria set forth in Rule 10A-3(b)(1) under the Act, subject to the exemptions provided in Rule 10A-3(c) under the Act). Finally, a Foreign Private Issuer that elects to follow home country practice in lieu of a requirement of Rules 5600, 5250(b)(3), or 5250(d) shall submit to Nasdaq a written statement from an independent counsel in such Company's home country certifying that the Company's practices are not prohibited by the home country's laws. In the case of new listings, this certification is required at the time of listing. For existing Companies, the certification is required at the time the Company seeks to adopt its first noncompliant practice. In the interest of transparency, the rule requires a Foreign Private Issuer to make appropriate disclosures in the Company's annual filings with the Commission (typically Form 20-F or 40-F), and at the time of the Company's original listing in the United States, if that listing is on Nasdaq, in its registration statement (typically Form F-1, 20-F, or 40-F); alternatively, a Company that is not required to file an annual report on Form 20-F may provide these disclosures in English on its website in addition to, or instead of, providing these disclosures on its registration statement or annual report. The Company shall disclose each requirement that it does not follow and include a brief statement of the home country practice the Company follows in lieu of these corporate governance requirement(s). If the disclosure is only available on the website, the annual report and registration statement should so state and provide the web address at which the information may be obtained. Companies that must file annual reports on Form 20-F are encouraged to provide these disclosures on their websites, in addition to the required Form 20-F disclosures, to provide maximum transparency about their practices.

Adopted Mar. 12, 2009 (SR-NASDAQ-2009-018); amended Apr. 27, 2009 (SR-NASDAQ-2009-040); amended May 20, 2009 (SR-NASDAQ-2009-049); amended June 16, 2009 (SR-NASDAQ-2009-052); amended May 14, 2010 (SR-NASDAQ-2010-060), operative June 13, 2010; amended Nov. 7, 2012 (SR-NASDAQ-2012-128); amended July 1, 2016 (SR-NASDAQ-2016-013), operative Aug 1, 2016.

(4) Limited Partnerships

A limited partnership is not subject to the requirements of the Rule 5600 Series, except as provided in this Rule 5615(a)(4). A limited partnership may request a written interpretation pursuant to Rule 5602.

(A) No provision of this Rule shall be construed to require any foreign Company that is a partnership to do any act that is contrary to a law, rule, or regulation of any public authority exercising jurisdiction over such Company or that is contrary to generally accepted business practices in the Company's country of domicile. Nasdaq shall have the ability to provide exemptions from applicability of these provisions as may be necessary or appropriate to carry out this intent.

(B) Corporate General Partner

Each Company that is a limited partnership shall maintain a corporate general partner or co-general partner, which shall have the authority to manage the day-to-day affairs of the partnership.

(C) Independent Directors/Audit Committee

The corporate general partner or co-general partner shall maintain a sufficient number of Independent Directors on its board to satisfy the audit committee requirements set forth in Rule 5605(c).

(D) Partner Meetings

A Company that is a limited partnership shall not be required to hold an annual meeting of limited partners unless required by statute or regulation in the state in which the limited partnership is formed or doing business or by the terms of the partnership's limited partnership agreement.

(E) Quorum

In the event that a meeting of limited partners is required pursuant to paragraph (D), the quorum for such meeting shall be not less than 33.3% of the limited partnership interests outstanding.

(F) Solicitation of Proxies

In the event that a meeting of limited partners is required pursuant to paragraph (D), the Company shall provide all limited partners with proxy or information statements and if a vote is required, shall solicit proxies thereon.

(G) Review of Related Party Transactions

Each Company that is a limited partnership shall conduct an appropriate review of all related party transactions on an ongoing basis and shall utilize the Audit Committee or a comparable body of the Board of Directors for the review of potential material conflict of interest situations where appropriate.

(H) Shareholder Approval

Each Company that is a limited partnership must obtain shareholder approval when a stock option or purchase plan is to be established or materially amended or other equity compensation arrangement made or materially amended, pursuant to which stock may be acquired by officers, directors, employees, or consultants, as would be required under Rule 5635(c) and IM-5635-1.

(I) Auditor Registration

Each Company that is a limited partnership must be audited by an independent public accountant that is registered as a public accounting firm with the Public Company Accounting Oversight Board, as provided for in Section 102 of the Sarbanes–Oxley Act of 2002 [15 U.S.C. 7212].

(J) Notification of Noncompliance.

Each Company that is a limited partnership must provide Nasdaq with prompt notification after an Executive Officer of the Company, or a person performing an equivalent role, becomes aware of any noncompliance by the Company with the requirements of this Rule 5600 Series.

(5) Management Investment Companies

Management investment companies (including business development companies) are subject to all the requirements of the

Rule 5600 Series, except that management investment companies registered under the Investment Company Act of 1940 are exempt from the Independent Directors requirement, the Compensation Committee requirement, the Independent Director Oversight of Director Nominations requirement, and the Code of Conduct requirement, set forth in Rules 5605(b), (d) and (e) and 5610, respectively. In addition, management investment companies that issue Index Fund Shares, Managed Fund Shares, and NextShares, as defined in Rules 5705(b), 5735, and 5745 are exempt from the Audit Committee requirements set forth in Rule 5605(c), except for the applicable requirements of SEC Rule 10A-3.

IM-5615-4. Management Investment Companies

Management investment companies registered under the Investment Company Act of 1940 are already subject to a pervasive system of federal regulation in certain areas of corporate governance covered by 5600. In light of this, Nasdaq exempts from Rules 5605(b), (d), (e), and 5610 management investment companies registered under the Investment Company Act of 1940. Business development companies, which are a type of closed-end management investment company defined in Section 2(a)(48) of the Investment Company Act of 1940 that are not registered under that Act, are required to comply with all of the provisions of the Rule 5600 Series. Management investment companies that issue Index Fund Shares, Managed Fund Shares, and NextShares, are exempt from the Audit Committee requirements set forth in Rule 5605(c), except for the applicable requirements of SEC Rule 10A-3.

Adopted Mar. 12, 2009 (SR-NASDAQ-2009-018); amended Aug. 18, 2009 (SR-NASDAQ-2009-078); amended Mar. 11, 2010 (SR-NASDAQ-2010-036); amended Nov. 7, 2014 (SR-NASDAQ-2014-020); amended Oct. 13, 2015 (SR-NASDAQ-2015-121).

(b) Phase-In Schedules

(1) Initial Public Offerings

A Company listing in connection with its initial public offering shall be permitted to phase in its compliance with the independent committee requirements set forth in Rules 5605(d)(2) and (e)(1)(B) on the same schedule as it is permitted to phase in its compliance with the independent audit committee requirement pursuant to Rule 10A-3(b)(1)(iv)(A) under the Act. Accordingly, a Company listing in connection with its initial public offering shall be permitted to phase in its compliance with the committee composition requirements set forth in Rule 5605(d)(2) and (e)(1)(B) as follows: (1) one member must satisfy the requirement at the time of listing; (2) a majority of members must satisfy the requirement within 90 days of listing; and (3) all members must satisfy the requirement within one year of listing. Furthermore, a Company listing in connection with its initial public offering shall have twelve months from the date of listing to comply with the majority independent board requirement in Rule 5605(b). It should be noted, however, that pursuant to Rule 10A-3(b)(1)(iii) under the Act investment companies are not afforded the exemptions under Rule 10A-3(b)(1)(iv) under the Act. Companies may choose not to adopt a nomination committee and may instead rely upon a majority of the Independent Directors to discharge responsibilities under Rule 5605(b). For purposes of the Rule 5600 Series other than Rules 5605(c)(2)(A)(ii) and 5625, a Company shall be considered to be listing in conjunction with an initial public offering if, immediately prior to listing, it does not have a class of common stock registered under the Act. For purposes of Rule 5605(c)(2)(A)(ii) and Rule 5625, a Company shall be considered to be listing in conjunction with an initial public offering only if it meets the conditions in Rule 10A-3(b)(1)(iv)(A) under the Act, namely, that the Company was not, immediately prior to the effective date of a registration statement, required to file reports with the Commission pursuant to Section 13(a) or 15(d) of the Act.

(2) Companies Emerging from Bankruptcy

Companies that are emerging from bankruptcy shall be permitted to phase-in independent nomination and compensation committees and majority independent boards on the same schedule as Companies listing in conjunction with their initial public offering.

(3) Transfers from other Markets

Companies transferring from other markets with a substantially similar requirement shall be afforded the balance of any grace period afforded by the other market. Companies transferring from other listed markets that do not have a substantially similar requirement shall be afforded one year from the date of listing on Nasdaq. This transition period is not intended to supplant any applicable requirements of Rule 10A-3 under the Act.

(4) Phase-In Schedule for a Company Ceasing to be a Smaller Reporting Company

Pursuant to Rule 12b-2 under the Act, a Company tests its status as a Smaller Reporting Company on an annual basis as of the last business day of its most recently completed second fiscal quarter (for purposes of this Rule, the "Determination Date"). A Company with a public float of $75 million or more as of the Determination Date will cease to be a Smaller Reporting Company as of the beginning of the fiscal year following the Determination Date (the "Start Date").

By six months from the Start Date, a Company must comply with Rule 5605(d)(3) and certify to Nasdaq that: (i) it has complied with the requirement in Rule 5605(d)(1) to adopt a formal written compensation committee charter including the content specified in Rule 5605(d)(1)(A)- (D); and (ii) it has complied, or within the applicable phase-in schedule will comply, with the additional requirements in Rule 5605(d)(2)(A) regarding compensation committee composition.

A Company shall be permitted to phase in its compliance with the additional compensation committee eligibility requirements of Rule 5605(d)(2)(A) relating to compensatory fees and affiliation as follows: (i) one member must satisfy the requirements by six months from the Start Date; (ii) a majority of members must satisfy the requirements by nine months from the Start Date; and (iii) all members must satisfy the requirements by one year from the Start Date.

Since a Smaller Reporting Company is required to have a compensation committee comprised of at least two Independent Directors, a Company that has ceased to be a Smaller Reporting Company may not use the phase-in schedule for the requirements of Rule 5605(d)(2)(A) relating to minimum committee size or that the committee consist only of Independent Directors as defined under Rule 5605(a)(2).

During this phase-in schedule, a Company that has ceased to be a Smaller Reporting Company must continue to comply with Rule 5605(d)(5).

(c) How the Rules Apply to a Controlled Company

(1) Definition

A Controlled Company is a Company of which more than 50% of the voting power for the election of directors is held by an individual, a group or another company.

(2) Exemptions Afforded to a Controlled Company

A Controlled Company is exempt from the requirements of Rules 5605(b), (d), and (e), except for the requirements of subsection (b)(2) which pertain to executive sessions of Independent Directors. A Controlled Company, other than a

Foreign Private Issuer, relying upon this exemption must comply with the disclosure requirements set forth in Instruction 1 to Item 407(a) of Regulation S-K. A Foreign Private Issuer must disclose in its next annual report (e.g., Form 20-F or 40-F) that it is a Controlled Company and the basis for that determination.

(3) Phase-In Schedule for a Company Ceasing to be a Controlled Company

A Company that has ceased to be a Controlled Company within the meaning of Rule 5615(c)(1) shall be permitted to phase-in its independent nomination and compensation committees and majority independent board on the same schedule as Companies listing in conjunction with their initial public offering. It should be noted, however, that a Company that has ceased to be a Controlled Company within the meaning of Rule 5615(c)(1) must comply with the audit committee requirements of Rule 5605(c) as of the date it ceased to be a Controlled Company. Furthermore, the executive sessions requirement of Rule 5605(b)(2) applies to Controlled Companies as of the date of listing and continues to apply after it ceases to be controlled.

IM-5615-5. Controlled Company Exemption

This exemption recognizes that majority Shareholders, including parent companies, have the right to select directors and control certain key decisions, such as executive officer compensation, by virtue of their ownership rights. In order for a group to exist for purposes of this rule, the Shareholders must have publicly filed a notice that they are acting as a group (e.g., a Schedule 13D). A Controlled Company not relying upon this exemption need not provide any special disclosures about its controlled status. It should be emphasized that this controlled company exemption does not extend to the audit committee requirements under Rule 5605(c) or the requirement for executive sessions of Independent Directors under Rule 5605(b)(2).

5620. Meetings of Shareholders

(a) Each Company listing common stock or voting preferred stock, and their equivalents, shall hold an Annual Meeting of Shareholders no later than one year after the end of the Company's fiscal year-end, unless such Company is a limited partnership that meets the requirements of Rule 5615(a)(4)(D).

IM-5620. Meetings of Shareholders or Partners

Rule 5620 requires that each Company listing common stock or voting preferred stock, and their equivalents, hold an annual meeting of Shareholders within one year of the end of each fiscal year. At each such meeting, Shareholders must be afforded the opportunity to discuss Company affairs with management and, if required by the Company's governing documents, to elect directors. A new listing that was not previously subject to a requirement to hold an annual meeting is required to hold its first meeting within one year after its first fiscal year-end following listing. Of course, Nasdaq's meeting requirement does not supplant any applicable state or federal securities laws concerning annual meetings.

This requirement is not applicable as a result of a Company listing the following types of securities: securities listed pursuant to Rule 5730(a) (such as Trust Preferred Securities and Contingent Value Rights), unless the listed security is a common stock or voting preferred stock equivalent (e.g., a callable common stock); Portfolio Depository Receipts and Index Fund Shares listed pursuant to Rules 5705(a) and (b); and Trust Issued Receipts listed pursuant to Rule 5720. Notwithstanding, if the Company also lists common stock or voting preferred stock, or their equivalent, the Company must still hold an annual meeting for the holders of that common stock or voting preferred stock, or their equivalent.

(b) Proxy Solicitation

Each Company that is not a limited partnership shall solicit proxies and provide proxy statements for all meetings of Shareholders and shall provide copies of such proxy solicitation to Nasdaq. Limited partnerships that are required to hold an annual meeting of partners are subject to the requirements of Rule 5615(a)(4)(F).

(c) Quorum

Each Company that is not a limited partnership shall provide for a quorum as specified in its by-laws for any meeting of the holders of common stock; provided, however, that in no case shall such quorum be less than 33.3% of the outstanding shares of the Company's common voting stock. Limited partnerships that are required to hold an annual meeting of partners are subject to the requirements of Rule 5615(a)(4)(E).

5625. Notification of Noncompliance

A Company must provide Nasdaq with prompt notification after an Executive Officer of the Company becomes aware of any noncompliance by the Company with the requirements of this Rule 5600 Series.

5630. Review of Related Party Transactions

(a) Each Company that is not a limited partnership shall conduct an appropriate review and oversight of all related party transactions for potential conflict of interest situations on an ongoing basis by the Company's audit committee or another independent body of the Board of Directors. For purposes of this rule, the term "related party transaction" shall refer to transactions required to be disclosed pursuant to Item 404 of Regulation S-K under the Act. However, in the case of non-U.S. issuers, the term "related party transactions" shall refer to transactions required to be disclosed pursuant to Form 20-F, Item 7.B.

(b) Limited partnerships shall comply with the requirements of Rule 5615(a)(4)(G).

5635. Shareholder Approval

This Rule sets forth the circumstances under which shareholder approval is required prior to an issuance of securities in connection with: (i) the acquisition of the stock or assets of another company; (ii) equity-based compensation of officers, directors, employees, or consultants; (iii) a change of control; and (iv) private placements. General provisions relating to shareholder approval are set forth in Rule 5635(e), and the financial viability exception to the shareholder approval requirement is set forth in Rule 5635(f). Nasdaq-listed Companies and their representatives are encouraged to use the interpretative letter process described in Rule 5602.

(a) **Acquisition of Stock or Assets of Another Company**

Shareholder approval is required prior to the issuance of securities in connection with the acquisition of the stock or assets of another company if:

(1) where, due to the present or potential issuance of common stock, including shares issued pursuant to an earn-out provision or similar type of provision, or securities convertible into or exercisable for common stock, other than a public offering for cash:

(A) the common stock has or will have upon issuance voting power equal to or in excess of 20% of the voting power outstanding before the issuance of stock or securities convertible into or exercisable for common stock; or

(B) the number of shares of common stock to be issued is or will be equal to or in excess of 20% of the number of shares of common stock outstanding before the issuance of the stock or securities; or

(2) any director, officer, or Substantial Shareholder (as defined by Rule 5635(e)(3)) of the Company has a 5% or greater interest (or such persons collectively have a 10% or greater interest), directly or indirectly, in the Company or assets to be acquired or in the consideration to be paid in the transaction or series of related transactions and the present or potential issuance of common stock, or securities convertible into or exercisable for common

stock, could result in an increase in outstanding common shares or voting power of 5% or more; or

(b) Change of Control

Shareholder approval is required prior to the issuance of securities when the issuance or potential issuance will result in a change of control of the Company.

(c) Equity Compensation

Shareholder approval is required prior to the issuance of securities when a stock option or purchase plan is to be established or materially amended or other equity compensation arrangement made or materially amended, pursuant to which stock may be acquired by officers, directors, employees, or consultants, except for:

(1) warrants or rights issued generally to all security holders of the Company or stock purchase plans available on equal terms to all security holders of the Company (such as a typical dividend reinvestment plan);

(2) tax qualified, non-discriminatory employee benefit plans (e.g., plans that meet the requirements of Section 401(a) or 423 of the Internal Revenue Code) or parallel nonqualified plans, provided such plans are approved by the Company's independent compensation committee or a majority of the Company's Independent Directors; or plans that merely provide a convenient way to purchase shares on the open market or from the Company at Market Value;

(3) plans or arrangements relating to an acquisition or merger as permitted under IM-5635-1; or

(4) issuances to a person not previously an employee or director of the Company, or following a bona fide period of non-employment, as an inducement material to the individual's entering into employment with the Company, provided such issuances are approved by either the Company's independent compensation committee or a majority of the Company's Independent Directors. Promptly following an issuance of any employment inducement grant in reliance on this exception, a Company must disclose in a press release the material terms of the grant, including the recipient(s) of the grant and the number of shares involved.

IM-5635-1. Shareholder Approval for Stock Option Plans or Other Equity Compensation Arrangements

Employee ownership of Company stock can be an effective tool to align employee interests with those of other Shareholders. Stock option plans or other equity compensation arrangements can also assist in the recruitment and retention of employees, which is especially critical to young, growing Companies, or Companies with insufficient cash resources to attract and retain highly qualified employees. However, these plans can potentially dilute shareholder interests. Rule 5635(c) ensures that Shareholders have a voice in these situations, given this potential for dilution.

Rule 5635(c) requires shareholder approval when a plan or other equity compensation arrangement is established or materially amended. For these purposes, a material amendment would include, but not be limited to, the following:

(1) any material increase in the number of shares to be issued under the plan (other than to reflect a reorganization, stock split, merger, spin-off or similar transaction);

(2) any material increase in benefits to participants, including any material change to: (i) permit a repricing (or decrease in exercise price) of outstanding options, (ii) reduce the price at which shares or options to purchase shares may be offered, or (iii) extend the duration of a plan;

(3) any material expansion of the class of participants eligible to participate in the plan; and

(4) any expansion in the types of options or awards provided under the plan.

While general authority to amend a plan would not obviate the need for shareholder approval, if a plan permits a specific action without further shareholder approval, then no such approval would generally be required. However, if a plan contains a formula for automatic increases in the shares available (sometimes called an "evergreen formula"), or for automatic grants pursuant to a dollar-based formula (such as annual grants based on a certain dollar value, or matching contributions based upon the amount of compensation the participant elects to defer), such plans cannot have a term in excess of ten years unless shareholder approval is obtained every ten years. However, plans that do not contain a formula and do not impose a limit on the number of shares available for grant would require shareholder approval of each grant under the plan. A requirement that grants be made out of treasury shares or repurchased shares will not alleviate these additional shareholder approval requirements.

As a general matter, when preparing plans and presenting them for shareholder approval, Companies should strive to make plan terms easy to understand. In that regard, it is recommended that plans meant to permit repricing use explicit terminology to make this clear.

Rule 5635(c) provides an exception to the requirement for shareholder approval for warrants or rights offered generally to all Shareholders. In addition, an exception is provided for tax-qualified, non-discriminatory employee benefit plans as well as parallel nonqualified plans as these plans are regulated under the Internal Revenue Code and Treasury Department regulations. An equity compensation plan that provides non-U.S. employees with substantially the same benefits as a comparable tax-qualified, non-discriminatory employee benefit plan or parallel nonqualified plan that the Company provides to its U.S. employees, but for features necessary to comply with applicable foreign tax law, is also exempt from shareholder approval under this section.

Further, the rule provides an exception for inducement grants to new employees because in these cases a Company has an arm's length relationship with the new employees. Inducement grants for these purposes include grants of options or stock to new employees in connection with a merger or acquisition. The rule requires that such issuances be approved by the Company's independent compensation committee or a majority of the Company's Independent Directors. The rule further requires that promptly following an issuance of any employment inducement grant in reliance on this exception, a Company must disclose in a press release the material terms of the grant, including the recipient(s) of the grant and the number of shares involved.

In addition, plans or arrangements involving a merger or acquisition do not require shareholder approval in two situations. First, shareholder approval will not be required to convert, replace, or adjust outstanding options or other equity compensation awards to reflect the transaction. Second, shares available under certain plans acquired in acquisitions and mergers may be used for certain post-transaction grants without further shareholder approval. This exception applies to situations where the party which is not a listed company following the transaction has shares available for grant under pre-existing plans that meet the requirements of this Rule 5635(c). These shares may be used for post-transaction grants of options and other equity awards by the listed Company (after appropriate adjustment of the number of shares to reflect the transaction), either under the preexisting plan or arrangement or another plan or arrangement, without further shareholder approval, provided: (1) the time during which those shares are available for grants is not extended beyond the period when they would have been available under the preexisting plan, absent the transaction, and (2) such options and other awards are not granted to individuals who were employed by the granting company or its subsidiaries at the time the merger or acquisition was consummated. Nasdaq would view a plan or arrangement adopted in contemplation of the merger or acquisition transaction as not preexisting for purposes of this exception. This exception is appropriate because it will not result in any increase in the aggregate potential dilution of the combined enterprise. In this regard, any additional shares available for issuance under a plan or arrangement acquired in connection with a merger or acquisition would be counted by Nasdaq in determining whether the transaction involved the issuance of 20% or more of the Company's outstanding common stock, thus triggering the shareholder approval requirements under Rule 5635(a).

Inducement grants, tax-qualified non-discriminatory benefit plans, and parallel nonqualified plans are subject to approval by either the Company's independent compensation committee or a majority of the Company's Independent Directors. It should also be noted that a Company would not be permitted to use repurchased shares to fund option plans or grants without prior shareholder approval.

For purposes of Rule 5635(c) and IM-5635-1, the term "parallel nonqualified plan" means a plan that is a "pension plan" within the meaning of the Employee Retirement Income Security Act ("ERISA"), 29 U.S.C. §1002 (1999), that is designed to work in parallel with a plan intended to be qualified under Internal Revenue Code Section 401(a), to provide benefits that exceed the limits set forth in Internal Revenue Code Section 402(g) (the section that limits an employee's annual pre-tax contributions to a 401(k) plan), Internal Revenue Code Section 401(a)(17) (the section that limits the amount of an employee's compensation that can be taken into account for plan purposes) and/or Internal Revenue Code Section 415 (the section that limits the contributions and benefits under qualified plans) and/or any successor or similar limitations that may thereafter be enacted. However, a plan will not be considered a parallel nonqualified plan unless: (i) it covers all or substantially all employees of an employer who are participants in the related qualified plan whose annual compensation is in excess of the limit of Code Section 401(a)(17) (or any successor or similar limitation that may hereafter be enacted); (ii) its terms are substantially the same as the qualified plan that it parallels except for the elimination of the limitations described in the preceding sentence; and, (iii) no participant receives employer equity contributions under the plan in excess of 25% of the participant's cash compensation.

(d) Private Placements

Shareholder approval is required prior to the issuance of securities in connection with a transaction other than a public offering involving:

(1) the sale, issuance, or potential issuance by the Company of common stock (or securities convertible into or exercisable for common stock) at a price less than the greater of book or market value which together with sales by officers, directors or Substantial Shareholders of the Company equals 20% or more of common stock or 20% or more of the voting power outstanding before the issuance; or

(2) the sale, issuance, or potential issuance by the Company of common stock (or securities convertible into or exercisable common stock) equal to 20% or more of the common stock or 20% or more of the voting power outstanding before the issuance for less than the greater of book or market value of the stock.

IM-5635-2. Interpretative Material Regarding the Use of Share Caps to Comply with Rule 5635

Rule 5635 limits the number of shares or voting power that can be issued or granted without shareholder approval prior to the issuance of certain securities. (An exception to this rule is available to Companies when the delay in securing stockholder approval would seriously jeopardize the financial viability of the enterprise as set forth in Rule 5635(f). However, a share cap is not permissible in conjunction with the financial viability exception provided in Rule 5635(f), because the application to Nasdaq and the notice to Shareholders required in the rule must occur prior to the issuance of any common stock or securities convertible into or exercisable for common stock.) Generally, this limitation applies to issuances of 20% or more of the common stock or 20% or more of the voting power outstanding before the issuance. (While Nasdaq's experience is that this issue is generally implicated with respect to these situations, it may also arise with respect to the 5% threshold set forth in Rule 5635(a)(2).) Companies sometimes comply with the 20% limitation in this rule by placing a "cap" on the number of shares that can be issued in the transaction, such that there cannot, under any circumstances, be an issuance of 20 percent or more of the common stock or voting power previously outstanding without prior shareholder approval. If a Company determines to defer a shareholder vote in this manner, shares that are issuable under the cap (in the first part of the transaction) must not be entitled to vote to approve the remainder of the transaction. In addition, a cap must apply for the life of the transaction, unless shareholder approval is obtained. For example, caps that no longer apply if a Company is not listed on Nasdaq are not permissible under the Rule. Of course, if shareholder approval is not obtained, then the investor will not be able to acquire 20% or more of the common stock or voting power outstanding before the transaction and would continue to hold the balance of the original security in its unconverted form.

Nasdaq has observed situations where Companies have attempted to cap the issuance of shares at below 20% but have also provided an alternative outcome based upon whether shareholder approval is obtained, including, but not limited to a "penalty" or a "sweetener." Instead, if the terms of a transaction can change based upon the outcome of the shareholder vote, no common shares may be issued prior to the approval of the Shareholders. Companies that engage in transactions with defective caps may be subject to delisting. For example, a Company issues a convertible preferred stock or debt instrument that provides for conversions of up to 20% of the total shares outstanding with any further conversions subject to shareholder approval. However, the terms of the instrument provide that if Shareholders reject the transaction, the coupon or conversion ratio will increase or the Company will be penalized by a specified monetary payment, including a rescission of the transaction. Likewise, a transaction may provide for improved terms if shareholder approval is obtained. Nasdaq believes that in such situations the cap is defective because the presence of the alternative outcome has a coercive effect on the shareholder vote, and thus may deprive Shareholders of their ability to freely exercise their vote. Accordingly, Nasdaq will not accept a cap that defers the need for shareholder approval in such situations.

Companies having questions regarding this policy are encouraged to contact the Nasdaq Listing Qualifications Department at (301) 978-8008, which will provide a written interpretation of the application of Nasdaq Rules to a specific transaction, upon prior written request of the Company.

IM-5635-3. Definition of a Public Offering

Rule 5635(d) provides that shareholder approval is required for the issuance of common stock (or securities convertible into or exercisable for common stock) equal to 20% or more of the common stock or 20% or more of the voting power outstanding before the issuance for less than the greater of book or market value of the stock. Under this rule, however, shareholder approval is not required for a "public offering."

Companies are encouraged to consult with Nasdaq staff in order to determine if a particular offering is a "public offering" for purposes of the shareholder approval rules. Generally, a firm commitment underwritten securities offering registered with the Securities and Exchange Commission will be considered a public offering for these purposes. Likewise, any other securities offering which is registered with the Securities and Exchange Commission and which is publicly disclosed and distributed in the same general manner and extent as a firm commitment underwritten securities offering will be considered a public offering for purposes of the shareholder approval rules. However, Nasdaq staff will not treat an offering as a "public offering" for purposes of the shareholder approval rules merely because they are registered with the Commission prior to the closing of the transaction.

When determining whether an offering is a "public offering" for purposes of these rules, Nasdaq staff will consider all relevant factors, including but not limited to:

(i) the type of offering (including whether the offering is conducted by an underwriter on a firm commitment basis, or an underwriter or placement agent on a best-efforts basis, or whether the offering is self-directed by the Company);

(ii) the manner in which the offering is marketed (including the number of investors offered securities, how those investors were chosen, and the breadth of the marketing effort);

(iii) the extent of the offering's distribution (including the number and identity of the investors who participate in the offering and whether any prior relationship existed between the Company and those investors);

(iv) the offering price (including the extent of any discount to the market price of the securities offered); and

(v) the extent to which the Company controls the offering and its distribution.

Adopted Mar. 12, 2009 (SR-NASDAQ-2009-018).

(e) Definitions and Computations Relating to the Shareholder Approval Requirements

    (1) For purposes of making any computation in this paragraph, when determining the number of shares issuable in a transaction, all shares that could be issued are included, regardless of whether they are currently treasury shares. When determining the number of shares outstanding, only shares issued and outstanding are considered. Treasury shares, shares held by a subsidiary, and unissued shares reserved for issuance upon conversion of securities or upon exercise of options or warrants are not considered outstanding.

    (2) Voting power outstanding as used in this Rule refers to the aggregate number of votes which may be cast by holders of those securities outstanding which entitle the holders thereof to vote generally on all matters submitted to the Company's security holders for a vote.

    (3) An interest consisting of less than either 5% of the number of shares of common stock or 5% of the voting power outstanding of a Company or party shall not be considered a substantial interest or cause the holder of such an interest to be regarded as a "Substantial Shareholder."

    (4) Where shareholder approval is required, the minimum vote that will constitute shareholder approval shall be a majority of the total votes cast on the proposal. These votes may be cast in person, by proxy at a meeting of Shareholders, or by written consent in lieu of a special meeting to the extent permitted by applicable state and federal law and rules (including interpretations thereof), including, without limitation, Regulations 14A and 14C under the Act. Nothing contained in this Rule 5635(e)(4) shall affect a Company's obligation to hold an Annual Meeting of Shareholders as required by Rule 5620(a).

    (5) Shareholder approval shall not be required for any share issuance if such issuance is part of a court-approved reorganization under the federal bankruptcy laws or comparable foreign laws.

(f) Financial Viability Exception

An exception applicable to a specified issuance of securities may be made upon prior written application to Nasdaq's Listing Qualifications Department when:

(1) the delay in securing stockholder approval would seriously jeopardize the financial viability of the enterprise; and

(2) reliance by the Company on this exception is expressly approved by the audit committee or a comparable body of the Board of Directors comprised solely of independent, disinterested directors. The Listing Qualifications Department shall respond to each application for such an exception in writing.

A Company that receives such an exception must mail to all Shareholders not later than ten days before issuance of the securities a letter alerting them to its omission to seek the shareholder approval that would otherwise be required. Such notification shall disclose the terms of the transaction (including the number of shares of common stock that could be issued and the consideration received), the fact that the Company is relying on a financial viability exception to the stockholder approval rules, and that the audit committee or a comparable body of the Board of Directors comprised solely of independent, disinterested directors has expressly approved reliance on the exception. The Company shall also make a public announcement by filing a Form 8-K, where required by SEC rules, or by issuing a press release disclosing the same information as promptly as possible, but no later than ten days before the issuance of the securities.

IM-5635-4. Interpretive Material Regarding Future Priced Securities and Other Securities with Variable Conversion Terms

Summary

Provisions of this IM-5635-4 would apply to any security with variable conversion terms. For example, Future Priced Securities are private financing instruments which were created as an alternative means of quickly raising capital for Companies. The security is generally structured in the form of a convertible security and is often issued via a private placement. Companies will typically receive all capital proceeds at the closing. The conversion price of the Future Priced Security is generally linked to a percentage discount to the market price of the underlying common stock at the time of conversion and accordingly the conversion rate for Future Priced Securities floats with the market price of the common stock. As such, the lower the price of the Company's common stock at the time of conversion, the more shares into which the Future Priced Security is convertible.

The delay in setting the conversion price is appealing to Companies who believe that their stock will achieve greater value after the financing is received. However, the issuance of Future Priced Securities may be followed by a decline in the common stock price, creating additional dilution to the existing holders of the common stock. Such a price decline allows holders to convert the Future Priced Security into large amounts of the Company's common stock. As these shares are issued upon conversion of the Future Priced Security, the common stock price may tend to decline further.

For example, a Company may issue $10 million of convertible preferred stock (the Future Priced Security), which is convertible by the holder or holders into $10 million of common stock based on a conversion price of 80% of the closing price of the common stock on the date of conversion. If the closing price is $5 on the date of conversion, the Future Priced Security holders would receive 2,500,000 shares of common stock. If, on the other hand, the closing price is $1 on the date of conversion, the Future Priced Security holders would receive 12,500,000 shares of common stock.

Unless the Company carefully considers the terms of the securities in connection with several Nasdaq Rules, the issuance of Future Priced Securities could result in a failure to comply with Nasdaq listing standards and the concomitant delisting of the Company's securities from Nasdaq. Nasdaq's experience has been that Companies do not always appreciate this potential consequence. Nasdaq Rules that bear upon the continued listing qualification of a Company and that must be considered when issuing Future Priced Securities include:

1. the shareholder approval rules {see Rule 5635}
2. the voting rights rules {see Rule 5640}
3. the bid price requirement {see Rules 5450(a)(1) and 5555(b)(1)}
4. the listing of additional shares rules {see Rule 5250(e)(2)}
5. the change-in-control rules {see Rule 5635(b) and 5110(a)}
6. Nasdaq's discretionary authority rules {see the Rule 5100 Series}

It is important for Companies to clearly understand that failure to comply with any of these rules could result in the delisting of the Company's securities.

This notice is intended to be of assistance to Companies considering financings involving Future Priced Securities. By adhering to the aforementioned requirements, Companies can avoid unintended listing qualifications problems. Companies having any questions about this notice should contact the Nasdaq Office of General Counsel at (301) 978-8400 or Listing Qualifications Department at (301) 978-8008. Nasdaq will provide a Company with a written interpretation of the application of Nasdaq Rules to a specific transaction, upon request of the Company.

How the Rules Apply

Shareholder Approval

Rule 5635(d) Provides, in Part:

Each Company shall require shareholder approval prior to the issuance of securities in connection with a transaction other than a public offering involving the sale, issuance, or potential issuance by the issuer of common stock (or securities convertible into or exercisable for common stock) at a price less than the greater of book or market value which together with sales by officers, directors, or Substantial Shareholders of the Company equals 20% or more of the common stock or 20% or more of the voting power outstanding before the issuance.

(Nasdaq may make exceptions to this requirement when the delay in securing stockholder approval would seriously jeopardize the financial viability of the enterprise and reliance by the Company on this exception is expressly approved by the Audit Committee or a comparable body of the Board of Directors.)

When Nasdaq staff is unable to determine the number of shares to be issued in a transaction, it looks to the maximum potential issuance of shares to determine whether there will be an issuance of 20% or more of the common stock outstanding. In the case of Future Priced Securities, the actual conversion price is dependent on the market price at the time of conversion and so the number of shares that will be issued is uncertain until the conversion occurs. Accordingly, staff will look to the maximum potential issuance of common shares at the time the Future Priced Security is issued. Typically, with a Future Priced Security, the maximum potential issuance will exceed 20% of the common stock outstanding because the Future Priced Security could, potentially, be converted into common stock based on a share price of one cent per share, or less. Further, for purposes of this calculation, the lowest possible conversion price is below the book or market value of the stock at the time of issuance of the Future Priced Security. Therefore, shareholder approval must be obtained *prior* to the issuance of the Future Priced Security. Companies should also be cautioned that obtaining shareholder ratification of the transaction after the issuance of a Future Priced Security does not satisfy the shareholder approval requirements.

Some Future Priced Securities may contain features to obviate the need for shareholder approval by: (1) placing a cap on the number of shares that can be issued upon conversion, such that the holders of the Future Priced Security cannot, without prior shareholder approval, convert the security into 20% or more of the common stock or voting power outstanding before the issuance of the Future Priced Security (See IM-5635-2, Interpretative Material Regarding the Use of Share Caps to Comply with Rule 5635), or (2) placing a floor on the conversion price, such that the conversion price will always be at least as high as the greater of book or market value of the common stock prior to the issuance of the Future Priced Securities. Even when a Future Priced Security contains these features, however, shareholder approval is still required under Rule 5635(b) if the issuance will result in a change of control. Additionally, discounted issuances *of* common stock to officers, directors, employees, or consultants require shareholder approval pursuant to 5635(c).

Voting Rights

Rule 5640 Provides

Voting rights of existing Shareholders of publicly traded common stock registered under Section 12 of the Act cannot be disparately reduced or restricted through any corporate action or issuance.

IM-5640 also provides rules relating to voting rights of Nasdaq Companies.

Under the voting rights rules, a Company cannot create a new class of security that votes at a higher rate than an existing class of securities or take any other action that has the effect of restricting or reducing the voting rights of an existing class of securities. The voting rights rules are typically implicated when the holders of the Future Priced Security are entitled to vote on an as-converted basis or when the holders of the Future Priced Security are entitled to representation on the Board of Directors. The percentage of the overall vote attributable to the Future Priced Security holders and the Future Priced Security holders' representation on the Board of Directors must not exceed their relative contribution to the Company based on the Company's overall book or market value at the time of the issuance of the Future Priced Security. Staff will consider whether a voting rights violation exists by comparing the Future Priced Security holders' voting rights to their relative contribution to the Company based on the Company's overall book or market value at the time of the issuance of the Future Priced Security. If the voting power or the board percentage exceeds that percentage interest, a violation exists because a new class of securities has been created that votes at a higher rate than an already existing class. Future Priced Securities that vote on an as-converted basis also raise voting rights concerns because of the possibility that, due to a decline in the price of the underlying common stock, the Future Priced Security holder will have voting rights disproportionate to its investment in the Company.

It is important to note that compliance with the shareholder approval rules prior to the issuance of a Future Priced Security does not affect whether the transaction is in violation of the voting rights rule. Furthermore, Shareholders can not otherwise agree to permit a voting rights violation by the Company. Because a violation of the voting rights requirement can result in delisting of the Company's securities from Nasdaq, careful attention must be given to this issue to prevent a violation of the rule.

The Bid Price Requirement

The bid price requirement establishes a minimum bid price for issues listed on Nasdaq. The Nasdaq Rules provide that, for an issue to be eligible for continued listing on Nasdaq, the minimum bid price per share shall be $1. An issue is subject to delisting from Nasdaq, as described in the Rule 5800 Series, if its bid price falls below $1.

The bid price rules must be thoroughly considered because the characteristics of Future Priced Securities often exert downward pressure on the bid price of the Company's common stock. Specifically, dilution from the discounted conversion of the Future Priced Security may result in a significant decline in the price of the common stock. Furthermore, there appear to be instances where short selling has contributed to a substantial price decline, which, in turn, could lead to a failure to comply with the bid price requirement. (If used to manipulate the price of the stock, short selling by the holders of the Future Priced Security is prohibited by the antifraud provisions of the securities laws and by Nasdaq Rules and may be prohibited by the terms of the placement.)

Listing of Additional Shares

Rule 5250(e)(2) Provides:

The Company shall be required to notify Nasdaq on the appropriate form no later than 15 calendar days prior to: establishing or materially amending a stock option plan, purchase plan, or other equity compensation arrangement pursuant to which stock may be acquired by officers, directors, employees, or consultants without shareholder approval; issuing securities that may potentially result in a change of control of the Company; issuing any common stock or security convertible into common stock in connection with the acquisition of the stock or assets of another company, if any officer or director or Substantial Shareholder of the Company has a 5% or greater interest (or if such persons collectively have a 10% or greater interest) in the Company to be acquired or in the consideration to be paid; or entering into a transaction that may result in the potential issuance of common stock (or securities convertible into common stock) greater than 10% of either the total shares outstanding or the voting power outstanding on a pre-transaction basis.

Companies should be cognizant that under this rule notification is required at least 15 days *prior* to issuing any security (including a Future Priced Security) convertible into shares of a class of securities already listed on Nasdaq. Failure to provide such notice can result in a Company's removal from Nasdaq.

Public Interest Concerns

Rule 5101 Provides:

Nasdaq is entrusted with the authority to preserve and strengthen the quality of and public confidence in its market. Nasdaq stands for integrity and ethical business practices in order to enhance investor confidence, thereby contributing to the financial health of the economy and supporting the capital formation process. Nasdaq Companies, from new public Companies to Companies of international stature, are publicly recognized as sharing these important objectives.

Nasdaq, therefore, in addition to applying the enumerated criteria set forth in the Listing Rules, has broad discretionary authority over the initial and continued listing of securities in Nasdaq in order to maintain the quality of and public confidence in its market, to prevent fraudulent and manipulative acts and practices, to promote just and equitable principles of trade, and to protect investors and the public interest. Nasdaq may use such discretion to deny initial listing, apply additional or more stringent criteria for the initial or continued listing of particular securities, or suspend or delist particular securities based on any event, condition, or circumstance that exists or occurs that makes initial or continued listing of the securities on Nasdaq inadvisable or unwarranted in the opinion of Nasdaq, even though the securities meet all enumerated criteria for initial or continued listing on Nasdaq.

The returns on Future Priced Securities may become excessive compared with those of public investors in the Company's common securities. In egregious situations, the use of a Future Priced Security may raise public interest concerns under the Rule 5100 Series. In addition to the demonstrable business purpose of the transaction, other factors that Nasdaq staff will consider in determining whether a transaction raises public interest concerns include: (1) the amount raised in the transaction relative to the Company's existing capital structure; (2) the dilutive effect of the transaction on the existing holders of common stock; (3) the risk undertaken by the Future Priced Security investor; (4) the relationship between the Future Priced Security investor and the Company; (5) whether the transaction was preceded by other similar transactions; and (6) whether the transaction is consistent with the just and equitable principles of trade.

Some Future Priced Securities may contain features that address the public interest concerns. These features tend to provide incentives to the investor to hold the security for a longer time period and limit the number of shares into which the Future Priced Security may be converted. Such features may limit the dilutive effect of the transaction and increase the risk undertaken by the Future Priced Security investor in relationship to the reward available.

Business Combinations with Non-Nasdaq Entities Resulting in a Change of Control

Rule 5110(a) Provides:

A Company must apply for initial listing in connection with a transaction whereby the Company combines with a non-Nasdaq entity, resulting in a change of control of the Company and potentially allowing the non-Nasdaq entity to obtain a Nasdaq listing. In determining whether a change of control has occurred, Nasdaq shall consider all relevant factors including, but not limited to, changes in the management, Board of Directors, voting power, ownership, and financial structure of the Company. Nasdaq shall also consider the nature of the businesses and the relative size of the Nasdaq Company and non-Nasdaq entity. The Company must submit an application for the post-transaction entity with sufficient time to allow Nasdaq to complete its review before the transaction is completed. If the Company's application for initial listing has not been approved prior to consummation of the transaction, Nasdaq will issue a Staff Determination Letter as set forth in Rule 5810 and begin delisting proceedings pursuant to the Rule 5800 Series.

This provision, which applies regardless of whether the Company obtains shareholder approval for the transaction, requires Companies to qualify under the initial listing standards in connection with a combination that results in a change of control. It is important for Companies to realize that, in certain instances, the conversion of a Future Priced Security may implicate this provision. For example, if there is no limit on the number of common shares issuable upon conversion, or if the limit is set high enough, the exercise of conversion rights under a Future Priced Security could result in the holders of the Future Priced Securities obtaining control of the listed Company. In such event, a Company may be required to re-apply for initial listing and satisfy all initial listing requirements.

5640. Voting Rights

Voting rights of existing Shareholders of publicly traded common stock registered under Section 12 of the Act cannot be disparately reduced or restricted through any corporate action or issuance. Examples of such corporate action or issuance include, but are not limited to, the adoption of time-phased voting plans, the adoption of capped voting rights plans, the issuance of super voting stock, or the issuance of stock with voting rights less than the per share voting rights of the existing common stock through an exchange offer.

IM-5640. Voting Rights Policy

The following Voting Rights Policy is based upon, but more flexible than, former Rule 19c-4 under the Act. Accordingly, Nasdaq will permit corporate actions or issuances by Nasdaq Companies that would have been permitted under former Rule 19c-4, as well as other actions or issuances that are not inconsistent with this policy. In evaluating such other actions or issuances, Nasdaq will consider, among other things, the economics of such actions or issuances and the voting rights being granted. Nasdaq's interpretations under the policy will be flexible, recognizing that both the capital markets and the circumstances and needs of Nasdaq Companies change over time. The text of the Nasdaq Voting Rights Policy is as follows:

Companies with Dual Class Structures

The restriction against the issuance of super voting stock is primarily intended to apply to the issuance of a new class of stock, and Companies with existing dual class capital structures would generally be permitted to issue additional shares of the existing super voting stock without conflict with this policy.

Consultation with Nasdaq

Violation of the Nasdaq Voting Rights Policy could result in the loss of a Company's Nasdaq or public trading market. The policy can apply to a variety of corporate actions and securities issuances, not just super voting or so-called "time phase" voting common stock. While the policy will continue to permit actions previously permitted under former Rule 19c-4, it is extremely important that Nasdaq Companies communicate their intentions to their Nasdaq representatives as early as possible before taking any action or committing to take any action that may be inconsistent with the policy. Nasdaq urges Companies listed on Nasdaq not to assume, without first discussing the matter with the Nasdaq staff, that a particular issuance of common or preferred stock or the taking of some other corporate action will necessarily be consistent with the policy. It is suggested that copies of preliminary proxy or other material concerning matters subject to the policy be furnished to Nasdaq for review prior to formal filing.

Review of Past Voting Rights Activities

In reviewing an application for initial qualification for listing of a security in Nasdaq, Nasdaq will review the Company's past corporate actions to determine whether another self-regulatory organization (SRO) has found any of the Company's actions to have been a violation or evasion of the SRO's voting rights policy. Based on such review, Nasdaq may take any appropriate action, including the denial of the application or the placing of restrictions on such listing. Nasdaq will also review whether a Company seeking initial listing of a security in Nasdaq has requested a ruling or interpretation from another SRO regarding the application of that SRO's voting rights policy with respect to a proposed transaction. If so, Nasdaq will consider that fact in determining its response to any ruling or interpretation that the Company may request on the same or similar transaction.

Non-U.S. Companies

Nasdaq will accept any action or issuance relating to the voting rights structure of a non-U.S. Company that is in compliance with Nasdaq's requirements for domestic Companies or that is not prohibited by the Company's home country law.

Governance

Audit Committee Charter Approved February 28, 2017 Nasdaq, Inc[28]

Organization

This Charter governs the operations of the Nasdaq, Inc. Audit Committee (the "Committee"). The Charter will be reviewed and reassessed, at least annually, by the Committee. The Committee shall be appointed by the Board of Directors in compliance with Article IV, Section 4.13(g) of the Nasdaq By-Laws and shall consist of three or more Directors, each of whom is independent of management. Members of the Committee shall be considered independent if they have no relationship that may interfere with the exercise of their independence in carrying out the responsibilities of a director as defined by the Securities Exchange Act of 1934.[29] All Committee members will be able to read and understand fundamental financial statements, including a balance sheet, income statement, and cash flow statement. At least one member must have past employment experience in finance or accounting, requisite professional certification in accounting, or any other comparable experience or background that results in the individual's financial sophistication, including service as a Chief Executive Officer, Chief Financial Officer, or other senior officer with financial oversight responsibilities or otherwise satisfy standards for financial expertise required for audit committees of companies listed on the NASDAQ Stock Market.

Statement of Policy

The primary function of the Audit Committee is to assist the Board of Directors in fulfilling its oversight responsibilities by reviewing the financial information, which will be provided to the shareholders and others, the systems of internal controls, which management and the Board of Directors have established, and Nasdaq, Inc.'s audit, financial reporting, and the legal and compliance process. Additionally, the Committee provides oversight of the Enterprise Risk Management (ERM) program including the risk governance structure, risk metrics, risk assessment and strategy as it relates to key risks, including regulatory, credit, operational, and technology and information systems, including cyber security. In so doing, it is the responsibility of the Committee to maintain free and open communication with independent auditors, internal auditors, ERM management, and Nasdaq, Inc.'s management. In discharging its oversight role, the Committee is empowered to investigate any matter brought to its attention with full access to all books, records, facilities, and personnel of Nasdaq, Inc. and the power to retain independent counsel, or other experts, and funding sufficient for this purpose.

Responsibilities and Processes

The primary responsibility of the Committee is to oversee Nasdaq, Inc.'s financial reporting process on behalf of the Board of Directors and report the results of these activities to the Board. Management is responsible for preparing Nasdaq, Inc.'s financial statements, and the independent auditors are responsible for auditing those financial statements. The Committee in carrying out its responsibilities believes its policies and procedures should remain flexible, in order to best react to changing conditions and circumstances. The Committee should take the appropriate actions to set the overall corporate policy for quality financial reporting, sound business risk management practices, and ethical behavior.

The following shall be the principal recurring processes of the Committee in carrying out its responsibilities. The processes are set forth as a guide with the understanding that the Committee may supplement them as appropriate. The responsibilities and processes of the Committee shall be consistent with the Exchange Act and the rules and regulations adopted by the SEC.

1. The Committee will meet at least four times a year, with authority to convene additional meetings as circumstances require. All Committee members are expected to attend each meeting, either in person or via tele-or-video conference. The Committee will invite members of management, auditors, or others to attend each meeting to provide pertinent information. Meeting agendas will be prepared and provided in advance to members, along with appropriate briefing materials. The Committee will meet periodically in executive session. Minutes will be prepared.

2. The Committee shall have a clear understanding with management and the independent auditors that the independent auditors are ultimately accountable to the Board and the Audit Committee, as representatives of Nasdaq, Inc.'s shareholders. The Committee shall have the ultimate authority and responsibility for the appointment, retention, approval of compensation, and oversight of the independent auditors. The Committee, where appropriate, will replace the independent auditors if the Committee determines that such a change would be in the company's and its stockholders' best interests. The Committee shall nominate the independent auditors to be proposed for shareholder ratification in any proxy statement. In addition, the Committee shall ensure the rotation of the lead independent audit partner every five years and other audit partners every seven years and participate in the selection of the lead audit partner.

3. The Committee is responsible for ensuring its receipt from the independent auditors, at least annually, of a formal written statement delineating all relationships between the auditor and Nasdaq, Inc., consistent with the applicable requirements of the Public Accounting

Oversight Board. The Committee shall actively engage in dialogue with the independent auditors with respect to any disclosed relationships or non-audit fees and services that may impact the objectivity and independence of the auditor and for taking, or recommending that the full board take, appropriate action to oversee the independence of the independent auditor. Additionally, the Committee shall review with the independent auditors any audit problems or difficulties and management responsiveness. The Committee shall prescribe what services are allowable by the independent auditors and approve in advance all services provided by the auditors (see Independent Public Auditor Services section). The Committee shall review all proposed Nasdaq, Inc. hires formerly employed by the independent auditors.

4. The Committee shall discuss with the Head of Internal Audit and the independent auditors the overall scope and risk-based plans for their respective audits, including the adequacy of staffing, compensation, and resources. Also, the Committee shall discuss with management, the Head of Internal Audit, and the independent auditors the adequacy and effectiveness of Nasdaq, Inc.'s internal controls, including systems to monitor and manage business risk, legal and ethical compliance programs, and financial reporting. Further, the Committee shall meet separately with the Head of Internal Audit and the independent auditors, with and without management present, to discuss the results of their examinations. The internal auditors shall report directly to the Committee and have free and open access to information deemed necessary by them to perform their assessments. The Committee shall provide oversight over the system of internal controls, relying upon management's and the internal and independent auditor's representations and assessments of the controls, and annually approve the internal audit plan, major changes to that plan, and the internal audit charter.

5. The Committee shall review and discuss with management the Company's Enterprise Risk Management process, including risk governance structure, risk assessment, and risk management practices and guidelines.

6. The audit committee will meet periodically with the internal auditors and assist the Board in its oversight of the performance of the internal audit function. The audit committee will also discuss with the outside auditor the responsibilities, budget, and staffing of the internal audit function. The Committee shall review the effectiveness of the Head of Internal Audit and the internal audit function, including assessing their effectiveness according to industry standards. The Committee will discuss the adequacy of resources and scope of the annual internal audit plan with the Head of Internal

Audit. Also, the Committee will review and concur in the appointment, replacement, or dismissal of the Head of Internal Audit.

7. Annually, the committee evaluates the performance of the independent auditor. As one of the inputs for this review, the committee receives and reviews, at least annually, a report by the Independent Auditors describing: (a) the Independent Auditors' internal quality-control procedures; and (b) any material issues raised by the most recent internal quality-control review, or peer review, or by any inquiry or investigation by governmental or professional authorities, within the preceding five years, respecting one or more independent audits carried out by the Independent Auditors, and any steps taken to deal with any such issues.

8. The Committee shall review the interim financial statements and earnings releases with management and the independent auditors prior to the filing of Nasdaq, Inc.'s quarterly report on Form 10-Q. Also, the Committee shall discuss the results of the quarterly review and any other matters required to be communicated to the Committee by the independent auditors under generally accepted auditing standards.

9. The Committee shall review with management and the independent auditors the financial statements to be included in Nasdaq, Inc.'s annual report on Form 10-K (or the annual report to shareholders if distributed prior to the filing of Form 10-K) and quarterly reports on Form-Q, including MD&A disclosures, their judgment about the quality, not just acceptability, of accounting principles, the reasonableness of significant judgments, and the clarity of the disclosures in the financial statements. Also, the Committee shall discuss the results of the annual audit, including the management letters, reports, and attestations prepared by management and the independent auditors to comply with the Exchange Act and any other matters required to be communicated to the Committee by the independent auditors under generally accepted auditing standards and SEC rules.

10. The Committee shall review and approve all related party transactions consistent with the rules applied to companies listed on the NASDAQ Stock Market.

11. The Committee shall have responsibility for, and oversight of, a confidential and anonymous process and procedures for the receipt, retention, and treatment of submissions regarding accounting, audit, internal accounting controls, and enterprise risk matters. All such submissions must be reported to the Committee.

12. The Committee shall provide oversight for the code of ethics program including the code, related policies, communication of the

code of ethics to employees, and monitoring employee awareness and compliance to the program.

13. The Committee shall oversee the adequacy and effectiveness of the regulatory and self-regulatory organization responsibilities of Nasdaq, Inc. and its subsidiaries; assess regulatory performance; and assist the Board and other committees of the Board in reviewing the regulatory plan and the overall effectiveness of regulatory functions.

14. The Committee shall review, and recommend to the Board for approval, the Company's regular cash and stock dividends.

15. An annual performance appraisal of the Audit Committee is conducted among the members and the results are reviewed by the Audit Committee.

Independent Public Auditor Services

The independent auditor is prohibited from performing any of the following services for Nasdaq, Inc:

- Bookkeeping or other services related to the accounting records or financial statements of the audit client
- Financial information systems design and implementation
- Appraisal or valuation services, fairness opinions, or contribution-in-kind reports
- Actuarial services
- Internal audit outsourcing services
- Management or human resources functions
- Broker or dealer, investment adviser, or investment banking services
- Legal services and expert services unrelated to the audit; and any other service that the Public Company Accounting Oversight Board determines, by regulation, is impermissible.

All audit and allowable non-audit services must be approved in advance by the Committee. However, the Chairman of the Committee is delegated authority to approve in advance audit and non-audit services by the independent auditor to support business development, consulting on accounting issues (subject to the aforementioned prohibitions) or tax consulting to the extent permitted by SEC rules, if such non-audit services do not exceed $300,000 in the aggregate between meetings of the Committee and the Committee is informed of such pre-approval by the Chairman at the Committee's next meeting.

21.19 Typical Exit Strategies

Common to all exit strategies is the concept of a large financial reward for an earlier risky investment in the venture. However, every exit strategy has advantages and disadvantages. Table 21.8 highlights both and may provide you with some considerations you have not thought of before. These exit strategies can take a business to its next stage. As your business transitions to the next stage, you may end your involvement or remain with the business in a new role.

21.20 Big Companies Stink at Innovation

Most established companies spend more money on acquisitions of startups than on R&D. For example, Cisco also prefers to "buy rather than build." According to Basil Peters[30] Fund Manager for Fundamental Technologies II, "It's also a great time to sell a business because large companies are sitting on loads of cash. This situation presents a problem for company management because shareholders want them to either invest the capital to create growth or distribute it to the shareholders as dividends. Distributing cash is considered an admission of defeat for tech company management because it shows they don't have any ideas about how to invest cash to increase shareholder value."

There has also been a remarkable growth in private equity buyout funds in the past several years. These funds are similar to what used to be called "merchant banks" years ago. These funds often buy companies for cash, operate them for a few years, make them highly profitable, and then resell them, usually for a significant gain.

Often, private equity funds will purchase a number of companies in an industry and increase their value by consolidating and realizing operating synergies and efficiencies. These funds are very active acquirers of companies in the under $30 million range.

It is logical that the optimum strategy for tech startups today is to design the company, and its corporate DNA, so everyone is aligned around the idea of a company acquisition in the under $30 million range. The good news is that these exits can often be completed in just a few years from startup.

Tech startups have a much higher probability of success than swinging for the fences and hoping for a big home run Nasdaq initial public offering. This exit strategy was nicely summarized in "The New Homerun" by Tom Stein[31] in *Mergers & Acquisitions Magazine*, when he said, "Startups must be content with hitting singles or doubles, that is, a buyout of [less than] $50 million."

TABLE 21.8

Exit Strategies Available to the Founder-Entrepreneur

Types of Exit Strategies (Harvesting)	Description	Advantages	Disadvantages
Merger with another company	A joining together of two previously separate corporations. A true merger in the legal sense occurs when both businesses dissolve and move their assets and liabilities into a newly created entity	Sellers may receive cash and/or stock, resources of both companies are combined, and some of the management may remain in place	New owners or executives may have different philosophies or ways of doing business. Original staff may have less control, and integrating the two cultures may be difficult
Acquisition by another company	An acquisition occurs when one entity takes ownership of another entity's stock, equity interests, or assets	Sellers receive cash or stock for the sale and management contract is negotiable for the owner to stay on during transition	It is not always appropriate for the business or employees, and the corporate identity or brand may diminish
Sale of the Company (To existing management, also known as a management buyout)	The company is sold to senior management, where all the assets are sold	Sellers may receive cash immediately or over time. Often business milestones (incentives) are attached to additional cash	May be difficult to find the right buyer at the right price, and changes in ownership may be difficult for employees
Franchise of the Company	The business concept is replicated and the company expands locally, regionally, nationally, or internationally	Franchisor receives cash for each franchise, current corporate management is maintained, and the enterprise sees an opportunity for large-scale growth	The process may be difficult and time-consuming, and the business concept may not be appropriate for franchising. Finding suitable location(s) may be complicated

(Continued)

TABLE 21.8 (CONTINUED)

Exit Strategies Available to the Founder-Entrepreneur

Types of Exit Strategies (Harvesting)	Description	Advantages	Disadvantages
Employee Stock-Ownership Plan (ESOP)	An **employee stock ownership plan (ESOP)** is an employee-owner program that provides a company's workforce with an ownership interest in the company. Employees receive shares or stock of the company over time	Key employees are rewarded for their contributions, receive incentives for staying with the company for a number of years, and share in the profits of the company they have helped to grow	The owner can borrow funds from the plan as a loan to the company, employees may lose their shares if they leave the company, and if the value of the company or company stock decreases, the employees share in the burden
Initial Public Offering (IPO)	An **initial public offering or IPO** is the first sale of stock by a private company to the public. IPOs are often smaller, younger companies seeking capital to expand their business	Shares convert to cash for investors, major shareholders control the company, and investors see potentially high returns	The company needs high growth to generate earnings and investors' interest, the process is costly, and the outcome is uncertain

TABLE 21.9

Advantages of an MBO for Selling Owner(s)

Rewarding those that made it all possible	By selling to your management, you are rewarding the people who helped make you successful
Selling to an informed and motivated buyer	Your senior team intimately *know* the business and growth opportunities better than anyone. They are likely to pay a reasonable price because they are confident in their knowledge of the company and their ability to execute growth strategies
Accelerated due diligence	The due diligence phase is typically faster and less intrusive when selling to the management. Senior management is already familiar with the ins and outs/ups and downs of your company Selling to an outsider will most likely take significantly longer to close a transaction relative to selling to the management team
Not exposing your competitive advantages to outsiders	If you try to sell your business to an outsider, you may have several potential suitors digging through significant financial and operational details, as they obviously need to know what they are buying

21.21 Selling to Your Senior Team

When it comes time for the owner to sell the business, the natural thought is to "sell to the highest bidder." This is often done as a part of the "auction" process. Sometimes this makes sense, but other times it does not. The advantages of selling to the highest bidder include a potential higher valuation. However, disadvantages may include your company's financials and customer lists being available to many interested suitors and maybe even your competitors.[32]

Selling to the highest bidder generally involves "going public." But going public as an exit strategy is a big endeavor. Your company has to be big enough to justify all the additional regulatory requirements under Sarbanes–Oxley. Initial public offering as an exit strategy is complex, time-consuming, and phenomenally expensive for a small company.

Is there a better way? As a possible exit strategy, owner-entrepreneurs may consider their senior team as potential buyers of their business. The technical term for this transaction is a management buy-out (MBO). There are several advantages to selling to your management team as a real exit option, and not a last resort, as listed in Table 21.9.

Notes

1. Bygrave, W.D., Timmons, J. (1999). Venture Capital at the Crossroads. University of Illinois at Urbana-Champaign's Academy for Entrepreneurial reference in Entrepreneurship. http://ssm..com/abstract=1496172

2. Price, R.W. Why is an exit strategy important for entrepreneurs? 2014 https://news. gcase.org/2014/06/19/why-is-an-exit-strategy-important-for-entrepreneurs-2/

3. Watson, J. and Everett, J.E. (1996). Do small retailers have high failure rates? Evidence from Australian retailers, *Journal of Small Business Management*, Vol. 34 No. 4, pp.45–62.

4. Roadmap for an IPO: A guide to going public 2015 PricewaterhouseCoopers LLP, a Delaware limited liability partnership. www.pwc.com/us/deals

5. Allison, S., Hall, C., McShea, D. (2008). *The Initial Public Offering Handbook: A Guide for Entrepreneurs, Executives, Directors and Private Investors.* Merrill Corporation, Publications Department, St. Paul, MN.

6. Allison, S., Hall, C., McShea, D. *The Initial Public Offering Handbook: A Guide for Entrepreneurs, Executives, Directors and Private Investors.* p 89. Merrill Corporation Publications Department St. Paul, Minnesota 2008

7. http://nvca.org/pressreleases/seventy-seven-venture-backed-companies-went-public-in-2015/

8. https://www.quora.com/Did-Google-buy-Android

9. https://www.cnet.com/news/google-buys-android/

10. http://www.investopedia.com/articles/analyst/03/111903.asp

11. Margolis, S. Optimal group size for decision making https://sheilamargolis. com/2011/01/24/what-is-the-optimal-group-size-for-decision-making/

12. http://www.intuitor.com/statistics/SmallGroups.html

13. Comment letter A letter from the SEC commenting in detail on the registration statement filed with the SEC, after its review of the initial registration statement or amendments to the filing.

14. Underwriters provide several services, including help with correctly assessing the value of shares (share price) and establishing a public market for shares (initial sale).

15. **Over-allotment option (or Green Shoe, "shoe")** An option that gives the underwriters the option to purchase up to 15% additional shares, on the same terms that they purchased the original shares, for a period up to 30 days after the initial public offering.

16. FINRA is the Financial Industry Regulatory Authority (formerly, the National Association of Securities Dealers, or "NASD"), which is the self-regulatory organization governing the conduct of the underwriters and broker-dealers in the IPO. before the offering may proceed

17. Regulation S-X includes and describes items of disclosure required to be included in the financial portion of the registration statement on Form S-1.

18. **Comfort letter** The letter from the company's auditors to the underwriters regarding the financial data and financial statements in the registration statement, which is delivered at pricing.

19. **Red herring** The preliminary prospectus, printed with a red legend on the side of the cover stating that the prospectus is subject to completion.

20. **S-1** The Form S-1 is the registration statement filed with the SEC to register securities for an offering. It includes the prospectus.

21. **S-K** Regulation S-K includes and describes items of disclosure required to be included in the nonfinancial portion of the registration statement on Form S-1.

22. **Road show** Representatives from the company meet with prospective investors (generally, institutional investors such as mutual funds, pension funds and the like) in various cities and make presentations about the company.

23. **Pricing** The determination by the company of the per share price at which the company will offer its stock to the public, after consultation with the under-writers following the road show and effectiveness of the registration statement.
24. Committee on Corporate Laws of the Aba Section of Business Law, Model Business Corp. Act § 8.25(a), at 8-26 (2008)
25. Standing committees are committees with a continued existence intended to consider all matters on an ongoing basis
26. The Business Roundtable, Principles of Corporate Governance (2016) www.businessroundtable.org/publications/index. aspx.
27. http://nasdaq.cchwallstreet.com/nasdaq/main/nasdaq-equityrules/chp_1_1/chp_1_1_4/chp_1_1_4_3/chp_1_1_4_3_8/default.asp
28. http://ir.nasdaq.com/corporate-governance-document.cfm?documentid=195
29. Directors shall meet the standards for independence set forth in Section 10A(m) of the Securities Exchange Act of 1934, as amended (the "Exchange Act"), the rules promulgated by the Securities and Exchange Commission (the "SEC") and Nasdaq Stock Market Rule 5605, as amended. The composition and respon-sibilities of the Committee also will be consistent with SEC guidance, and in particular with the SEC Order set forth in Release No. 34-37538.
30. Peters, B. Early exits. MeteorBytes Data Management Corp. 2009www.Early-Exits.com.
31. Stein, T. The new homerun: M&A instead of R&D and IPO's, *Mergers & Acquisitions Magazine, The Dealmaker's Journal* 43:1, 32–36, 2008.
32. Harnett, M. Have you considered a management buy out? http://exitpromise.com/considering-a-management-buy-out/

Index